This Great Symbol

(Culver Pictures)

This Great Symbol

*Pierre de Coubertin and the Origins of
the Modern Olympic Games*

John J. MacAloon

The University of Chicago Press
Chicago and London

For Madelyn and John

JOHN J. MACALOON is assistant professor in the Social
Sciences Collegiate Division and an associated faculty
member of the Committee on Social Thought at the
University of Chicago.

The University of Chicago Press, Chicago 60637
The University of Chicago Press, Ltd., London

© 1981 by the University of Chicago
All rights reserved. Published 1981
Printed in the United States of America
88 87 86 85 84 83 82 81   5 4 3 2 1

Library of Congress Cataloging in Publication Data

MacAloon, John J
  This great symbol.

  Bibliography: p.
  Includes index.
  1. Coubertin, Pierre de, 1863–1937.   2. Entrepreneur—Biography.   3. Olympic games—Philosophy.
4. Olympic games—History.   I. Title.
GV721.2.C68M32   796.4′8′09   80-21898
ISBN 0-226-50000-4

Contents

List of Plates

Preface

In Borges's story "The Chinese Mapmakers," the Yellow Emperor orders his cartographers to create the most accurate map of the kingdom possible. After years of labor, they present the lord with a triumph of their craft, a wondrous representation of the territory he rules. But the emperor is dissatisfied. Where entire mountain ranges are depicted, he wishes to discern individual peaks; where great rivers are charted, he would trace their tributaries as well. The mapmakers return to work. This cycle of success and rejection is repeated for decades, even generations. After each rebuff the royal cartographers halve the scale at which they work and double the size of their image, from 1 : 1000 to 1 : 500 to 1 : 250, until finally they succeed in creating a map whose scale is 1 : 1. They have followed orders and duplicated the world, and no one any longer knows which is the map and which is the territory.

This tale can be read as a parable of contemporary social science, portraying its aims and its follies. Certainly Borges's story neatly expresses the modern Olympic Games and what it is like, as a social scientist, to write about them. The Olympic festival is a global representation of human social process. Decade by decade, it has greedily reached out to encompass more territory, while at the same time drafting its established landscape in sharper relief. The anthropologist who attempts to map this map finds himself, like the Chinese cartographers, obeying an imperial command to work on a scale for which there is little precedent.

In scarcely eighty years, the Olympic Games have grown from a fin-de-siècle curiosity of regional interest to an international cultural performance of global proportion. Participants in the Olympic Games—athletes, coaches, officials, dignitaries, press, technicians, support personel, as well as artists, performers, scientists, and world youth campers attending ancillary events—now number in the tens of thousands, drawn from as many as 120 nations. Foreigners journeying to the host city number in the hundred thousands, total spectators in the millions, and the broadcast audience in the billions. According to reasonable estimates, 1.5 billion people—or about one out of every three persons then alive on the earth—watched or listened to part of the proceedings at Montreal through

the broadcast media. With the addition of a "guesstimate" of the newspaper audience and of those interested in the Games but prevented by
political censure or lack of facilities from following them, the figure rises to
something like half the world's population. Without the Soviet invasion of
Afghanistan and the consequent boycott, the television audience alone for
the Moscow Games might have exceeded two billion.

The faces of entire cities have been permanently altered by the Games,
and the impact of an Olympics on regional and national economies is now
prodigious. At Montreal, the debt alone exceeded $1 billion, if capital
expenditures are included. The total worldwide economic exchange occasioned by an Olympic Games is in the billions. The volume of symbolic
exchange, interpersonal and intra- and cross-cultural, defies quantitative
description, but is still more preponderant and arresting. The Moscow
imbroglio is only the most recent illustration of how the Games' symbolic
density draws them into the center of the political and ideological dramas
of modern life. As this volume will show, regimes and parties have been
variously rejuvenated or destabilized from the very first moments of
Olympic history, and a countermovement has progressed apace. The International Olympic Committee is presently considering a proposal, conditioned by events described in this book, that would make it master of a
sovereign state carved out from the territory of Greece. In short, the
Olympic Games are an institution without parallel in kind or in scope in
the twentieth century. Insofar as there exists, in the Hegelian-Marxian
phrase, a "world-historical process," the Olympic Games have emerged as
its privileged expression and celebration.

The Games' emotional power over individual dreams, not their impressive demography or political sociology, first compelled my interest in
them. In 1968, I was a collegiate runner, a journeyman, but just good
enough to fantasize about making the United States team. Troubled by
how much it mattered to me and moved by the courageous choices made
by others, particularly black athletes, in those heady days of the "Athletic
Revolution," I scoured the libraries for texts that would make sense of
these Olympic Games that were the common object of our confusion and
striving. The libraries yielded nothing of much use, no text that could be
said to contain a comprehensive interpretation of the Games, a satisfying
history of where they came from, or an explanation of why so many cared
so much. What little scholarly work there was to be found, tucked between the guidebooks, memoirs, technical reports, and official publications, invariably contented itself with some specialist's dram of concern
dipped from the sea of action and expression that is the Games. This
discovery was surprising and saddening to me: surprising because I then
thought social science (to which I was a stranger) an omnivorous beast
which investigated everything that moved; saddening because I took this

scholarly vacancy as further evidence of the contempt of "serious culture" for the ludic side of life, a contempt from which those of us who were having our most important experiences in sport felt ourselves daily to suffer.

Now, after some ten years of my own research, that absence seems readily understandable. I have learned something about Chinese map-making. The very qualities which make the Games intriguing—their scale, complexity, and multiple layers of meaning—make them resistant to comprehensive inquiry. More than any secret academic contempt, the built-in paradox of "serious play" throws up an additional barrier. And the concern for objectivity, method, and control that distinguishes social science from other disciplines seems to lead automatically to just the sort of particularistic Olympic studies that are so unsatisfying. To shift the metaphor from cartography to cuisine, the maxim of the Olympic researcher might well be, "He who tries to swallow the thing whole will find himself swallowed by it instead." I have spent some years in the pit of its stomach.

Yet despite enormous methodological problems my interest in the Games has remained holistic, essentially ethnographic and anthropological. This study is a history of the origins of the modern Olympic Games and a biography of their founder, Pierre de Coubertin. At the outset, I did not intend to write a book-length history, but the project fairly forced itself upon me, in its own right and as a necessary prolegomenon to other kinds of work. What passes for history in sociological and anthropological texts is generally embarrassing and irresponsible: embarrassing because such "historical" passages are often worthier of bad textbooks than of scholarly works; irresponsible because these sterile catalogues of names, dates, and -isms, juiced up with the odd quotation, destroy any sense of living sociocultural context in the very act of claiming to set one out. Few anthropologists would treat their living informants in the cavalier and conscienceless way they tend to treat those historical persons whose misfortune it is to turn up in their texts. There are serious issues at stake in the "structure vs. history" polemic, but too often it is a smokescreen for fundamental failures of energy and nerve. There are problems of evidence as well, but they cannot be insurmountable. Anthropologists and sociologists are not slow to laud the "ethnographic" quality of favorite historical works. But one rarely hears compliments flowing in the opposite direction. Not without justice does A. J. P. Taylor describe sociology as "history without the history."

For my own part, I could not write "history without the history," but that is hardly sufficient reason for a book unless tilting at windmills is one's pleasure. I felt compelled to understand how on earth someone came to the extraordinary idea that a group of people running around in short pants every four years had something to do with international understanding and world peace. And this is very much a story with a "someone." No modern institution so important as the Olympics owes its existence so fully to the actions of a single person. The history of the Olympic Games offers an exceptional case study of the encounter between collective social forces and unusual individual initiative (which is another matter anthropology must more concertedly take up if it is to make good its humanistic claims). Moreover, for all the vast changes that have accrued to the Games since their first celebration in 1896, they still bear indelibly—from their flag to their official ideology—the stamp of Pierre de Coubertin. It is impossible to understand the origins *or* the persistent "structure" of the Olympics without understanding this man, his personal drama and his milieu; how the themes of an era became the themes of a life, and were in turn embodied in a new cultural institution. Thus, it is in no sense a question of filling in the nineteenth-century "background" to a twentieth-century institution. Coubertin was in many important respects a transitional figure, a man in passage between his era and our own, and one of the strongest convictions that grows out of a study of the Olympic Games is that the nineteenth century has a profound and abiding hold over the twentieth. But it is precisely such abstractions that I have tried to avoid here, in part because they explain nothing, in part because they are all too common in previous works on Coubertin.

The story has been told only badly, or else in bits and pieces. There are, perhaps, a hundred texts that have something to say about Coubertin; nearly all of them are empty of content and style, hagiography or hagiolatry, not history. To the anthropologist, these works are interesting as ideological formations, but using them to this effect depends on first setting the story straight. Of the half-dozen serious studies of Coubertin and the early Olympic Movement, cited and discussed in this book, those of substantial length are often factually unreliable and arrive at no comprehensive and consistent interpretation. Those which are both reliable and revealing, including a pair of articles by a Third Republic historian of the first rank, restrict themselves to one or two aspects or moments of the story.

The pressing and, I dare say, public need for a responsible and detailed account of the pre- and early history of the Olympic Games has gone unanswered for a number of reasons. The story turns out to be delightful and compelling, but also rather complicated. Telling it requires a willingness to cross the boundaries of various academic disciplines: history, anthropology, sociology, psychology, literary criticism, and classical studies. I am grateful to the Committee on Social Thought of the University of Chicago, to whom this work was originally submitted as a dissertation, for encouraging such unpedigreed and cross-disciplinary enterprises.

Essential texts and other sorts of evidence are scattered widely throughout Euro-America. Many crucial writings of Coubertin were privately published, never circulated in England and the United States, and never broadly in France. Several of his commercially published articles occur in obscure journals, magazines, and newspapers found only in the best research libraries. The only Coubertin collection with any claim to comprehensiveness is the archives of the International Olympic Committee in Lausanne. During the summers of 1975 and 1977, I spent a total of two and one-half months there. I am grateful to Monique Berlioux, I.O.C. executive director, and to her staff, particularly Emmanuel Migraine, Judy Davis, and Rosemary Sandeman, for their hospitality and assistance. I also thank the Danforth Foundation for supporting me as a graduate fellow and the Wenner-Gren Foundation for Anthropological Research for indirectly making possible my 1977 return to Lausanne and my visit to Archaia Olympia and the collections of the Museum of the Modern Olympic Games. I am also indebted to the staffs of the University of Chicago Libraries, the Center for Research Libraries in Chicago, and the Library of Congress.

As a work of biography, this book is not a conventional one. My central concern is the creation of the Olympic spectacle, and I have focused on this dimension of Coubertin's life and thought in preference to, though not I hope at the expense of, other aspects of his story. Moreover, even after the necessary globe-trotting and pouring over hundreds and hundreds of pages of his writings, one is left without those materials most critical to the biographer's art. In the absence of extensive letters and private documents, not only of Coubertin but of his family and closest associates, telling this story is an act as much of reconstruction as of narration. It is here that I have had strategic recourse to concepts and methods borrowed from contemporary culture theory, sociology, and psychology. I have endeavored to turn anthropological kinship theory into an interpretive method, to get at the subjective meanings of Coubertin's genealogy and aristocratic heritage through the key cultural concepts of *prouesse* and *patronage*. I have made use of the sociological concepts of marginality and liminality, and have employed psychoanalytic and psychobiographical methods to explore the inner skin of the baron's familial dramas. In turn, these approaches are joined with recent processual symbolic analysis, with its attention to root metaphors and symbolic paradigms as interfaces between individual and social identities and projects.

In these efforts, I have taken as capital evidence Coubertin's heretofore neglected autobiographical novel, "Le Roman d'un rallié." In my treatment of this text, I have used standard techniques of literary criticism and comparison with other sorts of evidence as checks against the notorious tendencies of the cultural-category, psychobiographical, and symbolic approaches to run away with those who employ them. Whether I have succeeded in making a virtue of necessity by bringing social scientific concepts to bear on historical problems, the reader, as in all else, must judge. Should new documents come to light in the future, they will provide a test not only of my account of Coubertin's interior life, but also of this particular style of demonstrating the interpenetration of an individual struggle for identity, the social dramas of an era, and the creation of a new cultural institution.

I owe special gratitude to Victor and Edith Turner, who nurtured my desire to write about the Olympic Games during a period of doubt about the project. The full extent of my debt to Victor Turner's work will be more evident in a subsequent volume, but others who have known his teaching and friendship will recognize their inspiration throughout these pages. Not only did Ralph Nicholas read the manuscript closely, but his intellectual advice and example were crucial in the final stages of its preparation. Michael Schudson, Paul Wheatley, and James Redfield also read the manuscript, and conversations with Donald Levine, Natalie Davis, Bertram Cohler, Jan Goldstein, Cynthia Truant, Apostolos Kosmopoulos, and Istvan Balyi have contributed to sections of it. Acknowledgments of various kinds are owed to Thomas Buckley, Arjun Appadurai, Fred Marchant, Paul Antze, Beth Goldring, Richard Rand, Michael Vollen, Maribeth Vollen, Barbara Murphy, Roman Kokodyniak, and Gerry McGee. My debt to Tanya Sugarman MacAloon is greatest of all. Naturally no one but myself is responsible for the content of these pages. Unless otherwise indicated, all translations from the French are my own.

CHAPTER ONE

Introduction: Laocoon

Other notable philhellenes of Pierre de Coubertin's era had their names associated with one or another of the Greek mythic heroes: Schliemann and Odysseus, Nietzsche and Dionysus, Giraudoux and Hector. While Coubertin himself was not given to such poetic conceits, his life finds its classical sign and metaphor in the figure of Laocoon, whom Winckelmann, Lessing, Herder, Schiller, and Goethe had made into the very icon and "password" of European Hellenism.[1]

In a sense the Trojan priest belonged to the Coubertin family. The famous Laocoon statuary was discovered on Wednesday, January 14, 1506, on the estate of Felice de Fredi (di Freddis, de Fredy) near Rome.[2] Felice de Fredi, who later donated the marble group to the Pope,[3] is the earliest known member of the Italian noble line ancestral to the French lineage of Frédy (later Frédy de Coubertin), which appears to have branched off earlier, in the fourteenth century.[4] No child of Coubertin grew up without pilgrimages to the Vatican to see the statue, without reading the story again and again in their Virgils, and, in Pierre's case, without daily confronting the family connection to the ancients in his father's painting of the donation of the statue to the Holy Father.[5] Greek myth, aristocratic service, and the Catholic church joined in that image so prominently displayed in the family apartments on the rue Oudinot.

In the *Aeneid*, Laocoon, priest of Poseidon,[6] warns the Trojans against the Achaean horse. His spear thuds into its belly, and the horse's "vaults rang hollow." But the treachery of Sinon intervenes, and while Laocoon is offering sacrifice on the beach, two monstrous serpents rise from the sea to strangle and devour him and his two children. The Trojans, taking this as a final sign of Laocoon's sacrilege, proceed to their own ordained doom.

As a boy, Pierre de Coubertin is reported to have interpreted the myth to mean "the fate of those who too often tell the truth to those who cannot yet understand it."[7] It may also be read as indicating the fate of those who, blinded by moral passion to the fact that the gods they serve are themselves caught up in a larger web of destinies, fail to grasp sufficiently the

1

impact of their actions. Both readings capture much of the life of Pierre de Coubertin, as a private man and a public figure.

As E. M. Butler notes, the Laocoon group is a deeply "ironical symbol,"[8] an image of "noble simplicity and serene greatness" to its original admirers, while to modern detractors it belongs to "a theatrically rationalistic art such as only appears in this mingling of brutality and sensitiveness, of ice-cold calculation and dazzling craftsmanship in periods of decadence and decline."[9] Commentaries on Coubertin's life are polarized just so, either hagiographies or hagiolatries. Moreover, even among the two or three writers who have tried to understand before declaring themselves, judgments on the man's life and his creation have too often been substituted for one another. This too is reminiscent of Laocoon, whose eighteenth-century partisans were uncertain whether to see the statue through the story, or the story through the statue. And it mattered which. The literary communicants produced, in Butler's words, "a monument in which the effect of tragedy they (unlike the artists) strove to efface predominates on the whole."[10] Whether or not it so predominates over the life and main work of Coubertin, it is the purpose of this book to explore.

All of the themes of that life were oddly recapitulated in his death, on September 2, 1937, in a Geneva park, at the age of 74.[11] Through his final years, he had been resolute, though tortured by adversity, active and celebrated, yet marginal and alone. Each morning began with exercise, rowing on Lake Geneva or briskly marching through the gardens of Lausanne and Ouchy. After lunch, he would enter his study, precisely ornamented with souvenirs and testamentaries, to spend the afternoon composing still another hortatory pamphlet, historical notice, or charter for educational reform. But in his last years, he wrote for no certain audience, he rowed in circles, and he took his walks alone.

Coubertin's domestic life was a shambles and an agony. His once considerable fortune had long since been exhausted by his projects, depression, and war, and at the age of seventy-two, he sought paying work and failed to find it.[12] Mme. de Coubertin and he survived on the charity of friends and civic authorities, who honored them to keep them alive. Their rooms were small, but not inelegant, not unsuitable for French nobility. But they were donated rooms, and while in public the baron and his wife kept up a front of independence, in private they could not.[13] The baroness nagged him incessantly with their poverty and gained small revenge for her humiliation by denying him pocket money.[14] In his private diaries, he called her "*le chat*."[15] But their children's fates, rather than penury, were the real source of their great remorse. As an infant, the eldest, Jacques, had been forgotten in the sun, and the stroke he suffered left him hopelessly retarded through his fifty-six years of life.[16] The daughter, Renée, was a bright and artistic girl, a delight in a family of painters. But her father was perpetually away on his mission, and her mother, unhinged by guilt for the first-born, overwhelmed her until Renée fell prey to severe emotional disturbances, and never married or otherwise found peace with her life. The parents blamed each other and tried to find some solace in two nephews who served as surrogates for their own maimed children. Then they were killed at the front in the Great War.[17] These deaths had ensured that with Pierre the ancient line of de Coubertin would end.

His marriage had begun in rebellious love, as we shall see. One story has it that Marie Rothan won his heart with her faith in his grand scheme while others were scoffing at him.[18] Eyquem insists that, "in spite of her strange behaviors, her admiration and devotion for this man whom she tortured stayed unchanged until his death."[19] Perhaps, though in the 1930s she traveled often to escape him. She was away that final September.

All deaths in some measure highlight the ironies of the lives they end. The strangers who rushed to Pierre de Coubertin in the Parc de la Grange that day likely saw only a stricken old man in white whiskers and the frock coat of another era. They could not have perceived his interior struggle between domestic tragedy and public vocation; neither had most of those who read his books or listened to his speeches over the years. Coubertin was a confessional man only in the older, moral sense of the word. His celebrity, too, was not of the new twentieth-century sort; it attached more to what he had placed in the public world than to his person. Indeed, his creation had stolen his celebrity from him, in effect denying him that measure of personal adulation he desperately required in later years to assuage the sorrows of his family life. In exchange, he was given back not a retinue, but an eponym, something rarer and more lasting, but chimerical and dreamlike. To multitudes around the world he was and is known as le Rénovateur, the man who resurrected the Olympic Games, guided their rebirth, and set them on the road to becoming a global cultural institution of unprecedented kind and proportion. Though the idea was not his alone and did not originate with him, though his labors were assisted at every step by many others, no modern institution of comparable significance owes so much to a single man. Yet, in the end, that man could not find in it enough to satisfy his life.

Besides his familial misery, he was frustrated in his ardent desire to succeed as an *homme de lettres* and to be recognized by his native France. As Eugen Weber pithily remarks, speaking of the French celebration of the Coubertin centennial in 1964: "There were ceremonies, speeches, and a plaque was placed in the aula of the Sorbonne where, in 1894, Coubertin had won his greatest victory. Paris and a number of French cities named streets, squares, and stadiums after Coubertin. But Coubertin was dead."[20] Then, too, no one had been willing to supply him a portfolio for the "broader" educational and social reforms that obsessed him during his last thirty years: founding "workers' universities," teaching "universal history," and reestablishing the classical Greek gymnasium as the civic center of the modern town. He knew that he had failed with each of these, but, like Sisyphus, he could not stand down from the grandiose projects he carried with him into soberer and more "realistic" times.

But the most potent factor in his discontent, I think, was his inability to apprehend the meaning and to understand the role being assumed by the Olympic festival he had bequeathed to the modern world. Though slowed by age and circumstance, his social vision broadened through the '20s and '30s, and, having delivered the day-to-day administration of the Olympic Movement into other hands, he gained some distance from which to contemplate it. But in the final reckoning, his eyes remained too focused by the period in which he had forged an identity and the Olympics had been reborn, the 1880s and '90s. He failed to see that the Games had become not something different from, but something much more than, what he had intended. From a small public novelty of the Belle Époque, an athletic competition wrapped in a prepotent historical conceit and adorned with verdant social claims, the Games had been transformed in four decades into a crucible of symbolic force into which the world poured its energies, and a stage upon which it played out its hopes and its terrors, every four years.

Cause and effect, function, utility, program: these were the tendons of Coubertin's intellect, though his heart inclined in other directions. He was an unshakable rationalist, though he placed his rationalism and pragmatism in the service of the nonrational. His taste was for clear and distinct ideas, though it was the clarity and distinctness of his will that centered his life; and passion, not systematic thinking, his writings. Like so many of his generation and class, he tumbled between a philosophical idealism and a social pragmatism that he identified respectively with the French heritage and the England and America he observed and loved. Though he often celebrated and contributed mightily to what we might call "expressive culture," it was by the standards of "instrumental culture" that he weighed and judged and, in the end, misjudged his own life.

If, as is now widely opined, the problem of meaning is the problem of the twentieth century, then Coubertin remained rooted in the nineteenth. He knew what he wanted the Olympic revival to *do*, and he was perfectly capable of recognizing when it "did" other than intended. But he never saw through to puzzling about what the Games might *mean* in and of themselves. He never came to understand human creation, circulation, and interpretation of meaning as an autonomous—at least intellectually autonomous—activity and problem. Or, phrased more accurately, he could not analytically conceive of *meaning* as a form of *doing*, though his very identity and the nature of the Games themselves were conditioned by this relationship, as I will show. The questions he asked of the Games at the end of his career were the same ones he asked at the beginning: have they induced social reform, contributed substantially to world peace, reintroduced Western culture to its flesh, encouraged international understanding? Of course, these questions are finally the important ones, but as recent anthropology and social thought have recognized, answering them depends first upon discovering what events mean to the actors who produce and engage in them. As I shall demonstrate in a subsequent work, the Olympic Games are first and foremost an immense playground, marketplace, theater, battlefield, church, arena, festival, and Broadway of cultural images, symbols, and meanings. Whatever else they do— including such essentially nonsymbolic things as get people killed or save their lives, line or empty their pockets, ensure their happiness or steal it from them—the Games do because of their capacity to attract, amass, ramify, and distribute vast symbolic energies. Coubertin never understood this, and so, ironically, the true character of his creation escaped him. Like Laocoon, this was the real tragedy of his last years and days.

Eleven months before his death, Coubertin's voice echoed round the Berlin Olympic stadium through gramophone recording and loudspeaker.[21] The 110,000 assembled, an overseas radio network, and the first commercial television audience of any size heard him say: "The important thing in the Olympic Games is not winning but taking part. Just as in life, the aim is not to conquer but to struggle well."[22] The spectacle flowed on without further thought of him, and he, for his part, was no more capable than most of understanding the degree to which Olympism was locked in mortal combat with its very hosts during those Games. In a speech written for the closing of the Berlin Olympics, a speech no one asked him to deliver, he wrote: "The swayings and struggles of history will continue, but little by little knowledge will replace dangerous ignorance; mutual understanding will soften unthinking hatreds. Thus the edifice at which I have labored for half a century will be strengthened. May the German people and their head be thanked for what they have just accomplished. And you, athletes, remember the sun-kindled fire which has come to you from Olympia to lighten and warm our epoch."[23] It is easy to read this final testament as the pitiful delusion of a generous, but senile and romantic, humanist washed ashore among men who aim to conquer and not to struggle well. The truth is in every way more complex.

Coubertin was born with the Third Republic and came of age defending it against royalism, *revanchisme*, Boulangism, and radicalism. Fascism he never imagined, nor did he in the least suspect that the Third Republic would die just after him. In his writings and public life, moreover, he

maintained a curious and revealing compartmentalization. He publicized
the Republic, courted assignments from its ministries, sought the company of its politicians and statesmen, and celebrated their achievements in
the volumes of political history he wrote. Though he himself refused to
stand for Parliament, he seems to have considered himself, proudly and
with reason, a political man. Yet in his Olympic work, he regarded politicians as the enemy and proclaimed Olympism beyond ideology
altogether, even while manipulating political forces to his own ends and
promoting the "democratic" character of the Games and the Movement.
He could claim for the Games a central place in human affairs which he
knew to be eminently political and simultaneously act as if ideology and
politics were mere epiphenomena to be "transcended."

Coubertin never overcame, or indeed clearly recognized, this fundamental discontinuity in his thought, a discontinuity whose origins I will
explore. Yet even as it made him personally blind to certain of the real
relations between the Olympics and their shifting social contexts, this
failure of insight worked to the world's advantage. The dramatic embodiment of two competing world views—that men are what the social and
cultural structures they inhabit make of them; that men are what they
become when, for a time, they suspend those structures—is, at the most
general level, the source of the evocative power of the Olympic Games.
This same unfinished struggle dominated Coubertin's search for personal
identity, and he bequeathed it to Olympism. It was also staged a final time
in his obsequies.

After a private funeral, Coubertin was buried in the Bois de Vaux in
Lausanne, almost within sight of the present I.O.C. headquarters at
Vidy. But first, in accordance with instructions written into his will, his
heart was cut out of his corpse, placed in a white-satin-lined wooden box,
and sent to Greece. There, on March 26, 1938, a remarkable ceremony
took place at Archaia Olympia.[24]

Crown Prince Paul arrived to officiate. His sober military dress reflected the conviction of Metaxas and the throne as to the immediate peril
to Greece from the Germans, who were then annexing Austria. Paul's
uniform offered an ironic commentary on that which he had come to
Olympia to honor. The throne which he had refused in the stalemate of
1920 was to fall to him nine years later, in 1947, when his prestige as an
emblem of Greek national unity would afford him an important role in the
preservation of constitutional government in the midst of civil war. Yet it
was as honorary president of the Hellenic Olympic Committee and partisan
of Coubertin and the Olympic Movement that he came to Olympia that
day. From Paul's father and grandfather, without whose patronage and
enthusiasm the first modern Olympics would not have taken place in
1896, to Paul's son, who would become Olympic champion and I.O.C.

member in the 1960s, the royal family found in Olympism powerful symbols to meld the international character of their rule with the sincere desire to be accepted as "Greek" by the Greek people. Besides the patronage of Olympic Games, the other means they favored to this end was war. Paul's appearance in uniform could not but recall his father and his uncles happily leading the Greek army to disaster in 1897, just after and, perhaps, in part because of the success of the first Olympic Games.

After brief addresses by Count Berthier de Sauvigny, I.O.C. member in France,[25] Count Alexandre Mercati, Coubertin's old comrade in the making of the Athens Games, Count Henri de Baillet-Latour, the Belgian who was Coubertin's successor as I.O.C. president, and M. C. Georgopoulos, Greek minister of public worship, the heart was prayed over and blessed by an Orthodox priest. Then Paul, ascending member of the royal house of Schleswig-Holstein and crown prince of the Greeks by grace of plebiscite and foreign power, reverently lifted the heart from the altar. In deep concentration, he installed the relic of the French republican aristocrat, whose quite different fame resided equally in an interfingering of internationalism and Hellenism, in the base of a gleaming marble stele in the shadow of the mysterious Kronos hill within the sacred precinct.[26]

Coubertin's uncanny talent for symbolic invention showed even in these posthumous rites he ordered for himself. They have been called "a final piece of theatre,"[27] and certainly Coubertin may have wished, as did Renan, that his death would be "one of the finest moral spectacles of our age."[28] But something rather more and rather different was achieved in these strangely appropriate last rites. In them, *race, moment*, and *milieu*—the grand trinity of Hippolyte Taine, who had helped start Coubertin on his journey half a century before—were confounded one last time. So were the oppositions between pagan humanism and Christianity, the ancient and the modern, *prouesse* and hierarchy, marginality and aristocracy which figured so strongly in Coubertin's life and achievement. But great symbols do not merely confóund such binary oppositions, they wring emotional expression from them, exchanging logical and historical clarity for performative verisimilitude. In Pierre de Coubertin's necrophany, there was much "true-seeming." He had finally placed his heart where his heart was. Raised by nobles and notables, he was, in the end, buried by them. But if his achievements were born in privilege, it was their absorption into "popular" culture that ensured his memory.

CHAPTER TWO

Noble Works, Glorious Examples, Generous Sacrifices

~~~✦✦✦~~~

Prouesse *and* Patronage

Family tradition holds that the Frédys entered France and established themselves at Dreux, near Paris, prior to 1400.[1] This is reasonable speculation so far unconfirmed. All sources agree, however, that Pierre Frédy *dit* Sieur de la Motte was ennobled by Louis XI, whom he served as chamberlain, in March 1477. The original documents are described as "lettres écrites en latin, signé Lois, & plus bas, *Per regem*, Picot,"[2] and their seal is still held by the family in a perfect state of preservation.[3] The original warrant was registered with the Chambre des comptes on January 4, 1486, and the family was maintained noble in 1508, 1519, 1553, 1572, 1629,[4] 1661, 1668, 1700, 1717, and 1739.[5] In 1822, three weeks before Pierre's father was born, his grandfather, Julien-Bonaventure Frédy de Coubertin, was made hereditary baron by *lettres patentes*, in the general reorganization of privileges under Louis XVIII.

According to Bonald, "The aristocracy is the hereditary participation in legislative [policy-making] power; the nobility is the hereditary service to the executive [policy-enacting] power."[6] Coubertin's ancestors enjoyed roles of both sorts. Alphonse Frédy,[7] who died in 1553,[8] served as royal lawyer and judge in Montfort l'Amaury, and as *prévot provincial* for the constables and marshals of France, during the reigns of Francis I and Henry II. His third child by Marie Bluté, Jean Frédy (1518–98), was a Parisian merchant who made a fortune in the spice trade and used it to acquire the *seigneuries* of de la Verrie and de Coubertin, the latter (in the Chevreuse not far from Versailles) in 1577. From his second marriage, to one Catherine Boisdin,[9] there issued the second Jean de Frédy (1592–1677) who became senior counselor to Parliament. Of his children, two were notable: Médéric Frédy, seigneur de Coubertin (1625–87),[10] royal councilor, commissioner of war, treasurer general, and *payeur des rentes* at the Hôtel de Ville of Paris; and Michel Frédy, seigneur des Mallets (Mollets) (1629–85), who served as royal councilor and senior controller general of revenues at the Hôtel de Ville. When Médéric's son Martin Bernard (1658–1736), who succeeded to the offices of his father, died without male heir, the *seigneurie* de Coubertin went to François Frédy, seigneur des Mallets (1668–1742), eldest son of Michel.

François had a distinguished career as a soldier and a naval officer in the service of Louis XIV. Captain of the king's ships, he was raised to the *chevalerie* of Saint-Louis in 1712. The previous year, he had married Marie Morel, daughter of an official of the Paris law court and great-niece of Cyrano de Bergerac. With moneys amassed from the West Indies Company by a cousin, François built the château de Coubertin.[11] His son Pierre Frédy (1716–78) was appointed to the Cour des aides in 1744, and *his* son, François-Louis (1752–1807),[12] lawyer to Parliament, continued the privilege until the Cour des aides was suppressed by the Revolution in 1790. As "Citizen Frédy" and "Frédy *dit* Coubertin," François-Louis survived the Terror. Not so his paternal uncle, Henri-Louis Frédy de Coubertin, who was "exiled several times by *lettres de cachet* from Louis XVI for having told the king the truth, and guillotined in 1790 for having told the truth to the revolutionaries."[13]

Julien-Bonaventure Frédy (1768–1871), François-Louis's son, served Napoleon as a cavalry officer attached to the general staff. He became a subprefect and a consul at Cuxhaven in Germany, and later was aide de camp to the duke of Luxembourg. While it was the Bourbon Louis XVIII who awarded him the Légion d'honneur and made him hereditary baron in 1821, he did not hesitate to serve Louis Philippe as a bodyguard in the 1830s,[14] prompting one commentator to remark, "Les monarchistes seraient-ils plus royalistes que les rois?" This devotion to the crown, no matter who wore it, and his Freemasonry, were both rejected by the son born to Julien-Bonaventure and his wife, the daughter of the marquis de Pardieu. Charles Frédy, baron de Coubertin (1822–1908), was, as we shall see, a staunch legitimist and conservative Catholic—positions against which his own son, Pierre de Coubertin, would in turn rebel.

Pierre's mother's line was no less well stocked with notables. She was the daughter of Charles Gigault de Crisenoy (1787–1835) and his second wife, Euphrasie Eudes de Catteville de Mirville (d. 1887). Originally from l'Île-de-France, the Gigault family traced its patrimony to Étienne Gigault, the son of a hat merchant.[15] Born in Auxerre in 1695, he was made seigneur de la Salle in 1737, by Louis XV in whose court he served as councilor-secretary. His heir, Étienne-Pascal (1720–88), acquired the *seigneurie* of Crisenoy in Brie around 1754, and held appointments as royal secretary, controller general of audiences at the high chancellery, and *fermier général*. Achille-Étienne Gigault de Crisenoy (1756–1802) was a counselor at the Châtelet, a Parliament lawyer and in 1797, a deputy to the Five Hundred. His son, Étienne-Charles, Pierre de Coubertin's grandfather, chevalier of the Légion d'honneur and aide-major of the National Guard, was made hereditary baron in 1822, three months after the same privilege fell to the Frédys de Coubertin.

Pierre's maternal grandmother belonged to an ancient Norman family distinguished through the generations by its soldiers, first remembered from the Hundred Years' War. Mathieu Eudes fought at the battle of the Écluse, Regnault Eudes was ennobled in 1369, and Vincent Eudes was an officer in the guard of the archbishop of Rouen. Eight generations later, the military tradition continued with Alexandre-François Eudes de Catteville, knight of Saint-Louis, captain of the Compagnie des gendarmes dauphins, and, in 1784, *maréchal de camp*. For his services, he was made marquis de Mirville by Louis XVI. His son Alexandre-Pierre, Pierre de Coubertin's great-grandfather, fought as a major in the army of the Condé.

The *seigneurie* of Mirville, some two kilometers from Bolbec in Normandy, was a medieval fief, originally in the hands of one Guillaume Selles, from whom it passed in 1431 to the Dumesnildot family, ancient *nobles de race*. The du Bouillonnays (-ney), another very old Norman family (ennobled *aux francs-fiefs* in 1470), acquired it by marriage in 1592, and, in turn, one of their daughters brought it with her into the Eudes de Catteville in 1669. One hundred and seventy-seven years later, the château and lands of Mirville were the dowry of Pierre de Coubertin's mother. It was on this estate, rather than the paternal lands near Saint-Rémy-les-Chevreuse, that Pierre and his siblings spent their childhoods.[16]

Only the trunks of the Coubertin family tree have been coursed here. Pierre would have known also the branches (with their yet heavier load of distinguished gentlemen), additional houses and lands connected with his family by marriage, and other historical events and personnages associated with his ancestors. Further archival research should be undertaken to recover these.

But here the goal is not exhaustive historiography. While this genealogy is more complete than those supplied by previous writers on Coubertin, it is offered as assistance in a task overlooked by these authors. Each rather conventionally remarks that Coubertin's aristocratic heritage "weighed upon him," and, proclaiming the indubitable, each asserts that his family history influenced his work. But excessively simplistic and presentistic assumptions about "nobility," and outmoded notions of the "automatic" nature of socialization, have prevented any substantial, detailed understanding of the relationship between his heritage and his legacy.

As anthropologists have repeatedly demonstrated, genealogy is linked with much larger social interests than simple ancestor reckoning. In most social groups—peoples, classes, castes, movements, and so on—a family tree is not a mere map of blood ties, but an index and icon of the fundamental values which "blood" represents to that group. And, as a socializing agency, the performance of genealogy—reciting, disputing, verifying, and elaborating it, embodying it in images, coats of arms, portraits, documents, gestures, dress, and styles of comportment—provides recipes for action in accordance with these fundamental value orientations.

For a young French aristocrat, genealogy was both patrimony and project. By accident of birth, one's name gained mention in an already existing *récit*. But to ensure continued mention, one had to transform oneself from a name to a "name" in adulthood. Instructions for this transformation were found in the "descriptive" materials—in the French case, in the titles, positions, alliances, exploits, progeny, in roughly this order of precedence, joined to ancestors' names and dates in the genealogy.

In literate societies, "mentions" became additionally "places" or "spaces" in a written and illustrated document or chart. *Récits généalogiques* give way to *arbres généalogiques, chartes de noblesse*, and finally to *dictionnaires, annuaires, almanachs*, and (quoting the full title of a work to be cited shortly) *Archives généalogiques et historiques de la noblesse de France ou recueil de preuves, mémoires et notices généalogiques, servant à constater l'origine, la filiation, les alliances et les illustrations religieuses, civiles, et militaires de diverses maisons et familles nobles du royaume.*[17]

As has been pointed out recently, the relative fixity and consistency of the formal principles by which a document is constructed may influence the paradigms for behavior which the document "documents."[18] "Black sheep," for example, may be altogether elided from oral recitations of genealogy, but written genealogies less easily tolerate empty spaces. Lacunae become immediately marked and obvious. Moreover, "completeness" is added to such documents as a purpose and, therefore, as a principle of composition. Consequently, other strategies than elision must be devised for dealing with those ancestors who have deviated from the values and norms intended to be communicated by genealogy to the outside public and to the family young.

One such strategy relies upon the continued importance of oral narratives of family history in literate cultures. Not only do written documents never fully replace oral history in general, but in the particular cases of the not-yet-literate or those denied physical or intellectual access to documents, oral narrative (including exegesis of visual sources of information) is all there is. While the names, dates, birth orders, and so on, of the offending persons must appear in the written genealogies, all mention of them may be eliminated in oral narrative. Or else, if they must be mentioned to establish continuity of descent (as may be the case in nonliterate cultures as well), the speaker's greater control of emphasis and emotion will be used to distract attention from them.

Other strategies of selection and concealment depend upon the established cultural canons shared by written and oral genealogy alike. French noble genealogies always emphasize title and position at the expense of context. Exactly which sovereign was served by which *maréchal*, what the title *écuyer* meant in the sixteenth as opposed to the fourteenth century, the oscillations between ascriptive and achievement criteria for election to the Légion or to the Ordre de Saint-Louis, the number of appointments to the Cour des aides in the *ancien régime* (there were 345): such information is almost never provided by genealogical documents themselves. Thus is true history concealed, as well as revealed, by such "historical" documents. The triumphs of black sheep, no less than the failures of honored exemplars, may be made to disappear under the titles which they bore. And, of course, no information whatever is supplied in these documents as to the characters, personalities, and unique personal experiences—in short, the inner lives—of the "cherished" ancestors.

Where there is developmental conflict, however, such strategies of selective history employed by one generation may turn out instead to structure the curiosities of the next. When the fact of parental selectivity is itself consciously recognized by the young, they may be incited to discover charters for rebellious behavior lurking within the same official family history presented to them by their elders. We have noted how Pierre could cite the opportunism of his grandfather, "plus royaliste que les rois," against the legitimism of his parents. We shall see below how Pierre circumvented official family silence on a maternal great-uncle, a republican priest with "socialist" leanings, and made of him a psychological and literary ancestor-hero. But just as it is too simple to make of Coubertin a "product" of his class and caste, so also it will not do to make of him a straightforward rebel to his heritage. As always, the truth is more complex.

The final entry under Frédy de Coubertin in the 1975 Sereville and Saint-Simon *Dictionnaire de la noblesse française* reads, "To this family belonged the celebrated Rénovateur of the Olympic Games."[19] The last of his lineage, Pierre de Coubertin was the only member of it whose fame would outlive him. While the achievements for which he is acclaimed were without familial precedent and required breaking with aspects of his class, he, nonetheless, "belonged to the family." The persistent structure of values of the French aristocracy and its special fate in the flow of public life in nineteenth-century France must be characterized if the exact contributions of his heritage to his later life and work are to be understood.

Consider the following text, quoted at length from the preface to the first volume of Lainé's *Archives généalogiques et historiques*, published in 1828, at the height of the Restoration.

For civilized man, in whatever condition destiny has him born, it is a precious good which belongs to him alone and which no one else can take away. This sacred and inalienable property is conserved and increased by noble works, by glorious examples and generous sacrifices.

For it, the warrior is enflamed with an emulation which lifts his courage and his sang-froid even to heroism. For it, the magistrate keeps vigil over the sanctuary of the laws to maintain customs and public morality, and the man of genius reaches for the most sublime perceptions of human intelligence. For it, one sees the profound and conscientious jurisconsult offer the support of his eloquence and insight to the innocent and feeble oppressed, and the estimable savant enrich the domain of history and letters with tributes of a sound erudition. And, finally, for it, the distinguished artist adds a brilliant renown or important discoveries to those which already honor his native land, just as, in a career strewn with numberless reefs and dangers without glory, the dignified interpreter of Hippocrates still knows how to ennoble the touching labors of his useful ministry by his disinterested and noble compassion.

This property which nothing can measure, which time cannot limit, and of which each individual is jealous in proportion to the advantages received from it; this fortune which is inseparable from the man, and which the man never finds greater or more real than in misfortune, it is the ever-present shadow of his virtue, it is the measure of his honor and of the respect he enjoys in the world: it is his name.[20]

This text is revealing in part because of the situation of its author. Lainé issued from the middle bourgeoisie, was a soldier, then an industrial accountant. Aspiring to be an *homme de lettres*, in 1814 he entered genealogical research and publishing, a field then booming as noble families scrambled to reestablish titles and *preuves* lost in the Revolution, imperial *annoblis* fretted over their honors, and bourgeois usurpers sought to consolidate their status. After apprenticeships on other publications, Lainé struck out on his own with his *Archives*. Its success depended entirely upon the trust and good will of the noble families who supplied him with their histories and were the principal market for the books. His status depended upon his care with theirs and, above all, on their continued assurance that his conception of the aristocracy matched their own.[21]

In the text, one is struck first of all by the triangular relationship connecting "name" *(nom, honneur, vertu)*, "deeds" *(nobles travaux, beaux exemples, généreux sacrifices)*, and "vocation" *(guerrier, magistrat, homme de génie, jurisconsulte, artiste)*. This structural triangle became a paradigm for action for each new generation of aristocrats. Just as the *nom* which he acquired at birth consisted in the *honneur* accumulated by his ancestors' noble deeds in acceptable fields of action, so to maintain the family *nom* and to gain *honneur* for himself, the young nobleman had to select an appropriate vocation and to perform similar *nobles travaux*. But note that aristocratic *carrières* are not "careers" in the Weberian sense. Aristocrats are supposed to have vocations, not "professions," and certainly not "occupations."

Aristocrats are *guerriers* and not *soldats, magistrats* and not *juges, hommes de génie* and not *professeurs, jurisconsultes* and not *avocats, artistes* and not *peintres.* Aristocrats are called to activity by virtue of their positions. They are not to seek or to occupy positions in rationalized, bureaucratic, formal organizations, offering lifelong security, financial reward, and regular advancement according to fixed rules. Where their vocations bring them into contact with careerists and professionals, that is to say, those of the *classes moyennes,* they must take pains repeatedly to establish their *amateur* status: to demonstrate that they act disinterestedly for the love of the Faith, the Motherland, Nature, Art, Humanity. Actions based upon organizational routines and rational expectations bring no credit to an *homme de noblesse.* The only deeds which bring *honneur* and demonstrate *vertu* are those which belong to a special class of actions called *prouesses* ("feats of prowess").

Jesse R. Pitts, the American sociologist who was the first to emphasize the importance of *prouesse* in French culture generally and in the classical aristocratic ethos in particular, describes it as the search for spontaneous, irreproducible, unique, and conspicuous moral acts, undertaken for honor and not for utility. Though based upon "clearly defined and well-known" *principes* by which the wider society simultaneously recognizes the valor of the act, limits its disruptive potential, and appropriates its felicitous consequences, a feat of prowess is nonetheless a "conspicuously perfect—miraculous—solution by which one person triumphs over a unique situation."[22] *Prouesse* is a matter "of instinct, of intuition, and contingent opportunity," based on sociomoral "rootedness" *(enracinement).* It is not the result of rational deliberation on the basis of systematic knowledge, nor is it a mechanical response to organizational position. Indeed, Pitts argues, the cult of prowess is always in opposition ("dialectical" opposition, I would suggest) with a competing French ethos he terms the "doctrinaire-hierarchical" ("tout et tous, à sa place"),[23] and associates with (among other things) French formalism, demands for deductive chains of reasoning and ideological purity, the Civil Service, tendencies toward centralization of power, and the bourgeoisie as a class.

Such broad conclusions are controversial and need not concern us here.[24] But the concept of *prouesse* will repeatedly prove valuable in our attempt to understand Pierre de Coubertin's life and work in its proper cultural context. Lainé's text, in its very language no less than in its prescriptions, amply illustrates the significance of the cult of *prouesse* in the values of the traditional aristocracy into which Pierre de Coubertin was born.

The long list of his ancestors presented above can now be better felt as he would have felt it—in Lainé's image, as a long and "ever-present shadow" of virtue—and understood more as he would have been led to understand it. The titles, appointments, and offices of his ancestors would have been perceived by him not as ends in themselves, but as the signs of past, and the charters for future, acts of prowess. This is what genealogy, written and performed, official and rebellious, taught him to seek. When at the age of twelve he exclaimed to his mother, "I have a wild passion for France, and I am capable of translating it into sacrifices of every sort,"[25] his adolescent ardor expressed the aristocratic ethos of *prouesse*.

But value structures are no more static and monolithic than are the conditions and possibilities for actions which realize those values. Structures of value not only have a history, they live in history: a fact of which anthropologists and sociologists need continual reminder. The Lainé *préface* gives evidence of its particular moment of composition and of the changed and changing situation of its subjects/audience, as well as of the enduring value configurations of their class.

In the very first line we read that a man's name is a precious good "in whatever condition destiny [*le sort* and not *Dieu!*] has him born." While this quick nod toward the new equality, this acknowledgment that shop-keepers and schoolmasters (and peasants?) too have "names," is immediately swallowed in the following catalogue, Lainé returns in a page to make it explicit. "If the salutary and insatiable desire to distinguish himself, to stand out from the crowd, to wrest his name from the lot of shameful oblivion or to keep it unblemished and respectable incessantly goads the heart of the man of even the humblest rank, to what height of feeling must it not carry him whom birth has placed in a higher sphere."[26] Not only are certain post-Revolutionary claims acknowledged here, but such a use of lower class strivings to goad the nobility would have been abhorrent in similar documents from the *ancien régime*. Moreover, while Lainé has in mind the rallying of discouraged and disenfranchised nobles, his linkage of the cultivation of name-honor with the social "advantages received from it" implies a distinctively post-1789 explanation of the "dishonorableness" of the lower orders.

Lainé devotes pages, however, to denouncing, on all manner of grounds, revolutionary claims of full equality. "One knows," he writes, "how the Revolution realized the promises of this sorrowful and fatal delusion."[27] Nothing less would have been tolerated from him by his audience. At the same time, his refusal to entertain seriously the possibility of full return of noble privileges by the Restoration reflected the mainstream of sober opinion among the aristocracy of the 1820s and '30s. But it is hardly resignation which he counsels: "Nobility is no longer a privilege; it is a distinction, and even a burden, since, deprived of all past advantages, its obligations wholly remain. But this burden of a respectable existence and name is dear to those for whom honor suffices; it is dear to those who have reclaimed from the ancient heritage of their ancestors

nothing but a sword for the defense of the legitimate throne."[28] The
responsibility for *prouesses* has not only not disappeared, but its "dis-
connection" from social-structural privilege has given it added moral
beauty and weight.

Nothing could be more wrongheaded and presentistic than to see here
only empty rationalizations, attempts to put the best face on a bad situation. Such "native interpretations" are not merely rationalizations but
attempts to give meaning to traumatic events, and moral strategies for
social continuity and survival. Moreover, suggestions that after 1789, the
aristocracy were placed once and for all outside of the national life, totally
"isolated," "withdrawn," "anachronistic," simply discard history. The
monarchy of Charles X was not that of Louis XVI, but when Lainé's
words were written, there was nonetheless a Bourbon on the throne.

This is not in any way to suggest a homogenous aristocratic response to
the social and political circumstances of the period.[29] Indeed, there is a
signal ambivalence in the passage just cited, an ambivalence which neatly
reflects the dilemmas of action for the contemporary nobility. How were
they to interpret *faire des prouesses?* Did all deeds of honor, by honor
suffice? Or was it solely in the defense of the throne, by the sword if
necessary, that opportunities for prowess were located?

There is a revealing diatribe, revealingly banished to a footnote in the
Lainé text. After the celebration of the *guerrier* and the *magistrat* discussed
above, we suddenly find him attacking previous writers for over-
emphasizing "great men of war, celebrated magistrates, and illustrious
prelates" as "models for posterity." The real debt which France owes to
her nobility, he now insists, resides in its achievements "in the leisures of
peace." The foundation of cities, towns, churches, a multitude of religious
retreats, public refuges for the sick, the old, and the unfortunate,
establishments for primary education, *collèges,* and academies: "these are
the unrecognized fruits of this regime of privileges which the vulgar man
never speaks of without a certain consternation."[30]

Behind the elegaic bitterness lie an adjustment and a hortatory summons to the present day. Though he speaks of "charity and munificence,"
Lainé in fact recasts *noblesse oblige* into *patronage,* places it squarely in the
aristocratic tradition, and marks it as an option for the present-day aristocracy. *Patronage*—that is, organized acts of *prouesse* in which the lower
orders serve as direct objects and not as merely validating spectators[31]
—forms a second, alternative, and, in the context of the new order,
more dependable and widely available paradigm for virtue and action
through which aristocrats might claim a valued place in the changed conditions of national life while preserving continuity with their traditional
ethos. In response to social constraints and necessities that grow ever more
forceful through the middle decades of the nineteenth century, *patronage* is

steadily transformed from an avocation (appropriate for the retired or female noble and, perhaps, youngest sons) to a vocation as legitimate (or almost) as that of the *guerrier* or the *homme de génie* in the new order.

But even by Pierre de Coubertin's time, as we shall see, *patronage* never fully replaces the more classical solutions to the triangular drama of name, exploit, and calling. Already in Lainé, we can recognize the attempt to meld *patronage* with "unique moral acts" in a new, joint form of *prouesse*. Themes recessive in the conduct of traditional vocations gain emphasis and urgency. The "profound and conscientious jurisconsult" is distinguished not only by "his eloquence and insight" but also by his "offering of their support to the innocent and feeble oppressed." Moreover, vocations of once-questionable appropriateness gain a new pedigree. The physician, or rather, the "dignified interpreter of Hippocrates," may pursue "the touching labors of his useful ministry" because he *still* knows how to ennoble [them] . . . by his disinterested and noble compassion." As for the "estimable savant" who "enriches the domain of history and letters," we shall see how Pierre de Coubertin tried to combine such a public identity with the *patronage* of *collèges* and *lycées,* and how the novel and unorthodox realm of athletics, with its crystalline dynamics of structure and *prouesse*, delivered him his opportunity.

For Pierre's grandfather the sword and the throne yet sufficed. Through his military career, with its aura of prowetic service to the Motherland, Julien-Bonaventure maintained continuity of role and principle. Service to the throne took precedence for him over who sat upon it, Bonaparte, Bourbon, or Orleanist. However, for his son Charles, Pierre's father, honor lay solely in defense of the *legitimate* throne. Eight years old during the Revolution of 1830, Charles came of age with the July Monarchy and disliked it. While his father knew to prefer any monarchy to none at all, Charles had never lived without a king and thought he could afford to be more particular. Orleanism, in blood and in principle, seemed to him a regression which, far from preserving the monarchy from republican forces, delivered it to them. In his generation, and among men such as himself, the fatal split took place among the royalists. From the legitimism which supplied character and identity to his youth, Charles never deviated, even unto the death of the comte de Chambord in 1883. Moreover, legitimism developed from a political strategy in the 1830s and '40s into a distinctive subcultural milieu during the Second Empire[32] and the early years of the Third Republic.[33] It was in this milieu that Charles de Coubertin attempted to confine and to raise his children.

Unfortunately, little is known about Charles. No manuscripts, letters, or memoirs have come to light, and Pierre—for reasons we shall explore—never wrote directly about his father. It is impossible, therefore, to chart in any detail the course of his life and the progress of his opinions.

But his paintings contain valuable revelations, for painting was his vocation and the compass of his public existence.

The *Discovery of the Laocoon, Rome, 1506*, mentioned above, hung in the
Salon of 1846. He followed it in 1847 with *Scene of Frolic: Interior of a
Cabaret* and in 1848 with *Three Italian Poetries* explained as "the three
founders of Italian literature in the fourteenth century, Dante, Petrarch,
and Boccaccio, personified by the women they celebrated in song: Beatrice
is the symbol of religious poetry; Fiametta personifies free and light verse;
Laura, refined and lyrical style."[34]

There would be a short delay before Charles de Coubertin could enjoy
seeing his poetic women hang in the Louvre. On the very day of Ledru-
Rollin's election to the provisional government,[35] as "citizen minister of
the interior" he issued a proclamation subsuming the Académie des beaux
arts and the museums under his ministry and summoning the artists to
elect the Salon jury. It is doubtful that the baron de Coubertin joined the
conclave of March 5 (in which Cogniet, Ingres, and Delacroix received the
most votes).

After absenting himself entirely from the Salon of 1849, he was represented in 1850 by *Caravan Halt at the Wells of Beersheba in the Desert South of
Hebron* and *Episode of the Plague in Milan*. The latter, inspired by a passage
in Manzoni's *The Betrothed*, portrayed a woman suffering over her dead
child, and, likely, the artist's mood over the events of the day.[36] Though it
cannot be proved, Charles's absence from the first three Salons[37] after the
coup d'état of Louis Napoleon was likely a personal protest against this
regime which he detested, or at least against the congress of *le monde artiste*
with its functionaries.[38]

In 1857, he returned with three "Roman" paintings: *Pontifical Mass on
Christmas Day at St. Peter's in Rome, Promenades of a Roman Cardinal*, and
Fried Fish and Vegetable Stands in Rome. His reaction to the purchase of the
second of these canvases by Napoleon III himself has gone unrecorded.[39]
In 1859, Coubertin showed *Ballplayers in the Colosseum* and *The Last Born:
Woman of Chioggia*.

On July 3, 1861, Charles's work was decorated, though the *prix du salon*
with which his son's biographers have credited him[40] was in fact an honorable mention, one of 110 given that year.[41] The cited canvas was *The
Pontifical Cortege*, a "proposal for a frieze." Two other paintings were
shown in the same Salon, *The Pigeons of St. Mark's in Venice* and *Good Friday
in Palermo, Sicily*.[42]

The 1863 Salon catalogue lists *Death of Reverend Father de Ravignan*[43]
and, under "public monuments," a group of murals, *Holy Litanies*, commissioned for the choir of the Chevreuse church near the Coubertin estate.
In 1864 *The Martyr's Last Mass* was accepted and, in 1865, he showed *The
Death of Saint Stanislas Kotska*, destined for the Jesuit Gésu church on the rue
de Sèvres. That same year, he was made chevalier (the lowest rank) in the

Légion d'honneur by order of the very emperor he is said to have despised. Whether his commissions as a religious painter overcame the fact that he had never won a medal; whether, in his case, the Légion was an impersonal Napoleonic mechanism aimed to attract the support of another noble; what sort of behind-the-scenes politicking by his teachers and patrons went on; none of this is known. What is known is that he accepted. Just as the flame of legitimist opposition dimmed in the face of republican threat, so too it could wane in the matter of conventional royalist honors.[44] For very different sorts of *prouesse*, in a very different social context, Charles joined his father in the Légion. It was doubtless important to both of them.

Though *hors concours*, Charles continued to exhibit in the Salons of the Second Empire. He stuck to familiar themes with his *Saint Rose's Childhood* in 1867, and his *Departure of the Missionaries* (destined for the Séminaire des missions) in 1869. But he added portraiture to his repertoire in 1867 with *Portrait of Mme. la baronne de Coubertin* and with *Brother and Sister: Portraits* (Marie and Pierre) in 1868.[45]

Church, family, nobility, "La France," the classical heritage: these were the constant themes of Charles de Coubertin's paintings. Taken together they configured in the past and celebrated in the present a conservative moral geography which might conveniently be passed off as anachronism in the midst of far-reaching social change. Yet, as Robert Locke puts it, "What made the legitimists anachronisms in their society was not so much that they believed in a moral order but the specific moral order in which they believed."[46] In the 1860s, rather than the '70s about which Locke is writing, that "specific moral order" had far too many partisans to be passed off as mere nostalgia.

Nor will it do to see painting and painting such subjects as mere withdrawal. What looks like withdrawal from the outside often appears from the inside as resistance. Parisian painters were anything but a community of the withdrawn. While painting offered Charles a satisfactory outlet for the class ethic of *prouesse*, the Parisian artistic milieu was also a microcosm of the seething social and cultural currents of the day. Besides the examples of direct interest by the authorities in the Salons already given, mention may be made of the Salon des Refusés and of Napoleon striking Courbet's *The Bathers* with his riding crop. These were the days of Delacroix, the scandal over Manet's *Olympia*,[47] Cézanne, Renoir; but also of the comte de Nieuwerkerke[48] and the "triumphs" of academism, *le style Second-Empire*, and bourgeois tastes. It was the epoch chronicled by Castagnary and anatomized by Baudelaire. As for Charles de Coubertin, it is not surprising that he refused to convey his politics more directly in his art, say, by painting crowds of weeping Frenchmen surrounding Charles X as he sailed from Cherbourg.[49] To serve their designs for the future, men like Coubertin had, in the words of J. Lainé, "to confine themselves to recalling the monuments of the past without attacking the institutions of the present."[50] To do more would give comfort and ammunition to the *partis de mouvement*.

Castagnary gives Coubertin a single mention and that to fill out a list of "pensionnaires de la Villa Médicis," denizens of academic style and thought without a spark of originality: "One sees at a glance how painters like MM. Cazes and Michel Dumas, pupils of Ingres; Chazal and Coubertin, students of Picot; and Jobbé-Duval and Mazerolles, students of Gleyre are able to paint their mythological or religious scenes. These gentlemen carry on for their masters like the Macedonian generals carried on for Alexander the Great."[51] The evaluation of quality and the art-historical judgment of academism are right enough, but the politicomoral content of Coubertin's painting eludes the critic.

Baudelaire had a good word for Chazal,[52] for Coubertin not a jingle. Indeed, had Baudelaire even noticed the baron's painting, he would surely have numbered the artist among his "apes of sentiment."[53] But Baudelaire's raffish genius perceived in the great tradition of the schools an opening to the "heroism" and the "epic side of modern life."

> It is true that the great tradition has been lost, and that the new one is not yet established. But what *was* this great tradition, if not a habitual, everyday idealization of ancient life—a robust and martial form of life, a state of readiness on the part of each individual, which gave him a habit of gravity in his movements, and of majesty, or violence in his attitudes: To this should be added a public splendor which found its reflection in private life. Ancient life was a great *parade*. It ministered above all to the pleasure of the eye, and this day-to-day paganism has marvellously served the arts.[54]

Though Baudelaire might have been shocked at the application, this insight describes much of the aesthetic of the aristocratic journeyman Charles de Coubertin. The catalogue explication of *The Pontifical Cortege* apparently written by the painter, makes this plain: "Seated in his *sedia gestatoria*, surrounded by the officers of the Swiss and Noble Guards, the swords of the Catholic cantons, prelates and chamberlains of his court, preceded by a Roman senator, cardinals, patriarchs, and bishops of the Church, and followed by the superior generals of the religious orders, Pope Pius IX is carried processionally on all the principal feasts of the year to the foot of the great altar of Saint Peter."[55]

Pierre de Coubertin's rebellion would take him far from his father's world and his father's views, but much of Charles de Coubertin was carried over into his son's existence. Without approving, Baudelaire divined that the task of configuring modernity could seek its "figures" in the idealization of ancient life. While disapproving of Baudelaire, Pierre de Coubertin joined him in valuing "the true form of paganism."[56] For the

ecclesiastical processions of his father's paintings, Coubertin would exchange a vision of the ancient parade of the athletes into the Olympic
stadium. He would find his ministry to the pleasures of the eye not in
painted pictures, but in the living canvas of the modern spectacle. He
would make a career of drawing fanciful "ballplayers in the Colosseum"
off museum walls, out of art, and into motion. Performing anew, they
would play new games in new coliseums, to be put up in the center of
modern public life. Along the way, they would make of the "manly arts"
an art form, and claim it to be *the* democratic art form.

In the processions Coubertin would devise for these new "joueurs,"
social categories would pass in review. These would be nations, whole
nations, a whole world of nations, not the estates of the *ancien régime* or
the cities of a single language group. He would originate "a pilgrimage to
the past and a gesture of faith in the future" which belonged to "doing"
and not to "mere imaging." Instead of decorating chapels with noble
scenes of time past, he would seek to enlighten the schools, showing them
how to supply their students with "a robust and martial form of life, a
state of readiness on the part of each individual," a means of welcoming
modernity while transforming it into a noble scene.[57] He would perform
his acts of *prouesse* and *patronage* in favor of a moral order in which all could
partake of *prouesse* and *patronage*.

The End of the Notables

There was nothing instantaneous, predetermined, or predictable about
these visions and inventions. They issued from a long life course as complicated as that of any other human being.

Social scientists have lately employed the concept of "cohort" to mark
the chance intersection between historical events and the schedule of life
cycle stages which a culture prescribes for its members.[58] While the
academic sociologist or psychologist often chooses his cohort-marking
events arbitrarily, public cohort-reckoning is more selective and discern-
ing. Pierre de Coubertin belonged to a cohort recognized by Frenchmen as
especially significant. The landmarks which chart the cohort chart the
fundaments of the modern French experience.

Coubertin was born on New Year's Day, 1863, during the preparations
for the emperor's ominous adventure in Mexico. He reached the canonical
"age of discretion" with the national disaster at Sedan and on the eve of the
Commune. He received his first, solemn holy communion[59] as the constitution of the Republic was being debated. He gained his "maturity" as
the French bourgeoisie gained its, and he married and gave birth to children in the midst of the Dreyfus affair. His retirement on the morrow of

the triumph in World War I, and the coincidence of his funeral with the events which led to the death of the Third Republic have already been noted. The lives of his cohort spanned the vast social changes conventionally lumped under the rubric "modernization": the victory of the democratic political form, the industrialization of the economy, the spread of socialism and "the social question," the secularization of civil society, the absorption of provincial cultures into a national culture, the apparently paradoxical linkage of nationalism and individualism, and the rise of "modernism" in literature, music, and plastic art.

But cohort is only one ring of the circles of identity, and within that ring, there are distinct arcs of experience. The meanings perceived in public events and the meanings these, in turn, supply to constellations of individual lives are differentially configured by value patterns, class positions, and cultural milieus such as those we have been plotting for the mid-century French aristocracy.

The period which followed upon the debacle of the Franco-Prussian War was aptly and unforgettably styled by Daniel Halévy as "la fin des notables."[60] The phrase has since become a "household word,"[61] and it appears again and again in more recent histories of the period.[62] But the success of the phrase obscures the fact that the older generation of notables in the 1870s did not think themselves finished. What, in 1871, the radicals along with Marx saw as the "glorious harbinger of a new society,"[63] the republicans saw as their providence and their opportunity. But the monarchists too, and especially the legitimists, saw 1871 as their golden opening, and as the first elections served to demonstrate, there was nothing delusionary about this perception.[64]

It was a war which no group admitted to losing, yet it was also a war which everyone lost. Even as each party scrambled to blame the others[65] and thereby to claim its right to the future, there grew underneath a shared sense of common disaster and of common fate. Nothing in the life experience of the adults of 1870–71 had prepared them for this.[66] They had a difficult time admitting it, much less understanding it, and they fell back as soon as possible into that old habit "where—as if deliberately—a great nation applies itself to proving Rousseau wrong and Hobbes correct."[67] Still, something had changed and changed profoundly in the "preconditions" of the nation. It fell to their children, to the cohort of Pierre de Coubertin, to recognize, in their various ways, that change.

The Army of the National Defense served as a powerful symbol of this. In 1875, for the first and only time in his Salon career, Charles de Coubertin submitted a painting of a central, contemporary political event. Instead of the oblique messages behind his Pius IX's and his de Ravignan's, he painted the Army of the National Defense at Loigny on December 2, 1870, where eight hundred Frenchmen attacked an entire German division and were destroyed. But if some new feeling contributed to his acceptance of the Loigny commission, he quickly dispelled it with his interpretation of the event. Loigny, he carefully noted, was "the same ground where Joan of Arc repulsed the English"; the French soldiers were mostly Zouaves; and commandant de Troussures was "among the first to fall."[68] And to drive home his point, the following year he sent to the Salon a painting of *Louis XVII at the Temple*."[69]

Twenty years later, in a passage which stands out for its emotional exuberance in a work of otherwise measured tone, Pierre de Coubertin wrote of the Army of the National Defense:

> Gambetta announced himself as the second organizer of victory; at the summons of his voice, which rarely found nobler accents later on, confidence rose again in souls and hatred against the invader drew all hearts together. "Not an inch of our territory! Not a stone of our fortresses!" Jules Favre had said, and that haughty reply was repeated by each man in the depths of his own being. A great wave of patriotism had swept over France, solidifying it.... It was a heroic struggle. All the generous and noble ardor of the Gallic blood awoke: there was but one flag now; after the young men, the elderly enlisted, with joy in their eyes, happy to fight for a cause so just and holy; and when, at last, the ruin was complete, when Paris beseiged was on the point of perishing with hunger, when they were compelled to lay down their arms and confess defeat, France had the consolation of being able to assert, as in the time of Francis I, that all was lost, "save honor."[70]

"All is lost save honor," "the time of Francis I," soldiers "with joy in their eyes"—the old values of *prouesse* stare out from these phrases. But the passage recognizes engines of salvation where men like Charles de Coubertin could not see them: in a Jules Favre, not a commandant de Troussures; in the "noble ardor of the Gallic blood," not in the blue-blooded ardor of the Gallic nobility; in the depths of being of *each* man, in patriotism and not in conventional duty; under "but one flag now," the tricolor and not the white flag of the royal house. The universalizing, nationalizing character of these symbols and sentiments aptly signals the new meaning *la patrie* took on for the children of 1871.

Pierre de Coubertin's allusion to Francis I is really rather clever. The phrase "all is lost save honor" originates in a prison letter, written by Francis to his mother after the French defeat at Pavia in 1525. "Nothing remains to me but honor and life, which is safe."[71] Here Napoleon III is implicitly compared to Francis, described by one scholar as "at bottom... frivolous, profoundly selfish, unstable and utterly incapable of consistency or application."[72] While he founded the Collège de France and was a sincere patron of the arts, Francis's "mediocre, vacillating and foolhardy"[73] leadership carried France from defeat to defeat. The allusion, then, reinforces the central meaning of the Coubertin passage: honor resides at base in "La France," in the soul of her people; and the people will guarantee that honor against the dishonor of their sovereigns.

With such a view of Napoleon III, Charles de Coubertin would have agreed, but there is also in the allusion to Francis I a backhanded, probably unconscious, slap by Pierre at his father. The blood of Francis coursed in the veins of the comte de Chambord, whom Charles sought, in the 1870s, to have returned to the French throne. While his father associated Loigny with Joan of Arc's service to the legitimate monarchy, Pierre made the association with Francis I instead and saw the heroism of the National Defense as "La France" rising up to save the national honor from the perfidy and weakness of kings.[74]

L'Évolution française expressed the views of a man of thirty-three, but their origin may be traced back to Pierre's adolescence. This is a fact of some importance, for the life cycle stage at which individuals first self-consciously encounter historical events may itself influence the interpretations they place upon those events as adults. And when those interpretations are in conflict with those of parents, the origin of such disagreements may reside as much in general patterns of parent-child relations, family configuration, and birth order, as in straightforward differences of opinion. Among the social allegiances, political opinions, and moral standards of every adult are those which once served as "identity elements"[75] in the dramas of individuation within the natal family. While in Western cultures, at least among the propertied classes in periods of rapid social change, there seems to be a marked tendency for adolescents to see things differently than their middle-aged parents, we do not have to commit ourselves on the controversial topics of "adolescent rebellion," "identity crisis," and "generation gap" in order to recognize these in Pierre de Coubertin's development. Coubertin *himself* recognized them. Indeed, he was so convinced of, and wounded by, their place in his own adolescence that, in later years, he laid all manner of social upheaval squarely at the door of the "eternal misunderstanding which results from the difference of level between two generations and the centuries-old inability of parents to understand the illusions and to fathom the sentiments of their children."

This quotation is from "Le Roman d'un rallié," Coubertin's *autobiographie à clef*.[76] This text is virtually the only source for Coubertin's own subjective account of his adolescence and young manhood. Without it, it is impossible to give more than a mechanical interpretation of his early career. "Le Roman d'un rallié" offers all the problems of interpretation intrinsic to the genre. While an autobiographical novel, it is also a *Bildungsroman*, a work of political and social commentary, and a travelogue, all dressed round uncomfortably with a sugary love story. Its narrator editorializes as often as he narrates, and he fictionalizes as often as he remembers. Thus, any summary judgment as to what is fact and what is literary invention is quite impossible. The biographer who relies upon it must evaluate its events and episodes on a case-by-case basis, relying sometimes on extratextual sources of information, sometimes on patterns of evidence internal to the work, and sometimes on plain intuition.

In a passage describing the "intellectual misunderstanding which early on began to dig a pit between" Mme. de Crussène (Mme. de Coubertin) and her son Étienne (Pierre de Coubertin), the narrator suddenly, jarringly, takes wing into impassioned, even anxious, exhortation. It is worth quoting at length.

The day inevitably comes when in the human being you have engendered, something vibrates which must find an echo in you. Keep a constant ear out for it, in order to be able to respond to this attempt at unison. It may happen soon after the dawn, or later, nearing the midday [of life]. It will be only a very feeble sound and probably an unfamiliar one, because if our children are by chance smitten with the same things as we are, they [nonetheless] see them from different angles and they extol them in novel ways. And who knows how their future affinities awaken in them, what remote and irrational associations go on in the depths of their beings, perhaps some trifle which hasn't bothered anybody in an age affects them deeply!

Keep an eye out, because if they see that that fugitive trifle which troubles them has no response in you, separation begins. Thereon, they believe this terrible thing: that in them a force has been born which has never before existed, that they have created a new way of configuring or of appreciating things; and often the experience of a whole life will not be enough to disabuse them of this mad pretension and to make them see the emptiness of it. From this there follows a thousand disorders: the ill-arranged architecture and dangerous collapses of the social edifice, within which the man works without concerning himself with the buttresses constructed by his ancestors or with the risks he imposes on his descendants; the absolutist and intolerant view which supposes that science has attained its final destination and that the horizon has been pushed back as far as it will go; the useless and vain regrets, the exalted elegies given to the past by those who discontent and discourage the present and who, having no notion of the future, are incapable of seeking in it hope and consolation.

All this comes from the exclusivism with which each generation envelops itself. But the worst of all the evils engendered by this exclusivism is, perhaps, the moral crumbling it produces inside the family, the barrier it erects between the consciences and understandings of those whom nature has destined to succeed one another, to rely upon one another, to continue one another according to the logical and calm order of the universe. Once such a fissure is opened, no matter how imperceptible or insignificant at first, familial unity is shattered: this unity which resides neither in an identity of characters, nor even in a community of beliefs and views; this unity which fortifies, rather than weakens, the notion of the eternal evolution and the equivalence of generations, equal in their understandings and their efforts, if not in their results.[77]

On the heels of this deeply felt peroration, the narrator mentions a boyhood event which caused the "fissure" between Étienne and his mother to deepen. He is punished for refusing to stay seated at table "near a man whose ill-considered words had offended his nascent patriotism."

From that day on, [Étienne] knew that there were some subjects that it was better not to speak about with his mother, because he couldn't feel as she did and he hated to criticize her. They both followed their own path, holding out great tenderness for each other, but not understanding one another in the least and often wounding unconsciously.[78]

In a description of this incident earlier in the text, the offending visitor, an "exalted royalist" neighbor, galled the boy by asserting that "under the Republic, one was not proud to be French." Étienne "made a violent scene. . . . The Republic, for all he understood of it, was fated to be a very villainous thing; but, on the other hand . . . the idea that one could be ashamed to be called a Frenchman sickened his little heart." This incident "was quickly forgotten by the grown-ups, [but it] was not erased in his own memory." It remained that childhood episode with which Pierre marked the beginning of his "ferment of revolt."[79]

A second incident in "Le Roman d'un rallié" is located in early adolescence.

Étienne had always searched passionately in history for the unity of his *patrie*. Was this an instinct, or did it come from an earlier visit to the Versailles museum, when he was about fourteen? He still remembered his juvenile emotion when reading on the pediment of Louis XIV's palace the beautiful dedication inscribed there by the eclecticism of Louis Philippe: "To all the glories of France." What had captivated him most in the galleries were the last rooms, just recently opened up, where one saw, so to speak, history built up stone by stone. After Napoleon I, after the Restoration, after the July Monarchy, here were the Republic of 1848 and the Second Empire, entering in their turn. He detested . . . "l'homme de Sedan," but, without knowing quite why, he was fully at ease to find him there, as he was also at ease to find there a medallion of Gambetta, who had just died and upon whose tomb the passions of the day were conducting their wretched sabbath.[80]

Like the ora in a litany, notices of Étienne's self-enforced silence about those impressions, his inability to communicate them to a mother "who could not understand them," and his sadness at "the eternal divergence of the generations" follow each other immediately in the text.[81]

In his formal memoir of 1908, *Une Campagne de 21 ans*, Coubertin recalled that around the age of seventeen "nothing troubled my national amour propre more than the cohabitation in my pocket of coins bearing different effigies. Didn't this underline our repeated disorders and didn't it accentuate the ridiculous nature of our instability?" The mélange of effigies not only symbolically embodied the past, but also indicated to him the sole direction for France in the future. "Three monarchies, two empires and three republics in less than a century, that was a lot, even for a people with the resources of the French.... From then on, any new change [of regime], whether a restoration or some other, appeared to me to be fated to be nothing more than an expedient without a future."[82] There is no evidence that young Pierre ever confronted his mother with these coins and these words, as Eyquem would have us believe.[83] Perhaps he did, or perhaps he avoided the remorse of confrontation by keeping his views to himself.

Apparently, he accompanied his family quite voluntarily and without protest on their pilgrimage in 1879 to the Austrian village of Frohsdorf. Here the comte de Chambord, known as "Henri V" to intransigents like the senior de Coubertins, endured his exile. By the time of their arrival at the legitimist Mecca, Chambord's fate had already been sealed. His refusal to allow any conditions to be placed upon his return, his unwillingness to compromise with the Orleanists and thereby to secure the votes of the right-center in the National Assembly, and the "affaire du drapeau blanc" had doomed in advance any possibility of his restoration.[84] Indeed, the very day of the Coubertins' audience with him, the Loi Paul Bert, laicizing the *écoles normales*, passed the Assembly.[85] Such signs meant nothing to the elder Coubertins, nor did political "realities." Their faith in Chambord was religious, not political. Eyquem makes some very likely guesses about Pierre's reaction to Chambord. She suggests that Pierre arrived expecting to meet "a sovereign sure of himself and of his legitimacy, thinking only of his restoration, conspiring after, living for, nothing but his return to power."[86] This is the picture Pierre's parents had for years painted for their children, and Pierre's growing doubts about the wisdom and the possibility of a restoration hardly precluded his acceptance of their portrait of Chambord himself. As innumerable legitimist memoirs from the period make clear, royalists found a very different man at the end of their pilgrimage. Whether "pitiable," "sad," and "resigned" were the adjectives which really occurred to Pierre or not, Eyquem is likely correct that the appearance and behavior of the "king" gave the boy a shock which put an

end once and for all to even his "mauvais royalisme."[87] His disillusion
with his parents may have been as great as his disappointment with their
sovereign.

Earlier, in the discussion of Pierre's genealogy, allusion was made to
another important event of his adolescent years, an event about which
there is much fuller information. Some eleven pages of "Le Roman d'un
rallié" are devoted to young Étienne/Pierre's discovery of his black sheep
great-uncle, his clandestine researches into the man's career, and his boyhood identification with and cult of this mysterious *homme maudit*.

In the "Roman," this mother's mother's brother is referred to as "Monsieur de Lesneven,"[88] and described as an abbot, a comrade, and a disciple
of Lamennais. Lesneven died on May 1, 1851, "in final impenitence after
having followed till the end the path set out by the master."[89] "The end,"
in 1851, would include the democratic socialism, radicalism, and deistic
pantheism of Lamennais's prison writings and term as deputy in 1848–49,
and not just the earlier, liberal Catholicism of this foremost of pre–Third
Republic *ralliés*. Such a "path" would have drawn the anathema from
ecclesiastical authorities, and Lesneven is, indeed, described as living the
final six years of his life defrocked, exiled in a remote Brittany village, and
harassed constantly by the local bishop.[90] Having "given all to the
poor,"[91] he was left with nothing but his books and personal furnishings.
The day after his death, these were burnt, his house was demolished, and
Lesneven was buried in an unadorned and unmarked tomb on the joint
orders of the bishop and his sister-in-law (the wife of Charles-Jules Eudes
de Catteville de Mirville?).

Nothing would have been more offensive to legitimist families like the
Eudes, the Gigaults, or the Coubertins than to have had a follower of
Lamennais in their midst. The later generation of Coubertins surely reacted as did the "Crussène" descendants in "Le Roman d'un rallié": by
excluding even the man's name from the household and by attempting to
prevent their children from learning anything about him.[92] In the case of
Étienne/Pierre they were unsuccessful.

During Étienne's childhood, the narrator of "Le Roman d'un rallié" tells
us, the young nobleman knew "almost nothing" about his damned ancestor. The latter's pamphlets and newspaper articles had been removed from
the château library and "portraits of him had been carefully destroyed."
But one day, the boy discovered an unframed miniature of a "long-faced
and pale man with a fiery gaze and a tormented mouth" which had acci-
dently fallen behind some enormous folios in the library and was there
gathering dust.[93] The boy immediately guessed that it was a portrait of his
great-uncle and, not daring to carry it to his room "because of a sort of
superstitious fright," he concealed it "in a crack formed by the corner of
two pieces of worm-eaten wainscotting in a dim nook [of the room]."[94]

Étienne returned time and again "to contemplate the strange figure who so attracted him."

Later, about his fiftèenth year, his mother

> briefly revealed the painful secret and, [in words] he could still hear her saying, she added, "My child, perhaps you haven't noticed that the birthday of M. de Lesneven, October 30, is for me, each year, the occasion of a fast in which you can join me from now on if you wish. But I am not forcing you. Such memories are not appropriate for your youth and I will understand if you refuse to share in them."[95]

Lesneven's memory was not only not painful to the boy, but it excited his imagination, his curiosity, and his admiration. His mother's penitential fast "shocked him." He refused to join her in it and, thereafter, betook himself to church each October 30 to pray for his great-uncle, in spite of his mother's insistence on the futility of prayers for such an "eternally damned" soul. Throughout the remainder of Coubertin's adolescence, his curiosity about his *rallié* ancestor grew into an identification with him. The secret childhood rituals with which he surrounded "Lesneven's" memory later culminated in a clandestine pilgrimage to his grave. This intensely emotional and richly symbolic experience, which seems to have marked a turning point in Coubertin's young manhood, will be discussed in detail later on.

Juxtaposition of these five adolescent incidents—the offending luncheon guest, the visit to the Versailles museum, the matter of the coins, the audience with Chambord, and the discovery of the *rallié* ancestor— permits recognition of a striking congruence of structure underlying them all. Each episode concerns the confrontation between one or another of the domestic, social, political, and religious buttresses of his parents' legitimist world, Pierre's "typical" adolescent attitudes on issues such as patriotism and heroes, and the particular notions and choices that marked his attempt at individuation.

Moreover, each episode has the same psychological meaning. In each one, the boy is brought into conflict with his parents and faces the Hobson's choice of foresaking either their love and esteem or his own stubborn pride and self-respect. In each case, the boy attempts to solve the hurtful dilemma by discovering among his parents' own values and commitments a point of communication between their perceptions of the world and his own. The strategies of adolescence and his own precocious insight make him rather successful in this. But each time, his parents fail to see the extent to which he goes to avoid offense and breach. They accuse him of simple impertinence, patronize him, or ignore the merits of his arguments. In each instance, they repay their son's efforts to avoid hurting them by deepening the fissure between themselves and him.

The Republic might come to a bad end, but the "exalted royalist" had also defamed Frenchmen. Surely Pierre's juvenile sentiment and his parents' aristocratic heritage were in accord on the necessity of patriotism? They were not. As we saw in his father's interpretation of Loigny, *régime* and *patrie* were identified by his parents in the monolithic way of the *ancien régime*. Wasn't the Versailles museum dedicated by a king "to *all* the glories of France"? Couldn't Pierre's adolescent catholicism in his choice of heroes, his easy amalgamation of the Louis', Charles X, and Gambetta, find some echo in the "long view" taken by conservators of French tradition? It could not. To his parents, Louis Philippe was not a proper king, and Gambetta's glory was the glory of a brigand. The display of even his medallion at Versailles was abominable. Didn't the coins demonstrate that one must place one's trust in "the resources of the French people" and not in regimes? Didn't they show that changes of regime were foolish expedients and that a restoration would have no future? To the elder Coubertins, the effigies showed no such thing. Coins were "filthy money" and these arguments were Jacobinism with a pragmatic face. Couldn't one agree that Chambord was a hero by pitying his personal tragedy and admiring his alliance with "fate," without having to see in his exile a tragedy for France or to associate oneself with his interests? No, such a devotion to Henri V was impertinent and cowardly. Couldn't Pierre join in regretting his Mennaisist great-uncle's apostasy while still admiring his moral *prouesse* and praying for his soul? No, there is no *prouesse* in heresy (and none in adolescent independence). The man shamed his family, and the Church assured it that the heretic was damned forever.

While juxtaposition of these events discloses a persistent thematic and psychological structure, placing them in chronological sequence reveals the progressive making of a republican nobleman, a *rallié*. From a childish infatuation with "La France," untroubled by the complexities of political society, there grew with each new intrafamilial breach a more discriminating appreciation of circumstances and the popular will as historical forces, and a more informed conviction that the Republic is good in itself and "the only way for France."

Long after patriotism and republicanism were settled in Pierre's character and he had learned to measure himself in other mirrors than his parents provided, the concepts and habits of thought that are first discerned here as responses to the identity challenges of his adolescence continued to provide the landmarks of his intellectual and moral geography. The resolution of conflict by discovering "higher order" unities between the contending parties; the faith in the revelatory character of public symbols; and the distinction between regime (*gouvernement, idéologie*) and nation (*peuple, civilization, patrie*), a distinction transformed and sophisticated by the experience of his twenties: these commitments occupied the center of his adult world view.[96] They became core conceptual and analytical principles in the political histories he wrote and fundamental features of the design and conduct of the modern Olympic Games he invented.

The incidents discussed make clear Mme. de Coubertin's capital role in Pierre's moral development. Unfortunately, even less is known about her than about her husband.[97] In the "Roman d'un rallié," she is described as physically vigorous, radiantly beautiful, musically gifted, and possessed of a frank intelligence. While her evident prosperity gave a certain "haughtiness" and "instinctive coldness" to her mien, she was generous and warmhearted by nature.[98] She was celebrated in the salons of Paris during the winter social season, and the cultivated were pleased to be received in her home. She undertook "numerous works of charity"; in the country she visited the cottages of the poor, and one day a week at the family château, she distributed advice and medicines to an "interminable procession of tatterdemalions, cripples, and women with sick children."[99] She is said to have studied a little medicine for the purpose, but hardly enough to prevent a "radical" doctor, "who purveyed his politics more widely than his profession," from denouncing her to the local prefect for the "illegal practice of medicine." (Nothing came of this episode which, in its clash of *patronage* with bourgeois professionalism, is so revealing of the social climate of the day.) Her extreme piety and her rigid and uncompromising political views have already been described. But, as also noted, her son was so devoted to her that, even in rebellion, he went out of his way to avoid hurting this marvelous woman.

Altogether too marvelous, really. In the "Roman d'un rallié," Pierre so idealizes Mme. de Crussène that she is difficult to believe. This might be chalked up to want of literary craft (all the book's characters, whether patent inventions or the doubles of real persons, are flat and two dimensional) were it not for other facts which make a psychodynamic interpretation almost required.

In the novelette, the marquise is not only wealthy, compassionate, and beautiful, she is manless. Her father and brothers have died young (the hereditary curse of the apostate Lesneven is blamed), her husband has tragically perished shortly after the birth of their son. She cannot bring herself to consider remarriage and, since Étienne is an only child (the real Pierre had three siblings), he lives as the object of her total attention and affection. This love he returns in kind. Absence from her is a "painful burden," and the "terrible choice" between his mother and his sweetheart "tore apart his life."[100]

Without much fuller evidence, it is dangerous to make too much of Pierre's literary patricide, fratricide, and reconstitution of his family. But the altogether naive, transparent, and systematic character of these inventions, so patent they would seem like parody in a post-Freudian novel, recommends psychoanalytic interpretation. All the signs point to serious psychodynamic conflict folded into the psychosocial dramas of Pierre de Coubertin's youth.[101] Pierre himself supplied a powerful bit of evidence in the manner in which he chose to "kill off" his father in the "Roman." He has him fall December 2, 1870, on the battlefield at Loigny![102]

It would be misleading, however, to overemphasize the conflict and discord in Pierre de Coubertin's early years. As the baron himself noted in the "Roman d'un rallié," "blue skies" predominated over "gray skies" during his adolescence. Indeed, such familial antagonisms as we have been describing would not have so wounded and progressively estranged the boy had they not developed against a backdrop of general confidence and well-being. An adamantine sense of assurance distinguished Coubertin's adult career and prevented his final despair; it was rooted in the agreeable ambience of his privileged youth. Status, wealth, and leisure; the pleasures and mysteries of Mirville's stables, forests, and fields; the fond deference of the peasants and the companionship of their children; church feasts and Norman festivals; the sights and incidents on the yearly journeys to Rome; the fascination of the Parisian boulevards and the endless rounds of visitors and visiting, to and from the delightfully appointed Coubertin *hôtel:* Pierre grew up in an atmosphere of constant stimulation and amusement. School itself, for all of its discipline and sobriety, was an adventure.

The Heritage of the Jesuits

In October 1874, Pierre joined the first forty students of the new Jesuit *collège,* the Externat de la rue de Vienne. For decades the Mignon and Riant families, *grands bourgeois* with fortunes in metalwork, construction, and real estate, had tried to convince the Jesuits to open an *externat* ("day school") on a parcel of their property in the quartier de l'Europe. Jesuit finances and the political climate at last allowed Fr. Matignon, the Paris provincial, to recommend to the superior general in Rome acceptance of the Mignon gift. Pius IX himself is said to have blessed the enterprise by remarking, "Paris cannot fail to be converted with Notre Dame des Victoires at her center, Montmartre at the summit, and the Collège Saint-Ignace de la rue de Madrid between them."[103] The collège took this name when it moved from its temporary quarters in the Mignon *hôtel* on the rue de Vienne to new buildings in the rue de Madrid, constructed with a loan of one million francs from the Crédit foncier.[104] Construction was not completed until 1879. Pierre and his schoolmates received their lessons in an exciting disorder of carpentry and wet paint.

To Pierre's parents, the foundation of Saint-Ignace was, quite literally, a godsend. They believed with the founders of the collège that "Moral formation is, after faith and piety, the first concern of a Christian educational establishment."[105] Such establishments had been scarce for some time.[106] Though the externat's board was heavy with merchants, industrialists, and financiers, and in spite of the bourgeois origins of many of her pupils, the Coubertins trusted the Jesuits to inculcate in Pierre the proper attitudes toward the present as well as toward the past.[107] Moreover, it is probable that most of the bourgeois families associated with the collège belonged to what Robert Locke calls "the old Catholic bourgeoisie," a group which sent many legitimist deputies to the Assembly in the 1870s.[108]

Each day, students from the eastern *quartiers* arrived by omnibus; others were met by carriages at the pont de l'Europe or were delivered to Saint-Ignace by servants. Most were day students, but Pierre was among the *demi-pensionnaires* under the perpetual supervision of a Jesuit preceptor. Uniforms were mandatory at the collège. On Sundays, feast days, and holidays, gold-buttoned vest and short jacket in *drap de fer* blue were required. On weekdays, students were allowed to substitute a gray uniform, "the pants and, initially, the vests of which were in the style of Eton."[109] A special costume was worn for first communion. Tuition and fees were considerable.[110]

The institution's schedule reflected its commitment to "faith and piety." On Sunday mornings, communicants attended early mass, while their juniors were in catechism class; all then assisted at solemn high mass. On school days, attendance at 7:30 mass was required and daily communion encouraged. A former pupil recalled some twenty additional occasions of formal prayer each day.[111] First Friday devotions, the stations of the cross, the forty hours, three Marian cults (including the Immaculate Conception), particular devotions to the Holy Spirit, celebrations of Jesuit feast days and of the anniversaries of individual priests in the community, choir practice, and special ceremonies, as well as the ritual cycle of the festal seasons, added to the crowded and intense religious life of Saint-Ignace. Vespers closed each school day. The Coubertins prescribed such a vigorous ritual existence for all of their children; with Pierre they had an added reason to promote it. With two older sons on their way to acceptable "worldly" careers, Pierre was marked by them for the priesthood.[112]

But ritual training and pious devotion might be had in numerous clerical schools. What distinguished the Jesuit *collèges*, for both their clients and their enemies, was the distinctive "moral formation" offered within them. With the revival of the *collèges*, the ancient combat over "Jesuitical teachings" was resurrected in full. But now there raged behind it the battle between the "two Frances."

The legitimists considered evil inherent in man and this accounts for their unabiding pessimism. The worker's strike against his employer, the employer's neglect of his workers, the husband's infidelity toward his wife, the son's disrespect for the father—theft, war, and revolution, all were but particular manifestations of the greed, lust and unbridled ambitions that had dwelt in the hearts of corrupt human beings since the Fall. They believed the high-minded ideals expressed in socialist, red republican and liberal propaganda to be but a front for the baser motives of ambitious men or proof of the foolish misunderstanding of human nature by those of purer inspiration.[113]

In the 1870s, legitimist Catholics like the Coubertins delivered their sons to the Jesuits not only for the suppression of their passions, but also for the acquisition of that inner circumspection and subtle, logical reasoning that would allow them to resist the ideological blandishments of radicals, republicans, and "freethinkers." The Coubertins had a special desire to smother the incipient rebelliousness of their son.

For their part, the enemies of the Jesuits thundered against the moral casuistry of their schools on the triple grounds that it sterilized the spirits of valuable young men, reduced them to moral sheep, and turned them away from the Republic toward the reactionary, clerical party. Paul Bert, the Pascal of the 1870s, went to the trouble of translating from the Latin the entire *Compendium of Moral Theology and Cases of Conscience* of the Jesuit Fr. Gury in order to demonstrate to the French citizenry that a Jesuit

> does not know what is love, nor even decency, no more does he know what is delicacy, generosity, devotedness, friendship, personal dignity, civic duty, love of country: he ignores so thoroughly these noble things that he does not even know their name.... Everything that makes the heart of humanity palpitate leaves him cool. Do not speak to him of progress, of fraternity, of science, of liberty, of hope; he understands not: he rehearses, in his obscure corner, erroneous consciences, mental restrictions, shameful sins; and with all that he tries to compose I know not what electuary, in order to stupify and enslave humanity.[114]

The gate between the Externat Saint-Ignace and the street was a gate between two entire moral orders; for seven years Pierre de Coubertin entered and left by that gate.

It is against this background that the fierce debate over the curriculum must be understood. The curriculum at Saint-Ignace conformed closely to the *ratio studiorum* of 1832,[115] modified somewhat by the Ministry of Public Instruction through the instrument of the civil examining boards. In the *cours de lettres* (sixth form through *rhétorique*), which Pierre entered and completed, Latin and Greek grammar and composition were preeminent.[116] The ties between the classical curriculum and the bitter educational politics of the day are made plain in a proud boast of the comte de Fontenay, Pierre's former classmate at the Externat Saint-Ignace. "It is

thanks to such establishments as our school, whose existence is consecrated to the principle of freedom of instruction so dear to our families,
that there exist centers of Greco-Latin humanities, where there is dis-
pensed this strong classical culture we are happy to have received and
which will always find in us eloquent defenders."[117]

To Deputy Paul Bert, legitimist demands for "liberté de l'enseignement" meant clerical demands for the monopoly of teaching;[118] to Professor Paul Bert, accomplished Latinist though he was, the classical curriculum meant the suppression of the natural and social sciences of which
France and the Republic had so much need.[119] Since clerical education
meant classical education, the two issues were indivisible. However, to
another group of republican professor-reformers, men like Michel Bréal,
Jules Simon, and Octave Gréard, the problem was not the classical languages themselves, but the methods with which they were taught.[120]

Bréal was a member of the Institut, an accomplished classicist, linguist,
and pioneer of comparative grammar and semantics. The "heritage of the
Jesuits," especially its mechanical emphasis on grammatical formulas
which he called "the art of ignoring the reasons for things," distressed
Bréal no end. He complained that the institutions of the *dictée, correction,
thème,* and *vers latin* replaced careful *explication de texte,* imposed French
rather than native idioms upon the ancient Greek and Latin authors, and
permitted the art of writing to suppress "the art of discovering and observing facts, the art of comprehending and verifying the truth." Worst of
all, he argued, this superficially literary education made true knowledge of
antiquity impossible. "How can one wish that our youth learn to know
and to love antiquity when we serve it to them so chopped up into bits and
when the pleasure they might find in the little of it they see is every
moment disturbed by stylistic preoccupations and the exigencies of translation?"[121]

The crown jewel of the *cours de lettres* was the class in rhetoric.[122] The
students had drilled into them the principles and rules of formal rhetoric
which they then had to illustrate and to embody in Latin and French
discours. "To write a *discours*," as one critic succinctly puts it, "is to place
noble words into the mouths of great personages."

> The subject who speaks is always a great man: king, emperor, saint,
> scientist, or poet. What could such personages be made to say? Noth-
> ing, assuredly, that one could draw from daily life, but only mighty
> sentences... lofty sentiments.... These princes ignored reasons of
> state, jealousy, cunning tricks. It is politics minus Machiavelli. Honor,
> dignity, virtue, nobility, courage, sacrifice, renunciation of the world:
> one breathes a bountiful air on these heroic summits.[123]

The consonance between these exercises and the aristocratic value and
world view of *prouesse* is patent and obvious. The aims of Jesuit literary

and moral education and socialization into a distinctive class ethic again intersected. "The mask would finish, one thought, by devouring the face: by dint of dreaming up their *discours* the students would end by resembling the heroes they made speak."[124]

For contemporary and recent critics alike, matters turned out differently: the students were not fooled. Forced, however, to abjure reflection on "real life" and "condemned to fabricate, in everything they wrote, an artificial and ideal moral universe for which antiquity . . . furnished the materials,"[125] they were educated into a perilous double vision, a sort of moral schizophrenia. Finely wrought speeches, eloquent literary works, public displays of virtue: these were everywhere admired and nowhere to be trusted. This deep-seated ambivalence toward the tongue, the pen, the heart, and the eye all too easily resolved itself into scepticism or bad faith for those who, like the pupils of Saint-Ignace, aimed to succeed in a public order dominated by persons facile with words and images. Classical education "prepared the notables for their future situation. From Latin one went on to law; from rhetoric, to drawing-room conversation, to speech making in the general councils, to the political life."[126] "The hypocrisy of [adult] bourgeois morality was inscribed in the very heart of this education."[127] Of course, what critics regarded as "hypocrisy" the Jesuits and their defenders encouraged as Christian conviction: the irreconcilable gap between the world of the spirit and the corrupt realm of public life. Classical education taught how to be in the modern world, but not of it. Innocently delivered over to classical education as children, its adepts would struggle between these two estimations of it as adults.[128]

Reformers like Bréal, Simon, and Gréard pleaded for better relationships between teacher, student, and fellow students, as well as for new pedagogical methods. They abhorred the authoritarian discipline which Durkheim concluded to be the only truly original innovation of the Jesuits,[129] a disipline maintained through an exorbitant workload (8½ hours of class per day at Saint-Ignace), the intensive scrutiny of each individual child (maintained through the preceptor system),[130] and, above all, the rivalry fomented between the pupils.

> In order to train pupils in intensive formal work which was, however, pretty lacking in substance, it was not enough to be constantly concerned to contain and to sustain them: it was also necessary to stimulate them. The goad which the Jesuits employed consisted exclusively in competition. Not only were they the first to organize the competitive system in their colleges, but they also developed it to a point of greater intensity than it has ever subsequently known. Although today in our classrooms, this system still has considerable importance, nonetheless it no longer functions without interruption. It is fair to say that with the Jesuits it was never suspended for a single moment.[131]

Schoolwork involved a "perpetual hand-to-hand combat" and students were "on a veritable war footing with one another."[132] It was, Durkheim wrote with only a little exaggeration, "an academic organization which appealed only to egotistical sentiments."[133] Among the instruments of competition, Durkheim singled out the classical "games,"[134] the matched combats between pupils in the classroom, the persistent shaming and mortification of the weak, round after round of *concours* and prize givings, and the "academies" of the senior forms to which only the best pupils belonged.[135]

At the Externat Saint-Ignace, the three top students in each class were appointed to the academy. These elect had the "privilege and responsibility" to prepare independently for trimestrial examinations, to pursue supplementary studies leading to an *examen d'honneur*, and to give before the entire collège a special presentation of their honed labors.[136] Pierre was not only a member of the academy, he served as one of its officers.[137] This important fact reveals not only that he was a bright student who intensively absorbed Latin and Greek literature in the Jesuit mode, but also that he excelled in the extremely competitive regimen the Jesuits maintained in the school. Moreover, Pierre could not have displayed at school the political and religious independence he showed at home, for no such boy would have found himself in the academy. A rebel on his home ground, in the hierarchical and peer group environment of the collège, young Coubertin was, at least in his behavior, a conformist.

As a schoolboy, Pierre was surely aware, at least in general ways, of the political controversies surrounding his collège. That he recognized in medias res the problematic character of its curriculum and pedagogy seems more doubtful. He was likely too preoccupied with meeting the demands of his Jesuit masters, too hemmed in by *bachotage*, and too closely guarded by his preceptor[138] to be in any position to challenge the premises of Jesuit instruction. If he knew of Jules Simon at all, it was as a senator and cabinet minister. Of Bréal and Gréard he had likely never heard.

But within a decade of his *bachot*, Coubertin had found a vocation as an educational reformer, inspired by Philhellenism and that "constitutional cosmopolitanism" that Durkheim linked to Jesuit education,[139] but a reformer whose programs were in flat opposition to the pedagogy and scholastic organization of schools like his own in the rue de Madrid. In voice and in person, he joined the liberal, republican classicists, attaching to their now-established critiques his own special preoccupations with educational sport (competition, *prouesse*, classicism) and student self-government. By 1888, Coubertin had the ear of Simon and a platform in the "Comité Jules Simon"[140] which he organized and led. By 1890, Coubertin had attracted the patronage of Gréard, then rector of the Sorbonne,[141] and, in 1894, Coubertin and Bréal together invented the marathon race for the first modern Olympic Games.

A World of Contingent Opportunity

Coubertin's search for a public identity in the 1880s was full of fits and starts, and his pedagogical vocation remained an incomplete one. As an accomplished and attractive member of a wealthy elite, he was predisposed to see a world of many choices. At the same time, popular prejudice against aristocrats and his own aristocratic values and expectations conspired to shrink those choices, to make him feel constricted and uncertain about what to do with himself. Institutional situations conventional for young noblemen seemed either too reactionary for a *rallié* like Pierre, or else too routinized and compartmentalized for a young man resolved to perform great deeds of *prouesse* in favor of greater France. He could remain no longer than a year in any of the public institutions he tried in the 1880s, and, after that, he never tried again.

But doubly lonely, he could not quite manage to go it alone. Wealth, education, and social connections were considerable resources for plotting an autonomous, individual career. Yet these same resources were emblems of a social class and caste suddenly marginal in the new order of things. Coubertin suffered and lamented that marginality, but it left him solidary with no group, for he came to despise the escapism, and hedonism, and the vacant illusions of his brother aristocrats. Committed to performing great individual deeds, he was nonetheless desperate for some experience of community for himself, in an era of vibrant and vital solidarities. A string of committees and voluntary associations, each dedicated to one or another form of social *patronage*, offered him a taste of group allegiance and a wharf from which to launch his personal missions and on which to display the booty of those journeys. Coubertin spent the 1880s anchored to such committees; he spent the rest of his life creating them.

This hopscotch between independent initiatives, formal institutions of training, and voluntary associations began as soon as Pierre was released from school. Through the figure of Étienne in the "Roman d'un rallié," Coubertin recalled the freedom afforded his curiosity once he was liberated from his preceptor, as well as the mysteries of his new "double life."

> Books piled up around [Étienne]; he wanted to know the great works that moved humanity. He read them avidly, at random, noting in turn their profound emotions and their unforeseen deceptions. The authors on the Index and orthodox writers alike entered pell-mell under [his mother's] roof: the *Histoire du peuple d'Israel* [Renan] and the *Paroles d'un croyant* [Lamennais] were concealed behind the *Génie du Christianisme* [Chateaubriand], Voltaire and Darwin underneath Maistre and Bonald, *Gargantua* and La Fontaine escorted by Molière and *Don Quixote*.
>
> Étienne quickly abandoned balls, which he found monotonous, and the Folies-Bergère which he thought insipid. The pure pleasures of the

fencing school and the wholesome fatigue of horse and bicycle riding more suited his needs and his instincts. The feminine silhouettes that hastily and rarely crossed his life... vanished like shadows without leaving enervating memories.

What dominated him was curiosity. It showed itself in everything. Étienne gleaned scraps of knowledge even from the enemies of the social order. He would have liked to do more, to be able to change social milieu, to live different lives. But this eclecticism was his secret. He hid it so well beneath irreproachable appearances that hardly any of his intimates even suspected his double existence.[142]

Certainly his decision in 1880 to enter St.-Cyr, the French military academy, was above reproach. Paul, Pierre's eldest brother, had been a Zouave in the Papal Guard. His other brother, Albert, had graduated from St.-Cyr and was on his way to a colonelcy in the regular army. Like the priesthood, the army was a vocation and, having despaired of the monastery for him, Pierre's parents were doubtless happy to settle for the barracks.

Many Saint-Ignaciens, and the majority of the aristocratic boys among them, entered St.-Cyr, or else went to the army via the École polytechnique. While exact figures for Saint-Ignace are unavailable, Sainte-Geneviève, the Jesuits' smaller sister-school, sent between sixty and a hundred a year to St.-Cyr between 1870 and 1880.[143] Pierre's decision to enroll was surely influenced as well by conditions at the academy. The anti-Catholic and antiaristocratic biases and practices at St.-Cyr had peaked in the middle 1870s. The graduates of the Jesuit *collèges* were no longer so subject to harassment and shaming, and by 1876 were comfortable enough to take holy communion en masse at feast day services at the military schools.[144] Moreover, after the debacle of the Prussian war, the government's interest in reviving the prestige and confidence of the army was supported by broad spheres of public opinion. At the time of Pierre's entry into St.-Cyr, as David Ralston points out, France was undergoing a "military renaissance," and the social prestige of officers had, perhaps, never been greater.[145] To a considerable degree, this broad public interest in a revitalized army tempered republican prejudice against aristocrats within it.

However, Pierre resigned from St.-Cyr within a few months of his matriculation. Some years later, he attributed this sudden exit to his "divining a long period of peace [and] all the monotonies of garrison life before him."[146] Ralston draws attention to the raft of antiarmy novels, with their withering portraits of the demoralization of barracks life, which began to appear in the 1880s and '90s. Simultaneously, university intellectuals began "to expound on the antithesis between the goals of education, which aims at the development of the individual, and those of military life, in which the individual is submerged in the common body for the common good."[147] How directly Pierre was influenced by these new voices raised against what public opinion and his family endorsed is not clear. What is clear is that Pierre wanted action and distinction, and candidates were flocking to St.-Cyr in such numbers that peacetime distinctions were not easily achieved. Moreover, the sons of the middle classes, who composed a larger and larger proportion of the St.-Cyriens, did not share the class ethic of *prouesse*. An increasingly bureaucratized and routinized St.-Cyr conformed to the motivations and habits of these new trainees. Gentlemanly valor and daring were giving over to professional training and skill, a process abetted by the still-lively belief that the disasters of 1870 were tied to aristocratic styles of command and conduct. As a child of the defeat, Pierre undoubtedly supported the modernization of the army. And, as a budding *rallié*, he could endorse the demands for equality which, as Max Weber taught,[148] undergirded such bureaucratization. But as a young aristocrat obsessed by great deeds, he was bored and galled by the routine of St.-Cyr. Apparently, he found no intimacy with his fellow St.-Cyriens and so could not believe with T. E. Lawrence that "peacetime soldiering is still the best lay-brotherhood."[149]

For those commissioned in the army the prospects for distinction and advancement were no better, not only because of the likelihood of peace but also because of the contemporary conditions of the military organization. As Ralston has shown, before 1870, a man from St.-Cyr could expect to retire as a major or a lieutenant colonel, and rather early at that. Pierre had his brother Albert for example. But by Pierre's time, a St.-Cyrien lieutenant could expect to wait ten years to make captain, another ten to be promoted to major.[150] Pierre had stomach neither for this, nor for the unfavorable comparison it would bring with elder siblings toward whom he maintained a lifelong ambivalence and rivalry.[151] Other aristocrats made do in the army, but they were not the sort to attract Pierre to their company: "For a Catholic of strongly conservative beliefs, the Army was about the only career left wherein he might serve the State. Access to the civil service, the diplomatic corps, and the magistrature had been systematically made difficult for them. If the Army seemed to contemporary observers to be a stronghold of monarchist or Catholic [legitimist] sentiments, there were solid reasons for it."[152] Pierre was no legitimist, and he did not care to become, as he later put it, "a gentleman of the old world imprisoned . . . in the ruins of a dead past."[153] But by rejecting the army, Pierre severely circumscribed his chances for a career in any major public institution. His title and name were sufficient to bring down upon him the same prejudices and discriminations that the less enlightened members of his family and class better deserved. The diminished prospects for aristocrats would also play a role in his later rejections of the law and of official diplomacy as careers. As to the civil service, like any true nobleman, Coubertin gave no more thought to it than to a career in business.

In his 1908 memoir, *Une Campagne de 21 ans,* Coubertin remembered himself, upon his resignation from St.-Cyr, as having "brusquely resolved to change career in the desire to attach my name [!] to a great pedagogical reform."[154] The possibility assuredly occurred to him in 1882, as we shall see. However, the certainty with which the "resolution" is represented in this text owes more to retrospective autobiography than to the real state of affairs in Pierre's nineteenth year. A more accurate portrait of Coubertin's identity search in the eighteen or so months of "private study" and drifting after the academy is to be found in "Le Roman d'un rallié," in the description of Étienne's murky and overexcited state of mind after his brief military service.

Étienne was sick from being pushed toward action and not being able to act. Action, he saw it everywhere, in the most varied and attractive forms. What he unconsciously sought in his private studies were motifs for action, laws for regulating action and making it fertile. Without effort, human life seemed to him banal and society criminal. Effort gave all problems meaning and spurred on all toils.

And just such times as these open unlimited perspectives in the most opposing directions.... Tendencies and methods: everything is remaking itself. Other generations knew this uncertainty about tomorrow that agitates us. Others have seen rearing up before them these burdensome tasks which terrify us. But in the past more often than not, a man was paralyzed by these adverse circumstances. Or else his plan of attack was traced out for him in advance by some despotic authority, transforming him into a slave who accomplished or created nothing.

To foresee that tomorrow will be whatever we make it, to know that the slightest gesture, the least word, resolves itself into forces that accelerate or slow down the vast rotation: truly this is something to befuddle and intoxicate the individual. And, indeed, it does befuddle him. Action becomes his goddess. He doesn't erect an altar to her in the threshold of his house, but at the bottom of his heart he renders her a cult, a passionate, almost voluptuous cult.

Étienne felt strongly this general impulse. The more he grew into manhood, [the more] an irresistible need took hold of him and pulled him toward descending into the arena. But how? At almost every turn of the century, destiny, that great ironical thing, placed off to the side a fistful of men whom it condemned, for the privileges their fathers enjoyed, to lead an exceptional existence[155] and to suffer from it. They are seated as solitary spectators in a marble tribune covered with purple where their dignity binds them down. From [that tribune] they cannot descend without falling, and toward [it] the crowd no longer turns even its irritated glances. It leaves them there, a little astonished that they live on.... Aristocracies are slow to die. It will soon be obliged to pity

them, because honorable regrets and delicate scruples often make themselves the accomplices of pride and indolence.[156]

To stay up there counting the years, speaking of the old days and
distrusting the future—Étienne knew that he could not do it. But to
climb down, to separate himself brusquely from all his relatives by
scandalizing them, to deafen himself to his mother's pleadings, to ex-
pose himself to afterthoughts in order, perhaps, to fail lamentably in the
final accounting—he could never risk it. What then to do? To run away,
to resign himself, or to try to forget. . . . The hour for fleeing was
past.[157]

CHAPTER THREE

The Vision at Rugby Chapel

❧

An England of Frenchmen

One alternative to running away is traveling afar with a purpose. The superimposition of a physical journey upon an inner search for meaning practically guarantees the itinerant seeker that sense of action missing in his heretofore sedentary introspection. "Action," as Erving Goffman has elegantly defined it, consists in situations at once problematic and consequential, where risks are taken voluntarily, where things are not yet decided but where decision is felt to be imminent.[1] Travel is by nature full of such situations. The action of foreign travel easily amalgamates with feelings of psychological discovery, confrontation, risk, and resolution. The evident progress of the journey—tickets purchased, trains met, rooms secured, currency exchanged, sights seen, adventures "advented," and chance encounters fortuitously made—provides the traveler with apparent evidence and opportunity for the mental and moral progress he is really seeking. Even the failures, discomforts, and sufferings of journeys, because they are voluntarily undertaken and endured and because they promise "tales to tell" later on, are taken as signs of "getting somewhere." For a time at least, amorphous longings, overwhelming fears, and conflicting responsibilities are condensed and clarified in neat little dramas of character and condition. By coming into contact with the foreign and, to a degree at least, by placing oneself at its mercy, one contacts the foreign in oneself, and the familiar as well. This is why the journey and the voyage, taking to the road or to the sea, to the mountains or to the desert, have served as powerful root metaphors and valued practical strategies for psychological maturation, spiritual discovery, and overtures to social commitments among so many peoples.

This search for action as a release from his mental claustrophobia, his inability to figure out what to do with himself, impelled Coubertin to depart for England in 1883. This choice was hardly extemporized or random. Just as his identity quandaries were rooted equally in social and personal facts, so too his English tour was equally made out of cultural precedents and individual initiative. The habitual journeying of his child-hood, the traditional cosmopolitanism of his class, his wealth and status privileges prepared him to act the young baron on his tour. Whether openly or in mufti, he could freely experiment in a foreign land with that aristoc-racy which was an inescapable fact of his existence at home, and which made him both a rebel in his parents' house and a marginal man in the public life of the new France. At the same time, he was following a model valued by and perfectly continuous with the traditions of his class. Unlike the English, the French did not prescribe travel for its own sake to un-committed gentlemen. While seeking to find himself "out there," the *voyageur-littérateur* was expected to collect materials for books, so as to profit his nation and to "find himself an author" back home.

Generally speaking, the gap which today separates the "globetrotter,"[2] the vagabond, the tourist, and the "dharma bum" from the professional historian, ethnographer, or "writer" did not yet exist in nineteenth-century France. For members of educated French elites, it was rather expected that such personal identity quests as Coubertin's had public meaning and would bear public fruit. While his trip to England was in part a result of Coubertin's inability to settle on a vocation, it was also a step toward that literary vocation to which every French notable aspired at some level of his being. Coubertin went to England with a purpose: to make inquiries into the English educational system. His determined schedule of visits to the public schools and to the universities is evidence that this aim was conceived beforehand. But whether his resolve to "attach his name to a great pedagogical reform" really occasioned the trip to England or was rather its outcome is difficult to judge with the available evidence.

Sizable numbers of literary men had chosen England before him. Under the Restoration, scores of Frenchmen, and among them many aristocrats traveling informally and without portfolio, crossed the channel to tour Great Britain. They produced a large literature notable, as Ethel Jones has shown, for its preoccupation with an "almost unanimous admiration" for the English constitution and system of government.[3] Stendhal, for one, returned convinced that England's constitution was the source of her strength and that "the English government is the only one in Europe that appears to be worthy of being studied."[4] As Jones notes, particular aspects of English life arrested the visitors' attention: "First of all, it was the cult of tradition with its successful modifications. Next it was the preponderant part played by the aristocracy with, as consequences; the system of non-intervention on the part of the state, the private initiative, individual or collective, of the citizens, and the serious political education of states-men."[5] While criticizing the pride of the English aristocrats, men like Guizot, Polignac, Cottu, La Vaugruyon, Rubichon, and Stäel-Holstein envied their status as "guardians of liberty" and admired their talents as the leading political class. A favorite pastime of these Frenchmen was observing elections which they later described as "spectacles," "carnivals," and "saturnalias," at once amazing and horrifying to the visitors.[6] From these observations of political life, there emerged a popular stereotype of the English national character: "hardiesse à entreprendre, ténacité à conserver" ("bold to undertake, tenacious to conserve").[7] Many remarked in passing on the poverty and inequality of the "nation of machines," but writers like Custine, Sismondi, Gourbillon, and Blanqui, who focused on the suffering and upheaval of the industrial revolution, were in the minority.

The tradition of political anglophilia continued through the Second Empire and into the 1870s, as Theodore Zeldin has shown.

> Charles de Rémusat declared in 1865: "I confess willingly that the dream of my life has been the English system of government in French society." The "republic of dukes" of 1871–9 was deeply impregnated by Anglophilism, as were also liberal Catholics of the school of Montalembert, Orleanists like Passy and Odilon Barrot, and liberal economists like Leroy-Beaulieu and Michel Chevalier. The snag about a lot of Anglophilism, however, was that it involved admiration for the aristocracy, in one form or another, and that was difficult to reconcile with democracy. Most of the admirers of England were not democrats.[8]

This "snag" about the aristocracy and the birth of the Third Republic helped bring to the fore a countertradition of anglophobia that had been festering right along throughout the nineteenth century. Maistre, Genoude, Esquiros, Faucher, Ledru-Rollin, and Quinet variously despised the ignorance, tastelessness, Protestantism, empiricism, and crass materialism of the English: "To crown all its political and economic faults, England was boring: it was the home of spleen. Even the poorest Corsican was happier than the worker of Birmingham. The slave-like conditions of the factories, the endless hard labor, represented France's revenge for Waterloo. If Merry England ever existed, it must have been a very long time ago."[9]

Both of these traditions, of anglophilia and anglophobia, were joined in Hippolyte Taine's *Notes sur l'Angleterre*, written between 1859 and 1870 and published in 1871. His *Histoire de la littérature anglaise* (1863–69) was a greater and more enduring work, bringing literature firmly within the purview of "scientific" social history, but *Notes* was itself a gem, the capstone of the genre of "travelogue" written about England. Coubertin almost certainly read it before he departed for England in 1883, and without a doubt knew the book well by 1886,[10] when his own articles on England began to appear. This alone recommends a detailed sketch of Taine's work. But even more important, Taine's thought exerted powerful

direct and indirect influences over Coubertin throughout the 1880s and
'90s. Though it is difficult to see Coubertin as anyone's "disciple" in the
strict sense of the word—not because his was an original mind, but rather
because he was so eclectic a thinker—it was Frédéric Le Play who was
most obviously his master. But Taine's influence, while subtler and more
complicated, was also fundamental and enduring.

The *Notes sur l'Angleterre* transformed the hortatory travelogue into an
early and important approximation of modern ethnography. The book deserves wider attention than it has received among historians of social
science and social anthropologists concerned with complex societies. In it,
Taine refocused the "problem of the English" around the concept of national character. Taine's organicism, ironically to certain modern eyes,
brought him close to a Tylorean conception of "culture," though he did
not use the word in this sense. Taine's stance was, for his time, culturally
relativistic, and his insistence that all of the departments of social and
cultural life are connected into a "system" was still fairly novel. Taine's
judicious and subtly motivated comparisons between France and England,
while hardly putting an end to foreign travel as a shopping tour for social
reformers and engineers, introduced a standard of caution that even enthusiasts of the following generation, like Coubertin, could not ignore.
Above all, Taine's work condensed and expressed a newly modern milieu
in which science and humanism, nationalism and universalism, taste and
the popular will contended for dominance. All of these themes are represented in a passage from the *Notes* on the familiar matter of the English
constitution.

> The constitution of a nation is an organic phenomenon, like that of a
> living body. Consequently that constitution is peculiar to the state in
> question, no other state can assimilate it, and all it can do is to copy its
> appearance. For beneath these, beneath the institutions and charters,
> the bills of rights and the official almanacs, there are the ideas, the
> habits and customs and character of the people and classes; there are the
> respective positions of the classes, their reciprocal feelings—in short, a
> complex of deep and branching invisible roots beneath the visible trunk
> and foliage. It is these roots that sustain and nourish the tree and if you
> plant the tree without its roots it will wilt and fall to the first storm
> of wind. We admire the stability of British government; but this stabil-
> ity is the final product, the fine flower at the extremity of an infinite
> number of living fibers firmly planted in the soil of the entire country.[11]

Taine sought to turn up these fibers and roots and to understand English society as an organic whole. Though a bricolage from the vantage
point of recent social science, his method was quite new at the time and
excited the most lively opposition in the French intellectual establishment.
It was, in the main, ethnographic. Taine conversed and made inquiries of

all whom he met, sat for hours on park benches to observe, and rode third class on trains in order to overhear. All the while he took copious notes. He was self-conscious about moralizing instead of presenting positive facts,[12] and he sought to check and control his informants' statements through other informants and through statistical information when he could get it.[13] He tried to investigate as many sorts of neighborhoods, schools, parks, meetings, associations, social gatherings, and social groups as he could think of. Concentrating on "ordinary" representatives of social classes and opinions, he rarely mentions famous persons or events, and then only as illustrations of broad social currents discovered in his congress with the "typical." Like Tolstoy, Taine was an enemy, on philosophical and sociological grounds, of the great man theory of history.[14]

At the same time, however, Taine's style of ethnography is primitive and unsystematic by today's standards. He appears to have spent no more than a few weeks in England,[15] and while he seems to have conducted his inquiries for the most part in English, his spoken command of the language was notoriously bad. His contacts and companions were aristocratic and upper middle class. With them he conversed and deliberated. Most of the middle classes he merely encountered, and at the working class he did no more than look. Taine's companions in Manchester had police contacts, so with an escort provided, he felt free to tour the working class ghetto at night. But it would never have occurred to him to go alone or in mufti. On one occasion he is taken aback at the suggestion that he visit a reformatory school without proper letters of introduction (though, it must be said, he does go). In the case of the novelists and poets, he makes a notable and sometimes uncritical exception to his Tolstoyan principles, drawing on Eliot, Dickens, Thackeray, Browning, and Tennyson for much of his information and sensitivity to English life and culture.

Taine's methods formed the compass of Coubertin's, though the baron applied them haphazardly and without Taine's genius. Coubertin's commitment to "positive knowledge," shaky enough in his youth, gave way in his maturity to a gentle skepticism of the scientific spirit. Yet he retained a love of taxonomy and categorization, originating no doubt in his Jesuit education, but given new legitimacy by the intellectual atmosphere Taine helped to create in the Paris of the 1880s and '90s.

Taine saw national character as the outcome of his famous triad of *race, milieu, moment*. But Coubertin, like the sociologists of Durkheim's school, whose works he appears not to have known, grew increasingly skeptical later in life of the role played by hereditary factors in social and moral life. No doubt the reformer's presuppositions about the malleability of social arrangements and the "slings and arrows" he suffered as a "hereditary" noble played a larger role than careful thought in Coubertin's doubting of the Tainean concept of race. But, on the whole, Coubertin never strayed from Taine's emphasis on national genius and national character as the intersection of enduring physical and social dispositions with particular historical circumstances.

As much as any other Tainean text, the *Notes sur l'Angleterre* illustrate the tension between historical and what we should today call "structural" understandings of cultural life. Character, national or individual, is an additive phenomenon, says Taine. "Every sight we see, every emotion we experience leaves some small permanent mark on us, and these marks taken together comprise what we call our character."[16] Yet *Notes* is an ahistorical work, a synchronic portrait, in which Taine takes much less interest in the origin and development of English society, manners, and life, than in their present configuration. The most brilliant insights in the book are structural ones. For example, Taine connects the testimony of reformed sinners at Methodist revival meetings with English empiricism, the taste for evidence and "living specimens," as in zoology, at which the English excel.[17] In turn, Taine relates the English love of facts, "scientific industry," work discipline, and human misery.[18] In this he foreshadows Weber and E. P. Thompson, and joins Dickens and Blake in the forefront of his contemporaries. Yet these insights go unsystematized, and, above all, Taine sees no connection between English scientism as a cultural style and his own positivist values and orientation.[19] As one of the most important apostles of the nineteenth-century doctrine of "progress," Taine cannot entertain the possibility that the cure will itself worsen the disease. Coubertin, too, was a progressist, without Taine's sometimes morbid sense of human frailty and evil.

"Both evil and good," Taine wrote, "are greater [in England] than in France."[20] The principal features of English character were, he concluded, "the need for independence, the capacity for initiative, the active and obstinate will, the vehemence and pungency of the passions concentrated and controlled, the harsh though silent grinding of their moral machinery, the vast and tragic spectacle which a soul entire furnishes for its own contemplation, the custom of looking into the self, the seriousness with which they have always considered human destiny, their moral and religious preoccupations."[21] These qualities Taine found admirable and, in their native habitat, enviable.

But the English also revolted him. "I do not know how it is, but whenever I consider this English society, always, beyond the human head and the splendid torso, I find myself aware of the bestial and muck-befouled hind quarter."[22] The scatological metaphor, the most potent in a Frenchman's arsenal, recurs throughout the text. The poor, streaming through the London streets or pouring out of their hovels to watch a street brawl, are the "effluvia" of "a human sewer . . . suddenly clearing itself."[23] Foetid, scrofulous, livid, filthy, exiguous, bestial: these are his adjectives for the poor and their dwellings. Of the prostitutes of the Strand, he writes: "The impression is not one of debauchery but of abject, miserable poverty. One is sickened and wounded by this deplorable procession in those monumental streets...a march past of dead women. Here is a festering sore, the real sore on the body of English society."[24] Such descriptions of the poor—descriptions in which horror overtakes outrage, revulsion smothers pity, and, among doyens of progress like Taine, a note of blaming the victims creeps inevitably in—were common enough in French writing about England. What makes Taine's text unusual is his attention to the "hind quarter" of the gentry and aristocrats as well.

"The contrast between the natural and the artificial man is grotesque, as it is between the gentleman and the beast which bursts out within him."[25] The appetites of the whole English race are "violent and dangerous."[26] In England, "the physical animal, and the primitive man as nature makes him before handing him over to civilization, is of a stronger, rougher species."[27] Taine complained of residual English puritanism, but like the Puritans, Taine above all feared "the beast within."[28] Taine preferred sophisticated forms of sublimation to the culturally organized outlets for the direct expression of human brutishness that he found among the English.

English styles of drunkenness, the cult of fistfighting, blood sports, the "carnivorous" cuisine, the grosser aspects of upper class identification with horses, school athletics and excessive virility, licensed loutishness to inferiors and its social antonym, masochistic fawning and the "lackey-spirit" toward superiors: all of this repelled Taine. The innocence and propriety of the English upper classes in matters of sex pleased him morally; but on aesthetic grounds, he could not help lamenting the absence of sexual playfulness and sophistication. English honesty, authenticity, and plain-speaking surprised and delighted Taine, but he missed the artfulness, irony, and wit, the savoir faire of French conversation and manners. He found England not so much boring as melancholy:[29] neither tragic nor ludic enough, but among the middle and upper classes, sane and workaday.

Taine was all praise for the English sense of duty which he saw as the keystone of English public life. "The aim of every society," he wrote, "must be a state of affairs in which every man is his own constable, until at last none other is required."[30] But a note of nostalgia for the cults of honor and *prouesse*, the French functional equivalents of duty, echoes repeatedly through his accounts.

On the essential matters of class and class conflict, Taine was of divided mind. The seeming absence of class warfare in England contrasted disfavorably with the perturbations of class struggle in France, and French calls for "major surgical operations, advocated by certain people, rarely result in anything but making the patient worse than ever."[31] Yet he also saw that in England class divisions were more rigid and carefully marked, and class boundaries more viciously defended. Despite its inconveniences, in the end he preferred what he took to be the French egalitarian spirit. The gap between the English rich and the *"de facto* slaves" of the docks and the factories shocked him, and he asserted against it the relative prosperity and happiness of the French peasantry.

What then held the "closely woven fabric" of English society together? In addition to English "progress," sense of self-discipline and duty, stable political form, and the powers granted to public opinion, Taine credited the symbolic role of the monarchy, the admirable religious adaptations of the Anglican church, the civilizing role of the newspapers, and the residual traditions of feudal deference and service between master and man. But Taine placed the greatest stress of all on the English "spirit of association," the formation, by private initiative, of

> swarms of societies engaged in good works: societies for saving the life of drowning persons, for the conversion of the Jews, for the propagation of the Bible, for the advancement of science, for the protection of animals, for the abolition of tithes, for helping working people to own their own houses, for building good houses for the working class, for setting up a basic fund to provide the workers with savings banks, for emigration, for the propagation of economic and social knowledge, for Sabbath-day observance, against drunkenness, for founding schools to train girls as school teachers, etc., etc. It is enough to walk the streets or glance at any newspaper or Review to understand the number and importance of these institutions.[32]

Taine gives an approving paragraph to trade unions, but he devotes page after page to these middle class and, especially, aristocratic associations devoted to "patronage." Taine is practically obsessed to communicate to his French readers not only the importance of these institutions but also the distinctive spirit that animates them. In English aristocratic patronage, there is little, he claims, of *noblesse oblige*. Rather, "An Englishman rarely stands aside from public business; for it is *his* business, and he wishes to take a hand in its management. He does not live withdrawn, on the contrary he feels himself under an obligation to contribute, in one way or another to the common good."[33] The contrast with the French aristocracy is unstated, but everywhere implied in Taine's discussions of English patronage. It is made quite explicit in his contrast of the French *gentilhomme* and the English "gentleman." To simple minds, Taine writes, a gentleman is someone with a large private fortune, a considerable household of servants, and a certain outward appearance and life style. The better informed add in a liberal education, travel, information, and good manners.

But for real judges the essential quality is one of heart. Speaking of a great nobleman in the diplomatic service, B—— told me, "He is not a gentleman." Thomas Arnold, when travelling in France, wrote to his friends, "We see here few whose looks and manners are what we should call those of a thorough gentleman. . . . A thorough English gentleman—Christian, manly, and enlightened—is more, I believe, than Guizot or Sismondi could comprehend; it is a finer specimen of human nature than any other country, I believe, could furnish." Make ample allowances for the exaggerations due to national pride, and we still have here a very instructive document. For them a real "gentleman" is a truly noble man, a man worthy to command, a disinterested man of integrity, capable of exposing, even sacrificing himself for those he leads; not only a man of honor, but a conscientious man, in whom generous instincts have been confirmed by right thinking and who, acting rightly by nature, acts even more rightly from good principles.[34]

The whole of Coubertin's encounter with England is presaged in this passage. Coubertin, as we have seen, was driven in his twentieth year by aristocratic values. But all around him, in his family and peer group, he saw not "truly noble men" but *gentilshommes,* idle dandies or ignorant reactionaries "imprisoned in the ruins of a dead past." Taine assured him that in England he would find a different model of "nobility," a modern aristocracy "who, as citizens, are the most enlightened, the most independent and the most useful of the whole nation."[35] This is exactly what Coubertin found in 1883, and repeatedly thereafter, until by 1887, he had developed a profound identification with the English.

With this act of identification, Coubertin went far beyond Hippolyte Taine, the sober intellectual and provincial lawyer's son, who took England as a moral "spectacle,"[36] and the English as "good to think with."[37] Coubertin's alienation was more thorough, his life stage more vulnerable, his epoch fuller of a sense of crisis; his quest, therefore, more total and consuming. It reached a critical point in 1886, when Coubertin had a vision, a vision at the tomb of none other than Thomas Arnold, the dead master of Rugby School, whom Coubertin thereafter deified and took as his lifelong hero, prophet, and father-substitute. His vocation confirmed by this vision, Coubertin began in 1887 his "21-year campaign" to bring to France what he took to be Arnold's legacy: *la pedagogie sportive,* "athletic education," a "proven" method for the production of "Muscular Christians"[38] which, as a budding republican, Coubertin intended to extend not only to his own class, but to the bourgeoisie and, ultimately, the working class as well. The "Arnoldian system" of school sports, student self-government, and postgraduate athletic associations would, Coubertin felt assured, be the means by which France would "rebronze" *(rebronzer)* after the disasters of 1871, and would create a lasting democratic society as the English had. Coubertin himself, through tireless patronage, would be the apostle of this great reform. Audacious to his contemporaries, this prolonged adolescent's scheme seems all the more outlandish, even ludicrous, in the late twentieth century, when young men do not have such dreams or, if they do, do not dream of acting on them. At the end of his life, Coubertin would judge himself a failure with regard to France, but he never recanted or thought himself a fool. Along the way, he took up another dream, even more unlikely and outlandish: the resurrection on an international scale of the Olympic Games. This dream he succeeded in drawing into the world's waking life. Its seeds, too, were planted in his traffic between England and Paris, in 1883–87.

Peregrinations through the Public Schools

Taine devoted an entire chapter of the *Notes* to English education. The unhappy memories of his own school days,[39] the natural curiosity of a former *normalien* and sometime professor, the Demogeot and Montucci report of 1868, and the repeated statements of his informants that "all [that Englishmen] owe their children is an education"[40] led Taine to this special interest in English schooling. Taine visited Harrow, Eton, Oxford, and Cambridge, all in a matter of a few days. He had neither the time nor the interest to interview students, relying instead on Thomas Hughes's *Tom Brown's Schooldays* for his information on the inner life of the public schools.[41]

Coubertin, no less than Taine, smarted from the personal wounds of his *collège* days, though he was less concerned than Taine with the intellectual side of schoolboy oppression. Because Coubertin was as yet a foreigner to higher learning, his initial curiosity about English schooling was not spurred by professional interest but by the broad bodies of French public opinion which agreed that "after bread, education is the first requirement of the people."[42]

In England, Coubertin began on familiar ground, visiting first "some Polish friends" who were students at the Jesuit school of Beaumont, near Windsor.[43] However, it was the "famous public schools" he had come to see. In 1883, during a period of several weeks, he toured Harrow, Eton, and Rugby, in addition to Oxford and Cambridge. He may have visited others, but since he left no exact chronology of this, or subsequent, trips, it is difficult to reconstruct his itinerary. It is certain that Coubertin returned to England in the summer of 1886, his longest sojourn. (Though the evidence is unclear, he may have crossed the Channel at least once during 1884–85.) In 1887, he returned again in the autumn[44] and, thereafter, yearly. By 1887, he knew Wellington, Winchester, Malborough, Charterhouse, Couper's Hill Westminster, Toynbee Hall, Christ's Hospital, and various Catholic schools, as well.[45]

His methods of inquiry were those of Taine, though Coubertin applied them more energetically to the schools and later chided Taine for relying too much on Demogeot and Montucci instead of conducting independent investigations.[46] Coubertin would arrive at a school with letters of introduction,[47] have tea with the masters and invited pupils,[48] be conducted on a tour of the grounds and introduced to students,[49] and then generally left to himself to wander around, observing games and lessons, chatting with the boys, and joining them in chapel and at meals.[50] He later commented on the easy familiarity of the students with foreign visitors, a familiarity made easier in his case, no doubt, because he was barely older than they, neither physically imposing[51] nor pretentious, spoke decent English, and was, as a French baron, an object of curiosity himself. The masters likely remembered the stir caused by the publication in England of Taine's *Notes*,[52] and were pleased to indulge the new visitor, an ingenuous young Frenchman who so clearly liked everything that he saw. Coubertin kept up a correspondence with one Harrow master[53] and probably with others of his new acquaintances. These contacts served him anew on subsequent visits.

While Coubertin observed the public schools more closely than Taine, his reliance on *Tom Brown's Schooldays* was greater still. It may be said without exaggeration that Coubertin's "ethnography" of the public schools was devoted simply to verifying what he had read in Hughes's famous book. *Tom Brown* controlled not only the aim of his eye and the questions he asked, but also his judgment. Coubertin first read the book in 1875, when Girardin's translation appeared in the *Journal de la jeunesse*.[54] Taine had described the French *lycéen* as "in a cage where his imagination ferments."[55] *Tom Brown* appears to have seized the imagination of the impressionable boy of twelve, encaged in his *collège* in the rue de Madrid, like no other book. As a still-impressionable youth in his twenties, he carried his English-language copy "on all my peregrinations through the public schools of England, the better to help me bring to life again, in order to understand it, the powerful figure of Thomas Arnold and the glorious contour of his incomparable work."[56] How moved and ecstatic Coubertin must have been in 1883, as he rushed through Rugby school from one storied place to the next: the schoolhouse hall where East and Tom once took their meals; the same fireplace where Tom was roasted by Flashman; Martin's magpies still fluttering above the quadrangle and the little studies where he once kept his menagerie and conducted his chemical experiments; the lecture hall where Arthur broke down in recitation, so moved was he by the immortal lines of Homer; the close behind the chapel where Tom, in defense of his chum, once fought it out with Slogger Williams until Dr. Arnold emerged from the turret door (that one over there!) to break it up; the fives-court, the football field, and the great cricket ground where Tom captained the eleven to glory on his

last day at Rugby; and the chapel. Here, for the first time, young Coubertin gazed on the tomb of "the Doctor." "How wonderful that it all truly
exists," Coubertin must have thought over and over again to himself; "It's
all just so."

The substance of his "findings" at Rugby will be treated in detail below,
after we have set the context of the writings from which they are known.
His talks with the boys and observations of their sports convinced him
that the public schools were still run by Arnoldian principles, and more,
that the excesses of fagging and bullying had been put down. Already
predisposed to overlook Taine's reservations about the darker side of the
English character and the antiintellectualism and excessive physicality of
the public schools, Coubertin found nothing new to dampen his enthusiasm for them. Even his discovery that Arnold was little remembered
and remarked upon by the current set at Rugby gave him scant pause. In
1883, nothing disturbed the joyous fit between the results of his "serious
inquiry" and the needs of his heart. Perhaps he had never felt so independent and alive as during his first experiences at Harrow and Rugby.
But these experiences were not yet in full control of him. To his parents,
and as yet to a part of himself, he was still a young man on holiday. His
parents' hold over him was ebbing, but still strong enough that, at their
insistence, he took time out from his educational tour to pay a call on the
comte de Paris.[57] And awaiting him back in France was the business of
finding a suitable career.

Upon his return from England, he mentioned to his father the possibility of enrolling in the École libre des sciences politiques. "Do you wish
to become a diplomat?" asked the senior Coubertin. "No, father," replied
Pierre. "Then don't waste your time. You have refused entry into the
army; there is only one option left for you, the law." "Haven't I any other
alternative?" "There's no other for men of our milieu."[58]

For a final time, Coubertin bowed to his father's wishes and made a last,
half-hearted attempt at a conventional higher education. Putting Arnold,
Rugby, and school reform aside, he entered the Faculté de droit in 1884.
The outcome was predictable; he rarely went to class: "Legal studies were
horribly repelling to me. It was a torment to me, on the day of the annual
examinations, to have to put on my back one of those black robes with the
white sash that were then mandatory for the candidates. How I had gotten
into such straits, God only knows."[59] Coubertin later extolled English
fathers for not interfering with their sons' courses of study in the public
schools and universities.[60] How Coubertin must have wished for an "English" father! In 1885, he stood up to his father and quit the law, and it
seems that Charles de Coubertin never found anything but fault with his
son's subsequent projects and achievements. Probably, too, Coubertin *père*
belabored Pierre with the examples of his elder brothers, who had done

the proper things with themselves. We have seen how Pierre repaid them in kind later on, with the symbolic patricide and fratricides of "Le Roman d'un rallié." All this contributes to the view that Coubertin's growing worship of Thomas Arnold and his fraternal identification with Arnold's "children," the Rugby School boys, were psychodynamically, as well as morally, determined.

Coubertin then enrolled in the École libre des sciences politiques.[61] Taine would not have been surprised. He was counting on just such men as Coubertin for much of the student body of the École libre, which Taine had helped to found and still guided at a distance.

> I'm not worried that auditors will be lacking. Of the three thousand students of law in Paris, one reckons on seventeen hundred of them who, having ease or money, consider their studies as a supplement to their education and don't wish at all to become lawyers. They have leisure, especially during their first two years, and doubtless many of them, instead of taking a political opinion at random, will wish to learn before believing, to know before speaking out.[62]

These remarks appear in Taine's announcement of the aims and methods of the École libre, first published in the *Journal des débats* in 1871. That they aptly describe Coubertin in 1885 is made clear from what we know of him at the time and from his own celebration of the École libre in an American review in 1897.

> The school was intended to prepare young men for the civil service or diplomacy. It meant to provide the state with good financial surveyors and administrative officers. But the vast majority of those who heard the lectures of its improvised professors were improvised students, men of leisure, post-graduates, who felt eager to learn without a definite object. And so it happened that the school partook in some way of that purely scientific and sacred character of the Athenian gymnasiums.[63]

Coubertin's political and social views were indeed in formation in 1885, after the fashion Taine described in his article. The young baron did wish to know before speaking out. Boutmy, Vinet, and Taine had founded the École libre in reaction to the Sedan debacle, on one side, and to the Commune, on the other. As Taine put it:

> Not only didn't they dream of supporting a [political] party, but they wanted to keep the teaching outside of [ideological] theories. What they wished to do was to contribute to the knowledge of facts and of statistical, moral, diplomatic, military, commercial, legislative, and historical documents of every sort, without which no clear idea or worthy opinion on public affairs could be had. A well-brought-up Englishman or American possesses [the facts], we don't, and it's for this that we abstain from voting or else make up our minds like blindmen. Republicans,

absolutists, partisans of limited monarchy, socialists, whatever our
preferences, we need [the facts] to have confidence in our judgment and
to not mistake our choices.[64]

Notwithstanding the école's sincere commitment to positivist and value-
free learning (it was one of the earliest and most important approximations
of the modern "research" university), Orleanism was its dominant, albeit
implicit, ideology in the 1870s. By the middle 1880s, with the monarchy
defeated and the Republic relatively secure, the liberal education of the
école was provided in an atmosphere of moderate republicanism. Though
formally open to them, neither legitimists nor socialists would have found
the institution any more inviting than in the previous decade, and few, if
any, attended its courses.

The École libre was dedicated to training an elite, at once meritocratic
and ascriptive, "an elite," as Boutmy put it, "formed of men who by their
family situation or special aptitudes had the right to aspire to exercise an
influence on the masses in politics, in the service of the state, or in big
business."[65] Though it had only some two hundred and fifty students in
the 1880s, the école was well on its way to a monopoly over places in the
embassies, the state councils, and the civil service. It was already, in the
words of Marc Bloch, "the spiritual home of the scions of rich and
powerful families,"[66] though, as we have seen, Coubertin's family didn't
think so. For this reason too, the social and political milieu of the école
drew Coubertin like a beacon. A common dedication to influencing the
direction of French society allowed the uprooted children of the old aristocracy, like Coubertin, and the place-seekers of the bourgeoisie to mix
freely and comfortably in its halls.

But there were other reasons for Coubertin's matriculation at the École
libre. It was the most suitable institution in all of France for him to pursue
the inspiration of his English moral adventure. Though Taine was off in
retreat working on the final volumes of *Les Origines*, the spirit of the author
of *Notes sur l'Angleterre* still permeated the école. Émile Boutmy, its director and senior professor, was no less obsessed with England than Taine.
Boutmy subscribed quite thoroughly to Taine's views on the English, and
he extended and developed them.[67] In 1885, when Coubertin enrolled,
Boutmy was working on his article "Le Gouvernement local et la tutelle de
l'état en Angleterre."[68] The next year he wrote "L'Individu et l'état en
Angleterre,"[69] which was published in 1887, together with his *La Développement de la constitution et la société politique en Angleterre*.[70] In these texts
Boutmy was preoccupied with a favorite theme of Coubertin's, the English ethos of self-government. While interests in England and Germany[71]
predominated, the école promoted investigations of all "the states which
have an important place in the world."[72] Not merely a matter of individual professors' interests, the comparative approach was built in through-

out the curriculum, an approach "unique in its international outlook and its interests in foreign politics and institutions."[73] On top of this, some ten percent of the students were themselves from other nations, including Coubertin's former schoolmate at Saint-Ignace, the Englishman Austen Chamberlain.[74]

The original program of the École libre consisted in ten courses, each explicitly comparative: geography and ethnography,[75] diplomatic history, labor and wealth, history of political economy, finance, comparative law, administration, military history, constitutional history, and social theory.[76] By Coubertin's time, the program had been reorganized into four "sections" or departments of instruction (administration, diplomacy, economy and finance, and public law and history).[77] There were also several faculty "working groups," many supplemental courses, and conferences given by the Society of Former Students.

Coubertin appears to have enrolled in the public law and history section (also known as the *section générale*), but he freelanced around the institution. His earliest extant manuscripts are three dated 1885–86: "Droit administratif," "Les constitutions de l'Amérique et les États-Unis," and "Les constitutions françaises." These are almost certainly "course papers" for the école, the last one for Alexandre Ribot's "French constitutional law from 1791–1875." This course was given in 1885–1886, during Ribot's brief absence from Parliament. (In 1885, he had been instrumental in the fall of the Ferry ministry. In 1887, he returned as a deputy and later was five times prime minister.) Remembering his course at the école, Coubertin described Ribot as "a magnificent orator, an amazing person, speaking a language of impeccable form and elevated purpose. His integrity and his moral nobility were also widely respected."[78] To Coubertin, Ribot was typical of the "instructors of an unknown type" that Boutmy "created." "Many of them had lived what they were asked to teach; all had learned not merely from books, but from their own experiences."[79]

Eyquem reports that Coubertin was also devoted to the lectures of Albert Sorel and Anatole Leroy-Beaulieu, whom he described as "marvelous teachers whose instruction was not deformed by the slightest pedantry and who, in a clear style, furnished us with *novel* and *independent* views. . . . I left their courses filled with intellectual light."[80] Sorel was a well-known diplomatic and political historian, author of *L'Europe et la révolution française*,[81] and a leading figure at the école. Anatole Leroy-Beaulieu was a religious and political historian, author in 1885 of a text of undoubted interest to Coubertin, *Les Catholiques libéraux: l'église et le libéralisme de 1830 à nos jours*.[82] In his 1897 article on the école, Coubertin additionally singled out Léon Say, Vandal, and Levasseur. He may have taken courses from one or all of them. It is also not clear whether he actually studied with Boutmy.

Coubertin appears to have been an assiduous and energetic student at the École des sciences politiques. In his later years, he had nothing but compliments for the institution. Yet after he returned from England in the fall of 1886, Coubertin stayed away from its halls until 1898, when he himself lectured there.[83] Why did he drift away? He did not take a diploma nor, since he sought no government position, did he try for one. The administration of the école was only too happy to have auditors like Coubertin stay on indefinitely. His doubts about the technocratic and positivist underpinnings of the école did not develop until much later. Why, then, didn't he return? The answers lie, I think, in the very qualities of the École libre that attracted him in the first place.

It was, he wrote, "a school where students who are not *regular* students listen to professors who are not *regular* professors, and who dare to lecture on subjects that do not belong to the *regular* academic course."[84] The great service the école had rendered him was the legitimation of Coubertin's own "irregularity." For a socially marginal man like Coubertin, at odds with his class, his family, and his traditions, the École libre had provided a home, for, in those days, it was itself a liminal institution,[85] standing betwixt and between the academic and aristocratic establishments and the workaday world of bourgeois place-getting. But to stay around the école as an auditor would have been, for Coubertin, to surrender to his own marginality and uprootedness, in other words, to indulge them. He would have become only a more elevated version of the *flaneurs* and "*crétins* of the faubourg" whom he so despised among his own class.[86] The école had provided him with a cosmopolitan environment, populated by intellectuals, public figures, and "hungry" young men committed to inquiry into the cultures of other nations and to energetic discussion of the social problems of the day. But Coubertin was headed neither for the university, nor for the civil service; still he needed somehow to become "a regular guy." While he admired his teachers for combining books with prestigious public service, he was not yet one of them. And he wished to be. Moreover, for all of their pragmatism and sense of public duty, they were intellectuals and positivists. They had given him an arena in which he could preserve and nurture his fascination with England and her public schools. But Coubertin was a moralist, not a scholar; he wished less to study England than to transplant a piece of her to France. His sort of anglophilia was, in the end, very different from that of Taine, Boutmy, and Leroy-Beaulieu. There was no place for Coubertin's excesses of the heart at the École des sciences politiques. That he knew this and kept his dream to himself while a student at the école is made plain in his later writings. In those works, he typically reports every reaction, pro or con, by a famous personage to his reformist proposals. Yet there is not a single mention of any such conversations with his professors in 1885–86, or, indeed, any evidence that they took the slightest notice of him while he was their student. But two years later, Boutmy, Paul Leroy-Beaulieu, and Ribot knew very well of his scheme to bring English sport to the French schools. Approaching them not as a student, but as himself a public man, Coubertin drew their patronage, and he could then happily quote from a letter to him from Ribot, in which the latter "congratulated himself that such an important reform belongs to a former student of the École des sciences politiques."[87]

What altered in the meantime was Coubertin's resolve, his confidence, and his self-credibility as a potential reformer. In 1886, he was twenty-three years old, better informed, and fresh from the lectures of some notable minds. In 1883, his father's models for a proper career had been a drag-weight on his resolution. Now he had cut loose that anchor. At the École libre, social amelioration was a matter of everyday consideration, and not the mere fantasy of isolated youths. His juvenile notion to "attach his name to a great pedagogical reform" had survived his coming of age, and now there was nothing left but to act upon it, or to forget it. This was no real choice for Coubertin; he had little else in the way of an identity to fall back upon. In England, in 1886, his vision took possession of him.

On this trip he broadened his travel to Ireland, took a greater interest in political questions, and expanded his educational observations to popular education and to various Catholic schools. But the public schools remained his focus and, among them, it was still Rugby that drew him like a magnet. There, "in the twilight, alone in the great gothic chapel of Rugby, my eyes fixed on the funeral slab on which, without epitaph, the great name of Thomas Arnold was inscribed, I dreamed that I saw before me the cornerstone of the British Empire."[88]

Coubertin was not the first, only the first Frenchman, to fall into such a reverie in Rugby chapel. In his poem of that title, Matthew Arnold once conjured up and elegized the ghost of his father: "Solemn, unlighted, austere / Through the gathering darkness, arise / The chapel-walls, in whose bound / Thou, my father! art laid. / There thou dost lie, in the gloom / Of the autumn evening. But ah! / That word, *gloom*, to my mind / Brings thee back, in the light / Of thy radiant vigor, again."[89] Though it was written in 1857, Coubertin does not seem to have known the poem, nor indeed Matthew Arnold as any but a name.[90] Yet in his 1886 illumination, Pierre felt quite what Matthew expressed in "Rugby Chapel": "In such hour of need / Of your fainting dispirited race, / Ye, like angels, appear, / Radiant with ardor divine! / Beacons of hope, ye appear! / Langour is not in your heart, / Weakness is not in your word, / Weariness is not on your brow. / Ye alight in our van! At your voice; / Panic, despair, flee away."

Coubertin *did* know *Tom Brown's Schooldays*, and like a bible. In its final pages, Tom returns to Rugby to meditate in grief over the Doctor's tomb. Here was ample charter for young Coubertin's ecstasy some forty-four years later, "at the altar, before which he had first caught a glimpse of the glory of his birthright, and felt the drawing of the bond which links all living souls together in one brotherhood—at the grave beneath the altar of him, who had opened his eyes to see that glory and softened his heart till he could feel that bond."[91]

The Arnold Imago

Most writers on Coubertin begin their narratives in earnest here. Some, hagiographers typically, accept as historical fact whatever Coubertin subsequently wrote or said about Arnold.[92] Others, iconoclasts for the most part and equally naive, dismiss Coubertin's perceptions of Arnold as mere idiosyncratic invention, without any basis in fact, "a consciously created myth inspired by a writer of children's books."[93] The truth is more complex and deserves to be puzzled out.

Within months, Coubertin was back in France equating, in speeches and articles, the qualities of English schooling with the genius of Thomas Arnold, "the father of present-day English education."[94] Arnold, Coubertin proclaimed, "was the first to adopt and apply the principles which are the basis" not only of the public schools[95] but of the "manner in which any Englishman, rich or poor, raises his children."[96] The Arnoldian system, as Coubertin described it, was composed of moral development, athletics, and social education, in this order, and its two axial principles and methods were "liberty and sport."[97]

These notions do indeed hew closely to what T. W. Bamford calls "the Arnold legend" current in England in the 1880s.[98] We might leave the matter at this but for three reasons. First, not all of Coubertin's claims are unfair to the historical facts, and Arnold's, like any legend, contains its share of truth that must be drawn out. Second, Arnold was not just a legend to Coubertin, but an imago as well, a complicated psychological representation in which an external personage is blended with a set of condensed psychic needs and relations.[99] Coubertin's "Arnold" cannot be understood without taking this into account. Third, Coubertin's information about Arnold was not limited to what was "in the wind" about him in the 1880s and thereafter. Coubertin owned and read not only *Tom Brown*, but also A. P. Stanley's *The Life and Correspondence of Thomas Arnold*.[100] These two works by students of Arnold at Rugby played a well-known role in the growth of his legend, but they are not by any means false on the whole, and in important respects they contradict one another, the legend, *and* Coubertin's later version of it. It is necessary to know what Coubertin overlooked, as well as what he seized upon, in the eyewitness accounts that were available to him.

The difference between the Arnolds of *Tom Brown* and *The Life* owe principally to the very different experiences of Hughes and Stanley at Rugby. As his biographers tell us, Hughes was a rather ordinary boy, little noticed by the Doctor, and certainly not a member of his inner circle.[101] Hughes's love for Arnold and portrayal in *Tom Brown* of Arnold's "downrightness, exuberance, and kindness,"[102] his manly sensitivity to feelings, openmindedness and benevolence, and the more spiritual than religious character of his leadership and teaching were all derived from observation at a distance. Arnold was a lasting influence on Hughes's life, but as Mack and Armytage point out, the Doctor plays a surprisingly small role in *Tom Brown*, entirely offstage until the middle of the book and, in its final chapters, gaining influence over Brown only through the intermediary figure of the saintly Arthur.[103] *Tom Brown* is much more a book, and a descriptively accurate one, about school life than it is a book about Arnold, and this is how Taine had read it. Coubertin, on the other hand, absorbed everything good about Rugby into the figure of Arnold. While invited, perhaps, by *Tom Brown*'s final chapters, this was nonetheless a misreading that could not have gone forward without inner dispositions of his own. In Stanley's *Life*, however, Coubertin found testimony for identifying Rugby and Arnold.

> From one end of it to the other, whatever defects it had were his defects; whatever excellences it had were his excellences. It was not the master who was beloved or disliked for the sake of the school [as with Hughes], but the school which was beloved or disliked for the sake of the master. Whatever peculiarity of character was impressed on the scholars whom it sent forth, was derived not from the genius of the place, but from the genius of the man. Throughout, whether in the school itself, or in its after effects, the one image we have before us is not Rugby, but AR-NOLD.[104]

Stanley came late to Rugby, was rapidly promoted to the fifth and so escaped fagging altogether. He was "queer" enough to be respected and left alone by the rest of the boys, and his exceptional intelligence brought him immediately under the Doctor's eye and wing.[105] Thus his Rugby was very different from Hughes's.[106] Stanley idolatrized Arnold and was rewarded in kind. The effect was not particularly salubrious.

> Tom Hughes' failure to achieve intimacy with Dr. Arnold (along with the qualities that precluded such intimacy) saved him from the soul-shattering experiences that Clough, Stanley and even Matthew Arnold underwent. Dr. Arnold, who hated childishness, could not help putting pressure on his favorites to grow up prematurely, to develop an intellectual awareness and spiritual drives that were morbidly intense. As

a consequence, they were torn asunder when, without Dr. Arnold's aid, they had to face the realities of an adult world.[107]

Coubertin, who later celebrated *le régime Arnoldien* for fostering independence and preparation for the adult world, knew nothing concrete about the interior fates of Arnold's pupils. He had only Stanley's book to go on, and in it Stanley defends Arnold against these very charges. But it does not require too subtle a reading to discover in *The Life* Stanley's terrible fear of being overwhelmed by the Doctor, his persistent anxiety and morose apprehensions of failure to live up to Arnold's requirements. *The Life* bespeaks not merely hero-worship or idolatrous gratitude, but the pathological swallowing of a young man's ego by his teacher. Coubertin either missed this, ignored it, or balanced it off against the far healthier portrait of Thomas Hughes, that more ingenuous, airier, and, to Coubertin, more kindred soul. On the other hand, Coubertin wished to be overwhelmed, and with Arnold safely dead, he could accept Stanley's "sizing" of the man without having to suffer the personal consequences that Stanley did.[108]

Coubertin's selective reading of *The Life* was hardly limited to matters requiring exegesis. On page after page, Stanley insists and Arnold's letters demonstrate that the Doctor's first concern at Rugby was religious. Even before the headmastership was offered, Arnold was writing to Reverend George Cornish:

> If I do get it, I feel as if I could set to work very heartily, and, with God's blessings, I should like to try whether my notions of Christian education are really impracticable, whether our system of public schools has not in it some noble elements, which under the blessing of the Spirit of all holiness and wisdom, might produce fruit even unto life eternal. When I think about it thus, I really long to take rod in hand.[109]

And rod in hand he took, to make the school "an instrument of God's glory":[110] for "the business of a schoolmaster no less than that of a parish minister is the cure of souls."[111] He wrote: "My object will be, if possible, to form Christian men; for Christian boys I can scarcely hope to make. I mean from the natural imperfect state of boyhood, they are not susceptible of Christian principles in their full development."[112]

Coubertin celebrated Arnold's cautions to himself not to expect too much or to make rules the boys could not keep. Coubertin ignored Arnold's puritan obsessions with the "evil of boy-nature," "the nakedness of boy-nature."[113] Where common sense and ordinary persons saw pranks, misdemeanors, boyish high spirits, innocent frivolity and play, Arnold saw only "vices," "monstrous evil," "temptation and corruption," and "Satan," in "boys whose ages did not prevent their faults from being sins, or their excellences from being noble and Christian virtues."[114] Arnold's "absolute wrestling with evil"[115] and "deep consciousness of the invisible world"[116] were his own most distinctive personal characteristics. He had a streak of Manicheanism in him that could precipitate "severe rebukes for individual faults, showing by their very shortness and abruptness his loathing and abhorrence of evil."[117] Ironically, his boys may have suffered all the more for his generally liberal and compassionate outlook on England as a whole. "When he thought of the social evils of the country, it awakened a corresponding desire to check the thoughtless waste and selfishness of schoolboys."[118] Though his later chapel sermons softened in tone from the brimstone he served up early on, he never lost the conviction that "the spirit of Elijah must ever precede the spirit of Christ."[119] In his confirmation instructions, he made the boys say "Christ died for me" and not "for us,"[120] and, on occasion, he agitated his charges with the most morbid forms of memento mori. For himself and for them, he insisted that the "distance from attendance on a pupil's deathbed" to the classroom ought to be "slight."[121] "His education, in short," says Stanley, "was not . . . based upon religion, it was religious."[122]

Coubertin all but ignored what Arnold put first. "Religion," writes the baron, "holds a large place" in public school education, "but a place off to the side."[123] Protestantism is a "tolerant" and "very elastic form of worship which accommodates itself to the most diverse attitudes," and what Arnold called his "chess match with the Devil" was limited to Sunday School instruction. It was thought well for the boys to attend, but if they didn't care to, says Coubertin, "their wishes were faithfully respected."[124] With these remarks, the whole matter is dismissed.

Several reasons may be adduced to account for the baron's avoidance of Arnold's most important and indisputable pedagogical aim. Arnold's obsessions with boyish sinfulness and evil must have put Coubertin at least subliminally in mind of the residual Manicheanism of the Jesuits of his own *collège*, the very model of pedagogy he was seeking an alternative to in England. Though Catholic scruples are different from Protestant scruples, and the Jesuits employed different means to induce and to remedy them, the resemblance must have been altogether too close for Coubertin to acknowledge. Moreover, though a lapsing Catholic himself, Coubertin could not have found much to please him in Arnold's hatred of popery and railings against Roman perversions of the Gospel. Coubertin did not entertain, as Taine did, any particular admiration for the Anglican church or any desire to see France "protestantized." Having suffered himself from destructive school practices rationalized by religion and from the oppressive pieties of his parents, Coubertin was all too ready to overlook evidence of the same features in Arnold.

Again here, Coubertin seems to have traded Stanley for Hughes. In *Tom Brown*, God plays an even smaller role than Arnold, and the devil a

smaller role still. Tom Hughes, like Tom Brown, was too much a participant and appreciator of schoolboy misdemeanors not to see them for what
they were: boyish errors of judgment, reason, and character, perhaps, but
hardly damning sins. In *Tom Brown*, Hughes leads his readers to believe,
as he himself seems to have believed, that the Doctor was more apt to turn
a benevolently blind eye, knew full well and accepted that "boys will be
boys," and when called upon to punish, did so regretfully and with a light
hand. Hughes was a good-hearted and simple soul. He was prepared to
associate the good that boys did with great Christian virtues, but neither
their faults nor their natures with the devil. And even in its final chapters,
it is the schoolboy Arthur, and not Arnold, who is most demonstrably
preoccupied with religion in *Tom Brown*. The Arnold whom Stanley
described was a very different fellow indeed. Coubertin had to follow
Hughes, on this issue, if Arnold was to serve him as an imago, a father-
figure, and the inspiration and authority for a career as a secular reformer
among Frenchmen who wanted a dram of religion to sweeten the sauce,
but would have found it unpalatable had the real Doctor been known.

Finally, it must be noted that Arnold's commitment to "Christian education," though he pursued it more assiduously than other headmasters,
was the least distinctive feature of his pedagogy, little remembered and
little celebrated in the more secular clime of the 1880s.[125] As good Englishmen and churchmen, Stanley and Hughes demanded of a hero only
that he be unusually adept at great common virtues. Coubertin, with his
French aristocratic value of *prouesse*, needed him to be unique and original.

Arnold himself ranked second what Coubertin's "Arnold" put first, the
individual moral development of gentlemen. "The supreme goal of the
English masters," says Coubertin, "is to make men and to lead them,
thereafter, into improving themselves. Character and good method, that is
their aim."[126] It is, of course, quite misleading to separate Arnold's intense Christianity from the principles of morality, character, and conduct
he strove to inculcate in his boys, as Hughes to some extent, and Coubertin more fully, did. As Mack puts it, "The Tom Browns were a product of
Arnold's moral training, but they were never a direct embodiment of
Arnold's most exalted teaching."[127] Coubertin attributes the slogan "True
Manliness" to Arnold, but it belongs more properly to Hughes. To
Hughes, Christ was a virile, simple, and courageous fellow, a sort of
working class gentleman and regular old boy, one might say.[128] Arnold
wouldn't have had it this way, for to him, one could become a man and a
gentleman only through devotion to the surpassing figure of Christ. Arnold never would have settled for mere manliness without an overarching
devotion to the Divine Will. It is in this respect that "it is no exaggeration
to say that *Tom Brown's Schooldays* made the modern public school."[129]
Hughes reassured middle class parents who would have been put off by

Arnold's excessive religiosity, and it was Hughes, more than Arnold, who taught generations of students, parents, and trustees to take the development of strong and manly characters as the principal aim and result of public school education.

Still, Coubertin was not mistaken about the virtues the Doctor sought to instill. "Initiative, daring, decision, habits of self-reliance and blaming no one but oneself when one stumbles":[130] these were indeed Arnold's goals. Arnold surely would have endorsed the sentiments of honor, compassion, justice, and physical courage that inspired *Tom Brown*, though he would have hesitated, with Taine, over the maxim Hughes draws from them, a maxim that, for good or ill, still strikes a responsive chord in the heart of any male veteran of Anglo-American schooling: leave behind you "the name of a fellow who never bullied a little boy, or turned his back on a big one." Hughes's estimation, indeed love, of gentlemanly pugilism is well-known.[131]

Turning a blind eye on the matter of religion, Stanley completely confirms this perception of Arnold's models of character and conduct, and his preoccupation with turning out characters based on these models. Coubertin's sense of the importance of moral education in the public school is so strong that he virtually subsumed intellectual training under it, and so answered the complaints of Taine, Demogeot, and Montucci about the intellectual backwardness of English schoolboys. "To instruct is not to educate," says Coubertin. Frenchmen have deplorably confused the two notions. Among Frenchmen, "instruction is everything, education nothing."[132] The English suffer no such confusion. Since they understand well the difference, they are able to assign instruction and education to the appropriate stages of the life cycle. Between the ages of eight and twelve, Coubertin assured his audience, English boys work very hard and take the "serious" examinations required for entry into public school. But between twelve and sixteen, their characters are in formation, and so it is appropriate that in public school they do not have so much instruction, do not suffer from *surmenage* ("overwork"),[133] and are taught rather to instruct themselves. To be sure, they leave school knowing less about classical subjects than French *lycéens*, but they have been nonetheless "inculcated with the fundamental notions of all knowledge" and have been "given the habit of work."[134] Moreover, they get into and do well at Oxford and Cambridge where instruction becomes once again important. Again, one is left to infer, it is Arnold's wisdom that has arranged things so.

Arnold himself ranked intellectual training third among his goals at Rugby, and since, as we learn from Stanley, he saw it as of a piece with religious education, Coubertin's presentation is not entirely inapt. Moreover, scholars are quite in accord that it is not for his classroom innovations that Arnold ought to be remembered. Still, Arnold himself would not have been happy to hear Coubertin pass over the intellectual side of his pedagogy so lightly. Arnold was himself a serious, if indifferent, classicist, author of a commentary on Thucydides and a history of Rome. In biblical matters, he was a disciple and proselytizer of Bultmann, and one of the first to bring German criticism to the attention of the English. The classical authors were alive for him (though, revealingly, he did not care for the tragedies), and he was concerned that they became so for his students, though indeed for moral reasons. He believed that all of the great political and social truths that man might discover outside of the gospels were contained in the Greeks and the Romans. Stanley devotes many pages to his attempts to bring them out to his pupils.

Coubertin was himself a product of a classical education, and he found nothing unusual enough to interest him in Arnold's version of it. To trumpet it before a French audience would be to bring grapes, and an inferior species at that, to Burgundy. Again, he followed the lead of Thomas Hughes, who, like him, "always showed a predilection for action and common sense as against theory and for character as against intellect."[135] Despite the author's denials,[136] *Tom Brown* is a frankly anti-intellectual book. Hughes taught Coubertin what to pay attention to in Stanley, and that was the Doctor's and Rugby's emphasis on moral training.

Coubertin quotes Arnold's remark that "my aim is to teach boys how to govern themselves which is much better than to govern them well myself,"[137] and his stress on the Doctor's concern for individual responsibility is fair enough. But on the related matters of obedience and punishment, Coubertin was far too sanguine.

> There, discipline is understood as certain rules of internal order, and that's all. What the eminent bishop of Orleans [Msgr. Dupanloup] finds so necessary in French secondary schools, the English set aside as dangerous and against nature. They spurn that regimentation of every moment requiring nothing more than the practice of obedience—a virtue, such as it is, that they have never appeared to me to make much of, or even to grasp its nature. They shove aside preventative discipline which their instincts almost absolutely refuse to admit in the government or in the schools.[138]

However, it is not nearly so remarkable as Coubertin's virtual silence on that other "rod" Arnold had in hand. Tom Brown is himself caned by the Doctor, and in another episode Arnold, in perfect rage, strikes a boy who has misconstrued his Latin. Hughes is careful to say that this was the first and only instance in which Tom saw the headmaster strike a boy in class, and, in general, flogging by masters is treated as a light enough thing, and, where Arnold is concerned, a last resort. The fact is that in his middle

years at Rugby, Arnold had a public reputation as a brute, brought on by
a notorious case in 1832, in which he personally delivered eighteen vicious
strokes to an innocent and sickly boy.[139] Stanley gives no particulars on
this or similar cases, so Coubertin may not have known about them. But
Stanley does reproduce, and in detail, Arnold's defense of flogging as a
practice, and so gave Coubertin ample opportunity to recognize that Arnold saw physical punishment as something more than an unfortunate
necessity.

Arnold described the "beau ideal of school discipline" for younger boys
as the retention "on principle" of corporal punishment "as fitly answering
to and marking the naturally inferior state of boyhood, and therefore as
conveying no particular degradation." Rather than seeking alternative
punishments, Arnold preferred to "cherish and encourage to the utmost
all attempts made by the several boys, as individuals, to escape from the
natural punishment of their age." To his critics Arnold answered in a
colic, that their reservations on corporal punishment "originated in that
proud notion of personal independence which is neither reasonable nor
Christian—but essentially barbarian. It visited Europe with all the curses
of the age of Chivalry, and is threatening us now with those of
Jacobinism." Thereafter Arnold refused "to discuss the thickness of the
praeposters' sticks, or the greater or less blackness of a boy's bruises for the
amusement of all the readers of the newspapers."[140]

Though he could be cruel, Arnold was certainly not, on the whole, a
brutal man, and flogging may well have decreased during his tenure at
Rugby. Still, Coubertin's recommendation that "those who would au-
tocratically govern French *collèges* with an iron hand" ought to "meditate"
on the example of Arnold[141] seems smooth-faced. But like most urbane
Frenchmen, Coubertin had a perfect horror of corporal punishment, so it
required little effort for him to put Arnold's actual attitude on the practice
out of his mind. Taine had been shocked by the beatings he witnessed at
Harrow in the 1860s. He remarked upon how hard it would be to find, at
any price, French schoolmasters to undertake them. But he also noted that
flogging was accepted, even popular, with English boys, who preferred
it to other punishments and regarded canings as tests of courage.[142] In
his single mention of corporal punishments in "L'Éducation anglaise,"
Coubertin repeats, almost verbatim, these findings of Taine and leaves it
at that.[143] Thereafter, he seems to have imagined that flogging was a part
of the system Arnold was trying to reform.

Fagging, Coubertin also despised as a "species of slavery."[144] Stanley is
silent on the matter, but he does refer his readers to Arnold's "defense of
the general system of fagging" in the educational journals,[145] and no
reader of *Tom Brown* could mistake Arnold's position as mere tolerance of
the practice. Here too, Coubertin read selectively. Encouraged by his

observations and a letter from his friend, the Harrow master, Coubertin satisfied himself that abuses of fagging had all but vanished in the 1880s public school. Taine hated fagging because "by it English boys are urged along the way to which they already incline, in the direction of all those excesses entailed by their energetic temperaments—violence, tyranny, and harshness."[146] Coubertin admitted no such qualities in the English character. The only danger he recognized in the public school regime was the potential for promoting "egotism" in the boys, and this, he added, "was attributable more to the race than to the education."[147]

What Coubertin failed to see was that fagging and excessive flogging by senior boys were immediate corollaries of Arnold's promotion of the sixth form as his special agents in school life. Of this system, Coubertin fully approved, and he quoted Arnold at length on the matter: "I can neither theoretically nor practically defend our public school system, where the boys are left so very much alone to form a distinct society of their own, unless you assume that the upper class shall be capable of being in a manner *mesitai* between the masters and the mass of boys, that is, shall be capable of receiving and transmitting to the rest, through their example and influence, right principles of conduct, instead of those extremely low ones natural to a society of boys left wholly to form their own standard of right and wrong."[148]

One of the favorite principles of the English, Coubertin thought, was that "one never obtains good order without interesting the maximum number of persons in its maintenance." Echoing Taine, he continued: "The English thought that the best means" to keep "resistance to authority from becoming glorious" was "to have authority, or a piece of it, reside in the same milieu from which resistance was likely to issue."[149] Sharing power with the boys of the sixth accomplished this nicely and was, moreover, democratic in Coubertin's eyes. While he repeats Arnold's comparison of the praeposters and monitors with "officers in the army or navy," Coubertin preferred to hear in Arnold's admonitions to the sixth "the head of a constitutional government addressing his ministers." "When I have confidence in the Sixth, there is not a post in England I would exchange for this; but if they don't support me, I must go," Arnold said.[150] Arnold was always threatening the boys with leaving them. While this was hardly sufficient to disturb the conduct of the majority of boys, many of whom would have been glad enough to see him go, its effects on his favorites and on others who worshiped him must have been upsetting indeed.

Whitridge was more specific than Coubertin, and closer to the truth. Under Arnold's regime, the sixth form boys were "playing the part of the cabinet in a constitutional monarchy."[151] And the part of the constabulary too. Coubertin overestimated the liberty of the majority of boys in the public schools. The sixth was formally an elite of achievement, and any boy could aspire, in principle, to a share of its prerogatives. In practice, however, only a small percentage made it to the sixth at all, and, since this was perfectly well known, the many resigned themselves to being ruled without any chance of ever ruling. This may well have sapped academic motivation, and it surely contributed to the unauthorized fagging and bullying of the little boys by fifth form dead-enders. In short, what the school social system "modeled," with all of its strengths and injustices, was a liberal meritocracy.

Arnold's rule through the sixth was indirect, but it was rule nonetheless. As Stanley makes plain, Arnold valued the sixth not only as a means for creating respect for excellence, but also as "an efficient engine of discipline . . . and of diffusing his own influence through the mass of the school."[152] But the contrast with the regimented life of the French *lycéens* led Coubertin to an unbalanced interpretation. "The route that the French boy travels to emancipation is lined with high walls that imprison his gaze,"[153] he wrote. By contrast, public school boys did indeed seem to enjoy a minimum of surveillance and a maximum of "democratic" liberty and self-government.

What Coubertin most celebrated about the "social education" of the Arnoldian public school was its encouragement for boys to create and inhabit a society as homologous as possible with the adult world they would soon enter. "Education must be, I repeat, the preface to life. The man will be free; the boy must be so as well. He only requires to be taught to use that liberty and to understand its importance."[154]

It matters that the world is never hidden from the boys. Besides, to conceal evil is to underline it. In the same way that draping the painting of a nude will lead your sons to lift up the curtain and will give them a taste for what is prohibited.[155]

English schoolboys had the run of the town and the countryside, and Coubertin happily summoned up before his audience "that curious spectacle . . . of all the boys, large and small, passing by in squads up and down the streets, entering the shops, or running through the fields, never in uniform—that's for a barracks—but in fact all dressed the same, which more or less shows how little they care for elegance in their clothing."[156] The boys got up as they wished, either early to study or take a walk, or just in time to make class: "In any case, there's no bell to brusquely awaken you."[157] The English, "because they find *privacy* and *property* two powerful means of education,"[158] foresake dormitories in favor of the boys' having their own rooms, or at least a little study where they can work.

At the public school, the boys thus live surrounded by small objects that remind them of home and family. They take pleasure in decorating their little rooms. On the walls one sees pictures of their parents, their friends, and engravings of hunting scenes. Often there are flowers, pretty knick-knacks, some trophies.... This sanctuary is quasi-inviolable. The master crosses its threshold as rarely as possible, and then more as a visitor than a surveillant.[159]

Yet counsel is ready to hand if the boys care to seek it out, for each house has a master living in, and his family. This provides the boys continuity with their home lives. If in their juvenile commerce they get into debt, and their parents are not forthcoming, then they are forced to sell off their trinkets, and this teaches them to "calculate in advance the results of their actions."[160] Public opinion plays a great role, as it does in adult life, and therefore the masters encourage the boys to attend to their reputations: "The Debating Societies are not the least of the peculiarities of this system. These are, you see, assemblies where parliamentary procedures are scrupulously observed and where one practices public speaking.... You have to hear the debates to get an idea of the liberty of opinions there tolerated."[161] The boys are allowed to subscribe to illustrated magazines and to read popular novels. Rugby has its own "review," "created by Arnold himself,"[162] where the boys publish articles. "Do you see our boys from rhetoric class allowed to print their lucubrations in a journal?" asked Coubertin rhetorically. No, for "such liberty of opinion would be shocking in France because it would produce divergence in the family."[163] In England, "the cult of the home" is strong enough to tolerate differences of opinion, and the boys are encouraged to preserve their loyalties to family through long vacations and uncensored mail.

In sum, says Coubertin, "These English schools are true societies with their laws, their prejudices, their characteristic traits."[164] Consequently, a graduate of one of them "is familiar with the great social laws" because he has "seen them in miniature around him."[165] He prizes solidarity, is anxious to play a part for the common good, and is not easily smitten with ideologies. French boys are all the opposites because they have been locked up in an artificial world bearing little resemblance to the real one.

Though only the review is explicitly attributed to Arnold, Coubertin leaves the impression that the whole of this English system was fathered by him. It was not. Even the magazine may have been initiated by Clough and other pro-Arnold boys in the sixth to counter opposition to Arnold in the press and local public opinion.[166] Virtually all of these customs were traditional at Rugby before Arnold ever entered her halls. Some of them, as both Stanley and *Tom Brown* suggest, were preserved by the boys in opposition to Arnold's attempts to stamp out aspects of the old "constitution."[167] Others, like schoolboy commerce, he barely tolerated. But the main ones among them, privacy, property, liberty, family ties, and so on, he did indeed support within the limits of good order and his Christianity. In this sense, it is not false to see them as part of the "Arnoldian system" of social education.

The Whole Sum of Schoolboy Existence

Three aspects of Arnold's system remain to be discussed: the elitism of the public schools, their connection with the larger social dramas of England, and the essential matter, for Coubertin, of school athletics.

On the first issue, Coubertin's belief that the moral and social values of the public schools differed not in kind, but in degree, from English schooling as a whole has already been noted. He also argued that the public schools were, on closer look, not nearly so expensive as they seemed to French observers and, in any case, the expense was worth it.[168] He promoted the opening of the schools to ever lower ranks of the middle class, and noted the availability of merit scholarships.[169] (Coubertin seems not to have known about the Wraightslaw law suit over the charge that Arnold was driving out the local "foundationeers," that is to say, the scholarship students.) But he was not deceived as to the fact that public school education was upper class education. On the one hand, what he wanted for France was not the development of a separate system of elite private schools, but the incorporation of public school principles into the existing, state-run *lycées*. On the other hand, he defended the interior elitism of the Arnoldian public schools on the grounds that it was consonant with leading British ideas and repaid the general, common weal. These notions emerge most clearly in his full report on Arnold's controversial practice of readily expelling "unpromising boys": "The adjective 'unpromising' doesn't limit the application of this measure to those who are guilty of something, but to all who do not profit from their stay at school, because those who don't profit will also prevent others from profiting. This is not, therefore, a punishment."[170]

Arnold's frequent expulsions of boys caused great public controversy at the time, because of the apparent arbitrariness of the headmaster and his sometime refusal to allow the boys to state their sides of the case. While Stanley thoroughly defends Arnold on the matter, he provides enough clues to have given Coubertin some doubts on the undemocratic character of the practice. But Coubertin thought the practice laudable because the schools ought not to be "houses of correction," and parents ought not to be able to transfer to the schools their own responsibilities for "improving bad characters."[171] Above all, Coubertin wrote, this practice of Arnold's corresponds to the "very British idea" of "selection" and to the merciless realities of English life.

> If you know the English, you know that for the timid, the feeble, and the lazy, life is unbearable. In this jostling existence, they are cast aside, knocked down, and trampled. One discards them, they are nothing but a hindrance. Nowhere is selection more ruthless. There are two distinct races here [Taine again]: men of bold gaze, strong muscles, and assured bearing; and sickly men, of resigned and lowly mien, with the look of

the vanquished. Well, in the public schools as in the world: the weak are pushed out. The benefits of this education are available only to the strong.[172]

But a moral elite, such as that produced by the public schools, was, Coubertin thought, justifiable only to the degree that it contributed to the social and moral progress of the whole nation, to making the weak ones strong. "It's always an elite that one keeps in mind, for a small and superior phalanx always returns more than does widespread mediocrity."[173] On the one hand, this meant, to Coubertin, patriotic service in the government, the colonies, the diplomatic corps, the army, the churches, and so on. On the other hand, it meant dedication to social and political patronage of the sort Taine had celebrated among the English and Coubertin was embarking upon for the French. Coubertin thought Arnold such a man, and his school regime dedicated to turning out such men. Here, he came nearer to the truth about Arnold than he suspected, for he paid scant attention to Arnold's activities outside of Rugby.[174] The social philosophies of the two men were indeed similar in crucial respects, a fact that is rendered less startling when it is recalled that France in the 1880s was undergoing the sort of societal transformation that England had gone through fifty years before: the consolidation of an industrial order; the triumph of bourgeois, national culture;[175] the expansion of democratic political rights; and the making of the working class.[176]

At this stage of his life, and indeed through most of it, Coubertin understood a just society to require more than a democratic political form. France had that, but its people were not yet democratic "in spirit," as he put it.[177] A democratic people and a just society depended on the elimination of artificial inequalities in the social system. Like Arnold (and Taine and Le Play), Coubertin thought some inequalities natural, namely, those of morality, character, and achievement. Therefore, he did not oppose social stratification or class structure as such, but rather their present abuses, locking individuals into social positions through artificial means. Coubertin came to feel, as did Arnold, that "if there is one truth short of the highest for which I would gladly die, it is democracy without Jacobinism."[178] Like Arnold, he refused to accept violence as a legitimate means of social change, and this, together with his belief in individual property, made him a steadfast opponent of socialism through most of his life. Arnold hated the doctrines of laissez-faire political economy,[179] and Coubertin eventually grew to oppose turning men into machines by the exploitation of the unregulated market economy. Both, therefore, gave qualified assent to state regulation of the market and to workers' associations including, in Coubertin's case, trade unions. But neither opposed capitalism as such.

While both were "gradualists," especially to twentieth-century eyes, both were thoroughgoing reformers too. Coubertin could well have said, as Arnold did, "My love for any place or person, or institution, is exactly the measure of my desire to reform them; a doctrine that seems to me as natural now, as it seemed strange when I was a child, when I could not make out, how, if my mother loved me more than strange children, she should find fault with me and not with them."[180] In 1831, Arnold scandalized his peers by agitating publicly for the Reform Bill. In his second letter to the *Sheffield Courant*, he outlined the same liberal goals that Coubertin pursued a half-century later:

> The Aristocrat aims to reduce all ranks but his own, the Jacobin to reduce all ranks to the lowest level . . . our business is to raise all and to lower none. [Absolute] equality is the dream of a madman or the passion of a fiend. Extreme inequality or high comfort and civilization in some, coexisting with deep misery and degradation in others is no less a folly and a sin. But an inequality where some have all the enjoyments of a civilized life, and none are without its comforts—where some have all the treasures of knowledge and none are sunk in ignorance, that is a social system in harmony with God's creation in the natural world.[181]

Arnold's jeremiads against the gap between the rich and the poor brought down upon him the wrath of the Tory aristocrats and gentry who sent their boys to Rugby or to the other public schools. France did not yet know such industrial poverty, and Coubertin directed his energies against the general demoralization and the absence of patriotism, solidarity, and sense of common good in *la patrie* as a whole. Arnold continued to believe that the aristocracy could be reformed and that, with an equally reformed Broad Church, it would play a leading role in the amelioration of social conditions. Coubertin was less sanguine about the reform of the French aristocracy, though certainly he wished for it, and he shortly joined battle in favor of the separation of church and state in France, as against Arnold's radical identification of the two in England. Although there is controversy over whether Arnold indoctrinated the boys with his own political and social views,[182] he certainly attempted to instill a general sense of responsibility for the common weal and a particular sense of duty to the poor in the upper middle class students of his avowedly elitist education. Coubertin wanted the reformed French *lycées* to be first of all schools of patriotism and moral training. He seems to have thought, at first, that appeals to such "self-evident" values allowed him to circumvent the rabid and divisive political and ideological forces surrounding the issue of French school reform. But France was a republic, so patriotic schools meant schools committed to instilling republican values, and Coubertin declared for them.[183]

   Though public school education was for an elite, Arnold insisted that
education was for all. "Education, in the common sense of the word, is
required by a people before poverty has made a havoc among them; at that
critical moment when civilization makes its first burst, and is accompanied
by an immense commercial activity."[184] Such a "burst" was taking place
in France as Coubertin was beginning his public career, and he too
believed that education, of one sort or another, was for all and an essential
requirement for human dignity and social peace. He shortly accepted the
republican call for free, universal, and compulsory primary schools.[185]
The *lycée* system—though it needed to be expanded, to accept students
strictly on the basis of merit, and to develop scholarships for working class
children—neither could nor should be made universal or compulsory. But
institutions for the popular education of working class adults had to be
developed, under either private or governmental auspices. While the
secondary education of adolescents remained the focus of Coubertin's reformist proposals, he had an intense and lifelong interest in popular education. After "L'Éducation anglaise," the next article he published in
La Réforme sociale celebrated Toynbee Hall, a sort of university extension
offering classes in the Whitechapel slums of London, and in the 1920s he
was still proselytizing for *universités ouvrières.*
   In this, Coubertin seems not to have realized that he was also following
an Arnoldian tradition. Arnold had interested himself in the Society for
the Diffusion of Useful Knowledge in 1826, and in 1831 he founded the
Englishman's Register, a seven-penny weekly that hoped to attract working
class as well as middle class readers.[186] In 1839, he laid plans for a society
of men from all parties to collect and disseminate exact, statistical information on the conditions of the poor.[187] Arnold's followers went
further. Matthew Arnold's works on popular education have already been
cited. And the most famous Arnoldian of them all, Thomas Hughes,
joined Kingsley and Maurice to found the Christian Socialist Movement,
whose most notable achievement, after the organization of workers'
cooperatives, was the establishment of the first Working Men's Colleges in
London.[188] Hughes committed himself deeply to the work, but, less intellectual and pretentious than his friends, he felt that he had nothing to
lecture upon that the dockworkers and joiners who frequented the place
would find worth knowing. So with characteristic vigor and simplicity, he
instructed the workers in what he knew and loved best in the world after
family, God, and social justice: boxing, cricket, rowing, and football.[189]
Hughes thought this "the best social work he ever did," and the innovation
caught on. By 1880, athletic sports were broadly incorporated into patronage associations, liberal and Tory alike, whose programs were concerned with the betterment of the working classes.[190] This "return" of
athletic games to the lower orders was the third great movement in the
social history of English sport.[191]

Hughes had been present for the second "movement" as well—the expansion to the middle class of the aristocratic preoccupation with athletics in the context of the public schools of the '20s, '30s, and '40s. Indeed, through *Tom Brown*, Hughes became the most important interpreter of this development to greater England. Though much of the thought behind it may have been Charles Kingsley's,[192] the unabashed devotion to games was Hughes's alone. Together, the thought and the feeling made *Tom Brown* the still unsurpassed charter of sport as a mode of character formation and inculcation of bourgeois virtues. But the athletic traditions of the public schools were well in place long before Hughes or Thomas Arnold ever set foot in Rugby, for the public schools had played a role in the first act of the English social history of modern sport as well—the appropriation and transformation of village games and amusements by the aristocracy and gentry of the seventeenth and eighteenth centuries.[193]

Cricket is known as a popular boys' game as early as the sixteenth century, and by late Stuart times it had attracted the attention of the gentry and was becoming established as an organized, adult game.[194] By the mid-eighteenth century, its popularity had spread throughout the social strata, and protests were heard against the mixing of ranks at matches.[195] It was played at Harrow at least by 1768,[196] twenty years before the Marylebone Cricket Club, a convenient marker for the upper class usurpation of the game, was founded by public school graduates. That same decade, it came to Rugby.[197] In 1805, Lord Byron played for Harrow in the first match against Eton, and after another Eton-Harrow match in 1818, the opposition of school authorities was overcome and the "long series" began at Lord's in 1822. In 1827, the year before Arnold took up tenure at Rugby, the Oxford-Cambridge matches were initiated.[198]

Football, too, existing in innumerable regional variations, was an ancient village game, known well back to Elizabethan times, associated especially with Shrove Tuesday feasts. Some brand of football is mentioned as a public school amusement as early as the seventeenth century.[199] In 1820, it was still in a "primitive state," played at Harrow and Rugby but "not of absorbing interest,"[200] doubtless because of its lowly pedigree and roughish associations. But in 1823, the great "innovation" (though popular precedents abounded)[201] to which Rugby attached its name took place, when William Webb Ellis "with a fine disregard for the rules" took the ball in his arms and ran with it.[202] The "new" game was rapidly systematized, and its fame spread quickly. When Queen Adelaide visited Rugby in 1839, she asked to see it played, and one of those who scrummed up before her may well have been Tom Hughes himself.

As Whitridge pithily puts it, Arnold's only contribution to the craze for athletics was that he sometimes stood on the sidelines and looked pleased."[203] No "objective," unmotivated reader of *Tom Brown* or Stanley's *Life* could think it otherwise. In *Tom Brown*, the Doctor takes an occasional look-see at cricket and football. The only other direct connection between Arnold and games comes in the speech of Old Brooke, in which he feels called upon to reassure the doubting Schoolhouse boys that Arnold does not intend to prohibit team games. Stanley's equation between Rugby and ARNOLD can be extended to athletic games only by ignoring the evidence of Stanley himself. Cricket and football receive only one or two passing mentions in all the letters and sermons of Arnold that Stanley reproduces; Arnold certainly never mounts any brief for them. Stanley, too, notes that Arnold would now and then "stand in the school-field and watch the issue of *their* favorite games"[204] (emphasis mine). The only games it occurred to him to join in were the childhood pastimes of his offspring.[205]

Arnold was, to be sure, an adept of individual physical exercise, regularly enjoying walks, flower hunts, bathing, and riding.[206] He believed in a healthy body for a sound mind, motivated in part by the almost neurotic anxiety that "life and health [be] spared me" that one finds repeatedly in his letters.[207] But he also was inspired by the Greeks and by familiar notions of "hygiene." Insofar as he passively encouraged the athletic games he found in place at Rugby, it was for their fitness, recreational, and "gymnastic" values alone. As Stanley puts it, "The Greek notion of the *aretē mousikē* with the *aretē gymnastikē*, he thought invaluable in education, and he held that the freedom of the sports of the public schools was particularly favorable to it."[208] But which "sports" did the unathletic Stanley have in mind here? More likely bathing than cricket. The passage continues "and whenever he saw that the boys were reading too much, he always remonstrated with them, relaxed their work, and if they were in the upper part of the school, would invite them to his house . . . to refresh them." Recreation, in the original etymological sense is the dominant theme.

There was nothing unusual or innovative in these views. What has been said of Richard Baxter, Weber's and Tawney's archetypal Puritan of a century and a half before could be said of Arnold: "He was quite sure that man could take all the exercise that health and sanity demanded without indulging in sport as such."[209] The "real genuine joy,"[210] rapturous and animal, that the Toms, Brown and Hughes, felt at football would have brought out the Puritan in Arnold. East's pride that "there's been two collar-bones broken this half, and a dozen fellows lamed"[211] would have been condemned by the Doctor as irrational, loutish, and, to say the least, "unhygienic." His pupil's experience of the *illud tempus* and their sincere belief that football "is worth living for; the whole sum of school-boy existence gathered up into one straining, struggling half-hour, a half-hour worth a year of common life"[212] would have shocked Arnold as an impiety of monstrous evil and would have brought down the full weight of his anathema. Toward the association made by the "athletic Christians" between games and character,[213] patriotism,[214] moral training,[215] and adult duty,[216] Arnold would have been skeptical at best.

In sum, then, it was not Arnold but his students and their friends who formulated this social philosophy of middle class sport. An Etonian wrote in 1831, "I cannot consider the game of football at all gentlemanly. After all, the Yorkshire common people play it."[217] It was not until the 1850s at school, and the 1860s and '70s nationally, that class barriers fell to physical desire and both forms of football became widespread.[218]

Rowing is known as an informal but competitively organized recreation at Winchester as early as the 1740s,[219] but only after the university boat races were begun in 1829 did it become a notable activity at those public schools blessed with suitable riverine courses. Rugby was not one of them. Swimming, too, was a valued recreation of long standing, and *Tom Brown* shows its popularity at Rugby in the 1830s. But it was not until the middle nineteenth century that it began to be organized as a competitive sport, and then not widely.[220] Running at Rugby was typical of the other schools. It was popular in the early years of the nineteenth century, but "the boys tended to use the countryside as they found it rather than to make up a well balanced steeplechase course or measure out standard lengths."[221] Flat races at 100, 200, and 440 yards were known but poorly organized and not popular. As described in *Tom Brown*, "hare and hounds" and paper chases provided the competitive format.[222] The first regular bigside runs appeared in 1837, during Hughes's stay at Rugby. Fives, bat-fives, and quoits were old games at Rugby, but always minor ones.[223]

Pugilism, that is to say fighting as an organized contest, developed rapidly through the eighteenth century. The settling of workers' quarrels by fisticuffs, with some rules of fair play and betting among the spectators, is known at least as early as 1727. But boxing may have been part of the revived Cotswold Games in the seventeenth century. In the middle and later 1700s, the rules were systematized, "academies of Boxing" appeared, principles of "scientific" self-defense were laid down, and great matches were arranged. The combatants themselves were generally of humble origin, but the matchmakers, promoters, spectators, and gamblers were often gentry or aristocrats.[224] Gambling was the least concealed source of upper class interest. As Brailsford succinctly puts it, "if the Restoration carried a maypole in one hand, it also carried a purse full of stake money in the other."[225] By the 1770s, boxers had become national celebrities, and large matches drew thousands of spectators. This phase peaked in the 1820s, when George IV is reputed to have had an honor guard of prizefighters at his coronation,[226] and Tom Hughes took as his

first boyhood hero a fighter named Henry New.[227] By the 1840s, however, prizefighting had fallen into disrepute among monarchs and gentlemen alike. In his adulthood, Hughes loathed it as "as brutal and degrading
a custom as any nation could tolerate,"[228] while at the same time lauding
gentlemanly pugilism in the public schools and Working Men's Colleges.[229] The origin of sparring with gloves at the public schools is difficult
to date, though it certainly predated Hughes's time at Rugby and was
likely to have been taken up in imitation of the celebrated prizefighters
around the turn of the century, though prizefighters used gloves only
during practice. Only much later, after the Marquess of Queensberry
reforms of 1866 and the foundation of the Amateur Boxing Association in
1884, did boxing emerge as an aboveboard organized sport at the public
schools—in the 1890s, in the case of Rugby.[230]

From the eighteenth century through early Victorian times, the upper
classes' efforts to suppress the grosser popular sports were accompanied
by equally zealous efforts to protect their own blood sports against en-
croachment or moral criticism.[231] Foxhunting, game hunting, and angling
were the most controversial of these, especially during the period of the
Enclosure Acts and the fashionableness of "deer parks" set down amidst
the starving poor. Horse racing, or rather, owning and wagering on horses
ridden by hired men, was the other great animal "field sport," one with a
long pedigree. Schoolboy versions of these activities—keeping hounds,
hunting for rabbit and grouse, if not deer, and betting among themselves
on the great derby races—were established traditions in the public schools
of the eighteenth and early nineteenth centuries. Arnold endeavored to
suppress them upon his arrival at Rugby. This indirectly benefited athletic games by releasing more time for them, and it was Arnold's most and
only effective action "in favor" of them.

It was members of a succeeding generation of headmasters, like Edward
Thring, and not Arnold, who saw fit to join personally in team games and
athletic contests. Thring was headmaster at Uppingham until 1887.
"Mark me," he once wrote to his biographer G. R. Parkin, "cricket is the
greatest bond of the English speaking race, and is no mere game."[232] And
it was not Arnold, but his sworn enemy, J. H. Newman, who speculated
on the spiritual value of sport: "There are bodily exercises which are
liberal, and mental exercises which are not so. . . . It is absurd to balance,
in point of worth and importance, a treatise on reducing fractures with a
game of cricket or a fox-chase; yet of the two, the bodily exercise has that
quality which we call 'liberal,' and the intellectual does not."[233]

Of Newman's remarks on sport Coubertin might have been aware,[234]
and in the 1890s the names of Kingsley and Thring crept into his
speeches.[235] But throughout his life, Coubertin persisted in believing that
"Arnold himself loved and practiced sports," "admirably understood their

various aspects," especially their role "in moral hygiene," thought "intense physical effort" the best form of sport, and was himself "one of the muscular Christians."[236] From the first to the last, Coubertin insisted on laying at Arnold's door *la pédagogie sportive*.

In the memories of 1880s Englishmen, Arnold had indeed become associated with athletic games. But more than the "legend" is required to account for Coubertin's "mistake," for not only had the baron read the original sources, but he himself noted his cognitive dissonance upon finding in them scant connection between the Doctor and sport.

> To be sure, M. Taine and MM. Demogeot and Montucci strongly acknowledged that sport played a moral, and indeed a social, role in English education, but they didn't explain in what way this was done. The interior mechanism remained obscure. The English didn't help me at all to discover it; one could say that they themselves didn't perceive it. *My worst disillusionment* came from the fact that Thomas Arnold had nothing more to say about it than they did. I would have hoped, in the absence of a treatise on the matter, which no doubt the shortness of his life didn't leave him time to write, to have found in his letters and sermons some precise information. But no. The subject, implied throughout and, one knows, a preoccupation haunting the brain of the great pedagogue, was nowhere explicitly approached.[237] [Italics mine]

Coubertin's identification of Arnold with educational sport was an illusion in Freud's sense of the term: a deep and multiply determined wish fulfilled.[238] Coubertin needed a link between school reform, social and moral education, and athletic games; and he needed that link embodied in a single, distant, exotic, kind, and fatherly figure of patriotic and progressive genius to serve him as an imago and the new France as a model. Because he needed Arnold to be this man, so he made him to be.

Far from a "consciously created myth," to use the phrase of a writer on Coubertin already quoted, this was a complicated and largely unconscious solution for a young man whose own identity was on trial. Coubertin's refusal to be "dis-illusioned" in the face of contrary evidence, evidence he felt perfectly free to announce, adds weight to a contrary interpretation of Coubertin's "Arnold." After the remarks cited in the previous paragraph, Coubertin passes to *Tom Brown*. Hughes gave him his lead, *not* because Hughes identified Arnold and sport—as we have seen, he does nothing of the kind—but because Hughes did not feel, or feel called upon to note in his book, any dissonance between Arnold as moral leader of Rugby and Rugby sport as moral enterprise. Coubertin simply went the author of *Tom Brown* one better, by absorbing Hughes himself into the prepotent figure of Arnold.[239] That is why, in the hundreds of pages of his writings on sport and the English schools, Coubertin nowhere shows the slightest curiosity about Hughes, the man. Given the signal importance of *Tom*

Brown to his development, this is very odd indeed, unless it is understood
after the fashion I am suggesting. Coubertin could brook no rivals for
"Arnold's" legacy, nor, it seems, could he entertain the notion that the
greatness of Arnold's heirs was anything but a reflection in them of the
glories of their master. Such a condensation of a complex chain of associations into a single preponderant figure is one familiar solution to the
problem of cognitive dissonance.[240]

Another is to seek out and appeal to some very great, but tangential,
authority. This Coubertin did on a return visit to England in 1888,[241]
when he secured an interview with no less a personage than Gladstone.
"All that he told me of his schoolboy recollections," Coubertin reported,
"confirmed the bad opinion which I already held of the corruption existing
in the English schools" before Arnold's reforms "wrought a moral revolution of the most effective and admirable kind."[242] Gladstone, whom
Coubertin later celebrated as a "veteran boater,"[243] also announced with
great pride that "I don't believe there's a single spot on the Thames where
I couldn't tell you, in calm weather, the power of the current and the
depth of the water."[244] What were likely scattered replies to the disjointed
questions of the young foreign nobleman were later assembled by Coubertin into high testimony for his equation of Arnold's school reforms,
sports, and the strength of the British Empire. Thereafter, and often,
Coubertin appealed to the authority of Gladstone for his belief that far
more than Waterloo was won on the playing fields of Rugby and Eton.

> Arnold draws up . . . the fundamental rules of the pedagogy of sport.
> From Rugby, he affects the other public schools by the contagion of his
> example, without resounding phrases or indiscreet interference; and so
> the keystone of the British Empire is laid. I know that this point of view
> is not yet that of the historians nor of the British themselves, but I am
> content to have had it approved by one of the greatest survivors of the
> Arnoldian period—Gladstone. When I put the question to him, being
> afraid that I might be mistaken, he asked me for time to think the matter
> over, and having thought it over he said: "You are right, that is how it
> happened."[245]

The third well-known solution to cognitive dissonance is missioniza-
tion.[246] Whatever disconfirmation of wishful beliefs that Arnold's writings
might have threatened for Coubertin was utterly removed when, between
1886 and 1887, Coubertin set about in earnest the proselytization of
France for school sports on the English model.

Liberty, morality, character, patriotism, the common good, and devotion of an elite to less fortunate countrymen: these were the qualities
Coubertin admired in the Arnoldian public schools. But, he told his
French audience, "the role played there by sport" is "what appears to me
most worthy of notice in English education."[247] Sport was the inner

engine of the system, because "it reacts upon the whole."[248] It's role "is at once physical, moral, and social."[249]

> Sport is movement and the influence of movement on the organs is a thing well-known through the ages. Strength and dexterity have always been admired, by savage as well as civilized peoples, and one obtains them by exercise and practice. The successful development of physical qualities generally produces a happy equilibrium in the moral domain. *Mens sana in corpore sano* say the ancients.[250]

But the English are distinctive, says Coubertin, because they attach physical training to the highest values,[251] and English athletic games are the best form of physical training because of their ethical qualities.

In sport, liberty "is complete," because cricket, lawn tennis, and football are freely chosen by the boys and never imposed.[252] Sport accrues to the virtues of initiative, daring, decision, and self-reliance, and it "also has the effect of exalting courage."[253]

> All whom I questioned on the subject were unanimous in their answers: they have only to rejoice in the state of school morality, and they loudly declare that sport is the cause of it; that its role lies in pacifying the senses and calming the imagination, stopping corruption by cutting it off at the root and preventing it from being shown off, and, finally, in arming nature for the struggle.[254]

In Arnold's eyes, says Coubertin, nothing was worse than the mind's taking too great a lead over the body. "In its development, the intelligence must have an ample outer covering, one strong enough to contain it and to endure the stress of its expansion."[255] But physical games do more than contribute a healthy "casing"; they promote intellectual development itself. "It is said that the life of the thinker and the life of the athlete are opposed, the one to the other. For my part, I have often noticed that those who find themselves first in physical exercises are also first in their studies. The serious commitment in one area promotes the desire to be first throughout; for victory, there is nothing like the habit of it."[256] Moreover, says Coubertin, games have a classical pedigree, and so the English have shown them an excellent means to engage the boys in their classical studies. "The English believe in the necessity of enthusiasm at this age. But they also think that it's not easy, if it's even desirable, to lead the boys to being caught up in enthusiasm for Alexander or Caesar. The dust of Olympia [*la poussière olympique*] is still that which best and most naturally excites their emulation."[257] Though a passing remark, this is a revealing one. Athletic games on the "Greek" model are substituted for the "classical games" of Coubertin's own *collège*, that is, the acting out of events and episodes from the Greek historians, as a pedagogical tool. In Coubertin's published writings, this is the second reference to the Olympic Games.

The first occurs in a similar context in his premier article in *La Réforme sociale*, for the most part, a rehash of Taine's remarks on Harrow in the *Notes*.[258] Taine, however, was under no illusion that English sports faithfully transcribed Greek ones. Often, in the *Notes*, he comments on how badly "any classical form or idea" fares in England. "I am always discovering that London resembles ancient Rome, as Paris does Athens."[259]

Finally, Coubertin argues that athletic games "furnish a perfect terrain for social education." The boys are entirely responsible themselves for organizing athletic associations, collecting dues, electing officers, and "obeying them with a remarkable spirit of discipline." The president organizes matches and "makes 'toasts.'" The secretary convokes meetings, and the treasurer reports on the budget to the "general assembly." In short, says Coubertin, this is a "complete embryo of society."[260] And so, Coubertin concludes: "I believe that if some reforms might be hoped for in our system, it's only by this means [sport] that they might be introduced. I even fancy that I see a movement taking shape in this direction that could be utilized very advantageously."[261]

CHAPTER FOUR

Athletic Education

❧❧❧

Frédéric Le Play and the Société d'Économie Sociale

La Réforme sociale, in which the first statements of Coubertin's *pédagogie sportive* appeared, was the combined organ of the Société d'économie sociale[1] and the Unions de la paix sociale. Both organizations were founded and overseen by Frédéric Le Play, a complex man, and an important, thought generally neglected, sociologist and social philosopher of the mid-nineteenth century. Le Play's theories had a lifelong influence over Coubertin, who, as a very old man, wrote that "Le Play was, with Arnold, the master to whom my gratitude goes now that the night is approaching. To these two men I owe more than I can say."[2]

Le Play was born into a poor Norman family in 1806, the son of a minor customs official who died or disappeared when the boy was five. For some years Le Play lived in Paris with an uncle who presided over a Catholic and royalist salon. After schooling in Le Havre, Le Play came under the influence of Dan de la Vauterie, an engineer and land drainage expert, and returning to Paris, he passed rapidly through the Collège de France, the Polytechnique, and the École des mines, where he was the most brilliant pupil in a generation.[3] The school required its students to tour and report on mines and metalworks. In the company of a Saint-Simonian colleague, Le Play journeyed some four thousand miles through Europe.[4] The extensive diaries he kept and the descriptive reports he wrote were the prototypes for the case study methods he later pioneered, and these inquiries turned the skilled engineer and *technicien* toward social studies, labor questions, and industrial management.

In 1830, Le Play was seriously burned in a laboratory explosion at the École des mines. While he was in a hospital fighting for his life, the July Revolution broke out, and the combined personal and collective bloodshed worked a conversion in him. "I dedicated my life to the reestablishment of social peace in my country."[5]

What 1870 and the wounds of social marginality were to Coubertin, 1830 and a physical wound were to Le Play. In the '30s, he was an editor of the *Annales des mines,* a founder of the Statistical Commission on the

Metal Industry, and had carried out technical and social studies in Spain, Belgium, Russia, and England. These researches, many of them government funded, continued into the '40s and '50s,[6] when Le Play was professor at the École des mines and a well-paid manager of the vast iron and steel works of Prince Demidov in Russia.

Le Play was temporarily enthusiastic for the Revolution of 1848, and he served the provisional government as a member of the Luxembourg Commission for the Workers. But rapidly disillusioned by the regime, he turned conservative in his personal politics and skeptical of political solutions to social problems in his philosophy. In lines that recall the "episode of the coins" from Coubertin's own youth, Le Play wrote: "Since 1879, ten regimes have governed France. Each of these has been set up and then overthrown by force. These unstable and uncertain conditions are without parallel."[7]

Thereafter, governmental policies took precedence over governmental form in his thinking and actions, and, without qualms, he took a variety of posts under the Empire, including commissioner general of the 1855 and 1867 universal exhibitions, state councilor, and senator. He sought, often successfully, to influence the emperor's social and economic policies through personal contacts with him, through the intermediary of Prince Napoleon, with whom Le Play was friendly, and through publicizing the results of his own "scientific observations of human societies." These Le Play described as built upon "rules analogous to those to which my mind has been trained for the study of minerals and plants . . . a method that has allowed me to understand personally all the underlying currents of peace and disharmony, prosperity and suffering which are present in contemporary societies of Europe."[8]

Les Ouvriers européens, published in 1855, was the grand expression of this "monographic method," as it has come to be called by historians of sociology. Le Play was among the first to emphasize fieldwork in the modern sense of the term. "The time is not far distant," he wrote, "when the fact that an author has not moved out of his study will be sufficient refutation of his theory."[9] For periods of a week to a month, Le Play intensively interviewed, in their several languages, hundreds of working class families across Europe. Concerned above all with family stability, he reported on social networks, religious practice, and values, but concentrated the bulk of his attention on the collection of detailed family budgets. Not only were income and expenditures measurable and subject to statistical analysis, but, as Pitts (following Sorokin) has pointed out, Le Play thought that "all crucial family activities express themselves in momentary form which can be represented as a budget item."[10] Each field study was then written up as a separate monograph and subsequently collected into *Les Ouvriers*, a work crowned by the Prix Monthyon for statistics in the year of its publication. Le Play's method was not, how-ever, explicitly comparative, and this later occasioned much criticism.[11] Instead, he sought to generate a taxonomy of family types, associated with degrees of stability.

While he continued to promote case studies through the '60s and '70s, in works like *La Réforme sociale en France, L'Organisation du travail, La Paix sociale après le désastre*, and *La Constitution essentielle de l'humanité*,[12] Le Play elaborated a social philosophy in which the values of family, property, social peace, worker security, Catholicism, decentralization, and personal morality were offered as charters for societal reform. As Pitts has shrewdly pointed out, these two sides of Le Play were not in contradic-tion. Rather than a true commitment to empirical study and inductive theory building, the monographic method was "the invention of an anti-empiricist" who believed that "in his day only scientific descriptions of social realities would render self-evident the one way to social harmony and individual happiness."[13] Though more systematic in method and less dependent upon intuitive insight than Taine's ethnography, Le Play's was, in the end, kindred in spirit (though Le Play never flirted with cultural relativism, as Taine did). Coubertin had no interest in methodol-ogy and no patience for case studies. His methods were closer to Taine's, and he shared their common humanistic ethos.

Le Play attracted talented collaborators, whose monographs we find in *Les Ouvriers* and sister publications. In 1856, he founded the Société d'économie sociale to give form to their attachment and to recruit and train additional amateur sociologists in his methods. Brooke rightly com-pares the société to the numerous contemporary associations for the pro-motion of natural science.[14] The manifesto of the société ran as follows: "Friends of progress, but dreading disorder and sterile agitation, we sum-mon onto the ground of experience, fertilized by study and discussion, all those men who wish to render our country free, great, and prosperous."[15] Since he believed that exact knowledge contributed in itself to social peace, that private citizens had a role equal to that of politicians, bureau-crats, and professors in the search for class harmony, and that these goals transcended political ideology, Le Play insisted that "the same spirit always controls our meetings; that we are concerned with social facts, with exact observations and not with *a priori* theories; that politics and per-sonalities should always be strictly barred."[16] Le Play added that mem-bers did not vote on the conclusions of reports, leaving each free to make up his own mind. Of course, this also afforded Le Play himself more complete control over opinion. Like the École des sciences politiques, the société thought that "value-free" inquiry and the pursuit of the common good made it a nonideological institution.

However, in the 1860s, the société began to consider policy more directly in its meetings, and following the events of 1870–71, the Franco-Prussian War and the Commune, Le Play felt the need to spread his gospel more energetically. In 1872, he founded the Unions de la paix sociale to serve as the propaganda arm of the société, whose scientific reputation he hoped to protect through this differentiation. The unions were small study groups organized throughout France, and eventually in neighboring countries, each linked to Paris by a "correspondant." Potential members could apply for admission directly, but most were coopted. Members were duty-bound to read Le Play's books, "whose study is irreplaceable," to promote them and the journal *La Réforme sociale* in their local environs, and to recruit additional "zealous auxiliaries."[17] Membership in the société and the unions overlapped, and after 1882, a joint congress met annually for "general sessions, working and discussion groups, and 'social visits' to industrial establishments, farms, and public assistance projects."[18] The unions, too, invited all whose commitments were to greater France and not to particular social groups or ideologies.

In fact, both Le Play organizations were disproportionately conservative in the '60s and '70s, as scrutiny of the membership lists reveals. Many aristocrats and provincial *abbés*, drawn by Le Play's emphasis on family, Church, and the chastity of women, brought royalist commitments with them into the société. This trend continued in the '70s, when the unions lobbied against the anticlerical laws.[19] Others, influenced by one or another stream of social Catholicism, were attracted by the Le Play preoccupation with the gap between rich and poor. Despite the master's insistence that the sentiment of charity was "both honorable and stupid," because it did nothing about the roots of poverty and pandered to complacency of the corrupt upper classes, some of these members saw the société as continuous with the St.-Vincent-de-Paul societies they patronized.[20] Others, like Benoist d'Azy, an aristocrat and industrial director who for decades had sought to alleviate working class distress through paternalistic factory management, were drawn by this aspect of Le Play's thought. Benoist d'Azy was later a legitimist deputy, as were Anatole de Melun and Louis de Kergolay, and all three became vice-presidents of the société.[21] More slavish legitimists, aristocrats and bourgeois alike, joined simply because Chambord had let it be known that he favored Le Play's ideas.

But the société cannot simply be characterized as an organization of reactionaries. In the '60s, Saint-Simonians like Michel Chevalier played prominent roles in it; in the '70s, the center of gravity shifted to Orleanism, while many moderate republicans joined up. By Coubertin's time, this group was far stronger in the société than the holdover intransigents. Moreover, while some members railed against the socialists in société meetings, others joined Le Play in sincere and sometimes concerted efforts to find common ground with the left. For example,

Limousin, French delegate to the First International, was invited to speak about the congress of 1876 to the société,[22] an invitation that would never have issued from the seemingly more worldly École des science politiques.

In late 1883, Coubertin became one of the 2,731 members of the Unions de la paix sociale.[23] The following year, while dodging his classes at the Faculté de droit, he likely fulfilled the pledge to read Le Play's books, but there is no evidence that he took particularly active part in union meetings. During his days at the École des sciences politiques, he seems to have had little time for the Le Play group, but after abandoning the école in 1886, Coubertin joined the Société d'économie sociale as well, and became very noticeable at société and union sessions.[24]

The continuities between the école and the société make Coubertin's shift of venue for his project comprehensible: Le Play's theories were in favor at the école; école professors like Paul Leroy-Beaulieu had connections with the société; methodological and philosophical commitments were similar at both institutions; both were politically neutral but in fact dominated by the parties of order; at both, young *rallié* aristocrats and the bourgeoisie mixed freely; and both were founded and run by observers of England and were frankly international in outlook. But the discontinuities between the école and the société were important to Coubertin as well. While both were liminal institutions, poised between the academy, government, industrial elites, and the scientific community, the école was still a school, with formal courses, professors, degrees, and the like. As we have seen, these aspects of the école intimidated Coubertin somewhat. And rightly so. Even had a format for them been available, "Harrow School," "Cambridge," and "L'Éducation anglaise" would never have passed muster at the école. They would have been immediately overshadowed by the works of Taine and Boutmy, and the zealous anglophilia and precipitate calls for cross-cultural borrowing contained in them would have brought down severe criticism upon the audacious but inwardly unconfident Coubertin. His emotional resources, gathered in visions at Rugby chapel, could scarcely have withstood the attack of intellects greater than he. The société, on the other hand, was less formally and hierarchically organized. As a purely voluntary organization, it embodied social patronage, whereas the école merely favored it. The unions and the société had sufficient intellectual legitimacy to satisfy Coubertin's need to believe himself in the center of the French national debate, but the broader range of intellectual styles and competencies among the membership afforded Coubertin a more open atmosphere in which he did not feel intimidated. Here he could feel a sense of community with those he took to be a moral and social elite of a progressive sort, while opportunities for displays of his own *prouesse* were present. Reformist schemes, as long as they were salted with statistics and face-to-face experiences, received a hearing. In sum, the société gave Coubertin a relatively safe and supportive atmosphere in which to try his wings, and when he did, it assured him that he could fly.

"L'Éducation anglaise" was greeted by the president, Claudio Jannet, with expressions of pleasure over "this brilliant report, whose qualities exclude neither humor nor literary charm." It was, Jannet effused, "a very great joy to see a true talent showing itself in this way . . . confirming the great Le Play's conclusions on the subject of great importance." A few innocent and encouraging questions from the audience, the chair's fond hope that Coubertin would pursue the topic in a future meeting "that one couldn't wish to be more interesting and animated than the present one,"[25] and the baron was glad-handed into the Paris night, tipsy, no doubt, with his first public adulation.

Coubertin could scarcely wait to return the favor. Just as he had imported Arnold to France, he seized the first opportunity to export Le Play to England. In November 1887, seven months after "L'Éducation anglaise" appeared in La Réforme sociale, Coubertin stood before the Société nationale française de Londres, an association of French expatriates and officials posted to London, with a smattering, perhaps, of English francophiles, arguing for the introduction of Le Play societies into Britain.[26] This speech, which brought him more high praise from the société in Paris, contained a summary of Le Play's philosophy.[27] It demonstrates that, while he declared himself a disciple of Le Play as much because the société gave him adulation, legitimacy, and a platform, Coubertin was well acquainted with Le Play's system, and influenced in crucial ways by parts of it. Though Le Play was an intellectual guide to Coubertin, and not an imago as Arnold was, the baron did use quasi-religious language in expressing his hope that in London Le Play's "great light would shine through him."[28]

In London, Coubertin trumpeted Le Play's preference for social and cultural, rather than political, solutions to French problems; the divisibility of private political commitments from corporate social action; and the derivative significance of institutions.

> Our program will seduce you because it doesn't belong to any party or sect; because to adopt it, one doesn't have to sacrifice any belief or allegiance since it resolutely sets aside purely political remedies which our country has so often tried and which have caused so much bitter disillusionment. It is only too evident that no governmental contrivance will alone give the country what it lacks, stability and inner peace. Nothing can make up for the deficiency of true and conscientious social reform . . . it must be accomplished in ideas and customs before being realized in institutions.[29]

This orientation, for which Coubertin's adolescence, his family and social history had prepared the ground, deeply influenced him later in life. It played a role in his refusal to stand for Parliament, and it led to a compartmentalization in his thought and writing.[30] From these early days forward, Coubertin tended to keep his political commentaries separate from his writings on sport, education, and social reform. This habit surely paid dividends for the fledgling Olympic movement, but it also prevented Coubertin from arriving at a satisfying social theory of sport. Above all, it laid the basis for his mature belief that sport could and ought to stand outside of political and governmental interference. The International Olympic Committee that he would create to control international sport likewise had its models in "nonideological" institutions like the British patronage associations Taine celebrated, the École des sciences politiques, and, above all, the Société/Unions de la paix. Société precedents existed for all of the principles of I.O.C. organization: membership by cooptation; service to the "idea" and to "humanity" rather than to narrower segmental constituencies (the principle of "reversed delegation," he would call it); a "moral elite" that happened to be an economic and status elite as well; a "non-political" or privately political association (in the event, disproportionately conservative); emphasis on decision making by consensus rather than voting which in practice augmented the domination by the principal man (Coubertin himself); and jealously independent control over projects combined with the patronage of heads of state (as Le Play's societies had sought and received the patronage of Napoleon III in the 1860s, and of republican statesmen like Jules Simon in the '80s).

Into his own thought, Coubertin also absorbed Le Play's stress on *bonheur*, meaning individual happiness and peace. *Bonheur*, as Pitts puts it, "is a state of inner harmony, with a definite sensualist tonality, rather than an external goal like salvation."[31] As Zeldin notes, Le Play also associated *bonheur* with "satisfaction with the organization of society."[32] Coubertin was to place *bonheur* at the center of his Hellenism.

> Hellenism is above all the cult of humanity in its present life and its state of balance. And let us make no mistake about it, this was a great novelty in the mental outlook of all peoples and times. Everywhere else cults are based on the aspiration of a better life, the idea of recompense beyond the tomb, and the fear of punishment for the man who has offended the gods. But here it is the present existence which is happiness. Beyond the tomb there is only regret at the loss of it; it is a diminished survival.[33]

Just as *bonheur* lent a psychological dimension to Le Play's social theories, so it would add to Coubertin's psychology of sport a measure of counterpoint to his more common emphasis on sport's utilitarian, character-building values. Moreover, the later Coubertinian concept of "eurythmy" came to represent the interpenetration of individual *bonheur* with the aesthetic choreography of the Olympic festival.

But Le Play took *bonheur* to be the outcome of a successful struggle against original sin and corrupt human nature. Though no orthodox Catholic himself, Le Play counseled a return to the faith (especially to the Decalogue) as the only defense against human evil and vice. Just as Coubertin suppressed Arnold's Manicheanism, so too he never mentions this side of Le Play. The baron had a more optimistic conception of human nature, thought original sin a destructive doctrine,[34] and, far from seeking a return to Catholic practice, was on his way toward a "cult of humanity in its present life." Like Arnold, Le Play abhorred the evil in children, and he saw education primarily as discipline, "a judicious mix of force and persuasion."[35] Coubertin had nothing but distaste for such views, but he could not bring himself to argue against Le Play, to whom he felt he owed so much, so he took Dupanloup as his foil. Le Play was relatedly obsessed with the chastity and propriety of women, and Coubertin shared enough of this sentiment later to resist the introduction of women as Olympic competitors, thinking that it would be an "unseemly spectacle."[36] Le Play, moreover, took little interest in physical education, and none whatsoever in athletic games. The société cared nothing for sport either. No articles on such matters appeared in the Le Play publications prior to Coubertin's own, and not a single discussant of "L'Éducation anglaise" was interested enough to question or to comment to Coubertin on this central theme in his speech.

The stability of the family was Le Play's central concern as a sociologist and reformer. He classified families into three types: patriarchal, stem *(la famille souche)*,[37] and unstable. The second approximates what we should today call the joint family, and the third the isolated nuclear family. To Le Play the stem family was the desirable sort, since the patriarchal family was associated with pastoral peoples, and the nuclear family with social decline, industrial uprootedness, and the absence of *bonheur*.[38] As practical devices for the maintenance of stem families, Le Play preached paternal authority and testimentary liberty. He argued, falsely it now seems, that the equal division of property enforced by the Civil Code divided estates into such small and unviable holdings that family ties were severed and succeeding generations impoverished.[39] In defense, families reacted by reducing fertility, and this accounted for the decline of the French birthrate, a topic of feverish debate in the late nineteenth century.

In his London talk, Coubertin reviewed these theories, and in his later writings sided with Le Play on the inheritance and population questions. But in the sociology of the family itself, Coubertin never took more than passing interest. Certainly, he thought stable families a good thing, and he pitched his accounts of the "family atmosphere" of the English public schools to take advantage of this preoccupation of the société. But his own family history gave him ample reason to oppose Le Play's calls for re-

newed paternal authority, calls which also flew in the face of what
Coubertin admired most about English father-son relations.

The theories of industry Le Play developed were based upon his sociology of the family. He idealized the French family firm and gave a distinctively economic meaning to patronage: the acceptance of responsibility
for workers' general well-being by employers; provision of worker housing, education, medical care, and recreation; permanent employment,
pension schemes, incentive pay, and concern for working conditions; and
the autocratic, but benevolent, exercise of authority. (Le Play reserved the
term "paternalism" for traditional, pre-industrial labor organization.)[40] Le
Play wanted industrial patriarchs who "found in the traditions of their
family the origins of the happiness they enjoyed and the source of the good
they spread about them,"[41] and who, in turn, arranged their businesses on
the model of stem families. Le Play's romance of the family firm was
motivated above all by his hatred of laissez-faire economics, the system of
"hire and fire" which destroyed family life, produced a rootless, prop-
ertyless, nomadic and urban proletariat, defenseless against the greed of
employers. Adam Smith, he thought, was "a writer completely ignorant
of the practices of the workshops,"[42] and England, for all its "balance"
between the classes, had the most unstable employment system in
Europe. At all costs, France had to avoid that system of "free labor" that
was the foundation of all industrial evil. In his travels and monographs, Le
Play combed Europe for models of agricultural and industrial *patronage;*
and his followers in the société and unions, many of whom were themselves "patronal" industrialists or *rentiers,* carried on this project.

Coubertin was familiar with these views, and in his London talk he
chided landowners and capitalists who "often misconceived their duties,"
the first "by regarding land simply as an investment, the second by seeing
in labor nothing but a vulgar product."[43] As a *rentier* just come into his
own fortune,[44] Coubertin found in the Le Play philosophy a moral and
social justification for his own means of livelihood. It was a justification
delivered in a modern, even "scientific," form, rather than an appeal to the
ancien régime or to the cynical ennui and hedonism of his brother aristocrats.[45] Coubertin was content to live off his investments, while socially
"recycling" a great portion of them through his reformist campaigns and
works of *patronage.* Otherwise, there is no evidence that he took more than
superficial interest, as an investor or as a social thinker, in industrial and
labor relations per se. Personally, he saw no opportunities for *prouesses* of
the old aristocratic sort in business and finance, because of the inevitable
admixture of the profit motive. Just so, he refused to limit *patronage* to the
economic sphere, and his mature disavowal of homo economicus, that
view of man as essentially self-interested and acquisitive, took a form more
extreme than the more "modern" Le Play.

Ruralism, decentralization, and nostalgia for the "simple life" of the provincial North, were the other values that undergirded Le Play's economic program. As Zeldin remarks, "Le Play longed to return to the fishermen he had played with as a child, whose primitive husbandry, living off natural resources, ever remained his ideal."[46] Such Tolstoyan sentiments were particularly common among the nineteenth-century aristocracy, conducting their seasonal rounds between Paris and their country estates. Coubertin was deeply attached to Mirville and to the pays de Caux. Page after page of "Le Roman d'un rallié" lovingly romanticizes the character, manners, cuisine, music, and recreations of the local peasantry attached to his family château. No episode disturbs "Étienne's" kindness and consideration for them, or their solicitous deference toward him. As a boy in Mirville, Pierre first conceived, and thereafter renewed, his love of outdoor sports—riding, sailing, rowing, and running through the fields with the peasant children he conscripted as playmates.[47] Even after the tennis courts, boxing and fencing halls, Jockey Club, bicycle and bridle paths of Paris had claimed him, he continued to associate the joys of physical exercise with the open countryside of the Seine-Maritime.[48] In May 1888, he got himself appointed to the municipal council of Mirville, and helped administer local affairs until his resignation in September 1892. The municipal archives have yet to reveal what projects he interested himself in. The "Roman d'un rallié" mentions educational programs, public libraries, and the arrangement of local festivals,[49] but one readily imagines him meddling in everything where his *patronage* and *prouesse* might show. Later, in 1902–3, he wrote, edited, illustrated, and published the little *Revue du pays de Caux*, a journal of "literature and politics" aimed at informing the provincials about the "wide, wide world,"[50] while celebrating the rustic simplicity of the province. Coubertin was one of the many *rentier*-humanists who failed to perceive the contradiction between their love of regional life and their commitment to making a national French culture.[51] They failed to recognize themselves for what they were: "missionaries of modern urban culture,"[52] who transformed rural society in the very act of patronizing it.[53] Coubertin, for his part, never realized that, as in England, the modern sports he advocated would spread to the provincial lower classes only at the expense of the traditional amusements and festivals he enjoyed and thought to preserve.

The final great influence Le Play exerted over Coubertin was through his model of history. Le Play believed that history was a cyclical process, in which periods of renewal were followed by periods of decline. Progress was cumulative but uncertain and regularly interrupted. Coubertin forsook Taine's view for this one. Le Play drew from it pessimistic conclusions about the future of French society; Coubertin, on the contrary, found in it reasons for optimism, which he announced in the stirring finale to his London speech.

> I would like to evoke the image of our beloved motherland, though we are far from her. Among her children, there are too many who love her with a despairing love, who have lost their faith in her destinies. They see her in decline because she has behind her a very long past. They compare nations to individuals and believe them condemned to decadence and destruction just as inevitably as men are doomed to decrepitude and death. This theory appears to be justified by their instability; but this is only a theory and Le Play, that great observer of facts, that great enemy of theories, has overturned it victoriously. He has shown that the history of all peoples, old or young, is composed of alternations that are not at all fatal. Therefore, we who have this consoling thought, with an ardent faith and not a resigned courage, may speak the words which, I'm sure, are at the bottom of your hearts, as they are in mine: "Vive la France."[54]

The Black Menhir

That other great errand in the provincial wilderness, Coubertin's pilgrimage to the tomb of his damned ancestor, the Mennaist "abbé de Lesneven," seems to have taken place a few months later in 1888, at the height of his involvement with the Le Play societies and at the outset of his campaign to "rebronze" France. The narrator of the "Roman d'un rallié" takes great care to fix the episode in Étienne's twenty-fifth year; Coubertin was twenty-five in 1888.[55]

"For a long time, he had promised himself that he would make this pilgrimage," and "with growing emotion" and full of "tumultuous thoughts and contradictory impressions," he set out in secret from his parents' château, in the company of a stableboy who was an old childhood friend.[56] Leaving him off along the way, the young baron carries on alone, out onto the Crozon peninsula, knowing only to ask for "the Black Menhir,"[57] "an enormous druid needle bizarrely overhanging at the top" and "set in the middle of a clover circle."[58] The locals are able to direct him to it, and in its shadow, concealed in a little grove of oaks, he discovers the rude and ill-kept tomb of his great-uncle. Securing the key from a peasant farmer, he enters.

> Raised up in the middle was a very plain sarcophagus, adorned neither with a cross nor with any sort of inscription, an anonymous sepulcher that the moss and lichens were devouring. The young man's heart sickened, and tears came to his eyes. He went up to the sarcophagus and

placed a hand on its stone, as a promise to him who slept there to protect him against the scandalous ostracism that pursued him even in death. "An iron grill will replace this wall," thought Étienne. "I will build here a marble tomb topped by a cross and bearing an inscription, and all around it flowers will be maintained." And he added in a high voice as if the dead man could hear him, as if he wished to summon invisible spirits as witnesses, "This will be so done, because I wish it."[59]

Layer upon layer of rich symbolism is condensed in this event. At its core lay a real experience in 1888, but it was written down in 1898, four years after Coubertin's founder's pilgrimage to Archaia Olympia and two years after the Athens Olympic Games. The language and many of the symbolic associations that inform the episode belong to this later date, and it is not a simple matter to sort them out from the meanings the experience had for him in 1888. Moreover, for all of its autobiographical character, "Le Roman" is still a novel. Literary embellishments may have crept in, and these too are difficult to disentangle.[60] The anthropologist, like the historian, must try; but like the psychologist, he also appreciates that the alterations made by the literary imagination and the retrospective memory are often as revealing of the subjective meaning of key events as are the naked facts themselves.

Lesneven was a mediating figure for Coubertin, first of all between him and his family. The *abbé* was a family member, but one who had repudiated all of the reactionary values the family stood for. For his courage, independence, and rebellion, he had been cursed by his kin and damned to hell by his Church. Early in adolescence, Pierre had been torn by ambivalence toward his own parents and their world. He wished to love and to be loved by them, but felt rejected and confused by their reactions to his attempts at independence and compromise. For his efforts, he was treated as an ungrateful rebel. We have seen how the childhood rituals with which he surrounded the image of Lesneven embodied and expressed these conflicts.[61] In 1888, Coubertin's rebellion against his father and his father's designs for him was in full swing. Pierre had refused any acceptable career, rallied to the Republic, and spent his time in England or in the company of social reformers. As the philosophy and social composition of the Le Play groups show, he was still trying to effect compromises between the new world and the old world of his parents. But they were still intransigent, refused to acknowledge his efforts, or to take him seriously as a reformer dedicated to the greater good of France. Once again, the figure of Lesneven and the rituals at his tomb emerged to mediate these deep psychological and intrafamilial conflicts. In 1898, hard on the heels of his first great success and public legitimation, the narrative of the Lesneven pilgrimage takes center stage in a book in which Coubertin symbolically kills off his father and his brothers.

Lesneven is also an intermediary figure between Coubertin and his new masters, Arnold and Le Play. Arnold made Rugby School a surrogate extended family; Le Play built a social theory around such a family type; Lesneven was a real member of Coubertin's extended family. Like Arnold, Lesneven was a clergyman; like Le Play, a Catholic. Like both, he was driven by the gap between the rich and the poor. But Lesneven was a follower in a preexisting Christian socialist movement, who divested himself not only of his wealth but of all the trappings of his aristocratic heritage. It was left to certain disciples of Arnold and Le Play to veer to forms of Christian socialism, and they themselves enjoyed the lives of *grands bourgeois* and thought that a reformed aristocracy would lead the way to social progress. Arnold and Le Play were prestigious men, the leaders of "schools," guaranteed places in the histories of their nations, whereas, like the twenty-five-year-old Coubertin, Lesneven had excited only the barest local notoriety and was an indifferent intellectual. When Coubertin described Lesneven as "a battler, a sincere and righteous man, proud no doubt, and perhaps not very inspired, but noble in battle,"[62] he could well have been describing himself, his own strengths and fears, in 1888. But in 1898, when he wrote this down, Coubertin had accrued some followers and the beginnings of an international name for himself. In the "Roman" version of the pilgrimage, Coubertin takes command over his ancestor's memory and, after a fashion, usurps it. He has become his great-uncle's superior.

Manifested in the Lesneven episode is a root symbolic paradigm[63] that organized and gave meaning to Coubertin's experience in 1888. The Black Menhir was a powerful symbol of a rural, exotic, pagan past of great antiquity, persisting incongruously in the midst of a modernizing nation, a landmark in the wrong land. It is juxtaposed to another anomalous monument: a churchman's tomb, unmarked by any Christian emblem, the run-down, wayside resting place of a dead man, anonymous to passersby, but who, through his values and deeds, lived on as a central figure for Coubertin, who knew and bore his name. To Coubertin, this "unmarked" tomb represented the anonymity of the real forces that make history and a nation great, in contrast to the grand public monuments for mere celebrities or the passive puppets of fate. Coubertin's vow to transform this symbolic tableau that he discovered in remote Brittany was synonymous with his designs for himself. He aimed to achieve sufficient greatness to rescue himself from social invisibility and marginality, to leave the periphery for the center of French national destiny. His "rescue" of Lesneven, by providing him a marble tomb, an inscription and a proper cross, and floral markers of his continued fecundity, was not only a symbol, but probably also a magical act in Coubertin's building of his own monument. Two other details of the Lesneven episode are revealing. Coubertin does not even consider tampering with the Black Menhir,[64] and he forestalls the local farmer's plans to open a restaurant on the property, in order to draw the tourist bathers from Morgat. It horrified him to think that this "place consecrated by so much suffering and by such a poignant interior drama" would become a "center for picnics."[65]

Earlier experiences of Coubertin are echoed in this symbolic paradigm: the "monumental" history of his aristocratic family, especially its connection to the great Christian sanctuary at Rome through the bequest of that emblem of pagan civilization, the Laocoon statue; and Pierre's boyhood fascination with the Pantheon and the Versailles museum and his disagreements with his parents over who should be interred or celebrated therein. The Lesneven episode is also a symbolic transformation of his vision at Arnold's tomb, with its simple and uninscribed altar slab, which Coubertin took to be a monument to English national achievement, indeed, "the very cornerstone of England." Moreover, we know from *Une Campagne* that Coubertin entertained the notion of raising a grander monument to Arnold, perhaps in France.[66] Additionally, Coubertin may have taken part in société deliberations over the erection of a proper shrine to Le Play.

In the years between the Lesneven episode itself and Coubertin's narration of it in "Le Roman," this symbolic complex reappears several times: at George Washington's tomb in Mount Vernon, at Carnot's obsequies at the Pantheon,[67] and above all, at Archaia Olympia. Here, on his founder's pilgrimage in 1894, he had his second vision, while contemplating the broken stelae, toppled columns, and cracked pedestals poking up through the sands of the Alpheus plain in the moonlight. Here he found his own menhirs, white not black this time, the living ruins not of an anonymous people, but of the glorious Greek "ancestors." Here, in a little wayside grove of olives in the sacred precinct, the strange last rites he would order for himself would be conducted forty years later. Secular dignitaries and an Orthodox priest would place his heart, paganly dug out of his corpse, into a marble stele bearing no cross, but rather a Greek inscription, his name, and the eponym which guaranteed his memory in Western cultural history.

The Lesneven episode is a symbolic jewel, hung suspended between Coubertin's past and his future, radiating light in both directions. But the effect it had on him in 1888 is made clear in one passage.

> "This will be so done, because I wish it."
> What mysterious powers accordingly devolve on those who pronounce certain phrases at certain decisive hours. In taking this solemn pledge, Étienne felt himself another man or, rather, he felt himself to be *a man*. It seemed to him that the will power dammed up inside of him ruptured the dikes and flowed out through all his being.[68]

Coubertin had his vision, his program, and the will power; in 1888, he also discovered an avenue and gained a powerful ally.

The Comité Jules Simon

On May 21, 1887, Jules Simon gave the opening address to the annual congress of the Société/Unions de la paix. After introducing himself as a man "who had had the honor and pleasure to know the illustrious Le Play," Simon discoursed on education.[69] The republican warhorse and aged philosopher gave a capital performance.[70] Simon was then seventy-four, a former prime minister and senator, long-time member of the Institut and of the Académie française, and a respected educational reformer. By this period, he had lost most of his political influence, but remained a figure of great prestige, a "grand old man," something of a French Gladstone, Coubertin might have said. Simon once shrewdly described himself as "profoundly republican and profoundly conservative." His speech was witty, ironic, and impassioned, and he was repeatedly interrupted by applause and laughter from an audience that included Pierre de Coubertin. Simon raised his voice against *surmenage* ("overwork") in the French schools: the "forced labor" of the eleven hours of study a day, the sickly emphasis on rote memorization of catalogues of facts and ideas, the cult of examinations, and the destructive methods of the *discours* and the *thème* which discouraged any true knowledge of the classical civilizations. These complaints were familiar from his writings in the 1870s, but the metaphors in this speech were new and reflected ten years of rapid social change in France.

Such a schooling, Simon averred, did not produce an educated man, but "a cornerstore whose bins and shelves are full of all sorts of ideas whose worth he cannot judge and of facts whose authenticity he does not know." It "results in an enormous number of mandarins, for whom there must be found an enormous number of positions, which occasions, as a consequence, an enormous number of blunders and vast new expenses."[71] In his speech, Simon attributed all of the evils of what we should today call "the credentialing society" to school *surmenage*. He went so far as to claim that independent legislators—who considered "the interests of *la patrie* and of humanity," asked what evils a proposed law would prevent and what good it would do, and were solicitous as to its reception by the "nonruling classes who are rulers of the situation"—were those who had escaped *surmenage*. Legislators who considered laws solely with regard to their political and party appeal were those who had suffered from it.[72] One might well argue that Simon had things upside down, that the regimen of the schools was a *consequence* of the demands of a democratic, bureaucratic, market society, but his arguments reveal the extraordinary significance reformers attached to school *surmenage* in the 1880s.

Coubertin had himself attacked it in his "L'Éducation anglaise," delivered to the société only one month prior to Simon's address.[73] But the critique of *surmenage* was not what excited Coubertin about Simon's speech. Instead, it was Simon's attack on the moral character produced by the French schools and his declaration in favor of physical education that must have brought Coubertin to the edge of his chair.

> There is instruction, but no education. We create a *bachelier*, a *licencié*, a *docteur*, but a man? There's no question of it. On the contrary, fifteen years are spent destroying his virility. We give society a ridiculous little mandarin who hasn't any muscles, who doesn't know how to leap a barrier, to elbow his way forward, to shoot a gun, or to mount a horse, who is afraid of everything, who, to make up for it, is crammed with all sorts of useless knowledge, who doesn't know the most necessary things, who can't give counsel to anyone, not even to himself, who needs to be directed in everything.[74]

Physical health, Simon asserted, was impossible without physical exercise, based on "the science of hygiene" which ought to be "half of pedagogy." Instead, "we have almost entirely neglected the body in our materialist society. Who would have believed it, it's against common sense!"[75] And who has taken up the cause of the body—the materialists? No, said Simon, delighting in the irony. "It is to us, vile spiritualists, that the task of entreating for the body before the materialists of the municipal council and the Chamber of Deputies has fallen."[76] Years later in his memoirs Coubertin still vividly recalled what Simon said next.[77]

> The right which I demand back for our children is the right to play. You understand well that I am the implacable enemy of games of chance; I entreat for active games, what the English call athletic games. I am willing to have gymnastics, provided that you get rid of all your trapezes and your showman's apparatus; I accept military exercises which the boys like; but what I ask for, above all, are games, the development of physical strength in joy and liberty. Joy itself is my friend and my ally, the noisy joy of childhood and youth. I want races, wrestling, and ball games, in the open air, not in your pestilential halls, in the country air, if possible. I have no fear of a thump, given or received. If my boy so forgets himself as to whimper for a bruise or a black eye, I have my response all prepared: "You are a man!" I heal him with that, and he returns to the fray, that is to say, to joy and pleasure.[78]

Great applause greeted this declaration, and the loudest huzzahs no doubt were Coubertin's, for here was the great Jules Simon endorsing his own very program. In the *Campagne*, Coubertin wrote that this was the first

time any Frenchman had said such things. But it was not, of course.
Coubertin had said as much only a month earlier. However, the société
had greeted his plea for athletic games with polite silence, whereas Jules
Simon drew enthusiastic applause. The message was clear. Coubertin had
to gain Simon as an ally, to join forces with him, and to attract his
patronage. But he didn't move precipitously. Instead of rushing forward
in the first flush of enthusiasm, Coubertin waited until he had in hand the
results of his "survey" of the state of physical education in the *lycées* then in
progress, before he approached Simon in the spring of 1888.

This inquiry had begun with a visit to Georges Morel, director of
secondary education in the Ministry of Public Instruction.[79] Arriving
"without an introduction, or any special claims on his benevolence,"
Coubertin found Morel "greatly surprised by the strange request I presented him." But after a "conversation that apparently convinced him of
the sincerity of my intentions," Coubertin was given a circular letter that
"opened all the *lycées* of France to me." It was then the turn of the *lycée*
headmasters *(proviseurs)* to be taken aback. Quite accustomed to the parade
of official inspectors, they did not know quite what to make of Coubertin.
"They had never seen, I really believe, an investigator of my sort. I
confess that this role didn't amuse me very much. I performed it with
timidity. This timidity and a wise prudence in general led me to keep
quiet about my projects." This "timidity" is indicative of the continuing
marginality Coubertin felt, despite his personal resolve. Whenever he had
to deal on a face-to-face basis with those occupying the middle levels of
any public bureaucracy, in this case the *proviseurs*, he tended to clam up
and to lose both the audacity which allowed him to barge in on top officials
and the natural gregariousness which led him to mix freely with the boys.
This passage also reveals how psychologically unfit Coubertin was for
ethnography, wherever it required intensive contacts with those whose
class background or lifestyle differed radically from his own.

At the majority of the state *lycées*, he found nothing resembling true
physical education, and, therefore, kept his own designs to himself. But,
as president of the Association of Former Students at Saint-Ignace, he
lobbied the Jesuit masters for the introduction of athletics there.

> But the *non possumus* was absolute. The Jesuits had the pretension,
> precious little justified, of giving a complete physical culture in their
> schools, because many of them participated zestfully in the games of
> their students. But they resolutely limited themselves to games of a
> childish character and severely proscribed all sports susceptible of being
> governed by the boys themselves, which would lead them, on match
> days, to interacting with young men from the state or secular schools.[80]

Most of the other religious establishments he visited—Stanislas, Arcueil,
Bossuet, Fénelon, Massillon—neither had athletics nor were interested in

acquiring them.[81] However, Abbé Dibildos, director of Gerson and "a man of great spirit and heart, who feared no innovation and was completely devoted to his work," took a sympathetic interest in Coubertin's program. So did Fr. Olivier, master of Juilly on the outskirts of Paris, "a beautiful *collège*" which "reminded" Coubertin of the English public schools. There the boys rode horses and played in an "atmosphere that had something sportive and free" about it that charmed Coubertin.

Neither were Coubertin's encounters with the *lycées* entirely disappointing. At Sainte-Barbe-des-Champs, he saw little in the way of physical education, but the director, M. Morlet, found Coubertin's recommendations reasonable. At the École Alsacienne, he discovered "the first regular athletic association" in any French school. There athletic games "were held in honor, but the school officials appeared to fear that by attracting public attention to this aspect of their pedagogy, the good name of the institution would be harmed."[82] However, it was at the École Monge that he found real innovations in progress and, in the person of M. Godart, a kindred spirit and convert. Godart was not only the master of the École Monge, but also a member of the Conseil supérieur de l'instruction publique and the founder of an association for educational research, then supervised by Levasseur. Coubertin thought Godart a courageous soul who was "ever on the lookout for progress" and unafraid to apply reforms at the *lycée* he directed. Unfortunately, to Coubertin's thinking, neither Godart nor his association had "pushed their enquiries to the shores of England; therefore, the importance of muscular culture as a factor in moral improvement had escaped him."[83] When Coubertin first visited Monge, athletic games on the English model were unknown. However, Godart had looked to Germany and had instilled in the *lycée* "a permanent preoccupation with matters of hygiene." For example, Godart was convinced of the value of open-air activity, and each day the boys were taken by omnibus to the Jardin d'acclimatation, with whose officials he had made suitable arrangements, there to enjoy their recreation. But if Godart "was poorly acquainted with British pedagogy" before Coubertin's appearance, he certainly got an earful of it from the baron. And, according to Coubertin, "as soon as it was exposed to him, with customary lucidity he seized upon its considerable import; ardent and enthusiastic, he was soon ready to try to apply it."[84] Within months, the pupils of the École Monge were organizing sports associations, running races in the Bois de Boulogne, and attempting (with what success we do not know) to penetrate the mysteries of English cricket. Certainly, they enjoyed the effort, and Godart, for his part, so appreciated what he saw that he became Coubertin's first real convert.

Modest as they were, these successes reassured Coubertin that "much good will lay dozing under the unfortunately thick covers of organized

routine" in the secondary schools.[85] The antipathy and rejections he endured convinced him, on the one hand, that he should steer clear of the
religious schools for a time, and on the other hand, that most *lycée* headmasters were "veritable slaves" lacking all autonomy. Unless he could first
win over the Ministry and the Académie de Paris, the secondary schools
could never be turned toward *la pédagogie sportive*. He needed Jules Simon,
and with his "survey" for added legitimation, he went round to see the old
man.

According to Coubertin, they hit it off completely. "The accord between us was immediately sealed."[86] Not only were their ideas on athletic
education in general harmony, but "the approaching innovations at the
École Monge seemed to [Simon] a sufficient guarantee of success." Despite the "great orator's" resolve not to undertake new projects at the time,
so great was his interest in physical education that "he, therefore, promised me his support, all his support."[87] Simon placed his name, his prestige, and his contacts at Coubertin's disposal, to use in any way the baron
thought fit in advancing their common cause.

As we have noted in the Gladstone episode and will note again,
Coubertin not infrequently exaggerated the intimacy, interest, and adherence he received from the great men whom he sought out. But we have the
testimony of Simon himself as to the regard he felt for Coubertin. Simon
contributed a preface to Coubertin's *L'Éducation anglaise en France*, published by Hachette the following year. "I have only one regret," Simon
began, "that is not to be fifteen years old and a student at the École
Monge."[88] After refuting those "peevish" critics who insisted that the
Monge students' sports would endanger their chances for the baccalaureate, Simon wrote:

> One asks oneself whether it is M. Godart or M. Pierre de Coubertin
> who has made this marvelous discovery. M. Godart has set his world in
> motion. You can see the spectacle yourself—a good and beautiful
> spectacle—by wandering through the Bois de Boulogne, in the area
> bounded by the large lake, the Catelan meadow and the Jardin
> d'acclimatation.

On the other hand, Simon continued:

> M. Pierre de Coubertin directs no school. He is simply an amateur
> who doesn't wish to be a Platonic amateur. He intends to remake the
> French race. The same idea formerly came to William the Conqueror for
> the English race. In England, he found a broken and undernourished
> people. Being a good Norman, he had recourse to roast beef, and out of
> this malingering, scrofulous, and needy people, he quickly made the
> finest infantry and the best blacksmiths in the world. At least that's
> what Michelet claims, and I leave responsibility for this account to him.
> M. de Coubertin has no thought for beefsteaks because our boys don't

lack them, and it isn't his concern to go keep a watch on our pantries. But he visited the English universities and schools where cricket and rowing are institutions. He saw in the London parks the whole youth of both sexes on horseback. He knew that the German generals always had a profusion of good riders to pick from when they needed an aide-de-camp, whereas, with us, no one, or practically no one, rides. We barely have, here and there, a *jeu de paume*.

. . . The blood rose to M. Pierre de Coubertin's forehead because of this. Here is a defect to be repaired, a situation to be overcome, so he said to himself. And what is required to do it? State intervention? Not at all. Money? Not very much. . . . What therefore is required? Quite simply, to put athletic education in fashion.

Coubertin could not have written a better press release for himself. The great Jules Simon was endorsing not only his ideas and his patriotism, but also the very shape of his life as an independent, reformist amateur (in both the sociological and the etymological senses of the word). But the great man wasn't finished. Simon, who liked to boast that he was bourgeois, went on inter alia to shrive Coubertin of his aristocratic origins.

Our grandfathers had a remedy for their languishing schools, the academies where the young nobility practiced fencing and equitation. There was nothing similar for the bourgeoisie. A magistrate or a banker on horseback would have appeared ridiculous. Since the Revolution, the young nobility has disappeared, and their academies with them, and our young bourgeoisie would be just like the English of William the Conqueror, if M. Pierre de Coubertin and M. Godart had not come along to rescue them.[89]

Thus Simon quite meant it when he offered his name and prestige, and Coubertin wasted no time in putting them to use. With his familiarity with patronage associations and in a milieu once dubbed "la République des comités," it is scarcely surprising that Coubertin set about forming a committee. Its proper name was the Comité pour la propagation des exercises physiques, but Coubertin preferred to call it the Comité Jules Simon, the better to serve recruitment and publicity.

The roster of comité members is revealing. The first names one notices are those from Coubertin's past. By recruiting them into the comité, he was in effect triumphing over that past, stitching it together into an emblem of his present status as a recognized reformer. General Tramond, the commandant of St.-Cyr, Ribot and Boutmy from the École des sciences politiques, and M. Delaire, the current secretary general of the Société d'économie sociale joined up.[90]

Simon interceded with Octave Gréard, vice-rector of the Académie de Paris,[91] and on his heels, Georges Morel, the director of secondary education, M. Cauvet, director of the École centrale, and M. Perrot, director of the École normale supérieure, came in. Doubtless Simon's name assisted Coubertin in recruiting Victor Duruy, historian and former minister of public instruction,[92] Georges Picot, member of the Académie des sciences morales et politiques, and General Lewal, former war minister.

Godart brought with him his "intimate friends": M. Moutardt, inspector general of mines, Adolphe Carnot, Le Play's successor as inspector of studies at the École des mines, General Thomassin, then in command of the Fourth Army at Le Mans, State Councilor Dislère, M. Collignon, vice-director of bridges and roads, Geoffrey-Saint-Hilaire, director of the Jardin d'acclimatation, General Barbe, director of the École polytechnique, Senator Xavier Blanc, M. Marey, professor of physiology and Institut laureate, Drs. Brouardel, Javal, and Labbé, the latter of the Académie de médicine, and others.

Coubertin enrolled Dr. Fernand La Grange, author of *Physiologie des exercises physiques*, and Dr. Rochard, who had written on exercise as a remedy for *surmenage* in the *Revue des deux mondes*. He also enlisted the allies he had discovered during his survey of the schools, Olivier, Dibildos, and Reider of the École Alsacienne. M. Chaumeton, president of the Association of Students, also became a member. In a relatively unusual and forward-looking move, Coubertin recruited journalists as well. Patinot, editor of the influential *Journal des débats*, and M. Hébrard, senator and editor of *Le Temps*, were members, and M. Chincolle covered the comité for *Le Figaro*. The powers of the press were becoming particularly noticeable during this period. Coubertin shared several of the fears about the press common to his class, and later on he often had occasion to complain about journalistic conventions. But from the start, he also had great respect for the powers of the journalists, and from the beginning resolved to make use of them. His own need for recognition contributed to his dawning sense of the relationship between *presse* and *prouesse*. M. Fouret, the director of the Hachette publishing house who was to liberal educationists in France what Macmillan was in England, also attended comité sessions.

Coubertin additionally recruited the leaders of the few nascent sports organizations in France: Adrien Fleuret, president of the Union des sociétés d'aviron; M. Caillat, president of the Société d'encouragement au sport nautique; Janssen, president of the Club alpin; M. Richefeu, president of the Société de longue paume; M. de Villeneuve, president of the Société d'encouragement d'escrime; Napoleon Ney, president, and Georges de Saint-Clair, secretary, of the Racing-Club de France; the marquis de Mornay, president of the Société hippique; Paul Christman and J. Sansboeuf, of the Union des sociétés de gymnastiques; and Dr. Philippe Tissié, founder of the Ligue gironde de l'éducation gymnastique.[93]

According to Coubertin himself, "A certain number of these men were convinced and enthusiastic. The rest indicated no more than a benevolent sympathy toward the work. But each one represented some technical or social power through which he was prepared to second our efforts."[94] The baron had cast his net wide, drawing in as many notables from as many sorts of elites as he could. In part, this decision to recruit for prestige as well as conviction was an act of political shrewdness, ensuring the broadest diffusion of comité views while maximizing Coubertin's own role as the organizer of this divided house. In part, the strategy was owing to Coubertin's sincere belief that great causes transcended sectional interests. In part, it was the act of a man who had so thoroughly suffered from his marginality that when the opportunity to draw the attentions of notables to himself and his plans came, he naturally made the most of it.

The comité roster was catholic in another important respect. Partisans of all four of the developing schools of thought on physical education were included. The first centered on the hygienists: physicians, physiologists, and pedagogues committed less to a form of exercise than to an overall model of physical health. The second group were the devotees of gymnastics proper, that is, organized, prescribed, noncompetitive physical exercise. Some, like Tissié, were proponents of the Swedish school of Per-Hendrik Ling (1776–1839), with its emphasis on anatomy and the "organic" development of individual physical capacity. Others looked to Germany and were inspired more or less explicitly by the "natural" and collective exercises of Guts-Muths (1759–1839) or by the *Turnkunst* tradition of F. Ludwig Jahn (1778–1858), with its special inventions, the rings, the pommel horse, and the parallel bars, and more especially its *Volkstum* and nationalist fervor.[95] The third group was expressly premilitaristic. Generals like Thomassin and Tramond insisted that physical exercise for young men approximate as closely as possible to soldierly requirements and military virtues. The fourth group was the smallest. Led by Coubertin, it preferred English games and stressed character development, liberty, and social education.

As Coubertin was forming the comité, the boundaries between these "sects" were not at all so fixed as they were shortly to become. As a public issue, physical exercise was so new that schools of thought were only beginning to congeal. Moreover, the general values associated with physical education—health, patriotism, military preparedness, character development, and the socialization of a democratic elite—were broadly shared among the members and cross-cut interests vested in one or another physical regimen. For example, La Grange and Marey were leading physiological hygienists, whose work was informed by Claude Bernard's theories on internal equilibria. But they had already joined with Sansboeuf, a gymnastics official and disciple of Déroulède's militant Ligue des patriotes, in an 1887 commission to produce a manual for school gymnastics instructors. This document, when it appeared in 1889, prescribed an eclectic regimen of free exercise, gymnastic routines like rope-climbing, *jeux scolaires*, and mildly premilitary training.[96] The Alpine Club, which Janssen represented, had been founded in 1874 "under the impact of patriotic grief," and sought not only to promote *alpinisme*, but also to be "a school of physical energy and moral vigor," and to make young Frenchmen "more virile, and more apt to bear military life."[97] Jules Simon, as we have seen, tempered his enthusiasm for English games with a ready "acceptance" of natural gymnastics and military exercises. Indeed, he had supported the creation of the *bataillons scolaires* in 1882 (organizations for military and gymnastic drilling in all schools, roughly parallel to the English schoolboy militias of the 1860s and '70s), and his later preface to Coubertin's book missed no chance to extol the military benefits of school sports, although the expense of uniforms and proper rifles, the difficulty of finding retired soldiers to drill the little corps, and later the aftermath of the Boulanger crisis led in retrospect to viewing the *bataillons* as *une erreur patriotique* in sporting circles.[98] Godart's conversion to English games was also not so complete that he abandoned the hygienic and German gymnastic routines he had started at Monge.

Moreover, as patriotic republicans and of national unity champions all, comité members could certainly have been expected to confer peaceably with one another. Coubertin reproduced the now familiar claim that "we have recruited adherents of all parties, our work is in effect sheltered from all political quarrels."[99] In fact, the "shelter," such as it was, owed to drawing all of the members from the "parties of order" and skewing their "neutrality" toward the right.

In the event, Coubertin's ingenuous faith in comité consensus was not entirely misplaced. Through the course of its several meetings, the membership did manage to investigate *lycée* practices, to visit and rate existing installations, to formulate plans for new playgrounds and *parcs scolaires*, to discuss the organization of athletic competitions, to collect donations, to identify and encourage student sports initiatives, and, above all, to publicize the cause in the press.[100] But by the time the comité faded from existence this consensus had quite broken down. The greatest significance of the Comité pour la propagation des exercises physiques, for Coubertin and for the historian, was as an arena in which territories were staked out and defined, opponents drew up battle lines, and the French physical education movement was irretrievably shattered at the very moment of its crystallization. As Coubertin later put it, with notable understatement, "In retrospect, these [comité] names formed too polychromatic a mosaic."[101] That the center could not hold was indeed in part because of the personalities, ambitions, and interests of the members, but the fissioning of the little world of physical education was also a reflection of that larger breakdown of the fragile, opportunist consensus that had nurtured the early Republic and guided France back from her disastrous defeat.

That Coubertin failed to anticipate the conflicts between his roles as

organizer and partisan of a particular point of view is apparent in "Le
Remède au surmenage" and the "Lettre aux membres," the two documents with which he announced the comité to the Société/Unions de la
paix, on May 29, 1888, at the annual congress.[102] He was careful to point
out that three of the comité vice-presidents, Picot, Rochard, and Thomassin, and he, the secretary general, were members of the Unions de la paix.
He went so far as to claim that Le Play's ideas would never gain the
following they deserved until the reforms he was proposing for education
were placed into effect. Simultaneously, he was celebrating the broad
base of the comité and engaging in special pleading.

In the very act of complimenting medical men like Rochard, Coubertin
"frankly" expressed his doubts as to the worth of discussing an issue very
dear to the hygienists, the merits of direct vs. indirect lighting in class-
rooms.[103] In his earlier progress through England, Coubertin had ignored
the stream of physiological and hygienic thought best represented by
Herbert Spencer's popular *Education: Intellectual, Moral, and Physical.*[104]
We may be sure that the same skepticism carried over into Coubertin's
behavior in the chair at comité meetings, and that the natural scientists
and physicians felt increasingly isolated from the main lines of comité
debate and increasingly resentful of the young and scientifically ignorant
upstart who thought he could control it. In his later writings, Coubertin
showed no more than passing interest in the arcane experiments and
theories of the biologists and medical men.[105] The names of very few
physicians, physiologists, or experimental psychologists[106] appear on the
rosters of later Coubertinian associations, and this is an emblem of the
divorce between sports organizations and formal science that came to mark
Euro-American sports culture until the 1950s and '60s.

On the matter of military exercises, Coubertin threw down the gauntlet
(or rather, the cricket bat) even more directly.

> Messieurs, I have just said that the present [school] regime would pro-
> duce physical enfeeblement, often also, intellectual torpor, and always,
> moral collapse. Therefore, you can guess what I think of the project that
> consists in militarizing education and in furnishing through military
> exercises a counterweight to the fatigue of studies. Perhaps you will
> thus produce stronger muscles, but you are equally certain to produce
> still less open minds and more and more colorless characters. We have
> enough such sheep in our poor country; let us not be given any more of
> them. We'll get them sure enough by confounding two regimes not at all
> alike, military discipline and school discipline, or by bringing together
> two beings who don't at all resemble one another, the soldier and the
> schoolboy.[107]

Pacifism was an ideology of the left during this period, and Coubertin was
no pacifist in the sense later associated with his contemporary Romain

Rolland. Coubertin was not so much against war as for peace, and no less than the other members of the comité he wanted a strong army worthy of domestic and foreign respect and capable of ensuring against another 1870. But he was no *revanchiste* either, and this put him in opposition not only to several older comité members but also to many French "athletic" initiatives that were motivated to a great degree by the sentiment, if not the overt aim, of military revenge.[108] Comité debates over the status of military exercises galvanized these deeper conflicts, the more so since the members sat down to work in the midst of the Boulanger affair. In the "Rèmede au surmenage," Coubertin straightforwardly equated socialism and Boulangism as enemies to be overcome by the reforms the comité was to introduce.[109] No comité members were overt Boulangists, but the crisis was still very much undecided (Boulanger was not to flee to Brussels for eleven months), and even republican generals resented what they took to be the antiarmy sentiment of Boulanger's opponents.

In England the connection between good football players and good officers was lost on very few, but it had grown up "organically." School sports were long an independent tradition, and neither government ministries nor popular ideologues felt much need to link the two explicitly. Certainly no one thought to militarize the public schools directly. The "organic" approach was all Coubertin was seeking. As the inventor, later on, of the modern pentathlon, Coubertin was hardly opposed to *adult* sports derived from military models, but he wanted no part of these for schoolboys. Patriotism and character would suffice. But France had no tradition of schoolboy sports, and it did have the stinging memory of military humiliation. The generals and their allies wanted the knot between physical training and military requirements drawn tight. As the comité began its deliberations, these conflicts bubbled barely under the surface. By the early '90s, they had boiled over, and the militarists and Coubertin and his friends had fallen into rival factions.

For their part, the admirers of German gymnastics expressed the widespread opinion that the Turners had proved their worth in the making of a skilled and patriotic army. As Eugen Weber puts it: "Everyone knew that the Prussian schoolmasters had been the real winners at Sedan and, somehow, Father Jahn's gymnastics seemed easier to imitate than the playing fields of Eton."[110] In his addresses chartering the comité, Coubertin plumped English games while saying nothing about gymnastics, and this no doubt angered members like Sansboeuf. That this impolitic oversight was partially owing to ignorance is made clear in subsequent years, when Coubertin did comment on the Swedish and German gymnastics traditions and elaborated his own *gymnastique utilitaire* as an alternative to them.[111] But to Coubertin, gymnastics would never be much more than exercises for children, the handmaiden of adult sport, or else acceptable

when transformed into sports themselves. Even more important than the
military issue, the unfavorable contrast Coubertin drew between gymnastics and athletic games as action systems was responsible for this judgment. Coubertin's breach with Tissié both occasioned and focused his
opposition to gymnastics as the ruling model of physical education.

Tissié was an attractive and convincing man who made for a considerable rival in the comité. Like his Swedish masters, but also like the Carte-
sian classicists of the academy and the hygienists descended from Claude
Bernard, Tissié stressed equilibrium, *ordre et mesure,* as the aims of physical training. On the eve of the first comité session, Coubertin included this
concept among the desired goals of reform.

> Whatever importance I attach to sport in itself and for itself, I here avow
> that I consider it above all as a means, and, in agreement with all of the
> English masters and with more than one French master too, I expect
> from it three things. First, that it would reestablish, in our younger
> generations, the equilibrium between body and mind so long ruptured,
> that it would give them not short-lived strength but lasting health and
> that prolonged youth that permits a man to leave behind him a solid and
> finished achievement. The second is that it would avert, at a critical age,
> the temptations against which nothing in our present practice is effica-
> cious, that is, it would furnish a terrain of enthusiasm, procuring a
> healthy fatigue that appeases the senses and the imagination. . . . [The
> third is that] sport, gently and without sudden shocks . . . would forge
> voluntary association, and produce the spirit and leadership, good
> sense, and character. . . . It makes boys more like men.[112]

Thus there was some common ground between them, and doubtless their
early encounters were polite. But Tissié was dead set against what he saw
as the excesses of competitive sport, the very elements of enthusiasm,
liberty, and schoolboy association that Coubertin so vigorously endorsed.
Their rivalry grew, until by the early '90s, they were implacable enemies,
and when Coubertin again pleaded for athletic games at a conference of
the French Association for the Advancement of Science at Caen, in 1894,
Tissié strenuously attacked him and carried the day. The conference resolved "to encourage physical exercise, but to make war on sports in
school establishments."[113]

In reaction, as Boulongne has pointed out, Coubertin not only re-
considered his approval of equilibrium as a goal, but thereafter made his
own war upon it. *Mens sana in corpore sano,* he repeatedly insisted, was
"a refrain for prize day speeches . . . that isn't human, or at least it isn't
young! It's an old buffers' ideal. Equilibrium occurs in life as a result not
as a goal, as a reward not as a search."[114] *Mens sana* "is a simple hygienic
recipe based, like all prescriptions of the hygienic sort, upon the cult of
measure, of moderation, the observance of the golden mean. . . . But sport

is impassioned activity."[115] Whether or not Coubertin had rejected *ordre et mesure* in his aristocratic patrimony, he had certainly retained the value of *prouesse*, and he saw no *prouesse* in gymnastics, only in sport. Its distinguishing psychological feature, he would come to proclaim, was the tendency toward deliberate excess. "Sport is a physical discipline sustained by an enthusiastic addiction to unnecessary effort. Daring for the sake of daring, and without real necessity—it is in this way that our body rises above its animal nature." This is sport's "nobility, and even its poetry," "its essence, its object, and the secret of its moral worth."[116] For physical education he would create the motto *Mens fervida in corpore lacertoso*, and for the Olympic Games, he would adopt Didon's device, *Citius, altius, fortius*. In reaction, new Tissiés like Georges Hébert would rise up to condemn the Olympic Games as "an international muscular fair without educational value."[117]

The comité occasioned another, and still wider, fissure in the physical education movement, again reflecting larger social and ideological themes. Patriotism had itself become an issue, and "national unity" had given over to the split between the nationalists, who in the world of physical education insisted upon purely French modes of exercise, and the internationalists, who in sport saw no embarrassment to patriotism in the adaptation of foreign models. Across this divide, Coubertin faced a much more potent rival than Tissié, one Paschal Grousset who, within two months of the announcement of the comité, brought his own Ligue nationale de l'éducation physique into the field to oppose it.

Nationalism was, at this time, largely an ideology of the non-Marxist left, and Grousset had impeccable leftist credentials.[118] He had been the Commune's delegate for foreign affairs. Exiled to the penal colonies in 1871, he had escaped to England in 1874. There he lived as a writer, collaborating with Stevenson on *Treasure Island* and with Jules Verne on *Salvage from the Cynthia* under the pseudonym of André Laurie, and as a journalist, whose reports on English life were published under another pseudonym, Philippe Daryl, in friendly French papers, and later collected as *À Londres, Notes d'un correspondant français*. Amnestied, he returned to France in 1881, where in addition to writing on foreign societies he published a series of books on boy life, including a bowdlerized translation of *Tom Brown's Schooldays*,[119] altered to make it "more appropriate" to the mentality of French schoolboys.[120] His *Public Life in England*, a collection of articles published in *Le Temps*, was characterized by one critic as the work of "a patriot.... England is in some measure for him only an anatomical subject in which he seeks better to grasp the laws of the physiology of France, even at the cost of a vivisection."[121]

As Coubertin liked pointedly to remark, Grousset had shown no interest in sports in these works, but he was keen on school reform, and the announcement of the comité brought his nationalism into focus on the physical education issue. Marcellin Berthelot, the chemist and recently dismissed minister of public instruction, was to the ligue what Jules Simon was to the comité, its president and prestigious stalking-horse. Most of the ligue members, like the radical socialist Georges Clemenceau, were well to the left of the moderate republicans of the comité.[122] In July 1888, Grousset launched his attacks with a series of articles in *Le Temps*, later reprinted in *La Renaissance physique*. Grousset, as Eugen Weber puts it, thought "sport was good; but it should be taken with a French sauce."[123] *Jeu de paume* was a nobler game than tennis, football was really the ancient game of *barette* in modern guise, and only singles rowing was appropriate to "the very French respect for the individual."[124] Grousset's nativism did not reach very deeply into the true past of French popular games, the way J. J. Jusserand's *Sports et jeux d'exercice dans l'ancienne France*[125] was to do. But it did add an appealing populist note to Grousset's urbane nationalism. (Grousset shortly turned from *barette* to the *bicyclette* for his popular rallying symbol, and with the help of the bicycle vote, was elected to Parliament as a radical socialist in 1893. Coubertin was also to become an adept of the *folle bicyclette*.) But Grousset also had what Coubertin so far lacked: a taste for festivals in which sports competitions were to be embedded. Grousset called for the revival of the *lendits*, medieval student festivals, and two of these "great competitive pageants for the *jeunesse des écoles*"[126] were held in 1889 and 1890.

Grousset's campaign struck a bass chord in public opinion, and Coubertin was not slow to recognize the strength of the threat. He hurriedly tacked a chapter on the ligue to his *L'Éducation anglaise en France*, and in his memoirs Coubertin dealt at length with the challenge. Grousset, Coubertin wrote,

> affected to see in us nothing but obtuse anglomaniacs proposing "to import to France the school games of the United Kingdom, the way one imports pointing dogs or racehorses." From cover to cover in his book, he had returned to the same idea. . . . "Let us be French. Let us be it in the little things; above all let us be it in the great things, like the education of our children, if you desire for France to survive amid the wild animals that are roaring all around her."[127]

Coubertin not only read *La Renaissance physique*, but he recognized its potential consequences. "At that time, with it so often repeated that the ligue incarnated the national traditions in opposition to a comité that humbled itself before England, our work risked being compromised and the transformation of the general routine of our *lycées* according to Arnoldian principles, which I always firmly believed in and from which I expected great things, risked being rendered impossible."[128] The ligue's program, Coubertin averred, was stolen wholesale from the comité. The establishment of *parcs scolaires* with "playing fields, palestras, and racing tracks" (one on the grounds of the Tuileries palace, "burned precisely by the Commune so dear to M. Grousset"), the alteration of school holidays to make them more convenient for sport, a training school for coaches *(moniteurs):* these ideas had all been first proposed by the comité, Coubertin complained. As for the *lendits*, they were "deplorable festivals that, by loading multiple contests into a brief space of time just before exams, risked throwing disorder into studies and inaugurating a veritable physical *surmenage*, not to speak of their inconvenience, which caused great stir and excessive publicity from the pedagogical point of view."[129]

But Coubertin learned from Grousset. Next to the universal exhibitions, Grousset's *lendits* were most responsible for turning Coubertin's attentions to youth festivals. And, in the course of his 1888 articles, Grousset had called for the inauguration of French Olympic Games.[130] Coubertin never saw fit to mention this summons, but he surely was influenced by it. Moreover, between the lines of Coubertin's counterattacks against nationalism, one cannot fail to sense a grudging respect for Grousset,[131] and, perhaps, a regret that their respective political cultures kept them from an alliance in favor of sports. Grousset was soon too preoccupied in Parliament to continue his sports propaganda, and in the early '90s, the ligue, like the comité, dissolved into other sports associations. But Coubertin's combat with French nationalism was only just beginning. Especially after the Dreyfus affair, nationalism was reborn on the right, in a peculiarly virulent and chauvinistic form, and its archpartisan, Charles Maurras, became Coubertin's great enemy.

The irony could not have been greater, or more indicative of the times, for in 1887–88, Maurras was a fellow Le Play follower and promoter of Coubertin. In two review articles on education in *La Réforme sociale*, Maurras noted that Jules Simon was thinking "in unison with M. de Coubertin," and claimed that the educational remedies proposed by Maneuvrier in his *L'Éducation de la bourgeoisie sous la République* were "largely borrowed from the so very interesting observations reported from England by our colleague M. Pierre de Coubertin."[132] And when Grousset was menacing Coubertin with his nationalist campaign, Maurras counseled him. "It was not worth the trouble to take the cause of physical education forcibly in hand by giving ourselves over to 'acts of near violence,' said M. Charles Maurras, in order to occasion the failure of all these admirable projects."[133] But signs of the man Maurras was to become were already in evidence in the 1888 review, when he complained that Maneuvrier, and therefore, indirectly, Coubertin, cared too much for democracy and too little for "excellence" *(vertu)* in education. On his voyage to Athens in 1896, Maurras converted to royalism, reaction, and what was to be the

program of the Action française.[134] As we shall see, that visit coincided
with the first modern Olympic Games, and in a lengthy series of dispatches to a Paris newspaper, Maurras decried Coubertin as a "zealot" and
the "International of sports" as an "anachronism," "the profaning of a
glorious name," and a tasteless "mixture of races", whose only benefit was
to convince Frenchmen of the menacing barbarity of the Anglo-Saxon
nations.[135]

Barrès, too, "shadowed" Coubertin in the 1880s. Barrès had learned
from Taine and Le Play, dedicated an 1889 novel to "French schoolboys,
victims of an abominable discipline,"[136] and would soon undertake his
own pilgrimage of usurpation in Greece.[137] But Barrès cared nothing for
sport. By 1892, Barrès and Cassagnac, in Coubertin's words, "were leading a malicious campaign against us, accusing us at once of lowering the
level of studies, provoking physical accidents, and sowing in the schoolboy ranks immorality and indiscipline."[138] In 1906, Barrès again played the
"spoil sport." As one of a dozen "distinguished personalities of the arts and
letters" asked to comment on the benefits of the Olympic Games, he
groused that he preferred the theater of Sophocles.[139] It was left to later
disciples like Jules Jolinon to associate sport and Barrès's narcissistic *culte
du moi*,[140] an association Coubertin would have found offensive. Like
Maurras, Barrès was the partisan of a particularly vicious form of
nationalism, concerned to prevent the spread of "foreign influences" in
France. Coubertin's very identity was wrapped up as fully in his internationalism as in his patriotism, and his politics, no less than his apologies
for sport, came to be centered upon the conviction that patriotism and
internationalism were not only not incompatible, but required one
another. On this point alone, Ernest de Seillières's claim that Coubertin
was a political confrere of Barrès is wrong.[141] Coubertin also differed
radically with Barrès (and Maurras) on the monarchy, the role of the
Church, equality of opportunity, and the success of the Third Republic.
Though an anti-Dreyfusard, Coubertin was no anti-Semite, and points of
view he shared with Barrès—e.g., antisocialism, regionalism, and the
romance of the provinces—were broadly held social opinions. Both were
partisans of French "national energy," but so were Durkheim (*effervescence
collective*) and Bergson (*élan vital*), and one would hardly care to see *them* as
decadent protofascists.[142] The wonder about Coubertin is not that he
shared certain concerns with France's most notable reactionaries, but that
he managed to escape the ideological excesses to which they were led.
More than any other single factor, it was his internationalism that saved
him, an internationalism born of his adolescent search for a public mission
and brought into the open and tested in his struggle with Grousset.

CHAPTER FIVE

The Olympic Idea

America, 1889

It is hardly surprising, then, that in the midst of his combat with Grousset, Coubertin felt the need once again to revitalize himself on foreign soil, this time in the United States. Because of the Grousset campaign, he wrote, "I wanted to enlarge the circle of models to follow; there were also some across the ocean and, if a crisis of educational anglophobia was befalling us in France, we had at least the youth of the United States to provide as an example to our own."[1] While it was true enough, as he went on to claim, that few Frenchmen cared about the doings of the American universities at the time, broad interest in the U.S. was apparent in Parisian circles.[2] Boutmy, for one, had passed on from his English studies to an equal obsession with writing about the U.S., and many of the Le Play society members followed him in this. Moreover, Coubertin had in hand the results of another of his "surveys," this one a questionnaire on physical education practices and facilities, written in English and sent to schools and universities in England, the United States, and the British colonies, under the auspices of the Paris Universal Exposition (more on this below). Coubertin received responses from ninety schools and colleges in the U.S., and he allowed himself to be convinced that, even though none mentioned Arnold by name, all showed that his doctrines were held in great favor, and in the United States there were no "cracks in the pedagogical block constructed by his genius."[3] Assured in advance, he embarked for New York on the *Normandie* on July 17, 1889.

But this time he traveled not as an amateur, but as the holder of an official commission by the government, charged by the minister of public instruction to investigate the organization of the schools and universities of the United States and Canada. Jules Ferry, whom Coubertin admired more than any statesman of the Third Republic, apparently took a hand in securing him the appointment.[4] Coubertin paid his own expenses, but that was small cost to be traveling in the footsteps of Tocqueville, whose works Coubertin knew and admired and who had himself first embarked for America in the exercise of a governmental inquiry.

Coubertin was a vigorous tourist. In four months, he made a great circle, from New York, through New England, Montreal, Toronto, Chicago, down the Mississippi to New Orleans, and back through Florida, Virginia, Washington, and Baltimore to New York. The report which he made to the ministry was equally long-winded. Almost four hundred pages long, it was published as *Universités transatlantiques* in 1890, a work, as Boulongne describes it, "not very academic in form, half travelogue, half philosophical miscellany."[5] Paeans to the Brooklyn Bridge, Niagara Falls, and the raw youth of Chicago are interspersed with commentaries on the American character and spirit, the cult of George Washington, the "negro question," and the mistaken French impression that American energies are devoted solely to commerce. In an article in *La Réforme sociale*, Coubertin insisted that "the ambitions, strengths, and passions that fill the soul of a Yankee" are as strong for intellectual and scientific things as they are for money and business, and that it is mere chauvinism to think otherwise.[6] But above all, he was happily surprised to discover the democratic sentiments of American Catholics, and he devoted a whole chapter of *Universités transatlantiques* to presenting the French public with the American example of a church passionately committed to democracy while backing the separation of church and state and the liberty of religious practice. These experiences hardly turned Coubertin to personal piety, but they deepened his commitment to the *ralliement* and his opposition to the intransigents and royalists, softened his hostility to the Church and to his own Catholic heritage, left him better prepared than most of his countrymen for Leo XIII's *Rerum Novarum*, and set the stage for his later seeking of Vatican approval of the Olympic Games. Coubertin returned again and again to the topic, most notably in *The Evolution of France* where he offered his experiences as evidence for Tocqueville's claim that Catholics "formed the most republican and most democratic class in the United States," and adjured Frenchmen to learn from the American example.[7]

But Coubertin was hardly negligent of his official mission. Among the universities and colleges he visited were Amherst, Harvard, Cornell, Montréal (which he compared unfavorably with McGill), Chicago, Tulane, Virginia, Johns Hopkins, and Princeton, and he inquired about others from professors and alumni he met along the way. He took only superficial interest in curricula and courses of study, and his reports on "organization" were no more than mechanical (though he did take pains to tout the role of private philanthropies). His interests were sports and physical education, and no doubt more than one mandarin professor was taken aback to discover such concerns in an official emissary of the French government. On November 29–30, Coubertin participated in a conference on physical training in Boston, and the report of the proceedings supplies

interesting information both as to the state of American professorial debate on the matter and as to Coubertin's self-presentation and perception
of the American situation.

William T. Harris, United States commissioner of education, presided
over the conference, which took place at M.I.T. The "old physical education," he said in his opening remarks, thought it sufficient to train the
muscles under the command of the will, whereas "the new physical education" (whose pioneers he listed as Dr. Hitchcock of Amherst, Dr. Sargent of the Cambridge Hemenway Gymnasium, and Dr. Hartwell of
Johns Hopkins) pays attention to assisting the involuntary organs through
"voluntary action and motion." He begged the conference to consider
whether "use of the muscles by the will" served as well as free play for rest
and recreation from studies and sedentary occupations.[8] But the conferees
were for the most part professionals and officials concerned with those
forms of physical training Harris classed as "work," and the merits of free
play were hardly mentioned, much less discussed in the course of the
meeting.

Hartwell followed with a long peroration on physiology, toward the
end of which he declared himself. Physical training had to conform to the
tenets of liberal education which did not seek to train specialists for their
later intellectual, commercial, or industrial pursuits. Just so, it was not the
business of physical education to "train up ball-players, carpenters, clerks,
or professionals of any kind. General bodily training is the kind demanded."[9] Pastimes, sports, and gymnastics were credible forms of exercise, he said. However, without meaning to disparage athletic sports
which he acknowledged were popular with students and had favorable
moral effects, Hartwell insisted that games aimed merely at "pleasurable
activity for the sake of recreation," whereas gymnastics sought "pleasure,
health and skill." Athletics "bear so indelibly the marks of their childish
origin, they are so crude and unspecialized." Gymnastics, on the other
hand, "are more comprehensive in their aims, more formal, elaborate, and
systematic in their methods, and are more productive of solid results."
Then Hartwell introduced what was to prove a leitmotif of the conference:
the translation of the debate about proper forms of physical education into
consideration of the national character of the peoples who had invented
each system.

Gymnastics have been most popular and general among the most highly
trained nations, such as the Greeks of old and the Germans of today.
The most athletic and, at the same time, one of the most ill trained of
modern nations is the British. . . . An Englishman believes, and acts
upon the belief that you come to do a thing right by doing it, and not by
first learning to do it right and then doing it; whereas the Germans leave
little or nothing to the rule of thumb, not even in bodily education.[10]

There followed a paper by Heinrich Metzner, principal of the New York Turnverein, which, in the course of explaining the German system, touted it because "it has not been influenced by any other," and demanded "a fair trial . . . free of all prejudice" for it in the American schools.[11] Hartwell, seemingly perturbed by the unprofessional character and nationalistic overtones of Metzner's paper, jumped back into the fray with a historical overview of the German system in America. Jahn's popular gymnastics had sought to produce able defenders of the nation at "the time of Prussia's deepest humiliation and trial." Adolph Spiess, who was, "unlike Jahn, not a popular agitator," had adapted the system to the schools. In 1825, Dr. Beck and Dr. Follen, friends and pupils of Jahn, had brought the system to Round Hill School in Northampton, where it had great success until they left for positions at Harvard. In the 1860s, one Dio Lewis renewed the tradition at Lexington School, and, as Hartwell was careful to add, Lewis's outfit included "an iron crown for the head, which was decorated with the stars and stripes."[12] From such "reassuring" symbols, Hartwell turned to showing that the Turners had already achieved great success in the States. The North American Turnerbund presently had 30,000 members and owned $2 million worth of property, including 160 gymnasia and libraries with 53,000 volumes. One hundred forty gymnastics teachers had graduated from the movement's normal seminary in the States, and some 15,000 boys and 6,000 girls were currently enrolled in Turner schools in New York, Boston, Milwaukee, Chicago, and St. Louis. Testimonies from school board officials as to the successful use of Turner methods in the public schools were also supplied. Hartwell noted that the Turners were interested in more than gymnastics; their schools discussed political, social, and ethical questions, taught German language and literature, maintained theater and singing groups, gave "domestic training," and some had military cadet batallions. But he saw no need to reassure his auditors that such ethnic endeavors were not un-American, or to argue that they eased the passage of German nationals into American life. Moreover, while complaining of the ignorance of elite educational and governmental circles as to the great success of the Turnerbund, it did not occur to him that this "ignorance" might be based in class and ethnic prejudice. For Hartwell, it was the best system, and therefore should be adopted, and that was that.

The partisans of Sweden then took the floor. Claes J. Enebuske, Ph.D., who thought it best "to make a clean breast of it at the outset and own right up that I am not an American," suggested that the question of physical education "combines the thought and aim of ancient, literary, beauty-loving Hellas, of powerful, disciplinary, purpose-strong Rome, and of modern, intelligent, energetic America."[13] The sum of this peculiar cultural addition was Sweden. Nils Posse then delivered a lecture on the technical and practical merits of Ling and his school. A demonstration by a group of boys from the Boston German Turnverein had followed Metzner's and Hartwell's talks, and a demonstration by "a class of ladies under the care of Mr. Posse" now undertook to display the merits of the Swedish system. The earl of Meath then attested to the value of the Swedish system by announcing that it had appeal in Britain because it was cheap. Since apparatus was deemphasized, the taxpayers would accept it. Moreover, the Swedish gymnasts he had seen could not have been equaled "except by professional acrobats in our country." Dr. Seaver, superintendent of Boston schools, arose to speak for "Yale men."[14] "Our American needs are peculiar," he said.

> I believe one criticism can be made that is fair and honest,—that [the Swedish system] requires too much mental attention. The pupil must have his attention centered on the instructor at all times. The pupil has all the time to watch for the word of command. Here in America (it may be wrong, but it is true) we do not care a snap for any man's say so. We do not like to be ordered around to do anything. It always made me mad as a boy, and it still does, to have any one talk to me in a dictatorial way. I believe it contrary to American spirit and custom.[15]

"Yankee schoolma'ams" must help accommodate "the needs of Yankee boys and girls, as well as of Irish or German," the doctor carried on none too subtly. "I believe that if there is one thing where we Yankees surpass other people, it is our inventive ingenuity." We must and will develop what we do not have now, Seaver said, an American system of physical education that builds upon the others.

Dr. W. G. Anderson of the Brooklyn School of Physical Training still more loudly played the patriot.

> I am an American. It is natural, therefore, that I should defend anything that is American if it is worthy of defense.... The so-called American system is as scientific as that of Ling. Why should it not be? We begin where he stopped; we have his experience. I have much respect for the German and Swedish systems; I have had experience with both, but taken as they are, they will not suit the American people. We have ideas of our own.[16]

Coubertin must have been very disturbed indeed, as he sat through all of this. To be sure, here was consensus as to the general value of physical education, a consensus lacking as yet in France. The pragmatic question of "how," not "whether," dominated the debate. But the very combat between the German, Swedish, and "native" models that he had thought to leave behind him in France was here repeated in full. And, unbelievably, no one had risen to defend English athletic sports against the claims of gymnastics. Hitchcock of Amherst came close. After describing the

physical examinations and anatomy classes required of all students and
noting that the gymnasium was a place of "play and amusement," he
averred that "training in out-door sports is considered the most desirable."[17] But the demonstration that followed was a dumbbell exercise by a
group from the YMCA, after which the floor was taken by Dr. Alice Hall
of the Baltimore Women's College, who again took up the merits of the
Swedish system, and by Dr. Helen Putnam of Vassar, who reported that
sixty-three percent of the girls in the best schools received no physical
training whatsoever.[18] Whereupon the conference adjourned.

The next day brought more of the same thing. Sargent of Harvard
thought "athletic sports, kept within bounds and carefully regulated, are a
valuable adjunct to our system of physical training" and noted that the
Harvard authorities were trying to increase athletic facilities. But he was
careful to note that athletics were managed by the students themselves
(which Coubertin approved) and that the authorities "are in no way responsible for" them (which implied a certain reticence on the issue of their
educational value, about which Coubertin would have been dismayed).
The bulk of Sargent's paper was devoted to promoting the system of
pulley-weights he had devised for the Hemenway gym.

Late in the day, and after several muddled and undistinguished papers
clearly left for last, Coubertin was invited to speak. His speech displayed
much of the style that later made his discourses so effective in mobilizing
sentiments: charm that disarmed skepticism as to his purposes, an apparent humility that paved the way for exaggeration and self-aggrandizement
later on, a capacity for making his listeners feel part of a heroic conspiracy,
and a talent for usurpatory rhetoric through which opposing views appeared to be given their due when in fact they were circumvented. He
thanked the group for their "hearty welcome" which he neatly turned
from respect for "my unknown self" to respect "to my country, your sister
republic," thus preparing the ground for his later claim that since France
and America looked for the same sort of citizen ("free-minded, self-
governing men, who will not look upon the State as a baby looks upon its
mother; who will not be afraid of having to make their own way through
life"), they should naturally wish for the same sort of physical training.

The results of his boldness in consenting to speak, said Coubertin, "will
be to give you an unfair idea of the way we Frenchmen speak English. It
will also give you an unfair idea of the way we fulfil our duties." As an
official commissioner of the French government visiting this country's
colleges and universities, he ought not to be making any statement prior to
his official report. But, said Coubertin, building up a little suspense as to
what he might say, "I understand . . . that the French Minister of Public
Instruction is not here to-day, and I trust you will be kind enough not to
let him know what I have been doing in Boston!"

I was asked the other day what, in my opinion, American education was like. I answered that in some respects it looked like a battle-field where English and German ideas were fighting. While I fully acknowledge that from the physical point of view nothing can be said against the German system, I believe, on the other hand, that from the moral and social point of view no system, if so it can be called, stands higher than the English athletic sport system as understood and explained by the greatest of modern teachers, Thomas Arnold of Rugby. His principles are the ones on which was founded last year the French Educational Reform Association. I wish I could give you a detailed account of the work our Association is engaged in carrying out; it is no less than a general reform of secondary education.[19]

The members of the Comité pour la propagation des exercises physiques may well have forgiven Coubertin for endowing them with the rather grander title of the French Educational Reform Association, but many would have been surprised to learn that the comité was founded on Arnoldian principles, and several would have been quite outraged to hear it suggested that they were unanimous in their support of English games over other models. It was not the last time Coubertin was to speak with the imperial "we" when the rest of his supposed colleagues were not around to hear him.

Having denied the social and moral value of German gymnastics, he hastened to note that they were nonetheless good for children. The French, he said, had solved the primary school question and "the German methods have now only to be developed in all our primary schools and made the general rule."[20] But "we believe that the most important period in a boy's education is the one extending from his twelfth to his nineteenth year. During that period not only his brain, not only his body, but above all his *will* can be trained." For this only "a strong taste for manly games" would do. Gymnastics may also be pursued, but only if they are not compulsory and do not interfere with athletic clubs and societies. Not wishing to antagonize his hosts, Coubertin rather superficially complimented Hitchcock, Hartwell, and Sargent and reiterated that he was speaking of the secondary schools. He launched into a paean to Arnold, dropped Gladstone's name and his "testimony," and made the claim that the Arnoldian reform "has been one of the most important events in the life of the English people." It prepared the way for the bright period called the Victorian Era, "the chief characteristic being the wonderful influence of athletic sports on the moral and social qualities of boys."[21] His Exposition survey had shown, he added, "that all over the world Englishmen, who perhaps know very little about Arnold himself, were still holding to his views and ideas and believed them to be the best."[22] Moreover, "Arnold's precepts are followed" in recently founded American schools such as Groton, Lawrenceville, Berkeley, and others, a notion that would have probably come as a surprise to the masters of these institutions.

There was no discussion of Coubertin's speech, or any echo of it in the closing statements of the conference. But if his views failed to carry the day among the elite of American physical educators, it was not, as in France, because athletic sports were not yet far developed. On the contrary, the concerns of the American physical educationists were motivated in no small part as a reaction to the growing popularity of sports in America.

Numerous rowing clubs had appeared by the 1830s, especially in New York and Philadelphia.[23] In 1843, Harvard students took up the sport, with Yale juniors purchasing a boat the following year, and the two colleges began to race in 1852. In the College Union Regatta of 1859, Brown also crewed, and the University of Pennsylvania shortly entered the intercollegiate contests. In 1869, the first international contest took place on the Thames. Oxford beat Harvard, and the match was said to have been witnessed by a hundred thousand spectators. In 1871, the Rowing Association of American Colleges was formed, and sixteen crews participated in its 1875 regatta. In 1878, Columbia defeated Cambridge for the newly organized Visitor's Challenge Cup in England. By the time of Coubertin's visit, collegiate rowing was well organized and widely followed. There were, moreover, many amateur boat clubs outside of the colleges. The Atlanta Boat Club of New York had been founded in 1848, the Union Boat Club of Boston in 1851, and a half-dozen clubs united into the Schuylkill Navy in Philadelphia in 1858. Twenty-eight clubs met to define amateur status and rules, and united in the National Association of Amateur Oarsmen in 1873, and national regattas were held in Philadelphia, Troy, Detroit, Newark, Saratoga, Washington, and Boston in subsequent years. Professional rowing is known at least as early as 1838, when a Poughkeepsie club lost a $1,000 race to the Independents of New York. In the 1860s, a championship belt and prize money of several thousand dollars was awarded to individual champions in regattas in New York and Boston, and James Hamill, the most famous of the professionals, went to England for match races.

Yacht racing also dates from the 1830s, and the New York Yacht Club was founded in 1844. In 1851, the schooner *America* arrived at Cowes in England, where she took the Royal Yacht Squadron Cup before a huge shoreline throng, including Queen Victoria and Prince Albert who later inspected the ship. Later she won a match race against the *Titania*, England's best, and the cup she brought home became, in 1857, the famous America's Cup. Four challenges for her were turned back in the 1880s, though no race took place during Coubertin's visit. Sailing contests were limited for the most part to a monied elite, and did not penetrate collegiate sport until the twentieth century, but the newspapers and the general public took great interest in the international matches.

Track and field athletics in the modern form took shape in the 1870s. The New York Athletic Club was founded in 1868. It held meets every year thereafter, and staged "annual championships" beginning in 1876. In 1887, English athletes appeared and marks included a 10-second hundred yards, a 22-second 220, a 47.5 quarter, a 1:55.4 half, and a 4:21 mile. Other events included a hammer throw, a primitive shot put, a pole vault (11′5″), standing and running high and long jumps, 120-yard high hurdles, the 3-mile walk, and a 10-mile race, which had long been familiar from professional match running earlier in the century. These meets attracted many spectators. In 1879, the National Association of Amateur Athletics was formed with fourteen clubs as members. Collegiate athletes began to participate in large numbers in the early 1880s, and in 1885, the association passed detailed rules on amateurism. By 1889, many Eastern colleges had track and field associations, intercollegiate meets were established, and collegiate athletes were coming to dominate the sport.

The greatest of the collegiate sports was, of course, football, as in England, a widespread popular game whose many variations were only slowly organized by a common set of rules. The earliest college matches known were the infamous "Bloody Mondays" in which Harvard sophomores matched themselves against the freshmen. These began in 1829, and continued almost yearly until they were banned by the administration in 1860. Football early on consisted of two sides squaring off to kick an inflated bladder toward the opposing goal, and the matches attracted local attention beyond the college walls. Indeed, *Harper's Weekly* struck a populist note when, in 1857, it complained of the inadequacy of physical training at the elite colleges.

> That game of football, which we are happy to say is not yet extinct, ought to be a matter of as much concern as the Greek or mathematical prize. Indeed, of the two it is the more useful exercise. Here the English are vastly our superiors. . . . We had rather chronicle a great boat-race at Harvard or Yale, or a cricket match with the United States Eleven than all the prize poems or the orations on Lafayette that are produced in half a century.[24]

In 1869, the first intercollegiate game was played between Princeton and Rutgers, organized in part to decide a feud over ownership of certain Revolutionary War cannon. A second match the following year drew extensive press coverage, and the college authorities were forced to cancel the third day's play for fear of a riot. In 1869, Rugby Union rules were printed in the *Spirit of the Times* and shortly began to dominate the college game. An 1873 convention between Princeton, Columbia, Yale, Rutgers, and Harvard debated the matter, and in 1874, a team from McGill came to Harvard to play two games, the first according to the mixed American rules ("the Boston game"), the second as rugby. A return visit to Montreal was made by the Harvardians that same year, and in 1875, they played a rugby match against Tufts. In 1876, the Intercollegiate Football Association was founded by Harvard, Princeton, Columbia, and Yale which voted to adopt the rugby rules. By the late 1880s, intercollegiate football of roughly the modern American sort was thoroughly established and had begun to spread out from the Ivy League to other colleges and secondary schools. Huge throngs of spectators watched the matches between the great colleges, the press covered the games extensively, and they became important social events whose scale quite amazed Coubertin.

A cricket club was known in Boston as early as 1809, and the game was played, though never widely, in that city, New York, and Philadelphia. The New York Cricket Club won an international match and $500 from Toronto in 1840, and in 1844, the St. George's Club of New York, took $1,000 from an all-Canada eleven. Other matches with Canada took place in 1853, 1854, and 1856, and in 1859, an all-England team destroyed an all-America team at Hoboken. In 1872, W. G. Grace brought an all-star team to the States, and the Canadian-U.S. matches, interrupted by the Civil War, were resumed. In 1874, intercollegiate cricket was begun by Haverford and Pennsylvania. In 1878, an Australian team visited the United States, and in 1879, an American team from Philadelphia competed in England, Ireland, and Scotland. The *American Cricketeer* was founded in 1877, but significantly it shortly devoted more space to other amateur sports than to cricket. The old game had the patriotic interest of international matches as well as presenting opportunities for upper class socializing "in the English fashion." But otherwise, it was poorly provisioned for the struggle with its American cousin, baseball, a faster, simpler, more theatrical and spectatorial, and above all, more "American" game.

As early as 1856, baseball was being referred to as "the national game": "We feel a degree of old Knickerbocker pride at the continued prevalence of Base Ball as the National game in the region of the Manhattanese."[25] It too had many prototypes, including "town ball," "old cat," and "round ball," reaching back to the eighteenth century. Among the many early clubs was the "Olympic Ball Club" of Philadelphia in the early '30s. Abner Doubleday, who drew up a set of rules in 1839, has traditionally been credited with the fatherhood of modern baseball, though the evolution of the game took several decades. The Knickerbocker Baseball Club was founded in 1845, and teams were shortly organized throughout Manhattan and in the other boroughs, culminating in an all-star game between Manhattan and Brooklyn in 1853. In Philadelphia, the Minerva Club was

organized in 1857, the Keystone in 1859, and the Athletic in 1860. The
game had also appeared in the Midwest in the late '50s. The first National
Association of Base Ball Players was founded in 1859, as an amateur force
to counter the trend toward professionalism already in evidence. At its
convention in 1865, 91 clubs participated, and 237 were represented in
1867. The Harvard Base Ball Club was founded in 1864, and intercollegiate play and games against town clubs brought Harvard the un-
official "New England Championship" of 1865. Teams like the National
Base Ball Club of Washington made extended tours in the Midwest, competing in large cities and small towns along the way. The game had
become so popular in the late '60s that players required police protection,
as at the 1866 match between the Philadelphia Athletics and the Brooklyn
Atlantics for the "Championship of America." The crowd stormed the
field in Philadelphia, and the game had to be completed on Long Island
later on. This same popularity brought gate receipts, paid players, and
active recruiting, and professional teams were rapidly formed, including
the Excelsiors in Chicago in 1867, and, the most famous of all, the Cincinnati Red Stockings, in 1869. The amateur association disbanded in 1874,
leaving only the colleges as homes for organized amateur baseball. Town
fathers and businessmen, recognizing the civic and commercial value of
successful baseball teams, began to subsidize them in various ways, and
professional baseball grew rapidly. The National Association of Professional Base Ball Players was founded in 1871, and in 1876 it was
replaced by the National League, whose first members were the Philadelphia Athletics, the New York Mutuals, and teams from Hartford, Boston,
Chicago, Cincinnati, Louisville, and St. Louis, and whose first president,
Morgan G. Bulkley, was later governor of Connecticut.[26]

These are but the main lineaments of the extraordinary efflorescence
of participatory and spectator sport in the United States in the middle and
later decades of the nineteenth century. As in England, horse racing (the
first Kentucky Derby was in 1875, the Travers and Belmont stakes having
been founded years earlier) had mass popularity, and the Grand Circuit of
trotting races was established in 1873. James Gordon Bennett introduced
and promoted polo in 1876, and foxhunting became an obsession with the
upper classes of New York. The first Westminster Kennel Club dog show
took place in 1877. Shooting and angling and the other "field sports" had
become even more popular when faster transport opened the West to
gentlemen's "expeditions." Racquets were another significant upper class
sport—the New York Racquet Club was founded in 1863—until it was
largely superseded by lawn tennis, which developed rapidly in the '70s
and was, among the urban leisure classes, even more responsible than
baseball for the decline of cricket as a participatory sport. The American
Alpine Club was not founded until 1902, but already in the 1880s young,

wealthy adventurers were replacing soldiers and scientists as the vanguard of American mountaineering, and the press took more than reportorial interest. In 1886, for example, the *New York Times* sponsored an unsuccessful expedition to Mount Saint Elias in Alaska.[27]

Parallel with these upper class athletic sports, a host of popular recreations grew up in the 1870s and '80s. Tobogganing and ice skating made their way down from Canada. "Roller polo," or hockey on roller skates, was known in the early '80s. Ice hockey, whose origins lay in the old game of shinny, was not introduced until the later years of the decade. Shinny originated in part with native Americans, and lacrosse, another Indian game, also came in during this period, Yale playing a New York team in 1883. Jackson Haines revolutionized fancy skating, and toured Europe in 1864. Pairs skating was popular in the later years of the decade, and a skating congress was held in Philadelphia in 1868. Formal speed and fancy skating competitions began to be organized and, by the late 1870s, ice skating had become a veritable craze throughout the Northeast. Lake Placid began to emerge as a winter sports resort. Roller skating and bicycling became other urban fads of great popularity, the high-wheeled bicycle having been introduced from Europe at the Philadelphia Centennial Exposition in 1876. (The centennial was also the scene of the first great international target shooting match, Americans, Irish, Scots, and Australians competing with rifles at 800, 900, and 1,000 yards.) The New York Bicycle Club was organized in 1879, and the League of American Wheelmen in 1880. Cycling races, exhibitions, and congresses, as well as the invention of the rubber tire, assisted the development of the bicycle as a great symbol and practical mechanism of urban life in the later '80s. Long-distance walking and, especially, prizefighting were among the sporting contests promoted and staked by the middle and upper classes, with the working classes supplying the combatants and much of the public following. It is perhaps sufficient to mention the names of John L. Sullivan and Gentleman Jim Corbett to indicate the mass attention to boxing in the 1880s. Later in the decade, the Marquess of Queensbury rules began to replace the bare knuckles brawls of the earlier period, and the celebrity of Sullivan brought the sport to the attention of aristocratic Europeans. In 1888, the year before Coubertin's visit to America, Baron Rothschild imported Sullivan and Charlie Mitchell to slug it out on his estate in Chantilly.

In the city parks no less than in the private clubs and colleges, and in the rural towns no less than in the cities, no French visitor in 1889 could have failed to take note of the "sporting" character of the American nation. Coubertin, of course, was on special lookout for all this, and was quite taken with it. He returned to France a passionate publicist for the American way, the United States having to no small degree replaced England in his heart: "The Americans, no less avid for science as for wealth, are preparing for us the currents of the future. Their efforts are not always well combined, in their ardor they mix the wheat with the chaff. But perseverence and hard work triumph over all difficulties, and their progress must be for us the motif of a fecund emulation."[28] The spate of articles he would write on or for Americans (some half a hundred), his setting of "Le Roman d'un rallié" in the States and the engagement of his literary double to an American girl,[29] the pleasure he took in American Olympic successes, and the awarding of the third Olympic Games to the United States all testify to the degree of his "American rapture." It was based, of course, on far more than American preoccupation with sport. But he saw sport as a dominant emblem and instrument of the vitality, democracy, and happy blending of tradition and modern innovation which he found distinctive of the United States.

Even as he had polemically misrepresented the state of affairs in France to the physical educationists in Boston, so too his account of American practices and thinking was hardly objective. "At the moment when, in France, the preoccupation with giving physical education the important place it deserves is so vigorously apparent, it was interesting to have a look at a country in which the two most opposed systems of physical education are found: free games from England, and scientific gymnastics from Germany." The freedom of athletic games, he told his French audience, allows for gymnastics in the States, but "intolerance, on the contrary, is fundamental to German gymnastics, which knows nothing beyond ensemble movements, rigid discipline, and perpetual regimentation." Coubertin implied that the highest educational authorities in the States now recognized the dangers in the German system, which in any case had not sunk deep roots because "it is contrary to the genius of the country." Coubertin quite clearly was disturbed by certain aspects of American collegiate sport, but by a remarkable sleight of hand and with notable cheek, he attributed them to the partisans of gymnastics in the schools.

In the United States, a reaction is being prepared against [gymnastics], and it is possible to foresee the day when the presidents of the universities will take back from the directors of the gymnasiums the foolish powers they granted to them. These directors have a high hand not only over the bizarre apparatuses of which they are—or think themselves to be—the inventors, but also over games, because, being unable from the first to get rid of them, they usurp them to their profit, choosing among their pupils the strongest and most agile, to the training of whom they exclusively devote themselves. As a result, during the fair season, the university teams go from competition to competition; crowds press in to

see them struggle; enormous sums of money are wagered by their back-
ers and, as soon as the champions give themselves over to this exaggerated athleticism, their comrades keep aloof so as not to interfere with
their training. . . . This is a warning to us not to let physical education
take the scientific and authoritarian character that certain theorists,
caring more for principles than their application, friends of the rational
and ignorant of pedagogy, would like to give it.[30]

Hartwell had indeed founded the first "department of athletics" at Johns
Hopkins and was endeavoring to bring school sports under his control and
to turn its energies and resources to teaching gymnastics. But neither he
nor his kind could be held responsible for the abuses Coubertin ascribes to
him.

On the other hand, Coubertin assured the minister and the French
public, secondary schools are being founded in the United States which
are "inspired by the immortal doctrine of the great Arnold," and in which
"the program of Arnold is almost entirely reproduced." There athleticism
is being used "to produce firm wills and right hearts at the same time as
robust bodies," and "through liberty and the hierarchy of merit" boys are
being prepared for their role as "citizens of a free country."[31] He left his
readers with the impression that such schools were widespread and,
moreover, that the abuses of collegiate athletics would be overcome "from
the bottom up," when in actual fact, then as now, it was the secondary
schools which, in the matter of athletics, imitated the colleges. Coubertin
was not, however, so put off by the "exaggerated athleticism" of the
colleges he observed not to love its general results.

> At the same hour, in New York, in Chicago, perhaps in San Francisco,
> six or seven hundred [college graduate] Yankees sit around tables to
> celebrate gaily, to acclaim the alma mater and to sing the old songs
> which end with one of these bizarre cries of chopped syllables whose
> savage harmonies recall the novels of Fenimore Cooper. Each college
> has its own and it serves to encourage its champions in the regattas,
> football matches, wherever honor is at stake.[32]

Barely seven years later, those same college yells would echo through the
streets of Athens at the first modern Olympic Games.

Prior to his American journey, Coubertin had taken no more interest in
French noneducational sports organizations than to include some of their
presidents in the comité, or occasionally to make use himself of a fencing
or boxing or Jockey Club hall in Paris. But in the States, he was impressed
by the number and extent of these associations, particularly in New York,
and especially the New York Athletic Club. He described such clubs in
detail in *Universités transatlantiques*, their gymnasia, billiard parlors,
swimming pools, boating sheds, athletic fields, and the salons where

members "write and dine." He noted the role of the clubs in promoting track and field, fencing, boxing, and other competitions. On the upper class character of most of these facilities he had nothing to say, other than to assure his readers that dues were not particularly high. Coubertin was still operating on the assumption that any sports manifestation or association, no matter its particular constituency or class character, would provide leavening for physical renaissance of a nation as a whole. America he professed to find "full of true liberty" as against the Old World which was "hierarchical and complicated."[33] As a result, he bothered little with the hierarchies and social complications of the New World. Only much later in his career would he call for the revival of public gymnasia on the Greek model, where citizens of all age groups and classes could freely mix. Nor did he comment on the class character of particular sports. Cricket, he merely noted, was not in vogue; baseball was "extremely simple as to the rules, but very difficult in practice" and therefore not suited to French schoolboys; tobogganing, snowshoeing, and ice yachting were impossible in France owing to climate; whereas football was greatly popular and had everything to recommend it. He closed his report with an instruction to the minister as to the arcane wonders of the shower bath.

The 1889 trip was also significant for the personal contacts Coubertin made. In New York, he met Teddy Roosevelt, just then emerging from his political "retirement" after his defeat in the New York mayoral race of 1886. Roosevelt was already well known as the American equivalent of Charles Kingsley, a notable partisan of muscular Christianity, of sport, and of the association of manly virtues with patriotism and democracy. Coubertin professed to admire Roosevelt's promotion of boxing clubs in the poorer quarters of New York. The baron later dedicated *La Gymnastique utilitaire* to the hero of San Juan Hill, and had Roosevelt awarded one of the first Olympic Diplomas in 1905. The two men are said to have conducted a "regular and reciprocal" correspondence,[34] though details of it have yet to come to light.

Roosevelt had first taken up sport and outdoor adventure as a therapy for the weakness and sickly condition which marred his boyhood.[35] Coubertin had never been sickly, but his love of sport was probably motivated, in part, as a compensation for his physical size. He was, as Richard Mandell delicately puts it, "unusually small,"[36] no Toulouse-Lautrec to be sure, but in every group photograph smaller in stature than his colleagues and associates. Smaller, perhaps, than his brothers too. If evidence on this was available, we might be able to surmise that it contributed to his sibling rivalries. Toulouse-Lautrec, whose paintings of sporting scenes, particularly of his elegant father on horseback, bear poignant testimony to the artist's own physical condition, was quite forthcoming about it. Coubertin, on the contrary, never once makes reference to his size, and if this were not sufficient evidence that "it was on *his* mind,"[37] we shall later find a Paris newspaper insulting him with it in an effort to satirize his sporting initiatives.

Coubertin's other American contacts were strapping types. At the Physical Training Conference in Boston, Coubertin first heard the name of the Swedish colonel (later general) Victor Balck, an open-minded official of the Royal Central Gymnastic Institute in Stockholm, and Balck was later to be recruited as one of the founding members of the International Olympic Committee. So was William Milligan Sloane of Princeton, undoubtedly the most important acquaintance made by Coubertin during his 1889 journey. Sloane was the son of Scots Presbyterians, born in Ohio where his father was master of a small academy. After taking his undergraduate degree at Columbia, Sloane became interested in history while serving as secretary and assistant to George Bancroft. Having received his Ph.D. in philosophy at Leipzig, he was made professor of political science and history at Princeton, where Coubertin met him. Sloane was as deeply interested in France as Coubertin was in America. Later he published a book on the religious dimensions of French political history, and his best-known work was the four-volume biography of Napoleon which appeared in 1896, when he was called to the Seth Low chair of history at Columbia. But the exceptional overlap between his philosophical and social views and Coubertin's is best remarked in *How to Bring Out the Ethical Value of History*, published in 1898.[38] Sloane combined professorial bearing with great wit, a manly constitution, and a worldly outlook. The source of his interest in athletics is not clear, but he supplied Coubertin with a well-connected ally and supporter to serve the cause in America in place of the physical educationists whom the baron found so wanting. The details of Sloane's contributions to the Olympic movement will be brought out shortly.

True Tests and Living Pictures: The Exposition Tradition

If America gave Coubertin first evidence of the mass popularity of spectator sports, the 1889 Paris Universal Exposition alerted him to the attraction and symbolic power of international public spectacles.

From the salons of Louis XIV, to the displays of industrial products in the year VI, to the Napoleonic exhibitions of 1804 and 1806, to the 1849 Exposition of Agricultural and Industrial Products, regional and national exhibitions had a long history in France.[39] But the London Crystal Palace of 1851 was the first truly international exhibition, whose mass popularity (over six million visitors), coherent embodiment of Victorian culture, and determined ideology of industrial and moral progress made it the model which all subsequent universal expositions, including the French, strove to emulate.

Prince Albert's role in the Crystal Palace merits sociological comparison with Coubertin's in the Olympic Games. Though hardly as *déraciné* as Coubertin, Albert was also a marginal figure, a German prince in an English court, clearly second-fiddle to his wife, and openly mocked and even reviled by the London bourgeoisie for being himself too bourgeois. The "uncomfortably handsome" prince was portrayed by *Punch*, prior to the exhibition, as a beggar soliciting donations on the street to bankroll the project. "Station has brought me to the state you see; / And your condition might have been like mine, / The child of Banter and Raillery."[40] Albert seized upon the Crystal Palace as a means for regaining the center of English life, and the ideology he articulated for the exhibition bears all the characteristics signaled by Pareto as typical of elites in decline.[41] It also is similar in several regards to the philosophy of Olympism Coubertin later elaborated for the Olympic Games. The prince himself won a gold medal in 1851 for his designs for workers' housing (just as Coubertin, under a pseudonym, was awarded the Olympic gold medal for poetry at the Stockholm Games). Pareto, who spoke of French landowners who "extorted money from their peasants" and then gave a fraction of it to "People's Universities" without ever sensing any contradiction between their humanitarianism and the source of their wealth, would have seen Albert and Coubertin as perfect examples of the decadence he described. To a degree he was certainly correct. At the same time, by seizing on incipient or marginal cultural forms, such as exhibitions and sports, they, especially Coubertin, became important culture creators who elaborated new genres of cultural performance which were indeed "universalizing" and engaging of the energies of the new as well as the old elites, often in ways that neither innovator intended. In the French case, sports may well have served as "the opium of the classes" in the 1880s and '90s.[42] But they were to develop from that into a multiplex and complicated cultural form in the Western world, a form that is distinguished precisely by its cross-cutting of class, status, and ideological boundaries.

Prince Albert stated in his Mansion House speech of 1850 what was to become the official ideology of the Crystal Palace.

> Nobody . . . who has paid any attention to the peculiar features of our present era, will doubt for a moment that we are living at a period of most wonderful transition, which tends rapidly to accomplish that great end, to which, indeed, all history points—*the realisation of the unity of mankind*. Not a unity which breaks down the limits and levels the peculiar characteristics of the different nations of the earth, but rather a unity, the *result and product* of those very national varieties and antagonistic qualities.
> The distances which separated the different nations and parts of the globe are rapidly vanishing before the achievements of modern invention, and we can traverse them with incredible ease; the languages of all

nations are known, and their acquirement placed within the reach of everybody; thought is communicated with rapidity, and even by the power of lightning. On the other hand, the *great principle of division of labor*, which may be called the moving power of civilization, is being extended to all branches of science, industry, and art.

"The publicity of the present day," the prince continued, makes the discoveries of specialized knowledge "at once the property of the community at large" and leads to improvement of every "discovery and invention," offering "the stimulus of *competition and capital*" for increasing "the powers of production." "The Exhibition of 1851 is to give us a true test and a living picture of the point of development at which the whole of mankind has arrived."[43] The Crystal Palace was indeed an agonal and expressive cultural performance of a magnitude that even the prince did not anticipate. While many read its messages to be the ones the prince and his colleagues intended, what made the Crystal Palace so powerful a symbol and so provocative an event in Victorian cultural history was its calling forth of commentary, celebration, and criticism from every quarter and current of British social opinion. As *Punch* wrote: "All sorts of morals grow out of it, or are tacked on to it. You overhear them in the park; they obtrude themselves upon you in leading articles, they oust the weather in casual street encounters, they beguile the pauses of the quadrille and set the conversation a-going in a railway carriage."[44] For every celebrant of what Caron Atlas calls "the organic solidarity of the exhibition world,"[45] a critic appeared to denounce the exhibition as a new and frightening form of exploitation of industrial workers. Mayhew, for one, wrote: "Let these gentlemen themselves try their soft hands at labour for a day and they will feel how much easier and as the world goes, how much more profitable it is to trade on others labor than to labor for oneself."[46] Owen, too, wished to know, "If our means of increasing wealth are to be augmented by [industrial science], why not also the mode of distributing it facilitated?"[47] Owen and Fergus O'Connor saw the exhibition as a magnificent opportunity for disseminating socialist principles and distributed a series of tracts to that purpose. Paxton, like Albert, thought the exhibition: "brought men together in contact with each other thus rubbing off the rust of prejudice and ill will and cementing them together by feelings of amity and mutual consideration for each other's prosperity.... Fancy a brotherhood of nations!"[48] Engels himself, for a quite different cause, thought that "the exhibition of 1851 will sound the knell of English insular exclusiveness."[49]

But with equal force, others saw the exhibition as the triumphant expression of the superiority of the English over other nations, while the organization of the event in the form of competition guaranteed controversies in the judging which in turn afforded opportunities for nationalistic displays and chauvinist sentiments, especially toward the

French and the Americans. Kingsley was overwhelmed by his first sight of
the Crystal Palace, but later complained of "treachery" in inviting foreigners whose only purpose was to serve as the butts of English self-
glorification. Kingsley, too, worried that all this glorification of human
works distracted men from the worship of their God.[50] For as many as saw
the exhibition as evidence for the new alliance between industry, science,
and the arts, there were others who, like Ruskin, decried the amalgamation of painting and sculpture with furnaces, carriages, and chemicals
under the roof of the "Great Glass House." The mixing of the classes who
came in such numbers to be entertained, amazed, and instructed was
taken by some as further evidence of social progress, by others as an
abomination to decorum, and by others still as no true mixing at all but a
renewed assertion of social boundaries. In sum, the Crystal Palace was
indeed a crystal, reflecting and refracting the core values, social categories,
ideologies, and conditions of Victorian English life. All agreed that nothing quite like it had ever taken place before, and writer after writer struggled to discover some metaphor to express the unique character of this
greatest mid-nineteenth-century spectacle. One metaphor is of special
interest to us. In the *Spectator*, an anonymous journalist called the exhibition "this Olympic game of Industry, this tournament of commerce," and
Horace Greeley, too, referred to it as "the first grand cosmopolitan Olympiad of Industry."[51]

In their dominant ideology, their international character, their elaborate
opening ceremonies presided over by the head of state, their setting in a
public park dominated by a specially constructed architectural marvel,
and their careful attention to elaborate classifications of objects displayed,
the subsequent French expositions followed the English model. But self-
conscious attempts were made to improve upon it as well. Le Play, who
was responsible for the taxonomy of exhibits at the 1855 exposition, was
appointed commissioner of the 1867 fair by Napoleon III, who had visited
the Crystal Palace and took a very great interest in the French expositions.
Conscious of the criticism that in 1851 the products of labor had been
celebrated in London, but not the laboring man, Le Play introduced a
section called Économie Sociale into the 1867 Universal Exposition. Here
competitions were held for the best patronage schemes—insurance and
pension plans, medical care benefits, workers' education, recreation, and
housing. Free lodgings and cheap restaurants were provided for visiting
workers, who numbered in the tens of thousands. Jules Simon also took a
hand in the planning. Despite its great success, Le Play was distressed by
the carnival atmosphere and side-shows of dubious taste which intruded
upon the serious educational purposes of the 1867 fair. Thereafter, he
promoted museums and permanent educational installations in place of
these intermittent expositions.[52]

The 1878 exposition was the first that Coubertin, then fifteen years old, witnessed. Sixteen million attended, and the political significance of the event was lost on no one. Whereas the Crystal Palace had celebrated continuity and relief after the defeat of the Chartist movement, the 1878 exposition was an attempt to demonstrate to Frenchmen and the world alike that France had more than recovered from 1871, that the Republic was firmly established, and that under her France had acceded to scientific, technological, economic, and social parity with any other nation of Europe. So great was the desire to surpass the Napoleonic exhibitions that the public debt occasioned by the 1878 fair was little complained of, and segmentary political interests were briefly put aside in the name of the prestige of greater France. Though, like all the exhibitions, 1878 was a rich display of social cleavages as well as consensuses, it served as a mass, though transient, experience of solidarity in a Republic that had not yet managed to generate its own rituals.

Each exposition had become a rehearsal for the next, and Jules Ferry had begun planning for the 1889 Universal Exposition as early as 1880. He and successive ministers intended it as "a bold statement of confidence," not only to reconfirm the results of 1878, but to mark the centennial of the French Revolution, to consolidate its legacy, and to "affirm the apotheosis of liberalism" for the next decade.[53] But the Universal Exposition took place in the midst of severe challenges to the very values and traditions it aimed to celebrate. France continued in an economic slump through the '80s, and the government and exhibition planners could only hope that its industrial displays and technological wonders would restore economic confidence and boost flagging industries. As a celebration of the stability of the Third Republic, the exhibition was threatened by the Boulanger crisis which seemed to give the lie to this central theme. And several European nations, not caring to be drawn into confirming 1789, refused to send official delegations and exhibits, thus demonstrating France's continued isolation from the dominant configurations of European political power. While these conflicts tempered the "mood of euphoria and supreme confidence"[54] of the exhibition sponsors and ideologues, they nonetheless enriched the dramatic character of the event, ensuring that, as a cultural performance, it emotionally and ideologically incorporated the central social dramas of the day.[55] Over 32 million visited the exposition, whose popularity was so great that its run had to be extended well into November (some 1.5 million were foreigners).

The icon of the exposition was, of course, the Eiffel Tower, that great iron obelisk that transformed the skyline of Paris. It was the marvel of fair-goers and a dominant symbol of "the convergence of engineering and architecture, thereby subverting the traditional rift between life and art, technical exigency and culture."[56] The Crystal Palace and Le Play's iron and glass hall in 1867 had prepared the way. But these were functional buildings, and temporary at that, whereas the tower was a permanent monument whose cosmological and quasi-religious character was, therefore, more highly marked. The protest by those who would retain the "rift between life and art" was furious. Charles Gounod, Charles Garnier (who designed the History of Human Habitations exhibit), Alexandre Dumas, Victorien Sardou, Guy de Maupassant (who nonetheless thought the exhibition had "shown the world, just when it needed to be shown, the strength, the vigor, and the inexhaustible wealth of that surprising country, France"), Charles Leconte de Lisle, and Sully Prudhomme were among those who signed a petition against the tower in which they called it a "profanation," "a disgrace to Paris," "a black factory chimney," and an "odious column of riveted sheet metal."[57] From its summit, the tricolor beams of red, white, and blue passed like divine rays of grace over the 228 acres of the *ville lumière*. In 1878, electricity had been a sideshow curiosity at a single restaurant. In 1889, it was the wonder of the decade, the vehicle for the exhibition's root metaphor of "enlightenment," and the means by which the Champ de Mars was transformed into a nighttime "phantasmagoria."[58] More than any other single event in the late nineteenth century, the 1889 exposition revealed, in David Landes's phrase, "Prometheus Unbound."[59]

Silverman has noted that the entire groundplan of the exhibition was laid out on the model of a gothic cathedral, with the Eiffel Tower (itself modeled on the steeple of Notre Dame and incorporating *arcs de triomphe*) as the entry portal, the central axis lined with allegorical statues as a sweeping nave, culminating in the massive statue of Marianne (who, as a dominant symbol of the Republic, linked it symbolically with Mary and the heavenly polis) and the "impressive horizontal transcept" formed by the central dome and the Palace of Machines. The "cathedral of the nation" whose cupola was "reminiscent of St. Peter's" was decorated with panels narrating French national history, and enclosed national triumphs of manufacturing, science, and art.[60] The effect was not lost on contemporary observers. The Palace of Machines was referred to as the "sanctuary of industry,"[61] and new Alberts and Charles Kingsleys either celebrated these expressions of human genius as "divine instruments" or deplored them as sacrilege.

Like previous exhibitions, the 1889 Paris event was markedly polarized in structure. On the one hand, it was "an exercise in categorization and typology . . . the incarnation of Diderot's attempt to organize reality into a compendium of taxonomies."[62] As a "living encyclopedia," it embodied the rationality of the Enlightenment and the taste for classification and deductive reasoning so typical of French intellectual culture, here updated to include the discoveries of physical and social science. On the other hand, the exhibition afforded an arena for the release and enjoyment of "nonrational," ludic, even licentious emotions and behaviors, in short, for *bonheur*. It was a great festival, whose sober educational, commercial, and political purposes hardly detracted from its qualities as a mass and joyful entertainment. "The carnival atmosphere and a spirit of fantasy made the project known as a *cité féerique* ['fairytale city']."[63] At the same time as it rigidly organized the "sights" and the order in which they were to be seen, the exhibition was experienced by the visitors as a *grand spectacle* in which the eyes were, so to speak, "liberated" from the routine social organization of gaze. One went to see and to be seen, as one liked. Monod, one of the contemporary chroniclers of the exhibition, noted the consequent confusion as to "whether one would characterize the exhibition as a static, solemn *musée* or as a fantastic, bustling *foire* ['fair'],"[64] and a fair in the yet again doubled sense of a popular festival and a commercial market. As in 1851, so in 1889: participants and thoughtful observers alike sensed that the universal exhibitions were unique, that they utterly confounded the familiar classifications—or genres, as I call them elsewhere[65]—of cultural performance. The Olympic Games were to follow the exhibitions in this, as we shall see, and much of the secret of their cultural significance and mass appeal lies in this very thing.

Faced with the organization of socialist and anarchist working class movements, the republican organizers of the exhibition reintroduced and expanded Le Play's Économie Sociale section, and his efforts to accommodate workers and to display to them, through these conferences, exhibits, and arrangements, the esteem which greater France had for the working classes. For lack of something better, the section retained the Le Play themes of patronage, reconciliation, and social peace. Sixteen forms of workers' organization were represented, including syndicates and cooperatives, but paternalist schemes on the part of the state or private industrialists were emphasized.[66] Members of the Société d'Économie sociale and the Unions de la paix sociale found themselves suddenly, if briefly, at center stage.

A real innovation, for the French, was the colonial exhibit, whose aim was to convert public opinion to the government's expansionist, imperialist policy by advertising its successes. Arab, Oceanic, African, and Asian neighborhoods composed the "colonial city," through which the visitors passed on streets named "avenue de Gabon," "passage de Tonkin," "rue d'Haiphong," and so on. Whole buildings, including a Cambodian pagoda, a Tunisian casbah, and an Algerian mosque, were erected and "filled with the sights, sounds, and smells of a non-European world."[67] In previous exhibitions, people-watching, or what we might best call, in this context, "popular ethnography," had been limited to informal observations of foreign visitors by local spectators at the fair. But in 1889, people were added to artifacts in the exhibits themselves. Some 182 Asian and African natives were imported to occupy and to recreate their daily lives within the restored villages of the colonial exhibit. This aspect of the exposition proved exceedingly popular, and so set a precedent for all of the "ethnological zoos" of the twentieth century. Javanese dances and African craftsmen, no less than the exhibits of pre-Columbian and Buddhist art, were also to exert a powerful influence over subsequent French painting, sculpture, and design.

Garnier's History of Human Habitations, from paleolithic caves to Renaissance palaces, also included live actors in each. "The spectator could enter any of the habitats, and, according to the display, be greeted by a Scandinavian fisherman, a Roman glassblower, or a Russian peasant. These inhabitants even served the appropriate native refreshments."[68] The ancestry of modern theme parks, reconstructed pioneer villages, historical shows, Renaissance fairs, circus and Wild West show pageants, in which simulated natives engage in what Richard Schechner calls "the restoration of behavior," may be traced to here.[69]

In Buffalo Bill's Wild West Show, real Indians played themselves, or white stereotypes of themselves. Buffalo Bill's troupe made its first continental appearance at the 1889 Paris Exposition, whereafter it played to great crowds in Orleans, Macon, Lyon, St. Étienne, Valence, Arles, and Marseilles. From France it toured Spain, Italy (where the Pope received them and they camped temporarily in the Coliseum), Austria, Czechoslovakia, Germany, and wintered in Alsace-Lorraine. The next year the show returned to London and the Continent, and in the company of Indians were nineteen Sioux prisoners of war from the Ghost Dance rebellion.

The modern problematic of "authenticity" received one of its most significant early expressions at the 1889 exposition. As early as the fifteenth century, natives brought back from the voyages of discovery had been objects of curiosity and display in the courts of Europe. Thereafter, visiting delegations of native Americans attracted great crowds when their royal and gentry "hosts" allowed them to be seen in the streets. In 1762, four Iroquois sachems were forced onto the stage at a puppet show by the London mob which cried, "Since we have paid our money, the Kings we will have." In 1762, ten thousand rushed to the Vauxhall Gardens when word got round that three Cherokee chiefs were to pass there. That same year, the civic powers forbade that Indians be taken to places of public entertainment, and in 1765 the House of Lords passed a law forbidding the importation "without a proper License" of natives "under his Majesty's protection" for the purpose of public exhibition for fees. This after two Mohawks were displayed for a shilling at the Sun Tavern, Strand. In the 1840s, George Catlin failed to plump his exhibition of Indian paintings with a group of English actors dressed up as savages and performing war dances in the Egyptian Hall. Fortunately, another entrepreneur rented him the services of nine "Ojibbeways" he had in tow, and the public came in large numbers to see the real Indians perform (among other things) a ball game. When the promoter withdrew them to his own service, Catlin was left in the lurch until sixteen "Ioways" were turned up to replace them. The Indians, who breakfasted with Disraeli and camped and rode on the Vauxhall cricket ground, brought the crowds back for a time, until the press and public soured on the matter. (Two shortly died on Catlin's tour of the provinces, and the survivors he took to Paris.) Eskimos, Tahitians, Bushmen, Xosa, Zulus, and Chinese, not to speak of "Aztec Lilliputians" and a host of similar frauds were regularly paraded through London.[70]

The significance of the exposition lay in its opening to a mass public what had been largely the privilege of the rich or of the handful of officials and soldiers who had served in the colonies—the observation of "real" savages engaged in "real" savage life. Moreover, the prestige of the exposition not only assured authenticity, allaying public suspicion of commercial exhibitors and promoters, but it also brought the whole weight of bourgeois society to bear on legitimating this cross-cultural voyeurism in the name of science and the colonial march of Western civilization. Popular ethnography at the expositions was by no means limited to the savage races; it embraced the civilized nations as well, and afforded mass opportunities for generating stereotypes, images, and stories about rival peoples of Euro-America, and new nations such as Mexico, Brazil, and Argentina, each of whom exhibited for the first time in Paris in 1889.[71] In the very decades during which "scientific" ethnology and cultural studies were being organized by intellectual elites, "popular" or "mass" culture was formalizing and elaborating its own means to the same end. As we shall see, though under quite different forms and, lately, in the context of mass media and tourism, the appeal of the Olympic Games is based in no small part upon the continuing tradition of popular ethnography.

The Paris Exposition opened with two solemn ceremonies. It is doubtful that Coubertin witnessed the first, a state pilgrimage to Versailles, where Sadi Carnot, the ministers, and the deputies gave speeches and installed a plaque commemorating the foundation of the Estates General and then reviewed a military parade. The following day, May 6, Sadi Carnot led a procession down the Champs-Elysées, across the pont d'Iéna, through the arches of the Eiffel Tower, and up to the Marianne of the Republic at the door to the central dome. There, a great throng held back by honor guards and cuirassiers watched as Prime Minister Tirard "presented" the exhibition to the president who, in turn, lauded "a great century which has opened a new era in the history of humanity" and the blessings of the Republic. The great statue was dedicated, the Marseillaise was sung, and another military review (of special significance given the Boulanger crisis) took place. After it, Sadi Carnot declared the exhibition open.[72] His later commentary makes it clear that Coubertin witnessed these rites and that they impressed him mightily.[73] Many of their elements were to reappear in the opening ceremonies of the modern Olympic Games, most notably the entry procession (though of athletes and athletic officials, not politicians and soldiers), the flag raising and anthems, and the declaration of opening by the head of state of the host nation.[74]

Thanks to their connections with the moderate republicans in government and the exhibition organizing committee, Coubertin and his colleagues in the comité were able to outflank Grousset and the ligue through the exposition. The ligue appears to have had no role in it, whereas Coubertin's group proposed a "congress on physical exercises" (one of some sixty-nine international congresses on everything from lifesaving and postal rates to socialism) which took place in July, under the presidency of Jules Simon.[75] Five great sessions were held: one concerned with equitation; a second with gymnastics and shooting (an association which well represented Coubertin's position on the politics of physical education); a third on rowing and swimming; a fourth on *le sport pédestre*, including track and walking; and a fifth, during which Coubertin presented the results of his postal survey of the English-speaking world.[76] Informal sports displays were organized as part of the congress, largely under the initiative of Georges de Saint-Clair; French *lycées* contributed the competitors, but these games seem not to have attracted much notice amid the general hurly-burly of the exposition. Indeed, though Coubertin later plumped it up[77] (and in Boston left the impression that he had been secretary general to the whole education section of the exposition), and it did serve to attract some new French, and a smattering of foreign, colleagues to the comité cause, the congress left no great mark on the vast educational displays and spate of publications that issued from the exposition. However, one of the pedagogical monographs published by the directors of the overall section was Henri Marion's *Le mouvement des idées pédagogiques en France* which lauded British school sports in a Coubertinian vein.

The 1889 exposition provided Coubertin with his first experience of athletic games appended to an international festival/spectacle, devoted to the progress of science, art, and industry, in which new symbols and rituals, for all of their "inventedness," excited a sense of history such as no museum or book ever could.[78] Perhaps because he was out of the country for the last four months of the exposition, when the nobility and enthusiasm of its early days had worn thin; perhaps because he was, like any

pragmatic visionary, willing to seize upon any opportunity offered for the
realization of his projects, Coubertin was seduced by the exposition tradition. In 1900, 1904, and 1908, he was to allow the nascent Olympic
Games to be amalgamated to world's fairs, with almost disastrous consequences. But in 1889, he could not have foreseen the incompatibility of
these two great forms of nineteenth-century cultural expression. Then,
too, the Paris Exposition had brought the Olympic Games once again
before his mind. Under the Directoire, *jeux olympiques* had been held on
this same Champ de Mars, apparently as a democratic leveling device
in which competitors were recruited from all social classes. Although
Coubertin's first mention of this occurs in a text from 1894,[79] it is likely
that he became aware of the fact in 1889, when the public debate over the
exposition installations made the history of the Champ de Mars common
newspaper fare. Moreover, ancient Olympia itself was presented to his
view at the exposition. In the Palais des Beaux-arts, Victor Laloux had
taken the recent archeological finds of the Germans and made from them
an elaborate reconstruction of the buildings and monuments of Archaia
Olympia. With Yves-Pierre Boulongne, I do not doubt that Coubertin
lingered over this impressive exhibit.[80]

The Hour Had Struck

Even after the success of the Olympic Games and his own acceptance as
their Rénovateur were assured, Coubertin never felt concerned or self-
confident enough to set down a detailed record of how the idea was
planted and grew in his own mind. He left partisans and scholars to make
do with the following passage from his memoirs, written down some time
between 1906 and 1908, when the fate of the Games remained very much
in doubt.

Nothing in ancient history had given me more food for thought than
Olympia. This dream city, consecrated to a task strictly human and
material in form, but purified and elevated by the idea of patriotism
which there possessed as it were a factory of life-forces, loomed with its
colonnades and porticos unceasingly before my adolescent mind. Long
before I thought of drawing from its ruins a revivifying principle, my
imagination had been occupied in rebuilding it, in making the lines of its
silhouette rise again. Germany had brought to light what remained of
Olympia; why should not France succeed in rebuilding its splendors?
It was not far from there to the less dazzling but more practical and
fruitful project of reviving the Games, particularly since the hour had
struck when international sport seemed destined once again to play its
part in the world.[81]

This passage is unsatisfying and disingenuous in several respects. Certainly, we have every reason to believe that in the course of his classical education Coubertin several times encountered the ancient Olympic Games, and was touched by the magic and peculiar charisma of the phrase. But there is no evidence whatsoever that it gave him particular "food for thought." French and German science were indeed, as will be shortly noted, in competition for the fruits of Olympia during Coubertin's adolescence, but again there is no evidence that Coubertin's patriotism was early stirred by this scholarly combat, or that he had reinterpreted the ancient games themselves as patriotic performances in the 1870s or early '80s. As we have seen, his only mentions of the Olympic Games in his early writings are the two passing comparisons of English school games with the Olympics, remarks clearly in imitation of Taine.[82] Moreover, the notion of "life-forces" does not intrude upon his writings until the early '90s. From transient boyhood fantasies and occasional historical metaphors, it was anything but a short step to the "project of reviving the Games," and it was a longer stride still to actually setting that project in motion. Though Coubertin "forgot" or suppressed his memories of them, in the desire to establish his own priority, summonses to the Olympic project came at him from several directions between 1888 and 1892, when he first publicly declared himself.

The 1889 Laloux exhibit was but one manifestation of the broad European fascination with ancient Olympia, a fascination that extended well back into the Renaissance. Winckelmann was murdered in Trieste in 1768, while on his way to the site.[83] It had been "rediscovered" two years previously by Richard Chandler, an English antiquary sent to Greece by the London Society of Dilettanti.[84] While the exact location had been "lost" to Europeans, the peasants of Archaia Olympia and of neighboring Elis knew perfectly well where the ruins lay buried. In interviews I conducted in Archaia Olympia in 1977, local Greeks were still bitterly scoffing at the notion that Western Europeans "discovered" the site: "They had only to ask." In the early 1820s, Lord Stanhope followed his countryman to Olympia and mapped its topography. However, most Frenchmen, Coubertin included, attributed the true discovery of Olympia to the Morea expedition of 1828–29, and to Albert Blouet, who excavated part of the Temple of Zeus and, amid great adulation, returned fragments of its Heracles metopes to the Louvre.[85] The honor of bringing Olympia systematically to light fell half a century later to Ernst Curtius, professor at the University of Berlin. On January 10, 1852, Curtius delivered a lecture, or better, an exhortation on Olympia.[86] Among those who heard this speech were Friedrich Wilhelm IV and his son, the future kaiser, whose tutor Curtius had been. In 1874, with the kaiser's backing, Curtius concluded an agreement with the Greek government whereby, in return for bearing the cost and leaving all finds to Greece (a novel provision at the time),[87] the Germans were granted exclusive excavation rights to Olympia. Curtius began work in 1875, and by 1881, he had cleared the *altis* ("sanctuary," from a root meaning "sacred grove").[88] Though his final reports were published between 1890 and 1897,[89] the German government brought out yearly reports *(Die Ausgrabungen zu Olympia, Uebersicht der Arbeiten und Funde)* from 1875 to 1881. These were energetically devoured by scholars and journalists alike for, as one American professor put it, they revealed "discoveries of the highest interest and importance."[90]

In 1887, Victor Duruy issued an expanded three-volume edition of his *Histoire des Grecs*, which devoted some dozen pages to the Olympic Games, and included Curtius's plan of the site.[91] As noted above, Duruy was a member, though not an active one, of the Comité pour la propagation des exercices physiques, whom Coubertin described as a "great partisan of the first initiative" toward *lycée* sports.[92] But there are stronger reasons for suspecting that Coubertin studied Duruy's account of the ancient Olympics.

"The Gods are friends of the games," said Pindar. This sentence, which opens Duruy's account of Olympia is repeated word for word in Coubertin's "Olympia."[93] Their respective texts also contain the same rhetorical device, an invitation to the reader to undertake an imaginative journey. Duruy wrote: "Let us picture to ourselves that consecrated space [in front of the Temple of Zeus], crowded with altars, statues, and marble groups"; and Coubertin: "One may also repicture the approaches to the Temple [of Zeus], its steps and colonnades, and the multitude of structures which surrounded it: ex-votos, oratories, offertories, and sacrificial altars." "In the midst of this great concourse of men from all lands—some coming to see, or to be seen and admired; others to sell all kinds of commodities; others to attract public attention by their improvisations or by their ingenious sophisms—the Greeks gained their eminently social character." So wrote Duruy, and Coubertin, too, adjured his readers "to recreate in imagination the long avenues of plane trees along which there once came the athletes and pilgrims, the embassies and the commerce, all the traffic and all the ambition, all the appetites and vainglories of a civilization both more complex and more strictly defined than any which has followed it."[94] Then, too, artifacts, such as the discus of Iphitos bearing the text of the "Truce of God" (Coubertin, "the sacred truce"), and conventions, such as the qualifications for competitors, mentioned by Coubertin are to be found in Duruy's work.

These echoes might be charged to happenstance were it not for the fact that Duruy's ideas about the meaning of the Games formed an important part of Coubertin's "philosophicoreligious doctrine"[95] of Olympism later on. While noting that the competitons were limited to men and to free-born Greeks who had committed no dishonorable action, Duruy claimed that at the Games, "There was equality on condition of virtue and honor."

> Perfect equality prevailed at these games; neither birth nor fortune gave any man advantage. All, whether rich or poor, obscure or noble, might enter.[96]

Coubertin was not so sanguine about the "perfection" of this equality, but he was many times to insist that the Olympic Games were a "republic of muscles," in which, as far as possible, the only inequalities recognized were natural ones, transformed by the courage and spirit of the competitors into inequalities of merit. Duruy insisted upon the religious history and character of the festival, and also that the "games [themselves were] sanctified by religion."[97] Coubertin returned again and again to this theme. Olympia was a "cult center," he argued, and "the ancients would be astonished to find no expression or suggestion [in modern definitions of sport] of the religious idea of purification and sanctification."[98] The fifth century, said Duruy, "nourishing men's minds with strong religious thought, made worthy preparation for that in which the sentiment of patriotic duty was to work miracles."[99] Coubertin, who spoke of Olympia as "consecrated to a task strictly human and material in form, but purified and elevated by the idea of patriotism," redefined Hellenism itself as "above all, the cult of humanity in its present existence and state of balance."

> And make no mistake about it, this was a great novelty in the mental outlook of all peoples and times. Everywhere else, cults base themselves on the aspiration for a better life, on the idea of recompense and happiness beyond the tomb and the fear of punishment for him who has offended the gods. But here it is the present life which is happiness. Beyond the tomb there is only regret at the loss of it; it's a diminished survival.[100]

As for the gods of the Greeks, they are "magnificent men, but men—therefore, imperfect; for the most part wise; men of reason, and also of activity. They assemble, they are sociable, sporting, very individual, not very contemplative, still less bookish."[101] Having reinterpreted Hellenism as a religion of humanity with Olympia as its cult center, Coubertin would in turn insist that the "central idea... the essential principle" of neo-Olympism is that "like the athletics of antiquity, modern athletics is a religion, a cult, an impassioned soaring which is capable of going from play to heroism."[102] But such a view had to be imposed over what he called the "asceticism" of postclassical Western culture.[103] "In this secularized century one religion was to hand for this purpose; the national flag, symbol of modern patriotism, climbing to the mast of victory to

reward the winning athlete—this would carry on the ancient cult beside
the rekindled hearth."[104]

To Coubertin, ancient Olympia "with its memorable name became the
cradle of a view of life strictly Hellenic in form." In the eighth century,
when the Games were traditionally reckoned to have been founded,
"Homeric songs were recited in the popular assemblies of Syracuse."

> Everywhere the same tastes, the same habits of existence, the same
> human religion, the same bilateral cult of the things of the body and the
> things of the mind. At Olympia, the capital of ancient sport, couldn't
> one hear Herodotus reading a book of his history and see Aetion and
> Oenopidus, the one showing his paintings and the other his astronomi-
> cal tables: a powerful symbol of this marvelous tripod which supported
> Hellenic civilization, constituted by sport, art, and good citizenship, of
> this balance that it knew how to attain and to maintain between the
> individual and the city, between solidarity and personal interest.[105]

Duruy had voiced much the same views.

> It would not be too much to say that at these games the Greek genius
> was formed. . . . In the Greek world there was moral unity, but political
> unity remained unknown. At Olympia, at Delphi, men were brothers,
> they were Hellenes, they worshiped the same gods, they loved the same
> arts. . . . Outside the sacred territory, they were enemies again.[106]

While the site of ancient Olympia was a religious center as early as
Bronze Age, and perhaps, Neolithic times, the Games were "founded" in
776 B.C., according to later Greek tradition. It is indeed the case that the
Olympic Games, the Delphic Oracle, and Homeric poetry emerged together as pan-Greek institutions in the eighth century. This striking historical fact has yet to be understood, but the development of overarching
expressions of shared Greekness surely has to do with the simultaneous
emergence of segmentary city-states as the dominant sociopolitical
form.[107] There can be no question of a simple historical relationship between the ancient and modern Olympic Games, for in appropriating the
classical past, Coubertin and his colleagues distorted it to fit the modern
situation. But there is a remarkable structural relationship between the
sociocultural contexts of the ancient and modern Olympics. In the
nineteenth and twentieth centuries, the nation-state arose as the dominant
and segmentary form of social and political organization, and with it came
the modern Olympic Games as one, though the most notable, cultural
expression of "pan-human" (rather than "pan-Greek") unity.

At the ancient Olympic Games according to Duruy, shared activity in
shared forms generated powerful sentiments of commonality. "The sentiment of Panhellenism, so often forgotten, awoke in its strength at these
games"; and, short though it was, the Olympic truce "gave importance to

sentiments of peace and humanity."[108] Occasionally, practical political consequences followed: "More than once states were reconciled or made alliance in the midst of these solemnities, and the herald read aloud their treaty."[109] Coubertin was less sanguine about the Games than Duruy. The baron noted the "ups and downs and disturbances," the violations of the sacred truce, the disputes between the organizers, and the sometime corruption of the athletes in ancient Olympic history, none of the published descriptions of which "is completely correct or completely erroneous." He warned against "imagining antiquity in an oversimple way": "There were splendid festivals, brilliant successes, unforgettable spectacles, and at other times vulgarities, disorders, ill-arranged ceremonies, and disunited processions." But he also admired "the magnificent continuity in the celebration of the Games. The gravest events did not succeed in interrupting it."[110] This continuity, which was indeed extraordinary, he attributed to the noble qualities of the Games. What he failed to consider, equally with regard to the modern as to the ancient Games, was the role of conflict itself, of expressions of social dramas, oppositions, and combats, in accounting for the popularity, solemnity, and continuity of the ancient Games.

Like Curtius, Duruy, and most late-nineteenth-century commentators on the Greek heritage, Coubertin contrasted the "Dorian" and "true Greek" contributions. Sparta, to Coubertin, was "a sinister redoubt of Dorian barbarism" and a fundamentally "anti-Greek" state. "The Dorians cultivated gymnastics for their bodily, military, and disciplinary utility," whereas the Greeks since Homer's time "perceived in sport a mark of nobility...and a way to honor the gods." Whatever the Dorian contribution, "at Olympia, the cult of the games rapidly Hellenized itself."[111] The nineteenth- and early-twentieth-century equation between the Germans and the Dorians (and Sparta, in particular) is well known. These lines were written during the last days of World War I, and in them Coubertin was projecting, probably unconsciously, French attitudes toward Germany onto the superficially "objective" reading of Hellenic civilization. However, the equations between Sparta-Germany-gymnastics and Athens-France-athletic games hark back to and recapitulate yet again the struggles over physical education that were Coubertin's principal preoccupation in the 1880s and '90s.

The Coubertin texts which I have been citing date from after the Olympic revival in 1896, during a period when Coubertin was forced to condense, sharpen, and publish his ideas of the ancient Greek Games and their contribution to the modern festivals. But these ideas all appear in germ in his 1896 "Préface des Jeux Olympiques"[112] and I have no doubt that these notions first occurred to him between 1888 and 1892, when the European fascination with ancient Olympia was in full swing. Though it cannot be proved beyond a doubt that Duruy's book was a principal source for the organization of his ideas about the ancient Games and a medium through which the baron encountered the German results, this seems to me highly likely.[113] In any case, the Duruy text demonstrates the currency in Coubertin's social and intellectual circles in the 1880s of ideas about the Greek Olympics which came to play an important role in Coubertin's "neo-Olympism."

The archeological finds of the late nineteenth century represented the coalescence of classical humanism, modern science, and heroic, individual *prouesse* in another important respect. The archeologists used, or were reputed to use, classical literary sources as guides for excavation. A celebrated case of this took place at Olympia. Pausanias' *Guide to Greece* had had at best a mixed reputation in European scholarly circles, but on May 8, 1877, in the Temple of Hera, Curtius unearthed an extraordinary masterpiece, the *Hermes* of Praxiteles, at the exact spot where Pausanias said it to be.[114]

Heinrich Schliemann, that new Odysseus who claimed to owe his discovery of the Mycenaean tombs to his (mis)reading of Pausanias, and of Troy to his unshakable conviction as to the veracity of Homer, was the shining beacon of this new alliance between texts and tombs, literature and "scientific" adventure. Schliemann so succeeded in bringing the classical past to life in the public imagination that he became one of the most celebrated men in the late nineteenth century. As Leo Deuel puts it, "In two short decades, from 1870–1890, the names of Troy, Mycenae, Orchomenos, Tiryns—one after the other—lit up like torches against a dark winter sky. Bulletins from the ancient citadels captured the imagination in the manner of broadcasts of transatlantic monoplane crossings and ventures into space at a later date. From news of the day, the sensational scoops filtered into the consciousness of the age and became a cultural phenomenon."[115] This celebrity, almost as much as Schliemann's unscientific methods and reckless interpretation of his finds, enraged the professional authorities. But they profited from him as well, for more than any other figure Schliemann made archeology a popular science, and new prestige and financial backing fell to the professionals as a consequence. Especially after Dörpfeld joined him in 1882, and brought the scientific expertise he learned on the banks of the Alpheus to Schliemann's work at Tiryns and the second Trojan campaign, the opinion of the scholars became more tolerant and even respectful. Curtius, who had enraged Schliemann by beating him out for Olympia and for having once suggested that the Mycenaean finds were Byzantine and the "mask of Agamemnon" a representation of Christ, expressed his admiration for his countryman in 1891.

There was a time when learning was confined to cloistered rooms, particularly with regard to the study of ancient history. But it was the great merit of our Schliemann that he contributed a decisive breakthrough. How often we are told today that the lively interest in classical antiquity which inspired the age of Lessing, Winckelmann, Herder, and Goethe has died out. Yet with what excitement did educated people on both sides of the Atlantic follow every step of Schliemann. Did we not witness that, when doubt was cast on a result of his discoveries in *The Times*, a meeting was immediately summoned in London to debate before a large assembly the disputed points as if a burning issue of contemporary politics was at stake? It is irrelevant how many centuries may separate us from a bygone age. What matters is the importance of the past to our intellectual and spiritual existence. In the life of the mind, the most remote may become to us the closest and the most vital.[116]

So it was to be, with the Olympic Games, for Coubertin. The Olympic Idea coalesced in his mind at the very height of the Schliemann furor. Schliemann fought his final battle with his nemesis, Böttischer, at the archeological congress of the Paris Exhibition. Coubertin was away in America, but the affair was widely covered in the papers, like every other move Schliemann made. Though the references are all indirect, Coubertin's writings show that he too followed Schliemann's progress through the ancient world.

There were certain similarities between the two men. Both were wealthy amateurs (though Schliemann's money was earned in business, not inherited), and both were men of action, not scholars or men of letters given to careful reflection. Both faced opposition from academic authorities, and would exaggerate it when it suited their purposes. Both were shrewd politically and had a gift for publicity, and both were possessed by a classical dream. But Coubertin was not fanatical, as Schliemann was: he could not have been and have succeeded, for bringing to life a system of cultural performances is a very different thing indeed from unearthing material objects. Charm, tact, patience, vanity tempered by common sense: these were qualities of his personality without which Coubertin could not have succeeded. Schliemann lacked every one of them. Yet both men attracted the patronage of royalty and international notables. In 1871, Schliemann met Gladstone in England, and Gladstone was actively patronizing and promoting Schliemann's work in the very year when Coubertin came round to see him. On Schliemann, Gladstone wrote, "His enthusiasm called back into being the ancient spirit of chivalry."[117] Coubertin had come hunting the same sort of endorsement. Schliemann's high-handed demands and his arrogance alienated many

Greek scholars and bureaucrats, as well as Hellenes tired of having Homer read to them by Europeans. But the royalty and Europeanized elite applauded him. King George and Prince Constantine attended his coffin, into which copies of the *Iliad* and the *Odyssey* were placed, awaiting interment in a "stately mausoleum in Athens, inscribed 'TO THE HERO SCHLIEMANN,' dominated by a portrait bust, and encircled by a frieze showing Schliemann and workmen digging at Troy."[118] Four years later, in the atmosphere Schliemann had done much to create, the king and the prince began working with Coubertin to overcome governmental opposition to the revival of the Olympic Games, and during their celebration Schliemann's widow gave a party for the organizers. Forty years later, it was their descendant Prince Paul who would inter Coubertin's heart in the marble stele proclaiming his victory at Archaia Olympia.

Neither the idea of reviving the Games, nor actual attempts at it, were new when Coubertin undertook the task. Precedents are known from the United States, England, France, Sweden, Germany, and Greece. In the early seventeenth century, according to Dennis Brailsford, Robert Dover provided "a Homeric harpist" for his Cotswold Games, to give them "an Olympic character" and to attract the gentry to these essentially plebian festivals.[119] John Apostal Lucas has turned up a letter from one T. B. Hollis to President Josiah Willard of Harvard, written in 1788: "Our documents carry mention of an eventual rebirth of the Olympic Games in America. The friends of this latter [idea] want and pretend to be capable of it: after having acted according to Greek principles, they must practice Greek exercises."[120] The *jeux olympiques* of the Directoire have already been noted. In 1813, Barthold Georg Niebuhr, the great philologist and historian, is said to have

> planned a vast hall [in Rome] which, once properly decorated, could serve for the resumption of the Olympic Games. Later the project was modified to the construction of a hall where beggars could sleep and find a comfortable place.... The beggars wear clothing that recalls somewhat that of the Greeks and, after having regained their strengths, they would be able to resume the Olympic Games, all the more so since they would have so few rags to shed to be nude.[121]

Real attempts by physical educationists and sports lovers to revive Olympic-style contests shortly superseded such decadent and, perhaps, pederastic fantasies. As William Milligan Sloane later put it: "The sports-lovers were for the most part, though not entirely, men of the scholar class, the learned and thoughtful men who perfectly and thoughtfully understood the dangers of a narrow patriotism. It was but natural that their minds should recur to historic examples, and of these by far the most eminent was the Olympic Games, one of the forms in which Greek culture had for centuries expressed its unity."[122] Sloane's notions about patriotism and internationalism date from his associations with Coubertin, but he was certainly correct as to the regular associations to the Olympic Games made by sports enthusiasts in the earlier decades of the nineteenth century. Already in 1793, Guts-Muths had included a long section on the Olympic Games in his *Gymnastik für Jugend,* and by the time the second edition was published in 1804, he was flirting with the idea of a revival. However, the first true prototype of the modern Games emerged in Sweden in the 1830s, under the initiative of Professor Gustav Johann Schartau of the University of Lund.[123] In July 1834, he organized pan-Scandinavian games "in commemoration of the Ancient Olympic Games" at Rämlosa. Competitions were held in wrestling, high jump, pole vault, rope climbing, gymnastic exercises, and long and short-distance running. On August 4, 1836, the second "Scandinavian Olympic Games" were held in Rämlosa, and competitions for the best reading of compositions having to do with the Olympic Games were introduced. However, these Games did not catch on and were never held again.

There is no evidence that Coubertin was aware of these early Swedish 'Olympics,"[124] but in 1889, he became acquainted with another initiative, the "Olympic Games of Much Wenlock," that had been conducted in Shropshire since 1849. Coubertin's circular notice of the upcoming Paris Congress on Physical Training had been inserted in a number of English newspapers, and in response came a pamphlet from Dr. W. P. Brookes, a surgeon and magistrate, and founder and *archon* of the Wenlock "Olympic festival." Brookes offered Coubertin his fondest encouragements for the exposition congress and invited the baron to visit Wenlock at his earliest convenience. Coubertin responded and in October 1890, journeyed to Shropshire to see its forty-year-old "Olympic Games."[125] Brookes seems to have been the archetypal country squire, dedicated, one may imagine, to suppressing vice in his neighborhood, not by sermons, but by the creation of a festival to substitute for the older and "less noble" expressions of village gaiety. Coubertin was utterly bemused and delighted by what he saw. So much so that, having recounted the history of modern sports and gymnastics development in his 1897 article, including the Athens Games, he remarked that "such meetings are of an essentially modern character; the games are modern; modern are the rules, the dress, and the prizes. In Wenlock only something of the past has survived; it is safe to say that the Wenlock people alone have preserved and followed the true Olympian traditions."[126] This most unlikely remark, never again to be repeated, seems to have been occasioned by the inclusion of prizes for literary compositions and artistic works, the Greek banners, slogans, and songs, and, above all, "such displaying of etiquette and stateliness" as "no modern athletes" had ever known.[127] Coubertin's description is the most detailed one that has yet come to light.

> The morning rendezvous was at one of the two inns, the Raven or the Gaskell Arms. There the procession was formed. The herald came first on horse back, wearing a richly embroidered shoulder belt and a red velvet cap with white feathers, and carrying the banner of the association. Behind him were the committee and the officers and the Wenlock band playing a march. Then the school children singing hymns and casting flowers from their baskets and last the yeoman and the tilters riding their horses and bearing on their uniforms the association badge. Through the streets gaily decorated with flags and flower wreaths the procession would make its way toward the "Olympian field," where another kind of ceremonies was entered upon.

The playing ground, Coubertin thought, was beautiful for it setting, its grass tracks for footraces and equestrian sports, its cricket and lawn tennis grounds, its "large and comfortable stands," its "open-air swimming tank and its dancing lawn."

> But what makes it charming and unlike any other athletic field is the row of rare and beautiful trees that surrounds it. These have been solemnly dedicated to distinguished guests or to persons of high rank on some noteworthy occasion. The dedication of a tree was the ordinary prologue of the celebration: short speeches were delivered, a hymn was sung, and champagne was poured on the tree out of a large silver drinking cup that used to go round afterward from lip to lip of the officers of the day. Then the cortege was resumed and marched toward the grand stand in front of which the sports were to take place.

These were a motley lot, including tilting at the ring ("for which all the plucky young farmers of the neighborhood are always ready to enter their names") and tent pegging ("an exercise popular in India"), besides racing, cricket, and lawn tennis. Coubertin was not usually taken by such an amalgam, but the ceremonial and *bonheur*—indeed, what we might call the theatricality—of the Wenlock games quite distracted him. Brookes, he noted, was not without admiration for the Athenians, save for one thing: they lacked *galanterie*, allowing no woman into the stadium.

> This injury to the beauty and charm of the fair sex the old gentleman resented deeply. Not feeling satisfied with giving the ladies the best seats at the Wenlock festival, he had forced upon his countrymen the queer custom of having the champion tilter crowned with laurels by a lady. After the title of champion for the coming year had been solemnly proclaimed by the herald, the winner was ordered to kneel down before the lady who had accepted the duty of crowning him and to kiss her hand.[128]

Only rarely and of late have women crowned champions in the modern Olympic Games, but since the '20s, it has become a regular custom to have the prizes borne forward by young maidens from the host nation. This practice, and the idea of victory ceremonies themselves, were planted in Coubertin's imagination at Much Wenlock.

> The scene was, indeed, strange because of its derivation from three very different forms of civilization. The dress and the speeches were modern; the use of laurels and the quotations from Greek authors inscribed on the flags and banderoles were antique; the latter part of the ceremony was an homage paid to medieval ideas and theories.[129]

For all of its "strangeness," Coubertin found such syncretism tasteful and charming at Much Wenlock. The processional opening the Much Wenlock games likely added to the impressions he had already received from the opening solemnities of the Paris Exposition and contributed with them to the later opening ceremonies of the Olympic Games, and the performance inspired him to a meditation on festival patriotism.

> A man is bound to love and serve his country; it is not considered a duty for him to love and serve the smaller community where he was born or educated. The former feeling is pressed upon him, the latter grows up freely. Patriotism is a moral tie; local patriotism a more material one. The one is hereditary and general; the other is exceptional and depends on circumstances. You can love your country without even knowing it; you don't love a town or a village unless you have spent within its walls or fences the greater or most important part of your life. This is sufficient to explain why local patriotism decreases in proportion as patriotism grows strong. . . . The Anglo-Saxon race alone has succeeded in keeping up the two feelings, and in strengthening the one through the other. Local patriotism is not uncommon in Continental Europe, but there it remains platonic or selfish. It manifests itself by words not acts; *verba, non acta;* and if money is given or bequeathed for the purpose of erecting a public building or founding a museum or a hospital or a library, the motive will seldom prove a purely civic one.

The Much Wenlock sports festival joined local and national patriotism and was pure of motive. "This is the way Dr. W. P. Brookes did love Wenlock and the Wenlock people. He did not care for immortality and was a practical philanthropist."[130]

Coubertin cared very much for immortality, and for great festivals joining national patriotism with the still more "diffuse and enduring solidarity"[131] of humankindness. The few local sports competitions he organized in Paris aimed principally at building an infrastructure toward this larger goal, and he had refused to acknowledge the "local patriotism," of Grousset's *lendits.* Later on, claims made in the name of "local patriotism," that is, solidarity with subnational regional, ethnic, racial or political groups, were to become as strong a "threat" to the modern Olympic Games as nationalism itself, but it was the very isolation and self-contained character of the Wenlock "Olympics" that permitted Coubertin's enthusiasm for them, (as well, perhaps, as his failure to inquire into Shropshire working class attitudes toward them. We may well suspect that they had rather more ambivalent feelings toward "local patriotism" than did the farmers and gentry for whom such sentiments were happy luxuries). Brookes had tried and failed to export the idea. According to Coubertin, "Olympian festivals" under the same regulations had taken place in Birmingham, Shrewsbury, and Wellington, "but no regular movement was started," and they did not catch on.[132]

But through happenstance and intentional promotion, Brookes had brought the Wenlock festival to the attention of London society and eventually the Greek government and royalty. The Greek ode which won the 1860 lyric poetry competition (text by Mr. Douglas, editor of the *North Wales Chronicle*, music by Mr. W. C. Hay of Shrewsbury) was performed as a cantata the following year by the students of the Royal Academy of Music "with great success before a crowded audience" in London. Newspaper reports caught the eye of the Greek ambassador to England, who inquired of Brookes "whether any memento of an occasion so interesting to a descendant of the ancient Greeks could be furnished to him for transmission to his sovereign." On the eve of her husband's dethronement (in part for favoring Bavarian interests over Greek), Queen Amalia received from Wenlock a silver decoration awarded to victors and a silver belt clasp "worn by the female relatives of members of the [Olympian] society." In 1867, King George, who had succeeded as a constitutional monarch to the Greek throne, presented a £10 silver cup to the Wenlock association as a prize for the pentathlon. Finally, "Dr. Brookes . . . endeavored to promote a festival in Athens; many young Englishmen, he thought, would gladly avail themselves of such an opportunity of visiting the classical land." But again he failed: "The proposal was declined by the Greek government. A festival of this kind could hardly be planned as long as the [Coubertin's 1894] Paris Congress had not met to reorganize and revive the Olympian Games on a permanent and broader scale."[133] The real reason why this proposal was likely refused was that the Greeks already had their own "Olympic Games."

Was Coubertin aware of these previous Greek Olympics when he made up his mind to revive the Games? A passage in *Une Campagne de 21 ans* makes it clear that Brookes had made Coubertin at least partially aware in 1890. "At the time of King Otho and Queen Amalia, [Brookes] had sent to Athens a cup destined to be offered to the winners of the footraces decorated with the name 'Olympics' which took place on the occasion of some national anniversary I don't any longer remember."[134] This passage is a frank misrepresentation, for Coubertin was only too aware of the history of the pre-1896 Greek Olympics, when he wrote these lines between 1906 and 1908. They were being used by the Greeks in their claims against Coubertin in order to keep Athens as the permanent home for the revived Olympic Games. Moreover, if Brookes's first contact with the Greeks came in 1860, then the chronology of the pre-1896 Greek games about to be recited gives us reason to believe that Brookes posted his cup to King George and not to King Otho. Coubertin may indeed have been much more fully informed by Brookes in 1890 as to the previous Greek initiatives than the baron cared to remember, and the switch of sovereigns' names may be more defensive obfuscation.

These Greek Olympic Games were initiated by Evanghelos Zappas, a native of Epirus who had made a fortune on the Danube in what is now Romania. Like many Greek parvenus of the time, Zappas was impassioned for the ancient heritage, especially the athletic tradition, and he proposed to the king and the government a series of athletic festivals to be combined with industrial fairs. The latter never came about, but the first "Olympian Games" were held in 1859, at his expense. The results were less than salutary.

> The 1859 Games were held in a square—Place Louis—and in the streets of Athens, as no stadium was available. Confusion and chaos resulted. Although the King and Queen and many dignitaries attended, spectators were trampled on and injured by mounted police trying to keep the streets open for contestants, and athletes were arrested for acting like spectators. Boys and old men entered the competitions at the last minute and actually ran in some of the preliminary heats in order to get through police lines. A blind man presented himself to one of the officials for one of the events, using the opportunity to sing a song to the multitude, for which he was not recompensed. One of the runners dropped dead in a race. Events in the 1859 Olympics were the running broad jump, two unusual types of jumps involving ditches and leather bags, 200 and 400 meter dashes, 1500 meter run, discus throw, javelin, and rope-climbing.[135]

Zappas, however, was not discouraged, and upon his death he bequeathed his entire estate to the continuation of the games. A gymnasium and meeting hall, the Zappeion, was constructed from these funds, and "Olympic Games" were held again in 1870, 1875, and 1889 (there is confusion as to the year of the last festival).[136]

These events are recounted in an article published in *Cosmopolis*, an international review, in 1896. This article lauds Coubertin's role in the upcoming Athens Games, and Coubertin's own "Préface des Jeux Olympiques" appears in the same issue, which is further indication of the extent to which he hid his knowledge of the Zappas efforts earlier in the century.[137]

For the 1875 affair, we have the eyewitness account of J. P. Mahaffy, an Englishman who found matters little improved over 1859, despite the removal of the Games to the partially excavated Panathenaic stadium.[138] "The burden of great names and of a noble past seems to sit lightly on the modern Greeks," Mahaffy complained. The stadium was a "huge oblong stewpot," little suited for running. Its steep slopes made for good viewing, but when rows broke out ("as was inevitable when ten or eleven thousand people of all classes are gathered together") the combatants tumbled down the hill creating "an avalanche of human beings." The track was "pompously" lined with soldiers who paid no attention to containing the crowd, persons or dogs, who wandered about as they pleased. The 200-meter runners ("dressed in grey checked shirts, fashionable fitting grey trousers, and tight well-blacked spring-sided boots" which insured against good performances) had to thread their way around "a fat old lady with two cur-dogs walking up the course before them, and with whose right of doing so no one dreamed of interfering." The only event which seems to have come off without incident was the pole climbing; a pointing dog managed to enjoy an uninterrupted nap at the base of the pole. The discus was an ordinary wooden platter "like a bread plate," and the javelin consisted of an "ordinary broomstick" which only one competitor managed to send through the center of the target. The prizes were a crown of olive for first, an olive branch for second, and a bouquet of oleander for third. These prizes were ceremonially displayed "on a small table which was especially covered with a coffee-stained table-cloth." (Money prizes of 150 drachmas and 50 drachmas for first and second, respectively, were "distributed afterwards.")[139] But for all his satirical mockery, Mahaffy noted that "all Athens is perfectly satisfied," no one thought it out of place to employ all the old nomenclature of Greek games (the judges were *Hellenodicai*, the athletes *Olympionikoe*), and at the stadium "everybody looked very much pleased." The papers complained about the absence of the king and the judges' decisions, but were for the most part "in high delight and admiration" of the festival, which they pronounced "suggestive of ancient days" and "quite glorious enough for the greatest of national athletic feasts." Unfortunately, I have failed to turn up eyewitness accounts of the 1889 (?) festival, but improvements were likely made and the outpouring of civic joyfulness unabated. However, apparently for want of money and organization, these early Greek "Olympics" were thereafter discontinued. Coubertin would secure both to Athens in 1895–1896, but the Greek people were already well prepared to receive his initiative, as we shall see. And word of their efforts in the '70s and '80s had reached Coubertin at the very moment in which "the Olympic Idea" was forming in his head.

There were soundings closer to home, in Paris. The most important of these has already been mentioned, Grousset's call for a national Olympic Games. According to Gaston Meyer, Ferdinand de Lesseps, whose every word was closely followed by the Parisian public in the mid-1880s, called for the revival of the Olympic Games in 1885.[140] Demetrios Bikelas (Vikelas), a Greek intellectual living in Paris, was well known in French philhellenic circles for his passionate appreciation of French contributions to Greek independence.[141] Bikelas had been associated with the Zappas Olympic Games,[142] and he often proclaimed in print the importance of ancient Olympia in the classical world. In 1894, Coubertin met Bikelas and had the Greek installed as first president of the International Olympic Committee. In 1889–90, Coubertin became closely associated with Fr. Didon and General Février, whom he had drawn into his movement. Both men, as Boulongne notes, had been students at the seminary of Rondeaux near Grenoble, where both had been laureates of the "Olympic Games" which had taken place at that institution for over sixty years.[143] And Georges de Saint-Clair, member of the comité and a man with whom Coubertin was about to become even more closely associated, apparently himself called for the revival of the Olympic Games in 1885.[144] In short, the Olympic Idea was pressing in on Coubertin from many directions. His eponym, le Rénovateur, was to be earned not for dreaming up the idea of the revived Olympic Games, but for being the one to make the dream reality.

CHAPTER SIX

The Mighty Working
of a Symbol:
From Idea to Organization

❧❧✦✦✦

The U.S.F.S.A.

Coubertin's drive and personality, the resources of money, prestige, and social contacts he commanded, and his total investment[1] in his identity as a sports entrepreneur and reformer were essential to his success. In 1889, Coubertin repulsed an effort by certain citizens of Le Havre to get him to stand for Parliament. Despite the flattering character of the invitation, Coubertin turned it down in favor of his sports campaign, after consulting with Ribot. (Additional efforts were made in 1893 and 1898; these too he rejected.) As Eugen Weber has put it, "Coubertin meant what he said and that mattered."[2] But without his talents for organization and inspiration, the modern Olympic Games would not have been revived, or else would have been revived by someone else in a quite different form. These talents were honed on a double front between 1889 and 1894. On the one side, Coubertin shifted his efforts from general physical education to sports per se, placing himself at the center of attempts to organize the many, but diffuse French stirrings toward sport during the period. On the other side, he multiplied his international contacts and began to draw them together as the seed of the future International Olympic Committee. Coubertin saw these efforts as two sides of the same project. "Popularizing" sport in France depended, he wrote, on "internationalizing" it. "It would be necessary to organize contacts between our young French athleticism and the nations which had preceded us in the way of muscular culture."[3] But for these contacts to be possible in the first place, sports had to be popularized and sports groupings organized in France itself.

Developments in contemporary French gymnastics, shooting, military drill, alpinism, and walking have been described earlier. For the most part inspired by the bourgeoisie, these activities reached into the urban laboring classes on account of their patriotic and socially appeasing character, and the opportunities they offered for association and socializing in the transient and anomic world of industrializing France. In rural areas, traditional pastimes, animal sports such as cockfighting in the north and bullfighting in the south, and team games such as *hoquet* in Brittany and brutal forms of *soule* or *choule barette* (recalling the old English village "football" matches of Shrove Tuesday) remained popular in enclaves of peasant society as yet unacculturated by "greater" France.[4] Sport hunting, angling, and equestrianism remained de facto upper class pursuits, and many of the promoters of horsemanship, including members of Coubertin's comité, aimed to keep them that way. In the interesting case of the Paris Cirque Molier, equestrianists were aristocrats who performed (anonymously, it seems) before gentry and lower class audiences alike. But never at the same time. Separate performances were given for each class of patrons, apparently to prevent the *haut monde* from having to mix with their social inferiors.[5] As in England and the United States, horse racing, or rather, betting on horses, was a mass amusement patronized by the aristocracy, run by the middle classes, and bankrolled by the wagers of the lower orders. Professional boxing was becoming widespread, and the name of Carpentier was shortly to dawn over France. Bicycling was already assuming its status as the most popular and most notably French sport.[6] The first long-distance race, from Paris to Rouen, was held in 1869, and the first specialized sports journals, all devoted to cycling, arose at the same time in Paris. Amateur competitions, most dominated by Englishmen, multiplied in the '70s and '80s. In 1891, four Englishmen came first in the Bordeaux-Paris race, but Frenchmen won the 1,200-kilometer Paris-Brest-Paris ride that same year. The great cycling magazines and papers were begun: the daily, *Vélo*, in 1891 (sales of 80,000 by 1894); the weekly, *Bicyclette*, in 1894 (20,000 copies); and *L'Auto-Vélo* in 1901. The first regular sports column added to a fashionable literary and political review was Léon Blum and Tristan Bernard's "Critique de sport" in the *Revue blanche* in 1894. Significantly, from our perspective, Bernard built the first indoor bicycle stadium in France, in 1894, on the site occupied by Buffalo Bill's Wild West Show in 1889. The track was consequently known as the Vélodrome de Buffalo and was fashionable enough that Toulouse-Lautrec executed a famous painting of it. By 1891, there were 132,000 bicycles of one sort or another in France, though not until the turn of the century did cheaper models begin to transform cycling from a spectator to a participant sport for the working classes. In 1893, the cheapest model cost the equivalent of 1,655 hours' wages for a provincial factory hand; by 1911, 357 hours. By this time upper class interest had turned to the automobile, "one of the more exclusive sports destined in their turn to provide a public show."[7]

It is against this background that the rise of French athletics, which meant schoolboy athletics for the most part, has to be seen. In England, and to a lesser extent in the United States, schoolboys had developed their sports traditions well before adult authorities and patrons took notice of them. In France, on the contrary, early schoolboy initiatives were almost immediately seized upon, rationalized, and promoted by men like Coubertin, his colleagues, and his rivals. The players and their patrons were rarely allied in their motives, as Theodore Zeldin notes: "Many organisers of sport certainly believed that sport was a way of stimulating national prowess, improving health, taming violence, and disciplining youth. These ideals did not preoccupy most of those who actually played games. A history in terms of these ideals would largely overlook the element of totally disinterested enjoyment that motivated most participants."[8] At the same time, it will not do to overemphasize the intrinsic rewards of sport at the expense of those other "interests" it served for French *lycéens* and for adolescent males everywhere. A schoolboy rugby player of those days recalled the girls who watched, "their confused feeling that the young men in their English-style gear were no longer, at least for eighty minutes, under the control of their parents. Girls, even bourgeois girls, have an inclination for those who can reach a freedom to which they themselves cannot aspire."[9] Nor will it do to misconceive the payoff to *lycée* athletes accrued through the interest of adults, eager for morality or decorations. In the face of hostile headmasters and terrible facilities, a situation very different from that of England and the United States, schoolboy sports associations depended on the state and private patrons to second their initiatives. What concessions they managed to win in the '80s and '90s were almost always delivered through the intervention of men like Coubertin and Saint-Clair, aristocratic and middle class in origin, like themselves.

In the 1890s, Coubertin labored on behalf of a *lycée* cohort that would give France her first approximations of Thomas Hughes when they matured in the 1910s and '20s. Although the failure of organized sport to penetrate educational institutions in France, a failure widely commented upon in the last forty years, must be attributed in part to these men, who too often served the cause of sport only with their pens, and not, as Coubertin's (admittedly more monied, leisurely, and optimistic) circle had done, with their time and their social energies, these men never forgot their days as schoolboy athletes. In 1891, Charles Péguy persuaded the headmaster at his Orleans *lycée* to permit ("Association") football, and he led his team to victory over the rival *lycée* at Chartres. Upon moving to Paris, Péguy took up rugby at Lakanal[10] and captained the team in matches orchestrated by Coubertin. In the late '90s, the boys who later formed the famous *équipe des intellectuels* at the École normale—Jean

Giraudoux, Alain Fournier, Claude Casimir-Périer, Charles Tardieu, Alexandre Guinle—were learning their rugby from older schoolfellows.[11] Giraudoux was to celebrate sport, Coubertin, and the Olympic Games in his *Maximes sur le sport*, occasioned by contemplation of the 1924 Paris Olympics. Henri de Montherlant and Jean Prévost were to be his concelebrants.[12] These works, which went further toward admiring sport for its own sake than Coubertin ever did, afforded Coubertin his first and, in the event, his only luminous testimonials by leading men of letters. They also reflected the intense, though brief, fascination of literary and intellectual tastemakers with sport in France in the 1920s. This was a far cry indeed from the 1880s as remembered by Guillaume Apollinaire. "It was the fashion in those days to scoff at sports."[13]

Not, of course, among the handful of *lycéens* who organized the Racing-Club de France and the Stade français. Most of the earlier sports clubs had been short-lived experiments founded or dominated by resident Englishmen, including a Paris Rowing Club in 1853, the Havre Athletic Club founded in 1872, a Club de Coueurs in Paris in 1875, and the Paris Football Club in 1879. Inspired in part by these efforts, André Berthelot, the chemist's son, organized school chums for football and running in 1877. In 1880, Jean Charcot, the neurologist's son, organized games at the École Alsacienne. In 1882, remnants of these early groups, and pupils from Condorcet, Rollin, and the École Monge (the latter group a particular inspiration to Coubertin, as we have seen) founded "le Racing."

> Racing did not belie its name. Its terminology and style were borrowed from the turf. Runners were divided into stables, wore jockey costumes with colored sashes and caps, sometimes carried horsewhips to complete the pretense, idled in the "pesage," ran under assumed horse names in races whose titles were borrowed from Longchamps and Auteuil and whose results were bet on by the assembled sportsmen and their fashionable friends.[14]

In 1884, Lesseps became their *président d'honneur*. In 1883, Stade français, the other great interscholastic club, was founded on the Left Bank. In 1887, the two clubs, who had been competing in cross-country races, joined with the Association athlétic de Monge, les Francs-Coureurs, the Association athlétique Alsacienne, the Sport athlétique du Lycée Lakanal, and the Levrette of Janson de Sailly to form the Union des sociétés françaises de courses à pied. Georges de Saint-Clair served as its president, and represented the union on Coubertin's Comité Jules Simon, as previously noted.

In the name of the Jules Simon Committee, Coubertin had requested of Saint-Clair's union to organize the demonstration games for the 1889 exposition congress. The results left both men mindful of the union's limitations, and desiring that interscholastic meetings become annual affairs in several sports, they joined together to found, in early 1890, the Unions des sociétés françaises de sports athlétiques (U.S.F.S.A.). Others, like the comte de Pourtales, president of the Paris section of the Y.M.C.A., had a hand in it, but Coubertin as president and Saint-Clair as secretary general were fully in control. The union included rugby and Association football (with the former preferred), tennis, rowing, cycling, and flat and cross-country running. It offered member clubs an umbrella organization with solid connections at the top to arrange meetings, to lobby for facilities, and to vex recalcitrant headmasters. It also had its own publication, the weekly *Les Sports athlétiques.* Coubertin also had his own *Revue athlétique*, a publication that first appeared in January 1890, although Coubertin had been making arrangements for it as early as May 1889. The publishing house of Delgrave agreed to print and administer it, if Coubertin edited it gratis. At sixty-four pages a month, Coubertin found this "onerous," but he could hardly refuse, and for two years he kept up the task, writing some fourteen articles himself. By 1894, he had published some forty-one articles in *Les Sports athlétiques* as well. Together these two publications propagandized in favor of Coubertinian notions of sport and offered powerful weapons (in the little world of sport, that is) to those clubs and associations which allied themselves with the union in preference to Paschal Grousset's Ligue nationale. Grousset had not been shrewd enough to establish a publication of his own. Indeed, Saint-Clair and Coubertin managed to outflank the ligue at most every turn. Coubertin kept the Comité Jules Simon and the union formally independent of one another, and therefore managed to keep the potentially disruptive debates on matters of policy and philosophy which took place in the meetings of the former from disturbing the organization of "amical and virile [athletic] rendez-vous of the youth of France without distinction as to opinion" which fell to the latter. This decision presaged the later arrogation of policy to the I.O.C. while assigning the technical conduct of the Olympic matches to the International Federations. Grousset's group failed to differentiate, and with the battle turning from words to actions, the organization of rival athletic competitions, Coubertin's forces were at a distinct advantage.[15]

In June 1890, the U.S.F.S.A. put on a schoolboy regatta at Joinville-le-Pont. Coubertin recruited Gréard as honorary president, and no less than the naval minister as president of these competitions. Delegates from five rowing associations established the rules and oversaw the races. The prizes Coubertin secured from the minister of public instruction, the Société de l'Île Puteaux, and Sadi Carnot, the president of the Republic. Carnot's was a "good-sized" copy of the *Mercury* of Giambologna that cost some three hundred francs. Janson and the École centrale split the prizes between them. This meeting was a "brilliant success," according to Coubertin, far outpointing a rival regatta held by the ligue and only one rowing society, the Cercle nautique of Fleuret, who had gone over to the other side. The *Temps* thought this effort "more French" than Coubertin's, but otherwise the ligue lost the skirmish.[16]

The ligue made another capital error. It had a sizable budget of some 14,000 francs, but spent only some 2,850 a year on schoolboy competitions (the rest going for "administration and fake expenses," according to Coubertin).[17] The union was on paper poorer (though it had Coubertin's private fortune at its disposal), but it committed a larger proportion of its finances to organizing interscholastic matches. Its treasurer was Louis-Philippe Reichel, the highly visible president of the Amateur Bicycle Association, and so seemed to *lycéens* like Paul Champ to have schoolboy interests at heart more than the ligue. Then, too, ligue forces made a mistake by antagonizing M. Heywood, professor at Buffon and "the soul" of *lycée* football, by having his boys thrown off one of the playing fields of the Bois, apparently for no other reason than their mentor's alliance with Coubertin.[18]

The baron now sensed his advantage and, recognizing that no compromise was possible with Grousset on the nationalism issue, he refused to take part in a conference organized at the Sorbonne by Octave Gréard, whose purpose was to end the feud by merging the ligue and the union. Gréard sent Jules Simon to plead with him: "Peace, great God! When you're eighty years old, you'll be greedy for it like me." But Coubertin held fast, and refused to attend the conference. Despite a peeved letter from Gréard after its close, Coubertin reiterated the fundamental differences between the two organizations in *Les sports athlétiques* on March 21, 1891. This further angered Jules Simon, who wrote a letter of resignation from the comité which bore his name.[19] Coubertin flatly refused to accept it, and Simon did not pursue the matter. As Coubertin put it, "A frightening strait had been passed through." These bold moves by the baron, in which he risked everything, were revealing of his new self-confidence and courage. He was no longer a humble petitioner at the feet of the great; when he needed to, he could resist the very notables whose favor he was so good at currying and manipulating. This new temerity was to show itself plain in Athens.

The ligue was all but defeated and with it any chance of Grousset's organizing rival Olympic Games. But Coubertin had other battles within the U.S.F.S.A. on his hands. The rivalry between the Racing-Club and Stade français had grown fierce in 1890–91, and it threatened to dis-member of the union. Coubertin favored Stade, whose "sporting spirit" he thought superior to the other senior club. But he could not afford to lose Racing and sought instead to put Stade on an equal footing. He arranged

with the boys to have General Février installed as their honorary president
to match the prestige Racing accrued from Lesseps. To balance off Racing's traditional rights in the Bois, he secured partial, though not exclusive, rights for Stade to the playing fields of the Champ de Mars. which
had been made over for that purpose after the exposition, another example
of the "cultural succession" of sports over the physical territories of
exhibitions, a succession repeated many times over in the next half-
century after nearly every great exhibition in France, England, and the
United States. He also was careful to ensure that Stade was at least
equally represented in the competitions organized by the U.S.F.S.A.

The question of representation of the different sports in these affairs
supplied endless sources of contention within the union. Despite the fact
that "their psycho-physiological foundation is identical," the different
sports were seen by their partisans as inimical and opposed.

> The sportsmen of the nineteenth century were profoundly convinced
> that the technique of one sport was contrary to that of the next; they
> practically stood in the way of one another. The fencer would be de-
> based if he boxed. The rower had to be suspicious of the horizontal bar.
> As for the horseman of those days, the idea of footracing or playing
> football nauseated him. Only tennis, then in its heyday, and swimming
> didn't excite mistrust. [But] the former of these exercises was still
> nothing but an elegant pastime, and the latter a utilitarian practice
> recommended by general hygiene and safety in case of accident or the
> need for lifesaving.[20]

Coubertin might well have added the growing opposition between the
proponents of rugby and Association football within the union.[21] France
had yet to gain the ideal of the all-around athlete, which Coubertin
thought typical of England and held for himself. Moreover, grafted upon
the technical prejudices of the different sports were their differential
fashionableness and class and status connotations. Then, too, the officials of
each sport were competing for the as-yet-scarce financial and prestige
resources of the U.S.F.S.A., for themselves as well as for the clubs they
represented. Coubertin fought these forces of dissolution in his articles
and speeches, and in the gingerly way he ran U.S.F.S.A. meetings, all the
while charming and flattering the mutually hostile delegates. But, above
all, he sought with some success to "democratize" the actual sports competitions the union organized. This, plus the fact that the union was
becoming the only game in town, kept it together. Again these experiences
contributed to his later decisions to keep men committed to one sport
alone away from the centers of Olympic power and to select I.O.C.
members in part for their allegiance to "all sports for all."

Coubertin had another strategy for hostile *lycée* headmasters. On March
25, 1891, during one of their "annual visits to the Elysée," Coubertin and

Saint-Clair (with Heywood and General Lewal) were warmly received by Carnot. The president promised to appear, as a *simple promeneur*, during one of the union athletic fêtes in the Bois. On April 12, the morning of their athletic championships, the boys from Michelet notified Coubertin that their headmaster had decided not to attend. So Coubertin rushed over to the palace, reminded Carnot of his promise, and then betook himself to the Bois to await the president who arrived unannounced at three and stayed for an hour watching the races.[22] The headmaster was, of course, mortified, and warning was served to his peers.

Coubertin, meanwhile, seized every opportuniy on the international front. James Gordon Bennett, the second generation newspaper magnate and father of American polo, was conscripted with his yacht into a union regatta on June 4, 1891.[23] That same July, Racing welcomed a delegation from the New York Athletic Club, brought to Paris after a London tour. Racing called in Coubertin to arrange the festivities. Coubertin collected fifty francs each from several colleagues, but anteed up most of the thousand-franc budget himself. Coubertin dined with Whitelaw Reid, the U.S. ambassador to France, and after "many arguments" convinced him to preside over the competitions and banquet. Reid brought with him President Benjamin Harrison's daughter and granddaughter who happened to be visiting in Paris. The American athletes were somewhat taken aback by the primitive facilities of Racing. "But when the flags floated in the breeze and an elegant crowd filled up the sunny space, they pronounced themselves enchanted, and we parted from one another, after four days, the best friends in the world."[24]

Other international initiatives followed. In 1892 and 1893, Reichel labored for mutual recognition between his Association vélocipédique d'amateurs and the London National Cyclist's Union. In February 1893, Coubertin accompanied a Racing rugby team to London, and shortly he returned with a rowing team for the Henley Regatta. This crew was composed of members of the Société d'encouragement d'aviron and the Société nautique de la Basse-Seine, both organizations under the U.S.F.S.A. banner. On the second day of the regatta, an "unfortunate incident," as Coubertin described it, took place. The boat of the Thames Rowing Club veered off course and smacked into the French boat, knocking it in turn into one of the buoys marking the course. The French, who had been leading when the mishap occurred, were unable to catch up and lost the race. Coubertin, who had watched the affair from the judges' boat, found the French team confused about the incident when they first disembarked. But an hour later, the young men changed their ·minds and decided to file a protest. By reminding them that it would be bad form to accuse an English team of dirty tricks after they had been so well received on their first visit to Henley; that it could not be proved that the Thames club had struck them on purpose; that their change of mind an hour after the race would not be understood; and that they could take "moral benefit" from swallowing their disappointment, Coubertin managed to talk them out of their protest. The next day, the English newspapers lauded the sportsmanship and manliness of the French, and at the prizegiving ceremony they were roundly applauded and complimented by the regatta president for having given "a lesson not only in good sportsmanship but also in perfect courtesy."[25] But the boys were not placated and returned from Henley "discontented and hostile," on account not only of their defeat but also of "British cant." Neither Coubertin, who they must have felt betrayed them, nor their president, M. Dubonnet, could turn their minds "to proper ideas," and the Basse-Seine club shortly withdrew from the union. Coubertin hoped to cut his losses by returning to Henley the following year, but nothing came of it. However, an "international running championship" put on by Racing in the Croix-Catelan in July went off without a hitch, again with the help of Carnot, who seems to have received the winners in his office at the Élysée.[26]

Such were Coubertin's first experiences with the international competitions he hoped to institutionalize in the revived Olympic Games, a project he had publicly announced for the first time the previous November at the celebration of the five-year "Jubilee" of the U.S.F.S.A. The union was not, of course, five years old, but Coubertin back-dated it to include the Société de courses à pied, its forlorn ancestor. Coubertin enjoyed this little deceit immensely: we gave a birthday party, he said, and "switched the babies."[27] At least one "enemy publicist" noticed this "revised act of baptism," and thought that the celebration of a fifth anniversary was a little "ridiculous" and "pompous" in any case.[28] But Coubertin wanted a great occasion to issue his summons to Olympia, and by now he knew how to create one. After three days of lunches, cross-country races, and the dedication of a new Stade clubhouse, union members, officials, and invited dignitaries met on Friday, November 25, at 8:00 P.M., for a "solemn session in the amphitheater of the Sorbonne." It was, as Coubertin put it, "as sumptuous as our already meager budget permitted." After the Marseillaise, a Russian anthem in honor of the Grand Duke Wladimir, represented at the dinner by Prince Obolensky, and an ode to the union sung by a choir and declaimed by one M. Segond of the Odéon, Coubertin handed out prizes.

The three literary awards in the competition organized for the occasion went to a *lycée* headmaster and a director of an *école normale* for a text on the moral value of sport, and to "Paul Frédy," pseudonym of Pierre's older brother, for "an amusing verse comedy called 'Dante and Virgil at the Sports Union.'" As this is the only recorded instance of a member of Pierre's natal family taking an interest in his work, and he provides no details, perhaps Coubertin's engineering of the award to his brother was an attempt to win, rather than an emblem of, the latter's interest.

Next, Saint-Clair and Richefeu were decorated by the Ministry of Public Instruction, which awards, Coubertin is careful to note, he had solicited. Saint-Clair was not present, and though Coubertin makes excuses for him in *Une Campagne*, a note of defensive edginess sounds between the lines. The relations between the two men had soured. The details are not clear, but Saint-Clair may have felt, quite rightly, that Coubertin had usurped his work, and so he absented himself on the evening when Coubertin would call, as Saint-Clair had earlier called, for the revival of the Games. Coubertin was never a venal man, and only rarely a disloyal one. But he was ambitious, single-minded, and increasingly confident in his own abilities. Through the long course of his life, he had many colleagues, but few confreres; many acquaintances and not a few admirers, but few if any true friends.

Finally came the speeches: Georges Bourdon discussed sports in antiquity,[29] J. J. Jusserand, sports in the Middle Ages,[30] and Coubertin, sports in modern times. Coubertin's talk closed with a ringing summons. "Let us export rowers, runners and fencers; there is the free trade of the future, and on the day when it is introduced within the walls of old Europe the cause of peace will have received a new and mighty stay. This is enough to encourage your servant to dream now about the second part of his program; he hopes that you will help him as you have helped him hitherto, and that with you he will be able to continue and complete, on a basis suited to the conditions of modern life, this grandiose and salutary task, the restoration of the Olympic Games."[31]

But the summons failed to ring. "Naturally, I expected everything but what occurred. Opposition? Protestations, irony? Or even indifference? . . . Not at all. They applauded, approved, and wished me great success, but no one had understood. It was total, absolute incomprehension."[32] That evening, and through the following months, Coubertin was forced to ask his colleagues, "What do you have to say about the restoration of the Olympic Games?"

> The meaning of such an anachronism was not understood; it was thought that I had spoken symbolically. I had to take account of the fact that my audience, not having spiritually walked around the exedra of Herod Atticus and the tomb of Pelops as long as I had, placed the Olympic Games in their mental museum on a par with the Eleusinian mysteries or the Delphic oracle: dead things that could be revived only at the Opéra.[33]

What Coubertin neglects to mention is that many union members had heard the proposal before, from Grousset, Lesseps, Saint-Clair, and others. Since nothing had come of these suggestions, they had no reason to believe that Coubertin was serious. Moreover, he had not prepared the ground, as he later recognized. "Impossible to present the plan right off to opinion for, instead of resisting, it contented itself with smiling at it." He had presented no plan, only the magic words, which opened no doors in the souls of his union colleagues. Preoccupied with local and sectional sporting interests and familiar as they were with Coubertin, whom for all of his money, connections, and achievements they regarded, many with mixed feelings, as a peer, the U.S.F.S.A. was the wrong audience for the Olympic summons. Charisma is a property of a social field, the interaction between leader, audience, and setting. Coubertin was many things to this audience, but he was not charismatic. The Sorbonne pomp was effective for the national cause,[34] but too few emblems of the classical dream had been arrayed for it to have galvanized the Olympic project. Coubertin, his words, and the setting had not been "symbolic" enough. In fourteen months, Coubertin would return to the *aula* of the Sorbonne with a new audience, more groundwork, and a fuller plan: the spark would light and the modern Olympic Games would be born.

The Sorbonne Congress

In the meantime, as he always did when frustrated at home, Coubertin departed for the English-speaking world. In the fall of 1893, he left on his second trip to America. His immediate destination was Chicago—the Columbian Exhibition and its Educational Congress and Parliament of Religions. Msgr. John Keane, whom Coubertin had so admired after their 1889 meeting, played a prominent role in the latter, and may have been responsible for notifying Coubertin of it.[35] The parliament lasted seventeen days and created a very great stir. The historian of the Columbian Exhibition called it "the crowning event" of all the congresses held in association with the exhibition.[36]

Dozens of religious scholars and clerics spoke for their denominations, and for the most part refrained from attacking their rivals.

> On the platform sat men of all colors, of all races, from all quarters of the globe, and of all the faiths that during the ages have dominated the destinies of the human family. There were Christians—Protestant and Catholic, Roman and Greek; Jews and Mohammedans; Parsees, Brahmans, and Buddhists; followers of Confucius, and worshipers of ancestors; descendants of those antagonists who punctuated their conflicting assertions with the bullet and the bayonet, and of those who bore witness to their faith in the presence of the axe, the gibbet, or the stake; here gathered, they found their hands clasped in one unbroken circle as their upward gaze centered on one loving Father.[37]

Though prematurely optimistic and certainly unfair to the non-Christian participants, this conclusion ably reflected contemporary opinion about the parliament. It was an extraordinary event for the times, taken as an omen of international moral progress to match the material progress celebrated elsewhere in the exposition. Certainly, it must have inspired Coubertin further toward internationalism and the Olympic Games that would celebrate it in a far different way.

Coubertin appears to have taken no active role whatever in the parliament, or in the Educational Congress. His name does not appear in the records of either meeting; he was certainly not an official French delegate as Albert Shaw later claimed. But he was very busy elsewhere, promoting the Olympic Idea. In Chicago, Coubertin stayed at the "luxurious Athletic Club," spent a great deal of time touring the exposition which he found "grand and really beautiful," and renewed acquaintances from his 1889 trip.[38] He also visited President William Rainey Harper of the University of Chicago. Coubertin had called on Pullman, the "millionaire-philanthropist," and then on Harper, who "explained to me with a chilling emphasis that the superiority of his University derived from the fact 'that it functioned like a railroad company.'"[39] In 1893, Coubertin informed Harper of his plans for the revival of the Olympic Games. Harper apparently thought it a capital idea and the seeds were planted for the eventual award of the 1904 Olympic Games to the city and to the University of Chicago (though, as matters turned out, these Games were shifted at the last minute to St. Louis, despite loud protests by the Chicago student body and Harper's willingness to "pursue the matter to the end" if Coubertin wished him to).[40] After Chicago, Coubertin journeyed to San Francisco, where he frequented the Olympic Club ("of fated name"). Via Texas and Louisiana, he returned to the East Coast where, according to his account, he received an impressive welcome despite the fact that his *Universités transatlantiques* had failed to satisfy certain professors who "found the style a little airy and the content insufficiently elegiac."[41] At all of these stops, he promoted the Olympic Idea, but only at Princeton, where he spent three weeks with Sloane, was he able to make progress. At the end of November, Sloane convened in New York "the persons he judged most qualified to second us in our enterprise." Those assembled listened with interest to the plans for reviving the Olympic Games, but here Coubertin discovered the "senseless state of war" between the universities and the Amateur Athletic Union for control of amateur sport (a battle, incidentally, that today is still far from concluded) and hostilities between the sporting worlds of the American East and West. In France, no such struggle arose because, except for the occasional football match like that between the Schools of Medicine and Law in 1893, Coubertin and his associates failed to popularize sports in the universities per se. University men found their sporting outlets through the amateur clubs affiliated with the union.⁴² All Coubertin was seeking was "to accustom [American] public opinion to hearing the possible restoration of the Olympic Games spoken about." Sloane "alone was my counsel and confidant in all this business," and Coubertin credited Sloane's "ingenious activity" with achieving this result over the following two years.

Coubertin returned to Paris on the eve of his thirty-first birthday. Refueled by his American trip, he set immediately to work organizing the "Paris International Athletic Congress," scheduled for June. Adolphe de Palissaux had previously suggested a conference on amateurism, and a preliminary program had been approved by the officers of the union on August 1, 1893. Amateurism was a vexing question indeed: some thought the union ought to admit only pure amateur groups; others that both sorts should be represented but separate competitions organized; others that amateurs and professionals ought to compete with one another. Nor was the matter limited to the issue of prize money. Racing had early on adopted the 1866 British definitions of an "amateur," which excluded not only those who played for pay, but also all those who made their living through manual labor. To Coubertin, sport was to produce a moral elite, not a social elite. He was willing to be patient until sport trickled down from the scholarly and leisure classes to the masses, but from the beginning of his venture he stood for nothing else.⁴³ But Coubertin adapted the program further so as to produce a congress that would declare the rebirth of the Olympic Games. The union's prior approval allowed him to declare its sponsorship of the Paris congress, without having to consult further with union members. On January 15, a circular announcement was mailed to dozens of individuals and clubs in Europe, America, and the British colonies. Coubertin, Sloane, and C. Herbert were listed as the organizers. The latter was secretary of the British Amateur Athletic Association whom Coubertin had met the year before. He was, according to the baron, a taciturn man for whom the plan to revive the Games was neither "viable nor useful," but who had "a whole organised propaganda network at his disposal."⁴⁴ The text of the invitation read:

> We have the honor to send you the program of the International Congress which will meet in Paris on June 17 next, under the auspices of the French Union of Athletic Sports Clubs. Its aim is twofold.
>
> Above all, it is necessary to preserve the noble and chivalrous character which distinguished athletics in the past, in order that it may continue effectively to play the same admirable part in the education of the modern world as the Greek masters assigned to it. Human imperfection always tends to transform the Olympic athlete into a circus gladiator. We must choose between two athletic formulae which are not compatible. In order to defend themselves against the spirit of lucre and professionalism that threatens to invade their ranks, amateurs in most countries have drawn up complicated rules full of compromises and

contradictions; moreover, too frequently their letter is respected rather than their spirit.

Reform is imperative, and before it is undertaken it must be discussed. The questions which have been placed on the Congress agenda relate to these compromises and contradictions in the amateur regulations. The proposal mentioned in the last paragraph would set a happy seal upon the international agreement which we are as yet seeking not to ratify, but merely to prepare. The revival of the Olympic Games on bases and in conditions suited to the needs of modern life would bring the representatives of the nations of the world face to face every four years, and it may be thought that their peaceful and chivalrous contests would constitute the best of internationalisms.

In taking the initiative which may have such far-reaching results the Union is not trying to usurp a position of precedence which belongs to no country and to no club in the republic of muscles. It merely thinks that the clarity of its principles and its attitude, together with the high friendships both in France and abroad upon which it prides itself, justify it in giving the signal for a reform movement the need for which is becoming daily more apparent. It does so in the general interest and without any hidden motive or unworthy ambition.[45]

The "it" was, of course, Pierre de Coubertin.

Perhaps to shore up "once more my claim to be sole author of the whole project," the baron claimed in the same 1896 text that "the Program for the Congress was drawn up in such a way as to disguise its main object, 'the revival of the Olympic Games'; it merely put forward questions on sport in general."[46] While true enough for the preliminary program approved by the union in 1893, only one of whose eight articles mentioned the Olympic Games, the official program sent out in January 1894 made Coubertin's intentions quite clear. After seven topics dealing with amateurism, articles VIII, IX, and X boldly stated the Olympic project.

VIII. Possibility of restoring the Olympic Games—

Advantages from the athletic, moral, and international standpoints—Under what conditions may they be restored?

IX. Conditions to be imposed on the competitors—Sports represented—Material organisation, periodicity, etc.

X. Nomination of an International Committee entrusted with preparing the restoration.[47]

Acceptances were painfully slow in arriving. In mid-February, Coubertin went to London to drum up support. Sir John Astley put on a dinner at the London Sports Club, of which he was president. But only "a half-dozen personalities from the sports world," an "inert little fistful," showed up.[48] Astley, however, was enthusiastic, and Coubertin immediately appointed him one of the congress vice-presidents. Astley, a peer and a member of the House of Lords, was but one of the aristocrats and patricians whom Coubertin sought to include in the 1894 congress. Though the baron does not admit as much, members of his own social stratum seemed more likely to be enthused for the Olympic Games than the more sober bourgeois types who had failed to answer the call in 1892. But if Astley was also the author of a series of articles in *Nineteenth Century*, which called for Olympic Games strictly limited to high-born members of the English race, by one "J. Astley Cooper," who, like Maurras, later despised the Athens Olympics as "a hybrid, babel gathering," it is no wonder that after 1894, his name disappears from the Olympic Movement.[49]

The other names were carefully chosen to demonstrate the international character of the congress. From France there was Saint-Clair; his successor as union president, the vicomte Léon de Janzé; and G. Strehly, headmaster of the Lycée Montaigne. In addition there were George Adee, president of the New York University Athletic Club, for the U.S.; M. Ketels, president of the Belgian Federation of Walking and Running Clubs; Victor Balck, professor at the Central Gymnastic Institute, for Sweden; and F. Kemeny, director of the Royal School at Eger, for Hungary. The last two Coubertin had corresponded with, but had not yet met.

Coubertin thought it only natural that Casimir-Périer, then prime minister but also minister of foreign affairs, would serve as the congress president. But Casimir-Périer backed down from his initial agreement with Coubertin to open and close the congress because he feared certain diplomatic "inconveniences in so unusual a presidency." Coubertin then turned to the highly visible baron de Courcel, a senator and former ambassador to Berlin. Courcel was dubious at first, protesting that "no one was less athletic" than he, but Coubertin prevailed upon him, and according to the latter, Courcel grew confident and sympathetic for the work.[50]

Three organizers, one president, and eight vice-presidents were hardly enough for Coubertin's masthead. In addition to himself as "Commissioner General," Herbert, comte de Pourtales, M. de la Frémoire, vicomte de Madec, and Franz Reichel were listed as "officers," the latter for the press. Then there was the impressive list of "honorary members." With Charles Waldstein, an archeologist excavating Argos, as intermediary, King George of Greece and the Duke of Sparta were informed about the congress and accepted. So did the king of Belgium, the crown prince of Sweden, the Prince of Wales, Grand Duke Wladimir of Russia, the duke of Aumale, and several foreign political figures including A. J. Balfour, future British prime minister, whom Jusserand, then serving as French ambassador to the Court of St. James, managed to recruit.

But while this arsenal of luminaries was being assembled, old, familiar conflicts arose to threaten the congress. M. Cuperus, the president of the Union of Belgian Gymnastic Societies, saw red when he received his invitation to the congress. His federation, he wrote Coubertin, "had always believed and still believed that gymnastics and sports are two contrary things and has always fought against the latter as incompatible with its principles."[51] Not content with this, Cuperus mounted a "vigorous propaganda campaign" against the congress, in various European, and especially German, gymnastic circles. In the event, this campaign was not effective, but it greatly troubled Coubertin at the time, the more so since the issue of German participation in the congress had reared up in France. Sansboeuf, the old *revanchiste* and militant nationalist, threatened to withdraw all of the gymnastic clubs under his control if any Germans attended. According to Coubertin: "I found this not only hateful, but humiliating. . . . I don't know how to say how often, during my adolescence, I suffered from this attitude, this false and mean-spirited conception of patriotism imposed on my generation. Despite having grown up in the shadow of Sedan, I never felt the sentiment of defeat . . . [instead] the faith in a future different than the past, but not unworthy of it."[52]

Coubertin, by his own account, solicited German participation, by calling on the German embassy in Paris, where the military attaché, Colonel von Schwartzkoppen (the same man who later triggered the Dreyfus affair), supplied him with the name of Herr von Podbielski in Berlin. But the latter responded "as pettily as possible" to Coubertin's letter, and a public appeal in a Berlin sports journal produced no result. None of the other Germans, to whom Coubertin wrote without being acquainted, responded. Interest in athletic sport was growing in Germany at the time. (On June 18, while the congress was in session, the German emperor attended a regatta at Grünau, announced that he had his own rowing apparatus in the palace, urged the German universities to imitate the English as to rowing, and offered a prize for interuniversity matches.)[53] Certain Germans were thus willing to antagonize the Turners by soliciting sports contacts with France. Among these was baron von Rieffenstein, who on January 27, 1894, had written Coubertin from London, proposing matches between the French and athletes from Berlin. Coubertin invited Rieffenstein to the congress, where he was the only German present. Because he was not an "official" delegate, Sansboeuf did not take umbrage and agreed not to withdraw.[54]

Doubt is cast on the whole matter, however, by an interview Coubertin gave to *Gil Blas*, a Paris newspaper, on June 12, 1895, in which he was reported to have said about the Paris congress, "Only Germany, which—perhaps on purpose—was invited very late, frowned at us and refused to take part in the congress." The Greek royal family, he added, were on bad terms with the Hohenzollerns and "their sympathies were French."[55] These remarks were picked up by the *National-Zeitung* and created a storm, which failed to abate despite Coubertin's denial in that paper that he had ever said such things. Coubertin, as we shall see, was roundly embarrassed by the whole matter, which resulted in limited German participation in the Athens Games. Well into the spring few clubs had accepted the invitation to the congress. "Again and again we had to return to the beginning, invite, insist; the amount of letter writing we had to go through was appalling. Success came at the last moment."[56] Among the two thousand persons who attended the opening banquet on June 16 were 79 official delegates, representing 49 societies from 12 countries (England, France, United States, Sweden, Belgium, Greece, Italy, Spain, Russia, Hungary, Bohemia?, New Zealand?, Argentina?).[57] The declaration of restoration of the Olympic Games was a foregone conclusion. The day before the congress opened, an article by Coubertin entitled "Le Rétablissement des Jeux Olympiques" appeared in the *Revue de Paris*, presenting as faits accomplis all the particulars that the conferees were scheduled to debate, and announcing the first Games for Paris in 1900.

Two weeks earlier Balck had turned up with a mission from the Swedish government offering Stockholm as the site. On the ticket of admission to the opening session, Coubertin had changed the name of the conference to "The Congress for the Restoration of the Olympic Games," and before a vote had even been taken on the matter, a telegram was received from the king of Greece thanking Coubertin and the members for having declared the revival.[58] But the congress was not, for all of this, a sham. Coubertin shrewdly understood that if the Games were to attract an international participation and public they had to be unanimously declared in the name of an international body—literally unanimously, that is, with one soul and heart, enthusiastically, euphorically. Coubertin's genius lay in his recognition that great sentiments move men more than ideas, however "clear and distinct." At the Paris congress, he aimed, he said, "not to convince, but to seduce."[59] Roberto Da Matta has written that symbols are created by acts of dislocation;[60] so too, we may add, a taste for symbols appears in dislocated men. Coubertin's Catholic and aristocratic background and his marginality in the face of it; the trials he had endured as an adolescent; the reveries commanded in him by Arnold's and Lesneven's and Washington's tombs; the hyperactive, even desperate, seriousness with which he gambled on the representational world of sport and Olympia; the ceremonies of the Paris and Chicago expositions: all of these plus some inscrutable force of spirit had endowed him with a tacit understanding of the power of dominant symbols which he could never discursively articulate (in place of the utilitarian, instrumental language of his time) but could manipulate like few others. Doubtless to keep control of the congress, Coubertin did not ask a single franc from the union; all his money as well as his hopes was staked on the ceremonial banquets and fêtes of the Paris congress, on "every splendor which enhances the mighty working of a symbol."[61]

"In contrast to the usual practice, I wanted the principal solemnity to take place the first day to attract and to captivate public attention." From Gréard, now rector of the University of Paris, he once again secured the amphitheater of the Sorbonne:[62] "To show that something more than an ordinary sports conference was intended to be held, I insisted on our meetings taking place in the Halls of the Sorbonne. . . . It seemed to me that under the venerable roof of the Sorbonne the words 'Olympic Games' would resound more impressively and persuasively on the audience."[63] Particularly, we may imagine, on the foreigners, for whom the sumptuous decorations of this great cathedral space—Puvis de Chavannes' mural of the *Bois sacré*, the statues, portraits, inscriptions, and the rest—must have been impressive indeed.

After greetings by Coubertin and a "magisterial opening address" by Courcel, the poet Jean Aicard, whose gospel poem "Jésus" had made him fashionable "like a great blue butterfly flapping its wings on every Parisian dressing table,"[64] declaimed a composition on athleticism. Then, after more hortatory speeches and champagne, came the pièce de résistance, a performance of the "Delphic Hymn to Apollo." In 1893, the French School in Athens had discovered tablets inscribed with the ode and what turned out to be musical notation. Théodore Reinach, who was present this evening to provide a commentary, translated the verses, and the celebrated composer Gabriel Fauré wrote a choral accompaniment to the ancient melody. Earlier in the year, the composition had been performed to great acclaim in Athens, Constantinople, Brussels, and Paris.[65] For Coubertin's occasion, Fauré outdid himself. To the rich background of harps and a great choir, Jeanne Remacle of the Opéra sang the ode. According to Coubertin, the effect of these magic harmonies echoing through the amphitheater was "immense."

> The two thousand persons present listened in a religious silence to the divine melody risen from the dead to salute the Olympic renaissance across the darkness of the ages.[66]
> The sacred harmony plunged the great audience into the ambiance hoped for. A sort of subtle emotion flowed as the ancient eurythmy sounded across the distance of the ages. Hellenism thus infiltrated the vast enclosure. In these first hours, the Congress had come to a head. Henceforth I knew, consciously or not, that no one would vote against the restoration of the Olympic Games.[67]

The London *Times* concurred. "The plaintive beauty of the chords of the Greek 'Hymn' coming at the close of such constant references to the race that cultivated rhythm and music to the point of excellence beyond the achievement of all others served no doubt as the most constraining of all arguments in favor of the idea on which this Congress is engaged."[68]

At a plenary session the next day, the delegates were divided into two commissions. The first took up amateurism. Michel Gondinet of Racing was appointed president, Sloane and Todd of the English National Cyclists' Union were vice-presidents, and Mangeot of the Stade bordelais served as recording secretary. The second commission discussed the Olympic Games. Demetrios Bikelas, the delegate from the Panhellenic Gymnastic Society whom Coubertin hit it off with immediately, was placed in the chair. Baron de Carayon La Tour of the French Equestrian Society was named vice-president and Maurice Borel from the Île Puteaux club, secretary. All of these officials were handpicked by Coubertin, who was taking no chances. As a consequence of this leadership, the afterglow of the opening ceremonies, and the prestige and authority they accrued to Coubertin himself, the deliberations were, in his words, "thorough and calm,"[69] that is, subservient to the views of the baron and his intimates. With Sloane riding herd, the amateur commission had by the end of the week declared against the British restriction on manual laborers; distinguished between prize money and indemnities for expenses, banning the first and leaving open the second; decided against granting amateur status to salaried coaches and gymnastics instructors; and settled for a loose consensus instead of a strict amateur code that could not (and still cannot) be agreed upon and imposed internationally. On the Olympic side, as Coubertin succinctly put it, "They followed me almost without debate. I had successively voted the fundamental principles previously resolved in my mind." These included four-year intervals for the Games; exclusively modern sports; exclusion of competitions for children (Bikelas and Lieutenant Bergh of Sweden had been in favor of these); a permanent and stable International Olympic Committee whose members would represent Olympism in their respective countries and not the other way around; and what Coubertin called the "ambulatory" character of the Games, their passage from site to site.[70]

All through these discussions Coubertin had been stunning the delegates with fête after fête. To celebrate Racing's growth to five hundred members, he and Gondinet arranged a "summertime *soirée* as serene as we could have hoped." The playing field of the Croix-Catelan was illuminated by a thousand torches. The delegates sipped wine and watched footraces and fencing matches, punctuated by trumpet fanfares and military music "lilting through the woods," and ended with a fireworks display. A "lunch" and fencing exhibition was put on at the île des Loups; another, featuring a parade of yachts and rowers, was offered by Janzé at Puteaux. Then there was another banquet and a tennis championship in the

Luxembourg Gardens. To remind them of their own importance, Coubertin had the delegates formally received by Charles Dupuy at the Ministry of Interior, and by Champoudry, the president of the Municipal Council, who conducted them through the Hôtel de Ville.[71] The whole affair had been an enormous success. Coubertin and most of the delegates—if their subservient behavior is any evidence—arrived at the final ceremonies euphoric and a little dizzy.

These were held in the Jardin d'acclimatation's great gallery. Between inspiring speeches by Courcel, Bikelas, Villiers, Fabens, Bréal (who announced and offered a cup for the first Marathon race), Mangeot, and Rabier (who presented *palmes académiques* to Sloane, Palissaux, and Marcadet), the delegates delivered their unanimous vote for the restoration of the Olympic Games. And another great decision was made in the stirring heat of the moment. Through the course of the congress sentiment had grown that six years was too long to wait for the first Games. Apparently on June 18 or 19, Coubertin sounded Bikelas out about Athens for 1896.[72] In the midst of all the exuberance of the final session, the two men held a hurried conversation.[73] Then Coubertin arose to make the formal proposal, and the assembly proclaimed it, too, unanimously. The modern world would have its first international Olympic Games (and Bréal his race from Marathon to Athens) in less than two years. At last Coubertin rose to speak. He began by thanking "this congress which fulfills the hope of the first ten years of my adult life" for "the restoration of a 2000 year old idea which today as in the past still quickens the human heart."

> The Greek heritage is so vast, Gentlemen, that all those who in the modern world have conceived physical exercise under one of its multiple aspects have been able legitimately to refer to Greece, which contained them all. Some have seen it as training for the defense of one's country, others as the search for physical beauty and health through a happy balance of mind and body, and yet others as that healthy drunkenness of the blood which is nowhere so intense and so exquisite as in bodily exercise.
>
> At Olympia, Gentlemen, there was all that, but there was something more which no-one has yet dared to put into words, because since the Middle Ages a sort of discredit has hovered over bodily qualities and they have been isolated from the qualities of the mind. Recently the first have been admitted to serve the second, but they are still treated as slaves and made every day to feel their dependence and inferiority.
>
> This was an immense error whose scientific and social consequences it is almost impossible to calculate. After all, Gentlemen, there are not two parts to a man, body and soul; there are three, body, mind, and character. Character is not formed by the mind, but primarily by the body. The men of antiquity knew this, and we are painfully relearning it.[74]

Coubertin was certainly correct in asserting that precedents for all the ideologies of sport that he mentioned could be found in the texts from which the ancient cult of sport is known. And he could have said more. As the sociologist Alvin Gouldner has pointed out, Greek sport was but one manifestation of the agonal design, the taste for formal competitions, that was the paradigm of fifth-century urban Greek life.[75] Competition is the law and root paradigm of modern, industrialized, class-stratified society as well, and it is hardly surprising, in this added respect, that competitive sport should reemerge and prosper in such a sociocultural context. Although we find no, or scant, precedent in the Greek texts for modern notions of sport purely for its own sake, as good for nothing but its own autotelic rewards; sport as instrument for class struggle; sport as "universal language" and emblem of mankindness (Greeks played with Greeks, and thought the barbarians "barbarian," among other reasons, because they were incapable of noble games); and, of course, sport as itself organized "big business," it is not surprising that modern humanists, pedagogues, and practical men should rediscover this aspect of the Greek heritage that had been almost ignored in the classicism of the Middle Ages and the Renaissance.

Coubertin's remarks were unwittingly perceptive in another, related way. Only a few months before, Durkheim's *Division of Labor in Society* was published in Paris, and in it Coubertin's great contemporary argued that in complex, highly differentiated societies the collective representations that provide solidarity must of needs become more abstract, a view which is now axiomatic in social thought. Anthropologists have subsequently shown that even in societies of Durkheim's "mechanical" type, rituals whose task is to reunite socially or politically contending parties typically array symbols of overarching, generic, "abstract" identities for this purpose.[76] "Hellenism" was perhaps the only body of symbols and conceptions—at once sufficiently vague yet pristine, abstract yet minutely particular (in William Blake's sense), familiar yet exotic and inspiring, consensual yet multivocal—to have afforded the congress the means of putting aside for a time the oppositions and factions that characterized the developing world of modern sport. And Hellenism was to serve in turn as the thinly spread but strong symbolic glue which held nascent international sport together until the ideology of Coubertin's "neo-Olympism" could consolidate sufficiently to take its place.

Coubertin knew also that solidarity can be achieved among a divided "we" by creating a sense of a "they," and he sounded this note in his closing oration: "The adherents of the old school groaned when they saw us holding our meetings in the heart of the Sorbonne; they realized that we were rebels and that we would finish by casting down the edifice of their worm-eaten philosophy. It is true, Gentlemen; we are rebels and that is why the press which has always supported beneficent revolutions has understood and helped us—for which, by the way, I thank it with all my heart."[77]

The notion that character is formed primarily by the body is indeed a rebellion from the main lines of Western cultural tradition. But Coubertin and, still less, his auditors had hardly gone far toward asserting it. As Western intellectual history amply demonstrates, critiques of dualism are still a far cry from any true monistic position. As for the "old school," there is no evidence of anyone's having been "scandalized" that Coubertin's band of athletic humanists and sports officials held their meetings in the venerable Sorbonne. Nor is it clear that the press as an aggregate particularly "understood and helped." The results of Reichel's and Coubertin's efforts with the papers were mixed indeed. As was to be the case throughout his career, Coubertin and his projects received a more benevolent, or at least benignly neutral, treatment in the Anglo-American papers than they did in the French.

The *New York Times* of June 17 noted the opening of the "International Athletic Congress" by Baron de Courcel, "who presided over the Bering Sea arbitration." The *Times* correspondent inflated the number in attendance to three thousand "mostly delegates" and mentioned the presence of Sloane of Princeton. After noting that the delegates "would try to establish international athletic championships," the piece closed with a list of athletic events the conferees would witness.[78] The *New York Tribune,* clearly receiving dispatches from the same individual, added that among the three thousand were "senators, deputies, army officers, priests, university students, many men of science, and not a few women." The international athletic championships were to be "the old Grecian games in a modernized form." The *Tribune* reported that Courcel was frequently interrupted by applause and went on to note the appearances of Aicard, Remacle, and the Hymn to Apollo. While the *Times* reported on the Congress in the sports section, the *Tribune* included it in "international news." From its very first moments of life, Olympism has presented newspaper editors with a problem of conventions in news reporting. On June 20, the *Times* briefly noted the barring of professional athletes "from participation in the proposed Olympian games," and the Congress's general resolution against money prizes for amateurs. On June 24, both papers informed their readers that the congress had finished its work by electing a committee to organize the Olympian games, of whose members only Sloane, Herbert, and Lord Ampthill were mentioned by name. Coubertin's name never came up.

The *Times* of London did the matter up more thoroughly, sending their own correspondent (Mr. Dalzell), and devoting some 240 lines of print to it over a week's time. In its first report on June 18, the *Times* informed its readers that "the object was to propose in all seriousness the revival of the Greek Olympic Games." The congress had been talked about "for nearly a year."

> On November 27, 1893, representatives of Harvard, Yale, Princeton, and Columbia assembled under the presidency of Professor Sloane of Princeton and listened to the appeal of M. de Coubertin, the Frenchman who conceived this great project. M. de Coubertin has since written an article in the *Revue de Paris* which has attracted great attention.

The *Times* reporter clearly favored the restoration, but was cautious about the prospects for it. "Whether yesterday's great meeting will really be found to have been what its promoters have wished it is too early to say." But the imposing list of delegates "from almost every country" and the ceremonies ("simple and brief but in a high degree worthy of the object of the meeting") "certainly afforded grounds for hope." Noting the absence of an official German representative, the correspondent chided Germany for missing a chance for "a friendly demonstration toward France." On June 19, 20, and 23, the *Times* reported in detail the amateurism debates and resolutions and quoted in full the telegram from King George of Greece. In a final article on June 25, the paper provided a list of I.O.C. members and announced the scheduling of Olympics for Athens in 1896, and Paris in 1900. The handing out of decorations at the closing banquet was noted, but not Coubertin's speech.

The *Spectator* (June 23, 1894) was indifferent. It thought the Olympics would be a waste of money and as likely to produce spite as amity among athletes and nations, but generally concluded that the restoration of the Games was a "harmless whim." Paul Shorey, writing eleven months later in the *Forum*,[79] figured that "professionals, idle young amateurs of wealth, a few educators, and the least studious among our college youths" might take "genuine and unfeigned" interest, and the rest of the world would be "amused," but "the real leaders of life and thought" knew better than to imagine that the glories of the Greek gymnasium could be revived.

The coverage in *Le Figaro* was fairly typical of French reporting of the congress. On June 18, the paper noted that "a taste for sport grows day by day; 'polo,' 'tennis matches,' and 'yacht' races are all anyone talks about." *Figaro* had pretensions to fashionability, and it preferred to cover the sporting "high life" of the *haut monde*. In its front page society column of June 16, it noted with pleasure the party given the night before by the vicomte de Rochefoucauld for seventy Spanish, English, Russian, American and French polo players in Paris for the recently concluded international matches. (Coubertin is listed as one of the guests.) On June 17, the opening of the congress was barely noted. Under the heading "Les Jeux Olympiques," a cursory list of the dignitaries and the performances was given, but the writer cared mostly to share his amusement at the presence of one Choppy Warburton, a professional cycling trainer, in the audience. He was there, the reporter satirically pointed out, in the misguided hope of picking up some coaching tips.

On June 18, the Grand Prix and a tennis match between titled ladies at the Île Puteaux crowded mention of the congress down to a two-line remark about the cycling and tennis matches given in its honor. On June 19, *Figaro* waxed warmly over the upcoming Racing-Club soirée, giving full details of "this magical fête," but neglecting once again to provide any substantive coverage of the congress in whose honor it had been arranged. On June 20, in the course of inaugurating a new section, "La Vie sportive,"[80] the columnist Paul Meyer revealed the mocking hostility behind this prior neglect: "To satisfy that insurmountable need that impels him to meddle with and want to regulate everything, man invented congresses.... Say, if you will, that they have never served or will never serve to improve things much; moreover, that their goal is to emit mostly platonic resolutions that, most often, are not realized: but what does this matter to the conferees? They have done the work and that suffices for them. At bottom, [a congress] is a pretext for speeches accompanied by parties and banquets." Hearing the Apollo Hymn, seeing the Racing fête, and becoming "acquainted with the broad and patriotic ideas of the baron de Courcel" on sport: these were the only worthwhile results of the congress. Unfortunately, "its pretensions aren't limited to so little." It had to go and mix up poets and fashionable ambassadors in the silly business of amateurism. Amateurism, Meyer instructed his readers, was simply another matter of "classification," and "classifications are shackles, the opposite of progress." *Figaro*, the writer trumpeted, would cover all sorts of sport without bias.

Figaro had not yet mentioned Coubertin's role in the Congress, and the reason became clear in the issue of June 22, when Meyer pointedly remarked that Georges de Saint-Clair was "the promoter of athletic games in France." Whether Coubertin or his friends intervened, or whether there was a conflict between the editor and his correspondent over the matter, is not clear, but page 1 of the June 25 number included the following piece:

> M. de Coubertin dreamed of reestablishing the olympic games. The gathering of the international Congress which is presently holding its meetings in Paris owes to his efforts. Through his paper, the *Revue athlétique*... M. de Coubertin effected the union of all the sports and athletic societies of France and a large number of those of the new and old worlds. M. de Coubertin has asked the Congress to organize the first games at the Universal Exposition of 1900. [The paper seems unaware that the Congress had closed two days earlier with the Athens resolution.]

M. de Coubertin is not, as one would believe, an athlete. He is a small
man, but lively and on the go; his voice is shrill, but his gesture ready
and fluent. Untrained in gymnastic exercises, he is a literary type who
reserves all his strength for mental matters. It is, perhaps, because he
regrets not having been able to make his limbs supple and to strengthen
his muscles that he dreamed of flexing and strengthening those of his
contemporaries. Seneca, didn't he extol contempt for riches, he who
was ostentatious and rolling in money?

In the very act of acknowledging Coubertin's contributions, the paper
embarrassed him with his size and slandered his physical abilities.
Coubertin had never, so far as is known, taken part in formal athletic
competitions, but he had boxed, fenced, rode, sailed, cycled, rowed, and
engaged in all sorts of exercises, and he was proud of his *prouesses* in these
disciplines. To have his virility so insulted and to be cast as an effete
parvenu in the sports movement on the front page of a popular and fashionable newspaper must have wounded him deeply.[81]

Figaro would have left matters here but for a long letter of protest that
arrived on June 25 or 26. Signed "A Member of the Congress," it gave a
substantive account of the proceedings, corrected the paper's errors of
fact, and vigorously complained that "the moral side of our work appears
to have escaped you." *Figaro* printed it whole on June 27 (but without
defense or apology) because Meyer strongly suspected that Saint-Clair had
penned it, and, as he wrote, "as I have often said, and it pleases me to
repeat, he is the true innovator of athletic sport in France and creator of
the Union to whom goes the honor of having made the educational world
understand that physical education is the necessary complement to intellectual and moral instruction."[82]

Despite these reactions in the press, mixed in the foreign papers, disappointing in the domestic, the congress itself had been a total sucess from
Coubertin's point of view. He had closed his final speech with a flourish:
"If I were to go on, this gay champagne would evaporate with boredom. I
therefore hasten to give the word again, and lift my glass to the Olympic
idea, which has traversed the mists of the ages like an all-powerful ray of
sunlight and returned to illumine the threshold of the 20th century with a
gleam of joyous hope."[83] In a lantern-lit parade, Coubertin and the delegates had marched tipsily out into the Paris night, and doubtless Coubertin's euphoria lasted to the following evening when came the news that
Sadi Carnot had been assassinated at an industrial exhibition at Lyons.
France was plunged into shock, mourning, and acts of vengeance against
whatever Italian countrymen of the assassin were foolish enough not to
board up their businesses and stay indoors.

Coubertin was especially grieved; he had known Carnot personally,
admired him, and was more than grateful for the interest the president

took in his projects. From "Le Roman d'un rallié," we know that Coubertin attended the public funeral, and later, in *The Evolution of France*, the
baron elegized Carnot in the highest terms. His grief was tempered, however, by the funeral rites and by the outpouring of sympathy from
France's traditional enemies. Carnot was a martyr whose death "conferred
upon the Republic the supreme consecration." Carnot's "blood has crim-
soned the summits of the Republic. The men of humble origin who have
made it were all rendered great by the dagger of Caserio, and ancient Gaul
felt, as she gathered round that tomb, that her new destinies and her free
institutions had received baptism before the eyes of nations and of
kings."[84] The *National-Zeitung,* whose hostility to things French Coubertin was personally to feel, went so far as to wonder "what international
means can be put into operation to fight the enemies of Humanity."[85]

Coubertin's conviction that the restored Olympic Games would serve
as one such means and his faith in the efficacy of symbolic performances
were deepened by Carnot's murder and funeral. Far from distracting or
dissuading him from the Olympic mission, these events, coming as they
did on the heels of the Sorbonne congress, seem to have impelled him
forward. There is no direct evidence for it, but it is hard not to suspect
that some deep, perhaps unconscious, psychological association between
Carnot's mission and his own was formed in Coubertin's psyche during
these days. When he met with Callot and Sloane in Bikelas' Paris apartment later in the week, he was doubtless much sobered, but no less
resolute.

The Conquest of Greece

There was sufficient cause for sobriety. The Sorbonne declaration, a
far-flung and largely honorary I.O.C., the king's telegram, and no more
than the hope that congress delegates would proselytize for the Games
upon their return to their respective countries: these were the scant resources they had to work with. Unlike Meyer and *Le Figaro,* Coubertin
understood the symbolic power of congresses, their capacity for supplying
emotional veracity to grand ideas; but organizing congresses was a simpler
matter than organizing an international public festival. The local and
single-sport international competitions that Coubertin had taken a hand
in arranging were hardly cause for confidence in his ability to organize
an Olympic Games. Nothing like it had ever taken place in the modern
world, and Greece—the real Greece, not the philhellenic and neoclassical
dream-Greece—was to Coubertin a great unknown.

He prevailed upon Bikelas to accept the presidency of the I.O.C.,
having decided that the office should be held by a native of the country

holding the Games. He would take the chair for 1896–1900, when the Games would go to Paris; Sloane for 1900–1904, when the third games were planned for the United States.[86] Coubertin had three reasons for this decision, which would prove to be a shrewd one. First of all, the Greek Bikelas would serve as stalking horse to the Greeks, defusing, the baron hoped, whatever nationalist feelings might be aroused by the European origins of the project. Second, "Everything that could consolidate the international character of the cycle about to be initiated appeared to me to be of the first importance," and the revolving presidency was a step in this direction. Third, the baron had no intention of surrendering real control. As he had done with the U.S.F.S.A., he reserved for himself the position of I.O.C. secretary general, "more interesting than most presidencies because the mainsprings of active administration" came with it.[87]

The roster of the I.O.C. itself had been handpicked by Coubertin and so voted by the congress he had enthralled. Besides himself, Callot, Sloane, and Bikelas, Balck had been elected for Sweden, General Boutowsky for Russia, Jiri Guth-Jarkovsky for Bohemia, Franz Kemeny for Hungary, Herbert and Lord Ampthill for England, Professor José Zubiaur for Argentina, Leonard Cuff for New Zealand, Count Maxime de Bousies for Belgium, and Count Lucchesi Palli (shortly replaced by the duke d'Andria Carafa) for Italy. Several of these were paper members only; they hadn't even been present at the Paris congress, and Coubertin neither required nor desired them to play an active role in I.O.C. decision making. "I needed elbow room for the whole period of the debut, because multiple conflicts couldn't help but appear. . . . It was desirable to seize the helm."[88] The original I.O.C., he later wrote, "was already what it would be for thirty years—and still is—composed of three concentric circles; a small nucleus of active and convinced members; a nursery of members of good will who were capable of being educated; and finally, a facade of more or less useful men whose presence satisfied national pretensions while giving some prestige to the group."[89] Moreover, to protect the consolidation of power and leadership in himself and his intimates, the baron established the principle of the I.O.C., as a "self-recruiting body" (in English).[90] The irony of such an organization at the head of a movement claiming to serve democratic aspirations and values was never lost on Coubertin. Embodied and represented in it was Coubertin's own social experience as an aristocrat searching for a role in modern democratic social life; a social elite, which he preferred to think of as an elite of moral prestige, an elite of *prouesse*, "disinterested high priests of the Olympic Idea," as he later would call them, organized to serve collective aspirations that, to him, cross-cut class and status lines. But the concentration of power in the hands of a self-selecting few had pragmatic benefits as well; in this respect, Coubertin was more "English" than "French," a practical man willing to compromise general principles for the sake of success. His previous "battles for physical education" had taught him this. And whatever else one thinks of it, this organization "worked." I am convinced that if I.O.C. members had been more "constitutionally" elected, say by the most important sports bodies in each nation, or if Coubertin had submitted each decision to a postal vote by the members, certainly the 1896 Games and most likely the whole series of modern Olympics as we know them would never have taken place.

Coubertin's experiences with the *Revue athlétique*, which, as we saw, had given him an edge over Grousset and whose worth even *Figaro* had acknowledged, led him to begin publishing immediately a short series of bulletins to serve as "press releases," making up for the inadequacies of congress coverage in the papers. They were also useful as organizational charters during the period of preparation for the first Games, and as insurance that the congressional "we" spoke his voice. The second *Bulletin* contained this passage, which well reflects Coubertin's intentions and fears in the months following the Sorbonne declaration.

> Our thought, in reviving an institution which had disappeared for so many centuries, is this. Athleticism is taking on an importance that grows each year. Its role promises to be as considerable and durable in the modern world as it was in the ancient world; moreover, it reappears with new characteristics: it is international and democratic, as a result, appropriate to the needs and ideas of the present time. But today as in the past, its action will be beneficial or noxious according to the party which organizes it and the direction in which it is oriented. Athleticism can put into play [an unselfconscious metonym whose import altogether escaped the author] the most noble as well as the most vile passions; it can develop disinterestedness and the sentiment of honor as well as the love of gain; it can be chivalrous or corrupt, virile or bestial; finally, it can be used to consolidate peace or to prepare war. But nobility of sentiments, the cult of disinterestedness and honor, the spirit of chivalry, virile energy and peace are the first needs of modern democracies, whether they are republican or monarchical.[91]

Thus, the Games were worth the risk. In his public statements Coubertin was, through his life, an irrefragable and aggressive optimist: good would and did outweigh the evil which flowed from the Games. But as this passage indicates, even in the beginning he was no fool. Those ugly incidents, evil pleasures, and ominous manipulations occasioned by the Games—those which he recognized at least—dismayed but never really surprised him. What he could never see, given the nineteenth-century, utilitarian, progressist cast of his mind, was that the dramatization of evil and conflict at the Olympics would prove an essential component of their global triumph.

On July 3, a second telegram arrived from Athens, this one from an aide de camp of Crown Prince Constantine. "The duke of Sparta has noted with great pleasure that the Olympic Games will be inaugurated in Athens. I am certain that the king and the prince will accord the celebration of these Games their patronage."[92] The little nucleus in Paris doubtless received this as good news, how good they could not have foreseen at the time. Otherwise all they had to go on were Bikelas' reputation and contacts in Athens. "Preceded by a number of personal letters accompanying the first issues of the *Bulletin*,"[93] Bikelas left for Athens in the early autumn. Coubertin, it was understood, would follow shortly.

On October 4, Bikelas wrote that "from Brindisi to here, all my countrymen whom I met spoke to me with joy about the Olympic Games," and Coubertin was noting dispatches to the same effect sent by the correspondent of *Le Temps*.[94] The day after his arrival in Athens, Bikelas called on Prime Minister Charilaos Tricoupis and found him, so he wrote Coubertin, "disposed to do everything possible for the success of the enterprise" despite the fact that he would have "preferred" that the matter had never cropped up.[95] But in subsequent missives, Coubertin sensed that Bikelas had been the victim of "grand illusions" as to Tricoupis' true intentions and that the prime minister was really "poorly disposed" to the Games and "had already decided to do everything to keep them from taking place."[96]

Coubertin's hunches were perfectly correct. In the words of two recent historians, Tricoupis' "purposeful leadership was derived from the indignation of the urban middle class at the corrupt confusion of public administration."[97] Fiscal conservatism, internal industrial development, and shrinking Greece's huge national debt had been the cornerstones of his policy ever since he had formed his first government in 1875, and won his first parliamentary majority in 1881. In May 1892, he had been returned to office on this platform, but with the foreign debt eating up one-third of the nation's income and the disastrous fall in world prices for currants, he had been compelled in 1893 to admit that Greece was bankrupt. In these conditions, the Olympic Games were proposed to him, and it is no wonder that he saw in them only further public expense and the likelihood of incurring additional losses of prestige in foreign capitals already hostile on account of the reduction of interest payments to their investors.

Meanwhile, Bikelas proposed to build an organizing committee around the Zappas Commission, which "contains only my friends" and was presided over by a politician whom Bikelas knew from the Panhellenic Gymnastic Society and, possibly, from the earlier "Zappas Olympics," Étienne Dragoumis. (It was then the fashion among more cosmopolitan Greeks to use the French versions of their given names, in Dragoumis' case Étienne for Stephanos, a practice that provides an index to cultural tastes and status aspirations.) The Zappas Commission had control over the Zappeion gymnasium and the ruins of the Panathenaic stadium, had been charged by Zappas' will with organizing athletic competitions but prevented from doing so when the Romanian government froze the merchant's assets, and, so Bikelas assured Coubertin, "would serve as an intermediary between ourselves and the government."[98] Bikelas arranged for a meeting of the commission, but before it could convene he was called back to Paris by a death in his family.

In Paris, Coubertin had been busy consulting with sports officials on the technical aspects of the athletic competitions to be held, but all the while he had been growing restive and concerned about the state of affairs in Athens. He had already decided to go there himself, when Bikelas arrived in Paris. Coubertin "hardly had time to confer with Bikelas" (whose "valiant nature refused to be discouraged even in the sorrowful circumstances")[99] before taking the fast train to Marseilles and boarding the steamer *Ortegal* for Piraeus. During the voyage, Coubertin was "disquieted and joyous, but more joyous than disquieted, as I always was on the eve of action."[100] There was every reason to be anxious.

The Zappas Commission had met without any representative of the I.O.C. present. Dragoumis, who was Tricoupis' political ally, caused the commission to decline the Games, and he wrote Coubertin to this effect. The letter crossed the baron in the Mediterranean, though Coubertin received a copy shortly after disembarking in Greece. In it, Dragoumis warmly and sincerely thanked Coubertin and the Sorbonne congress for awarding Athens the Games, which "wouldn't fail to produce in Greece a stir of satisfaction and to raise sentiments of gratitude at the same time." But "how could [our government] dream of placing itself at the head of the movement, to send out invitations, to take initiatives dictated by interest in the success of a great international festival at the moment when, finding itself in the throes of a great economic crisis, it believes itself obligated to face the most grave external complications." Moreover, Dragoumis asserted: "It would be false shame not to acknowledge that in a new country where there is still much to do before attaining the full range of conditions essential to the existence of a civilized people, the exact notion of what you call 'athletic sports' does not exist." Yet in "deference to its past," you want Greece to arrange "games organized on a new and extremely complicated basis." Inaugurate the "peaceful modern competitions" in Paris, Dragoumis advised: Paris, "with its immense resources," its proximity to the great centers of civilization where "aided by well-organized societies" and with the added "magnificence" of opening the century, "one can be assured of success."

Monsieur le baron. . . . It will be easy for you to understand how strong
is our regret at having to decline an honor graciously offered to our
country and to lose at the same time an opportunity to associate our
efforts with those of elite men who preside over the work of restoring a
glorious ancient institution. Aware of the feeble means presently at the
disposal of the Greek people and convinced that the task exceeds our
resources, we haven't had the liberty to choose.[101]

The letter did nothing to dissuade Coubertin from his mission. An 1896
Olympics and, though a contingency plan for Hungary existed,[102] an
Athens Olympics were fixed ideas by the time he set foot in Greece. At
the outset of his "conquest of Greece," as he liked to call it later, he was
plainly insensitive, like so many European "philhellenes" before him, to
the needs of the Greek people when these appeared to conflict with their
noble past. Men like Coubertin could not, and in many cases still cannot,
understand how the great monuments of the classical age might seem to
many Greeks to be stones around their necks: stones that Western Europeans were fond of tipping over into the sea. Tricoupis and Dragoumis
thought the Olympic Games a wonderful idea, but, to them, it was European markets and industry that Greece needed, not European games. But
Coubertin persisted in believing that ulterior motives—what these might
have been he never specified—lay behind their arguments.[103] This, even
after Tricoupis, who was to be the tragic figure in this drama, took an
extraordinary and self-effacing step to convince him.

Coubertin's first day in Athens had been filled with "luminous and
unforgettable hours."[104] He had gone around the city leaving his card,
and in the company "of some young enthusiasts who quickly became his
friends," he had made a "pilgrimage" to the ruined stadium where he was
thrilled to see the "famous passage by which the athletes formerly entered."[105] On the next morning, while Coubertin was conferring with
Maurouard, the French chargé, in the baron's hotel, Tricoupis arrived
unattended and unannounced. It was a remarkable gesture which "put
aside all protocol," and a risky one at that. A prime minister so effac-
ing himself before an uninvited foreigner without portfolio could have
offered ammunition for Tricoupis' enemies. But Coubertin—audacity,
chauvinism, his own sense of sacred mission?—was unimpressed.
Tricoupis was "cordial," restated his arguments, and closed by inviting
the baron to "take a look, examine, study our resources at your leisure:
you will convince yourself that it's impossible!"[106]

In the days following, Coubertin did "see for himself" and was convinced to the contrary. Instead of a backward nation struggling to discover
its place in the "civilized" world, Coubertin was "astonished" to find
"Hellas" "first so alive and next so traditional." "The Greek resurrection
seemed to me such a miracle that it imposed respect," and gave the lie to

Western European writers who had portrayed Athens as "an overgrown little market-town."[107] With Durkheim and so many other French children of 1871, Coubertin believed that a society is "above all the idea which it forms of itself."[108] Material and social progress depended on shared representations of national character and purpose, not the other way around. For the Greeks this meant recovery of the classical heritage in modern form and recognition of its role in drawing Greece into the center of international life. "I believe that Hellenism has a great role to play in the world. Liberated, it rapidly casts off its dross and becomes itself again. Material strength would return to it little by little, and it has lost none of its moral strength."[109] Since, to Coubertin, the Greek revival was attributable to just this reappropriation of the past, holding the Olympic Games could mean only further progress, for to celebrate the Olympic Games, he said, was "to make both a pilgrimage to the past and a gesture of faith in the future."[110] Though sober politicians and weak-kneed conservatives like Tricoupis could not see it, Greece required nothing so much as this.

In his peregrinations around Athens, Coubertin convinced himself that "the people" were united in support of hosting the Games. "The warmest partisans of the Olympiad were found among the merchants and coachmen of Athens. Shopkeepers who knew French [what sort were these?] interrogated me with a growing interest."[111] One day, according to Coubertin, while he was riding with George Melas, son of the mayor of Athens and the baron's new ally, the coachman suddenly climbed down and addressed his companion: "Mr. Georgie, I'm going to explain to you how your friend must deal with Tricoupis."[112]

But it was the young men of the leisure classes and not the "people" with whom Coubertin made his rounds. Besides Melas and Count Alexandre Mercati,[113] the son of the director of the Ionian Bank, Spiridon Antonopoulos, the secretary of Bikelas's Panhellenic Gymnastics Society, helped to assure the baron that Dragoumis had been mistaken as to the sporting character of Athens. There were, after all, two gymnastics and athletic clubs, a fencing association, a rowing club, and several cycling societies in Athens alone.[114] As to facilities, Coubertin pronounced the Zappeion rotunda "marvelous" for the fencing matches, and the cavalry grounds sufficient for the equestrian events, as were Phaleros Bay for the yachting and rowing, and the bay of Zeos for the swimming and diving. There was no velodrome, but the Greeks had been talking about building one anyway. Gymnastics and track and field would take place in the stadium, whose shape presented "an unfortunate anachronism," but whose "venerable soil" more than compensated. At this stage, he had "contented himself with rebuilding it in his imagination, while sitting on a picturesque slope," but had no thought of attempting to return it to its antique splendor. A few wooden benches and a temporary tribune would do.[115] All this allowed him to cook up a "budget," not surprisingly modest, to show the authorities how cheaply it could all be done.

Since the 1880s, Greek politics had been a de facto two-party system. Tricoupis' "Constitutional" party had revolved in office with the opposition party led by Theodoros Delyannis (Deligiannis). The latter's power lay with the educated, cosmopolitan elites, and its policies were expansionist, adventurist, fiscally liberal, and devoted to military strength and *enosis:* recapturing those areas of greater Greece in foreign hands. This was the meaning of "Panhellenism" in contemporary Greek political vocabulary, and what many Greeks heard when men like Coubertin employed the slogan. These commitments alone might have inclined Delyannis' party in favor of the Olympics, but with an election likely in a few months, Tricoupis shaky in his seat, and his opposition to the Games now well known, Delyannis was not slow to let out that he supported them. The papers made much of the issue. A cartoon in *Romos* portrayed Tricoupis and Delyannis in oversized boxing gloves slugging it out over the question of the Olympics.[116] "I had thrown a football between two political teams," said Coubertin.[117] In his memoirs, the baron claimed that he did not try to take advantage of the situation, offering as evidence the fact that he had "beseeched" M. Rhalli, Delyannis' lieutenant, not to put the matter to a vote in Parliament.[118] After all, the Paris congress had reiterated Coubertin's position that the Olympics were outside of and not to be mixed up with politics. But such denials, we may be sure, were disingenuous in the extreme. If Coubertin tried to avoid a legislative vote, it was for tactical reasons only (Tricoupis had, after all, a majority), and in his "visits to politicians and journalists"[119] Coubertin, doubtless subtly but concertedly, manipulated the situation to his advantage and felt perfectly justified in doing so.

There was another "team" on the field, ready to seize the Olympic "football" and run with it, the royal family. In 1875, "with that sense of political realism that distinguished him from his predecessor,"[120] King George had invited Tricoupis to form his first government despite the latter's criticisms of the regime. For the next twenty years, the monarch had profited most and rested least during the years Tricoupis governed. Delyannis' policies and political allies were felt to be far more trustworthy with regard to the security of the monarchy. Now with Greece in such perilous straits, the royal family had all the more reason not to regret the prospect of Delyannis' return to power. On top of this, Crown Prince Constantine was eager to test his muscles in anticipation of ruling, and that meant demonstrating his independence from and willingness to gainsay the prime minister. With his father away in Russia at the funeral of Alexander III, Constantine was serving as regent while the Olympic controversy raged, and it gave him an opportunity. Moreover, as European royalty reigning precariously over an "oriental" people, the royal family were always on the lookout for chances to demonstrate their "Greekness" and their prowess in embodying it. Often enough, this took the form of classical conceits, the identification of the sovereign with his people through symbols of their "shared" classical past. The royal family had patronized the "Zappas Olympics," and both George and Constantine had sent congratulatory telegrams to the Paris congress. In two years Constantine would be eager to show his worth by leading his father's subjects in war; for now, he would settle for leading them in sport. Moreover, a dynasty that had from the beginning depended upon international favor could hardly be hurt by such an international festival as a French baron now came to propose.

Introduced by Mercati, who had been Constantine's boyhood friend, Coubertin held "a series of interviews" with the prince. Coubertin found him "very poised, very wise, and at the same time, I sensed, very enthusiastic; the duke of Sparta, so to speak, sowed confidence all around him."[121] So strong were his feelings about the Games that Constantine consented immediately to serve as president of the organizing committee Coubertin was laboring to establish.

Coubertin had now outflanked Tricoupis on two sides. Whether the prime minister really felt threatened or else simply was satisfied by Coubertin's declaration in their second meeting that he was "ready to proceed without official sanction" is not clear. In any case, he gave the baron a "promise of neutrality" which Coubertin accepted without for a moment believing.[122]

The baron's gifts as an organizer lay in a deft sense of timing that in retrospect could seem uncannily shrewd. The opposing interests he had set in motion were useful in the short term, but could themselves wreck the project if allowed their full head. They had to be tempered with appeals and invitations to corporate solidarity offered in the name of history. At a well-attended meeting of the Parnassus Literary Club, whose very name suggested empyrean disinterestedness, Coubertin was careful "not to allude to the disputes" about the proposed Games "in the political world."[123] Instead, he took the audience on a tour of his own version of the world history of sport. The honor for inventing it, he said, belonged to your "forefathers," since Egypt and India knew little of it. In ancient Greece: "Muscles and ideas coexisted . . . in brotherhood, and it seems that this harmony was so perfect as even to unite youth and old age. Your ancestors, as a general rule, knew neither the extravagances of the adolescent nor the peevishness of old men [so much for Alcibiades and Socrates alike!]: the art of living was at its apogee, and the art of dying followed from it quite naturally; people knew how to live without fear and to die without regrets for the sake of a changeless city and an undisputed religion—something which—alas!—we know no longer." The Roman circus and Christianity dealt death blows to athletics, which are now being reborn in the nineteenth century, said Coubertin.

> If we begin to study the history of our century we are struck by the moral disorder produced by the discoveries of industrial science. Life suffers an upheaval, people feel the ground tremble continually under their feet. They have nothing to hold on to, because everything around them is shifting and changing; and in their confusion, as though seeking some counterpoise to the material powers which rise like Cyclopean ramparts about them, they grope for whatever elements of moral strength lie scattered about the world. I think this is the philosophic origin of the striking physical renaissance in the nineteenth century.

This is the earliest concerted statement on Coubertin's part of what was to become a persistent theme in his own and Olympic ideology, that sport is an antidote to the evils of industrial civilization. Heretofore, he had emphasized the role of sport, particularly English sport, in promoting national strength, which included industry and industrial science. Certainly the argument played well in an Athens afflicted by incipient industrialization.

Next he reviewed the two traditions of contemporary physical education, claiming that gymnastics (Sparta—Prussia after Jena—France after Sedan—the U.S. after the Civil War) is preparation for war, whereas "sport for the individual" (Athens—Arnold and Kingsley—clubs throughout Europe and South America—Athenian clubs that "compare favorably with many well-known clubs in Western Europe") prepares for peace. "Peace," he said, "has become a sort of religion whose altars are tended by an ever-growing number of the faithful."

Unlike the ancient Olympics, "the lofty aim, the whole patriotic and religious apparatus which once surrounded the festivals of youth" has been lost to the modern world. But the moral content that will keep athletics from "sinking into the slough of commercialism" is to be found in democracy and internationalism. Modern athletics are "becoming . . . democratic" because "the social revolution [is] already accomplished among men and perhaps shortly [is] to be accomplished among things also." Internationalism, "understood, of course, in the sense of respect for and not destruction of native countries," arises from "fast transport and easy communications" and from "the great need for peace and brotherhood which is welling up from the depths of the human heart."

> Healthy democracy, wise and peaceful internationalism, will penetrate the new stadium and preserve within it the cult of disinterestedness and

honor which will enable athletics to help in the tasks of moral education and social peace as well as of muscular development. That is why every four years the revived Olympic Games must give the youth of all the world a chance of a happy and brotherly encounter which will gradually efface the peoples' ignorance of things which concern them all, an ignorance which feeds hatreds, accumulates misunderstandings, and hurtles events along a barbarous path toward a merciless conflict.

Though well calculated to inspire the audience to a corporate mission and to gain their adherence to the Games proposal, this speech was also a sincere expression, in miniature, of all the themes which Coubertin was later to elaborate as the ideology of neo-Olympism: that Olympic Games model democratic social arrangements; that athletic competition between nations contributes to peace; that what he would soon call "true internationalism," that is, respect for and celebration of national, cultural differences, rather than "cosmopolitanism," the extirpation of such differences, was to be served by the Olympics; and that ignorance is the chief enemy of peace and brotherhood and the Games serve an educational function that I have proposed to call "popular ethnography."

Having lifted his audience to the heights, Coubertin now hastened to reassure them as to the challenges before them on the ground. The Games would entail "a minimal expenditure—about 150,000 francs—which would soon be more than recovered," and he listed the facilities which Athens had already available. He closed by warning against the fear of Greek defeats at the hands of strangers in the competitions themselves. "Dishonor would not lie in defeat, but in failure to take part. You may be sure that in working for the cause of sport you are working for your country."[124]

The issue of holding the Games had become so public that the newspaper *Asty* published Coubertin's speech in full, and the baron pressed home his advantage with a letter to the editor. Reviving a tactic used in his closing address to the Sorbonne congress, he thanked not only *Asty*, but "the entire Athenian press that has given me a sympathetic and encouraging welcome," when in fact the press had been as divided as the politicians over the matter. The tide was turning in his favor, but the issue was far from settled. Cleverly, however, he assured *Asty*'s readers that "the question of the Olympic Games is henceforth decided and an accord has been reached." Only questions of responsibilities and arrangements remained. While noting that Tricoupis was "unable to involve the government," Coubertin altered the premier's pledge of neutrality to a "benevolent following of our efforts." An organizing committee was soon to be formed, and Coubertin announced that it would "appeal to the patriotism of your countrymen" for subscriptions to cover the modest expenses of the "great solemnity." Coubertin closed the letter with his own goad to Athenian nationalism. "In our country we have a proverb saying that the word 'impossible" isn't French; someone told me this morning that it was Greek. I don't believe that at all."[125]

Coubertin and his friends handpicked the persons invited to the meeting to organize a committee. The crown prince judged himself unable to attend because of his duties as regent, but the rest assembled in the Zappeion on November 24. "Happily," said Coubertin, "I was already practiced in these sorts of loose assemblies which must flatter, anesthetize, and precipitate matters in turn.... The prior patronage of the royal prince prevented anyone from daring to dispute the principle" of hosting the Games.[126] The program of competitions Coubertin had brought with him from Paris was duly approved, and with it the organization of each according to the rules of one or another national sports body. This was another of Coubertin's ploys to ensure the international look of the Games.[127] Next officers were elected to serve under Constantine. The vice-presidents were Colonel Mano, Commander Soutzo of the Cavalry, Mr. Retzinas, the mayor of Piraeus, and Étienne Scouloudis, a deputy and former cabinet minister. Mercati and Melas were the committee's secretaries, and Paul Skouses, its treasurer. The dates for the Games were fixed for April 5–15. Coubertin foresaw that in 1896 the Western and Greek Easters would by happenstance coincide, and alive to the powerful symbolic theme of resurrection, he scheduled the resurrected Olympic Games to open on Easter Monday.

With matters now decently arranged and in trusted hands (Bikelas was due back shortly to oversee), and with public opinion shifting noticeably in favor of the Games, Coubertin felt free to depart for Paris. Along the way home, he made his founder's pilgrimage to Archaia Olympia. What thoughts danced through his head as the slow train wound across the isthmus, along the sea, and into Patras we can only guess. In Patras, the baron was "warmly welcomed" by the local gymnastics society, and with one of its members as a guide, he set off immediately for Pyrgos, the hills above, and Olympia. In this "solitude so propitious for reflections," he arrived "late in the evening" at the village and its little railroad station whose "modernism" was modest enough "not to trouble the majesty of the holy city and the pious reverie of those who visited it as pilgrims to history." "I remember the footpath that climbed snakelike up the little hill where the museum and hotel were located. A pure air, perfumed with scents, blew up from the banks of the Alpheus. For a moment the moonlight animated a vaporous landscape, then a starry night fell over the two thousand years with which I had come to seek stirring contact." Because of the hour, "I was forced to wait until dawn to discern the outlines of the sacred landscape of which I had so often dreamed."

The next day, from my window, I kept watch for the sunrise, and as soon as its first rays had crossed the valley, I rushed toward the ruins. Their smallness—owing on the one hand to the restrained proportion of the buildings and, on the other, to their crowdedness (this absence of open spaces so characteristic of Greek and Roman civilization, which is in striking contrast to Persian conceptions)—neither surprised nor deceived me. It was a moral architecture I was going to gather lessons from, and it magnified every dimension. My meditation lasted all morning, while only the noise of the bells of the flocks on the way to Arcadia disturbed the silence.

All morning long I wandered in the ruins.[128]

Pierre left no more detailed account of what he saw and felt that morning in either volume of his memoirs. This leads one commentator to suggest that Olympia made no "specific impression" on him.[129] Not only is this contrary to the texts just cited and to all that we know about Coubertin's personality and spirit, but there are also other texts which give evidence for quite a different interpretation. In his 1929 lecture "Olympia," Coubertin refers to himself as "drinking in the spectacle" of the holy place and sitting "on the wooded slopes of Mount Kronion at the hour when beyond the Alpheus the rising sun begins to touch the swelling hills with gold and to lighten the green meadows at their feet."[130] These are certainly "specific" impressions. Later on in the same text, this time as a literary reverie, he describes picnicking on the site of the exedra of Herod Atticus, "succumbing to the soft incitement of earth and sky," thinking he could imagine "the joyful cries of the ephebes in the gymnasium" and could see "an attendant climbing the steps of the main sanctuary to feed with incense the tripod placed at the foot of Jupiter's statue, the work of the immortal Phidias. That traveller down there taking notes—could be it Pausanias, the benevolent editor of a guidebook that will later enable us—much later—to identify and rediscover the Hermes of Praxiteles at the very spot where he had mentioned it as being present?"[131]

The text is ambiguous whether these particular fancies are those that came to him during his meditation that day; but if not these, then doubtless others like them. With the possible exception of Delphi, Olympia is for modern visitors the most conducive of all the Greek sites to redreaming and acting out in imagination her ancient dramas. The layout of the ruins, their isolation, and the excellent while unobtrusive reconstruction by the Germans contribute to this effect: but the "familiar" character of sport is most responsible. On the morning when I first saw Olympia, for example, a sudden shower cleared guards and tourists from the ruins. On the excuse of shelter from the rain, I gathered myself under the remaining

arch of the tunnel that served as the liminal boundary between the *altis*
and the stadium. Through it the athletes had once emerged, nervous and
numb for the trial; from the reassuring company of trainers and priests to
the open space and the light, to the fanfares and crowd roar, with blinking
eyes open outward yet focused within, to the pure moment of decision
and, for some, destiny. Such a passage is impressive in any case. To an
athlete who has already worked himself into a hyperstate of emotion and
attention, it can be overwhelming in its joy and terror, his severest trial.
As I huddled there on the boundary between these twice-two worlds,
powerful flashbacks to similar moments in my own athletic career—in the
tunnels of Franklin Field, Madison Square Garden, and a dozen lesser
passageways—came unbidden upon me. My body remembered so vividly
that I felt strong urges to vomit and to run. The first I resisted, the second
I could not. Though embarrassed that I too should fall prey to such
conceits and irrationally fearful that in this act I would somehow compromise my anthropological and historical training, I shook and strutted
myself to the starting line in the old way, conducted the old ceremonials
I thought I had forgotten, took a false start to increase the drama, then
sprinted the 200-meter length of the ground. By the end of the trip, a
lighthearted cackle of joy and pleasure had replaced my embarrassment
and solemn seriousness. I congratulated myself at not having pulled a
muscle running like that in street boots.

As I ambled back toward the *krypte*, amused at myself, two Frenchmen,
stripped to the waist and on the same mission, came dashing by. I was to
witness this scene a hundred times in the following week, played out by
old and young tourist/pilgrims of several nationalities. A guard told me he
had orders to prevent such behavior, lest it do some vague damage to the
stadium or be "disturbing of order and quiet." But the guards had long
since given up trying to enforce the rules. "How can we," said my in-
formant, "they all want to do it."

The stadium was not cleared when Coubertin visited. He had no such
flashbacks to take possession of him and, in any case, the baron would
have been more protective of his dignity. But in casual conversations with
German, American, Yugoslavian, Swedish, and French tourists, I found
but one or two who did not readily own up to the less demonstrative sorts
of meditative re-creation that had occupied the baron. As to the effect
these experiences had upon him, he left a concise but perfectly clear
notice: "On [that] morning in November, 1894, I became aware in this
sacred place of the enormity of the task which I had undertaken in proclaiming five months earlier the restoration of the Olympic Games after an
interruption of 1500 years; and I glimpsed all the hazards which would
dog me on the way."[132]

I class this event among Coubertin's visions, though it was, it seems, a kind of "anti-vision," a sobering experience, and transformative for just that reason. The *metanoia* induced in the baron that morning lay less in another flight of ecstasy than in a kind of enstasy, an awareness, perhaps for the first time, of the true "enormity of the task," and therefore of the role he had chosen for himself. The symbolic paradigm of his illuminations at Arnold's and Lesneven's (and Washington's and Carnot's) tombs was here recapitulated in a new form. Those had been experiences of a private call to a vocation, this was the confirmation of a vocation already publicly under way. As if to abrogate the reality principle, to over-compensate for the absence of "real world" plausibility and assurances, visions of the call nearly always are marked by a psychic exuberance, even arrogance. While no less transformative, visions of confirmation, where the realities of the situation are better known and the "hazards" are as familiar as the glories, tend to be psychically calming, even humbling. My guess is that on that luminous morning in November, Coubertin became aware not only of the enormity of the task but also, and with a shudder, of the enormity of his hubris in arrogating it to himself. It is this which accounts, I think, for the absence of long-winded evocations of the moment in his later writings. We might have had such texts had he visited Olympia earlier in his career, or even on his way to Athens to battle for the Games. But, as it turned out, he reached Olympia in the thick of things, fresh from confronting the all-too-real forces guarding the portal between the ancient Games and the modern world. And there was reason to believe that he had triumphed over those forces; this was what pro-tected him against the paralyzing effect the sheer silence and inertia of the ruins and their "lesson in inner modesty" might otherwise have had on his will. The last phrase is from his second journey to Olympia thirty-three years later, another experience of confirmation, though this time of achievement, not just of vocation. He had won, like Arnold and Lesneven, his own "proper monument," a marble stele erected by the Greek gov-ernment in the sacred *altis* to honor and celebrate publicly his achievement in reviving the Olympic Games.

> On a morning in April, 1927, I waited there in a kind of devout con-templation for the hour when the hand of the minister of education would draw back the Greek and French flags veiling the dazzling marble erected to attest success. And when in the course of the ceremony I had to reply to the homage of the representative of the Greek government, my first thought was to salute those who have not succeeded in life despite their best efforts, because fate has set its snares against them; the recollection of their disquieting *cortège* affords a lesson in inner modesty and in the emptiness of what we call merit.[133]

In a further passage of the same vintage, he returned to the theme of the emptiness, for himself, "of what we call merit."

> Perhaps one will judge that these remarks are inspired by pride. But if I have a high opinion of and take great pride in the work that was given to me to accomplish, I recognize no merit in it for myself. Merit begins there where the individual, obliged to struggle against himself or against excessively disfavorable circumstances, wins victories over his own temperament and, as it is said, succeeds in "subduing his fate." Favored by lot in many respects, sustained unceasingly in the face of my task by a kind of internal force from which it happened that I searched in vain to escape, I count no such victories to my credit.[134]

These sentiments are frankly conventional for addresses at testimonials and the conclusions of memoirs, and there is in them false modesty on the part of a man who had jealously guarded and zealously promoted his own role as Rénovateur. But they are not, for all that, dishonest or insincere, for when Coubertin wrote these texts, his personal life had become a tragedy. Laocoon had caught up with him, and it was this that made him so keenly aware of "the emptiness of what we call merit." These antinomies were symbolically encoded in his final, posthumous act: his heart was sent off to Olympia, while his corpse stayed behind in Lausanne to be joined in the grave by his wife and his children. The seeds of his tragedy were planted in the very years, 1895–98, of his triumph.

Pl. 1. Young Baron Pierre de Coubertin in sport clothes (*Presse Sports*)

Pl. 2. Pierre and Marie de Coubertin (*Courtesy of M. Geoffroy de Navacelles*)

Pl. 3. The fledgling International Olympic Committee, meeting in Athens during the Games. From left, Dr. Wilhelm Gebhardt (Germany), Pierre de Coubertin (France), Jiri Guth-Jarkovsky (Bohemia), Demetrios Bikelas (Greece), Franz Kemeny (Hungary), General A. Boutowsky (Russia), Colonel Victor Balck (Sweden)
(*International Olympic Committee Archives*)

Pl. 4.   Georges Averoff, a wealthy Alexandrian Greek, who became "the new Herod Atticus" by bankrolling the Stadium reconstruction. This monumental statue of him was placed at the Stadium portal and dedicated on Easter Sunday, the eve of the Games. *(Brown Brothers)*

Pl. 5.   Reconstruction of the Panathenaic Stadium for the first modern Olympic Games *(Librairie Jules Tallandier)*

Pl. 6.   Despite great distances, the absence of mechanical loudspeakers, and the utter novelty of such athletic competitions, the opening day crowd watched them intently *(Brown Brothers)*

Pl. 7.   Robert Garrett, Jr., of Princeton, winner of the discus and the shot, second in the long jump, and third in the high jump *(Brown Brothers)*

Pl. 8.   Albert C. Tyler of Princeton, second in the pole vault *(Brown Brothers)*

Pl. 9.   William W. Hoyt of Harvard and the Boston Athletic Association, hurdles competitor, and winner of the pole vault *(Brown Brothers)*

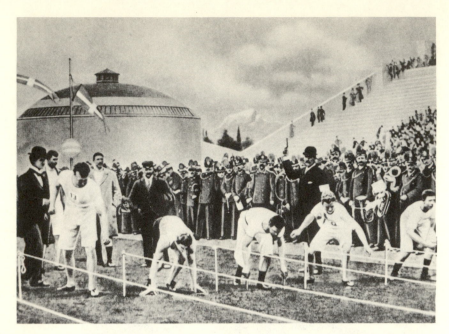

Pl. 10.   The 100-meter final. From left, A. Halkokondylis (Greece), T. Burke (USA, first place), F. Hofmann (Germany, second), A. Szokolyi (Hungary, third), F. Lane (USA). Note the variety of starting postures *(Historical Pictures Service, Inc., Chicago)*

Pl. 11.   The newly constructed velodrome on the plain of Neon Phaleron *(Ekdotike Athenon)*

Pl. 12.   Start of a cycle race in the velodrome *(International Olympic Committee Archives)*

Pl. 13.   Illustration from *Le Petit Journal* in Paris, captioned "Athens Olympic Games: Our compatriot Masson, winner of the bicycle race." In fact, Paul Masson won three races, all in the velodrome, none on bumpy lanes in the shadow of the Acropolis. This embellishment, and his fanciful costume, heroic posture, and celebration by dandy and peasant alike were common themes in Euro-American press illustrations. © *Archives SNARK*

Pl. 14. The start of the Marathon race on the outskirts of the village with that storied name *(International Olympic Committee Archives)*

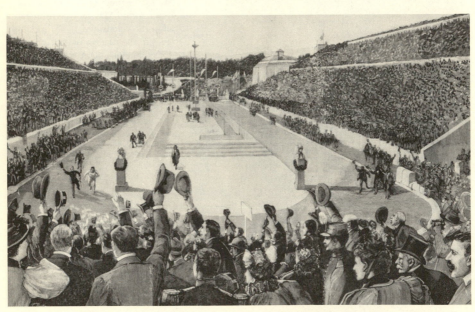

Pl. 15. Illustration, widely reprinted in the Americas, of the epic moment of Spiridon Loues' victory in the Marathon *(Historical Pictures Service, Inc., Chicago)*

Pl. 16.   In the aftermath of his victory,
"one heard nothing but the name of Mr.
Spiridon Loues, and one saw nothing but
his picture." In this rare and evocative
photograph, Loues is posed, Greek flag in
hand, by some of his celebrants.
(Brown Brothers)

Pl. 17.   Athletes and dignitaries assembled for the awards ceremony. Coubertin (arrow) was denied a
place of honor on the dais. In a photo taken later in the ceremony, he is still staring at the ground.
(Ekdotike Athenon)

Pl. 18.   Loues and other victors laden
with their prizes *(International Olympic
Committee Archives)*

Pl. 19.   The American team (James B. Connolly with stick in the right foreground) with Loues and Princes Constantine and George in uniform *(International Olympic Committee Archives)*

CHAPTER SEVEN

An Indescribable Spectacle

~~~

Fever in Waiting

After another round of speeches and the Marseillaise in Patras, Coubertin put to sea. His vessel stopped at Corfu, where he received the good wishes of Abbot Boulgaris, the archimandrite of the monastery there. From Brindisi, he took a train to Naples, where he addressed a meeting of the Philological Circle on December 7, a meeting called by the duke of Andria, I.O.C. member in Italy, whom Coubertin was meeting for the first time. His speech on the ancient and modern Games— doubtless the same one that had been such a success in Greece—was a failure here, "a sword pass in the water." "Evidently," Coubertin took note, "away from the harmonies of the Hymn to Apollo and the silhouette of the Parthenon, the evocation of the Olympic Games lacked efficacy."[1] It was a lesson he would relearn several times in the coming months, sometimes humorously. A former colleague on the Mirville Municipal Council asked him in all seriousness whether "the *feux olympiques* gave off good light and whether [Coubertin] was satisfied with this new [form of] illumination."[2] In the very course of the Athens Olympics, a lady assured Coubertin that she had already seen the Olympic Games in her native San Francisco. "It was very lovely," she said; "Caesar was there,"[3] referring to a theatrical, stage-show pageant "Olympia" that toured England, Paris, and the States in the 1890s. And Coubertin continued to endure the barbs of "cultivated persons" who were fond of jocularly inquiring of him whether in the new Games, as in the old, female spectators were to be barred so that the competitors could be naked.[4] For as many as battled in earnest over the Olympic revival, there were equal numbers who treated the whole business as Grand Guignol. For as many as took inspiration from Puvis de Chavannes's *Bois sacré*, there were others who delighted in Toulouse-Lautrec's *Parodie*.

Fifteen days after the baron's departure, Bikelas returned to Athens,[5] and thereafter kept Coubertin regularly informed by letter. No sooner was the Frenchman gone than Scouloudis convened the other organizing committee vice-presidents, convinced them that Coubertin's budget was a

fraud and that expenses would be much higher, and announced that the
government would refuse to approve a lottery to finance the Games.
They, therefore, could not be held, and the committee's duty was to
dissolve itself. A report was drafted to this effect and carried to Constantine. "M. Scouloudis had thought he could intimidate him by this
collective step. But the Prince calmly laid the report on his desk and said
that he would study it at leisure. Thus he very shrewdly left the matter in
suspense; his mind, however, was already made up."[6] The same day the
matter was put to Parliament. Among the speakers for the Games were
Deputies Papamichalopoulos, Extafias, Embiricos, and Zycomalas.
Dragoumis and Scouloudis spoke for Tricoupis and the opposition. Delyannis kept silent for which, according to Coubertin, the papers took him
"vehemently" to task the next day.[7]

Just after the New Year, the Tricoupis government fell. Coubertin was
careful to note that the immediate cause was unconnected with the Olympics (though he remembered it as an incident during a labor strike, instead
of a dispute over military discipline, as it was),[8] but the baron intimated
that the Olympic issue played an important if indirect role. In this, he was
quite correct, for Tricoupis' opponent over the military issue was Constantine, who was using the Olympics simultaneously to assert his independence and opposition to Tricoupis and to draw to himself the popular
appeal the prime minister had already lost through his fiscal policies.
Coubertin avers that Tricoupis, in his interview with the king, asked the
latter "to choose" between his prime minister and his son.[9] I have not
found confirmation of this in contemporary documents, but we may be
sure that Tricoupis complained of Constantine's meddling, and Coubertin's source may have been King George himself. The sovereign met with
Coubertin in Paris in July and spoke "with visible pride of the qualities
of which the Prince showed proof in the organization of the Games."[10]

Upon Tricoupis' resignation, Constantine seized the initiative for the
Games. He immediately dismissed the organizing committee's vice-
presidents, appointed Timoleon Philemon, a former mayor of Athens, as
secretary general, added two more of Coubertin's allies, Constantinos
Manos and G. Streit, as secretaries to serve with Melas and Mercati, and
named his brothers, Prince George and Prince Nicholas, as heads of the
working commissions.[11] The interim government hastily approved an issue
of special Olympic postage stamps, proceeds from whose sales would go to
the Games. Appeals for donations went out to wealthy Greeks living
abroad. Subscription by such men to public projects was already an
established tradition in Greece, and success came immediately. The merchant Schilizzi of Constantinople gave 10,000 drachmas, which the wealthy Athenian Syngros, to whom Coubertin had earlier appealed,
matched. Donations arrived from the Greek communities in Alexandria,

London, and Marseilles, and by February 19, Philemon wrote Coubertin that 130,000 drachmas were already in hand. But it was Constantine himself who located and pressured the man who became, as Coubertin and others liked to put it, "the new Herod Atticus" of the Athens Olympics.[12] This was Georges Averoff, a shy and retiring man of fantastic wealth living in Alexandria. Averoff agreed to bankroll the bold project of rebuilding the Panathenaic stadium in all its antique glory. In the end it was to cost him some 1 million drachmas (about 110,000 current dollars). The old quarries of Mt. Pentelicon (Pentelē) were reopened for the purpose, and soon hundreds of laborers, working two shifts, were busy clearing the stadium site in preparation for installing the new blocks of gleaming white marble. The architect Anastas Metaxas drew up the plans and supervised the work in consultation with the German and French archeological academies. The only genuflections to modernity in their ambitious plans were the decisions to widen the track by removing a few rows of the ancient seats, and to fabricate it of cinders, for which a London grounds keeper was called in as consultant. Discovered in earlier excavations were two Hermes statues which had escaped the Turkish lime kilns; these were subsequently installed as turning posts. A great statue of Averoff, to be unveiled on Easter Sunday the following year, was commissioned for the entrance to the stadium.[13]

The announcement of the Averoff philanthropy unleashed a great outburst of civic pride, triggered more donations, released organizing committee funds for other projects, and, by creating jobs (and the opportunity for profiteering), gave Games partisans ammunition in the propaganda war over the wisdom of hosting an international festival in times of fiscal disaster. Between summer 1895 and the following spring, the progress of the stadium restoration provided Athenians with a living symbol of the coming rebirth of the Games and embodied and focused their growing anticipation of them (see pl. 4). In the winter and early spring of 1895, that is, during the electoral campaign, the publicity and feverish beginnings of the project focused the opposition between the two contending political parties over the Olympic Games.

In April, Delyannis soundly defeated Tricoupis, who, broken in health and spirit, immediately retired from politics. The history of Greek politics over the previous fifteen years, and the nature of the general situation in 1895, make it clear that Tricoupis would have lost even if Coubertin had not come calling with the Olympic proposal. But the Games offered Tricoupis a convenient symbol of his fate, and Coubertin was probably correct in asserting that the great statesman "bore a real grudge against the Olympic Games."[14] The timing of his departure for Nice on the eve of their opening in 1896 was probably not accidental. The news of Tricoupis' death in Cannes arrived in the midst of the Olympic celebration on April

11, "during an evening of great festivity, amidst the pomp of light and music," as Coubertin coldly put it, without a shred of compassion or second-thought.[15] In an irony both final and tragic—given the calamities that were shortly to befall Greece, calamities prepared by or abetted by Tricoupis' opponents, the partisans of the Games—his funeral took place in Athens on April 23, "while the city was still decorated with flags and garlands after the celebration of the Olympic Games."[16]

The "conquest of Greece" did not in itself ensure that athletes and spectators from the various nations would indeed come. This task fell largely to Coubertin in Paris. Though the invitations to participate went out from Athens over the signature of Philemon, the secretary general of the organizing committee, it was Coubertin who prepared the lists of individuals and clubs to be invited, and he spent a good deal of time lobbying behind the scenes to guarantee they would arrive. His success was mixed indeed.

As by now we would anticipate, in France Coubertin met resistance and ultimately failure. In the fall of 1894, he had formed the "French National Olympic Committee" (F.N.O.C.), the prototype of all subsequent national Olympic Committees (N.O.C.s) which were to be and still are, with the I.O.C., the International Federations (I.F.s), and the Olympic Games organizing committees (O.C.O.G.s), the components of Olympic organizational structure. As its honorary president, he secured Félix Faure, former naval and commerce minister. Eugene Spuller, former minister of foreign affairs and recently resigned minister of public instruction, Courcel, Gréard, Bréal, Lebaudy, d'Estournelles, Mézières, and Paul Bourget, whose novels Coubertin especially admired for their sports themes, were other notables on the committee. The rest of its members were officials of the various sports federations. Despite the fact that Faure acceded to the presidency of France on January 17, 1895, and Léon Bourgeois, who had earlier lent his presence to at least one of Coubertin's athletic fêtes, to the premiership in November, "the government ignored the movement. A subsidy for French athletes to go to Athens? What a pretension!"[17] As for the sports officials, they immediately returned to form. The president of the cycling commission, M. Baltazzi, refused to commit himself without assurance that at least thirty competitors would show up in Athens, and Damala, the secretary of the committee on nautical sport, demanded of Coubertin a definite list of the nations and clubs already inscribed for the Games before he would take action. Merillon, the president of the Union of Shooting Clubs, resigned from the F.N.O.C. in protest and vowed to boycott the Olympic Games because "shooting was to be incorporated and encased as a [mere] branch in an ensemble of sports" at Athens, and because the Olympic organizers had the gall to propose making his union "an appendage of their Committee."[18]

As it turned out, only a motley handful of French athletes—a long-

distance runner, two cyclists, and four or five fencers—took part in the
Athens Games.[19] Coubertin was no more successful in his attempt to
draw the interest of French artists through the commission of Puvis de
Chavannes to design the Olympic certificates to be given as prizes. After
looking over photographs and drawings of Greek scenes in Coubertin's
apartment, Puvis "stupified" the baron by rejecting the commission because he (one of the most celebrated of neoclassical painters) found it
"impossible to hellenize himself sufficiently" to do it.[20] Jules Chaplain did
consent to design the medals—a "splendid composition, one of the most
perfect he ever executed, with a head of Olympian Jupiter on one side and
the Acropolis on the other"[21]—but Coubertin reaped no publicity for the
Games from it. Even his design for the velodrome, based upon a tour and
inquiries of the designers of the one at Arachon, was rejected by the
Hellenic committee in favor of copying the velodrome in Copenhagen.[22]
The baron had more success arranging tours at reduced rates for tourist/
spectators. He and two associates secured a Paris-Athens round trip, first
class for three hundred francs; and an additional crossing from Marseilles
on the steamship *Senegal* was made by at least two hundred persons. The
ubiquitous agency of Thomas Cook secured exclusive rights to arranging
the tour, but as Coubertin was sadly compelled to note, very few Frenchmen took advantage of it.[23]

Coubertin had been "pestering" I.O.C. members to constitute N.O.C.s
in their respective countries, but few succeeded in doing so. Balck wrote
from Sweden that the crown prince was taking an interest and that he was
working hard, but he acknowledged his unease and could give Coubertin
no better reassurance than that "everything possible will be done."[24] As it
turned out, only one Swedish athlete and four Danish athletes appeared.
From Russia, Boutowsky wrote that the newspapers found physical education unworthy of notice, and that he was encountering total indifference
as to the Games.[25] The Belgian sports clubs retained their hostility to
Coubertin from 1893, and vowed not to participate in the Games.[26] On
the Continent, only Hungary, with its little N.O.C. led by Kemeny and
Count Czaky, pressed forward enthusiastically, despite the disappointment of not hosting the Games themselves. Kemeny won government
backing for a team of eight competitors, doubtless because of the regime's
interest in demonstrating its autonomy to the Hapsburgs on the occasion
of the Magyar "millennium." Though some Swiss, Austrian, and Bulgarian athletes were to turn up at the last minute, some to win medals, they
came as individuals. Coubertin failed to incite any corporate initiatives in
these countries, or in Spain, Italy, Portugal, or Holland. The one Italian
athlete, Carlo Airoldi, who decided to compete walked the entire distance
between Milan and Athens to get into shape, only to be refused entry,
apparently because he had no amateur credentials.[27]

G. S. Robertson, the Oxford athlete who delighted the Greeks and

Coubertin by reciting an original ode in ancient Greek and Pindaric style during the awards ceremony, blamed the failure to secure a representative English team squarely upon the "French organizers," that is, upon Coubertin. In a remarkable oversight, only French and German texts of the program and rules were posted to England. An English-language version, published by a commercial printer, did not appear until shortly before the Games were to begin. Herbert and Ampthill, upon whom Coubertin was obviously counting, had no "present connection with the Universities." This was particularly unfortunate since, as Robertson wrote: "Of all Anglo-Saxon athletes those at present in residence at Oxford and Cambridge were the most likely to be able to take part in the meeting. The Easter Vacation was exactly suited for a visit to Athens, and the English University man would, of all men, require the least pressure to induce him to pay a visit to Greece." But the Cambridge Athletic Club made nothing of the German invitation they received, and an "obscure notice" posted up at Oxford and a paragraph in an "unimportant Oxford journal" attracted little attention.[28] Moreover, "If one wrote to the central committee, one was liable to be told that all information could be attained by subscribing a considerable sum to the journal of the committee."[29] Perhaps incredulous that difficulties should come from the nation of Thomas Arnold and confident not only in Herbert and Ampthill but also in Manos, who was a sometime student at Oxford, Coubertin was slow to recognize the English situation. Too late did he send "hurried letters to the principal British newspapers, appealing for the cooperation of the main English [athletic] clubs." "In general," according to Coubertin, "the papers accompanied the publication of these documents with reflections that were sympathetic but mixed in with bits of irony; they didn't believe in the Olympic Games; on the contrary, they extolled pan-Britannic games and called for their organization without delay."[30] Direct contacts with the university clubs were not made until the month before the opening of the Olympics.

As a result, the six athletes "who did go, did not go as representatives of any club, but, for the most part, as private pleasure-seekers."[31] In Athens, their number was augmented by Edwin Flack, an Australian who was a member of the London Athletic Club, by Mr. Boland, an Oxfordian who happened to be living in Athens and who entered the tennis competition, and by two "servants" at the British embassy. Appealing to the old British amateur rules, certain Englishmen present tried to prevent their entry on the grounds that they were servants. But, said Robertson, who, like other more sporting Britons, was terribly embarrassed by this, "no one could cast the slightest slur on their amateurism," and the I.O.C. overruled the English gentlemen and admitted the two men to the cycle race from Marathon. According to Robertson, they were leading and would have won the race had not fate decreed that they collide with each other, leaving the way open for a Greek.[32]

Robertson's pique over the English showing was exacerbated by the appearance of what he took to be "a fully equipped team of American athletes," turned out through "the natural enterprise of the American people and . . . the peculiarly perfect method in which athletics are organized in the United States."[33] Triumph after athletic triumph fell to the Americans in Athens, but in fact the team was formed largely through circumstance, was thought by Americans to be anything but "well equipped,"[34] and departed to much less clamor than had the Yale athletes bound for Oxford in 1894.[35]

At Princeton, Sloane secured academic leave for four athletes who were juniors at the college: Robert Garrett, Jr., Francis A. Lane, Albert Tyler, and Herbert Jameson. Garrett was the son of a wealthy Baltimore banker who agreed to foot the bill not only for his own son, but for the entire Princeton contingent.[36] Coubertin had been acquainted with the Boston Athletic Association during his American trips. This, and perhaps Sloane's urging, caused an announcement of the Games to arrive at B.A.A. headquarters. However, according to Ellery Clark, the decision of the B.A.A. to send a team began as a joke. At an association meeting in January 1896, Arthur Blake, the recent winner of a local race, jocularly remarked, "Oh, I'm too good for Boston. I ought to go over and run the Marathon, at Athens." A well-to-do stockbroker named Arthur Burnham heard the remark and promptly offered to finance a team, and Oliver Ames, the governor of Massachusetts and B.A.A. patron, also offered to contribute.[37] The B.A.A. delegation consisted of Blake and William Hoyt, Harvard alumni; Clark, a high jumper and Harvard undergraduate; Thomas Burke, a sprinter and alumnus of Boston University; and Thomas Curtis, a hurdler from M.I.T. and Columbia College.[38] James B. Connolly from the Suffolk Athletic Club was also currently enrolled as an undergraduate at Harvard; but while Clark was given leave because of his high academic standing, the dean threatened Connolly with dismissal should he make the trip. The young triple jumper is said to have replied with typical gentlemanly pluck, "I am not resigning and I am not making application to reenter. But I *am* going to the Olympic Games, so I am through with Harvard right now."[39] The rest of the American contingent was composed of two Boston marksmen, Sumner and John Paine, then captains in the army, a swimmer, Gardiner Williams, who paid his own way, the Princeton trainer Scotty McMaster, and manager John Graham from the B.A.A. (See pls. 7–9, 19).

The question of German participation unfolded amid the outrage triggered by the inflammatory remarks purportedly made by Coubertin in an interview, which I referred to earlier, to the effect that he had deliberately discouraged German participation in the Sorbonne congress. From the outset there had been no question of at least some German representation at the Games. Prince Constantine was married to the kaiser's sister, and the Greek ambassador to Berlin had constituted a committee with the chancellor's brother as president and Dr. Wilhelm Gebhardt as secretary. Gebhardt, who was in regular correspondence with Coubertin[40] and who was appointed by the latter as I.O.C. member for Germany in 1895,[41] had royal patronage on his side and was busy organizing a team when the storm broke. The reprinting of Coubertin's purported remarks in late 1895 in the *National-Zeitung*, together with the refusal by one of the great German gymnastic clubs of the Greek organizing committee's invitation to the Games, "provoked a veritable tempest" in Greece as well, as the Athens correspondent of *Le Temps* wrote his paper on January 4. Exactly when Coubertin learned of it or from what source is not clear, but he threw himself into action immediately.[42] Letters denying these "insane" allegations were posted to Constantine, Gebhardt, the Greek ambassador in Berlin, and the *Zeitung*. On January 5, Coubertin received a long letter from Rangabé, the ambassador, who began by remarking on the gravity of the situation. He had received, he said, over fifty newspaper articles from throughout the German empire. But, he continued, the *Zeitung* had published Coubertin's denial, albeit with some "uncivil but trifling remarks" which the ambassador interpreted as "covering its retreat." Moreover, a translation had been sent to all the major newspapers. Gebhardt was taking Coubertin's denial to the chancellor who, one could be confident, would personally show it to the emperor, who, after all, "desires the maintenance of good relations with France." Some days later, the German Olympic committee met, and Gebhardt felt confident enough that the matter was blowing over to send Coubertin the committee's "unanimous sympathies and wishes for success in the common effort." A copy of this message was also delivered to Jules Herbette, French ambassador to Berlin.[43] Time, however, was working against Gebhardt. Unable to secure a postponement of the Games until the fall from Coubertin[44]—who did not wish to forsake the Easter symbolism and who, in any case, had lost control to the Greeks over such matters—Gebhardt was able to produce only three athletic competitors and ten Turners for the Athens Games.

Throughout the German controversy, Coubertin had heard nothing directly from the Greek organizers. Finally, on February 7, Philemon sent a laconic telegram to Paris: "Hellenic Committee never believed words attributed to you initiator renaissance Olympic Games." A "warm letter" followed. But "it was a little late for this assertion to convince me," said Coubertin. From Gebhardt, the baron had learned that Philemon had tried to use the German hubbub as a pretext to suppress the I.O.C., a "temporary mechanism that no longer had reason to exist."[45] Having earlier telegrammed the Germans as to the complete independence of the Greek organizing committee,[46] Philemon saw no reason not to make it so. The calming of the German situation caused Philemon not to "abandon his black design," as Coubertin put it, but rather to go at it more subtly. With Greek public opinion now so enthused, construction for the Games so feverish, and the Greeks naively confident that hordes of foreign competitors and tourists were busy making plans to descend upon Athens (Coubertin "did not dare" to tell them that no more than "a hundred athletes" and a "few thousand foreign spectators" were likely to come),[47] nationalism and factional interest dictated that Coubertin be eliminated from the picture. Philemon's letter "was the last manifestation of Athenian recognition; sure of success, they had no more need of me; I was no more than an intruder recalling by my mere presence the foreign initiative. From this moment on, not only was my name no longer mentioned but each one appeared to make it his business to help efface the memory of the part played by France in the restoration of the Olympiads. Most of those whom, the year before, I had gathered around the new-born work avoided meeting me or affected not to recognize me."[48] Having set Greek national pride so thoroughly in motion in favor of the Games, Coubertin was now to suffer personally from it. As we shall see, the merciless campaign to cast him out continued through the Games themselves. In the very moments of his triumph, he was treated as a pariah, and the Greeks themselves were later to imperil his Olympism by attempting to seize permanent control of the Games for themselves.

Why through all of these potentially fatal difficulties did Coubertin remain in Paris? Why had he not, as was his habit, traveled to foreign capitals to intervene personally, to flatter, cajole, inspire, and manipulate? As to the Greek campaign against him and the I.O.C., he became apprised of it only four months before the scheduled opening of the Games, too late to do very much. And, he was doubtless shrewd enough to give the Greeks their head. The recruitment of teams and tourists, however, might well have profited from his polished publicity techniques: convening conferences, appealing to notables, seeking out the press. It apparently never occurred to him to march into the lion's den, Germany, Belgium, or Holland: his boldness had its limits. But why did he not take to the stump in England, at least? Probably because there were other strong claims upon his attention during these fifteen months.

On March 12, 1895, he married Marie Rothan, the daughter of Gustave Rothan, a bourgeois of Alsatian Protestant background. In 1847, Rothan had begun a career as a diplomat, and under the Second Empire he had

served as plenipotentiary minister, largely in Germany and Italy. After
the fall of Napoleon in 1870, Rothan took up writing history. His first book,
Les Origines de la guerre de 1870, was published in 1879; six volumes of diplomatic memoirs followed, the last of which appeared in 1890, the year of
his death. What limited contemporary interest these works excited owed
to their inside view of diplomatic negotiations during the 1860s.[49]

Eyquem, unfortunately without documentation, claims that Rothan
and Charles de Coubertin, Pierre's father, were well acquainted, that the
two families "often received one another," and that Pierre and Marie
together heard their fathers castigating "Zola, Wagner, Manet, everything
modern and egalitarian."[50] While the elder Coubertin was a staunch
legitimist and might have looked askance at Rothan's service to the emperor, there is nothing in Rothan's books that would have led the baron to
close his door to the diplomat. Both were, indeed, haters of everything
modern. However, what lends credence to Eyquem's claim is that Rothan
was an avid and well-known collector of paintings, whose collection had
been several times publicly exhibited, whose tastes were congruent with
those of the painter Coubertin, and who was likely to have encountered
the baron in the fashionable salon and gallery world.[51]

Pierre seems to have seen Marie infrequently after these early meetings,
but, according to Eyquem, she was present in the audience during the
ill-fated Sorbonne meeting of 1892, when Coubertin's first call for the
Games fell upon deaf ears. Marie could have had no other reason for being
present except an interest in Pierre himself, and, as he dejectedly left the
hall, she is said to have rushed up and reassured him, "Your idea remained
beyond their understanding. It will be necessary to make it enter in there
little by little. But this time their reactions are of no importance."[52] This
declaration of faith and interest from a woman, in such circumstances,
must have struck Coubertin through and through.[53] "Their encounter had
been *the* encounter," declares Eyquem rather solemnly but aptly, given
later events and what we know of Coubertin's soul. Over the next two
years, though they saw each other only "from time to time" (Coubertin
was away in America for part of the period), "an almost daily correspondence was established between the two." In it, Coubertin is said to
have recounted in detail "his actions, projects, successes, and irritations,"
and she, in her answers, to have spoken only of him.[54] Given the pro-
tracted courtship, Eyquem was certainly correct that "between them, love
hadn't had that imperious appeal that overthrows all lucidity."

In his public projects, Coubertin knew how to be persistent yet patient,
alternately to flatter and inspire, to set in motion the most romantic fancies
and the most common interests. Was he now subject to such a campaign?
It seems difficult to explain otherwise the incongruity between Marie's
intelligence, ambitiousness, and sternness of character (which she dis-

played to all who subsequently knew her)[55] and the one-sided nature of their correspondence. Then too, she could afford to be patient. Marie was already in her thirties, unmarried, fatherless, and of doubtful means. She was passably pretty, with large and striking eyes that reflected her doleful and provocative moodiness, soft skin, and a strong constitution, yet short enough for Coubertin. But she was hardly a beauty.[56] For Pierre's part, it is not clear whether he had his doubts, was too absorbed in his projects, or else not given to precipitous, febrile passion in love, unlike in reform and sport. In any case, their love grew steadily into mutual respect and dependence, and in October 1894, he announced their engagement to his parents. They were, of course, outraged, as he must have known they would be. Indeed, no small part of Marie's attraction, we may guess, lay in her foreignness to all that his parents represented. She offered him a final act of rebellion. The fact that she appeared to credit his projects while his parents, in whose home he had been all the while living, ignored or condemned them only added to her Protestantism, her Alsatian background, her age, and her *roturier* origins. Whatever feelings Charles de Coubertin might once have entertained for her father were hardly sufficient to reconcile him to this. In his answer to their objections, Pierre returned to the old strategy of his adolescence, appealing to history and to higher-order identities: "All this is perfect; Alsace is a province torn away that must be loved more than the others; I am a Christian, so are the Protestants. Doubtless, there was a time when our family was *roturier* too. And she and I are old enough to know what we are doing."[57] These arguments, as had similar ones fifteen years before, only angered his parents further, and, barely a few days later, Coubertin shipped on the *Ortegal* for Greece: another act in which the Olympic project simultaneously gave him the chance to flee from his domestic heritage.

Whether his parents had mellowed toward the marriage by the time of his return we do not know, but may well doubt. Surely they were horrified that it took place in a Protestant church.[58] (See pl. 2.) Unlike his other acts of rebellion, this one was to end badly. Likely as not, the first year of his marriage was as promising as most, but before long it began to decline into the ill-starred, combative, and, perhaps, venal entente which scarred his later years. On the very eve of his triumph in Athens, Laocoon was rising.

Besides settling into marriage, Coubertin stayed in Paris to write political history. Prior to 1895, he had published a half-dozen articles in the field and had tried his wings as a political and social commentator in conferences in out-of-the-way places like Birmingham and Bolbec. But in 1895, he devoted himself in earnest, closed down the *Revue athlétique*,[59] sent nothing to *Les Sports athlétiques* (he shortly resigned from the U.S.F.S.A.), and, indeed, for the first and only year between 1886 and 1937, published nothing at all. In October and November, he gave a series of "popular conferences" on international politics at the Hôtel de Ville in Le Havre,[60] but it was the writing of *L'Évolution française sous la Troisième République* that commanded his energies in 1895 and early 1896.

It was to prove his finest work; nowhere in the two thousand pages of general and political history that he produced over the next thirty years was he again to approximate the measured tone, the literary style, and the unified vision of *L'Évolution*. His subsequent works were typically simple chronicles, collages of opinion, or undigested congeries of facts. Of his books, *France since 1814* and *Pages d'histoire contemporaine* were collections of newspaper articles without any organizing conception, and his four-volume *Histoire universelle* was so uninspired a summary of world history that he had to subsidize its publication and reduce himself to handing out copies in the vain hope that someone would take notice of it. But *L'Évolution* was conceived all of a piece, devoid of the abstract perorations and failure to discriminate the important from the unimportant that mar his later works. Above all, it is controlled by an underlying Tolstoyan-Tainean vision, what Albert Shaw, in his introduction to the American edition, summarized as "the essential unfolding of the latent capacities of the nation itself for its own self-ordering and self-direction.[61] Upon this deeper theme, Coubertin pivoted "a strong argument to show that, thus far, in the life of the Third Republic, the quick responsiveness of ministries to the veerings of public opinion as exhibited in the chambers has made for strength rather than weakness."[62] The argument was not delivered discursively, but embedded in concrete narrative, which gives the book a certain moral charm.

Coubertin must have had very great hopes for the book, given the great and unusually disciplined energy he put into it at a time when the Olympic Games could have commanded all of his attention. Despite the fact that his campaign for French educational reform had enjoyed mixed results at best, and despite the fact that success in Athens was anything but assured, Coubertin's ambitions had grown. He must have been helped to endure the scandalous absence of Frenchmen and the pariah treatment to which he personally was subjected during the Athens Games by the confident expectation that with the appearance of *L'Évolution française* in July, he would be recognized and celebrated as a historian and literary man in his native country.

But it was not to turn out that way; instead, the reception of the book was to begin a lifetime of literary disappointment and frustration. The most favorable comment the book received was a brief notice in the *Revue politique et parlementaire*. Calling the book "an intermission in his works on physical education," the reviewer complimented Coubertin on the "alert and compact style" of his portraits of contemporary statesmen, on his "interesting digressions" on colonial history and political education, and on "the real moderation" yet "extreme frankness" of his judgments. But the reviewer was clearly skeptical of Coubertin's attempt "to analyze everything that has taken place in France between 1870 and 1894." The book, he said, was likely to raise some "curious polemics." In particular, it would "assuredly astonish those who aren't acquainted with the sensibility of the younger generation and the complete liberty of mind with which it appraises men and events."[63]

La Réforme sociale also heard the voice of the younger generation in *L'Évolution française*, but to a different effect. The journal in which Coubertin had got his start mocked his book for its naive optimism, ignorance, and forgetfulness.

> Here is a book written from the point of view of "pure" opportunism, but made to please, we think, the younger generations, and perhaps, to develop in them what is called "the new spirit," that which could be called more simply a timid return to good sense. Certainly it will be otherwise received by those who, older than the author, lived through the disasters and dissensions from which the Republic emerged in the previous years.

Adding insult to injury, the reviewer unfavorably contrasted Coubertin's sanguine account of French foreign relations with the "sad" and "wonderful pages" of Gustave Rothan, Coubertin's own late father-in-law. While complaining of Coubertin's "visible predilection for the disastrous work of Jules Ferry," the reviewer did acknowledge that there was "more than one successful passage" on various policy questions. Yet, he concluded, there is not perhaps a single page which does not "disconcert and shock the reader with an unexpected contradiction." "M. de Coubertin congratulates the Republic for considering itself the heir of *all of France* and for not having repudiated *any* of its traditions! Whoever has listened to the official harangues or paged through the school textbooks will ask himself who is mocking whom here."[64]

Had more liberal reviewers risen to his defense, Coubertin might have chalked up these sentiments to the increasingly reactionary character of the Société d'économie sociale. But his friend Demolins, leader of the breakaway Le Play group, took no notice of the book in the pages of *La Science sociale*, and more liberal journals ignored it as well. In the midst of the Dreyfus affair, France, liberal or conservative, was in no mood to hear that everything was going along fine, that cabinet and party instability were inconvenient but necessary while the French were becoming a truly democratic people. This is not to say that all optimists fared as badly as Coubertin. Durkheim, with whose work it is always useful to compare

Coubertin's, was in the midst of his own overly optimistic fancies about representative politics as a cure for anomie.[65] But Durkheim was far and away a finer intellect, a respected, if controversial, university professor, with his own journal and a devoted group of students. Moreover, his optimism was squarely based upon a coherent social theory, not, as was Coubertin's, upon a diffuse and highly personal synthesis between aristocratic values and the modern temper, a synthesis embodied in the motto Coubertin had chosen for himself: "Voir loin, parler franc, agir ferme" ("See far, speak frankly, act firmly").[66] Then too, a host of better writers were filling the bookstalls and magazines with treatments of the same problems, and how many Parisians were prepared to take seriously as a historian and *littérateur* a man whose only claim to public notice had been a campaign to convince them of the moral value of athletic sport? Coubertin was once again a man out of season. By the time Parisian opinion might have recognized the generosity and sensibleness of his book, it had been, like most works of current history written by unknowns, quite forgotten.

With his bride and his dreams of literary glory, Coubertin departed for his appointment in Athens. His marriage and his hopes as an author were destined to end badly; the Games were destined to prosper and to win for him the eponym le Rénovateur. With the Olympic Games, he was for the first and only time in his life a successful innovator in the vanguard of his contemporaries. Not until 1912 would it occur to Durkheim to call for "new feasts and ceremonies . . . to serve for a while to guide mankind."[67]

The Heaving Heart of the Multitude

Coubertin arrived to find Athens awash with enthusiasm and anticipation. A festival spirit had thoroughly claimed the city. "All the public buildings were draped in bunting; multicolored streamers floated in the wind; green wreaths decked the house-fronts. Everywhere were the letters O.A., the Greek initials of the Olympic Games, and the two dates B.C. 776, A.D. 1896, indicating their past and their present renaissance."[68] Hundreds of Athenians, triply liberated from work by Easter, Independence Day, and the Olympics, traipsed off to the stadium to review the state of preparation, worried with each other over tickets and provisions, gossiped and poured over the latest rumors in the papers. Through streets echoing with music from the many little bands tuning up, they coursed in search of glimpses of arriving foreigners, who were themselves out to see and be seen. The most popular of these attractions were the Hungarians, who, as one English observer noted with some jealousy, were "possessed of the art of self-advertisement to a very high degree." "They and their blue and white ribbons seemed to be ubiquitous; if one did not meet them driving in a cab with the Hungarian flag at the mast-head, one found them blocking the traffic in a compact line stretched across the Rue de Stade."[69]

Greece itself had been "seized with a remarkable fit of athleticism." Impromptu contests unfolded "almost at every street corner. Sometimes one discovers infants putting a rude weight some six times too heavy for them; at other times one finds every man and boy in a quarter of the town long-jumping, with a policeman and a soldier to keep the course clear."[70] The authorities, too, it seemed, were persuaded "that the old times had come around again when there was nothing more serious to do than to outrun, outleap, and outwrestle."[71]

If every man and boy could suddenly give himself up to street-corner play, so too could they claim the right to judge the size and muscles of the foreigners and to compare them with those Greeks who were to represent them in the Games. The Greek throwers Gouskos and Versis had already emerged as folk heroes. Compatriots made it their business to turn up at their practice sessions to marvel and speculate, or else were certain to pass by the café on Constitution Square where each night Gouskos drank wine and held court.[72]

Added to the natural joy of release from work and domestic cares, the liberation of the streets, inversion of authority, the curiosity to see the foreigners, and the amusing novelty of athletics were still stronger emotional and historical themes. The timing of the Games fairly piled symbols of religious, political, and ethnic resurrection upon the Greeks, linking national pride and resurgence with emblems of international recognition. Not only was April 5 the Greek Easter Sunday—"as usual celebrated with pomp and noise . . . , the law prohibiting the sale of large torpedoes being in abeyance on that day"[73]—it happened to coincide with Western European Easter Sunday, an icon of Christian unity given material form by the much noticed association between the Dominican Fr. Didon and Orthodox patriarchs during events at the stadium. To top off Easter morning, Princess Marie announced her betrothal to Grand Duke George of Russia, an alliance which caused even more than the usual celebration given Russia's strategic position in the unending struggle of the Greek people with the Turks. Easter morrow was not only the day of rebirth for the Games, it was Greek Independence Day. The holiday was always the occasion for military parades, patriotic speeches, displays, and rejoicings, but "perhaps since its institution it never assumed such magnificence"[74] as it did with its linkage to the restoration of the Olympics. "This made a congeries of holidays almost bewildering to one wishing to be quite sure what he was celebrating, and gave to the period of Easter a character befitting the name given it by the Greeks, 'Lambri,' the brilliant."[75] A congeries, indeed, but not a patchwork: the same dominant themes and

festive emotions cross-cut and united all three public celebrations. The
trying circumstances Greece found herself in in quotidian life not only did
not detract from these themes, but made them more resonant. Nothing
like it had been known by modern Greeks,[76] and the new Olympic Games
basked in the "brilliance" of this extraordinary density of symbolic energies. The sustained and almost unmarred good feeling of the subsequent
Olympic Games owed as much to this general atmosphere as it did to the
attractiveness of "the Olympic Idea" and to the actual events themselves.

As Richardson realized, Easter and the Olympics were further linked
by a particular ritual. "Easter itself was made the *proagon* to the Games by
the unveiling of the statue of Averoff."[77] Despite a heavy rain that thoroughly drenched them, several thousand turned out for this ceremony in
the square outside the stadium. The statue of the "new Herod Atticus"
was a larger than life-size study in white marble, portraying Averoff
in frock coat with classical draping, right hand extended in a gesture that
seemed to be showing Athenians to their seats (see pl. 5). As Constantine
unveiled it, cries of "Long live Averoff!" and "Long live the nation!" broke
out. "Eyes grew moist with tears, hats were tossed in the air on all sides,
and an indescribable current of enthusiasm flowed through all the
ranks of these thousands of spectators."[78] Next, a wreath was laid by
Valaoritis, president of the Philharmonic Society of Athens, also endowed
by Averoff's generosity. Then, in a gesture that "electrified the crowd,"
the ubiquitous Hungarians, led by Kemeny, stepped forward and laid an
immense laurel wreath, trimmed in their national colors and inscribed in
Greek and Hungarian "To the Benefactor of the Olympic Games [from]
the Magyars." To the cheers and cries of "Long live Hungary!" the Hungarians responded with their "national hurrah."[79] Constantine and his
brothers then departed to the first of the many ovations they were to
receive over the next ten days. "Little by little" the crowd too trailed back
into the city for an evening of expectant celebration.

On that morning, Coubertin had heard mass in the Catholic cathedral,
where the sermon was preached by his friend Didon, who had journeyed
to Athens for the Games. Whether the baron was present for the stadium
dedication is unclear. On the one hand, it would not have been like him to
miss it, but on the other hand, he did not discuss it in his writings. The
day before, he, Balck, Kemeny, and Bikelas had convened in Coubertin's
rooms in the stylish Hotel Grande-Bretagne to grouse about the inadequacies of other I.O.C. members,[80] and doubtless too about the now-
obvious attempt by the Greek organizers to isolate and draw all attention
away from the I.O.C. On the morning of the opening ceremonies,
Coubertin, Balck, and Kemeny were joined by Boutowsky, Gebhardt,
and Guth-Jarkovsky. Bikelas, the only one of them who had a real role
with the organizing committee, was occupied elsewhere. As if to reassure

themselves that they were still in some command, the little I.O.C. discussed whether to award the 1904 Games to New York, Stockholm, or Berlin.[81] (See pl. 3.)

Meanwhile, outside the staid dignity of the Hotel Grande-Bretagne, the hubbub was building toward its first crescendo.

> From the early morning on, the movement and animation which reigned in Hermes and Stade streets and in Constitution Square, offered an indescribable spectacle. At every moment, there resounded joyous musical airs sent up by the Philharmonic societies of Zacynthos, Leucados, Larios, Patras, etc., who had come to take part in the festivities of the Olympic Games and who had all betaken themselves at that moment to Constitution Square. About 11 o'clock, the royal family and the foreign princes present in Athens went to the metropolitan cathedral, where a *Te Deum* was sung. All along its route the royal cortege was wildly applauded.[82]

While the groundlings chased the king through the streets, the well-to-do were chasing after tickets. No advance sale had been arranged, so all morning the organizing committee offices in the house of Melas, the mayor, were "literally beseiged by an immense crowd."[83] The tickets were cheap enough, one drachma for the upper tier, two for the lower (about 12¢ and 24¢),[84] but the demand was proving so great that "numerous and noisy" groups formed around those shrewd enough to arrive early to buy up whole blocs to resell. Scalping had made its appearance in Greece, and though "the police were obliged to intervene to prevent all attempts at speculation,"[85] it is doubtful that they had much success.

By noon, an immense crowd "of all ages and conditions" began "to flow toward the Stadium." Vehicles careened through the streets and continuous trains from Piraeus brought visitors staying on ships into the city.[86] "It was a joyous and motley concourse. The skirts and braided jackets of the *palikars* contrasted with the somber and ugly European habiliments. The women used large paper fans to shield them from the sun, parasols, which would have obstructed the view, being prohibited."[87] The sun shields were not needed as "clouds hung heavy and dark over the Stadion all afternoon."[88] Once again, however, the weather failed to dampen the festival spirit. Band music and the "piercing cries of the refreshment vendors"[89] punctuated the effervescent murmur of the streaming mass.

Yet amid the great and animated throng, "the most perfect order never ceased to reign."[90] "We never observed any confusion or disagreeable incidents of any kind," said Robertson, who chalked it up to Greek national character. "The Greeks are a patient people and allow themselves to be organized. The committee were fortunate in not having to deal with a north-country football crowd."[91] The policemen, horse guards, and soldiers had not to keep order but to organize it. On Olga and Herod Atticus boulevards, they prevented all but the carriages of the invited officials from approaching the stadium. Soldiers checked tickets at two locations and served as ushers, guiding the spectators to their seats[92] in the new "temple of athletic sports,"[93] which filled up an hour before events were scheduled to begin.

> The decoration of the Stadium was really splendid. At the entrance, were elevated masts topped by flags and ornamented with escutcheons; on each side of the facade were tripods copied from ancient art; all around the circumference of the Stadium were flagstaffs decorated with coats-of-arms; at each end of the sphendrome, the Hermes discovered in the ruins were placed. The tiers were covered with little cushions on which the spectators sat. In the arena and on the racing field, members of the diverse commissions, the senior officials, and other functionaries promenaded back and forth. The musicians next made their entry and played various pieces.[94]

"Brilliance" under dark and overcast skies; gay music against a background of sonorous murmuring; perfect order in mass disordering; exuberant decorations amid architectural lines of antique simplicity: in color and language too the scene afforded absolute contrasts relieved by little outbreaks of chromic and conversational joy. The predominantly dark clothing of the assembled framed in white Pentelicon marble[95] made eyes flow all the more to the plumes and flowers on the ladies' hats, the sashes and decorations on the soldiers' uniforms, the bright colors of the flags floating overhead, and the dull green center of the arena. Though "nineteen-twentieths of the mass were Greeks," "all the tongues of Europe were heard,"[96] and we may well imagine the pleasure and amusement when some common idiom—French, English, smiles, or gestures—allowed neighbors to communicate their impressions to one another.

It was an assembly such as had never been seen in the modern Mediterranean. Since it was constructed in stands and not seats, the capacity of the stadium was difficult to estimate, but all contemporary observers placed it between 40,000 and 70,000. Richardson guessed the number inside to have been "40,000 or more ... enough to stir that deep feeling caused by the presence of a multitude, the feeling which made Xerxes weep at the Hellespont."[97] Others, noting that all of the completed tiers of seats were filled, suggest a higher total. A throng at least again as large covered the surrounding hills, packed the square outside the stadium, as well as the neighboring streets. Szymiczek estimates the total crowd at 80,000;[98] Mandell at 120,000.[99] The true figure was probably somewhere in between. Until it was surpassed four days later—the day of the Marathon—it was one of the largest single assemblies for a peaceful celebration ever gathered in the modern world. It is difficult for us, who are used to such crowds, to imagine the impression made by such a mass of humanity, all the more so since it was the spirit of participation that drew them. (In these days before loudspeakers and radio, no more than a handful could have heard a word of the speeches and proclamations.) But we are helped by recalling that Athens had at the time a population of scarcely 130,000.[100] An entire city had been practically emptied, transported, and reassembled. It was, the official report repeated, "a magic spectacle."[101]

A little before three o'clock, a murmur from the square outside grew into a roar and cascaded into the stadium. The royal party had driven up. In the company of the king and queen were Princess Marie and her new fiancé, Princess Sophie, the king of Serbia, and the widow and daughters of Crown Prince Rudolph of Austria.[102] They were met by Constantine and his brothers, Delyannis and the Cabinet, the Greek organizing committee, and the I.O.C., including Coubertin. Revealingly, instead of the "I.O.C.," the official report notes the presence of "members of the various commissions" in the reception party. I.O.C. members were being treated as heads of their national delegations or else as technical officials, little more.[103] After flowers were presented to Olga and Marie, the procession entered the stadium to the strains of the Greek national anthem and the roar of the crowd now on its feet.[104] King George led the way in the uniform of an infantry general.[105] As he walked the length of the stadium, "accompanied all the way by the acclamations of this mass, he is said to have declared his emotion to have been so great that he could with difficulty compose himself for the great historic act of reopening the Olympic Games after they had been in abeyance for fifteen centuries."[106] Well might he have been moved: it was the greatest demonstration of popular approval during his entire reign. "The moment was gripping and the spectacle, indescribable," echoes the refrain of the official report.[107]

Reaching the tribune, the procession was greeted by "the court ladies and functionaries, the diplomatic corps, and the deputies."[108] The king and the queen, who was dressed all in white, took their places on the two marble thrones draped with red velvet. To their right sat the Cabinet, the deputies, the Orthodox bishops, "and some foreign ecclesiastics among whom was the celebrated Fr. Didon."[109] To the left sat the court, the foreign diplomatic corps, and "the representatives of the foreign commissions,"[110] back among whom was Pierre de Coubertin.

After a moment, Constantine arose, faced his father, and addressed a speech to him. He began, in Coubertin's bitter words, by "touching on the origin of the enterprise."[111]

Sire, the execution of the resolution of the International Congress of Paris, that the Olympic Games would be celebrated for the first time in Athens, imposed on our country [the task] of giving birth to and making these Games prosper.

Constantine then mentioned the obstacles overcome and Averoff's gift, hinted at his own capital role, and lost no chance to emphasize the royal tutelage of the great event.

> May God wish it, O King, that the restoration of the Olympic Games will draw closer the ties of reciprocal friendship between the Hellenic people and other peoples, whose representatives we are pleased to welcome here for the celebration of the Olympic Games. May God make it reanimate bodily exercises and national sentiment and contribute to forming a new generation of Greeks worthy of their ancestors.
>
> With this hope I pray Your Majesty to deign to proclaim the opening of the Olympic Games, which are going to be conducted under such happy auspices.[112]

At that, the king rose, and "in a sonorous voice,"[113] "sealed the restoration of the Olympic Games by pronouncing the sacramental formula."[114] "I proclaim the opening of the first international Olympic Games at Athens."[115] The crowd did not need to hear in order to know what had been done, and it let out a deafening cheer. Cannons roared and "a release of pigeons filled the stadium with their joyous flight."[116] Coubertin's pique at being so neglected was forgotten amid this extraordinary scene which he more than anyone could appreciate. "It was a thrilling moment. Fifteen hundred and two years before, the Emperor Theodosius had suppressed the Olympic Games, thinking, no doubt, that in abolishing this hated survival of paganism he was furthering the cause of progress; and here was a Christian monarch, amid the applause of an assemblage composed almost exclusively of Christians, announcing the formal annulment of the imperial decree; while a few feet away stood the archbishop of Athens, and Fr. Didon, the celebrated Dominican preacher, who, in his Easter sermon in the Catholic cathedral the day before, had paid elegant tribute to pagan Greece."[117] To Coubertin, it was a moment of pure *illud tempus* in which history and myth broke through to captivate and suffuse the present, a moment for which he had struggled for years and which justified his whole previous life. The edge of whatever self-pity he might still have felt over his treatment by the Greeks was further taken off when Gebhardt, the German, leaned over to him and said in English, "All that is your work."[118] Four more times, Coubertin was personally to witness the recreation of this glorious moment. After the debacles of 1900 and 1904, the heads of state were again to pronounce the "sacred formula" amid such pomp and symbolic splendor, in London, Stockholm, Antwerp, and Paris, in 1908, 1912, 1920, and 1924. But with one important difference: it would not be the head of the Games organizing committee who invited them to do so, but the president of the I.O.C., Pierre de Coubertin.

After London in 1908, the procession was to become a procession of the athletes. At these first opening ceremonies, the competitors, save those who were shortly to compete, were arrayed in two lines in the center of the arena. It is not clear whether they made a formal entry. The Olympic Hymn which now followed, was also to enter the tradition of Olympic opening ceremonies, along with the cannonade and the pigeons. That hymn, performed "as soon as silence had been reestablished,"[119] had been specially commissioned by the Hellenic organizing committee. The composer was Spyros Samaras; the lyricist, the influential poet and novelist Costis Palamis.[120]

> Immortal Spirit of antiquity, father of the true, the good, and the beautiful, descend, appear, shed over us thy light, upon this ground and under this sky, first witnesses to thy glory.
> Give light and vitality to these noble games: throw imperishable floral crowns to the victors in the running, wrestling, and discus, and with thy light animate hearts of steel! In thy light, plains, mountains, and seas shine in a roseate hue and form a vast temple to which the nations throng to adore thee, O immortal Spirit of antiquity.[121]

Samaras himself led the huge massed orchestra—composed of the army, navy, municipal, and provincial bands, augmented by strings—and the chorus of one hundred and fifty voices.[122] "The composition of Samaras obtained complete success. The melody, soft and slow at the beginning, growing little by little more animated, and finishing in a triumphant crescendo joining all the voices and instruments, produced the most grandiose effect. The hymn was frenetically applauded by the audience. All the spectators, and the King himself, demanded an encore; the applause was redoubled at the conclusion of the second performance."[123]

Today, we would speak of the spectators "settling back into their seats" for the games that followed. Few in the crowd, however, had ever seen a formal athletic contest. As the official report put it, "The curiosity of the public was at its height."[124] The genres of ritual and game were not yet marked as distinct performance types in the Olympics. For the first day, at least, the whole was likely experienced as a single continuous performance. Until the trumpet sounded, only the splitting up of the bands and their distribution into the stadium tiers—"from where, in the intermissions, they played marches"[125]—marked the transition to the games themselves.

The first competitors, the 100-meter men, entered the arena through the tunnel. I have already discussed, in reference to Olympia, the impression this journey through liminal space universally makes on athletes. Robertson waxed poetic about its special character at Athens.

The competitor, as he hurried through the gloom of the ancient tunnel, the Crypte, which led from his quarters on the hill behind to the arena, if he possessed a particle of imagination, felt himself now to be a Phayllus or a Phidippides, about to accomplish feats to excite the amazement, and arouse the suspicions, of all future times, now a martyr of the early Christian ages, whom a lion or a bear awaited where the gloom gave way to the sunlight.[126]

Clad in longish, loose-fitting shorts and light woolen jerseys with numbers "corresponding to the order of entry"[127] affixed to them, twenty-one contestants made their way to the starting line. There to greet them were the Ephors[128] and the *Hellanodikes*. While the Ephors were all Greek, the *Hellanodikes*, or jury, were international. Prince George presided over Kemeny, Gebhardt, Fabens, Manos, and R. Finis, an Englishman. Overseeing all was Constantine, who, as every eyewitness report avers, busied himself about everything. Constantine marched about in the uniform of an artillery officer, George, in that of a naval captain. Said Maurras, "These two princes brought all sorts of memories to mind. One could compare them to the sons of Nestor in beautiful Pylos, or to Prince Polydamus."[129] The starter was S. Arvanitis, and the official timekeeper, Charles Perry, an Englishman; that a Greek sent competitors off and an Englishman measured their performance is an appropriate symbol, in microcosm, of the history of Western athletic sport. Three heats were run, each won by an American: Lane, Burke, and Curtis.

The first final of the day was the triple jump, an event little known in England, but practiced in the United States and Greece.[130] The Frenchman Tuffère was leading the competition, with the Greek Persakis in second place, when it came the turn of James Connolly of Harvard and Suffolk. He took the crowd aback by tossing down his cap a meter or so beyond Tuffère's mark. Who but an American collegian could have committed an act of such arrogance? It was reminiscent of those athletes who used to arrive at Olympia with their already carved victory statues in tow. Robertson, for one, knew his myths too well to have ever tempted the gods of the stadium with an act of such hubris. But Connolly, the indifferent student and Yankee Protestant, either knew little history or cared little for it, and he shortly made good his boast, leaping 45'11¾", just beyond the cap.[131] "It's a miracle, It's a miracle!" voices in the crowd were said to have proclaimed.[132] The Olympic Games had their first champion since Barasdates of Armenia, who is said to have won the boxing in 369 A.D.[133]

The first victory ceremony was then conducted. The American flag, followed by Connolly's number, was run up the central mast at the entry portal of the stadium by Greek sailors stationed there for the purpose. In these first Olympics, the victory and prize-giving ceremonies were separate, the latter conducted en masse on the final day. Not until the 1932 Los Angeles Games were the two combined into the definitive victory ceremony we know today.[134] The throng applauded, but its attentions were jarred and drawn away by unknown sounds. The sailors from the *San Francisco*, students at the American School in Athens, and the rest of the American team were delivering themselves lustily of college and club locomotive cheers. The Greeks had never heard anything quite like it, and were apparently astonished by this exotic cultural form of adulation. By the end of the week, it was all too familiar to them, amusing, and, according to most reports, rather popular. The crowds were said to request these performances from Americans they met in passing in the streets, and even to have attempted to join in. Maurras, for his part, despised the yells as barbaric, as he despised everything American he saw at the Games. "In ancient Athens," he pointedly remarked, "the Scythians were good for nothing but policemen."[135]

Next, heats in the 800 meters were run, to the consternation of Robertson and surely others, there being scarcely nine competitors.[136] The preliminaries were won by the Australian "Englishman" Flack and the Frenchman Lermusiaux, whom the Americans found altogether amusing. When asked how he managed to train simultaneously for the 100-meter, 800-meter, and Marathon, for all of which he was entered, Lermusiaux responded, "One day, I run a leetle way, vairy queek. Ze next day, I run a long way, vairy slow." In the 800 meters, as in all his races, he added white gloves to his toilette. When asked about this, he replied, "Ah-hah! Zat is because I run for ze king."[137] The legend of Lermusiaux doubtless had gained something in the telling by the time anyone got round to writing it down. Though neither was party to the other, what Maurras was doing to the Americans in his reports to Paris, the Americans were doing to the French, in the person of Lermusiaux, in their reports back home.

After the 800-meter heats, all attention turned to the discus, which promised the first Greek victory. Not only was it the most recognizably classical and Greek of the events, but the municipal attraction and hero Versis was entered. Nowhere else in the world was the discus practiced or even known, but eight foreign athletes, drawn by its classical allure, entered anyway. Among them was Garrett of Princeton. Some months earlier Sloane had sent him to the library to peruse volumes on classical antiquity. Garrett then tried throwing "what he thought was a reproduction of a classical discus. It was a slug of metal some twelve inches in diameter, an inch thick, and was, it developed, entirely unwieldy."[138] Garrett abandoned the notion. But once in Athens, he happened upon a specimen of the discus, two kilos in weight, and rather more aerodynamic. The day before the event he asked Coubertin whether he ought to enter, fearing that he would appear "pretentious and ridiculous" in a competition for which he had never trained. But the baron, who took a special interest in Sloane's charges, encouraged him.[139]

Each competitor had three throws. Versis retired after two, leading the contest at 94'5". P. Paraskevopoulos then delighted the crowd by throwing 95'. But Garrett dashed their hopes by hurling the plate 95'7¾". However, when the stars and stripes were run up, and the "P-R-I-N-C-E-T-O-N, Rahs!" broke out, the crowd displayed the generosity and good sportsmanship that all who witnessed the Games took pains to comment on.

How had Garrett "beat the Greeks at what was regarded as their own game?"[140] Coubertin attributed the victory to the "perfection of his general bodily preparation."[141] Robertson was more specific and nearer the truth. "The American won simply because he was accustomed to the throwing of weights, and knew how to bring his strength and weight to bear on the missile. The Greek had brought the knack of throwing to greater perfection, but one could see that he did not know how to apply any large portion of his strength to the throw."[142] Whether or not, as Olympic folklore has it, the Greeks adopted their style from contemplating Myron's *Discobolos*, they threw prettily, but entirely with the arm. In matter of strength, therefore, the 95' of Paraskevopoulos was a greater achievement than the 95'7" of Garrett. But Garrett cared nothing for style, only for victory. He let "Yankee practicality" and what Coubertin often aptly referred to as "muscular imagination" dictate his crouch and spin technique.

The final events of the day, the 400-meter heats, were won by two more Americans, Burke and Jamison. As Richardson wrote:

> It is no wonder that the victories of the Americans became the talk of the town. The Hungarians, who alone wore a distinctive mark on the street—straw hats with uniform bands—had scored the first point in the favor of the populace. . . . And they remained popular all through the festival. But now they were relegated to second place. The American athletes were the heroes of the hour. They were lionized and followed by enthusiastic crowds wherever they went in the evening. One paper accounted for their prowess by the consideration that in their blood "they joined to the inherited athletic training of the Anglo-Saxon the wild impetuosity of the red-skin."[143]

The papers also reported them to be employing special "American prayers."[144] So began the spate of popular ethnography and national character reckoning which flowed through this and all subsequent Olympics and which, as I shall argue in another volume, is not the least cause of the immense significance of the Olympics.

The second day opened with more of the same. Curtis and the Englishman Goulding took the hurdles heats; Clark (20'10"), Garrett, and Connolly, the first three places in the long jump;[145] and Burke (54.2) and Jamison, the 400 meters. In the shot put, the Greek disappointment of the previous day was not only repeated, but compounded by a terrible mistake.

The favorite was Gouskos, "whom the crowd called Hermes for his fine form and motions."[146] But on his very first throw, Garrett got off an effort of 36'9¾", and Gouskos could never match it. With each of his throws, the Greek improved, "owing to his careful imitation of his American rival,"[147] but his last put fell a scant ¾" short. Meanwhile, the crowd could scarcely perceive this, and convinced that "Hermes" had triumphed, it let out a joyous roar that convinced the sailors at the victory mast. When they ran up the Greek flag and Gouskos' number, the crowd took the victory as official and roared anew, only to sink into murmurs of bitter disappointment when the blue and white was lowered in favor of the stars and stripes. "For the first time one felt the real heaving of the heart of the multitude. . . . The revulsion of feeling which came with the speedy correction of the error was all the more painful."[148] Surely, many had begun to fear that Greece should never have her *Olympionikes*. Yet, as Robertson wrote: "The behavior of the crowd under very trying circumstances was most exemplary. . . . This may have been partly due to their temperament, which is not in the least emotional [both other writers and subsequent events gainsay him on this]; but it must also be attributed to a great extent to gentlemanly feeling."[149] The Americans softened the blow by putting up a cheer for Gouskos, but Richardson likely comes nearer the truth about the peculiar "gentlemanliness" the Greeks showed the Americans.

> The closer the tie and the more intimate the acquaintance the sharper often was the rivalry.
> The Americans were . . . evidently great favorites with the audience, partly, perhaps, because they lived so far away as to take the place occupied in Homer by "the blameless Æthiopians," almost beyond the sphere of their jealousies and antipathies. An old priest who sat two seats in front of me kept turning and asking with smiles, "Is that one of yours?" adding, after an affirmative answer, "Yours are doing well."[150]

How constant all this has remained through the history of the Games. In each one, the host audience seems to single out one foreign team for special kindness and attention. Most often, it has indeed been a people exotic, distant, and unthreatening. In recent Olympics, the Africans have filled the role, beginning with that "blameless Æthiopian" Abebe Bikela, who won the Marathon, barefoot, in the streets of Rome.

And, too, during my field work in Montreal, I found Richardson's scene with the priest repeated time and again. There is a natural assumption that every member of the audience is glad for his own, and neighboring foreigners in the stadium are solicitous for each other's champions. It is an unwritten but elaborate code of Olympic spectatorial etiquette. But, of course, there are spoilsports too; and they were present in Athens. A Greek sitting next to Maurras informed him in bad English that in the cycling, "one of my compatriots, M. Flamand, had won the prize. I read on his face that he was certain that he would be giving me extreme pleasure." But Maurras was deep in his funk over the Games, embarrassed by the invisibility of the French, and hating all things Anglo-Saxon, including English spoken by a well-intentioned Greek. "I gave him my best thanks in the idiom of Shakespeare, which I took good care to mutilate. Alas!, even distorted, what could the Muses have said, hearing such a conversation under their hill."[151]

Neither national character nor sociological explanations of Greek generosity appealed to the *Spectator*. To the degree that it concerned itself at all with the reaction of modern Greeks, it attributed that reaction to a mistaken and misguided nativism. "Of all the modern nations, the Greeks, having no particular present, care most to reconnect themselves with their own glorious past." But there was "nothing classical about the celebration" of the Games.

> One wonders what Pericles would have said if he could have known that when the Olympic games were revived two thousand three hundred years after his death, nearly all the honours of the first day would be carried away by barbarians from a continent the existence of which he had never dreamed, and would, indeed, with his notion of the limits of the ocean, have regarded as impossible. If he knew all that was known in his time he may have speculated for an instant on the conceivable existence of a far-away island in the Atlantic, inhabited by monsters or by demi-gods, but of a vast continent under the same conditions as our own he can have had as little idea as he had that the unknown land would be populated by Britons and Iberians, or that they would have so mastered the secrets of nature that they could send accounts of a victory or defeat at Athens instantaneously under the ocean to their own abodes. The expansion of the world as he knew it by continuous discovery, and the contraction of the world through new methods of communication are perhaps the greatest material changes which have occurred since his time, and one wonders whether he would have welcomed the prospect of them, or regarded it only as something which fatigued his mind and terrified him for the future of his race. "The barbarians, then," he would have thought, "are to capture the gods, to win by their favor new worlds, to tear down fire from heaven, to beat us even in the struggles of the stadion; what will become of Greece?"[152]

The modern Greeks did not, of course, think like Pericles, nor did classical conceits limit their enjoyment of the performances themselves. But they did devoutly wish for a Greek victory in the stadium, and their extreme hospitality, sportsmanship, and good feeling toward the Americans would not, perhaps, have survived too many more Yankee triumphs. As Richardson noted, "The danger now was that if the few American spectators made too much demonstration, this good-will might be turned to envy."[153]

One such "dangerous" episode occurred when the Greek papers began running the story that, after his victory, Garrett had telegraphed Princeton: "Guskos [sic] conquered Europe, but I conquered the world." A reporter subsequently confessed that he had invented the telegram, "but he took great pride in it; for he said it was what Garrett ought to have said."[154] By the time the story "made its way through the salons and cafes of Athens" to Maurras, Garrett had been transformed into Connolly and the message into "The Greeks conquered Europe, but I conquered the whole world." This gave Maurras a special opportunity for his barbed wit. "I've always said that Tarascon was an American city."[155]

In the festive atmosphere of the "salons and cafes" that week, the good spirit might have survived even this, but, most mercifully, the final three events of the second day were won by non-Americans. Jensen, the Dane, took the two-handed weightlifting (245¾ lbs.), and the Englishman Lawrenceton Elliot, the one-handed (156½ lbs.). Moreover, during the competition, Prince George, "an easily recognizable figure, owing to his height and athletic build," "lifted with ease an enormous dumb-bell and tossed it out of the way. The audience broke into applause, as if it would have liked to make him the victor of the event."[156] In the 1500 meters, the final contest of the day, Flack, the Australian (4:33.2),[157] beat Blake, the American (4:35.4), with Lermusiaux third. With the passage to the mast of the Danish flag and the Union Jack, ideology at last promised to be matched in performance, or as Coubertin put it, "the international character of the institution . . . well guarded by the results of the contests."[158]

On Wednesday, competitions opened in other sports and other venues away from the stadium, and the index of Olympic champions broadened further to other nations. The king and the queen opened the shooting contest at Kallithea, the latter by firing the first ceremonial shot from a flower-draped rifle. There were 150 Greek and 10 foreign entries,[159] so nothing was decided that day. Eventually the Paine brothers were to win the 25-meter and 50-meter pistols, and three Greeks, S. Phrangoudis, P. Karassevadis, and G. Orphanidis, the 25-meter rapid-fire pistol, the 25-meter military revolver, and the 200-meter rifle shot, respectively.

I have found no account of the attendance at the shooting, but it was probably slight. The velodrome, however, was filled to its capacity[160] on Wednesday. The king inaugurated the new facility on the plain of Neon Phaleron, and, "on the coldest day since February,"[161] Léon Flamand (Flameng, by some accounts) won the 100 kilometers despite a terrible fall near the end. During the race, according to Eyquem, the Greek Colettis' machine required repair, and Flamand halted to await his rival. This brought cries of "Zito Flamand" and "Vive la France" from the crowd,[162] and inaugurated a particular genre of sportsmanly display later repeated in several Olympics. On subsequent days, Flamand was joined in victory by his countryman P. Masson, who took the sprint and the 2,000 and 10,000 meters, and by an Austrian, Felix Schmall, who covered 315 kilometers in the twelve-hour race. The road race, held toward the end of the festival, was won by a Greek, A. Konstantinidis, who covered the 54-odd miles in 3:22:31. (See pls. 11–13.)

Tennis eliminations opened Wednesday as well, at the courts of the "Athens Tennis Club." Attendance here seems to have been sparse,[163] limited no doubt to foreigners and the handful of well-to-do Greeks who had seen the game played in the fashionable quarters of the Continent. Eventually, Boland, the Englishman, emerged victorious in the singles, and in an episode rare in Olympic history, he combined with the German Thraun to win the doubles. I have found no other example of an "international" competitive unit in the Games, such is the Olympic commitment to the organizational and symbolic representation by nation-state alone.

The fencing also had begun in the Zappeion, and in the course of several days, before a small audience of notables often including the king, E. Gravelotte of France and the Greeks Iannis Georgiadis and L. Pyrgos won the épée, the saber, and the épée for *professeurs* (coaches) respectively.

Athenians awoke Thursday morning to find Pentelicon "covered with snow nearly down to its base, an event probably unparalleled for this time of year."[164] The cold, a brief lull in interest, and the scheduling of only one running event (the 800 meters, won by Flack in 2:11 over a Hungarian) amid the gymnastics greatly reduced the stadium crowd.

The first events were the team parallel and horizontal bars, and the team long vaulting. A Greek squad offered the little band of Turners their only competition, but Hofmann's Germans were readily declared the winners. According to Maurras, after the results of the first competition were announced, "the entire crowd was on its feet crying 'adika! adika!' ('injustice! injustice!')." The Greeks, says Maurras, "thought the judges to have judged poorly."[165] According to one eyewitness the Greek squads appeared to have "kept better form,"[166] but, as Robertson and Mandell point out, the crowd was ignorant of "the recondite rules of turning competition."[167] Then, too, as is still the case today, the "subjective," group judging of gymnastics left room for disagreement.

The victories of this day depended on the judgements of a committee, and however fair the award might be, it was after all, a matter of opinion, and the spectators seeing that the award resulted sometimes from discussion and compromise, kept their own opinion, which was sometimes at variance with that which found expression at the mast-head. The real athletic contest is that which is decided by measurements and time-keeping beyond the possibility of dispute, affording results which the spectators can see for themselves. Such is pre-eminently the run. This, in the present Games, as always and everywhere, evoked the keenest attention.[168]

Next came the individual events, won by the Germans Flatow (parallel bars), Weingärtner (horizontal bar), Schumann (long vault), and the Swiss Zutter (pommel horse). The Greek crowd had quickly returned to its customary good feeling and sportsmanship. "Nevertheless, the good work of two or three of these german [sic] and prussian [sic] barbarians ended by winning general admiration," wrote Maurras. "That's because they had no French contestants before them. Realizing this, I was able to abandon myself to the common sentiment."[169]

If the gymnastics troubled the crowd because of the judging and Maurras because the winners were German, they bothered the trackman Robertson because they were not athletic. He vigorously protested against the idea of the equality "of the different branches" of sport, that Coubertinian dictum on whose account the baron ironically was defending his old nemeses, the gymnasts. Wrote Robertson:

> The climax was perhaps reached in connection with the vaulting horse. There were two olive branches, medals and diplomas granted for this exercise, one for leaping the horse, the other for maneuvering upon a horse with pommels. The...first...seemed to the athletic and un-gymnastic eye to be puerile,...the second...little less so.... Yet the winners received the same olive branch as the winner of the 100 meters; even the seconds in these absurd gyrations gained the same laurel branch as the second in the Hurdles. They were proclaimed Olympian victors, they returned to their native Germany and Switzerland with a halo of glory, while the second in the 1500 meters, for instance,... had to recross the Atlantic bearing with him the consciousness of merit alone.

Robertson wanted the gymnastics combined into an all-around event, for "an Olympic wreath is far too precious a thing to be squandered on good form in hopping over a horse or swarming up a rope."[170]

Unless, perhaps, it fell to a Greek. For this is how, at last, the Greek flag rose to the summit of the mast. I. Mitropoulos won the iron rings, and the crowd, smallish though it was, shook the stadium with its joy. "Then the difference was made manifest between generous applause hitherto bestowed on foreigners and real delight in victory, all the more intense for the long delay and disappointment. Then it was that if the seats had not rested upon solid earth they might have come down. The young victor after being carried about on the shoulders of the crowd went on to the dressing-room kissed by his father and his brother as he passed them. At last the Greeks had an Olympionikes."[171] Andriacopoulos soon followed with a victory in the rope climbing, and word of the Greek victories in the shooting came shortly thereafter. But as Richardson put it with notable understatement, "Greater things were yet to come."[172]

While the athletic events were "the kernel of everything,"[173] celebrations of different kinds kept the festival spirit burning brightly through the town.[174] "Every night while the games were in progress the streets of Athens were illuminated. There were torch-light processions, bands played the different national hymns, and the students of the university got up ovations under the windows of the foreign athletic crews."[175] There were also "nocturnal festivities on the Acropolis, where the Parthenon was illuminated with colored lights, and at the Piraeus; where the vessels were hung with Japanese lanterns."[176] These street fêtes were open to all the strollers of the cité féerique. Many banquets were also given for notables, Olympic officials, and athletes. "The mayor of Athens gave one at Cephissia, a little shaded village at the foot of Pentelicus. M. Bikelas, the retiring president of the international committee, gave another at Phalerum. The king himself entertained all the competitors, and the members of the committees, three hundred guests in all, at a luncheon in the ballroom of the palace."[177] There were also "some intellectual accompaniments of the occasion," as Richardson noted. Sophocles' Antigone "was presented twice at Athens and once at the Peiraeus in the original text, with music for the choruses by Mr. Sakellarides, a Greek well-versed in Byzantine music, who also with his fine voice and boundless enthusiasm officiated as chorus leader." The newspapers made merry at Sakellarides' pretensions, and "for the first hour of the first presentation the theatre was in a hub-bub, but Sophokles silenced it." The music was not only not bad, but "achieved a triumph." However, Richardson was dismayed that the actors playing Kleon and Antigone "put little soul into their parts," and so "a fine opportunity was lost."[178] Richardson also mentioned a "procession of native and foreign scholars" to Konolos, where, "with appropriate ceremonies," wreaths were laid on the "somewhat neglected monuments of Karl Ottfried Müller and Charles Lenormont."[179] All this allowed the professor to satisfy himself that "the visiting contestants were forced into contact with history, and their visit to Greece was an education."[180]

Egine Loues

For all the ludic celebration of the athletes at the evening fêtes, focusing festively roused spirits upon the next day's contests, and for all the novelty of the *agones* themselves, which made them objects of joyful curiosity as much as distinctive performances with their own determined and "serious" mood and style, the festal and agonal dimensions of *bonheur* and *prouesse* had not yet fully interpenetrated. Moreover, since the opening day, the awesome, spectacular quality of the Olympics had dwindled. The crowd had disaggregated into social segments with their own performances—banquets, theater, scholarly ceremonies, small-public matches such as tennis and fencing—or else into a heterogenous mass by the centrifugal action of the festival, which engaged all but never focused their corporate attentions. In addition, the sense of ritual connection with transcendent forces, divine or historical, had only here and there recurred since the opening ceremonies on Monday. In language I will employ extensively in another work, the performative genres of game, rite, festival, and spectacle had not yet coalesced into a single, unified experience of feeling and meaning.[181] Had such a moment not transpired, we have every reason to suspect that subsequent Olympic history would have been different indeed. But on Friday, in one dramatic, epic event—the Marathon—that moment came.

In certain respects, the climax had been scripted in advance. Since Bréal first proposed it at the Sorbonne congress, Coubertin assiduously promoted the Marathon race in all his Olympic speeches, programs, and announcements. Not only was it "on the schedule," but the classical conceit behind it had so fully taken root that no contemporary commentator saw fit to challenge its "authenticity." Neither the professional classicist Professor Richardson, who celebrated the Games, nor the skeptical columnist of the *Spectator*, who criticized them for being insufficiently classical, expressed the slightest doubt about the race's pedigree. In fact, of course, it was chartered in wishful legend, more than in history.

The ancient Greeks, with their implacable sense of the golden mean, would have judged a formal race of such length barbaric and abominable, with neither goodness nor beauty in it. The *dolichos*, the longest of the ancient running events, never extended beyond 4,800 meters at Olympia,[182] twelve laps of the track (24 stades) and not a road race. Which is not to say that ancient runners on a mission did not cover great distances. Indeed, it is said of Argeus, *dolichos* winner at the 113th Olympiad in 328 B.C., that he announced his own victory in Argos the very same day.[183] There are also many indications in the Greek texts of heralds and couriers traversing great distances to deliver military or civic dispatches. Here, of course, lies the origin of the Marathon legend. Herodotus gives the name

of Pheidippides to the herald sent to summon the Spartans to battle at
Marathon. He is said to have covered the 160 miles in less than 48
hours.[184] A second episode has to do with an Athenian who, returning
from abroad, ran out to join the army in time for the battle, then ran back
to Athens to pronounce the famous words *chairete, nikōmen* ("Rejoice, we
conquer"), whereupon he expired on the spot. Plutarch gives him the
name of Eucles,[185] but other names are known. At least as early as Lucian,
the two episodes were joined in memory, and Pheidippides became the
hero who announced Athens's and Greece's greatest victory.[186] In this
form, the classicists and poets of the eighteenth and nineteenth centuries
received and maintained the story.[187] By transforming it into a formal
contest, Bréal and Coubertin "revived" the run from the village of
Marathon to the Panathenaic stadium, a distance of about 24 miles, 1,500
yards, down along the sea, through Raphena, Pikermi, Stavros, and
Chalandri, although more recent scholarship makes it seem probable
that the original route was the longer and more hilly one from Tymbos
(the tomb of the Athenian dead) west through the hills, past the ancient
shrine of Dionysus, around Pentelicon, and down to Athens through
Kephesia and Maroussi.[188]

By the day of the race, interest in the Marathon had grown monumental. Robertson reported that "this event was reckoned the chief feature of
the meeting, and in many ways it deserved its position. It possessed
greater historical interest than any other of the competitions, and was, no
doubt, also the greatest criterion of endurance."[189] Richardson too noted
that "the run from Marathon was felt by all the Greeks to be the principal
event of the Games," calling it "the one coveted honor."[190] There is ample
evidence that these were not retrospective opinions. The Friday crowd
was immense, surpassing that of opening day. The stadium was full "to its
utmost capacity, i.e. with 50,000 people."

> But outside and above the enclosing wall of the Stadion, especially on
> the west side, where the hill runs up much higher than this wall, were
> congregated from seven to ten thousand more, poor people, a sea of
> downturned faces, reminding one of those old Athenians who, not
> getting into the theatre, contented themselves with "the view from the
> poplar." Many more stood outside the entrance to the Stadion, just
> across the Ilissos, on ground even lower than the floor of the Stadion,
> where they could see nothing of what was going on inside, but could
> only catch something of the spirit of the occasion from proximity. On
> Friday probably nearly one hundred thousand people were massed in
> and about the Stadion [all contemporary observers concur]; besides
> which the whole road to Marathon was lined with spectators.[191]

Since no one was able to estimate the numbers of this latter category, it is
impossible to place an upper limit on the crowd size. We are safe in
thinking that at least 120,000 had turned out for the event.

They had come in the devout hope of witnessing a Greek victory. Coubertin reported that "as the great day approached, women offered up prayers and votive tapers in the Churches, that the victor might be Greek!"[192] Rich Athenians were said to have pledged great sums of money to any Greek who could win the Marathon, and Maurras reports that on the eve of the race, one "Mlle. Y.," said to be the most beautiful daughter of the Athenian bourgeoisie, "publicly pledged her heart and her hand to the victor, if he was Greek."[193] The Marathon had become "a truly national test,"[194] and, added Richardson, Greek "national pride would have been deeply touched at losing it."[195] As Maurras wrote: "A sort of mystical sense had become attached to it. Fear and hope made the hearts of our assembled Athenians flutter. Not only in the Stadium, but the surrounding hills, the roads and streets, trembled with anxiety and fever."[196] According to some, Greeks had begun practicing for the event as much as a year earlier.[197] The summons had reached well out into the provinces. "Even in the remote districts of Thessaly young peasants prepared to enter as contestants."[198] The rumor that three such lads had died in training for the terrible and semisacred ordeal did nothing to diminish the "mystical sense" that surrounded it.[199]

As the Games approached, trial races were held over the distance, and a Greek team led by Charilaos Vasilakos was selected. But so great was the Greek obsession to win the Marathon that the officials violated the rules—entries being officially closed—and held a second qualifying run. According to Robertson, "A few days only before the Games the Greek authorities seem to have become alarmed at the prospect of foreign competition in the Marathon Race, and especially at the fame of Mr. Flack, and, like Nicias before the last sea-fight at Syracuse, thought that perhaps they had not yet done all that was possible."[200] But Flack, by Robertson's own account, had not arrived in Athens until March 31, and his victories in the 800 and 1,500 meters were well before him. It may be doubted that it was he who spurred the Greek committee to its "quite exceptional" tampering with the rules. And on this, Robertson seems to protest too much. It is not clear that any foreign competitor who wished to stand for the race at the last minute would have ben denied. In any case, among the entries added after this second trial was one Spiridon Loues. The Greeks now had their best enlisted for the struggle.

But for all its "scriptedness," the Marathon was anything but a "ritual game" in the anthropological sense of a game whose outcome is known in advance.[201] A race of such length, under such psychological conditions, was an utter novelty. None of the foreigners had ever tried it, and training, in the strict sense, was unknown. The Western European "experts" were so sure of its dangers that Coubertin and his colleagues would have cancelled it had not the idea taken such passionate and total hold over everyone.[202] The competitors mounted the carriages on Thursday night to carry them to Marathon for a race that had taken on epic themes and proportions. The claims of justice were all on the side of the Greeks, but against them were arrayed the claims of skill, as the drama of the discus had shown. Against the claims of romance were arrayed those of physiology. All this pivoted on the legs and lungs, the *prouesse*, of a handful of anonymous Greeks. Their names were barely known, not a one of them a "pre-hero" like Gouskos or Versis. Few Athenians and none of the foreigners had laid eyes on any of them.

"Not a one of us," said Coubertin, "believed that the winner would be [a Greek]," though he, like everyone else, longed for this. As Giraudoux was to remark about the Olympic Games, behind every actual winner there often stands a moral winner. In the first Marathon, it was devoutly wished that these two victors would be the same man, but in modern athletic contests, where no one is sure if gods still care to intervene, the prize would go to the "best" man, and there was no cause for confidence that the best man would prove a Greek. But here was another great irony. For once, the philhellenes failed to look for omens in the ancient texts. Had they returned to their Plutarchs, they would have found, after his description of the first courier from Marathon, the following passage: "Suppose that some goatherd or shepherd upon a hill or height had been a distant spectator of the [battle] and had looked down upon the great event, too great for any tongue to tell, and had come to the city as a messenger, a man who had not felt a wound nor shed a drop of blood, and yet had insisted that he should have such honors as Cynegeirus received, or Callimachus, or Polyzelus..."[203] Had they looked to this passage, they might have convinced themselves that a Greek victory was not assured, but was fated.

The stadium events opened with gestures of good will toward the Greeks "by the American athletes displaying little Greek flags besides their own and the distinctive marks of orange and black for Princeton and the unicorn's head for the Boston Athletic Association."[204] A parade of American victories followed. Burke took the 100 meters in 12 seconds, with Hofmann, the German, just behind (see pl. 10). Next Clark (5'11¼"), Connolly, and Garrett repeated in the high jump their previous "slam" in the long jump, with the latter two exchanging places. In the 110-meter hurdles, Curtis (17.6) edged out the favorite, Grantley Goulding of England. This defeat rankled Robertson, who persisted in believing his countryman "the better hurdler." "His defeat was due partly to the fact that the race was run on cinders, in the American style, to which he was unaccustomed, and partly to a mistake at the start, which lost him at least two yards."[205] Not a single world record was broken in the track events at the 1896 Games. Robertson was surely right in attributing this in large part to the conditions and layout of the track. It was too soft on top and too hard underneath (the cinders not having had time to settle and water being unavailable to treat it), and the tightness of the turns around the ancient *Hermes* was so pronounced that the 400-meter runners had almost to come to a stop to negotiate them. Robertson thought that the layout cost three seconds in the 400, four seconds in the 800, and eight seconds in the 1500.[206]

The pole vault, which began next, "was immeasurably drawn out by the bar being lifted inch by inch for Greek competitors, long before the Americans, Hoyt and Tyler, had felt called upon to take off their 'sweaters' and really compete."[207] The skein of American victories must have transported the mood of the immense crowd of Greeks back to opening day. Doubtless, the Greek competitors in the hurdles, the high jump, and the pole vault served momentarily to distract the crowd's attentions, but the real drama was unfolding elsewhere. As everyone knew, the runners had left Marathon at two o'clock. "The one hundred thousand people waiting for them in the Stadion could know nothing of the stages of the contest,"[208] and the vaulting of Hoyt and Tyler could do little to assuage the "trembling anxiety and fever."

> In the Stadium, the spectators were plunged into all the anxieties of waiting. After 4:30, the impatience could no longer be withstood. In spite of all the interest presented by the various phases of the pole vault, it couldn't long hold the attention of the crowd. All of a sudden the rumor spread that the Australian Flack was coming first: the news had been carried in by the German bicyclist Geedrich. A sorrowful mourning spread over every face and the general discouragement translated itself into a long silence.[209]

But shortly thereafter Major Papadiamantopoulos, the starter of the race himself, galloped up to the stadium and was seen to rush toward the royal boxes and excitedly blurt out a message to George. "The king, exceedingly agitated, half rose and no one around him could keep his seat."[210] "Elleen! Elleen!"[211]: it was a Greek.

> The news soon spread with the speed of light, an immense Vivat! rose from every breast to the sky; at the same moment resounded the cannon that announced the arrival of the Greek victor. The spectators then no longer understood anything, neither caution, nor order, nor remonstrance; everyone was on their feet staring fixedly toward the entrance to the Stadium; the same emotion reigned outside of the enclosure, and when the prefect of police on horseback, entirely overcome with emotion, announced that a Greek was the victor, this news was received with uninterrupted acclamations.[212]

Maurras described the incomparable scene this way:

> An enormous agitation shook the masses, an immense *Nenikikamen!*

"We have won." The bourgeois Athenians [were] as enthusiastic as the
humblest laborer, the old as the young. Flags were wildly waved, cries
and singing conveyed the magnetic joy of a people. . . . Each one knew,
but each one wished to see. Animated by the wind, the great shadows of
the cypresses and pines that limited the view from the Stadium, at that
moment, undulated less grandly and less profoundly than the human
forest spread out over every slope.[213]

The joy of the crowd doubled and redoubled, but in such moments of
absolute and dramatic fulfillment, the eye is the sole organ of belief.[214] "At
the end of several minutes which seemed like centuries, a certain movement was noticed at the Stadium entrance, where the officers and committee members had hastened to betake themselves."[215] A roar came
flowing down Herod Atticus Street and burst into the stadium, and with
it came its source, a tiny figure, "dressed in a jersey of blue and white, the
colors of Greece,"[216] "sunburnt and covered with dust."[217] It was Loues.

Some twenty-five contestants had toed the line in Marathon, three
hours earlier (see pl. 14). Papadiamantopoulos had made his speech and
fired his pistol at three minutes, thirty seconds, before two o'clock. Maurras
supplies this precise time.[218] Since there is no reason for him to have
invented it and since, of course, he was not present in person at the start,
he must have got it from the papers the next day. Its recording there is
indicative of the pains taken to fix every detail of the great national
triumph in the public memory.

Escorted by a cavalry squad, a hospital wagon, and cycle-mounted
seconds and officials, the runners took off, and Lermusiaux burst immediately into the lead. The first ten kilometers were slightly downhill
and the Frenchman kept up a furious pace. "Along the route, the inhabitants of the different Attic villages stationed themselves, awaiting
with lively interest the passing of the runners whom they saluted and
encouraged without distinctions as to nationality, and to whom they
offered refreshments."[219] Through Nea Makri, Agios Andreas, and
Raphena, the runners passed. This second ten kilometers was only
slightly uphill, and Lermusiaux did not relent. It is said that he reached
Pikermi, twenty-two kilometers and over halfway, in fifty-five minutes,[220]
an extraordinary pace by any standard. By Pikermi, he had fashioned a
three-kilometer lead over Flack, his nearest rival. Behind Flack came
Blake, the American, Kellner, the Hungarian, and the pack of Greeks, led
by Lavrentis of Maroussi, Loues' fellow villager. Loues himself was well
back and was said by the official report to have taken a glass of wine in
Pikermi, inquired about those ahead of him, and "affirmed with the most
perfect conviction that he would catch and pass them."[221]

From Pikermi, the route turned uphill, with a hundred fifty meters of
altitude to be gained in ten kilometers, and the pace and physical agony

began to take their toll. Blake, his feet bloody and his mind confused, dropped out scarcely a kilometer beyond Pikermi, and a number of Greeks abandoned the race as well. Kellner and Lavrentis slowed, and Vasilakos overtook them. A Greek was now in third place, but well behind the leading two. Up front, Lermusiaux was coming back to Flack. The Frenchman was still leading at Karavati, whose peasants crowned him with a floral wreath under a triumphal arch they had erected for the occasion.[222] The priests, here and there along the route, who offered incense from their thuribles,[223] were likely present in Karavati too, but their prayers did Lermusieux no good. Just beyond the village, the incline increased, and he began to drift about and stagger. A countryman named Guisel rode too close on his bicycle and knocked Lermusiaux down. As he struggled to rise, Flack went past him and into the lead.[224] The pace Lermusiaux had set had been suicidal, and his condition must have been awful indeed. But with a final act of courage, he rose and carried on. At the thirty-two-kilometer mark, near Agia Paraskevi at the very summit of the course, Lermusiaux "staggered, fell, and was carried to one of the vehicles following the runners."[225]

Lermusiaux was a comic figure no longer. The little man, whom the Americans had mocked for his white gloves and training methods, had delivered himself of an extraordinary act of courage and endurance. Lacking the training and skill of his Anglo-American rivals, he had audaciously tried to steal the race. The crown delivered him at Karavati was richly deserved, and the Greek villagers who sportingly offered it to him could not have realized that the Frenchman's destiny was to make their own fondest dream come true. For Flack was now in front; it was now that he sent Geedrich, the bicyclist, off to the stadium with the awful news. But the effort of keeping contact with Lermusiaux and, finally, of passing him had taken its toll. Loues, accompanied "by what one might call an honor guard" of peasants from his village,[226] had passed Kellner and the other Greeks and little by little was gaining on the exhausted Australian. At Chalandri, thirty-three kilometers from Marathon and only nine from Athens, Loues caught him and went into a lead of about twenty strides.[227] They ran like this for the next four kilometers, each agonized by his own legs and lungs and by the presence of the other. A little before the village of Ampelokipi, Loues put on a short burst, and Flack could take it no longer. He let go, staggered, and fell, "and was carried unconscious to a vehicle."[228]

As the cannon boomed, Loues was on the outskirts of Athens, barely three or four kilometers from the stadium. During his battle with Flack, Kellner had gone briefly into third, but later was passed by Vasilakos and Belokas. Greeks were now running strongly in the first three places. A Greek was going to win the Marathon. And it would be Loues. Vasilakos threatened once to draw close, but Loues put on another burst, and was in the end to beat his countrymen by seven minutes and seven and one-half minutes respectively.

On through the streets of Athens Loues came. Mad with joy, the crowd thickened at every stride, "saluting the victor and heaping encouragements upon him."[229] The wonder is that he was not smothered, that the horse guards and soldiers managed to open a path for him to get through. There are no moments in all of sport like the run-in of the Olympic Marathon, when the leader comes alone. With no rivals to bother about, he is occupied only with his strides, his breathing, and what thoughts he can muster, what feelings he can feel. At once a survivor and a hero, an emblem of triumph and exhaustion beyond the imagination of ordinary men, a figure tiny and frail as he patters down broad concrete avenues surrounded by screaming masses who push in obsessed to have a glimpse of him, the *Marathonomaque* occasions a storm of joy and extreme pathos that billows up like a thunderhead toward the sky and, like the blast of air in the vanguard of an avalanche, flows down the street in front of him. Such things have been known in subsequent Olympics, but it is doubtful that anything approaching that wave of feeling and meaning that Loues pushed in front of him down Herod Atticus Street has ever occurred again. "Elleen! Elleen!" A Greek had won the first Marathon.

Loues' feelings as he entered the stadium are unknown, but there are ample descriptions of the crowd's. "The spectacle that the Stadium then presented was really indescribable. . . . The atmosphere resounded on every side with unending cries of victory. Women waved their handkerchiefs, the men their hats; little Greek flags, carefully concealed until now, were unfurled; quite beside themselves, the people demanded that the band play the national hymn. A delirious enthusiasm took possession of everyone; the emotion won over the foreigners, who, in various languages also acclaimed the happy victor."[230] Loues was still running "fresh and in fine form,"[231] persuading Coubertin that "psychic forces play a far more effective role in sport than has been attributed to them."[232] Robertson, too, was amazed by Loues' appearance. Ever the practical Englishman, he refused to accept the "absurd misrepresentation" that victory had been "reserved for the heaven-gifted and nature-nursed Greek athlete," but Robertson himself could come to no full explanation: "It certainly seemed to the impartial spectator that the winner was nothing of a runner. He arrived in the Stadium with a stride of a foot or so, but apparently not much exhausted. . . . We can only explain the fact by supposing that the winner succeeded by monumental perseverance at a moderate speed, though, strangely enough, his time for the distance [2:58:50] was really first rate."[233]

Loues, whose "brisk advance" toward the finish line "was found sublime,"[234] was immediately joined by the crown prince and Prince George who ran the length of the stadium with him, "the one on his left, the other on his right."[235] (See pl. 15.) They may have thought to protect him from the crowd, but more likely they were caught up in the emotions of the moment and themselves overwhelmed by "the redoubled roars" of the mass. "O Nikitis! O Nikitis! Zito!" ("The victor! The victor! Long live the victor!") As Maurras put it, "There wasn't a son of a good Greek who didn't rise to acclaim the *marathonomaque*,"[236] and the princes must have felt themselves, at that moment, the sons of good Greeks. "The usually quiet king himself had meanwhile nearly ripped off the visor of his naval uniform cap in waving it wildly in the air."[237] "He appeared poignantly moved."[238] As Loues arrived at the finish, "the stalwart Crown Prince, the president of the Games, and the still more stalwart Prince George, the referee, led or rather almost carried, this victor before the royal seat in the Sphendrome."[239] At this "spontaneous gesture,"[240] "some aides-de-camp rushed forward and effusively embraced the victor,"[241] and Loues "would have suffocated,"[242] had not "the two Princes joined by Prince Nicholas lifted Loues up and carried him for an instant in triumph."[243] Years later, Coubertin still "conserved the impression" of this scene as "one of the most extraordinary spectacles that I can remember."[244]

As the little peasant rode on the shoulders of his princes, white doves were released into the sky, and the Greek flag followed by his number 17 was lifted to the masthead. This new "apparition excited [more] frenetic applause."[245] The Greek people, said Maurras, "succumbing to the drunkenness of history, took consciousness of itself."[246] The Greeks were not the only ones who "succumbed." In these extraordinary, Pindaric moments, moments in which *prouesse* and *bonheur* thoroughly suffused, foreigners, philhellenes and tourists alike, seem to have shared a profound identification with the Greeks and so with the "Greekness" of their own histories. Loues' victory was "held almost beyond the reach of envy."

> Pity it would have been had a foreigner won this race. None felt this more keenly than the foreign athletes themselves. All who were present will remember the commotion of the crowd in the Stadion in that moment of victory as one of the greatest scenes of their lives. In the gentle light of the sun of Attica, as it inclines toward the horizon, a light not known elsewhere in the world, the magnificent gift of Averoff, the new Stadion—and yet the old—receives its real dedication. Athletics were crowned in it as never before in modern times. Here was inspiration for a painter.[247]

Those athletes who later wrote about the Games bore Richardson ample witness. Robertson thought the five thousand who watched the Yale-Oxford track meet of 1894 made proportionately more noise, but "the *coup d'oeil* [here] was indeed surpassingly fine," and "the whole scene can never

be effaced from one's memory."[248] When Connolly, that supposed Tarta-
rin of Boston, opened his new career as a writer with a novelette about the
1896 Games,[249] it was Loues' exploits and not his own that he sought to
enshrine. The scene left its mark on the intellectuals present as well. It has
been suggested of Maurras that his humiliation at the showing of French
athletes at the Games played an important role in turning him to
royalism.[250] Far more certain is that his later conviction that "France had
need of symbols, as opposed to the abstract ideas with which its republican leaders had bemused it,"[251] was forged in his experience of
Loues' victory. "Thus," he said of it, "must each nation know how, op-
portunely, to reason irrationally [déraisonner]."[252]

Since no scholar competent in the language has yet surveyed contemporary newspapers, journals, archives, and letters, we have no direct account
of the Greek interpretation of these events besides the official report. But
we do have the evidence of Greek behavior, as reported by it and by
Western Europeans and Americans. Coubertin reported that the lady
standing next to him in the stadium "unfastened her watch, a gold one set
with pearls, and sent it" down to Loues. "An innkeeper presented him
with an order good for three hundred and sixty-five free meals, and a
wealthy citizen had to be dissuaded from signing a check for ten thousand
francs to his credit."[253] According to Maurras: "Rich men got up a subscription to honor him. A café was signed over to him. A thousand gifts
were showered on him. A lady from Smyrna attached a gold chain to his
neck."[254] Richardson reported that one man offered Loues 25,000
drachmas and another, 100 drachmas a month for life. "Everybody in
Athens wanted to get hold of him and give him something—watches, suits
of clothes, freedom of barber shops and cafés for life."[255] By giving the
extraordinary gift of his victory, Loues had placed the Greek people in his
debt, and these feverish attempts "to get hold of him and to give him
something" represented celebration of his victory through the idiom of
exchange, rather than quid pro quo attempts to "pay him off." By all
accounts, Loues refused these gifts. Coubertin chalked this up to "the
sense of honor, which is very strong in the Greek peasant," and noted that
Loues "saved the non-professional spirit from a very great danger."[256]
Richardson thought Loues acted "from a desire to keep his amateur
standing as an athlete, and perhaps run again from Marathon in 1900."[257]
The first explanation seems predicated more on aristocratic than peasant
notions of "honor," though it is understandable why Coubertin, having
witnessed an extraordinary act of *prouesse*, had recourse to it. The second
explanation would be more plausible but for the facts that the concept of
"amateur athletics" had arrived in Greece with the Games and was hardly
widespread, and that Loues, as far as is known, never presented himself
again for another Olympic Marathon, or, indeed, for any other inter-

national long-distance race. Loues' real motives for declining to become a rich man remain not the least of the mysteries surrounding this epic figure.

Only one Athenian is recorded as having wished to take something back, rather than giving to the victor. That was the unfortunate "Miss Y." who had promised her hand to the winner should he be Greek. Since she had naturally expected, or else had heard, that most of the Greeks entered were "young men of good mien, belonging to excellent families, students, officers," there was little risk in her engagement. But sport had proved more democratic, in this instance, than she expected, and "a little herdsman" had won the prize. In tears, she told Maurras that now "no one in Athens knew how the adventure would turn out." Maurras, evidently enjoying the joke, noted that "Mademoiselle Y. appeared embarrassed by her laureate."[258]

While class endogamy survived the experience of communitas that Loues—and Bréal, Coubertin, Lermusiaux, and the rest—created, little else did; while romantic love in the end turned tail on romantic wager, this was the only subplot in the Marathon Romance that did not arrive at its scripted conclusion. In the days and nights that followed, "One heard nothing but the name of Mr. Spiro Louys, and one saw nothing but his picture," as "the name of this happy victory rose to the skies."[259] (Pl. 16.)

After the flag-raising ceremony and the arrival of the other Greeks and Kellner, who finished fourth, Loues retired to the dressing room. The stadium program resumed, but "the rest of the competitions offered no great interest; a certain number of spectators left; the hour was already late."[260] This, according to the official report, but Richardson reports that King George took special interest in the denouement of the pole vault. After Hoyt had won the competition, the sovereign requested that he try 3.30 meters which the American vaulted over "to the King's evident satisfaction."[261] And Maurras claimed that the remainder of the crowd did take considerable interest in the wrestling bouts which began after Hoyt concluded his victory. Through "ruse and agility" the little Greek Christopoulos defeated the "expert and methodical brute" Jensen, the Dane. In a second David-and-Goliath scenario, the German Schumann, a Turner, pinned the Englishman Elliot, who refused to accept his defeat in a sportsmanlike manner and had to be seen from the field by the princes. When next it was proposed that Christopoulos be matched against another Greek, Tsitas, the crowd protested: "No, no! Oki, Oki, Oki! The sacrilege couldn't be allowed, a match between men of the same language and blood wasn't wanted."[262] Maurras greatly admired this spontaneous Greek protest, but apparently the match took place anyway.[263] Tsitas, who won, lost the final to Schumann the following day. Swimming, cycling, shooting, and tennis events concluded on Saturday, Sunday, and Monday. There were some notable victories and amusing incidents. One centered on the American swimmer Gardiner Williams. He strutted and preened for the start of the 100 meters, and when the gun went off, took a great leap into the water, only to emerge screaming "Jesus Christ, I'm freezing!" whence he rapidly betook himself back to the float.[264] Hajos, the Hungarian who won this and the 1,200 meters, thereby becoming the first of his nation's long list of Olympic heroes, was to win another gold medal years later in the newly inaugurated Olympic artistic competitions. (His design for the Budapest swimming stadium took the architecture prize.) But it was all anticlimactic. Loues' victory had brought dramatic closure to the first modern Olympics, and the public could barely be distracted from celebrating and interpreting his and their triumph.

On the evening of his victory, Loues seems to have enjoyed his celebrity only briefly before "he hurried away to his native village to share his happiness with his most intimate friends."[265] It is not clear whether he was present in the city on Saturday, when hordes of Athenians scurried about seeking a glimpse of him, but on Sunday, he reappeared for the king's banquet. "Dressed in fustanella," he "bore himself with becoming modesty, but with composure even in the presence of the king." After the banquet, "he was met at the door by his father, who, as they drove slowly through the streets, enjoyed his son's glory so visibly that one hoped that it might be as continuous as that of one of the old Olympic victors, and that he might remain also as modest as before the victory. If he does fulfil the latter wish, his victory in this will be even greater than that already won."[266]

The evidence we have suggests that Loues did indeed win this "second victory," and his self-effacement and seclusions, followed by sudden reappearances, only added to the myth making that would have, in any case, surrounded his person. Like witnesses to extraordinary events everywhere, Greeks and foreigners rapidly fell to filling in Loues' story for him. As Richardson noted, "A cycle of myths is already growing up about him. It is not uninteresting to be present at this genesis of myths in which the newspapers play a considerable part."[267]

Who was Loues? That he was twenty-four years old and from Maroussi was known to all, but some made him a poor shepherd,[268] others a "well-to-do farmer,"[269] and still others said that he lived comfortably off the proceeds of water carrying from a well to which he had rights. These social placements were turned to account for his victory itself. It was said that his physical fitness was owing to his coursing after his flocks or, alternatively, his packing water up and down hills. Other versions downplayed his physical preparation in favor of the spiritual. Richardson reported one variant of this: "Just before going out to Marathon on Friday [there is no evidence that Loues did not go with the rest on Thursday afternoon], he is said to have taken the sacrament from the priest of his native village, saying that he wished to invoke the aid of heaven in his great struggle."[270] Coubertin preserved and spread another variant: "He prepared himself by fasting and prayer and, it is said, passed the final night before candle-lit icons."[271] Another story soon grew up in which speculation on his family background and his reasons for refusing gifts were absorbed into a familiar folktale motif. It was said that he wished only for royal clemency for his brother who was in prison. "But since he has asserted in print that he has no brother in prison, and since others have asserted for him that he has no brother at all, that myth is for the present disposed of as far as Athens is concerned; but who can stop a fiction that is gone out into all the earth?"[272]

Connolly took these themes, added others, and wove the tale of Loues into a little, nineteenth-century *Roman de la rose*. Loues is not merely a poor peasant in Connolly's story, but a veritable child of nature, an "idler" devoted to the rocks and forests. His physical strength was gained not in shepherding, farming, or water carrying (Connolly makes the Maroussi water privilege Loues' desired reward for his victory), but in hunting and gamboling through the hills and serving (like Pheidippides) as a messenger in the army. Loues is said to have enlisted out of patriotic fervor against the Turks and refusal to accept the settled life. Upon his discharge, he is persuaded to the Marathon by his godfather, Euripides, a shoemaker and village Socrates devoted to the glories of the ancient past. Loues, for his part, is devoted to Marie, a peasant girl whose "beauty had flowered like a rose bush in May."[273] Her father, however, prefers the tall, handsome, and better-off Vanitekes from Megara, who, in Connolly's romance, is substituted for Vasilakos as Loues' great rival in the upcoming Marathon. Having witnessed an intimate scene between Vanitekes and Marie, Loues doubts his chances until a red rose and a blue and white rosette, "the colors of Greece,"[274] fall to him from her window.

Loues shows no great promise in training at Athens and barely makes the team when, "torn apart with pain and dread, shame and fear, hope and despair," he manages a final burst in the trial run. Collapsing at the finish line, he is carried away by Gouskos, whom Connolly makes his boyhood friend, a lover of wine and a "great-souled" brute turned nativist by the admiral who recruited him for the weight events.[275] The identification Connolly reports between Gouskos and Prince George—their great size and "common" naval service on the same ship—may well have been a popular one at the time. It is, of course, an identification based on social inversion with the body as mediator between the royal naval captain and the peasant seaman. The same sort of social inversion and unification of opposites took place when the princes bore Loues on their shoulders before the throne, and later, when the king at his banquet acted as if it were Loues who had given the affair. The "director" (coach), however, has marked Loues out: "There is that in his features which tells me that he needs but the occasion to do a great deed." After hearing from Loues that he was called Ergoteles in the army, after a four-time winner of the *dolichos* celebrated in one of Pindar's odes, the director is still more intrigued. "Stay by us, Loues, for surely you are possessed of the true spirit. They are to be many, the chance is slight among them all; but who knows, my Loues, that you shall not win."[276]

But Loues is lovesick, and the day before the race, he breaks training and runs to Maroussi to see Marie. Lying about in the hills, he "reviewed all the years, the years and years, the beautiful years of his boyhood," until Marie appears like a vision before him and wakes him with a chaste little kiss right out of a medieval romance. Together they confess, receive communion, and light tapers to the Virgin Mary in the village chapel. After Loues frightens his sweetheart with a pledge to "win or die," she presents him with a small Greek flag, which she "kisses rapturously," and a blue and white ribbon, both of which she sews on his racing jersey right over the heart. To these gages, she next adds a red rose in exchange for the withered remains of the earlier roses that fell from the window. This new flower, Loues sews into a "scapula" to wear as an "amulet" during the race. Marie coyly inquires about "Madam Herikler," Maurras's "Mlle. Y.," whom Connolly makes into a rich, beautiful widow. But this love play only further confirms her devotion to Loues, and so provisioned, he heads off for Marathon with eyes that "flamed like the sword of an archangel."[277]

The identification of romantic love and love of country is the symbolic theme controlling the first part of Connolly's narrative; the identification of the competitors with their respective national characters governs his often amusing interpolations in the treatment of the race itself. The Frenchman (Lermusiaux, but not named) comically gads about at the starting line, trying obsessively to induce the other competitors to drink from his bottle of cognac "to the health of their respective countries." Perhaps in deference to his own ethnic roots, Connolly introduces, among his several "added starters," an Irishman who serves as the Frenchman's foil. After putting down a huge meal, the big and "droll" Irishman quotes Homer on the merit of drink and, so as not to make a liar of the poet, has a swill with the Frenchman, and later another. "For the glory of the sport then, Frenchie, one more hooker. And may the devil paralyze your legs if you bother me again."[278] Loues, the child of Greek nature, is meanwhile taking an "outdoor nap" under a tree, "a page from his old life," all the while musing on "Marie's kiss still on his lips." At the gun, the Frenchman "with a backward look and a call of defiance, went off like a wild goat in the lead," followed by the Irishman, "leaping like the puck of his own fairy tales to the challenging call." Loues' strategy of falling to the back is represented as an eminent cross of "Greek" qualities: the wisdom of moderation, mathematical reasoning ("he well knew his [reserve stock of energy] would decrease in geometrical ratio to the demand beyond the normal"), and peasant "intuition" that gave him "clear knowledge of his larger self."[279]

The Frenchman goes down in a café, having run in exhausted, put down several cognacs, and then, unable to rise from his chair, stayed there "shouting gay songs senselessly." "Goodby, Frenchie," says the Irishman, "goodbye, and good luck to you, though you and your cognac-healths and your wild bog-leaping have been the ruin of me, I fear." And so it is, for he shortly succumbs to bleeding feet. As for the American, Connolly has him last beyond the Aussie, when in truth Blake went down well before Flack in the actual race. Loues smiles at the American as he is carried to the cart: "such was his humiliation . . . that he was motioning to the guards to draw off his jersey, on the breast of which he wore the flag of his country. That flag he did not want seen on him, as he, a defeated man, was being driven into the city." Into Loues' mind, Connolly puts this thought about the scene: "Truly, this pride of country, it adorns like a laurel wreath. No wonder the Americans are a great nation."[280]

The rest of Connolly's novelette goes much like this. I have treated it in detail to fill out the Loues legend, but also to show how in literature—as in newspapers, folklore, proverbs, and gossip—Olympic performances are retold in a way that typically incorporates popular ethnography and accrues mythic, historical, literary, and religious motifs, often of surprising sorts. In later studies I will demonstrate how broad this process is, and I will argue that no small part of the significance of the Olympics lies in the opportunities provided for popular storytelling, cultural commentary, and metacommentary. In this matter, as in so many others, what is familiar in the later history of the Olympic Games was present in their beginning.

Arguably, no subsequent Olympic victory has had the epic quality of Loues', and Connolly's overwrought and precious narrative lacks the epic character of the naked string of facts themselves. Here art—at least bad art—proved less than life, and only with Loues' arrival in the stadium does Connolly's tale provoke the same emotions as the original. The fictional presences of Euripides, Marie, and Gouskos do not disturb us, for the eyewitness accounts suggest that in those magic moments those present felt themselves transformed into symbolic types. Nor do the expressions of awesome joy by Connolly's characters distract us, for we already know that the real scene was "truly indescribable" and, therefore, no fictional description can distort it. The false step that breaks this happy intersection between kinds of narratives comes when Connolly has the king bestow a medal on the victor and Loues request that the sovereign not pin it on "the heart side—that was sacred to Marie's token."[281] However, with his Tolstoyan final scene—of Loues toiling up the hill with his

goatskins of water toward his little home where Marie waits at the door
and from which his children come running down the road to meet
him[282]—verisimilitude and embellishment seem once again to coincide.

Without Loues, the Athens Games would have had no epic hero, no
master symbol to condense and express so richly so many ideological,
sociological, and historical themes. Though such things cannot be proved,
it seems to me that the Olympic Games would have been less likely to
survive the traumas of the next twelve years had not the symbolic capital
of the first Marathon and those "indescribable" and "unforgettable" moments in the stadium that Friday been there to draw upon. While it is not
clear how thoroughly he recognized it, Coubertin had found his most
potent ally in the peasant from Maroussi. Indeed, it may fairly be said of
Loues that, more than any man but Coubertin, he created the modern
Olympic Games.

Besides social background and kinds of achievement, the alliance between the two men enfolds other striking oppositions. Coubertin, who
was an invisible man at these first Olympics, would eventually win for
himself the title of Rénovateur. Every four years, his name and this
eponym would be ritually invoked by an international public. But
Coubertin never inspired myths, properly speaking, and even after the
Games had become irrevocably associated with his person, he remained an
invisible man in his native land. At the first Games, Loues the "nameless"
peasant became the center of attention and a national hero. Over the
decades, his status in Greece has "declined" into that of a historical folk
hero. But the name of Loues has been enshrined in the very language
itself. Loues was transformed into a proverb: *egine Loues,* "he became
Loues," or as an imperative, "become Loues," or "turn into Loues." Other
variants have the sense of "taking off like" Loues. In this way, Loues'
memory is invoked not only on Olympic occasions, but in the most banal
events of everyday life. ("As soon as the cop stopped interrogating him at
the intersection, *egine Loues.*")[283]

Not until forty years after his great triumph was Loues to be seen again
by an international audience. In 1936, Carl Diem and the German organizing committee made no great effort to bring Coubertin to Berlin, but
Loues they had to have. Still trim and wiry despite his sixty-four years,
Loues was drawn into the composition of another master symbol in
Olympic history, a symbol far different from the one he created and
became in 1896, a symbol not of joyous rebirth, but of a troubled loss of
innocence. During the opening ceremonies, the peasant from Maroussi,
dressed in fustanella and smiling his modest smile, carried forward a
bouquet of flowers and presented them to Adolph Hitler. Like Coubertin,
Loues was surely ignorant of the full import of these events. Whether, also

like the baron, Loues was fortunate enough to die before his nation, which he had helped to make "conscious of itself," was torn by invasion and civil war, is not known.

Endgames

These events lay unimagined in the future as the Athens Olympics wound to their close. The remarkable success of the festival and the results of its competitions were celebrated and confirmed on two principal ceremonial occasions, the king's banquet on Sunday and the prize-giving rituals on Wednesday.[284] At both, Coubertin was another face in the crowd.

At 10:30 Sunday morning, King George, attired in his admiral's uniform, strode into the great ballroom of the palace, where 250 invited guests awaited him. They included the majority of the athletes, the organizing committee, the international committee, foreign chargés and coaches, members of the commissions, and representatives of the domestic and foreign press. As always, the Hungarians and the Americans stood out. "Conforming to the invitation, each came to lunch wearing street clothes; an American even wore short bicycling culottes; only the Hungarian athletes wore black evening dress." But the most noticed figure of all was the winner of the Marathon. "Loues, in national costume, was the object of general attention."[285]

After the Corfu Philharmonic Society played the national anthem and Samaras' Olympic Hymn, the king welcomed the guests and sat down among the princes and cabinet ministers. Then all had at the meal.[286] Eating roast beef and drinking wine with the rest sat Pierre de Coubertin. According to prior plan, he had assumed the presidency of the I.O.C. at a meeting on the previous Wednesday, but the campaign to ignore him continued apace. M. Larroumet, the *Temps* correspondent, had caused a minor stir when, in an early dispatch, he had referred to the "Olympic Games just restored by one of our countrymen, M. de Coubertin." Toward the close of the festival, one Stephanopoli, the editor of the *Messager d'Athènes*, wrote in his paper: "One thing has surprised us in this country of great-hearted memory; that's that gratitude and felicitations with regard to the success of the Olympic Games have been addressed to everyone except to him who was their promoter." For this "courageous intervention," Coubertin was grateful, as he was for the one instance in which a member of the royal family indirectly acknowledged his existence. At Bikelas' luncheon for the foreign athletes, the crown prince had Foreign Minister Skouses propose a toast to the baron and appeared to join in with "significant eagerness." Coubertin thought this "a delicate gesture," but it was precious little indeed.[287] In his memoirs, the baron was inclined to be generous. "The care that the Greeks took to 'suppress' me on every occasion pained but did not astonish me. Because the evolution that unfolded in their minds rendered their attitude comprehensible, sincere, excusable."[288] We may well doubt that he was so sanguine about it at the time, and, according to Eyquem at least, his wife was positively seething.[289]

Why, with success behind them, had the Greeks not felt safe in allowing Coubertin at least a modicum of recognition? If he did not already suspect, the baron had the reason made perfectly clear to him in the king's banquet toasts. That very institution which, from *Tom Brown's Schooldays* to the Sorbonne congress, Coubertin had admired and turned to his advantage was now to be used against him.

As the dessert was served, George rose, lifted his glass, and pronounced his first toast in French.

> Gentlemen, let me tell you of the joy that we all felt in seeing you come to Greece to take part in the Olympic Games. By the population's acclaim for you, you've been able to convince yourselves of the gladness with which the Hellenic people have received you. I take this further opportunity to express my warmest congratulations to the victors. In a few days, you'll be returning to your respective countries. Here, I don't say *adieu*, but *au revoir*. I pray you to remember us well and not to forget the enthusiastic emotion that we all felt at the arrival of the Marathon winner in the Stadium. The Queen is unfortunately ill, she regrets not being able to be present today; she charged me with her salutations to all of you. I drink to your health and reiterate my sincere thanks to you.[290]

The king's every phrase was punctuated by applause,[291] and, according both to the official report and to Coubertin, after his final words (and, we may imagine, a little hurried translation), a storm of cheering broke out. "The Americans cried 'Hurrah!' the Germans, 'Hoch!' the Hungarians, 'Eljen!' the Greeks, 'Zito!' the French, 'Vive le Roi!'"[292]

The sovereign was hardly through. When "after a fairly long interval silence was regained,"[293] George again lifted his glass and began a second toast, in Greek this time, a toast Coubertin did not care to report in his own 1896 summary of the Olympics. "Gentlemen, the restoration of the Olympic Games in their classical cradle has been crowned with the most complete and unexpected success. I am also charmed to be able to congratulate and thank today all those who have worked to secure this marvelous result." First on the list was his own son, Crown Prince Constantine, for having been convinced of the "national utility" and patriotic character of the venture and for having "presided over the work with so much distinction and surmounting by his indefatigable and persevering activity the obstacles that could have prevented success." Next Georges Averoff, "the emulator of Herod Atticus," was thanked, and next Princes

George and Nicholas, "who organized and directed the sports competitions in the conviction that they were accomplishing a patriotic deed." Then Philemon was congratulated for working "even to the detriment of his health" with "a zeal and enthusiasm beyond all praise." As for the Greek and foreign champions, who "enhanced the fame of the Games" and "honored the Hellenic arena," "I am convinced," said the king, "that upon leaving Greece, the foreign champions will make known the progress of our country and the great labors accomplished in a relatively short time to assure the success of the Games."

If Coubertin still held any hope for a storybook reconciliation, he was quite mistaken, for the king's honor roll was at an end. Not even Bikelas received a mention. The reason became suddenly clear as George, with the audience raised to a celebratory fever, proceeded to drop his bombshell. "Mother and wet-nurse of gymnic Games in antiquity, Greece, having undertaken to celebrate them again today under the eyes of Europe and the new world, can, now that success had surpassed every expectation, hope that the foreigners who have honored her with their presence will appoint our country the peaceful meeting-place of the nations and the permanent and stable home of the Olympic Games. With this desire, Gentlemen, I drink to all."[294] There it was, an *au revoir* indeed. One wonders what disturbed Coubertin most at that moment, the trap that had been sprung on him and which represented the destruction of his most cherished designs for the Olympic movement, or the storm of applause and acclamation which attended the king's proposal.

As it subsided, the obsequious Philemon was first on his feet. Philemon's response, which was said to have deeply moved the king,[295] crowned the sovereign champion in an oratorical contest and included a political note that was to prove ominously prophetic: "The diamonds which have just fallen from your mouth, O King, shine so brightly that they throw the most victorious eloquence into the shade. Perhaps by sincerity and enthusiasm one can add to them. In this moment you have shown, O King, that you understand the lofty meaning of the title you bear, you are the King not only of the Hellenes of free Greece but also of the Hellenes living in the unredeemed Greek lands. I thank God for having permitted me, before my eyes close in death, to witness this glorious spectacle."[296]

The Games had proved of capital assistance to George in his need as a foreign monarch to prove himself to and win the loyalty of his subjects, especially at a time of economic crisis. His second need was for emblems of endorsement by the Western European nations that had helped to impose and maintain the monarchy in the first place. The next speaker was a European journalist, not an ambassador or head of state, but under the circumstances, it was enough. Hughes le Roux was a correspondent

for *Figaro*, who in his dispatches to that paper led its readers to believe that
he and the king were on personal, if not intimate, terms. Now he proclaimed that Loues and the princes had won for Greece and her king new
subjects from beyond the realm, and he implicitly seconded the royal
proposal to keep the Games permanently in Athens.

> Sire, it's not only for those of my race and blood that I ask permission
> to raise my glass. It's for all those whom you reunited and welcomed
> here. All of us carried here this desire: "May it only be that one of our
> own wins the Marathon cup."
> But when we saw appear, at the entry to the Stadium, this peasant
> who came first, there wasn't one of us, from whatever nation, who
> didn't tremble with joy. We felt that the Greek earth had run under her
> son to give him the victory. It had to be a Greek who came to say:
> "Forget what divides you. The barbarians are repulsed. Civilization
> triumphs a second time."
> In that moment, when your two sons took this child of Greece into
> their arms, when they presented him to you, Sire, there were no longer
> foreigners or Greeks in the Stadium, there were only your subjects.[297]

If, in these harrowing moments, Coubertin took cold comfort in the
thought that, through the enthusiastic Hughes le Roux, *Figaro*, the baron's
old nemesis, was reporting the Olympics in a favorable light, he was, for
the most part, mistaken. Four of Hughes le Roux's articles did eventually
make front page (April 13, 17, 21, 22), for a total of eight columns. But
only the first two concerned themselves directly with the Games—the
third was an appeal for government support for the French School at
Athens, and the fourth was a paean to King George—and in them
Coubertin's name was not mentioned. The article of April 13 praised the
modernity of Greece, Averoff, the great heart of Lermusiaux of Racing,
the Americans, with whom Hughes le Roux had shipped and, in contrast
to Maurras, quite liked and admired in a Tocquevillean vein,[298] and the
"almost sacred character" of the opening ceremonies. Hughes le Roux's
descriptions are filled with religious language. The foreign spectators were
"pilgrims come from the four corners of the globe." The stadium on
Marathon day was "a colossal vessel carrying an entire generation of
men toward some Promised Land." Just before Loues' appearance, the
stadium was filled with a "profound silence like a church."
    But this article was followed immediately by a full page of Caran
d'Ache's cartoons lampooning the Olympic Games and French participation in them. Entitled "Discobolus and Why He Didn't Win the Olympic
Games Prize," the cartoons feature a portly provincial from Marseilles
named Marius, who brags to his café confreres that he'll win, packs a
metal pie plate, a bottle of wine, and a little linen, and heads for Athens.
Upon arriving, the first thing he does is to have his name engraved "in

many known languages" on his "discus," to which the now-empty wine bottle is attached by a string. In the stadium, Marius, in his jersey with a big "M" for Marseilles on it, explains to his startled fellow competitors that, with his name on the disc and his address in the wine bottle, he is sure to have the implement returned to him when he throws it out of sight. In the final drawing, Marius is being hounded away by contest officials, but, as the caption notes, back in Marseilles he tells his buddies that the entire Hellenic committee "begged" him not to compete so that he wouldn't "humiliate Greece."

This juxtaposition on the pages of *Figaro* of divine representation and worldly parody, Hughes le Roux's article and Caran d'Ache's cartoons, immediately recalls Puvis de Chavannes's *Bois sacré* and Toulouse-Lautrec's knowing parody of it. Both "double visions" admirably express French reactions to the Olympic Games and the "two cultures" that lay behind their invention and interpretation.

As for the paper's substantial sports sections, Coubertin's old enemy Paul Meyer gave no more than seven short paragraphs over a twelve-day period to Olympic news, less ink than devoted in any two issues to listing the notables "spotted" at the previous afternoon's horse races. Turf and professional cycling continued to dominate *Figaro*'s coverage, and during this fortnight a French fencing competition, the "national" football championship (ironically won by a team called "l'Olympique" over Racing), and an international football match between France and Edinburgh received more press than the Olympic Games. Bracketing simple information and a few results of the contests, mostly inaccurate,[299] were one or two positive comments—Loys' [*sic*] victory in the marathon was "remarkable, stupefying really"; the fêtes left nothing to be desired[300]—and several more negative ones. Fewer competitors than expected had turned up, the yachting and rowing were consequently canceled, the Greek organizers had made a mess of things and Coubertin (the only mention of him) had failed to do anything about it, although his efforts in this regard were acknowledged.

Among the news items that fell between Hughes le Roux's front page features and the sports columns and, so to speak, mediated between the Olympics themselves and the social and cultural dramas that surrounded them (Tricoupis' illness and death in Cannes, the announcement of Princess Marie's engagement, celebrations in Athens and Paris of Greek Independence Day), only one mentioned the Games explicitly, and this in an ambiguous fashion. On Monday, April 6, *Figaro* noted that in an address Fr. Didon had remarked on "the Olympic Games as a peaceful festival of great international importance," but, the paper concluded somewhat incongruously, "his magnificent discourse raised immense enthusiasm for France." As for Coubertin, the irony could not have been greater when, on April 9, the paper noted the promotion of his brother to "commandant of the cavalry section of St.-Cyr."

When Hughes le Roux sat down after his speech, the correspondent of the London *Times* next took the floor.[301] Neither his name nor his toast was recorded, but from his dispatches we may be certain that he entered no protests against the king's perpetual claim on the Games. Through him, the *Times* offered its readers the most complete, accurate, and judicious coverage of the Athens Olympics in any foreign newspaper, and also the most sober and factual. Beginning on April 6, with a long and accurate review of events leading up to the Games, a review in which Coubertin's role was amply portrayed, the *Times* carried daily factual summaries of the competitions, ceremonies, and banquets with little in the way of literary embellishment, moralizing, or interpretation.[302] The correspondent's reports of the Games were altogether positive, but with none of Hughes le Roux's spiritual enthusiasm. The *Times*'s man was even restrained when it came to Loues' victory, though he did confess that "the scene baffles description."[303] The paper carried his Olympic reports in the foreign affairs and not the sports section, and, by juxtaposing them with his more overtly political dispatches, the editors showed themselves more shrewd. For example, only the *Times* treated the presence of the king of Serbia as something more than a royal social occasion, noting the presence of the Serbian minister of war in the king's retinue and suggesting that behind the scenes "on the present occasion," important discussions between the two monarchs were being held over the Macedonian question and the common threat posed by Bulgarian initiatives in Romania.[304] Though I have not discovered any records of the discussions of the Macedonian and Bulgarian questions between the two kings during the Games, we may be sure that they took place, beginning a long tradition of private diplomatic negotiations between heads of state and diplomats who put on a public face of "innocent" attendance at an Olympics. It is a tradition that continues today and is as important a feature of Olympic politics as the more direct political impact of the Games themselves.

The final *Times* article on the Olympics on April 16 was followed by a terse report of growing terrorism between Christians and Turks on Crete, though no one as yet suspected that a connection would be made between the Olympic festival and the future of the island, though that very connection had been presaged in Philemon's toast. Only in his last dispatch did the *Times* correspondent allow himself some editorializing. After a detailed description of the prize-giving ceremonies, he concluded with a call for compromise between the king and the International Olympic Committee (Coubertin was not mentioned by name, nor had he been since the article of April 6) over the location of future Olympics, a proposal whose outlines will be given below.

Whether, as he followed the royal party and the rest of the guests into a drawing room for coffee,[305] Coubertin's mind was already racing ahead to such compromises, or whether he felt thoroughly outflanked and undone, we do not know. Until 3:30 Sunday afternoon, "the King conversed familiarly with all the guests, and spoke with an entirely special favor to the winner of the Marathon and his old father."[306] To his American readers, Coubertin described this as "a really charming scene, the republican simplicity of which was a matter of wonderment particularly to the Austrians and the Russians, little used as they are to the spectacle of monarchy thus meeting democracy on an equal footing."[307] But, again, we may doubt that his joy in this scene and the overall success of the festival quite canceled out his maltreatment, the possible theft of the Olympics from him and his friends, the "traitorous" endorsement of the proposal by his countryman in his country's name, and the abetting of it by journalists whose papers, he would later complain, treated the Games as a "sparkling and picturesque news-item...but not at all as an institution which the conditions of the future rendered worthy of debate."[308] While the London *Times* gave the Olympics substantial coverage on the foreign affairs page, and *Figaro* treated it scantily as a "feature story," the *New York Times*'s modest coverage wandered through the front page, and the editorial, sports, and college news sections. The paper, which had no special correspondent in Athens, treated the Olympics exclusively as a sports event, reporting on April 8, that "One thing is believed to have been established and that is that the future of the Olympian Games has been decided, and that they will henceforth take their place among the noted events of the athletic world." Even as a sports event, however, the Olympics received far less coverage than either professional baseball or preparations for the coming Ivy League collegiate seasons. Had the Americans not won so many events, the Olympics wouldn't even have been a "news item" for the *New York Times*.[309]

By his own account, Coubertin decided to play dumb over the next two days, though we may imagine that his discretion was as much forced as strategically chosen. "To yield or to resign myself. I there and then decided to do neither. On the other hand, however, resistance wasn't at all easy under the circumstances. I decided to play the imbecile, the man who didn't understand. I pretended to ignore the royal discourse under the pretext [of not understanding the king's Greek]. I also ignored the document signed by the American athletes supporting the King's initiative."[310] This "memorial" was signed not only by the athletes but "also by many resident Americans" in Athens.[311] It read:

We, the American participants in the International Olympic Games of Athens, wish to express to you, to the Committee, and to the people of Greece, our heartfelt appreciation of the great kindness and warm hospitality of which we have been continually the recipients during our stay here.

We also desire to acknowledge our entire satisfaction with all the arrangements for the conduct of the games.

The existence of the Stadion as a structure so uniquely adapted to its purpose; the proved ability of Greece to completely administer the games; and above all, the fact that Greece is the original home of the Olympic Games; all these considerations force upon us the conviction that these games should never be removed from their native soil.[312]

As Richardson noted, this missive had special significance, since the I.O.C. had already let it be known that the 1904 Games would be held in the United States. Without Sloane present to represent the I.O.C. to the American team and to temper its enthusiasm for Greece, the most prestigious athletic nation at the Games could be claimed for the king's party. There was no strong I.O.C. member for England, and Robertson's views on the issue, which may well have represented the sentiments of the British athletes, could offer Coubertin scant comfort.

The French regard themselves as the nursing-fathers of the first Olympic Games. They consider the permission granted to Greece to hold the first meeting at Athens as a special favour, which is bound up inseparably with the stipulation that the next Olympic Games shall be held in Paris in 1900. It seems likely that Greek enthusiasm, aided by considerations of sentiment and propriety, might under ordinary circumstances carry the day against French contentions. The Greeks would be supported by the whole body of scholars and lovers of antiquity and by most educated athletes. Unfortunately the French have a most powerful ally to support their claims—their great Exhibition. Even supposing that the Greek arguments prevailed, we cannot doubt that Paris would hold a rival international meeting. In that case we much fear that Paris and modern display, within a moderate distance of Central Europe, would prevail against Athens and the soberness of antiquity in the remoter East. The opposition between the claims of utility and of taste and sentiment in this matter seems to be irreconcilable: on the one side we have the probability of a truly representative international meeting, conducted on purely modern lines, in a modern arena unconnected with the memories and glories of the age which has provided models of grace and strength for all time, on the other we find the possibility of non-representative competitions, held in a spot which, with every beauty of form and position, is connected with all the magnificence of that golden age of athletics, whose ideals it should be the object of these international gatherings to promote. The opposition is so sharp that it would be fair to describe it by asserting that these games, if held in Athens, would be Olympic but, we fear, not international; if held elsewhere than at Athens, international but not Olympic.[313]

I have quoted Robertson's reasoning at length because events were to prove it correct. The claims of philhellenism and of modern, international sport, so happily married at Athens, were indeed shortly to begin to part company.

Meanwhile, the I.O.C. members in Athens were themselves beginning to weaken. Said Coubertin: "Many of my colleagues asked themselves if we had any choice but to bow [to the king's wishes] and dissolve ourselves. They feared, if we didn't act spontaneously in this direction, we'd be forced to it in some way by universal opinion."[314] Later in the week, when Coubertin did begin to take action against the widely supported royal design, he did so without the advice and consent of his I.O.C. "colleagues." "Monarchism," he pithily remarked, "was dominant among them," and they "alarmed themselves" over his apparent impertinence.[315] But the baron, who cherished and manipulated protocol, was never one to stand on it when he felt cornered. Cornered he was, and resolute.

"I had all the leisure, in the space of mental solitude where everyone had left me, to examine the legitimacy of [the Greek] aspirations."[316] There was none, he concluded, first of all for reasons like those adduced by Robertson. The Games had not been sufficiently international—the vast majority of spectators were Greek, a "great number" of nations were represented but by very few individuals—and were unlikely to become so if the Games stayed in Athens—not a single railroad line connected Greece and the rest of Europe, boats to Piraeus were few, and expenses in the city high. Second, Greece would not be able to manage the expense in the absence of profits from a considerable number of foreign tourists. Third, "political difficulties" could well "surge through these same Olympics" and destroy the regular succession of festivals. The fourth reason, he did not care to state openly, but it was apparent nonetheless. If the Greeks kept the Games, it would be the end of his own connection with them. "I did not hesitate to convince myself that to fix the seat of restored Olympism in Greece in a definitive and exclusive fashion would be equivalent to the suicide of *my* work" (emphasis added).[317] Coubertin may have already been planning his campaign in the international press "to assert once more my claim to being sole author of the whole [Olympic] project,"[318] and the first Olympic congress in 1897 in out-of-the-way Le Havre, where an international body of sports officials and luminaries would be led to endorse tacitly his leadership of the movement. His doubts about Greece's ability to organize the Games permanently were reasonable enough; he had proved his own capacities as an organizer and inspirational figure; and his vision of the Olympic future was the broadest and most daring of all, including his conviction that the Games had to be "ambulatory" to win true international standing. Thus, objective right and practicality were, in large part, on his side, but intense, personal need surely played a major

role in his resolution to fight during his last days in Athens. The Olympics
and his own sense of psychosocial identity were now inextricably bound
together, and he doubtless expected that the 1900 Paris Games would give
him what he most desired in life, honor in his own country.

On Monday and Tuesday Coubertin appears to have kept his own
counsel, still "playing the imbecile" toward the king's party. But to the
crown prince's subtle hint of rapprochement, Skouzes' toast,[319] Coubertin prepared his own delicate but self-assertive signal, a letter to the king
which the baron also posted to the newspapers.

> Sire,
> In assuming the presidency of the International Committee of the
> Olympic Games, I hold it my first duty to address thanks to the august
> sovereign of all Greece. By the efforts of his sons, led by the noblest of
> them, the work which I had dared to urge upon him has been accom-
> plished.
> Two years ago, when the Paris Congress opened, Your Majesty
> deigned to send me a telegram of encouragement. May I be permitted
> to recall to Him today that my hopes are accomplished and that the
> Olympic Games are reestablished. In presiding over their restoration,
> Your Majesty has given me and my colleagues the right to count further
> on his benevolence in the future.
> Deign to accept, Sire, the hommage of my most profound respect and
> my unalterable gratitude.[320]

Finally, Coubertin felt prepared to hold what he called "a long conversation," and Richardson (who acknowledged Coubertin to be "perhaps
more than any other man the originator of the whole project of the revival
of the Olympic Games"), a "semi-official conference," with Constantine.[321] The *New York Times* (April 16, 1896) reported that the encounter took place Wednesday evening after the prize-giving ceremonies,
but this dispatch cannot be trusted since it also reported that agreement
was reached to hold the next Games in Athens.[322] On the contrary, no
agreement was reached, and Coubertin had come not to surrender but to
propose a compromise. Since the London *Times* reported the proposal in
full with its coverage of the awards ceremonies from a dispatch dated
April 15, the meeting may have taken place Tuesday night or Wednesday
morning.

What Coubertin proposed to Constantine was "the establishment of
Panhellenic competitions which would be intercalated within the series of
international Olympiads."[323] The first of these "Athenaea" would be held
in 1898. Writing a decade later, Coubertin claimed that "the Prince had
already thought of this and he showed himself very partial to such a
solution. It appeared to equally please His Majesty who gave me the
warmest welcome when I went to take my leave of him."[324] However, this

passage is a disingenuous misrepresentation, written in the shadow of the
so-called "interim Games," held in Athens in 1906. Unless the crown
prince and the king were themselves playing cat and mouse with Coubertin in these face-to-face meetings, any interest they showed in his proposal
was predicated on his offering full Olympic Games in Athens every four
years. He was not, and we have Richardson's testimony that they were
not fooled: "It did not require much perspicacity on the part of the Greeks
to see that [Coubertin's offer] was only a seeming compliance, and that the
'Athenaia' would be overshadowed by the games at the great capitals
which would bear the name 'Olympic Games.' With them it was 'Aut
Caesar, aut nullus'."[325]

The London *Times* too (April 16, 1896) made it very clear that the issue
was not at all settled, that the idea of intervening Panhellenic festivals was
favored only by the "members of the International Congress now in
Athens," and that without the title "Olympic Games" and inclusion in the
Olympic series, the Athenaea would "degenerate into a purely local celebration." Instead the *Times* proposed making the Olympics fully biennial,
with every other celebration in Athens. This same proposal was to be made
to the I.O.C. some months later by Bikelas himself, in response to
Delyannis' more radical proposal, passed by the Greek legislature, of
keeping the Games exclusively in Athens.[326] But Coubertin was to remain
adamant. His old friend Bikelas and his new ally Delyannis were to fall
from his favor, and the baron's repeated insistence later on, that Constantine stayed willing to go along with his wishes, is doubtful at best.
Beneath the brilliant awards ceremonies, these controversies seethed, and
the forces which were in the end to determine that there be no Athens
Olympics in 1898 or 1900 simmered.

Thousands had turned up on Tuesday for the final ceremonies, but the
rain fell mercilessly, and "the crowd dispersed after an hour of fruitless
waiting under umbrellas."[327] On Wednesday, however, "the weather itself seemed to join partnership with the feast: the sun rose beautiful and
radiant."[328] This alliance of nature and ritual sent Maurras into one of his
poetic reveries. "The air was delectable and, from the great fissures that
age, wind, and dust had opened in the mass of these beautiful trees, the
garden cypresses exhaled breaths of cassis and oleander.... On this
morning, some wispy companies of clouds marched along by the wind
occasionally covered the sun. This took nothing away from the
magnificence of the ceremony."[329]

The whole scene fittingly recalled the grandeur of the festival's opening.
"From the first hours of the day, the Stadium began to offer the imposing
spectacle of the Games."[330] Notwithstanding the previous day's disappointment, the crowd returned in huge numbers. "Toward the approaches flowed an immense crowd; by 10 o'clock, the spectators were

almost as numerous as on the day of the Marathon."[331] And, according to Maurras, their "popular enthusiasm" was as great as on the epic day of Loues' victory: "'Zito's' were cried. Doves were released. Little blue and white flags were waved in the air."[332]

Led by the "paternal and solemn" king,[333] the royal family entered and took their places at 10:30. The queen was still indisposed but the retinue was augmented by the newly arrived Mohammed Ali-Pacha, brother of the Egyptian khedive.[334] In a gesture of social incorporation, the gates were then opened to all those without tickets still waiting in the forecourt. When they had filled the remaining stands, the ceremony began with the national anthem.[335]

Next the Oxford student G. S. Robertson (the official Greek report "promoted" him to professor) approached the sovereign and read his "Pindaric" composition. "In this ode, full of elevated thoughts and which breathed the most ardent philhellenism, the poet celebrated the glory of the Olympic Games. The King lent his most profound attention to the reading of these beautiful verses, whose conclusion brought enthusiastic applause."[336] Coubertin found this a "charming incident." "Music had opened [the Games], and Poetry was present at their close: and thus was the bond once more renewed which in the past united the Muses with feats of physical strength, the mind with the well-trained body."[337] For his effort, Robertson was awarded a laurel branch. This was the "prize" referred to in the title of his article which has been repeatedly cited, though Robertson does not make this explicit for his readers. Perhaps later on he realized how readily he would have traded it for the olive branch of athletic victory which he failed to achieve. But at the time it was doubtless sufficient, helping render "the scene unsurpassed and unsurpassable." Later, too, he would reflect more soberly on the question, but in these moments he was converted to keeping the Games in Greece. "The feeling of absolute entrancement with the beauty of the sight, the rapture of sensation, and the joy of recollection, which overmastered all who shared in this spectacle, found vent in ardent wishes that the Olympian games should be reserved to dignify Athens and to be gloried by her glory. No one, while under the glamour of the moment, could have ventured to oppose this suggested reservation."[338]

The king stepped forward on a raised, white wood dais to begin the presentation of awards. With him stood Constantine, with Philemon, Melas, and Captain Hadjipetros, the herald, a little off to the side, and the council of ministers and the rest of the royal party and government delegation standing or seated behind.[339] The rostrum formed one side of a rectangle composed by the athletes and officials standing beneath it on the stadium floor. The athletes were on the flanks, and facing the dais some twenty feet away, the organizing committee officials, military officers, and the international committee stood three deep in formal lines. In the photo-graph reproduced in plate 17, Coubertin can be made out clearly, the smallest man in the front rank, next to a white-whiskered fellow in a tan overcoat. The photographer caught the baron in a telling pose, leaning on his cane, and looking down and away from the dais upon which most other eyes are fixed.

On the platform, just to the left of the king, stood a table piled with the branches of olive cut from the sacred *altis* at Archaia Olympia, the silver medals engraved by Chaplain, and the large certificates designed by Gyzis. Along with special cups and sculptures for a few selected events, these were the prizes for the victors. The second-place finishers received laurel branches and bronze medals, and every competitor received a com-memorative medal engraved by Nikiforos Lytras.[340] Those who won more than one victory were given additional olive branches.

As Richardson noted, the prizes were meant to emphasize again "the amateur spirit of the occasion." The olive branches had no monetary value, but were the "one prize which an Olympionikes might well covet."[341] The olive wreath had been the prize at the ancient Olympic Games, and the laurel crown at the Pythian. Maurras spoke of "this mystical laurel" and "the solemn olive [frond]," the first holding "a young and charming nymph captive in its smooth and immaculate stem," the second, with its "subtle and pure leaves . . . intimately blending the light into their gray shadow."[342] When the ceremonies were concluded, the crowd rushed "to appropriate the remainder of the pile of branches. Every twig and every leaf was treasured up as a souvenir of the occasion."[343]

In structural contrast but symbolic harmony with these perishable, wild plant prizes were the imperishable medals of precious metal, silver, and bronze, with their symbolic associations of riches, nobility, luster, and timelessness. But the modest monetary value of the medals is intention-ally contrasted with their value as art and artifact. "On one side of the medal is the Acropolis, with the Parthenon and the Propylaea; on the other a colossal head of the Olympian Zeus, after the type created by Phidias. The head of the god is blurred, as if by distance and the lapse of centuries, while in the foreground, in clear relief, is the Victory which Zeus holds on his hand. It is a striking and original conception"[344]—one which iconically symbolized the connection between the ancient past and victory in the modern Olympic Games.[345]

When each victor's name was pronounced by the herald, he mounted the dais by the carpeted, right-hand stairs, "bowed before the King, who addressed to him some words of congratulation, gave him the diploma, medal, and olive branch, and shook his hand, after which the *olympionikes* bowed again" and left the platform by the left-hand stairs.[346] Awaiting him at the bottom were his heavily laden fellow victors. The crowd roundly acclaimed each victor, but especially enthusiastic "testimonies of sympathy" were reserved for, among the foreigners, the Hungarians, the Americans, and the German Schumann, all of whom "were wearing Greek insignia on their chests."[347] Among the special prizes, the French fencer Gravelotte took away a silver cup given by the Athenian Club, Karassevadis and Phrangoudis, a richly ornamented rifle and pistol respectively, and Garrett, a silver cup and a marble bust of Athena, presented to him by Princess Sophia.

Then came the moment the crowd had come to witness and be part of. As Loues' name was called and the little peasant in his fustanella began to mount the platform, the whole stadium became "a scene of indescribable excitement."[348] "The amphitheater resounded with applause which redoubled when doves trailing ribbons of the national colors were released as a symbol of joy from a large number of grandstands. Flags floated in the air, hats and handkerchiefs were waved, eyes filled with tears, and the foreigners were struck dumb in the presence of such a spectacle."[349] As Richardson described it, "The appearance of Loues was again the signal for the crowd to turn frantic with joy. . . . Flags and flowers literally filled the air."[350] (See pl. 18.)

Besides his medal, diploma, and olive frond, Loues received the silver cup, ornamented with waving grain, and inscribed in Greek "Olympic Games, 1896, Marathon Race, Given by Michel Bréal." There was another "cup" as well. Some time before the Games opened, Ionnis Lambros, a wealthy collector of antiquities, had written to the crown prince. "The magnificence which the Marathon race is summoned to give to the Olympic Games joined with the archaeological character of this terrible ordeal, whose winner will be so worthy of envy, has suggested to me the idea of offering as the most appropriate of prizes, an ancient vase taken from my collection and representing a *dolichos* contestant running under the eyes and supervision of the Hellanodikes."[351] The crown prince duly accepted the prize and on this day handed it to Loues who later, according to Richardson, "with rare good sense, presented [it] to a museum."[352]

After completing the awards to the victors, the second-place winners were called to the rostrum one by one. This finished, Wilhelm Gebhardt, the German member of the I.O.C., stepped forward to present the crown prince with a laurel wreath "knotted with ribbons in the colors of Greece and Germany." Constantine answered Gebhardt's "warm allocution" with a "few words of thanks in German."[353]

Next, "in conformity with the program," the athletes formed up for a triumphal procession around the stadium.[354] The elegant and handsome Manos served as *Hieropomp*, leading the march, top hat in one hand, walking stick in the other. At the head of the procession, set off from the others, came Loues. "Joyous and full of glory,"[355] "agitated and deeply moved," he "thanked the crowd which acclaimed him by his gestures and continuously waved a little Greek flag which one of the spectators had handed him."[356] After Loues came the Americans, the Hungarians, the French, the Germans,[357] then presumably the rest of the laureates. All marched "with slow steps" to the choruses of "triumphal marches" played by the various bands, until the tour of the stadium had been completed and all stood again in front of the king.[358] After the Olympic Hymn was played a final time, he rose, embraced his son Constantine, and in a loud voice called out: "I proclaim the closure of the first Olympiad."[359]

CHAPTER EIGHT

Conclusion:
Flags and Flowers

After a final burst of prolonged applause, the royal party left for the palace and the crowd began slowly to file out. But the mass still overflowed with *bonheur* and *effervescence collective*. The closing ritual had not fully succeeded in organizing, expressing, and releasing the crowd's emotions. "A little afterward, a demonstration spontaneously organized itself," that would culminate in a performance that symbolically inverted the closing ceremonies.

> The crowd, led by Philemon and the Council of Twelve, accompanied by diverse musicians and by Stadium ushers carrying the flags of the nations represented at the Games, made for the Palace where it acclaimed the Crown Prince. He appeared on the balcony, accompanied by his two brothers, Princes George and Nicholas. On behalf of the Organizing Committee, Mr. Deligeorgis presented him with a laurel crown and warmly addressed him. The Crown Prince responded with some words of thanks which closed with his crying out "Long Live Greece!" Orphanidis [the shooting winner] then made a speech to him in the name of the *olympionikes*, to which His Royal Highness responded in like manner.[2]

Orphanidis then gave an olive wreath to each of the princes. Some of the crowd later passed on to the offices of the Olympic Committee, where Philemon, Bikelas, and Papamikhalopoulos were acclaimed,[3] but it was Constantine who was the premier object of their adulation and affection. It was he whom they had wished to crown "Olympic champion" in this spontaneous rite of reversal. In an important sense, Constantine *was* the victor of these Games. Their success delivered to him, and through him to the whole ruling house, a public favor he had not previously enjoyed. Coubertin, who had no special reason to plump the crown prince during the dispute over the venue for the next Olympics, described it in full.

> A local and immediate consequence of the games may already be found in the internal politics of Greece.... It was the first time that the heir apparent had had an opportunity of thus coming into contact with his future subjects. They knew him to be patriotic and high-minded, but

they did not know his other admirable and solid qualities. Prince Constantine inherits his fine blue eyes and fair coloring from his Danish ancestors, and his frank, open manner, his self-poise, and his mental lucidity come from this same source; but Greece has given him enthusiasm and ardor, and this happy combination of prudence and high spirit makes him especially adapted to govern the Hellenes. The authority, mingled with perfect liberality, with which he managed the [Olympic organizing] committee, his exactitude in detail, and more particularly his quiet perseverance when those about him were inclined to hesitate and to lose courage, make it clear that his reign will be one of fruitful labor, which can only strengthen and enrich his country. The Greek people now have a better idea of the worth of their future sovereign: they have seen him at work, and have gained respect for him.[4]

As we have repeatedly noted, Coubertin was willing to mobilize political forces to serve the Olympic restoration, as indeed he had to be. Here, it is evident how eager he was in the aftermath of the Athens Games to further their prestige by promoting those internal political consequences to which he was favorable.

The royal family's ascendency, of course, meant Delyannis' ascendency. On this Coubertin was silent. The former seemed to belong in his mind to national, historical, even "spiritual" politics (to "metapolitics," as we might say today), the latter to some more venal category, party politics, or the "politics of the politicians." In *The Evolution of France*, the book he had just completed on his native country, he was perfectly able to recognize and interpret the relationship between the two domains. In Greece, for the time being at least, he blinded himself to it. Was this solely because the Olympics were the focus of his attention here, and the Olympics for a time had suspended sectional interests and had absorbed them into broader, overarching social identities? Or was it also because on one side of the opposition stood kings and princes?

Maurras took what he saw of George and Constantine as capital evidence that France, too, must have her king. Coubertin could not have been more hostile to this view. He had alienated himself from his family because of it, and he dedicated all of his writings on French history to demonstrating its idiocy and foolhardiness. But Greece was a foreign, underdeveloped, "dream" nation; George was someone else's king. It is not hard to suspect that Coubertin's one-sided promotion of George and Constantine was socially and psychologically overdetermined. Behind it lay, in part, an opportunity to reconnect safely with the values and aspirations of his natal family and social milieu without any danger of converting to them. Coubertin would repeatedly claim that the Olympic Games allowed individuals to experience and gain knowledge of exotic political systems. Ironically, the "exotic" system Coubertin encountered in Athens was the world of his parents.

When this dimension is added to Coubertin's simple gratitude for the royal family's instrumental role in the Games, it is easier to explain why, in his first writings after them, there is not a single note of fear that the new royal prestige gained from the Olympics might endanger constitutional limits on the monarchy or lead to disastrous policies aimed at consolidating its new public esteem. This "forgetfulness" is all the more startling since, in his 1896 text, Coubertin pointed exactly in the direction from which disaster would come.

After noting that the Olympic Games "have made a breach in the heart of the nation," just as in former times cities made breaches in their walls to admit their returning Olympic champions, Coubertin wrote: "When one realizes the influence that the practice of physical exercises may have on the future of a country and on the force of a whole race, one is tempted to wonder whether Greece is not likely to date a whole new era from the year 1896. It would be curious indeed if athletics were to become one of the factors in the Eastern question. Who can tell whether, by bringing a notable increase in vigor to the inhabitants of the country, it may not hasten the solution of this thorny problem."[5] At the time he penned this passage, Coubertin could not appreciate the weight of his own words. Doubtless he meant only to publicize the Games by linking them with that issue which most regularly brought Greece to the attention of the Western European press. What cues he picked up we cannot say with certainty, but during the Games, the papers were reporting renewed terrorist acts on Crete and, as previously noted, Philemon made a not-so-oblique reference to Panhellenism and *enosis* in his toast at the king's banquet. Eleven months after the Games and three months after the passage just cited appeared in an American periodical, Greece was at war with Turkey, triggered by events on Crete.

By such phrases as "the force of a whole race" and the "vigor of a country," Coubertin meant both physical prowess and patriotism, which he saw as intimately connected. Patriotism and nationalism he differentiated. Patriotism was the love of one's country and the desire to serve her; nationalism, the hatred of other countries and the desire to do them ill. This distinction was common enough in the social thought of the era, and it had deep roots in Coubertin's earlier experiences. The "rebronzing" of France was patriotic, *revanchisme* was nationalistic. His battles with Grousset were fought over this issue, and he was in the midst of a break with Maurras, for whom patriotism and nationalism were the same thing. The events which followed the Athens Games were to cement the distinction in his mind and in his later writings. He bequeathed it to neo-Olympism and the Olympic movement as a fundamental ideological feature. Ever since 1896, the modern Olympics have stood as focal performances of the problematic relationship between patriotism and nationalism in the modern world of nation-states: is it possible to love and serve one's country without hating her rivals? Is it possible to judge hatred of rival nations as something other than patriotic duty?

What Coubertin meant to promote here was the Greek patriotism which flowed from the Olympic Games. What he failed to appreciate was that, for broad populations of Greeks, patriotism meant *enosis,* and *enosis* meant nationalist hatred against, especially, the Turks. The Games did, indeed, become "one of the factors in the Eastern question," but far from "hastening the solution to this thorny problem," they exacerbated it.

Since no historian has yet turned detailed attention to the role of the 1896 Olympics in precipitating the Cretan war, it remains difficult to judge the degree of their effect. One might reasonably argue that the war would have taken place in any case. Certainly, with Tricoupis dead, there was no one to lead the opposition and to counsel restraint. But with Delyannis in power, Tricoupis' party forced into the shadows, and, above all, the royal family on the ascendant—matters in which the Olympics had played a role—events were surely hastened. Loues' victory and the showing of the other Greeks may or may not have generated an illusion of national physical preparedness. The satisfaction of the international officials and athletes with the Games and their gestures of support and good will toward the Greeks may or may not have produced the illusion that the Powers would back any Greek political initiative. But it cannot be doubted that the success of the Games fomented national sentiment.

However, from aroused national sentiment to a declaration of war is a very large step indeed, rarely taken without intermediary groups and institutional pressures. Bourchier has proposed just such a mechanism. "The revival of the ancient festival, which drew together multitudes of Greeks from abroad, led to a lively awakening of the national sentiment, hitherto depressed by the economic misfortunes of the kingdom, and a secret patriotic society, known as the Ethnike Hetaerea, began to develop prodigious activity, enrolling members from every rank of life and establishing branches in all parts of the Hellenic world."[6] The Ethnike Hetaerea was founded in 1894 by young officers upset with governmental neglect of the army. We may recall Constantine's quarrel with Tricoupis over this very matter. As Tricoupis was falling from power, the society was fomenting irredentist rebellions in Macedonia. "The outbreak of another insurrection on Crete supplied the means of creating a diversion for Turkey while the movement in Macedonia was being matured; arms and volunteers were shipped to the island, but the Society was as yet unable to force the hand of the government."[7] But in the months after the Olympic Games, the Ethnike Hetaerea grew rapidly in strength, until "perhaps three-quarters of the army's officers belonged."[8] Delyannis for a

time tried to hold back, but the society had strong influence over the
ministers and with the royal family who were not particularly ill disposed
to a war which would, they thought, be easily won and contribute further
to their new glory and prestige. The society triggered the Canea outbreak
on February 4, and Delyannis announced the abandonment of official
neutrality.

On February 10, a naval fleet commanded by Prince George left for
Crete. On February 14, Colonel Vassos landed an army near Canea and
declared the occupation of Crete "in the name of King George." Contrary
to Greek expectations, the Powers showed themselves hostile, producing
"the utmost exasperation at Athens; the populace demanded war with
Turkey and the annexation of Crete."[9] Constantine now assumed command of the Greek armies in Thessaly and, with the collusion of Delyannis and doubtless of the crown prince,[10] society irregulars attacked
Turkish outposts. On April 17, one year after the closing of the Olympics,
Turkey declared war.

The war lasted thirty days, and Greece was humiliated. The Greek
government was bankrupt; its troops were no match for the German-
trained Turks; the Powers prevented any state from coming to her aid; and
her commanders, including the royal ones, were hopelessly inept. The
settlement imposed by the Powers was remarkably lenient—autonomy for
Crete under Turkish sovereignty, with Prince George later appointed
governor; minor border adjustments in Thessaly; an indemnity to the
Turks—but the war was in every way a debacle for the Greek nation.
Delyannis refused to resign and was dismissed by the king, but until
Venizelos, Greece was not to find a political leader to rally her destinies.
The king and, especially, Constantine were widely blamed for the
disaster, and a fever of antidynastic feeling broke out. As a further
humiliation, the country's finances were placed under the control of an
international commission. Needless to say, there would be no Olympic
Games in Athens in 1898 or 1900.

Greece would indeed "date a whole new era from the year 1896," just as
Coubertin suggested it might. But the date would come to mark both the
triumph of the Games and the tragedy of the war, and, to this day, it is not
recalled except with the most profound ambivalence (as is made plain in
the current public debate in Greece over proposals to return the Games
there permanently).

In France, as we know from Coubertin himself, popular opinion turned
against Greece for the first time in a generation, and by war's end, the
Olympics were widely blamed "for having greatly contributed to and
serving as a screen for the preparation of the bellicose initiative."[11] To his
Souvenirs d'Amérique et de Grèce, which appeared in July 1897, Coubertin

hastily added a sentence or two in effect blaming the Powers for the disaster.[12] A decade later in his memoirs, he was somewhat more forth-coming. He insisted that the Cretan movement was the "spontaneous outcome of circumstances, and that there was no proof whatever that the leaders of Panhellenism had assembled in Athens "under the cover of sport." On the royal family's role in the Games and the war, he said nothing. However, he did admit that the Games had hastened the flow of circumstances. "I consider it beyond a doubt that the success of the Games somewhat intoxicated opinion and gave the Hellenes a dangerous confidence as much in their own forces as in the good will of foreign nations."[13]

In the conclusions to his 1896 summary of the Olympics, Coubertin had written: "Should the institution prosper,—as I am persuaded, all civilized nations aiding, that it will,—it may be a potent, if indirect factor in securing universal peace."[14] Coubertin was eventually forced to rec-ognize, in the aftermath of the first Olympic Games, that they could also be a potent, if indirect, factor in the destruction of regional peace.

The baron's immediate judgment on the pacificatory nature of the Olympics was based first of all on the high patriotism of the Athens athletes and the absence of nationalistic displays among them. He saw no reason to doubt the continuation of this in the future. "When they come to meet every four years in these contests, further ennobled by the memories of the past, athletes all over the world will learn to know one another better, to make mutual concessions, and to seek no other reward in the competition than the honor of victory. One may be filled with desire to see the colors of one's club or college triumph in a national meeting; but how much stronger is the feeling when the colors of one's country are at stake! I am well assured that the victors in the Stadion at Athens wished for no other recompense when they heard the people cheer the flag of their country in honor of their achievement."[15] The Athens Games had indeed supplied ample evidence in support of this Pindaric judgment. The Olympics were indeed destined always to encourage the belief that athletes do *represent* their countries, to make people cheer for other peoples' flags, and to demonstrate the possibility of patriotism without nationalism in the dominant behaviors of the athletes. But in this respect too, the 1896 Games were an incomplete indication of what was to follow. In Paris in 1900 and London in 1908, Coubertin was personally to discover that Olympic athletes were not constitutionally immune to chauvinistic, nationalist displays toward their brothers. In turn, such displays would lead to challenges, on the part of countrymen and foreigners alike, as to whether athletes truly represented their countries. The relations between athletes, no less than between the broader social groups from which they issue and which they represent, would more fully model, throughout Olympic history, the *problematic* of patriotism and nationalism rather than its *resolution*.

Coubertin's assertions about Olympic pacification were secondly derived from the educational value of the Athens festival. His notion of international harmony was fundamentally rationalistic; war and peace were matters of knowledge and ignorance. "Wars break out because nations misunderstand each other. We shall not have peace until the prejudices which now separate the different races shall have been outlived. To attain this end, what better means than to bring the youth of all countries periodically together for amicable trials of muscular strength and agility?"[16] In his other enterprises, Coubertin assigned a capital role to formal education in the quest for knowledge of the "others" and, thereby, peace with them. The Olympics offered popular education or, to be more precise, "popular ethnography," as I have called it. As we have seen, the Athens Olympics drew athletes, officials, and spectators alike not only into making contact with foreigners but into condensing, expressing, and exchanging images and judgments on exotic national characters, social institutions, and styles of life. To men like Coubertin, Richardson, Connolly, and Hughes le Roux, the outcome was altogether salubrious. In the language of Durkheim, they concluded that in the Athens Olympics "social density" had indeed produced "moral density."

Maurras judged matters differently. He had arrived at the Olympics prepared to despise them for their "cosmopolitanism, which is nothing but a confused mixing of nationalities reduced [to nothing] or destroyed."[17] Such race mixing, leveling of social and cultural differences, and expressions of common humanity filled Maurras with a visceral disgust. He saw in them the destruction of all boundaries of history, taste, morality, and reason. The Olympics, he was certain, would be a master episode of repulsive cosmopolitanism.

But "from the moment I unpacked my suitcase" and "went to judge it with my own eyes," Maurras underwent, so he said, a "conversion." "Never was there offered a more favorable occasion [than the Olympic Games] for exactly distinguishing cosmopolitanism...from internationalism which supposes first of all the maintenance of the different national spirits."[18] Time and again, the Games demonstrated to Maurras that there "was nothing to fear from the side of cosmopolitanism," because "in our day, *when several distinct races are thrown together and constrained to interact, they repel one another, estranging themselves in the very moment when they think they are blending.*"[19] To Maurras, this happy effect was all the more powerful at the Olympics, where masses of persons ordinarily socially distant came together. "No, countries aren't yet socially dissolved. War isn't dead yet. In former times, peoples interacted through ambassadors. These were intermediaries, buffers, which the new order of things tends to suppress. The races, released from the earth's gravity, served by steam and electricity, are going to interact without proxies, to insult one another mouth to mouth, and to turn one another's stomachs. The ancient *ludus pro patria* will be all the more necessary."[20] A cosmopolitan assembly "has become the happy battlefield between races and languages. Nature, against which one conspired, has made the sovereignty of her laws all the better understood."[21]

The Games, Maurras was certain, would convince all Frenchmen of what they had convinced him: the ugliness and stupidity of modern Greeks compared with their glorious ancestors, the idiocy of republican government as against the solemn dignity of monarchy, the barbarianism of these "absurd peoples, the English, Germans, and above all, the Yankees."[22] But the Anglo-Saxons were not only absurd, they were powerful and dangerous. "Nationalism is a noble passion,"[23] and the Anglo-Saxons were possessed of it. The French must have it too, and the Olympics would help to convince them. To Maurras internationalism was the best guarantor of nationalism, and nationalism and patriotism were identical. This was, in miniature, the ideological program of the future Action française.

Coubertin would later oppose the Action française; in the period immediately following the Athens Games, he insisted still more vigorously that internationalism was a bulwark against ignorance, chauvinism, and war. To this end the baron refined his concepts, and the 1898 article in which they appeared revealed the close attention he had paid to his associate-turned-nemesis Maurras's formulations. "Does Cosmopolitan Life Lead to International Friendliness?"[24] hinges on the baron's *own* distinction between "cosmopolitanism" and "true internationalism." His discursive treatment is worth citing at length. With it he not only took issue with Maurras and bequeathed a fundamental stance to the Olympic Movement, he recapitulated, as well, much of his own biography.

> Cosmopolitan life is no longer an insignificant fact, an eccentricity of a few elegant women who, while they live in Paris, have their linen washed in London or betake themselves periodically from Spain or Germany to Biarritz or to Spa. Nowadays the whole aristocracy of Europe leads that sort of life. It scales the mountains of Switzerland or of the Tyrol, makes yachting trips to the fiords of Norway, shoots grouse in the highlands of Scotland, goes to Bayreuth to hear Wagner's operas and to Monte Carlo to lose its money; it spends Holy Week in Seville and the Carnival in Nice, ascends the Nile in a *dahabeah*, and coasts down the frozen slopes of St. Moritz on toboggans in winter. And it is not pleasure alone which makes them come and go thus; they pass from place to place in order to drink the waters here or there, to consult a celebrated physician in Amsterdam, or to undergo a surgical

operation in Munich at the hands of a famous surgeon. Men of letters and artists have followed the footsteps of the leisured classes and have taken to traveling. Paul Bourget hastens from Oxford to Corfu, and his principal work is a vast monograph on the New World. Ibsen and his disciples get their plays acted even in Italy, while Gabriele d'Annunzio, like his German colleague Sudermann requests the French reviews to consecrate his success. A magazine in three languages [*Cosmopolis,* to which Coubertin contributed] has been founded which is published simultaneously in Paris, London, and Berlin. The painters, in their turn, transport their brushes and colors not only for the purpose of bringing home with them distant landscapes, but in order to make portraits; and while a whole colony of American artists live in Paris, Benjamin-Constant and Chatran go off to Washington to reproduce the features of beautiful women. As for the scientific men and journalists, a whole series of congresses draws them from their native lands and gives them an opportunity to wander all over the civilized world.[25]

Moreover, "the railroad and telegraph" have rendered these journeys accessible not only to "persons of leisure" and to academic and artistic elites, "but to business men and actors" as well. (It is interesting to note that Coubertin uses the word "aristocracy" in both its French and its broader American senses.)

Does this cosmopolitanism lead to international friendliness in a world desperately in need of it? Coubertin's answer is no. First of all, social distance is not really overcome.

The first thing that strikes me is that all these people who mingle do not penetrate each other. Each one leads in his home the life of his own country, remaining the slave of his own petty habits. An English company—the same one which owns the Hotel Metropole in London—has built very near Cannes an enormous hotel which is filled with English people. Why do they go there instead of to other hotels equally as well, or even better, situated? Because the wallpapers, the furniture, the staffs, even the fenders, all come from London; because they gave bacon for breakfast in the morning and toast and muffins at afternoon tea; because, in short, they provide themselves with the illusion of being on the shores of the Mediterranean without having left England. What do Frenchmen who are passing through London seek at the Hotel Savoy unless it is French cooking and French servants?[26]

Second, these habits produce deadly illusions and "false conclusions" based on superficial "appearances of the daily life of the citizens" which are "infinitely deceptive."

What connection can possibly exist between the fact that the Americans drink iced water and eat fried oysters and their methods of government and education? Would they be any less good republicans if they ate macaroni, and would the Russians change their character if they ceased to like caviar? Now, I greatly regret that I am obliged to note the fact that the information possessed by many cosmopolitans concerning the peoples whom they have visited does not exceed that range of ideas.[27]

Third, such travelers do not even bother to make those observations that might disconfirm their expectations and prejudices, as with a French "authority" on the Americans who insisted to Coubertin that "the family does not exist among them. They live in hotels!"[28]

Fourth, cosmopolitans do not read or otherwise study for their journeys. "Study—this is the true secret of international friendship; ignorance maintains prejudices; study alone expels them. In order to understand a country it is not enough to see it live; its present state must be compared with its recent past. . . . For this history is indispensable, and especially the political history of the present century. . . . I would like to say that it is regrettable that one should visit a country before he has made such a study."[29]

Fifth, cosmopolitans lack imagination: "For my part, I have searched the point where I always try to get outside of myself, in a way, when I have to judge an international question. I say to myself: 'What would I think about Cecil Rhodes if I were an Englishman? What would be my opinion of India if I were a Russian? What would I desire in the East if I were a Hungarian? What would be my colonial ideas if I were a German?' And I think that in our modern world this manner of forming one's judgment is the only one which affords any chance of arriving at the truth and consequently of doing any good."[30]

"True internationalism" on the contrary, is to be found with those who go out among the peoples they visit, who do not recreate the habits and society of their own land in foreign ones, who do not judge by material appearances, and who seek to test their prejudices and expectations by careful observation. True internationalists are those who study the histories of the countries they visit and who try to imagine the world through foreign eyes. "Therefore," said Coubertin, "my conclusions are very clear. In order that cosmopolitan life should beget international friendliness, that life must be intellectual, not material. The fact that people live in a foreign country does not banish their prejudices against that country, and very often, on the contrary, it gives rise to new ones. And as for the society which, by reason of its customary existence, gets called cosmopolitan society, it is generally not greatly to be recommended. It displays many vices, much corruption, and it is not even of use to serve as a link between the different countries. One gains nothing by contact with it; it can teach you nothing; it is not good for anything. Properly speaking, cosmopolitanism suits those people who have no country, while internationalism should be the state of mind of those who love their country above all, who seek to draw to it the friendship of foreigners by professing for the countries of those foreigners an intelligent and enlightened sympathy."[31]

These passages might well serve as summaries of the first thirty-five years of Pierre de Coubertin's life. As subjective autobiography, they itemize most of his charges against his parents and his social class, and they recount the ways in which he felt he had broken with them and the means he had employed in doing so. As materials for objective biography, these passages again reveal a man on the boundaries between two worlds, for Coubertin was and remained, by his own definitions, both a cosmopolitan and an internationalist.

Coubertin absorbed Maurras's "internationalism" into his category of "cosmopolitanism," cross-national contacts that assert differences and divide men from one another. To Coubertin, true internationalism certainly involved the discovery and experience of social and cultural differences. However, far from dividing and repelling men from one another, national differences were to be celebrated as different ways of being human; their recognition was the first step toward peace, friendliness, and what the baron would later call *le respect mutuel*.[32] Upon this view of things, Coubertin would build a philosophical anthropology which he could never in his life fully explicate, in part because his loose habits of mind ever prevailed (he could not even use the terms "cosmopolitanism" and "internationalism" consistently in his later writings), in part because he lacked a concept of "culture" appropriate to the task. It remained for Marcel Mauss to pick up where Maurras and Coubertin left off and to draw the concepts of patriotism, nationalism, cosmopolitanism, and internationalism into a coherent social anthropology of the nation-state.[33] But Coubertin grew ever more convinced that "humankind" exists because of, not in spite of, cultural differences, and that the task of "the best of internationalisms" was, in the phrase of the anthropologist Ruth Benedict, "to make the world safe for differences."[34]

In his article on "cosmopolitan life," Coubertin did not discuss Olympic Games, but other texts make amply clear his conviction that the Olympics promoted true internationalism over cosmopolitanism. He regarded Olympic athletes as internationalists almost by definition, and like the athletes, he thought, Olympic officials were necessarily drawn by the athletic contests themselves into rich contact with the cultures of their foreign opponents and comrades. Most foreign spectators too, he dared to presume, even if they had arrived in Athens on another cosmopolitan round, had been lured into real interaction with the Greeks in the stadium, and, in turn, in the hotels, taxis, restaurants, and streets of Athens. Rather than superficial observations that merely confirmed such prejudices as the backwardness of Greece, the majority of all three groups of foreigners had had provocative experiences of the true state of the Greek nation. Most, Coubertin also seemed to assume, had studied Greece in school and would continue, after the festival, to read and to think about Hellas, ancient and modern. Moreover, identification with Loues and the joy of the Greek people in the stadium had helped foreigners to see the world "through Greek eyes."

The first Olympics convinced Coubertin of what he was already convinced. Such encounters, in which real cultural differences were discovered and celebrated, had led foreigners to true experiences of common humanity, from their shared emotional reactions to epic events to their recognition of the common, if multivocal, Greek heritage which "united" the peoples of the civilized world. Sport had indeed served, as Giraudoux later put it, as "the Esperanto of the races," a common tongue which simultaneously permitted its "speakers" to discover the real and important differences between their "native languages." Though in different locations, with different dominant themes, and in the face of new problems, subsequent Olympics, their founder had faith, would continue to serve true internationalism.

While Coubertin's views of the Athens Games were to no little extent apodictic and colored by his role as their founder and spokesman now fighting for organizational and ideological control, his interpretation was hardly a complete, wish-fulfilling illusion at total variance with the course of events. As we have seen, the Athens Games did, in many respects, unfold as an epic romance, and the subjective judgments and descriptions of several eyewitnesses lend credence to the baron's own. At the same time, we have seen ample evidence to support a different interpretation. Coubertin's own behavior—from his ignorance of the two Greek languages to his narrow perception of Greek politics—is alone sufficient illustration of the persistence of cosmpolitanism in the midst of this festival of internationalism. As to overcoming stereotypes and superficial notions, we may remember how American victories were attributed to Yankee prayers and cross-breeding with Indians, and Greek victories to the blessing by gods of nature's children.

But the Games surely did move masses of men to attend, to talk, to think, to feel, and to interpret—to tell stories about themselves and about the "others," organized around mutually focal events. This much may be said with certainty, and it is no little thing.[35] Rationalists like Coubertin and many of his critics could never comprehend what is now common wisdom among anthropologists, social thinkers, and, perhaps, the majority of modern men. For better or for worse, stereotypes and superficial notions most generally control the actions of men and women, and a second look often enough reveals that such notions are not so superficial at all. From the very first, the Olympic Games have been a feast of storytelling, of the making and exchange of cultural imagery. One cannot begin to judge the "quality" and the effects of such images and stories unless, in condensed, dramatic, and unselfconscious form, they are first exposed to public view. For hundreds of thousands of Greeks and a few hundred Euro-Americans, the Olympic Games served this purpose in 1896. Barely eighty years later, they would so serve one-third to one-half of the populace of the earth.

Coubertin's notions of patriotism, internationalism, humanistic religion, and non-European cultures would grow more sophisticated in his later years. But in 1896, he was convinced once and for all that the Olympics generated "true" knowledge of other peoples, and so never bothered to think more carefully about the nature of that knowledge. Thirty years later, he could still write: "To ask the peoples of the world to love one another is merely a form of childishness. To ask them to respect one another is not in the least utopian, but in order to respect one another it is first necessary to know one another. . . . Universal history is the only genuine foundation of a genuine peace. . . . To celebrate the Olympic Games is to appeal to history.[36]

Maurras, too, was certain that the Games would help the nations to know one another's pasts and presents, but that this knowledge would divide and repel them. Even without the despicable future that lay ahead for Maurras, it is difficult to find any sympathy for his view that for the sake of preserving her special destiny, a nation ought to keep on a perpetual footing of war with her rivals. But on another count, it is not so easy to dismiss Maurras. His belief that the recognition of and dramatic encounter with cultural differences necessarily divide human groups from one another certainly finds as much support in the human record as does Coubertin's opposing view.

Modern ethnology has gone so far in exposing cultural differences undreamed of in the 1890s that today the very possibility of true cross-cultural knowledge has been challenged. The fundamental question of modern social science, and of anthropology in particular, may be stated quite succinctly: is there such a thing as Man or are there only men? One and a half billion men and women now pose themselves the very same question during the Olympic Games. The modern social sciences and the Olympic Games were born of the same historical era; it is hardly surprising that their root problematics are identical. In this volume I have used social scientific concepts and methods to illuminate the origins of the Olympic Games. Perhaps it is now evident that Olympic history illuminates the origins of modern social science.

During the very period when received humanistic notions about the essential unity of mankind have come crashing down around us, we have seen those political and economic interconnections between nations that Marx called "world-historical process." Hegel had meant something different by the phrase. Notions like "civilization," the Western or Eastern "mind," "bourgeois culture," "working class culture," even "twentieth-century monoculture" ("Coca-Cola-Marx," as the French pundits say) have lost little of their currency. Yet, concurrently, our era is one of renewed awareness of particularistic boundaries of race, language, ethnicity, and religion; boundaries that have not and will not disappear. Our world seems to be shrinking and expanding simultaneously. This is the true world-historical process, a doubly dialectical process, and the Olympic Games have emerged as its privileged celebration.

Consequently, it is not surprising that the answer to the question of whether the Olympic Games unite men, as Coubertin thought, or divide them, as Maurras insisted, has been from the very first that they do both.

There is, of course, a fourth possibility of which the *Spectator*'s anonymous critic took account in 1896.

> International athletics, we see in the newspapers, are to furnish "new bonds to bind together the nations"; but if they are only bound as the Greek States were, the advantage will not be conspicuous. The probability is that Olympic games, ancient and modern, had and will have the effect of games merely, that is, of distractions, innocent or otherwise according to circumstances, from the peremptory work of the world. They are not worse than other amusements, and being enjoyed in the open air and under thousands of eyes, they are probably better than some of them. . . . That is about as much as it is as yet justifiable to say.

But the author could not prevent himself from giving the lie to his own claim that "mere games" stand outside of "the peremptory work of the world." "Rather," he concluded, "a population of football players than a population devoted, like the Chinese, to cards, or like the Bengalees, to gossip."[37]

Competition, consecration, enjoyment, and wonder are primary modes of human action, orchestrated by, and in turn orchestrating, ideological, social, and psychological formations. These modes of action and experience are particularly condensed in discreet genres of cultural performance: games, rites, festivals, spectacles. The Athens Olympics were composed of performances of each kind, but demarcated and elaborated to different degrees.[38]

The games of these Olympic Games were the most clearly and con-sensually framed of the performances. By contrast with such prototypes as the Wenlock, Zappas, and Rämlosa Olympics, the 1896 Games had a unity and integrity of rule, purpose, and form. Yet, as we have seen, participants and spectators were still repeatedly faced with dilemmas of typification: Greeks did not quite know whether to take the hurdles as circus comedy or muscular contest; British athletes refused to classify

Turner-style gymnastics as sport; no one knew in advance whether the Marathon was an athletic contest or a semireligious ordeal, and few were entirely certain after it. Spectatorial structures of attention, etiquette, and evaluation, no less than the athletes' and officials' codes of performance and judgment, were often enough ad hoc. Even persons from national cultures with long histories of amateur athletic games were often brought up short by the novelty of these Olympic games. It would be several decades before "games" would really consolidate as a cross-cultural category of performance, bearing with it, in more or less consensual and predictable form, all the properties that Gregory Bateson and Erving Goffman have taught us to recognize in culturally framed performances.[39]

The rituals of these first Olympics were far less differentiated. A congeries of ritual symbols—solemn music, processions, flights of birds, sacred plants, flags, mythic and divine images, invocations, crownings, wreath laying, statue dedications—populated the opening, victory, and awards ceremonies. Ordered in time, space, and intention, they reproduced the universal schema of rites of passage discovered by Arnold van Gennep and elaborated by Victor Turner.[40] Moreover, all those present for the Olympics came from cultures in which the categories "ritual" and "ceremony" were highly marked. But were these particular performances rites or ceremonies? In other words, were they experienced and understood as causing and consecrating profound social and spiritual transformations, or merely as confirmations of transitions whose sources lay elsewhere?

It is difficult to say. Ample evidence has been brought forward to suggest that, in Olympic rites, many individuals encountered sacred forces, whether understood in conventional religious terms, or after the fashions of Durkheim and Paul Tillich. But the data are far too incomplete to ensure that many more did not associate these performances with ceremonies of state or such prototypes as the openings of the universal expositions. The Olympic rites were, after all, more novel than the Olympic games, perhaps even sui generis. Moreover, the boundaries between the rites and games were not elaborately marked. The ceremonies and contests on opening day were likely experienced as one continuous performance; the victory ceremonies were but crude, punctuating appendages to the stadium events; and the awards ceremony centered almost fully on the distribution of prizes to the athletes rather than on an elaborate ritual act of closure and reaggregation with mundane social life. Religious forces were called into account as factors in athletic success—weakly, in the case of the Americans, strongly, in the case of Loues—as often as in descriptions of the ceremonies proper. The linguistic markers "festival" and "spectacle," and mood signs of joy and awe-full wonder, are more common than markers of "ritual" and solemnity in the accounts of the ceremonies.

The street festivals that were framed within the opening and award ceremonies and that adhered to and agglutinated the athletic contests were still more open-ended, spontaneous, and unbounded. The organizers had decorated the city, little more. Athens was *en foire* because sentiments of joy and the desire for enjoyment overflowed into unconsecrated space and unorganized time. These *festspiele* were the play of the people—not focused, competitive, or solemn, but free. Years later, Coubertin would write: "If anyone were to ask me the formula for 'Olympizing' oneself, I should say to him, 'the first condition is to be joyful.'"[41] This endorsement of the festival frame and consequent efforts to organize and bound it grew out of the spontaneous experience of Athens.

"Spectacle," as we have seen, was a term used repeatedly by eyewitnesses to characterize Olympic performances in 1896. But the spectacle had not yet condensed into a discreet genre of cultural performance. The evidence lies in the recurrent use of the adjective "indescribable" to modify the noun "spectacle," as if to deny the substantive qualities, the "thingness" of what the word represented. "Spectacle" was as yet an expression of pure quality, of awesomeness and grandeur to be wondered at, not a nominative category of performance. This, too, would come later in Olympic history and, more broadly, in the history of Western culture as a whole.

Cultural performances do not simply express human experience, they constitute it. In this work, I have traced the creation of new kinds of performances out of the historical dramas of particular social groups and individuals. The history of subsequent Olympics—from the "disasters" of 1900 and 1904, to the transitional Games of 1906 and 1908, to the triumphant Olympics of 1912 and 1924, through their coming of age in 1932 and 1936—is a story of the simultaneous differentiation, elaboration, and lamination of the performative genres of game, rite, festival, and spectacle. In another volume, I will try to demonstrate that the development of this new "ramified performance system" accounts more than anything else for the fantastic global interest in the Olympics and its emergence, over all rivals, as *the* dramatic celebration of world-historical process.[42] Here I shall merely suggest, on the evidence of the Olympics, that whatever is born and survives as cultural "tradition" is that which is performed. Born into the world as a unique performance system, the Olympic Games not only express but constitute the experiences of particular social groups and individuals.

One of these, of course, was Pierre de Coubertin. After the awards ceremonies, still further banquets, group photography sessions, and ceremonial leave-takings took place. (The American athletes were conveyed to their ship by a particularly enthusiastic Greek crowd.) It is not clear whether Coubertin took part in any of these celebrations. At the end of the week, he left with his bride for Paris, stopping along the way to show her Corfu. As he left Athens, newspaper editorials and insulting letters continued to accuse him of being "a thief, trying to strip Greece of one of the historic jewels of her raiment." But on Corfu, he enjoyed "an enchanting tranquility without a shadow of remorse coming to trouble my philhellene's conscience."[43]

> Throughout the provinces and the Greek isles, little boys amused themselves after school by "playing olympic games." After running, leaping, and throwing some pebbles for fun, they formed themselves into processions, and the biggest among them grew solemn and handed out olive branches to the others. This symbolic gesture, accomplished for the first time in Athens after so many centuries had passed, put them into unconscious contact with their great heritage vaguely perceived. This poetic play in the divine countryside of Corfu was my last vision of the first Olympiad.[44]

To his wife, still complaining of his treatment by the Greeks, Coubertin is said to have insisted that these children's games were praise enough and a real sign that the modern Olympics had been born.[45] Baronne de Coubertin, too, was pregnant.

Jacques de Coubertin was born later that year, though the month has not been ascertained. The child could have been conceived before they left for the Games or else during the Olympics themselves. Given reigning upper class medical notions and habits of confinement, it is doubtful that the baronne would have accompanied her husband had she known that she was pregnant. But by the time they languished on Corfu, Pierre and his wife must have realized that in the year he had given birth to the Olympic Games, his thirty-third year, he would also beget a human child and, as they wished and it turned out, an heir.

Coubertin arrived back in Paris with a triple sense of fertility. As to the Games, he said, it was time "to work to assure them a progeny."[46] He penned his *Century Magazine* article and sent it off to the United States; for France, he readied *Souvenirs d'Amérique et de Grèce* which Hachette would bring out the following year; and he set to preparing the first Olympic congress for Le Havre in 1897, intended to reunite under his tutelage and on his home ground, the sporting authorities of Europe. Each of these efforts was aimed to "assert once again my claim to be sole author of the whole [Olympic] project," at once to outflank the Greeks and to prepare the way for his personal triumph in Paris in 1900.

L'Évolution française sous la Troisième République was due to appear in July 1896. With this book, into which he had put such energies, Coubertin was certain he would win major recognition as a historian among French intellectuals and literati. Arrangements for an American translation were shortly made. Eight articles interpreting French culture and politics to the Americans were readied for the *American Monthly Review of Reviews* over the next eighteen months, and five on "The Formation of the United States" simultaneously prepared for the fashionable *Nouvelle Revue*. So confident was the baron in his coming emergence as an intellectual and political broker between France and America, as an informal but independent and respected diplomat, that when inquiries concerning his standing for Parliament arrived from Le Havre in June 1896, June 1897, and March 1898, he turned them down flat.

We may well surmise that the birth of his son seemed to him a strong assertion of his manhood, evidence to his parents of the wisdom of his independence and judgment in the past. Through the grandchild, he would win back their affections which he had so often alienated, but on his own terms. Having his own son would put an end to their long treatment of him as a misguided, impulsive child.

Over the next three years all these fertile hopes were stillborn.

As we have already seen, *L'Évolution française* was panned by the few who noticed it, and the United States edition met no further success. Despite the plumping of his American editor, no one found any reason to invite "the new Tocqueville" back to American shores, where he never set foot again. By 1900, Coubertin's career in the *Monthly Review of Reviews* was over, and he was reduced to posting complimentary copies of his privately published *Chronique de France* to uninterested American universities. In France, neither *Souvenirs* nor his articles on American life found any favor. Whatever personal satisfaction he felt in his 1898 lectures on the topic before a small audience at the École des sciences politiques was likely small compensation for his failure to join the intellectual elite. Indeed, by the end of the century, his brief career in the academic and fashionable literary journals of Paris was over. Thereafter, only the newspapers found any place for his musings on politics and international relations. The political historian had been reduced to political journalism. It was not long before Coubertin the author returned to where he had started: to books on school reform and tracts on sport in the *Revue olympique* and *L'Éducation physique*, little magazines he bankrolled for himself.

We don't know whether the presence of the infant Jacques had begun in 1897 to work the transformation in Coubertin's affective family relations that he wished for. But the tragedy that befell the boy in 1898 clearly put an end to any progress that may have been made. Left alone too long in the sun, the infant suffered a stroke that left him a hopeless, monstrous idiot for the rest of his days.[47] Laocoon had returned to harm his heirs claiming one child as he would later claim the other. Plunged into grief, Pierre de Coubertin sat down to write "Le Roman d'un rallié," with its patricide, its fratricides, its pathological mother claim, its population of transparent sexual symbols, its compensatory fantasies of conquest and delight: its recapitulation of his own childhood and adolescence with a new "happy ending" revolving around not Olympic Games or educational reform, but a conventional political career. And, too, with its pubescently perfect, storybook romance between a gifted, prowetic French nobleman and a young, beautiful, Catholic, American girl. With the tragedy of the firstborn, the marriage of Pierre de Coubertin and Marie Rothan began to come apart.

Family tragedy and psychological turmoil played their roles in Coubertin's failure, between 1898 and 1900, to win back and consolidate his control over the upcoming Paris Games. Other forces were arrayed against him as well. With his earlier fascination with the universal expositions, he had laid a trap for himself and for the Olympics. The happy, almost spiritual resolution of contending political interests at the 1889 Paris Exposition and the marked internationalism he saw in the 1893 fair on the shores of Lake Michigan led him to expect the same results in 1900. The Olympics would be the capstone of the 1900 Exposition and millions of fairgoers would be captivated by the same experiences that had so moved thousands in Athens. He had failed to recognize that the Athens success had depended in no small way on the Games' independence from such commercial extravaganzas. The second Olympic Games in Paris were fated to be just a sideshow, lacking the boundaries of space, time, and intention required for focal performances.

Coubertin realized the danger too late, when the exposition bureaucrats who knew little about sport and less about the Athens Olympics had seized control of arrangements and made a hash of them. With his high political contacts dead or retired, the baron could exert no internal influence over the exposition planners. With no time to build a coalition of prestigious notables, bourgeois officials in the ministries, and French sports authorities—a coalition he could not have built in any case—Coubertin tried a maneuver that was, at once, an act of desperation and of social regression. He assembled a new committee composed almost exclusively of titled aristocrats that attempted to organize an Olympics independent of the exposition. For this he was vilified in the press, his committee fell apart, and the Games were forced to "submit...to a humiliating vassalage" in the exposition.[48] Some of the athletic performances in Paris were of a higher standard, but otherwise little of the legacy of Athens was preserved. In the second disaster in St. Louis four years later, when the Olympics were again an appendage to a world's fair, even that little remnant of historic capital was erased.

Not until the 1912 Stockholm Games did the Olympic Movement fully regain its strength and begin to make good on the promise of Athens. The wonder is that during these sixteen years Coubertin did not give up and the Olympic Games did not vanish, to be remembered only as a fin-de-siècle curiosity. Pierre de Coubertin's greatest display of *prouesse* came during these dark years. Even more than the "noble works, glorious examples, and generous sacrifices" that led to the Athens Games, these patient, persevering, and not very heroic efforts earned him the right to his eponym le Rénovateur. And the survival of the Olympic Games through this period testified eloquently to the need the modern world had, and has, for them.

22?
Sat. night
7:30

Notes

![decorative ornament]

Chapter One

1. E. M. Butler, *The Tyranny of Greece over Germany* (Boston: Beacon, 1958), pp. 71, 11–81, passim.

2. C. C. Van Essen, "La Découverte du Laocoon," *Mededelingen der Koninklijke Nederlandse Akademie van Wetenschappen* 18 (1955): 291–305.

3. Julius II, not Leo X, as Carl Diem and Mandell and Eyquem, who mistakenly follow him, have written. Carl Diem, "Pierre de Coubertin's Ancestry," *Bulletin du Comité international olympique*, January 15, 1952; Marie-Thérèse Eyquem, *Pierre de Coubertin: L'Épopée olympique* (Paris: Calmann-Levy, 1966), p. 13; Richard Mandell, *The First Modern Olympics* (Berkeley: University of California Press, 1976), p. 50.

4. The exact relationship between the Italian and French lines is in doubt. See Yves-Pierre Boulongne, *La Vie et l'oeuvre pédagogique de Pierre de Coubertin* (Ottawa: Leméac, 1975), pp. 40–41.

5. The canvas appeared in the Salon of 1846. The catalogue contains the following exegetical note from Winckelmann, apparently supplied by Charles Frédy de Coubertin himself. "This group was discovered by Félice de Fredi in the substructures of the Palace of Titus, near the underground vaults today called the Sette Sale. César Trivulce, in a letter to his brother Pomponius, says that the Cardinal Saint Peter in Chains offered six hundred gold *écus* for it, but that Fredi refused to sell and offered it to Pope Julius II, who had it transported to his villa, near the Gate of the People, and from there to the Vatican. Michelangelo, having presented Félice de Fredi to the Sovereign Pontiff, the latter, in testimony to his gratitude, accorded him a right over the entrances to the gate of Saint John Lateran, and later Leo X named him his apostolic secretary." Société des artistes français, *Salon, 1846* (Paris: Musée Royal, 1846), p. 51.

6. In other versions, of Apollo.

7. Eyquem, *Pierre de Coubertin*, p. 14. She also claims that young Pierre associated Laocoon with Christ, though no documentation is provided.

8. Butler, *The Tyranny of Greece*, p. 81.

9. Egon Friedell, quoted ibid., p. xi.

10. Ibid., p. 81.

11. There is some confusion as to the date in the literature. Otto Mayer (*À travers les anneaux olympiques* [Geneva: Callier, 1960], p. 159) and Eyquem (*Pierre de Coubertin*, p. 288) supply it accurately. Boulongne first gives December 2, but later corrects himself (*La Vie et l'oeuvre*, pp. 70, 380). Richard Mandell erroneously has it as September 25 in *The First Modern Olympics* (p. 173), though in an earlier and more successful book (*The Nazi Olympics* [New York: Macmillan, 1971], p. 283) the correct date is given.

12. Boulongne reports that he aspired either to a chair at the University of Lausanne or to an administrative post with the Suez Canal Company (*La Vie et l'oeuvre*, p. 70), though the

latter fantasy seems to belong to the period of World War I, when Coubertin's fortune, by his own estimate, was reduced by 30–50 percent. (See his 1915 letter to Count Blonay, cited by Eyquem, *Pierre de Coubertin*, p. 222.) In his will, dictated on August 5, 1935, he recorded his failure in bittersweet words: "On the other hand, my repeated efforts to obtain some paying position have all failed, as it frequently happens to those who having always labored gratis, suddenly find themselves with the obligation to search for paying work" (ibid., p. 283). His "choices" of university teaching and international business are ironic and revealing; he had no qualifications for either, having lived a life marginal and ambivalent with respect to formal institutions.

13. When a "Fonds Coubertin" of some fifty thousand francs was assembled by the International Olympic Committee in response to an urgent appeal by his friend Dr. Messerli of Lausanne, the baron acknowledged with thanks but refused to receive the money personally, asking instead that it be conserved for his children (Mayer, *À travers les anneaux*, p. 155). His friend and confidante the countess de Montmort, a pioneering social worker and founder of the French Girl Scouts, was also active in raising funds for him (Eyquem, *Pierre de Coubertin*, p. 232).

14. Eyquem, *Pierre de Coubertin*, p. 282.

15. "The cat" (ibid., pp. 222–24). These diaries and agendas to which Eyquem had access are no longer available to scholars. Boulongne has established that they were intentionally destroyed by surviving relatives of Coubertin some time in the late 1960s, perhaps out of pique at the "indiscretions" in Eyquem's work (*La Vie et l'oeuvre*, pp. 62–63, n. 26).

16. The accident took place in 1898. The scripture on his stone in Lausanne reads, "Happy are the pure of heart, for they shall see God."

17. "I'm worried for the bird [Renée] that 'the cat' never ceases to repeat is sick on my account, although there isn't even an appearance of truth in it" (1922 diary entry, in Eyquem, *Pierre de Coubertin*, p. 265). The mother of Bernard and Guy de Coubertin, wife of Paul, Pierre's older brother, was also killed during the war, in the bombing of Saint-Gervais.

18. Eyquem, *Pierre de Coubertin*, pp. 131–32, 158.

19. Ibid., p. 223. Baronne de Coubertin died in 1963, at the age of 104. The degree to which her "admiration" for her husband extended to the Olympic Movement is difficult to determine. In response to I.O.C. condolences on her husband's death, she wrote, "I will continue to follow with the highest interest all the minutes and articles having to do with his Olympic work" (Mayer, *À travers les anneaux*, pp. 160–61). However, there is little evidence that she did so beyond what politeness required for one sustained by the charity of the Movement.

20. Eugen Weber, "Pierre de Coubertin and the Introduction of Organized Sport in France," *Journal of Contemporary History* 5 (1970): 26.

21. The last Olympics Coubertin attended were in Paris in 1924, Games notable for their placidity, joy, the participation of leading artists and poets, and the central place the baron occupied in them. Coubertin never saw, and so failed to appreciate, the extraordinary transformation the Olympics underwent in the '30s, when they arrived at truly spectacular proportion and were drawn into the center of international political, ideological, and commercial life.

22. Though it is his most oft-quoted statement, half of it originated with the archbishop of Pennsylvania in a benediction at St. Paul's during the 1908 London Games. See Pierre de Coubertin, "The 'Trustees' of the Olympic Idea," 1908, in Pierre de Coubertin, *The Olympic Idea: Discourses and Essays*, ed. Carl-Diem-Institut and Deutschen Sporthochschule, Köln, rev. Liselot Diem and O. Anderson, trans. John G. Dixon (Stuttgart: Hofmann, 1967), p. 20.

23. "Speech by Baron de Coubertin at the Close of the Berlin Olympic Games," 1936, in *The Olympic Idea*, p. 136.

24. See Mayer, *À travers les anneaux*, pp. 166–67.

25. And a distant relative by marriage. Pierre's father's mother's mother was a Berthier de Sauvigny.

26. Evidence for this description may be found in photographs held by the Museum of the Modern Olympic Games, Archaia Olympia. The stele was later moved to its present location in the "Coubertin grove," outside the *altis*, and bounded on four sides by the stadium, the International Olympic Academy, Kronos, and the area of Mycenaean *tholos* tombs.

27. Mandell, *The First Modern Olympics*, p. 173.

28. H. W. Wardman, *Ernest Renan: A Critical Biography* (New York: Humanities, 1964), p. 206.

Chapter Two

1. Cf. "Généalogie de Pierre de Coubertin," assembled by his great-nephew Geoffrey de Navacelle and published as Annexe III in Boulongne, *La Vie et l'oeuvre*. This very useful document supersedes the haphazard list of ancestors found in previous works on Coubertin. However, it requires clarification and supplementation, particularly with regard to Pierre's maternal line. This may be found in A. Révérend, *Titres, anoblissements, et pairies de la Restauration, 1814–1830* (Paris: Champion, 1903), 3:177–79. Additional information on Frédy de Coubertin may be located on pp. 92–94 of the same text and in F. A. de La Chesnaye-Desbois, ed., *Dictionnaire de la noblesse de la France*, 3d ed. (Paris: Schlesinger, 1866), 8:624–27. Caution must be taken with this source, however. While biographical information and dates are generally accurate, the "splitting" of the twice-married Jean Frédy, the first seigneur de Coubertin, into two persons has left the first five generations in the genealogy utterly confused. A. Révérend, ed., *Annuaire de la noblesse* (Paris, 1893), 49:384–85, contains additional materials on the cadet lines. There are, of course, many general accounts of the French nobility. One of the most useful for the anthropologist seeking "native categories and classifications" as they change over time is *Le Second Ordre* (Paris: Éditions du Grand Armorial de France, 1947).

2. *Dictionnaire*, p. 624.

3. Boulongne, *La Vie et l'oeuvre*, p. 38.

4. *Lettre de relief* for a *dérogeance* (*Le Second Ordre*, p. 135). I have been unable to discover with certainty the cause of this forfeiture, which must have taken place between 1573 and 1628 (see below, n. 9).

5. This list is compiled from the *Dictionnaire*, p. 624, and from various other sources.

6. Quoted in E. de Sereville and F. de Saint-Simon, eds., *Dictionnaire de la noblesse française* (Paris: Contrepoint, 1975), p. 15.

7. Boulongne and de Navacelle make him the son of the first Pierre Frédy (*La Vie et l'oeuvre*, p. 42), while the third edition of the *Dictionnaire* (p. 624) makes him a grandson. Given the difficulties mentioned above in note 1, I credit the former account, though the dates give pause.

8. Elsewhere, 1556. *Dictionnaire*, p. 624. In 1519, Alphonse Frédy was released from the *franc-fiefs* (Révérend, *Titres*, p. 93).

9. The first wife was a cloth merchant's daughter, and Catherine Boisdin seems to have been a *fille bourgeoise* as well. Though there is no exact proof, these morganatic marriages may have caused the *dérogeance* mentioned above (n. 4). Boulongne mentions that "in spite of the merchant status of the father, the patents of nobility were to be renewed by Louis XIII" for Jean II de Frédy (*La Vie et l'oeuvre*, p. 42). Since Louis XIII reigned from 1610 to 1643, these "lettres de noblesse" must be the *lettres de relief* of 1629.

10. Boulongne gives 1624–1788. While the latter is clearly a misprint, I have found no reason for the year's variance between these dates and those given above from the *Dictionnaire*, p. 625.

11. Eyquem (*Pierre de Coubertin*, p. 15) attributes the construction to Médéric Frédy "in the twelfth century." Both date and person are wrong.

12. Boulongne insists that François-Louis was born in 1772, but all the sources are against him. Cf. *Dictionnaire*, p. 626; Révérend, *Titres*, p. 93.

13. *Pierre de Coubertin*, p. 15. There are two problems with the date. The first guillotine was not set up in Paris until 1792, and since he was the second younger sibling of Pierre Frédy and almost certainly was not born before 1718–19, he would not have been 73 at the time of his execution as Mandell claims (*The First Modern Olympics*, p. 51). Either he was not guillotined in Paris, or he was not 73, or he was both and the execution did not take place until 1792 or thereafter. Perhaps capitalizing on his "sacrifice," the progeny of Henri-Louis styled themselves "comtes de Frédy," during the Restoration. As noted above (chap. 1, n. 25), later Frédys de Coubertin were related by marriage to the first martyr of the Revolution, Berthier de Sauvigny, the intendant of Paris.

14. Eyquem, *Pierre de Coubertin*, p. 15.

15. There appears to be no relation between this family and that of Gigault de Bellière et de Belfond, ennobled in 1489.

16. As Boulongne aptly stresses, Pierre considered himself a Norman. All the lines of his spiritual geography remained emotionally anchored in the Pays de Caux. *La Vie et l'oeuvre*, p. 39.

17. P. Lainé, *Archives généalogiques et historiques de la noblesse de France ou recueil de preuves, mémoires et notices généalogiques, servant à constater l'origine, la filiation, les alliances et les illustrations religieuses, civiles, et militaires de diverses maisons et familles nobles du royaume* (Paris: Chez l'auteur, 1828, 1850).

18. Jack Goody, *The Domestication of the Savage Mind* (Cambridge: Cambridge University Press, 1978).

19. P. 452.

20. Pp. 1–2.

21. As Lainé himself asserts, ibid., pp. 20–21. His son tells us that: "To his eyes, historical names were a national treasure whose defense was everyone's business. Also, the scandalous usurpations made in this matter were outspokenly attacked by him." Lainé *père* is known to have entered the lists against the pretensions of the house of Marconnay to the name of de Chastillon. In turn, Lainé was periodically the object of "libels directed against him by jealousy or wounded vanity." All this was to be expected of one who would convince the legitimate nobility that he was not an *avocat complaisant*, but a *juge conscientieux*, worthy of the privilege of establishing and defending their history. J. Lainé, "Avertissement," in *Archives généalogiques et historiques* 11 (1850): 6. Besides the nature of the author and his audience, the celebratory, almost ceremonial character of this text recommends it for the present purpose. For a more conventional history of the nobility in the 1830s and '40s, see André Jardin and André-Jean Tudesq, *La France des notables*, 2 vols. (Paris: Seuil, 1973) and André-Jean Tudesq, *Les Grands Notables en France, 1840–1849*, 2 vols. (Paris: Presses Universitaires de France, 1964).

22. Jesse R. Pitts, "Change in Bourgeois France," in Stanley Hoffmann, et al., *In Search of France* (New York: Harper Torchbooks, 1965 [orig. pub. Harvard University Press, 1963]), pp. 235–304.

23. Ibid., p. 239. In ethnoscientific terms, we might say that *prouesse* and *tout à sa place* are the French "emic" equivalents of Weber's "etic" categories of "charisma" and "rational-bureaucratic" authority. Whether the French would agree on an "office *(place)-prouesse*" is problematic, and they seem in "emic" accord with critics of Weber who have pointed out "traditions of charisma." The value and authority of *prouesse* are certainly "traditional" in the French aristocracy.

24. Among the objections of François Goguel ("Six Authors in Search of National Character," in *In Search of France*, p. 375), is that Pitts's account fits Parisian and not French

culture. Subsequent historical research amply bears this out. (Cf. Eugen Weber, *Peasants into Frenchmen* [Stanford, Calif.: Stanford University Press, 1976], and Maurice Agulhon, *La République au village* [Paris: Plon, 1970].) Pitts derives his value configurations both from doctrines of Catholic theology and from observed secular behavior. His failure to analyze the relationship presents methodological problems. Indeed, most of the difficulties with his paper are intrinsic to all studies of civilization which take the "national character" ("world view seen from the outside," Ralph Nicholas, pers. comm., 1977) approach. Notable among these is the tendency to overestimate the systematic character of value orientations in complex, pluralistic societies.

25. Eyquem, *Pierre de Coubertin*, p. 11.

26. *Archives généalogiques et historiques* 1:2.

27. Ibid., p. 4.

28. Ibid., p. 7.

29. There were, of course, reactionary notables who called for a full restitution of noble privileges, which "seemed to them an act of strict justice, of mere equity which it was manifestly impossible that the king should refuse them." Pierre de Coubertin, *France since 1814* (New York: Macmillan, 1900), p. 9.

30. *Archives généalogiques et historiques* 1:3, n. 1.

31. Pitts writes that for the author of *prouesse*, "His act is validated in his own eyes when the spectator to it acknowledges the irresistible appeal of both the man and the deed" ("Change in Bourgeois France," p. 243).

32. Octave Aubry, *The Second Empire*, trans. Arthur Livingston (New York: Lippincott, 1940).

33. Robert R. Locke, *French Legitimists and the Politics of Moral Order in the Early Third Republic* (Princeton: Princeton University Press, 1974).

34. *Salon, 1848*, p. 77.

35. February 24, 1848. Pierre de Coubertin later described Ledru-Rollin as a "Jacobin" linking such bourgeois as Dupont de l'Eure with socialists like Louis Blanc in the fusion of the two provisional governments. *France since 1814*, pp. 146–47.

36. The picture went eventually to the Laval Museum. Ulrich Thieme, *Allgemeines Lexicon der bildenden Kunstler* (Leipzig, 1912), 7:565.

37. 1852, 1854, 1855 (Exposition universelle).

38. Given the nature of his painting and the election of his teacher, Picot, to the jury in 1849, refusal is virtually ruled out as the cause of his absence. While a shortage of submissable work—perhaps under the pressures of the day—is a more plausible alternative, it still is less likely than intentional withdrawal.

39. The purchase is reported by Eyquem (*Pierre de Coubertin*, p. 13), but it is not noted in the customary fashion in the Salon catalogue of 1857. If not by *commandé*, then how was it purchased? The details might illuminate Charles's attitudes toward the emperor.

40. Eyquem, *Pierre de Coubertin*, p. 13.

41. *Salon, 1863*, p. xiv. The ceremony took place in the Palais de l'Industrie, presided over by Count Walewski, the minister of state, who gave a long and pretentious speech. It would be interesting to know whether Coubertin attended.

42. The catalogue exegesis reads, "A Christ, in wax, seated beneath a window in each corner of which appears an angel bearing one of the instruments of the passion, is carried in procession each year on the evening of Good Friday" (*Salon, 1861*, p. 86). For a comment on this, see below, pp. 20–21. The picture was acquired by the Paris Luxembourg Museum.

43. As explication, the painter supplied a quote from Fr. de Ponlevoy's biography of Ravignan. His corpse draped in "simple white" and "ornamented" with a large crucifix, radiated his "majestic and serene beauty" (*Salon, 1863*, p. 59).

A deputy attorney general in the Royal Court of the Restoration, Gustave François Xavier de Ravignan caused a sensation when he retired to the seminary in 1822. In 1828, he was ordained a Jesuit priest and left France for Switzerland during the Revolution of 1830. There he taught theology and began to win celebrity as a preacher. In 1836, he was called to the pulpit of Notre Dame where his Lenten sermons and retreats became fashionable (*Conférences du R. P. de Ravignan* [Paris: Poussielgue-Rusand, 1860]). He wrote a spirited defense of his order, *De l'Existence et de l'institut des Jésuites* (Paris: Poussielgue-Rusand, 1844) and otherwise sought to influence the religious policy of Louis Philippe. His opposition to the July Monarchy led to an attempt to draft him as a deputy in 1848, but he refused to be slated. A staunch legitimist, he allied himself with Msgr. Dupanloup, Montalembert, and Berryir against the Falloux law and the teaching of pagan classical literature in the public schools. Though forbidden by his superiors to join Dupanloup on the editorial board of *L'Ami de la religion*, he remained active behind the scenes in the legitimist opposition to Napoleon III. See *New Catholic Encyclopedia*, s. v. "Ravignan, Gustave François Xavier de." Since he died in 1858, Ravignan could not have been active in the 1863 elections as Aubry claims (*The Second Empire*, p. 270). Ponlevoy, whom Coubertin quoted, was the Jesuit provincial of Paris from 1864 to 1873.

44. In 1828, Lainé had written that "the Légion d'honneur appeared as the signal and first proof of a coming return to ancient doctrines" (*Archives généalogiques et historiques* 1:5). While those who awarded it in the 1860s had anything but "ancient doctrines" in mind, those who received the honor might well pretend to themselves otherwise.

45. Does Eyquem confuse this painting with *The Departure of the Missionaries* by placing the figures of Pierre and Marie in the latter canvas? *Pierre de Coubertin*, p. 13.

To a later period belongs Charles's academic self-portrait, reproduced by Eyquem and aptly described by her. "From his poised visage, cross-sected by a thick mustache, softened by white sideburns, his eyes pierce the canvas, eyes vivid, intelligent, and cold (ibid., pp. 12–13).

46. *French Legitimists*, p. 270.

47. The name is, of course, suggestive of our topic. While there is no direct relationship between the painting and the Olympic Games (Manet never mentions ancient Olympia; Pierre de Coubertin never remarks on the painting), there is a connection nonetheless. The French expedition to Greece in 1828 was accompanied by a "scientific commission" that, in Pierre de Coubertin's words, "had the honor of being the first to ransack the spoils of Olympia" (*France since 1814*, p. 74). As described in detail in a subsequent chapter, this and later archeological episodes excited the public imagination and added a new emotional charge to that provided the name "Olympia" in the classical education of the schools. This is evident in the critic Jules Claretie's outrage at Manet's painting. "Who is this odalisque with a yellow belly? A degraded model picked up I don't know where and who has the pretention to represent Olympia. Olympia! What Olympia?" Cited in S. C. Burchell, *Imperial Masquerade: The Paris of Napoleon III* (New York: Atheneum, 1971), p. 219. Claretie later participated in a 1906 "conference on the arts and letters" held by Pierre de Coubertin in the Comédie-Française to secure the blessings of the French art world for the revived Olympic Games.

48. Director general of the imperial museums.

49. See below, pp. 22–23, 32.

50. *Archives généalogiques et historiques* 11:5.

51. James A. Castagnary, *Salons, 1857–1870*, 2 vols. (Paris: Charpentier, 1892), 1:127.

52. Charles Baudelaire, *Art in Paris 1845–1862: Salons and Other Exhibitions Reviewed by Charles Baudelaire*, trans. and ed. Jonathan Mayne (London: Phaidon, 1965), p. 27.

53. Ibid., p. 98.

54. Ibid., pp. 116–17.

55. *Salon, 1861*, p. 86.

56. Pierre de Coubertin, "Olympia," 1929, in *The Olympic Idea*, p. 110.

57. Pierre de Coubertin, "A Modern Olympia," 1910, in *The Olympic Idea*, p. 34.

58. E.g., Glen Elder, *Children of the Great Depression: Social Change in the Life Cycle* (Chicago: University of Chicago Press, 1974). Erik Erikson's *Childhood and Society* (New York: Norton, 1950) remains the classic work in English on life cycle stages, despite its serious flaws.

59. The traditional French practice was *communion solennelle* at the age of twelve years, a pattern which endured even after the proclamation of *Quam singulari* by Pius X in 1910. G. Jacquemet, ed., *Catholicisme hier, aujoud'hui, demain*, 7 vols. (Paris: Letouzey, 1949), 2:1383–86. At the externat de la rue Madrid, the Jesuit *collège* Pierre attended, first communion was the great event of the sixth form. After a full year of preparation and a three-day retreat, the boys went down on their knees in the school parlor to beg forgiveness from their parents. On the morrow, the feast of the Ascension, they communicated for the first time. Institut supérieur de théologie, Enghien, Belgium, *Les Éstablissements des Jésuites en France depuis quatre siècles*, 5 vols. (Wetteren, Belgium: Meester, 1955), 2:1402.

60. Daniel Halévy, *La Fin des notables* (Paris: Grasset, 1930). *The End of the Notables*, trans. Alain Silvera and June Guichardnaud (Middletown, Conn.: Wesleyan University Press, 1974).

61. Alain Silvera, Introduction, *The End of the Notables*, p. ix.

62. E.g., Jean-Marie Mayeur, *Les Débuts de la IIIe République, 1871–1898* (Paris: Seuil, 1973), chap. 1.

63. Karl Marx, "The Civil War in France."

64. Estimates of the number of legitimists in the National Assembly of 1871 vary from eighty to two hundred. Locke, after reviewing the evidence, arrives at an approximate figure of 176. Another 187 deputies were either Orleanists or Bonapartists, giving the monarchists 363 out of 689 seats. There were 106 titled deputies, and Locke demonstrates the close association between legitimist ideology and aristocratic social class. *French Legitimists*, pp. 36–70.

65. Or the generals: that marvelous habit which the Greeks institutionalized and which an army of Tolstoys will never erase.

66. None had been alive in 1789, few in 1812, and, in any case, this was different. France had lost to an invading outsider.

67. Eugen Weber used this marvelous phrase to describe 1848, but it fits, at least as well, the 1870s. Eugen Weber, *A Modern History of Europe* (New York: Norton, 1971), p. 789.

68. *Salon, 1875*, p. 78.

69. *Salon, 1876*, p. 64. The painting depicts the famous dialogue between the child king and Simon the cobbler (quoted by Coubertin from A. de Beauchesne). "Capet, if the Vendéens come to deliver you, what will you do to me?" "I will pardon you." Royal *prouesse* at an early age!

70. *L'Évolution française sous la Troisième République* (Paris: Hachette, 1896). I am quoting from the authorized English translation by Isabel Hapgood, *The Evolution of France under the Third Republic* (New York: Crowell, 1897), p. 6, and will do so throughout. I have checked the translation against the original and find it faithful. Moreover, as Albert Shaw notes in his introduction to it (p. iv), Coubertin "extended and revised" the English edition.

71. Jules Isaac, *Encyclopedia Britannica*, 13th ed., s.v. "Francis I."

72. Ibid.

73. Ibid.

74. There is another provocative layer to the symbolism of Francis I. He was a great lover of "violent exercises... tournaments, masquerades, and amusements of all kinds." "Hunting, tennis, jewelry, and his gallantry were the chief preoccupations of his life." (Ibid.) At the very moment he seized upon the image of Francis, Pierre was attempting to transform sports and physical exercises from idle pastimes of the bejeweled and gallant rich and from mere amusements, to forms of moral training available to all. And the medieval tournament was one of the strands of adolescent inspiration which lay behind the revival of the Olympic

Games. The first modern Games took place the same year that *L'Évolution française* appeared, as we shall see.

75. The phrase is used here in the same sense as it is employed by its originator, Erik Erikson.

76. Georges Hohrod [Pierre de Coubertin], "Le Roman d'un rallié," *La Nouvelle Revue* 116 (February 15, 1899): 577–601; 117 (March 1–April 15, 1899): 44–68, 222–47, 452–82, 650–84. Unfortunately, most writers on Coubertin have either ignored this account, or else have merely mentioned its existence in a catalogue of his works. Ironically, some of these same writers have unwittingly depended on it. Eyquem, almost always without citing her source, drew extensively, though piecemeal, from "Le Roman d'un rallié." Mandell, in his *The First Modern Olympics*, takes incidents and anecdotes from Eyquem, without checking their source, and thus does not realize that it is "Le Roman d'un rallié" upon which he is relying. Boulongne does seem to have read the work, but makes little use of it.

77. "Le Roman d'un rallié," pp. 453–54.

78. Ibid., pp. 454–55.

79. Ibid., 599–600. I have no doubt that the episode of the "royalist slanderer" was a real event in Coubertin's childhood. There is one discrepancy between the two descriptions of it in "Le Roman d'un rallié." In the first one, his punishment is the loss of his dessert and not the lunch of "dry bread" claimed in the second. But this little slip adds to, rather than detracts from, the evidence that this is a factual event. The later exaggeration reveals the emotions the episode held for Coubertin (as do its repetition and its contexts in the "Roman"), and he makes no such slips in the patently fictional episodes of the work.

80. Ibid., pp. 666–67. Again, though the interpretation placed upon the event in the passage cited is perhaps more definite than a young adolescent's might be, I am certain that the impression conveyed is faithful and that the episode itself actually took place. The context and the coloring of the passage make this clear. There is a problem of chronology, however. Gambetta died in December 1882. Pierre makes Étienne six years younger than himself, so Étienne was indeed "around fourteen" on the morrow of Gambetta's death. But Pierre himself was twenty in 1883. That the visit to Versailles took place then is unlikely. Pierre hardly would have described his patriotic emotions at twenty as "juvenile." The evocative visit to the museum probably did take place around Pierre's fourteenth year, that is, around 1877. The presence of a medallion of Gambetta on display at Versailles already in 1877 is hardly surprising, even though he was still very much alive. In the 1870s, Gambetta was acknowledged, even by his enemies, as the savior of France. That Pierre's intransigent parents did not so regard him hardly prevented the boy from accepting him as a hero. The passage from *L'Évolution française* cited above (p. 23) shows how Coubertin retained this conviction even when, as a political historian, he became more circumspect about the role of circumstances in Gambetta's greatness.

81. The presence of this coda is an emblem of the strong feelings which the episode aroused in the author. It is another bit of evidence that the visit to the Versailles museum was a real event in Pierre's youth.

82. *Une Campagne de 21 ans* (Paris: Librairie de l'Éducation Physique, 1908), p. 1.

83. *Pierre de Coubertin*, pp. 10–11. Eyquem takes severe literary license by assembling these three episodes (without citations) and rendering them as a single "dialogue" between Pierre and his mother. Eyquem's embellishments include "quotations" which are, on the evidence, purely her own inventions. For example, after the "three monarchies, two empires" passage, she has Pierre say, "Certainly, I would give my life to have the King returned, but I am ready to slap the face of whoever insults the Republic." While the Pierre of the "luncheon offense" might well have expressed himself this way, the addition flatly contradicts the altered view of the sixteen or seventeen-year-old who had come to see a restoration as "nothing more than an expedient without a future."

84. Halévy, *La Fin des notables*, pp. 42–54. Emmanuel Beau de Loménie, *La Restauration*

manquée: L'Affaire du drapeau blanc (Paris: Éditeurs des Portiques, 1932); D. W. Brogan, *France under the Republic* (New York & London: Harper, 1940), pp. 77–93;Locke, *French Legitimists*, pp. 10–33, passim. We may note in passing the extreme importance of flag symbolism in the days of Pierre's youth. About the "affaire du drapeau blanc" he later wrote, "Behind the color of the flag were concealed profound divergences of opinion and irreconcilable antagonisms" (*L'Évolution française*, p. 30). It was a lesson about the multivocality of dominant symbols which he sometimes forgot in his later celebration of flags as symbols of national unity at the Olympic Games.

85. August 9, 1879.

86. *Pierre de Coubertin*, pp. 22–23.

87. In his own later writings, Coubertin was inclined to be generous about Chambord. "France may be grateful to him for not having prolonged, by a restoration which could not have endured, the uncertainties and expedients of previous governments. When he died . . . , he carried with him to the tomb, the respect of all parties" (*L'Évolution française*, p. 40; see also pp. 38–40).

88. The name is italicized in the original ("Le Roman d'un rallié," p. 599). Lesneven is the name of a city in Léon in Brittany and of a clerical college there. We may surmise that the figure concealed behind this name was a pupil or teacher at the school, the abbot in the town, or all three.

89. Ibid., p. 598. In the Boulongne/de Navacelle genealogy (*La Vie et l'oeuvre*, Annexe III), Pierre's mother's mother, Euphrasie Eudes de Catteville de Mirville is shown to have a brother Charles-Jules. But this man married and had a daughter and, therefore, cannot be the offending abbé. I have been unable to locate a more complete genealogy of the Eudes de Catteville de Mirville family. On the off-chance that Pierre further disguised the matter by substituting a maternal grandmother's relative for a maternal grandfather's, I have checked the Gigault de Crisenoy line too, but no such person appears in this genealogy either. A rather thorough search of Lammenais's books and letters, of *L'Avenir*, and of the secondary sources on the Mennaisist movement has turned up no mention of an Eudes de Catteville de Mirville or a Gigault de Crisenoy. "Monsieur l'abbé de Lesneven" may have been a rather less significant figure in Mennaisism than the "Roman d'un rallié" portrays him. Or else the abbé may have been known by some other name than Eudes (or Gigault). Or both of these possibilities may prove true when "M. de Lesneven" is finally identified. Everything about the episode in "Le Roman d'un rallié" points away from the third possibility, that the figure of Lesneven is entirely invented.

90. The village is not named in the "Roman," but the minutely detailed itinerary of the boy's pilgrimage to the site leads to the Finistère, through the town of Chateaulin, out onto the Crozon peninsula, and to what appears to be the hamlet of Pen-ar-run. The tomb is said to lie in the shadow of the "Menhir Noir," and this could very well be the "dolmen de Liaven." However, there are so many ancient megaliths in the immediate area that it is impossible to know for sure. I am convinced that this is the real location of the ancestor's tomb—there is no other reason for the minutely detailed directions to it that Coubertin provides in "Le Roman," pp. 475–76. The only fictionalized aspect of the episode is the time it took to get there by carriage and foot from his real family's château in Mirville. Brittany was the center of the Mennaisist movement, and there is no reason to surmise that the ancestor lived out his days in Normandy. Moreover, a "M. Hamel," maritime commissioner at Brest, is said to be Lesneven's only friend at the end of his life.

91. Ibid., p. 481.

92. In "Le Roman," Lesneven's apostasy is described as a "hereditary curse" upon the Crussènes, and they ascribe the series of tragic deaths that befall the family to it as God's punishment. Just as these deaths are fictional, so too the family belief in a hereditary curse operating mysteriously is probably a literary exaggeration.

93. Ibid., p. 599.

94. Ibid. Such minute and careful description is not typical of Coubertin's demonstrably fictional prose. He had a clear image of a real place before his eyes when he wrote this passage. It is one more bit of evidence that this is an actual boyhood event.

95. Ibid.

96. He was hardly unusual in this. It is enough to mention the names of Barrès, Maurras, Rolland, Péguy, and Bourget to point out that many members of his cohort became preoccupied with the same dichotomy, though they were led to it from different social roots and developmental routes than was Coubertin.

97. This is hardly surprising given the general sexual asymmetry of documents from the period.

98. "Le Roman d'un rallié," pp. 243–47, passim.

99. Ibid., p. 452.

100. Ibid., p. 238.

101. Classical psychoanalysis has too rigidly insisted upon the infantile origins of such conflicts and complexes. I make no such claims here.

102. On this evidence alone, Eyquem (Pierre de Coubertin, p. 10) suggests that Charles de Coubertin actually fought at Loigny. While this possibility cannot be definitively ruled out, it is in every way doubtful. Our earlier discussion (see above, pp. 22–24) of the symbolism of Loigny in father-son relations amply explains the battle's presence here.

103. Les Établissements des Jésuites en France 3:1396.

104. For a description of the buildings and grounds, see ibid., pp. 1399–1400.

105. Ibid., p. 1403.

106. In 1865, less than 10 percent of the secondary students in the Department of the Seine were enrolled in ecclesiastical schools. By 1876, in part thanks to renewed Jesuit activity, the figure had risen to 20–29 percent. The laic laws and the larger student population drove the figure down to 10–19 percent by 1887. Antoine Prost, Histoire de l'enseignement en France, 1800–1967 (Paris: Armand Colin, 1968), p. 38.

107. Recall Charles de Coubertin's association with Frs. de Ravignan and de Ponlevoy, see above, pp. 281–82, n. 43.

108. French Legitimists, pp. 71–80. The number of aristocratic students at the collège declined rapidly during the forced secularization of the 1880s.

109. Les Établissements des Jésuites en France 3:1401.

110. Between 1880 and 1900, demi-pensionnaires paid 600–800 francs in the cours élémentaires, 1000–1100 francs in the cours de lettres, and 1100 in the cours supérieurs. Ibid., p. 1406.

111. Canon Couturier, quoted ibid., p. 1401.

112. According to Eyquem (Pierre de Coubertin, p. 14), Mme. de Coubertin supplied the child with miniature censors, altar candles, and chalices to play with. The Jesuits, of course, could not have been more pleased than to have such parental approval for encouraging a boy toward holy orders. In the thirty-four years of Saint-Ignace's existence, two dozen of its pupils entered the secular clergy, forty entered Jesuit novitiates, and ten more joined other religious orders. Les Établissements des Jésuites en France 3:1420.

113. Locke, French Legitimists, p. 141.

114. La Morale des Jésuites, 3d ed. (Paris: Charpentier, 1880). I quote from the English translation by the publisher, The Doctrine of the Jesuits (Boston: Bradbury, 1880?), p. xxxv. This edition includes transcripts of Paul Bert's speeches to the chamber in June and July 1879, complete with the interruptions shouted from the right. As much as any other single text, this debate on the "Loi Paul Bert" reveals the passions and the character of the controversy surrounding institutions like Saint-Ignace.

115. For details, see Les Établissements des Jésuites en France 1:1489–90.

116. French language, literature, and history; arithmetic, geometry, and algebra; and geography were taught as well. Living foreign languages (German and English), if available,

were not encouraged. Pierre later wrote excellent English, but we know from Albert Shaw, his American editor, that he did not acquire it until "after attaining manhood" (Introduction, *The Evolution of France*, p. xiii). When he acquired his more slight facility with German is not clear.

117. Quoted in *Les Établissements des Jésuites en France* 3:1405.

118. *The Doctrine of the Jesuits*, pp. 505, and 500–514, passim.

119. Bert was an experimental physiologist and zoologist, a student and editor of the great Claude Bernard. Bert taught at the Faculté de sciences. In the course of the 1879 debate he praised the École libre des sciences politiques, which Pierre de Coubertin was shortly to attend, and the newly founded École d'anthropologie. Ibid., p. 528.

120. Jules Simon, *La Réforme de l'enseignement secondaire* (Paris: Hachette, 1874); Octave Gréard, *Éducation et instruction* (Paris: Hachette, 1887). Bréal spoke for them all when he wrote in his influential manifesto *Quelques Mots sur l'instruction publique en France* (Paris: Hachette, 1872): "Misfortune has it that questions in France are always posed in an absolute manner. One debates whether Latin and Greek are useful studies or if it's better to suppress them. But few dream of asking themselves whether the manner in which we conduct the study of the ancient languages is best suited to obtain the intellectual profit that society would be right to demand of it" (p. 5).

121. Bréal, *Quelques Mots sur l'instruction publique en France*, pp. 171–95, passim. Thirty years later, Durkheim put the case more strongly. "Antiquity had to be uprooted from its historical setting in order to be exploited [by the Jesuits]." *The Evolution of Educational Thought*, trans. Peter Collins (London & Boston: Routledge and Kegan Paul, 1977), p. 266. Durkheim quite correctly judged that Bréal's humanism was still literary and not yet scientific (p. 323), but Durkheim failed to recognize how his own summons to an *enseignement des choses* had been anticipated by Bréal's (*Quelques Mots*, pp. 106–125). Though their inspiration lay elsewhere, positivist educators were more indebted to the linguists and integral textualists than either they or subsequent historians of ideas have recognized. (A curious reversal of the contemporary relations between anthropologists and linguists.)

122. At Saint-Ignace, two years of rhetoric were taken by pupils aiming to go directly to the baccalaureate examinations. Those who took the *cours supérieurs*, a two-year course in philosophy and natural science (mathematics, physics, chemistry, and natural history), prior to the *bachot*, stayed but one year in rhetoric. Since Pierre did not sit for his exams until 1880 and then received both *baccalauréats*, *ès lettres* and *ès sciences* (the twelve month wait between the two exams was not instituted until later that year), he must have followed the latter course of study.

123. Prost, *L'Ènseignement en France*, pp. 52–53.

124. Ibid., p. 53.

125. Ibid.

126. Ibid., p. 55.

127. Ibid., p. 53.

128. For an excellent history of the entire controversy see Clément Falcucci, *L'Humanisme dans l'enseignement secondaire en France au XIXᵉ siècle* (Toulouse: Édouard Privat, 1939).

129. *The Evolution of Educational Thought*, p. 265.

130. "It was wise to get to know the child well in order to be able to help in the development of his nascent personality. The Jesuits studied him rather in order to stifle more effectively his sense of himself." Ibid., p. 264.

131. Ibid., p. 260.

132. Ibid., p. 264.

133. Ibid.

134. Whole classes were divided into Carthaginians and Romans, with the best pupils awarded the roles of *imperator* and *praetor* and encouraged to lord it over the lowly infantry.

135. Ibid., p. 260.

136. *Les Établissements des Jésuites en France* 3:1405.

137. At a reunion of former students of Saint-Ignace on March 7, 1937, Pierre "recalled with remarkable clarity a certain fable of La Fontaine [the "favorite author of France," Bréal noted sarcastically, *Quelques Mots*, p. 742] recited and mimed by three persons during a class session. At the appropriate moment, I emerged from underneath a piece of furniture representing the den of the animal whose role I played; this must have taken place in 1876, in the fourth form taught by Fr. Froger. In the ensuing years there were other, more serious performances: pieces of tragedy in costume, with hot wine in the wings; then sessions of the Academy that Jean de Courcy presided over with a magnificent commander's ribbon affixed to his chest, while I held under my arm the secretary's superbly bound archives, containing the minutes of our meetings." Quoted in *Les Établissements des Jésuites en France* 3:1405. This quotation is interesting in that the Jesuit compilers of the history of the externat could quote Coubertin without seeing fit to mention his adult achievements in their discussion of illustrious former pupils. The Olympic Games were apparently unjesuitical.

138. A Jesuit priest whom Coubertin remembered as a "subtle logician," a "disciple of Saint Anselm much devoted to proving the existence of God," and "an enemy of all enthusiasm." "Le Roman d'un rallié," p. 600.

139. *The Evolution of Educational Thought*, pp. 263–64.

140. "The Committee for the Propagation of Physical Exercises in Education," endorsed by the Conseil supérieur de l'éducation on May 31, 1888.

141. Gréard was skeptical of the pedagogical value of sport, but, perhaps in the hope of turning the young baron's schemes in more conventional directions, Gréard permitted Coubertin the use of the Sorbonne's Great Hall. As we shall see, this was a symbolic resource of great importance in the early days of the Olympic Movement. Cf. Boulongne, *La Vie et l'oeuvre*, p. 187.

142. P. 601. There is some irony in Coubertin's use of the word *eclecticism* here. The overtones of dilettantism and superficiality which the word has taken on in both French and English are exactly opposite of the intended meaning. Yet, throughout his early life, Coubertin read widely, but never deeply. He was never a scholar in the strict sense of the term, but a moralist whose intellect was of a practical and not a theoretical cast. And, as we shall repeatedly see, his interest in and acquaintance with differing lifestyles were never enough to lure him far from aristocratic milieus.

Such passages remind one of *Étienne Mayran*, Hippolyte Taine's disguised autobiography. In it the horrors of the regimen at Saint-Honoré, the Paris *collège* Taine attended, are contrasted with the intellectual fervor, the enthusiasm for books and ideas, especially Greek ones, and the free interior life which Étienne enjoyed upon release from school. "Above all, he no longer felt isolated, he lived intimately with a vital meaning that never left him without emotion. Cold stoicism, painful resignation, had disappeared. A fertile and tumultuous flood of great desires had covered over and drowned them. . . . In this first rush, he imagined that all pursuits were going to be easy for him and that, the dike once ruptured, the flood of discoveries would flow as it had in the first days." *Étienne Mayran*, ed. Blossom L. Henry (New York: Prentice-Hall, 1931), pp. 110–11. Were it not that Taine's novel did not appear till 1910, one would suspect a genealogical relationship between his Étienne and Coubertin's, for as we shall see, Taine was an important early influence on the baron.

143. *Les Établissements des Jésuites* 3:1362.

144. Ibid., pp. 1365–66.

145. *The Army of the Republic* (Cambridge: M.I.T. Press, 1967), pp. 19, 84.

146. *Une Campagne de 21 ans*, p. 2.

147. *The Army of the Republic*, pp. 258–59.

148. "Bureaucracy," in *From Max Weber: Essays in Sociology*, ed. and trans. H. H. Gerth and C. Wright Mills (New York: Oxford University Press, 1946), pp. 196–244.

149. Letter to Mrs. G. B. Shaw, 1932, quoted in John E. Mack, *A Prince of Our Disorder* (New York: Little, Brown, 1976), p. 324. Lawrence's "contentment" in the R.A.F., of course, followed upon and would have been unthinkable without his years of prowess in the deserts and capitals of Arabia. The Coubertin of 1880, three years away from his first trip to England and more than a decade away from the sight of Greece, ought to be compared with the Lawrence of 1905, beginning his tours through France in search of Crusader castles, four years away from the Middle East. The lives of these two men deserve systematic comparison. Like their most notable achievements, their lives are reversed, mirror images of one another.

150. *The Army of the Republic*, p. 256.

151. In "Le Roman d'un rallié," Étienne is an only child (and, recall, fatherless) who laments (none too convincingly) the absence of siblings.

152. Ralston, *The Army of the Republic*, p. 229. Ralston is referring to a slightly later period here, but the scandal surrounding the examinations for the École polytechnique in 1876 illustrates the same condition of opinion in political circles during the period of Pierre's preparation for St.-Cyr. The examination results were annulled when it was claimed that Jesuit pupils had been supplied with the questions in advance. A parliamentary commission of inquiry was impanelled, with Gambetta leading the prosecutors and Albert de Mun leading the defense. Though charges were later dismissed, republican fears about the number of legitimists acceding to St.-Cyr and to the Polytechnique and thence to the army were hardly allayed. *Les Établissements des Jésuites* 3:1366–67.

153. "Le Roman d'un rallié," p. 681. There is a notable, unintended irony in this remark. Coubertin wrote it just after bringing to life the vision he had in the ruins of ancient Olympia.

154. P. 2.

155. *Une existence d'exception*. I have rendered the phrase literally in order to retain the ambiguity suggested by the French. The same ambiguity is employed in the category "exceptional children," in which our school authorities include both mental prodigies and the disabled and retarded.

156. While the subject is Coubertin's state of mind in 1882, the metaphors chosen to describe it belong to 1898. The arena, the purple-draped marble tribune full of aristocrats, the crowd of spectators who may or may not glance at them: the recently completed first modern Olympic Games in Athens had to be the source of these strikingly visual images in Coubertin's mind's eye, here converted and generalized into metaphors for his whole life course. The descent of the crown prince of Greece into the arena to lift up in celebration Spiridon Loues, the Greek shepherd whose victory in the first Marathon race produced an extraordinary public ecstasy, provided the embryonic Olympic Movement its most important early symbol, as we shall see. And, of course, it was the Olympic Movement that ultimately provided Coubertin himself with his "descent from his descent" into the thick of modern life.

157. "Le Roman d'un rallié," pp. 45–46.

Chapter Three

1. "Where the Action Is," in *Interaction Ritual* (New York: Doubleday Anchor, 1967), pp. 149–270.

2. By the 1890s, *le globetrotter* was a well-entrenched item in French vocabulary. For example, the anonymous author of the introduction to "Le Roman d'un rallié" uses it to refer to Étienne.

3. Ethel Jones, *Les Voyageurs français en Angleterre de 1815 à 1830* (Paris: Boccard, 1930), p. 183.

4. Quoted ibid., p. 182.

5. Ibid., p. 183.

6. Ibid., p. 195.

7. Stäel-Holstein, quoted ibid., p. 183.

8. *France 1848–1945*, vol. 2: *Intellect, Taste, Anxiety* (Oxford: Oxford University Press, 1977), pp. 101–2. See also "English Ideals in French Politics," *Cambridge Historical Journal* 1 (1959): 40–58.

9. Zeldin, *France 1848–1945*, 2:109. It is interesting and ironic that neither conservative nor liberal French critics perceived the role played by the English counterrevolution against "Jacobinism" in the creation of the working-class conditions they so quickly and rightly denounced. On this, see E. P. Thompson's *The Making of the English Working Class* (New York: Vintage, 1963).

10. Pierre de Coubertin, "Les Universités anglaises: Cambridge," *La Réforme sociale* 12 (1886): 601–2; "L'Éducation anglaise," *La Réforme sociale* 13 (1887); 634, 644, 647.

11. *Notes on England*, trans. Edward Hyams (London: Thames & Hudson, 1957), pp. 161–62. A crucial and destructive compartmentalization follows here. I do not know that Taine wrote on colonial policy. But many who, like the young Coubertin, followed his lead in denying the transplantability of political and social institutions between civilized nations failed to grant the same dispensation to colonial peoples.

12. Ibid., p. 197.

13. Ibid., pp. 137, 207.

14. As a matter of principle as well as of tact, Taine refused to quote from conversations with the famous. He makes an exception of Thackeray "because he has since died" (p. 196). Coubertin was also an enemy of the great-man theory of history, but he name-dropped whenever the occasion presented itself.

15. Taine is known to have visited England in 1859, and again in 1871, when *Notes* was published. Hyams (Introduction, pp. xxii–xxiii) produces good evidence of a third visit in 1862. In his text, Taine associates length of stay with familiarity, but does not apply the principle to himself. He does not even report the duration of his visits, leaving the matter to the puzzlement of scholars.

16. *Notes on England*, p. 197.

17. Ibid., p. 191.

18. Ibid., p. 134. Taine fails to sort out the relationship between national ideology, world view, and national character (world view seen from the outside). He writes: "Every nation takes the type which best manifests the national genius and serves the national needs, consecrates it and puts it on a pedestal. That is why public opinion, the common conscience [one of Durkheim's many debts to Taine shows here], says to every Englishman: 'Work, take a hand in some useful undertaking; if you do not, you are not a man, and have no right to self-respect'" (p. 65). Whose interests are taken as the "national" interest? Who controls the nation's self-perception and the perception of outsiders? What conflicts might there be between "national genius" and "national needs"? What constitutes the "best" manifestation? Unlike Marx, Taine little troubles himself with such questions.

19. The best known of Taine's positivist forays in the *Notes* is his chapter on English "types," categories of Englishmen amalgamated from physiognomy, humoral theory, personality, and style. Taine sees "types" not simply as analytical constructs, but as entities in the world ("Since I have arrived here, I have been *collecting* types, adding them to those I collected last year," p. 39, my emphasis). The strategy is interesting for its attempt to cross-cut class, status, age, and sexual categories, and for its incipient transformationalism, a kind of psychological grammar. But it goes nowhere, neither organizing new observations nor amounting to any theory. The types serve Taine most often to explain away apparent contradictions, for example, between the red- and hot-blooded nature of the English and their cold-bloodedness (*sang-froid*) in the face of danger or challenge (p. 50). This romance

with classification, with its incipient determinism and deemphasis of individuality, has, of course, industrial equivalents.

20. Ibid., p. 38.

21. Ibid., pp. 268–69.

22. Ibid., p. 100.

23. Ibid., pp. 31, 29.

24. Ibid.

25. Ibid., p. 36.

26. Ibid., p. 99.

27. Ibid., p. 47.

28. See Edward T. Gargan, Editor's Introduction, in Hippolyte Adolphe Taine, *The Origins of Contemporary France* (Chicago: University of Chicago Press, 1974), p. xvi.

29. *Notes on England*, pp. 18, 228, 263.

30. Ibid., p. 25.

31. Ibid., p. 134.

32. Ibid., p. 168.

33. Ibid. Taine is careful to discriminate this central meaning of English patronage—the exchange of good works for feelings of satisfaction of moral duty—from other, peripheral patronage exchanges. On the one hand, he ridicules the older sense of aristocratic mores by reporting an anecdote wherein an obsequious shopkeeper inquires of his middle class customers. "What kind of cheese do you 'patronize,' Madam?" (p. 195). On the other hand, he is aware of "patronage" in today's familiar political sense, the exchange of favors for votes (p. 184), but this, he makes clear, is an aberration. Taine is no fool on the economic underside of upper class good works. He does not doubt that the profit of the nobility and the gentry "is used less to relieve the poor than to enrich the rich. But in compensation the rich are natural born leaders, benevolent, and recognized as such" (p. 138). He does, however, overlook the religious payoff that, in no small way, underlay upper class English patronage.

34. Ibid., p. 145.

35. Ibid., p. 144.

36. The word is used a dozen times in the *Notes*, an important fact to which I will return in a subsequent work.

37. In the phrase of Lévi-Strauss who, by way of Durkheim, owes a debt to Taine.

38. A phrase which Coubertin sometimes translated (and transformed) into "athlétisme chrétien." "L'Éducation anglaise," p. 642.

39. See *Étienne Mayran*.

40. *Notes on England*, p. 5.

41. Hughes's purpose of representing "the most common type of a little English boy of the upper middle-class" was consistent with Taine's own methodology. "The book thus conceived," Taine wrote, "enjoyed an enormous success. Youths and grown men, all recognized themselves in the book, and we may make use of it ourselves while recognizing, with its author, that Tom's portrait, if not actually flattering, was certainly benevolently drawn" (ibid., p. 106).

42. The words are Danton's. Coubertin quotes this "profound saying" in his *Notes sur l'éducation publique* (Paris: Hachette, 1901), p. 1.

43. *Une Campagne de 21 ans*, p. 2. For Coubertin's description of the "mixed education" at Beaumont see "Les Collèges anglais: Harrow School," *La Réforme sociale* 12 (1886): 473.

44. See Coubertin, "Courrier d'Irlande: Les Difficultés de la situation," *La Réforme sociale* 13 (1887): 235 n. 1, 240; and "Toynbee Hall: Le Patronage social à Londres et les étudiants anglais," *La Réforme sociale* 14 (1887): 227. On the 1887 visit, see Boulongne, *La Vie et l'oeuvre*, p. 57.

45. All are discussed in his *L'Éducation en Angleterre* (Paris: Hachette, 1888), his first book, much of it a collection of earlier articles in *La Réforme sociale*.

46. *Une Campagne de 21 ans*, p. 2.

47. From English contacts, such as Austen Chamberlain, his former classmate at Saint-Ignace, or from officials at his previous stop.

48. "L'Éducation anglaise," p. 636.

49. "At Eton, in one of the 'boarding houses,' I recall having knocked at the door of a boy I was acquainted with. I was conducted there by a master's daughter who entered with me and put an end to the chit-chat. My young host was just returning from cricket." Ibid.

50. Eyquem presents a long reconstruction of Coubertin's days at the public schools (*Pierre de Coubertin*, pp. 33–52). It is entertaining and accurate in spirit. But it is a reconstruction, mixing events that clearly belong to 1886 (the Irish visit, Toynbee Hall) into a purported description of the 1883 trip. This creates an artificial and inaccurate impression that Coubertin's mission came to him suddenly and all-of-a-piece.

51. See below, pp. 127–28.

52. Serialized in the *London Daily News* in the late 1870s.

53. "L'Éducation anglaise," p. 639. Eyquem identifies him as one Meredith Brown (*Pierre de Coubertin*, p. 34).

54. Coubertin, *Une Campagne de 21 ans*, p. 2.

55. *Notes on England*, p. 106.

56. *Une Campagne de 21 ans*, p. 3. Coubertin also owned a copy of the 1880 London edition of *Tom Brown at Oxford*, and both books were treasured possessions till the end of his life. Boulongne, *La Vie et l'oeuvre*, p. 111, p. 22.

57. Reported by Eyquem, *Pierre de Coubertin*, p. 51. Though no citation is given, Eyquem could not have invented this episode. Moreover, it is perfectly consistent with what we may imagine to be his parents' views at the time. Chambord died in 1883, and the legitimists had no choice but to turn to the other branch of the royal family. That Coubertin discussed English schools with the comte (ibid.) is another sign of his attempts to build bridges between the old and new worlds.

58. Eyquem reproduces this conversation from "unpublished manuscripts," ibid., p. 54. As previously noted (see above, chap. 1, n. 15), Boulongne has established that these manuscripts were later destroyed by Coubertin's surviving relatives. It is impossible, therefore, to verify this conversation.

The whole matter of Coubertin's unpublished letters and papers is controversial. John Apostal Lucas (pers. comm., Lausanne, 1975) told me that materials he had seen in the I.O.C. archives during the early 1960s had subsequently disappeared, "probably returned to and destroyed by the family." However, in 1975, M. Emmanuel Migraine, I.O.C. archivist and librarian, denied to me that any such removal had ever taken place. In my research at Château de Vidy, I turned up few unpublished materials not already known to Coubertin scholars from Boulongne's bibliography.

59. Eyquem, *Pierre de Coubertin*, p. 54.

60. See "L'Éducation anglaise," p. 646. And for the contrast with French fathers, see *L'Éducation anglaise en France* (Paris: Hachette, 1889), pp. 180–81.

61. Courses at the école began in November, so it could have been in late 1884 that Coubertin enrolled.

62. Hippolyte Taine, "Fondation de l'École libre des sciences politiques," in *Derniers Essais de critique et d'histoire* (Paris: Hachette, 1894), p. 96.

63. Coubertin, "The Revival of the French Universities," *American Monthly Review of Reviews* 16 (1897): 56.

64. Taine, "Fondation de l'École," pp. 79–80.

65. Quoted in Zeldin, *France 1848–1945*, 2:343.

66. Quoted in Gargan, Editor's Introduction, p. xxxvi. As Gargan notes, Bloch thought that the heritage of the école played an important, and destablilizing, role in the later fortunes of the Third Republic.

67. For an excellent summary of Boutmy's views on England, see Zeldin, *France 1848–1945*, 2:105–8.

68. *Annales des sciences politiques* 1 (1886): 165–203.

69. Ibid., 2 (1887): 435–522.

70. *La Développement de la constitution et la société politique en Angleterre* (Paris: Plon et Marescq ainé, 1887). Other Boutmy articles on England followed at the rate of one a year through the '80s, and more slowly in the '90s, when Boutmy, like Coubertin, turned his attentions to the United States.

71. In the pages of the *Annales des sciences politiques*, Lucien Lévy-Bruhl was to Germany what Boutmy was to England. Coubertin seems not to have noticed Lévy-Bruhl. To the degree that Coubertin read on Germany, it was probably to his future associate Michel Bréal that he turned. Bréal's *Excursions pédagogiques: Un Voyage scolaire en Allemagne* (Paris: Hachette, 1882) was a document very like Coubertin's *L'Éducation en Angleterre*, and it included a chapter devoted to German physical education. Here then is another strand in the network of reformers Coubertin was becoming enmeshed in. The liberal classicists of the university establishment, like Bréal, were becoming internationalists themselves in the 1880s. Bréal (and Simon) provided the link between classical Greece and modern, international educational practice, a connection missing from the *École des sciences politiques*, whose commitment to positivist learning pushed the classical heritage into the background. (Boutmy's first book, published in 1870, concerned Greek architecture, but, once the école was founded, he never returned to these waters.) As mentioned above, Coubertin joined with Bréal in 1894, to invent the Marathon race.

72. Taine, "La Fondation de l'École," p. 80.

73. Zeldin, *France 1848–1945*, 2:343.

74. *Annales des sciences politiques* 1 (1886): 307–10.

75. To Taine, "ethnography" was defined as the study of "the natural boundaries, the races, languages, and religions of the principal states." "La Fondation de L'École," p. 80, from which this course list is taken.

76. "Histoire des théories contemporaines relatives à l'organisation des sociétés." About this course, Taine writes: "It is valuable to know one's adversaries, their motive, their principle, and their power. From Baboeuf to Saint-Simon and Fourier, from Proudhon, Louis Blanc, and Cabet to the Internationale, many sorts of millenniums have been constructed on paper, and we know what ravages they've made in uncultivated brains led by half-cultivated ones." The course also treated millennial religious sects in order to dismiss them. Among the "supportable or, at least, arguable" social theories taught was that of Frédéric Le Play, an important fact as we shall see. Ibid., pp. 94–95.

77. A fifth, colonial section, designed to recruit and train administrators for the French colonies, was added in 1887. See *Annales des sciences politiques* 1 (1886): 477, 485–86.

78. Coubertin, "Mes mémoires," *Ms*, 1936. The full text is printed in Boulongne, *La Vie et l'oeuvre*, pp. 455–61.

79. Coubertin, "The Revival of the French Universities," p. 56.

80. *Pierre de Coubertin*, p. 54, citing unpublished manuscripts.

81. *L'Europe et la révolution française* (Paris: Plon, Nourrit, 1887).

82. *Les Catholiques libéraux: L'Église et le libéralisme de 1830 à nos jours* (Paris: Plon, Nourrit, 1885). His best-known work is perhaps *Les Juifs et l'antisémitisme: Israel chez les nations* (Paris: C. Levy, 1893). But was it really Anatole Leroy-Beaulieu, and not his brother Paul, whom Coubertin so admired during his student days? Paul Leroy-Beaulieu, a well-known economist and later a deputy, had written a book on England (*L'Administration locale en France et en Angleterre*, 1872), addressed the école banquet in June 1886, and the following year inaugurated the colonial section with a series of lectures. Though I have been unable to confirm it, he may very well have taught a new course in 1885 or 1886. In his 1897 paean to the école, it was Leroy-Beaulieu the "economist, business, and practical man," that is to say

Paul Leroy-Beaulieu, whom Coubertin remembered as so important to the school. Was this because, in the interim, Paul Leroy-Beaulieu had been briefly associated with Coubertin's project, and so was favorably remembered? Or was it because he was indeed Coubertin's teacher in 1885–86? Eyquem is quite definite that it was Anatole Leroy-Beaulieu who was Coubertin's teacher, but since the manuscripts she says she is citing are no longer extant, it seems safest to conclude for the time being that Coubertin knew both men at the école.

83. How triumphant Coubertin must have felt when he returned to give these five lectures in the very halls where a dozen years earlier he had sat unknown, listening to men "with names." The fifth of his lectures, "Philosophie de l'histoire des Etats-Unis," was published in *La Revue bleue* 35 (June 4, 1898): 708–15.

84. "The Revival of the French Universities," p. 56.

85. My use of the terms "marginality" and liminality" follows that of Victor Turner. See *The Ritual Process* (Chicago: Aldine, 1969); *Dramas, Fields and Metaphors* (Ithaca: Cornell University Press, 1974); and Victor and Edith Turner, *Image and Pilgrimage in Christian Culture* (New York: Columbia University Press, 1978), pp. 249–51.

86. "Le Roman d'un rallié" is all we really have to go on for picturing Coubertin's social life away from the école. Though the evidence is scant and dicey, it seems clear that Coubertin was no hermit in 1885–86. Since he was still living at his parents' home in the rue Oudinot, he was in constant contact with their visitors at dinner parties, salons, and the like. Given his conflicted relations with his parents and their set, he may have absented himself as much as possible in the evenings. The "Roman" suggests that, however much he disapproved, he did indeed join in the usual amusements of his peer group. This must have made him exceedingly uncomfortable in yet another way, for, as Zeldin points out, the styles of aristocratic and upper middle class "high life" had been "Anglicized." "Dandyisme," English clothes, "bifteck" and "cocktails" at "Le Jockey-Club," turf sports, "flirting" with the girls: all had penetrated Parisian leisure (*France 1848–1945*, 2:102–3).

While these developments may have inspired, or even gratified, Coubertin, they must have also given him moments of severe self-doubt. Could his moral commitment to English ways, and his "serious" discussions of English institutions each morning at the école, be no more than rationalizations of the "playacting" at being English, conducted by the *gentilshommes* each evening on the Faubourg? Though we have no evidence for it, my guess is that he was often bedeviled by "what is real and what is pretense" in his own and his class's imitation of the English. His later distinction between "cosmopolitanism" and "true internationalism," discussed in the final chapter, may have in part been inspired by such early experiences.

87. *Une Campagne de 21 ans*, pp. 26–27 n. 1, 25, 27.

88. Ibid., p. 5. This was an "additive" or "cumulative" vision, for in this passage Coubertin makes clear that he had had this experience in Rugby Chapel several times. It seems to have grown in intensity each time until, in a flash one day, it quite overtook him. Many, perhaps all, such visions—intense psychospiritual experiences of revelation/conversion—are of this cumulative nature. The paradigm of the prophet-reformer's life is typically set in motion and controlled by two visions, the first, the conversion or call, the second, the confirmation and communication of the program. Coubertin's second vision awaited him at Archaia Olympia in 1894.

89. Matthew Arnold, "Rugby Chapel," in *The Works of Matthew Arnold*, 15 vols. (London: Macmillan, 1903), 1:269.

90. That Coubertin, so interested in the father, took no notice of the son, is curious indeed. Matthew Arnold was not only a philhellene and, by Coubertin's time, a famous critic, but he was also a school inspector. In 1859, he passed Taine in the Channel, on his way to make an inspection of the French school system. His *The Popular Education of France* was published in 1861. In 1863–64, he came out with *A French Eton; or, Middle Class Education and the State*, a work whose title expresses Coubertin's very project and whose conclusions

would have gratified and confirmed the baron's own. This massive trilogy, now entitled *Democratic Education*, was completed in 1868, with the appearance of Arnold's *Schools and Universities on the Continent*. (The first two parts are republished as vol. 2, and the third as vol. 4, of *The Complete Prose Works of Matthew Arnold*, ed. R. H. Super [Ann Arbor: University of Michigan Press, 1962, 1964].)

Coubertin never mentions these works, nor did he make any known attempt to contact Matthew Arnold in London in 1883, 1886, or 1887. (Arnold died in 1888.) His lifelong silence on Matthew Arnold is frankly deafening, all the more so since Charles Kingsley was known to Coubertin (though confusedly, as a contemporary of Thomas rather than of Matthew Arnold) at least as early as 1894 ("Athletics in the Modern World and the Olympic Games," *The Olympic Idea*, p. 8), and Coubertin is reputed to have called on that lifelong enemy of Arnold *père* and *fils*, Cardinal Newman (Eyquem, *Pierre de Coubertin*, p. 49, citing unpublished documents). Though it fits well enough with Coubertin's customary unwillingness to read, or to read systematically, the leading intellects of his day or to search carefully for precedents in the literature (what reformer does?), his avoidance of Matthew Arnold does not square with his habit of barging in on the famous who have something, even remotely, to do with his projects. One cannot help suspecting that Coubertin had a wish, perhaps not conscious, to protect his own vision of Thomas Arnold from what other "truer" sons might have to tell him. If so, then his "ignorance" of Matthew was of a piece with his lack of interest in learning anything of the real Thomas Hughes, and with his selective reading of A. P. Stanley. More on these below.

91. Thomas Hughes, *Tom Brown's Schooldays* (London: Macmillan, 1878 [1857]), p. 375. "And let us not be hard on him," the passage continues, "if at that moment his soul is fuller of the tomb and him who lies there, than of the altar and Him of whom it speaks. Such stages have to be gone through, I believe, by all young and brave souls who must win their way, through hero-worship, to the worship of Him who is the King and Lord of heroes." This is an autobiographical note, and the pious Hughes, writing to his own son and for the moral improvement of English boys, could not help but add it. Coubertin would not have so cautioned himself. He was "winning his way" to a worship of humanity and not to a rededication to the Christian god, and, as we shall also see, his concern was to strip the Arnoldian legacy of its dogmatic religiosity, not to accommodate it.

92. Bill Henry, *An Approved History of the Olympic Games* (New York: Putnam, 1976 [1948]), pp. 5–7; and Otto Mayer, *À travers les anneaux olympiques*, pp. 10–11, are but two of the many who credulously accept, as "true believers" in Olympism, what Coubertin said of Arnold. While more elaborate, Eyquem's account in *Pierre de Coubertin* is little improved in this regard.

93. Mandell, *The First Modern Olympics*, pp. 58–60. The first point stands against everything we know about Coubertin and is based on a crude disjunction between "myth" and "reality"; and the second is also simplistic. *Tom Brown* is more than a children's book, and Thomas Hughes was more than a writer of such.

John Apostal Lucas, a febrile partisan of the Olympic Movement, also consigns Coubertin's Arnold to self-created illusion in "Baron Pierre de Coubertin and the Formative Years of the Modern International Olympic Movement, 1883–1896" (Ph.D. diss., University of Maryland, 1962). Eugen Weber ("Pierre de Coubertin") does not consider the issue, leaving Yves-Pierre Boulongne (*La Vie et l'oeuvre*, pp. 111–24) the only author who attempts to sort responsibly between the legend and the fact. Unfortunately, Boulongne (following Jacques Ulmann, *De la gymnastique aux sports modernes* [Paris: Vrin, 1971], and Peter MacIntosh, *Sport and Society* [London: C. A. Watts, 1963]) considers only Arnold's role in sports and not his larger place in pedagogical history. Boulongne knows the sources of Coubertin's information about Arnold but does not investigate them.

94. "L'Éducation anglaise," p. 635.

95. Ibid.

96. Ibid., p. 632.

97. Ibid., p. 636.

98. *Thomas Arnold* (London: Cresset, 1960), pp. 175ff.

99. My use of the term *imago* is psychoanalytical, but in the combined senses of Freud and Jung.

100. From Boulongne (*La Vie et l'oeuvre*, pp. 114, 120) we know that Coubertin owned the 1882 edition of Stanley's *Life* (London: Murray; first published in 1844, two years after Arnold's death), as well as the more obscure *The Life of Dr. Arnold* by Emmena Jane Worboise (London, 1885). That he read Stanley in the 1880s, while his views on Arnold were in formation, is established without a doubt by his 1887 article "L'Éducation anglaise." Though he does not mention Stanley by name, the Arnold letters that he cites were published nowhere else than in Stanley's *Life*. Moreover, certain passages referring to episodes during the Doctor's headmastership are virtual paraphrases of Stanley. Later, in *Une Campagne de 21 ans* (p. 3), Coubertin asserts that he read extensively Arnold's "letters and sermons." While several volumes of sermons were indeed published in England, my sense is that he knew these also from Stanley's citations of them.

101. Edward C. Mack and W. H. G. Armytage, *Thomas Hughes* (London: Ernest Benn, 1952), pp. 20–25.

102. Ibid., p. 96.

103. Ibid., pp. 22–23.

104. A. P. Stanley, *The Life and Correspondence of Thomas Arnold* (New York: Appleton, 1845), p. 73.

105. Edward C. Mack, *Public Schools and British Opinion 1780–1860* (London: Methuen, 1938), p. 240.

106. When *Tom Brown* was published, Stanley wrote, "It is an absolute revelation to me: opens up a world of which, though so near to me, I was utterly ignorant." Quoted ibid., p. 306. Hughes, for his part, expressed amazement, in the preface to later editions of *Tom Brown*, that some found Rugby boys "a solemn array," "turned into men before their time," and "a semi-political, semi-sacerdotal fraternity," p. xiv.

107. Mack and Armytage, *Thomas Hughes*, p. 23. Matthew Arnold sounded this forlorn note in "Rugby Chapel": "For fifteen years, / We who till then in thy shade'/'Rested as under the boughs / Of a mighty oak, having endured / Sunshine and rain as we might / Bare, unshaded, alone, / Lacking the shelter of Thee."

108. For details, see R. E. Prothero [R. E. P. Ernle], *The Life and Correspondence of A. P. Stanley* (New York: Scribner, 1894).

109. Stanley, *The Life*, p. 34.

110. Ibid., p. 61.

111. Ibid., p. 73.

112. Ibid., pp. 61–62.

113. Ibid., p. 112.

114. Ibid., p. 73.

115. Ibid., p. 30.

116. Ibid., p. 29.

117. Ibid., p. 110.

118. Ibid., p. 69.

119. Ibid., p. 104.

120. Ibid., p. 99.

121. Ibid., p. 86.

122. Ibid., p. 73.

123. "L'Éducation anglaise," p. 633.

124. Ibid., p. 641.

125. Not until Lytton Strachey's withering portrait of Arnold in *Eminent Victorians* (London: Putnam, 1918) did his extreme religiosity retake its proper place in the popular image of Arnold.

126. "L'Éducation anglaise," p. 634.

127. Mack, *Public Schools and British Opinion*, p. 240.

128. *True Manliness: Selections from the Writings of Thomas Hughes*, ed. E. E. Brown, Introduction by James Russell Lowell (Boston, 1880); see also the series of lectures *The Manliness of Christ* (London: Macmillan, 1879).

129. Mack and Armytage, *Thomas Hughes*, p. 100.

130. "L'Éducation anglaise," p. 643.

131. *Tom Brown's Schooldays*, p. 311. "Boys will quarrel, and when they quarrel will sometimes fight. Fighting is the natural and English way for English boys to settle their quarrels. What substitute is there, or ever was there, amongst any nation under the sun?... As to fighting, keep out of it if you can, by all means. When the time comes, if it ever should, that you have to say 'Yes' or 'No' to a challenge to fight, say 'No' if you can,—only take care that you make it clear to yourselves why you say 'No.' It's a proof of the highest courage, if done from true Christian motives. It's quite right and justifiable if done from a simple aversion to physical pain and danger. But don't say 'No' because you fear a licking, and say or think it's because you fear God, for that's neither Christian nor honest. And if you do fight, fight it out, and don't give up while you can see or stand" (p. 299).

Arnold thought little of fighting to settle quarrels, and he sought to put a stop to it. The speech of old Brooke in *Tom Brown* notwithstanding, Arnold probably did not think much of the regular sparring in the houses either. This, too, Hughes found a very good practice (p. 280). On the first sort of fighting, Coubertin is silent. On the second sort, he agreed with Hughes that boxing gloves are "the surest keepers of the peace." Years later, Coubertin would defend boxing as an Olympic sport against all the humanitarian critics, and would admire Theodore Roosevelt's wisdom for promoting boxing matches in the rougher sections of New York, while he was president of the Board of Police Commissioners.

132. "L'Éducation anglaise," p. 634. This distinction was well known in French pedagogical circles. It gave Octave Gréard the title for one of his books.

133. Ibid., p. 652. *Surmenage* ("overwork") became, as we shall see, the rallying cry of many school reformers, Coubertin included, in the 1880s and '90s in France.

134. Ibid., p. 634.

135. Mack and Armytage, *Thomas Hughes*, p. 13.

136. Ibid., p. 96.

137. "L'Éducation anglaise," p. 635.

138. Ibid., p. 633.

139. Bamford, *Thomas Arnold*, pp. 49ff.

140. *The Life*, pp. 78, 85.

141. "L'Éducation anglaise," p. 635.

142. *Notes on England*, pp. 108–9.

143. "L'Éducation anglaise," p. 638.

144. Ibid., p. 639.

145. *The Life*, p. 79, n. 1.

146. *Notes on England*, p. 109.

147. "L'Éducation anglaise," p. 646; see also p. 639.

148. Stanley, *The Life*, p. 82; Coubertin's translation is in "L'Éducation anglaise," p. 639.

149. Coubertin, "L'Éducation anglaise," p. 639.

150. Stanley, *The Life*, p. 81; cf. Coubertin, "L'Éducation anglaise," p. 639.

151. Arnold Whitridge, *Dr. Arnold of Rugby*, Introduction by Sir Michael Sadler (New York: Henry Holt, 1928), p. 109.

152. *The Life*, p. 80.

153. "L'Éducation anglaise," p. 637.
154. Ibid.
155. Ibid.
156. Ibid.
157. Ibid.
158. Ibid., pp. 637–38.
159. Ibid., pp. 637–38.
160. Ibid., p. 639.
161. Ibid., p. 641.
162. Ibid.
163. Ibid.
164. Ibid., pp. 647–48.
165. Ibid., p. 646.
166. See Mack, *Public Schools and British Opinion*, pp. 312–13; see also Bamford, *Thomas Arnold*, pp. 104–5.
167. Stanley, *The Life*, pp. 75–77.
168. "L'Éducation anglaise," pp. 647, 651.
169. Ibid., p. 651.
170. Ibid., pp. 635–36.
171. Ibid.
172. Ibid., pp. 646–47. Some have tried to make of Coubertin a crude Social Darwinist. This passage is about as close as he ever comes, and it is ambiguous. Selection was a "very British idea," and as an anglophile, he admired almost everything English. But nowhere in his writings doe she attempt to apply such ideas to France, or in general to promote them. He certainly did not admire the division of England into "two races," and no crude Social Darwinist believed it possible to uplift all of the weak through the patient labors of the strong. In any case, it is not even clear what Coubertin understood by "selection"—probably no more than competiton and struggle, which he did think characteristic of his era, as indeed they were.
173. Ibid., p. 636.
174. Ironically, it seems. For while Bamford is perhaps too Whiggish on Arnold's educational achievements, he is quite right that Arnold ought best to be remembered for his political and social agitations. See Eugene L. Williamson, Jr., *The Liberalism of Thomas Arnold* (University, Ala.: University of Alabama Press, 1964).
175. See Weber, *Peasants into Frenchmen*.
176. In the sense of E. P. Thompson, *The Making of the English Working Class*.
177. *L'Évolution française*, pp. xxix–xli, passim.
178. Quoted in Mack and Armytage, *Thomas Hughes*, p. 43.
179. Mack, *Public Schools and British Opinion*, p. 265.
180. Stanley, *The Life*, pp. 245–46.
181. Quoted in Bamford, *Thomas Arnold*, p. 45.
182. Stanley insisted that Arnold did not indoctrinate the boys with his own political and social views. Bamford, on the other hand, finds merit in the charges at the time that Arnold did indeed seek to win over students to his "Radical" beliefs. Mack (*Public Schools and British Opinion*, pp. 292ff.) comes down somewhere in the middle.
183. It is in this sense that I take his remark, made in 1936, that it was in 1887 that he "rallied once and for all" to the Republic ("Mes mémoires," p. 457), the same year from which he dated his "21-year campaign" for school reform.
184. Letter to the *Hertford Reformer*, quoted in Raymond Williams, *Culture and Society 1780–1950* (New York: Harper & Row, 1966), p. 114.
185. "Secular" was the fourth item in the slogan. Coubertin wanted the separation of church and state, but he opposed anticlericalism as politically divisive, including the sup-

pression of the Jesuit *collèges* in the early 1880s (including his own in the rue de Madrid). This tension he solved by an educational pluralism. He wanted the state-run schools secular (though Christian in tone) and the Church free to organize its own parallel institutions.

186. Bamford, *Thomas Arnold*, pp. 30, 37, 152–53.

187. Arnold was rationalist (and foolish) enough to believe that upper class indifference to the poor was occasioned chiefly by ignorance of the real conditions among them. Coubertin's seeming ignorance of these plans of Arnold's is ironic, because Frédéric Le Play's monumental *Les Ouvriers européens* (Paris, 1855) was just such a work, and the Société de l'économie sociale, Coubertin's platform for his Arnoldian reforms, was devoted originally to exactly such ends.

188. Mack and Armytage, *Thomas Hughes*, pp. 76–80.

189. Hughes's means of paternalistic service to the poor brought him rather closer to them than his colleagues. At the Working Men's Colleges, his pupils took care not "to hit the gentleman on the nose." But at one of the subsequent Working Men's Institutes, Hughes took quite a beating from a "burly dokker." Mack and Armytage, *Thomas Hughes*, pp. 79–80.

190. By 1880, 24 percent of the 334 football clubs and 21 percent of the cricket clubs in the Birmingham area alone were church-sponsored or affiliated. Aston Villa (1874), Bolton Wanderers (1874), Wolverhampton Wanderers (1877), Everton (1878), and Queen's Park Rangers (1885) are but a few of the storied football clubs founded in this way. MacIntosh, *Sport in Society*, pp. 72–73.

This is not to say, of course, that all working class athletic initiatives in the middle and late nineteenth century were inspired by the middle class. Throughout the early decades of the century, popular recreations and games had been under attack and suppression in the names of religion, public order, and industrial work discipline. But a heroic resistance movement had kept them very much alive, and sport figured often as a form of social protest against the changing industrial order. Robert Malcolmson, *Popular Recreations in English Society* (Cambridge: Cambridge University Press, 1973); Brian Harrison, "Religion and Recreation in Nineteenth Century England," *Past and Present* 38 (1967): 98–125; E. P. Thompson, "Time, Work-Discipline, and Industrial Capitalism," *Past and Present* 38 (1967): 56–97, and *The Making of the English Working Class*; Thomas Henricks, "Sport and Social Distance in Pre-Industrial England," Ph.D. dissertation, University of Chicago, 1977.

Later in the century, reformers and philanthropists turned from the suppression of blood sports, gambling, and festival games to the new strategy of supplanting them with more seemly and useful leisure pursuits for the lower orders, namely their own organized versions of athletic games. In the eighteenth century, such aristocratic and gentry patronage of lower class athletics had been limited to "occasional dramatic interventions," such as "prizes offered for some race or sport." E. P. Thompson, "Patrician Society, Plebian Culture," *Journal of Social History* 7 (1974): 390. Here, however, was a much more explicit and determined effort to colonize working class leisure itself. In all three periods, workers had their own reasons for accepting or rejecting what was proffered to them.

191. This development was not completed until well into the twentieth century. Cricket lost much of its class character in the 1960s, leaving equestrianism and sailing as the only sports with a reasonably long pedigree still tied exclusively to the upper classes.

192. The two men were so intimate, and so like-minded on this question, that it is difficult to sort out who most influenced whom. The doctrines of these "muscular Christians" receive their most programmatic statement in Kingsley's *Health and Education* (London: Macmillan; New York: Appleton, 1874), a book surely influenced by *Tom Brown* and by Hughes's labors at the Working Men's Colleges. On the other hand, the hero of Kingsley's *Westward Ho!*, published in 1855, two years before *Tom Brown*, was himself a glorious and right-intentioned athlete. Amyas Leigh was a public school boy transported anachronistically back to Elizabethan times where he did battle for queen and empire. Among his other sporting pursuits, he boxed at school and "hardly considered that he had done his duty in his calling if

he went home without beating a big lad for bullying a little one." *Westward Ho!* (London & Toronto: Dent, 1906), p. 18. This is Tom Brown's very own motto.

193. In addition to Malcolmson, see Dennis Brailsford, *Sport and Society Elizabeth to Anne* (London: Routledge & Kegan Paul, 1969) and Henricks, "Sport and Social Distance." These three "movements" in the development of modern sports are drawn with broad strokes. There was, of course, a good deal of variation according to period, region, and particular game or recreation.

194. Brailsford, *Sport Elizabeth to Anne*, pp. 59, 209–10.

195. Malcolmson, *Popular Recreations*, p. 41.

196. Mack, *Public Schools and British Opinion*, p. 40.

197. Ibid., p. 45.

198. MacIntosh, *Sport in Society*, p. 66.

199. Mack, *Public Schools and British Opinion*, p. 40.

200. Ibid., p. 85.

201. Especially East Anglian "camping." See Malcolmson, *Popular Recreations*, pp. 35–36.

202. Ellis was a prefect and town dweller. Bamford speculates, admittedly without evidence, that his ludic deviance might well have been an expression of revenge for the bad treatment accorded the poorer and lower-status "townies" by the schoolboys living in. *Thomas Arnold*, p. 187. For contemporary accounts of the event, see W. H. D. Rouse, *A History of Rugby School* (London: Duckworth, 1898), p. 218.

203. *Dr. Arnold of Rugby*, p. 109.

204. *The Life*, p. 113.

205. Ibid., p. 63.

206. Ibid., pp. 66, 143.

207. Ibid., p. 63.

208. Ibid., p. 86.

209. Brailsford, *Sport Elizabeth to Anne*, p. 219.

210. *Tom Brown's Schooldays*, p. 107.

211. Ibid., p. 96.

212. Ibid., p. 109.

213. "As endless are boys' characters, so are their ways of facing or not facing a scrummage at football." Ibid., p. 105.

214. "Meet them like Englishmen, you School-house boys!" Ibid., p. 109.

215. "Why did we beat them? . . . Because we've more reliance on one another, more of a house feeling, more fellowship . . . each of us knows and can depend on his next hand better. . . ." Ibid., p. 121.

216. "A battle would look the same to you, except that the boys would be men and the balls iron; but a battle would be worth your looking at for all that, and so is a football match.". Ibid., p. 104.

217. Quoted in Mack, *Public Schools and British Opinion*, p. 85.

218. The Football Association was founded in 1863, and the Rugby Football Union in 1871.

219. Mack, *Public Schools and British Opinion*, p. 40.

220. In 1869, the first national swimming association was founded. In 1875, a swimming pool was built at Rugby, though diving for eggs, coins, and plates was favored over races. In the 1880s, diving for style came in, and in the 1910s and 1920s, water polo and interschool races. J. B. Hope Simpson, *Rugby since Arnold* (London: Macmillan; New York: St. Martin's, 1967), p. 288.

221. Hope, *Rugby since Arnold*, p. 273.

222. By 1845, Etonians had regularized the steeplechase (humans hedge-jumping and brook-leaping in imitation of horses), and in 1850, at Oxford, Exeter undergraduates transformed it into the first modern hurdles race, at 140 yards. In the 1860s, the prototypes of

modern track and field were born, the Amateur Athletic Club was founded, and flat racing became popular at Rugby. Of course, "pedestrianism"—matched walking or running races whose principal interest was gambling—were well known in popular society throughout the period. Ibid., and MacIntosh, *Sport in Society*, pp. 67, 60–61.

223. Rackets did not appear there till 1864, lawn tennis till 1877. Simpson, *Rugby since Arnold*, pp. 279–86.

224. Malcolmson, *Popular Recreations*, pp. 42–43; Brailsford, *Sport Elizabeth to Anne*, pp. 103–4, 206–7, 216–17.

225. Brailsford, *Sport Elizabeth to Anne*, p. 216.

226. MacIntosh, *Sport in Society*, p. 60.

227. Mack and Armytage, *Thomas Hughes*, p. 9.

228. Ibid., p. 98.

229. Hughes's attitudes make particularly visible the social and cultural forces that would precipitate the later-nineteenth-century distinction between "amateur" and "professional" sport. In late medieval and Renaissance times, individual sports had been used as explicit means of marking and maintaining social boundaries; for example, the sometime reservation of tennis as the exclusive privilege and property of the royal court. James I's *Book of Sports*, reissued by his son, was a weapon against Puritanism and, in that cause, loosened the de jure, if not the de facto, partitioning of particular "game cores" as class property. As we have seen, through the next two centuries—at least with regard to games like cricket, boxing, and football—the social stratification of sports became less a matter of game cores than of distinctive versions of the same games developed and claimed by particular social groups.

Hughes's position on boxing is instructive on the sporting "liberals" of the mid-nineteenth-century upper class. He thought it proper and beneficial for worker and gentleman alike, but only when pursued for moral education, fenced round with elaborate rules of fair play and decorum, and practiced according to scientific techniques—in other words, only in its upper class version. While Hughes was one of the few gentlemen who ever thought of stepping into the ring with a worker, he did so only in the relative "privacy" of the Working Men's Colleges and Institutes and would never have thought of boxing in public. Prizefighting, thus, offended men like Hughes on multiple counts: it was done for money; it easily degenerated into a brawl; and it was a public spectacle. The distinction between "amateur" and "professional" was developed first of all to codify these moral judgments. "*Amat*-eurs" competed for the love of the activity and its intrinsic moral and physical benefits. They were not to have competed for money in the past, intend to do so in the future, or take principal roles of any kind in events where money changed hands. They also had to place themselves under the authority of the rules as arbitrated by the "guardians" of the amateur order, the athletic associations. On the face of it, then, the amateur/professional classification cut across class lines. But the associations were typically composed of aristocrats and gentry, who could and did juggle the rules to keep the sports conformable to upper class models and to control social access to amateur events. Moreover, a second set of criteria, that no person who had engaged in paid manual labor could be an "amateur" at athletic sport, later effectively closed it off to the working classes. Hughes would not have approved of this, and neither did Coubertin, as we shall see.

230. Simpson, *Rugby since Arnold*, pp. 286–87. Interestingly, wrestling, though an organized and popular sport among the rural lower orders, never penetrated the public schools, or indeed the adult aristocracy, perhaps for reasons that D. H. Lawrence would have appreciated.

231. The attack on bull-baiting, cockfighting, and the like was not conducted without a good deal of class hypocrisy, for many genteel folk themselves patronized them. See Malcolmson, *Popular Recreations*, pp. 45–46, 122–26; Harrison, "Religion and Recreation," pp. 102ff.

232. *Life and Letters of Edward Thring*, 2 vols. (London: Macmillan, 1898), 2:305.

233. The whole passage reads: "There are bodily exercises which are liberal, and mental exercises which are not so. . . . Such, for instance, was the palaestra, in ancient times; such the Olympic Games, in which strength and dexterity of body as well as of mind gained the prize. In Xenophon we read of the young Persian nobility being taught to ride on horseback and to speak the truth; both being among the accomplishments of a gentleman. . . . Manly games, or games of skill, or military prowess, though bodily, are, it seems, accounted liberal; on the other hand, what is merely professional, though highly intellectual, nay, though liberal in comparison of trade and manual labor, is not simply called liberal, and mercantile occupations are not liberal at all. Why this distinction? Because that alone is liberal knowledge, which stands on its own pretensions, which is independent of sequel, expects no complement, refuses to be informed (as it is called) by any end, or absorbed into any art, in order to duly present itself to our contemplation. The most ordinary pursuits have this specific character, if they are self-sufficient and complete; the highest lose it, when they minister to something beyond them. It is absurd to balance, in point of worth and importance, a treatise on reducing fractures with a game of cricket or a fox-chase; yet of the two, the bodily exercise has that quality which we call 'liberal,' and the intellectual does not."

After placing medicine, diplomacy, pastoral theology, and natural science in the "distinct class of the Useful" as opposed to the "Liberal," Newman continues. "Whenever personal gain is the motive, still more distinctive an effect has it upon the character of a given pursuit; thus racing, which was a liberal exercise in Greece, forfeits its rank in times like these, so far as it is made the occasion of gambling. All that I have been saying is summed up in a few characteristic words of the great Philosopher [Aristotle, *Rhetoric*, I, 5]. 'Of Possessions,' he says, 'those rather are useful, which bear fruit; those *liberal which tend to enjoyment*. By fruitful, I mean, which yield revenue; by enjoyable, where *nothing accrues of consequence beyond the using*.'" *The Idea of a University*, 10th ed. (London: Longmans, Green, 1893 [1851]), pp. 107–9. The muscular Christians agreed about gambling, knew the Greek distinctions, and were personally able to enjoy sport for itself. But their justifications of it were utilitarian, utilitarian with regard to the highest "fruits."

Here the modern debate on the nature and cultural value of play and games begins in earnest—"modern" because it is exceedingly problematic whether the Greeks meant what Newman says they did. For all the nicety of Aristotle's philosophical distinctions, it is doubtful that he would have cared to claim that the Greeks pursued their racing and other games for enjoyment alone. And Plato, in the famous passage in the *Laws* recommending that "life should be lived as play, playing certain games," hastens to add that in this way men will win their battles, placate their gods, and fulfill their duties as citizens. Moreover, the segregation of enjoyment from the "fruits of action" meant something rather different in fifth-century Athens than it did in nineteenth-century London. Sport for its own sake, particularly where it is ideologically overdetermined and not merely a set of logical categories, is a modern rallying cry. In Homer, Athens, and Olympia, the utilitarians of the moral sort could and did find ample "precedent" for their views as well. These were the waters Coubertin was shortly to voyage. He embarked with the muscular Christians, while keeping an eye peeled for Newman, sailing on the horizon.

234. See above, pp. 294–95, n. 90.

235. There is no indication that Coubertin ever visited Uppingham or knew Thring personally, but Parkin's biography includes a long citation (pp. 139–40, n. 1) from a speech of Coubertin ("one of the most vigorous educational thinkers of modern France") in which the baron lauds Thring's educational philosophy along lines that suggest that Coubertin was acquainted with Thring's *Education and School* (London: Macmillan, 1867). In this work, Thring takes Hughes a step further and tries to break down the division between work and play at public school. "It is the separation of the parts of life that makes the difference, the cutting life in two halves, as if a boy's choice lay between manly games *or* learning; when the choice is really to take both, like bread and wine; for if bread strengthens man's heart, the oil

and wine of games make him a cheerful countenance. Life is not all bread, and each helps the other" (pp. 33–34). On Kingsley, see chap. 3, n. 90. It is tempting to suspect that Coubertin at some point read *Health and Education*, but the baron's confusion as to Kingsley's dates is evidence to the contrary.

236. *Une Campagne de 21 ans*, p. 6. For the persistence of these views see *The Olympic Idea*, pp. 8, 46–48, 58, 94, 103, 113.

237. *Une Campagne de 21 ans*, p. 3. Coubertin's real objection to Taine was not the latter's failure to understand the English school sports, but his disapproval of the obsession with them. Though Coubertin did not risk criticizing Taine by name in his early speeches and articles, the arguments against sports that Coubertin counters in them are taken directly from the *Notes on England*, wherein Taine claimed that "education on these terms is not unlike that of the Spartans, it hardens the body and it tempers the character. But as far as I can make out, it often produces merely sportsmen and louts" (p. 111).

238. Sigmund Freud, *The Future of an Illusion*, trans. James Strachey (New York: Norton, 1961), pp. 30–31.

239. During 1883, 1886, and 1887, Hughes was in the United States attending to the fortunes of his utopian, cooperative community at New Rugby, Tennessee, a community, incidentally, with its own "Arnold school" and in which sports played a prominent role (Mack and Armytage, *Thomas Hughes*, pp. 227–47). So Coubertin would have had difficulty tracking Hughes down. But there is no evidence that he even cared to try.

There is a further irony in Coubertin's studied ignorance of Hughes, for they were true brothers in another way than their shared love of games and their belief in the moral values of athleticism. As his biographers remark, "That Hughes, who so typically was a follower, not an innovator, should single-handed have created a new literary genre, is not the least of the mysteries surrounding *Tom Brown's Schooldays*" (ibid., p. 91). Coubertin, too, was in most ways typically a follower. That he should, almost single-handedly, create a new genre of cultural performance is not the least of the mysteries surrounding the Olympic Games.

240. Leon Festinger, *A Theory of Cognitive Dissonance* (Evanston: Row, Peterson, 1957).

241. The date is established in Coubertin's "Speech to the Conference on Physical Training," 1889, in Isabel C. Barrows, ed., *Physical Training* (Boston: Press of George H. Ellis, 1890), p. 114.

242. "Are the Public Schools a Failure? A French View," *Fortnightly Review* 78 (1902): 980.

243. "Gladstone, vieux canotier," *Journal des débats*, July 9, 1893.

244. "La Force nationale et le sport," *Revue des deux mondes* 7 (1902): 917.

245. "Olympia," 1929, in *The Olympic Idea*, pp. 113–14.

246. Festinger, *A Theory of Cognitive Dissonance*; Leon Festinger, Henry W. Riecken, and Stanley Schachter, *When Prophecy Fails* (Minneapolis: University of Minnesota Press, 1956).

247. "L'Éducation anglaise," p. 642.

248. Ibid., p. 633.

249. Ibid., p. 642.

250. Ibid.

251. Coubertin quotes with approbation a motto he found in *Tom Brown*: "Fear God and make 100 kilometers in 100 hours." "There you certainly see," he says, "an association of ideas in which sport is treated with honor, where it is placed in the same rank as the fear of God." In the same breath, he also noted more practical payoffs. To the English, "time is money," and sickness "is loss of time." Ibid., p. 643.

252. Ibid., p. 638.

253. "As for the evangelical command to turn the left cheek when you've been struck on the right, it is little practiced there, but replaced by the motto of the United Kingdom, 'If you strike, I'll strike.'" The "other side of this coin," says Coubertin, "is that energy can degenerate sometimes into harshness and brutality." Ibid., pp. 643, 645.

254. Ibid., p. 644.

255. Ibid., p. 643.

256. Ibid., p. 644. This is a strike at Taine who, citing Plato, did believe the lives of the athlete and the thinker incompatible. *Notes on England*, p. 120.

257. "L'Éducation anglaise," p. 644.

258. "And, in effect, if these games didn't have such a powerful organization, if the boys weren't as impassioned for them as the athletes of ancient Greece were for the Olympic games, Harrow tomorrow would be given up to disorder and the day after that would vanish for good." "Les Collèges anglais: Harrow School," p. 473. "It is obvious," Taine had written about university crew races, "that such a triumph must be as highly prized as the palms of antiquity's Olympic Games" (*Notes*, p. 122). And earlier, in a passage even more suggestive for Coubertin's later career, Taine wrote, "I have been told of a band of eleven cricketeers who actually went to play in Australia, as formerly athletes went from Punt or from Marseilles, to Olympia. There is, then, nothing surprising in it if adolescents become enthusiastic over games backed by such authority (*Notes*, p. 104).

259. *Notes*, pp. 9, 26.

260. "L'Éducation anglaise," p. 645. "Toastmaking" may seem an odd function for Coubertin to single out, but he had in mind, I suspect, old Brooke's moving elegy after the Schoolhouse football victory in *Tom Brown*, and, as we shall see, toastmaking was neither the least, nor the least effective, of Coubertin's own arts in the athletic associations he created or led.

That Coubertin nowhere discusses, in these early manifestoes, the connection between sport and military training is not accidental. As we shall also see, he labored against French reformers who wished to employ sport solely in such a cause. War and colonial expansion were separate phenomena to Coubertin. The latter he celebrated in England, and hoped to see for France, and he drew the connection between sport and the English colonial empire. "And then there are the colonies, that career of expatriation so well suited to the English, who everywhere they go carry 'Old England' with them. When one's a 'squatter' in New Zealand or a planter in America, one finds oneself well off to have received in the public schools such a strong physical and moral education. Muscles and character are there the first objects of necessity. If the principal cause of our colonial impotency lies in our deplorable system of inheritance, it nonetheless seems to me that education is also quite responsible." Ibid., p. 646.

261. Ibid.

Chapter Four

1. Originally known as the Société internationale des études pratiques d'économie sociale; later and today as the Société d'économie et de science sociale.

2. Unpublished ms in the I.O.C. Archives. Quoted in Boulongne, *La Vie et l'oeuvre*, p. 96.

3. This precis follows M. Z. Brooke, *Le Play: Engineer and Social Scientist* (London: Longman, 1970).

4. By the end of his life, Le Play is thought to have traveled some 175,000 miles through all the countries of Europe. Zeldin, *France 1848–1945*, 2:954.

5. Quoted in Brooke, *Le Play*, p. 8.

6. His *La Constitution d'Angleterre*, 2 vols., 2d ed. (Tours: Mame, 1875 [1845]) focused on industry, but was a general study of English life whose conclusions were broadly congruent with Taine's thirty years later. See Zeldin, *France 1848–1945*, 2:957, for a summary.

7. Quoted in Brooke, *Le Play*, p. 8.

8. Ibid.

9. Quoted in Zeldin, *France 1848–1945*, 2:954.

10. Jesse R. Pitts, *International Encyclopedia of the Social Sciences*, s.v. "Frédéric Le Play."

11. Durkheim rudely dismissed Le Play as a minor figure, and fiercely attacked the latter's *sociographie microscopique* as a mindless compilation of undigested facts, unconducive to generalization to broader social structure. Such criticisms are fair enough, but the Durkheimians were among those who "never left their studies," and they are noticeably silent on this side of Le Play's method. Several of Durkheim's arguments had precedents in Le Play, and Halbwachs employed the family budget method in his *L'Évolution des besoins dans les classes ouvrières* (Paris: Alcan, 1933) without giving Le Play his due. The Durkheimians were middle class, often Jewish, professorial, and anticlerical, while the Le Playites were generally upper class, Roman Catholic, independent, and conservative. These differing cultural milieus account for much of the hostility between the two schools. (Doubtless, too, these facts help to account for Coubertin's ignorance of Durkheim, despite the important intersections between their projects.) Not until Philippe Ariès was any formal attempt made to synthesize the two sociological traditions. For these conflicts and criticisms, and more recent defenses of Le Play's creativity, see Pitts, "Frédéric Le Play," pp. 87–89, and Brooke, *Le Play*, pp. 134–40.

12. *La Réforme sociale en France*, 3 vols., 4th ed. (Tours: Mame, 1872 [1864]); *L'Organisation du travail* (Tours: Mame, 1870); *La Paix sociale après le désastre* (Tours: Mame, 1871); *La Constitution essentielle de l'humanité* (Tours: Mame, 1881).

13. "Frédéric Le Play," p. 88.

14. *Le Play*, pp. 120–22.

15. Le Play, *La Constitution essentielle*, Appendix 3, p. 339.

16. Quoted in Brooke, *Le Play*, p. 28.

17. Le Play, *La Constitution essentielle*, Appendix 3, p. 342.

18. Ibid.

19. Evelyn M. Acomb, *The French Laic Laws, 1879–1889* (New York: Columbia University Press, 1941), p. 21.

20. Brooke, *Le Play*, p. 71. Before 1870, the principal rival society was Armand de Melun's revealingly named Société d'économie charitable. Coubertin agreed with Le Play on the matter of charity. Like the English Christian Socialists, Coubertin wanted to help workers help themselves through education.

21. Locke, *French Legitimists*, pp. 67–69.

22. Brooke reproduces parts of this illuminating speech (*Le Play*, pp. 130–31). Limousin took his presence before the société as a sign of progress in class relations. First, "you have wanted, you members of the ruling classes, to have on social questions the opinion of a member of the lower classes"; and the "second is in the rise in dignity of the class to which I belong, of which this honor done to me is proof. It is a step on the road to equality and the end of classes. . . . Yesterday, you rose in the world by ennoblement, today by enrichment . . . now the new fact, in my opinion, is the presence among you of a representative of a group of men who have come out of the masses without enrichment." Limousin then proceeded to list those aspects of labor policy where he thought socialists and Social Catholics had common ground.

23. He is listed as "admis avant Jan. 1884" in *La Réforme sociale* 7 (1884): 24.

24. Besides the speeches and articles being cited, Coubertin served as secretary for a working group at the 1887 joint congress, spoke up frequently in group debates, and later led société members on a visit to a reformist *lycée*.

The year 1886 was a difficult year for the société. Le Play had died in 1882, and without his steady hand, the société drifted, in the eyes of his two most brilliant pupils, Edmond Demolins and Henri de Tourville, too far toward philosophical debate and social prescription of the very sort represented in Coubertin's speeches. They wanted a strictly scientific association, and, in 1885, broke away to found the rival Société internationale de science sociale, which, in 1886, commenced publication of *La Science sociale*. See Brooke, *Le Play*, pp. 131–32, for an account of the schism. Later on, however, Demolins associated himself with Coubertin's work and even founded a French boarding school which explicitly copied the

English public school. Coubertin did not support him in this. See Coubertin, "The Olympic Games and Gymnastics," 1931, in *The Olympic Idea*, p. 120.

25. "L'Éducation anglaise," pp. 649ff.

26. A. M. Chauffourier, "the dean of French industrialists," presided over the meeting. The vicomte Saint-Genys and M. de la Chaussée represented the French embassy. The speech was apparently delivered in French and is known from an anonymous report, "Une Conférence à Londres," in the December 15 number of *La Réforme sociale* 4 (1887): 621–22.

27. Says the anonymous reporter, "The works of M. de Coubertin on English education haven't been forgotten here, and we don't have to recall the vital and brilliant allure of his thought, united to solid observations always supported by the facts. These qualities guaranteed success, and the speech was, indeed, widely noticed. The English press, without distinction as to political opinion, mentioned it, and many extracts were reproduced by the various newspapers" (ibid., p. 621). These press reports would make interesting reading, but I have been unable to discover them.

28. Ibid., p. 622.

29. Ibid., pp. 621–22.

30. Coubertin was deeply interested in politics and wrote often and voluminously on political questions. In the pages of *La Réforme sociale* itself, he discoursed on the Irish question under the ceremonial cover of an objective presentation of crime statistics. His stand was so excessively reactionary—a diatribe against Parnell, the National League, and the boycott movement—that the president of the société mildly rebuked him for seeing only one side of the political equation. These youthful excesses were occasioned by his idolization of the English, his denial that the Irish were a separate race (and therefore of their right to a separate nation), and his hatred of all forms of revolutionary violence. "Right may perhaps be on the side of the Irish (personally I doubt it); but the means employed to make it triumphant are execrable." "Statistiques irlandaises," *La Réforme sociale* 15 (1888): 668; see also "Courrier d'Irlande: Les Difficultés de la situation."

31. "Frédéric Le Play," p. 85.

32. It was this aspect of the concept that Durkheim picked up in his discussions of *anomie*. Zeldin, *France 1848–1945*, 2:955.

33. "Olympia," p. 109.

34. His most explicit statements on original sin appear in *Notes sur l'éducation publique*, pp. 14–15.

35. Le Play, *La Réforme sociale en France* 1:448. What Coubertin set himself against was not the necessity of moral education, but the view that children were evil little monsters and Le Play's parallel characterization of miscreant adults as "overgrown children" (ibid.).

36. "The Philosophic Foundations of Modern Olympism," 1935, in *The Olympic Idea*, p. 133.

37. Multigeneration households seated on family land, which kept one son home to manage an undivided estate, while the others, provided with portions and sent out on their own, were tied to the family seat as a sort of ceremonial center. Le Play (like Taine) thought this family type the source of England's strength and fecundity. *La Réforme sociale en France* 1:463.

38. On the theory and its fate, see Brooke, *Le Play*, pp. 132–34.

39. See Pitts, "Frédéric Le Play," p. 86.

40. See Brooke, *Le Play*, pp. 21–39, 88–97.

41. Quoted in Zeldin, *France 1848–1945*, 2:957.

42. Quoted in Brooke, *Le Play*, p. 89.

43. "Une Conférence à Londres," p. 622.

44. In a 1964 interview with Yves-Pierre Boulongne, Mme. Zanchi, former secretary of the I.O.C. who knew Coubertin personally, estimated his inheritance at 500,000 gold francs in the form of deeds and endowments. This figure represented the assessed value of the Coubertin *seigneurie* which fell to Pierre's eldest brother, and Zanchi reasonably concluded

that Pierre's legacy would have been of equal value. *La Vie et l'oeuvre*, pp. 55–56, n. 23. Gaston Meyer arrives at a similar figure in *La Phénomène olympique*, p. 8. Based on 1888 exchange rates, Coubertin's inheritance was worth approximately $97,250; in inflated 1979 dollars, approximately $730,816 (cumulative C.P.I. series). My thanks to James L. Rowe, Jr., of the *Washington Post* and Professor Donald McCloskey of the University of Chicago for assisting with these calculations.

As to the actual yearly income from these holdings, we know only that it amounted to something less than 100,000 francs. In *Une Campagne de 21 ans* (p. 8), Coubertin remarks on how useful was his fortune when he took up his reformer's banner. But, he adds, "It is certain that if my income as a young man had been raised to 100,000 francs a year, I would have had every means for leading one of those flashy campaigns that, translating itself into appropriate foundations, creates rapid conviction across a country. The results of such campaigns, however, aren't very lasting. And then, if I had had such sums at my disposal, would I have succeeded in using them well? I doubt it, and I thank heaven for not having bestowed them on me."

45. Pundits naively accused Le Play of attempting to bring back the feudal order, and critics have been fond of quoting Sainte-Beuve's characterization of Le Play as a "Bonald reincarnated." Sainte-Beuve did indeed pen the shrewdest contemporary criticism of Le Play, but the full quotation is that Le Play was "a Bonald reincarnated, progressive and scientific." Whereas Bonald "desired a return to the past" of the *ancien régime*, "Le Play is of a totally new generation; he belongs par excellence to modern society.... If he conceived a reform, it was only on the heels of experience, and, in combining the ways and means, he proposes with all the living forces of present-day civilization, without intending to suffocate them or to inhibit development." *Nouveaux Lundis* (Paris: Calmann-Lévy, 1884), 9:180–81, 189.

As Zeldin puts it (*France 1848–1945*, 2:959), Le Play's "tragedy was that he was taken up only by the conservatives."

46. Zeldin, *France 1848–1945*, 2:955–56.

47. He so loved his earliest sporting adventures that the names of his favorite horse ("Rob Roy") and boat (*Tam Tam*) have come down to us.

48. His intense physical memories were as much responsible for his argument that French *lycées* ought to be dispersed in the provinces as were his faith in the English public school model and the practical matter of the availability of land for playing fields.

49. "Le Roman d'un rallié," pp. 456–57.

50. Ibid., p. 681. In English in the original.

51. See Eugen Weber, *Peasants into Frenchmen*. Among the interesting articles in Jacques Beauroy, et al., eds., *The Wolf and the Lamb: Popular Culture in France from the Old Regime to the Twentieth Century* (Saratoga, Calif.: Anma Libri, 1976) are several that offer information relevant to Coubertin: Michael R. Marrus, "Folklore as an Ethnographic Source: A 'Mise au Point,'" pp. 109–26; Eugen Weber, "Who Sang the Marseillaise?" pp. 161–74; Robert J. Bezucha, "The Moralization of Society: The Enemies of Popular Culture in the 19th Century," pp. 175–88; and B. H. Singer, "The Village Schoolmaster as Outsider," pp. 189–208.

52. Michael Marrus, quoted in Bezucha, "The Moralization of Society," p. 183.

53. In the "Roman d'un rallié," Étienne is represented at a farmhouse *veillée*, where he is asked for his advice on decorations for an upcoming festival. But in the course of this discussion, his mind wanders to the *belles réformes* he has in mind for the unsuspecting provincials. "But, my God, how far from them Brittany was, and how poorly prepared to receive them. [Étienne] could no longer understand how he had been able to conceive the anomaly of a modernized Brittany, open to progress. The idea of a committee meeting presided over by Fr. Antoine, or a communal library administered by [the farmer] Pierre Braz, made him laugh." But, if such things did not come to pass, "the Republic would be nonsense" (pp. 456–57).

54. "Une Conférence à Londres," p. 622.

55. Since the journey is accomplished in the snow, we may further locate it in the first or last months of the year.

56. "Le Roman d'un rallié," p. 477. In the "Roman" version, Étienne is just back from an extended stay in America, whereas the real Coubertin had recently returned from England. Awakened for the adventure, Jean-Marie, the peasant companion, calls out "with his habitual familiarity," "This is a happy surprise; I was beginning to miss all this, I thought that you no longer loved *les fantaisies.*" Ibid., p. 474.

57. See above, pp. 28–29, 285 n. 89–90, for details on Lesneven, the exact location of his tomb, and the evidence for this pilgrimage as an actual event.

58. "Le Roman d'un rallié," p. 477.

59. Ibid., p. 480.

60. Still, on these grounds, I have refused to include the Lesneven visit on the list of Coubertin's visions, despite the fact that it is so portrayed in the "Roman." In the carriage from Chateaulin, Étienne dozes, and has "visions with the clarity of dreams." Smiling benevolently, but otherwise looking just like the miniature his nephew had discovered in his boyhood, Lesneven awaits the pilgrim on the threshold of his antique manor. "The *abbé* holds a book between his hands, raises a finger to his lips, and makes a sign. Étienne understands that the 'others' are sleeping and mustn't be awakened." Together, they climb to the summit, Lesneven appearing to float above the ground. There they approach the Black Menhir. Étienne is "brusquely recalled to reality" by the coachman's voice: "It's here, Monsieur." Étienne awakens to see before him the Black Menhir, exactly as it had appeared in the dream (pp. 477–78).

Its patently conventional symbolism and its all too obvious position in the narrative make it clear that this "vision" is a literary invention. Even its author was not convinced by it; he proceeds to argue that Étienne had never been there before, that even if he had seen engravings of such places, there were many druid ruins and this one was very particular, and so on. In short, he protests too much. But, like others of its kind, this embellishment of the story reveals the emotional significance that it had for Coubertin.

61. See above, pp. 28–29.

62. "Le Roman d'un rallié," p. 481.

63. A set of symbol vehicles and motifs that processually condense and express a persistent structure of associations and themes. See Turner and Turner, *Image and Pilgrimage*, pp. 248–49, for a related usage.

64. For centuries, throughout Brittany, it had been a practice to usurp the Neolithic and Gallo-Roman remains, by destroying them, erecting churches or chapels over them, or by carving Christian symbols upon them.

65. "Le Roman d'un rallié," p. 482. Étienne bribes them to give up their plans. It is interesting to note how this act contradicts the Le Play dictum that the small businesses opened by peasants and working men would help them to maintain their stem families and assist them in entering the modern economy.

66. *Une Campagne de 21 ans,* p. 6.

67. These events are described in "Le Roman d'un rallié," pp. 60–61, 682–683. Coubertin explicitly connects these episodes. Carnot's cortège rolls "toward the Pantheon where *la Patrie,* in its turn, promised immortality. There, at the top of the steps, under the enormous peristyle, the remains of the great man were interred . . . the flags were lowered before this symbol of the national vitality: Frenchmen died, France never died. . . . A tomb! Étienne saw again those where he had dreamed. The one over there on the banks of the Potomac, George Washington's, and the near one, on the shore of the Breton sea, the unfortunate abbé de Lesneven's: the one man forever illustrious, the other forgotten forever; the one man celebrated throughout the world, the other damned by his peers. But who knows? Perhaps they were equal before God for the purity of their intentions and the merit of their acts. . . . Is it

because Celts love death that they poeticize it, or only because their ancestors were mistreated by life? In any case, he, their descendant, had an ear for the voices that came forth from sepulchers, and the dead had made him understand the meaning of life" (p. 683).

68. Ibid., p. 480.

69. "L'Éducation," *La Réforme sociale* 13 (1887): 676–88.

70. His many contacts with the Le Play societies are not surprising. Among his many educational writings, *La Réforme de l'enseignement secondaire*, to which we have already referred, is the most germane.

71. "L'Éducation," pp. 681, 677.

72. Ibid., p. 683.

73. At the next year's société congress, Coubertin gave a speech entitled "Le Remède au surmenage et la transformation des lycées de Paris." *La Réforme sociale* 16 (1888): 241–49, reprinted as the first chapter of *L'Éducation anglaise en France*.

74. "L'Éducation," p. 682.

75. Ibid., p. 677.

76. Ibid., p. 678.

77. *Une Campagne de 21 ans*, p. 10.

78. "L'Éducation," p. 678.

79. The following account is drawn from *Une Campagne de 21 ans*, pp. 11–14.

80. Ibid., p. 13.

81. As Coubertin notes, Fr. Didon, a liberal and controversial priest, was then associated with Arcueil, but was "then absorbed in his functions as a preacher and author." Later Didon turned to education, introduced sports into Arcueil in 1890, and became a friend to Coubertin and the Olympic Movement. The motto which he offered to the Arcueil athletes, *citius, altius, fortius* ("swifter, higher, stronger") was taken over by Coubertin as the motto of the Olympic movement.

82. Ibid., pp. 12–13. Jean Charcot, the future celebrated arctic explorer, son of the famous neurologist who was Freud's teacher, was the schoolboy most responsible for the games at Alsacienne. In 1909, Coubertin had Charcot, "our true apostle," awarded the ninth Olympic Diploma. Coubertin, "Speech at the Award of the Olympic Diplomas," 1909, in *The Olympic Idea*, pp. 21–22.

83. *Une Campagne de 21 ans*, p. 12.

84. Ibid.

85. Ibid., p. 13.

86. Ibid., p. 24.

87. Ibid.

88. "Preface," pp. v–vi.

89. Ibid., pp. ix, xi.

90. This list is drawn from "Lettre aux membres de la Société d'économie sociale et des unions," *La Réforme sociale* 16 (1888): 252; and from *Une Campagne de 21 ans*, pp. 24–29.

91. Gréard was a dubious adherent. As Coubertin later put it, "I didn't feel that Gréard was able to support physical exercise out of conviction, but only out of the instinctive desire in him to canalize and to direct to his liking every stream that found a way to flow across his territory." Jules Simon was of the same opinion. Coubertin quotes a letter from Simon: "I have always believed that [Gréard] would shelter us a bit. But no. He is a damnable rector" (*Une Campagne de 21 ans*, p. 14). But Coubertin knew that all he really needed from Gréard in 1888 was the impact his name would have on the headmasters; and later, he was happy to settle for the keys to the Great Hall of the Sorbonne that Gréard would have in his pocket.

92. Under the Second Empire, when, in 1869, he had decreed gymnastics obligatory in the private schools. There had been several such governmental initiatives. In 1793, under the urging of Lepeletier and Robespierre, the Convention had declared in favor of school gymnastics. In 1845, Duruy's predecessor as minister of public instruction, M. Salvendy, had

created a commission to study gymnastics teaching. In 1850, gymnastics became optional in the private schools, and, in 1854, mandatory in the *lycées*. After Duruy's initiative, Jules Simon, in 1871, and Jules Ferry, in 1880–81, attempted once more to enforce these decrees. But they were never honored save in the breach. On these efforts and the reasons for their failure, see Eugen Weber, "Gymnastics and Sports in *Fin-de-Siècle* France: Opium of the Classes?" *American Historical Review* 76 (1971): 73–76.

Duruy responded to Coubertin's invitation, "I resided too long in ancient Greece, among a people who knew how to form great poets and the best soldiers in the world, not to approve the innovations so intelligently introduced at the École Monge. . . . I am too old and too faltering in health to be an active member of a committee which already unites the most enlightened masters of national education." But he gave his permission to put his name on the list "if you think it useful." Coubertin thought it very useful. His aristocratic background had left him with great respect for the powers of *noms*. *Une Campagne de 21 ans*, p. 25, n. 1.

93. The names of some dozen other members have come down to us. Edward Maneuvrier and Demolins were the most important of the later adherents of the comité.

94. *Une Campagne de 21 ans*, pp. 26–27.

95. These systems are summarized in Jacques Ulmann, *De la Gymnastique aux sports modernes*, a text which also provides a general history of European physical education doctrines. Names like Rousseau, Pestalozzi, Amoros, and Basedow do not appear in Coubertin's work until later when his ideas were already formed. Hence, I have chosen not to deal in detail with this wider tradition.

96. A later edition in 1891, perhaps under the shadow of the Boulanger affair, banned explicitly military training. On this document, see Boulongne, *La Vie et l'oeuvre*, pp. 214–15.

97. Quoted by Eugen Weber, "Gymnastics and Sports," p. 72. Weber goes on to note that despite its high dues the Club alpin had some 7,000 members by the turn of the century. ("The Age of Mountaineering," as Whymper with his customary understatement liked to call it, was in no small way English-inspired.) More populist associations like the Bordeaux Société des marcheurs touristes de France, founded in 1885, also thought of themselves as patriotic organizations, in this case promoting "the study of our country" and the training of resourceful army guides.

98. Ibid., pp. 74–75.

99. "Lettre aux membres," pp. 251–52.

100. Press coverage certainly did not produce a groundswell of public opinion in favor of physical education, but it did have another important consequence in the domain of language itself. In the later nineteenth century, the word "sport" was still confused with horse-racing and the like (see Eugen Weber, "Gymnastics and Sports," pp. 77–79). Popular acceptance of its use as a generic term for athletic games came about, in no small part, through the newspapers.

101. *Une Campagne de 21 ans*, p. 26.

102. The congress was presided over by Paul Leroy-Beaulieu in the great hall of the Société de Géographie. That morning, Coubertin had led some members on a tour of Lakanal, the model *lycée* of the Third Republic. That afternoon, he delivered "Le Remède au surmenage," and then had handed round the "Lettre" announcing the comité.

103. "Le Remède au surmenage," p. 243.

104. *Education: Intellectual, Moral, and Physical* (London: Watts, 1861). A few vague references to Spencer appear in Coubertin's later writings, but the similarities between their pedagogies are general at best. Certainly no direct influence may be claimed.

105. Vague organic metaphors, quite current in any event, were the closest approach Coubertin ever made to a biological theory of sport. The medical approval he sought for his projects was later far outweighed by the skepticism toward "the culture of science" that appeared in his thought.

106. For example, Coubertin paid no attention to Alfred Binet, the intelligence-testing pioneer, who in the early '90s published studies on chess players and in 1898 (with V. Henri) *La Fatigue intellectuelle* (Paris: Schleicher), a huge and well-publicized monograph on *surmenage*.

107. "Le Remède au surmenage," p. 243.

108. Weber counts as many as ten paramilitary gymnastic and rifle clubs, with an active membership of 1,800, in 1887 Bordeaux alone. "Gymnastics and Sports," p. 73.

109. "Le Remède au surmenage," p. 249.

110. "Gymnastics and Sports," p. 73.

111. See Coubertin, *Notes sur l'éducation publique*, pp. 126–216. Also *La Gymnastique utilitaire* (Paris: Félix Alcan, 1905) and *Essais de psychologie sportive* (Lausanne: Payot, 1913).

112. "Le Remède au surmenage," pp. 248–49.

113. Quoted in Boulongne, *La Vie et l'oeuvre*, p. 242.

114. "Seventh Olympic Letter," 1918, in *The Olympic Idea*, p. 57.

115. "Une Campagne de 35 ans," *Revue de Paris* 11 (1923).

116. *Pédagogie sportive* (Paris: Crès, 1922), p. 64. "Address delivered at the Opening of the Prague Olympic Congress, 1925," in *The Olympic Idea*, p. 96.

117. Georges Hébert, *Le Sport contre l'éducation physique* (Paris: Vuibert, 1925), p. 94.

118. This sketch is drawn in part from Eugen Weber, "Pierre de Coubertin," pp. 10ff.

119. André Laurie [Paschal Grousset], *La Vie de collège en Angleterre* (Paris: Hetzel, 1881).

120. *Une Campagne de 21 ans*, p. 9. I have not seen the volume, and so have been unable to check Grousset's treatment of the athletic episodes.

121. Philippe Daryl [Paschal Grousset], *Public Life in England*, trans. Henry Firth (London: Routledge, 1884). The quotation is from the translator's preface, pp. v–vi. This work is a more careful, but in every way less inspired, echo of Taine's *Notes sur l'Angleterre*. There is not a word about athletic games in it.

122. Eugen Weber, "Pierre de Coubertin," p. 13.

123. Ibid., p. 11.

124. Quoted ibid., p. 12, from a Grousset-inspired article in *Le Temps*, which attacked Coubertin personally for advancing team games.

125. *Sports et jeux d'exercice dans l'ancienne France* (Paris: Plon, 1901).

126. Eugen Weber, "Pierre de Coubertin," p. 12.

127. *Une Campagne de 21 ans*, p. 42.

128. Ibid. Marey, Hébrard, and Fleuret shortly went over to the Ligue nationale.

129. Ibid., p. 50.

130. *La Renaissance physique* (Paris, 1888), p. 256.

131. It is difficult not to suspect that Grousset was partially the inspiration for the figure of Vilaret, Étienne/Pierre's alter ego in "Le Roman d'un rallié." In the book, Vilaret is a left-leaning, up-from-obscurity journalist whose "sober yet flowery" writing Étienne admires, and a deputy who convinces the young nobleman to stand for Parliament.

132. Charles Maurras, "Les Nouveaux théoreticiens de l'éducation et l'école de la paix sociale," *La Réforme sociale* 14 (1887): 546; "Un Plan de réforme de l'éducation française," *La Réforme sociale* 15 (1888): 476. No wonder that Coubertin thought Maneuvrier's book "remarkable" (*Une Campagne de 21 ans*, p. 26). If Maurras was not exaggerating Coubertin's effect on Maneuvrier, then the latter's calls for athletic games and student sports associations while he was chairman of an official subcommission on secondary education (see Eugen Weber, "Pierre de Coubertin," p. 13) also were inspired by the baron.

133. *Une Campagne de 21 ans*, p. 50.

134. William Curt Buthman, *The Rise of Integral Nationalism in France* (New York: Columbia University Press, 1939), p. 243.

135. These "Lettres des Jeux Olympiques" appeared originally in *La Gazette de France*,

April 15, 17, 18, 19, 20, 22, May 29, 1896, and were republished in *Anthinéa* (Paris: Flammarion, 1901) and *Le Voyage d'Athènes* (Paris: Flammarion, 1929). Citations are from the latter edition, pp. 56–59. This text will be treated in detail below.

136. Cited in Weber, "Pierre de Coubertin," p. 7.

137. Barrès's journey to Greece took place in 1900, and is described in his *Le Voyage de Sparte* (1906). It was at Olympia, Barrès wrote, "that I got my clearest idea of ancient Greece." But in his contemplation of the ruins he saw something rather different than Coubertin did. "I saw the city-states as so many breeding studs who came to put to the proof in the stadium the form of their offspring." *L'Oeuvre de Maurice Barrès*, ed. Club de l'honnête homme (Paris: Plon, 1967), 7:296.

138. *Une Campagne de 21 ans*, p. 73.

139. Among the others were Coubertin, Bréal, Gabriel Hanotaux, and Spiros Lambros. Their longhand testimonies appear on a curious parchment titled in Greek "The New City" and displayed at the Museum of the Modern Olympic Games in Archaia Olympia. Perhaps the document is an artifact of the Conference of Arts, Letters, and Sports that Coubertin organized at the Sorbonne in 1906, but this is unclear.

140. In *Le Joueur de balle* (Paris: Reider, 1929), as noted by Weber, "Pierre de Coubertin," p. 15.

141. *Un Artisan d'énergie française, Pierre de Coubertin* (Paris: Henri Didier, 1917).

142. Alex Natan, a recent commentator, crudely and sensationally claims that Coubertin was a thoroughgoing "reactionary and aristocrat of the *ancien régime*" and a political thinker to be "considered a forerunner of totalitarianism" ("Sport and Politics," in J. W. Loy and G. S. Kenyon, eds., *Sport, Culture, and Society* [Toronto: Macmillan, 1969], p. 207). Natan also implies that Coubertin's thought was influenced by Nietzsche. The fact is that Coubertin never read and only once mentions Nietzsche. As Weber points out ("Pierre de Coubertin," p. 15), it was Paul Adam, an ally of Coubertin, who in his *Morale des sports* (Paris: Librairie mondiale, 1907) tried to connect sport and the Nietzschean "will to power." Weber and Boulongne summarize Coubertin respectively as an "enlightened reactionary" and a "bourgeois liberal." That there is little to recommend one shorthand over the other merely shows that Coubertin, like most men, was possessed of views which do not easily amalgamate under simple labels.

Chapter Five

1. *Une Campagne de 21 ans*, p. 42.

2. See Zeldin, *France 1848–1945*, 2:128–38, for a review of French attitudes toward the U.S.

3. *Une Campagne de 21 ans*, p. 39.

4. According to Coubertin, Ferry responded favorably to *L'Éducation en Angleterre*, a copy of which the baron sent to him. Ferry not only wished him well in the States but pronounced, "With you, one is assured of having observed nothing but what there is, and of having it observed well." "No approval ever caused me so much joy as this one did," wrote Coubertin. *Un Campagne de 21 ans*, p. 42. For Coubertin's admiration of Ferry as a statesman, see *The Evolution of France under the Third Republic*.

5. *Universités transatlantiques* (Paris: Hachette, 1890); Boulongne, *La Vie et l'oeuvre*, p. 109.

6. "Universités transatlantiques," *La Réforme sociale* 20 (1890): 182–84. Several reasons may be adduced for Coubertin's drifting away from the Société/Unions de la paix. He was increasingly busy with the comité and about to take over direction of the U.S.F.S.A. The *Revue athlétique* and *Sports athlétiques* offered new outlets for his writings, as did the newspapers which now opened to him on account of his new prestige. Moreover, though he continued to make use of société contacts, he had failed to interest the Le Play groups as a whole in

athletic education. In addition he was growing more circumspect about the politics of Le Play and his followers. In 1906, on the occasion of the fiftieth anniversary of the société, Coubertin published a long review of Le Play's work. While complimenting it in general, Coubertin complained of how "the unions assumed a hateful appearance of reaction" and that Le Play had failed to dissociate them clearly from "all reactionary tendencies" and to attract "republicans on equal footing with monarchists." "Le Play, réformateur et sociologue," *La Chronique de France* 6 (1906): 158–73.

7. The locus of these observations was the newly founded Catholic University of America in Washington, D.C. Working apparently from press reports, Coubertin had already characterized the university in *La Réforme sociale* 16 (1888): 349–51. In 1889, he met and was utterly overwhelmed by its rector, Msgr. John J. Keane, who began by hoping that Coubertin was not a royalist, "because you'd be wasting your time analyzing us." Keane, said Coubertin, "was American to his fingertips and afraid of nothing," and "his modernism would bring terror to the hearts of European Catholics." Coubertin also quoted extensively from the speech of Msgr. Spalding, the bishop of Peoria, delivered the previous year during the dedication of the Catholic University and in the presence of Cardinal Gibbons. Coubertin called it "the most magnificent and at the same time the most audacious discourse that ever passed the lips of a Catholic priest." "'Let us congratulate ourselves,' cried the bishop in an explosion of patriotism, 'for having proved by the facts that the respect for the laws is compatible with civil and religious liberty; that a free people can prosper and grow without a Sovereign and without war; that the Church and the State can act separately for the public good; that government by the majority, when men have faith in God and science, is after all the most just and wisest government. . . . We have the right to aspire to that happy moment when no man will be condemned to merciless labor without reward; to the time when no distinction will any longer exist between individuals.'" He also heard similar things said by Msgr. John Ireland in Baltimore on November 10. To be sure, Coubertin also told his French audience that "there aren't many over there who speak like Msgr. Spalding," but, he added, "there are many who think as he does." *Universités transatlantiques*, pp. 306–11, passim. In this respect at least, Albert Shaw's proclamation of Coubertin as "the new Tocqueville" was not entirely remiss.

8. "We all know the difference between play and work. In our play, caprice governs, and there is real repose for the will. But in work, the will takes the body and mind and puts them under forms prescribed by others or under such forms as it has adopted for itself in its rational hours. . . . Play is not inhibitory. . . . It is the source of the development of individuality through spontaneity. The individual through play learns to know, to command, and to respect himself, and to distinguish between his own impulses and inclinations and those of others." *Physical Training*, p. 3.

9. Ibid., p. 17.

10. Ibid., p. 20.

11. Ibid., p. 27.

12. Ibid., p. 31.

13. Ibid., p. 36.

14. "This is a day when Yale men are not in public," Seaver began. "Princeton put us in the hole yesterday, and I do not know when we will be able to come out!" This is apparently a reference to an intercollegiate football game, and the irony is that Seaver felt so strongly about it, but found no place whatever for school athletics in his subsequent remarks.

15. Ibid., pp. 53–54.

16. Ibid., p. 54.

17. Ibid., pp. 57–59.

18. Later on Dr. Carolyn C. Ladd of Bryn Mawr College and Miss Lucille Eaton Hill, Director of Gymnasium at Wellesley, made special pleas for the physical training of girls,

who are forced to give up playing with the boys when they become "young ladies" in high school, and therefore are neglected as to physical education in the majority of schools. Miss Hill added that this problem can be remedied only "by *women*" (ibid., pp. 79–80). Hearing women professionals debating in open forum with men about physical education was a completely new experience for Coubertin. In France, such a thing was unheard of. But Coubertin saw no reason to comment on it. Later on he took passing interest in physical education for girls and thought that the private practice of proper sports by women was all right. But he was a thoroughgoing Victorian when it came to women's athletics in public, and as I have mentioned, women were admitted to the Olympic Games over his strong objections.

19. "Speech to the Physical Training Conference," ibid., p. 112.

20. Ibid., p. 113.

21. Ibid., pp. 114–15.

22. Ibid., p. 115.

23. Here I touch on only the highlights of competitive sports development in the nineteenth-century United States. Many volumes have catalogued this development, including Herbert Manchester's *Four Centuries of Sport in America 1490–1890* (New York: Derrydale, 1931), from which many of these details are drawn. No synthetic scholarly account of American sport in the nineteenth century has yet appeared.

24. Quoted ibid., p. 129.

25. *Spirit of the Times*, quoted ibid., p. 127.

26. For an interpretation of the social history of baseball in subsequent decades, see Steven R. Reiss, "Professional Baseball and American Culture in the Progressive Era" (Ph.D. diss. University of Chicago, 1974).

27. For a good history of American mountaineering, see Chris Jones, *Climbing in North America* (Berkeley & Los Angeles: University of California Press, 1976).

28. *Universités transatlantiques*, p. 361.

29. On the contemporary fascination with American women, see Zeldin, *France 1848–1945*, 2:129–31.

30. *Universités transatlantiques*, pp. 365–67.

31. Ibid., p. 368.

32. Ibid., p. 183.

33. "Le Roman d'un rallié," p. 110.

34. Boulongne, *La Vie et l'oeuvre*, p. 110.

35. For Roosevelt's notions of manly virtue, patriotism, and Americanism, see *American Ideals and Other Essays Social and Political* (New York: Putnam, 1897).

36. Mandell's physical description of Coubertin from photographs is difficult to surpass. "His mustache was splendid. It was carefully pruned, with sumptuous tendrils that swooped out to wisps at the end, beyond the width of his canted ears and broad, asymmetrical forehead. He looked like a whiskered cat destined for a long life. . . . His heavy eyebrows and piercing eyes were always dark. In fact, his eyes were so dark as to appear to be without pupils. They were a bit popped, with Italian verve. . . . Dazzling and aggressive, they were the eyes of a man continually gauging the possibilities for action . . . this man with a peppy organ-grinder's good looks." *The First Modern Olympics*, pp. 49–50.

37. Ibid., p. 49.

38. William Milligan Sloane, *How to Bring Out the Ethical Value of History* (Chicago, 1898); *Life of Napoleon Bonaparte*, 4 vols. (New York: Century, 1896); *The French Revolution and Religious Reform* (New York: Scribner, 1901).

39. For a concise overview, see Richard D. Mandell, *Paris 1900: The Great World's Fair* (Toronto: University of Toronto Press, 1967), pp. 3–24.

40. Caron Atlas, "The Crystal Palace," M.A. thesis, University of Chicago, 1980.

41. In contrast to Plato, who held that aristocratic elites were distinguished by their vision

of the social whole when they were in power, Pareto argued that old elites displayed sentiments of altruism, humanitarianism, and universal solidarity precisely when they were in decline. "The new elite is full of vigor and strength, the old one is worked out; the new elite, bold and courageous, proclaims "the class struggle," the old one childishly praises "solidarity." For Pareto, such subjective sentiments of universal humanitarianism were inevitably decadent, first of all because they caused "greater weakness and lack of energy" among the group which held them, and second because these sentiments are typically "inflated, artificial, and false ... more seeming than real." *The Rise and Fall of Elites: An Application of Theoretical Sociology*, ed. with an introduction by Hans L. Zetterberg (Totawa, N.J.: Bedminster, 1968), pp. 67–68, 82, 100.

42. Eugen Weber, "Gymnastics and Sports," pp. 95ff.

43. Theodore Martin, *The Life of His Royal Highness the Prince Consort*, 2 vols. (New York: Appleton, 1880), 2:205.

44. *Punch* 20 (1851): 233.

45. "The Crystal Palace," p. 31.

46. Henry Mayhew, *1851: or, The Adventures of Mr. and Mrs. Cursty Sandboys and Family* (London: David Bogue, 1851), p. 153.

47. Robert Owen, *Robert Owen's Journal* 1 (1851): 97.

48. Quoted in C. H. Gibbes-Smith, *The Great Exhibition of 1851* (London: Victoria and Albert Museum, 1964), p. 21.

49. Friedrich Engels, *Socialism: Utopian and Scientific* (Chicago: Charles Herr, 1918).

50. Yvonne Ffrench, *The Great Exhibition of 1851* (London: David Bogue, 1951), p. 207.

51. *Spectator* 24 (May 3, 1851): 419; Horace Greeley, *Glances at Europe* (New York: Dewitt Davenport, 1851), p. 21. I am grateful to Caron Atlas for pointing these passages out to me.

52. Mandell, *Paris 1900*, p. 17. On the relationship between world's fairs and the growth of museums in the United States, see Neil Harris, "Museums, Merchandising, and Popular Taste: The Struggle for Influence," in Ian Quimby, ed., *Material Culture and the Study of American Life* (New York: Norton, 1978).

53. Debora L. Silverman, "The 1889 Exhibition: The Crisis of Bourgeois Individualism," *Oppositions* 8 (1977): 71–91.

54. Ibid., p. 71.

55. The concept of "social drama" is Victor Turner's, discussed in *Schism and Continuity in an African Society* (Manchester: University Press, 1957). I will treat it, and its relationship to "cultural performance," in detail in a subsequent volume.

56. Silverman, "The 1889 Exhibition," p. 71.

57. The petition is excerpted in Mandell, *Paris 1900*, pp. 19–20. The Maupassant passage is cited in Silverman, "The 1889 Exhibition," p. 78. For a recent reinterpretation, see Roland Barthes, *La Tour Eiffel* (Paris: Delpire, 1964). Coubertin called these artists "narrow-minded" but their petition "honest." *Evolution of France*, p. 230, n. 1.

58. Silverman, "The 1889 Exhibition," pp. 74, 80.

59. David S. Landes, *Prometheus Unbound* (Cambridge: Cambridge University Press, 1970).

60. Silverman, "The 1889 Exhibition," pp. 74–75.

61. Mandell, *Paris 1900*, p. 20.

62. Silverman, "The 1889 Exhibition," p. 78.

63. Ibid., p. 74.

64. Cited ibid., p. 82.

65. See my "Cultural Performance, Culture Theory" and "Olympic Games and the Theory of Spectacle in Complex Society," in *Rite, Drama, Festival, Spectacle: Rehearsals toward a Theory of Cultural Performances* (Philadelphia: Institute for the Study of Human Issues, forthcoming).

66. Silverman, "The 1889 Exhibition," p. 81.

67. Ibid., p. 77.

68. Ibid., p. 80.

69. "The Restoration of Behavior," in *Rite, Drama, Festival, Spectacle*.

70. Richard D. Altick, *The Shows of London* (Cambridge: Harvard University Press, 1978).

71. Coubertin did not comment directly on the Colonial or Habitations exhibits, or on the people-watching of the *flaneurs*. But he did wax poetic on the student festivals of the University of Paris. "Everywhere, in those days of mirth, were seen the satin cap of the University of Bologna, the felt hat of the scholars of Padua, the long scarf of Geneva and Lausanne, the braided cap of Liège and Brussels, and the silver fringed cap of the graduates of Oxford; the divers emblems of the Universities of Edinboro, Lund, Upsala, Copenhagen, Florence, Coimbre; the doublet, the sword and spurred boots of the students of Budapest." However, if this festival of foreign students indeed occurred between August 2 and 12 as he says it did, he could not have seen it in person, since he was in the States. *The Evolution of France*, pp. 231–32.

72. This description is taken from Silverman, "The 1889 Exhibition," p. 74.

73. After the opening ceremonies, he said, "all the world of Paris knew that the reality surpassed the dream." *Evolution of France*, p. 231.

74. Among other exposition symbols that may have served as proto-types for Olympic symbols are the medals awarded to the winners of the industrial competitions. Medal-giving, of course, was a long-established practice, particularly in military, artistic, and royal contexts. The official medallion of the 1900 exposition depicts the Marianne of the Republic bestowing a wreath on a representation of *Homo faber*, man the maker, seated amid his tools over the rays of the rising sun. The Olympic medal was not to be fixed until 1928, when the design consisted of an unnamed Greek goddess extending the Olympic wreath of victory to be won by the athlete, over a representation of the ancient Coliseum. Earlier designs approved by Coubertin had also included these symbolic elements. On the exhibition medallion, see Silverman, "The 1889 Exhibition," p. 81. Silverman says that the Marianne is bestowing her garment, but the illustration of the actual medal seems to show a victory wreath in her outstretched arm.

75. For its history and list of officers, see Coubertin, *Une Campagne de 21 ans*, pp. 37–40.

76. Unfortunately the text has not survived.

77. See Coubertin, "L'Exposition athlétique," *Revue athlétique* 1 (May 25, 1890).

78. "In vain had the men of 1789 been cast in bronze to adorn the public squares; in vain had all which could recall their exploits been collected in museums; in vain had it been repeated in every key that they had found the world out of joint and with a vigorous thrust had set it right for a series of ages,—all this was said without conviction [by the promoters of the exhibition], as if to acquit their consciences, and the throng did not listen. All absorbed with the joy of resurrection, it compared present prosperity with the anguish of the past; it experienced that 'sentiment of life and pride which Lazarus must have felt when he rose from the grave' [de Vogüé]. How far away was that unlucky day when the French, vanquished, despairing, had found themselves face to face with 'a whole France to be made over!' [Zola]. This work had been accomplished in the twilight; the Exposition suddenly set it forth in broad daylight." Coubertin, *The Evolution of France*, pp. 232–33.

79. "Le Rétablissement des Jeux Olympiques," *Revue de Paris* 1 (May 15, 1894): 171.

80. Though he could not have heard Paul Monceaux's speech on the ancient games, as Boulongne suspects, since he had left for America four days before it was delivered. *La Vie et l'oeuvre*, p. 152. Monceaux was the excavator of the site of the Isthmian games near Corinth; see "Fouilles au sanctuaire des jeux isthmiques." *Gazette archéologique* 9 (1884): 273–85, 353–66.

81. *Une Campagne de 21 ans*, pp. 89–90. My translation, for the most part, follows Dixon's in *The Olympic Idea*, p. 1.

82. See above, pp. 81–82, 304 n.258.

83. Winckelmann's interest in Olympia was excited by plastic art (see Butler, *The Tyranny of Greece over Germany*, pp. 11–48). Others, like Gilbert West, came to the games through poetry. *Odes of Pindar; to Which Is Prefixed a Dissertation on the Olympick Games*, 4 vols. (London: Willett, 1749). Newman, as we have seen, was drawn by philosophy to contemplation of the Games, see above, pp. 78, 302 n.233.

84. M. I. Finley and H. W. Pleket, *The Olympic Games: The First Thousand Years* (New York: Viking, 1976), p. 2.

85. "... the Morea Expedition, to which we owe the discovery of Olympia. (For all trace of it had been lost for centuries: the mud brought down by the Alpheus and the Cladeus, which meet at the foot of the ruins, had completed the work of natural convulsions [earthquakes, especially in the sixth century] and human barbarism. Nothing remained to mark the scene where so much glory, so much passion, and so much energy had been spent.)" Pierre de Coubertin, "Olympia," p. 107.

86. Ernst Curtius, *Olympia: Ein Vortrag* (Berlin: Wilhelm Hertz, 1852). Curtius lauded the Greeks for their equal attention to mind and body, cited Herodotus, Plato, and Pindar, recalled the Heracles and Pelops/Oenomaus foundation legends and the Iphitos/Lycurgos truce, and from Pausanias he listed the catalogue of monuments and sculptures waiting to be unearthed. It was truly a treasure to tempt a king, which it did.

87. According to Ludwig Drees, *Olympia: Gods, Artists, and Athletes* (New York: Praeger, 1968), p. 7.

88. Except during the world wars, the Germans have continued working at Olympia right up to the present day. Dörpfeld and Kunze were Curtius's immediate successors. Generations of German students have been raised to think of Olympia as a part of the German patrimony. This passion was especially evident in the symbolic innovations created for the 1936 Berlin Games. Today Germans outnumber the tourists of other nations at Olympia.

89. Ernst Curtius and Friedrich Adler, eds., *Olympia: Die Ergebnisse der von dem Deutschen Reich veranstalteten Ausgrabung*, 5 vols. (Berlin: A. Ascher, 1890–97).

90. Charles Eliot Norton, "The Dimensions and Proportions of the Temple of Zeus at Olympia," *Proceedings of the American Academy of Arts and Sciences* 5, n.s. (1878): 147. Another American who immediately took up the German results was Charles Thomas Newton, *Essays on Art and Archeology* (New York: Macmillan, 1880).

91. Victory Duruy, *Histoire des Grecs*, 3 vols. (Paris: Hachette, 1887); 1:791–802. The plan of Olympia was actually drawn by Dörpfeld, who was then Curtius's student.

92. "Second Olympic Letter," 1918, in *The Olympic Idea*, p. 53.

93. *Histoire des Grecs* 1:787; "Olympia," p. 109. Finley and Pleket refer in passing to "the Pindaric ideology of Greek athletic competition" (*The Olympic Games*, p. 131). This has been spelled out in detail by C. M. Bowra, who discussed Pindar's preoccupation with "the part of experience in which human beings are exalted or illumined by a divine force ... a marvelously enhanced consciousness ... which was the end and justification of life." *The Odes of Pindar* (Baltimore: Penguin Classics, 1969), pp. xii, xvi–xvii. Though I cannot agree with Bowra's contention that Pindar was little interested in games as such—reading the *Odes* as an athlete, I find too much verisimilitude and poetic attention to athletic detail to believe this—Bowra is certainly correct that Pindar was, above all, entranced by the revelatory quality of the athlete who, in the moment of victory, appeared as an *axis mundi* for the divine, the social, and the psychological realms to pivot on. Though Coubertin has no such precise and succinct formulation of this Pindaric ideology, it lay at the core of his "neo-Olympism."

94. *Histoire des Grecs*, 1:800; "Olympia," p. 108. These descriptions might equally well be applied to the nineteenth-century exhibitions.

95. "Olympia," p. 107.

96. *Histoire des Grecs* 1:797.

97. Ibid., p. 790.

98. "Olympia," pp. 108–9.

99. *Histoire des Grecs* 1:801.

100. *Histoire universelle*, 4 vols. (Aix-en-Provence: Société de l'histoire universelle, 1919), 2:34.

101. Ibid., p. 35. This, too, recalls a passage from Duruy, though it is about men not gods. After quoting Xenophon to the effect that philosophers are worth more than Olympic victors, who are not thereby better able to rule a state, Duruy says nicely, "This is true; but at Marathon and Thermopylai would the hair-splitters of the school of Elis have done better than did Miltiades and Leonidas?" (*Histoire des Grecs* 1:801).

102. "Olympia," pp. 118–19.

103. "Olympia not only disappeared from the face of the earth; it disappeared from the realm of man's intelligence. Asceticism was dominant. By that I do not mean at all that Europe was suddenly peopled by ascetics; the situation must not be understood in that way. But a belief spread abroad—conscious or unconscious, precise or vague, but at all events recognized and respected even by those who do not conform to it—that the body is the enemy of the spirit, that the struggle between them is an inevitable and normal state of affairs, and that no effort should be made to reach an agreement enabling them to pull together in governing the individual. . . . Olympism, doctrine of the brotherhood of body and spirit, and asceticism, doctrine of the enmity between them, have never succeeded in understanding and hence respecting one another—and since they both contain seeds of abuse capable of degenerating into downright evils they are fated to clash and follow one another in power like mere political parties, absolute and violent. . . . Moderation and the middle way are always utopias. The law of the pendulum applies to everything." Ibid., p. 112.

104. Ibid., p. 116. I will deal in detail in another work with Coubertin's flirtation with a religion of humanity. For a terse synopsis see my "Religious Themes and Structures in the Olympic Movement and the Olympic Games," in F. Landry and W. A. R. Orban, eds., *Philosophy, Theology, and History of Sport and of Physical Activity* (Miami: Symposia Specialists, 1978), pp. 161–70.

105. "Olympia," p. 107; see also *Histoire universelle* 2:39–40.

106. *Histoire des Grecs* 1:800, 802.

107. See A. M. Snodgrass, *The Dark Age of Greece: An Archeological Survey of the Eleventh to Eighth Centuries BC* (Edinburgh: Edinburgh University Press, 1971), pp. 416–36.

108. *Histoire des Grecs* 1:790, 798.

109. Ibid., p. 798.

110. "Olympia," pp. 107, 111. Finley and Pleket's *The Olympic Games* offers a useful contrast between modern visions of the ancient Games and their true character. However, their comments on Coubertin are not based on a wide reading of his works, and certain of them—such as the degree to which Coubertin took account of ancient Olympic abuses—may be challenged. On the ancient Games, see also E. Norman Gardiner, *Athletics in the Ancient World* (Oxford: Clarendon, 1930) and H. A. Harris, *Greek Athletes and Athletics* (Bloomington: Indiana University Press, 1966).

111. *Histoire universelle* 2:37–38, 45.

112. *Cosmopolis* 2 (1896): 146–59.

113. Only once, to my knowledge, does Coubertin mention Curtius by name, and this in regard to the number of cities in the fifth-century Athenian League. *Histoire universelle* 2:51. Nor does he ever cite Duruy's text; Alfred Croiset, Salomon Reinach, Albert Thibaudet, and Jean de Crozals are the sources mentioned in this 1919 text, though none with respect to Olympia. This might be good evidence for discounting the effect of Duruy's book on Coubertin were it not for his systematic covering up of the exact sources of inspiration which led him to the Olympics.

114. Coubertin celebrated this event. "Olympia," p. 113.

115. *Memoirs of Heinrich Schliemann* (New York: Harper & Row, 1977), p. 7.

116. Ibid., pp. 7, 352–53. Butler called Schliemann, "Winckelmann *redivivus.*" *The Tyranny of Greece over Germany*, pp. 301ff.

117. Deuel, *Heinrich Schliemann*, p. 352.

118. Ibid., pp. 310, 346.

119. *Sport and Society*, pp. 103–4.

120. "Baron Pierre de Coubertin."

121. This, according to a letter from Bettina (Brentano) von Arnim to her brother, cited in Boulongne, *La Vie et l'oeuvre*, pp. 147–48.

122. Quoted ibid., p. 239.

123. Tadeuz Biernakiewiez, "Un Précurseur de Pierre de Coubertin: Gustav Johan Schartau," *Kultura Fizycna* (Warsaw) (September 1964); Yves-Pierre Boulongne, *La Vie et l'oeuvre*, pp. 143–44.

124. At least until much later in his career. As Boulongne notes (p. 144), there is a passing reference to *jeux du Nord* in the 1906 edition of his *La Gymnastique utilitaire*.

125. *Une Campagne de 21 ans*, pp. 52–53; "Les Jeux Olympiques de Much Wenlock," *Sports athlétiques* 1 (December 25, 1890); "A Typical Englishman: Dr. W. P. Brookes of Wenlock," *American Monthly Review of Reviews* 15 (1897): 62–65.

126. "A Typical Englishman," p. 63.

127. Ibid., p. 64.

128. Ibid., pp. 64–65. A striking photograph of the victor in his riding garb and spurs, with the laurel wreath on his head, and kneeling humbly before the lady, as Brookes approvingly looks on, is included in this article.

129. "Theory," it is worth remembering, is derived from a Greek word meaning, originally, "spectator at an athletic games."

130. "A Typical Englishman," p. 65.

131. The phrase is David Schneider's.

132. "A Typical Englishman," p. 65.

133. Ibid.

134. P. 53.

135. John V. Grombach, *Olympic Cavalcade of Sports* (New York: Ballantine, 1956), p. 7. Grombach was a member of the 1924 United States Olympic team, and later of the United States Olympic Committee. Unfortunately he does not indicate his sources for this description, and I have been unable to discover them.

136. Otto Szymiczek ("The Revival of the Olympic Games," in *The Olympic Games through the Ages*, ed. Nicolaos Yalouris [Athens: Ekdotike Athenon, 1976], p. 290) gives it as 1887. The display at the Museum of the Modern Olympic Games at Archaia Olympia makes it 1888. Grombach is firm in dating it to May 18, 1889. In any case, the memory of "Olympic Games" was still fresh in the minds of Athenians when Coubertin began his campaign there in 1894.

137. J. Gennadius, "The Revival of the Olympian Games," *Cosmopolis* 2 (1896): 59–74.

138. J. P. Mahaffy, "The Olympic Games at Athens in 1875," *Macmillan's Magazine* 32 (1875): 324–27.

139. Ibid., p. 326.

140. *La Phénomène olympique*, p. 10.

141. Demetrios Bikelas, *La Grèce byzantine et moderne* (Paris: Fermin-Didot, 1893), pp. 247–71.

142. Grombach, *Olympic Cavalcade*, p. 9.

143. *La Vie et l'oeuvre*, p. 152.

144. Georges Bourdon, *L'Encyclopédie des sports* (Paris: Librairie de France, 1924), p. 147; Gaston Meyer, *La Phénomène olympique*, p. 10.

Chapter Six

1. Boulongne, *La Vie et l'oeuvre*, pp. 81–82. Though he claimed otherwise in his formal memoirs, "Le Roman d'un rallié" suggests that, on occasion, he regretted his decision. Could he have won election?

2. "Pierre de Coubertin," p. 19.

3. *Une Campagne de 21 ans*, p. 89.

4. Eugen Weber, *Peasants into Frenchmen*, pp. 382–83; Zeldin, *France 1848–1945*, 2:683–85.

5. Paul Bouissac, pers. comm., 1977.

6. This account of bicycling follows Eugen Weber, "Gymnastics and Sports," pp. 79–82. See also his forthcoming book on the Tour de France.

7. Ibid., p. 82, n. 29.

8. *France 1848–1945*, 2:682.

9. Pierre MacOrlan, cited in Weber, "Pierre de Coubertin," p. 23.

10. Weber, "Gymnastics and Sports," p. 87.

11. Ibid., p. 90.

12. Jean Giraudoux, *Maximes sur le sport* (Paris: Grasset, 1928); Jean Prévost, *Plaisirs des sports* (Paris: Nouvelle Revue française, 1926). Prévost, like Giraudoux, had become enamored of sport in school. In 1924, he spent a great deal of time in Coubertin's company during the Games, interviewing Pavo Nurmi and other athletes. Montherlant's *lycée*, on the other hand, had nothing in the way of sports, and the biweekly hour of gymnastics was avoided by most of the boys. When, at the age of nineteen, he sought to remedy this lacuna in his education, he was directed by the editor of *Auto* to Coubertin's Comité d'éducation physique (a 1914 successor to the Comité Jules Simon) under whose auspices he trained in the Parc des Princes (with Carpentier's brother as coach) and enjoyed "camaraderie with the *garçons du peuple*" who composed much of the membership. *Les Olympiques* (Paris: Gallimard, 1954), pp. 8–9. This work was originally published in 1924, and entered for the prize in poetry at the 1924 Olympic Games. Coubertin is said to have regarded it as "the *Iliad*" of sport (Eyquem, *Pierre de Coubertin*, p. 260), but the gold medal was awarded to another by the jury (which included Gabriele D'Annunzio, Maurice Barrès, Paul Claudel, Giraudoux, Blasco Ibanez, Edmond Jaloux, Selma Lagerloff, Maurice Maeterlinck, Anna de Noailles, Marcel Prévost, Albert Thibaudet, and Paul Valéry, the last subsequently known for his great love of sport).

13. Quoted in Weber, "Gymnastics and Sports," p. 78.

14. Ibid., pp. 82–83, from the account of Georges Bourdon, one of the founders of Racing.

15. Coubertin, *Une Campagne de 21 ans*, pp. 43, 47.

16. Ibid., pp. 49–50.

17. Ibid., p. 57.

18. Ibid., p. 56.

19. "I don't have to appeal to the Council about it. Besides, you are the association all by yourself, I recognize it. You founded, developed, and directed it. Therefore, I give you my resignation and ask you to communicate it to these men." Ibid., pp. 57–58.

20. *Mémoires olympiques* (Lausanne: Bureau international de pédagogie sportive, 1931), p. 10.

21. Weber, "Gymnastics and Sports," pp. 83ff.

22. *Une Campagne de 21 ans*, pp. 59–60. A photograph shows Godart, Franz Reichel, the footballer, L.-P. Reichel, Carnot, and Coubertin, all in top hats and frock coats, watching the races.

23. In 1895, Bennett donated to the U.S.F.S.A. a silver cup for the champions of Association football. Weber, "Gymnastics and Sports," p. 84.

24. *Une Campagne de 21 ans*, pp. 60–61.

25. Ibid., pp. 83–84.

26. Ibid., pp. 86–87.

27. *Mémoires olympiques*, p. 8.

28. Ibid.; see also *Une Compagne de 21 ans*, p. 73.

29. Bourdon was later to publish articles on Hellenism and a book on Russia.

30. Jusserand was later the author of a history of French sport, a text already mentioned, and he became ambassador to the United States.

31. *Une Campagne de 21 ans*, p. 90. Reprinted in *The Olympic Idea*, p. 1.

32. *Mémoires olympiques*, p. 9.

33. *Une Campagne de 21 ans*, p. 90.

34. The 1892 "Jubilee" publicized the union. Within months it had enrolled its hundredth member club, competitions like those previously described multiplied, provincial branches were organized, and the union was well on its way to becoming established as *the* national amateur sports body. Coubertin's personal efforts in Normandy were far less successful than his Parisian ones. He had been laughed at by his colleagues on the Mirville Municipal Council when he proposed communal games, and in 1892, he had resigned. An invitation to the fencers and gymnasts of Bolbec to perform in Mirville had come to nothing, and when, in 1893, he offered a cup for fencing and running competitions between Bolbec and Fécamp, the latter municipality refused this "sterile agitation." Ibid., pp. 87–88.

35. Keane's participation in this ecumenical meeting was in part responsible for his later dismissal as rector of the Catholic University, in the midst of Leo XIII's crackdown on American liberal "neo-Catholicism." Coubertin seems not to have been apprised of these subsequent events. See P. H. Ahern, *The Life of John J. Keane* (Milwaukee: Bruce, 1955), pp. 120–78.

36. Rossiter Johnson, *A History of the World's Columbian Exposition*, 4 vols. (New York: Appleton, 1898), 4:221–37.

37. Ibid., pp. 221–22.

38. *Mémoires olympiques*, pp. 15, 61.

39. Ibid., p. 61.

40. Ibid., p. 63. A search by Byron Trott of the Harper archives at the University of Chicago has yielded no further record of their conversations.

41. Ibid., pp. 15–16.

42. *Une Campagne de 21 ans*, p. 92.

43. At the 1894 congress, he and Sloane lobbied vigorously against the British definition of "amateur," and carried the day with respect to Olympic competition. The British, because they were eager for international competition, were forced to come around. While it would be some years before the older class preserves were wiped away in England and among her imitators, their death knell was sounded by the growth of international amateur sport in the '90s. On Racing, see Weber, "Gymnastics and Sports," p. 86.

44. *Une Campagne de 21 ans*, p. 91; *Mémoires olympiques*, p. 13.

45. "Bulletin du Comité international olympique," July 1894, reprinted in *Une Campagne de 21 ans*, pp. 91–92, and in *The Olympic Idea*, pp. 2–3.

46. "Les Jeux Olympiques, 776 av. J.C.–1896," in *The Olympic Idea*, pp. 13, 14.

47. *Mémoires olympiques*, pp. 14–15, reprinted ibid., p. 5.

48. *Une Campagne de 21 ans*, p. 93; *Mémoires olympiques*, p. 16.

49. For Astley, see Manchester, *Four Centuries of Sport*, pp. 197–98; for "J. Astley Cooper," see Mandell, *The First Modern Olympics*, pp. 32–33, 178.

50. *Une Campagne de 21 ans*, pp. 94–95.

51. Ibid., p. 94.

52. *Mémoires olympiques*, p. 17.

53. *Times* (London), June 19, 1894.

54. *Une Campagne de 21 ans*, pp. 93–94.

55. Cited in Mandell, *The First Modern Olympics*, p. 93, from German sources.

56. "Jeux Olympiques," p. 14.

57. *Une Campagne de 21 ans*, p. 97

58. "Very sensible of the act of M. de Coubertin, I beg him, as well as the members of the Congress, to receive, with my sincere thanks, my best wishes for the reestablishment of the Olympic games." *Times* (London), June 23, 1894.

59. Quoted in Eyquem, *Pierre de Coubertin*, p. 135.

60. "Carnival on Multiple Planes," in *Rite, Drama, Festival, Spectacle*.

61. This unselfconscious but very apt locution (cited in *The Olympic Idea*, p. viii) is from a later comment on the design of the Olympic festival.

62. Gréard was not an official member of the congress, perhaps because of his earlier tiff with Coubertin over the Ligue nationale, but the rector "came down from his apartment several times to take part" in its sessions. *Mémoires olympiques*, p. 19.

63. "Les Jeux Olympiques," *The Olympic Idea*, p. 13.

64. According to a contemporary English observer. Edmund Gosse, "Current French Literature," *Cosmopolis* 2 (1896): 671. Coubertin had indeed secured Aicard through Mme. Adam, a fashionable hostess who was a friend of the baron. *Une Campagne de 21 ans*, p. 96.

65. Théodore Reinach, "Une Page de musique grecque," *Revue de Paris* 1 (1894): 204–24.

66. *Une Campagne de 21 ans*, p. 96.

67. *Mémoires olympiques*, p. 18. While Hellenism infiltrated the vast enclosure, its occupants simultaneously "infiltrated" Hellenism, much as the dark line of nineteenth-century Parisians including the artist himself wandered into the *bois sacré* in Toulouse-Lautrec's 1884 *Parodie* of Puvis de Chavannes's mural which now surrounded Coubertin's assembly.

68. *Times* (London), June 18, 1894.

69. *Une Campagne de 21 ans*, p. 98.

70. *Mémoires olympiques*, pp. 19–20.

71. *Une Campagne de 21 ans*, pp. 96–97.

72. Ibid., p. 98. The *Times* (London), June 20, 1894, makes it clear that the decision to hold a Games in 1896 "in one of the European capitals" was taken on June 19.

73. Mandell, *The First Modern Olympics*, p. 91, but without citation.

74. "Speech by Baron de Coubertin at the Paris Congress, 1894," in *The Olympic Idea*, pp. 6–7.

75. Alvin Gouldner, *The Hellenic World: A Sociological Analysis* (New York: Harper Torchbooks, 1969), pp. 41–77.

76. Especially Victor Turner's analyses of Ndembu rituals, *The Forest of Symbols* and *Schism and Continuity*.

77. "Speech at the Paris Congress," p. 7.

78. This in an issue that devoted some ten full columns (1¼ pages) to sports, particularly horse-racing, baseball, and cycling.

79. "Can We Revive the Olympic Games?" *Forum* 19 (1895): 317–23. I am grateful to Richard Mandell (*The First Modern Olympics*, pp. 91–92) for notice of the *Spectator* and *Forum* articles.

80. Prior to this date, a column called "Le Sport" was devoted primarily to horse-racing, with a subhead, "Les Sports athlétiques" for all the rest. After June 20, "La Vie sportive" included subsections on turf, cycling, and athletic sports, including professional and amateur, with student and adult games under the latter.

81. His reaction has gone unrecorded, but it must have been with a sweet sense of revenge that he became a columnist for *Figaro* and wrote seventy-three articles for its pages between 1902 and 1906, treating mostly of history and politics, but also of his own role in sport. These articles were collected as *Pages d'histoire contemporaine* (Paris: Plon, 1908).

82. Neither Coubertin nor Saint-Clair are mentioned by name in the letter, whose authorship remains a fascinating little mystery. Perhaps Meyer had been tipped off or recognized Saint-Clair in its lines, but Saint-Clair had been shunted to a minor role in the congress and,

unless he was embarrassed by *Figaro*'s slighting of Coubertin in his favor, it is hard to imagine why he would have taken the trouble. Anyone familiar with Coubertin's modus operandi would immediately suspect that *he* had written it, but the style is not his. Could Franz Reichel, the "press officer," have been responsible for it?

83. "Speech to the Paris Congress," p. 7.

84. Pp. 270–71.

85. Quoted in the *New York Times*, June 26, 1894.

86. *Mémoires olympiques*, p. 21. In the event, Sloane refused the presidency in 1900, and Coubertin remained in the office until his "retirement" from the I.O.C. in 1925.

87. Ibid.

88. Ibid., p. 20.

89. Ibid., p. 23. This is still an apt description of the present I.O.C., though important changes have been made. The size of the "third circle" has shrunk, the first and second circles have been more or less formalized in the executive board and the commissions, the post of "secretary general" has become the "executive director," who is not an I.O.C. member but an exceedingly powerful "staff" person, and the president's powers, though not his visibility, have been circumscribed somewhat in recent years.

90. Ibid. Here he compares it to the Henley Regatta Committee, but its larger prototypes were the patronage associations he had come of age with.

91. Ibid., pp. 22–23.

92. Quoted in *Une Campagne de 21 ans*, p. 108. It is interesting to note, if the transcription is accurate, that the Greeks, unlike most of the Euro-American newspapers, capitalized the words "Olympic Games" from the outset.

93. *Mémoires olympiques*, p. 23.

94. *Une Campagne de 21 ans*, p. 108; *Mémoires olympiques*, p. 23.

95. *Une Campagne de 21 ans*, p. 109; *Mémoires olympiques*, p. 24.

96. *Une Campagne de 21 ans*, p. 109.

97. John Campbell and Phillip Sherrard, *Modern Greece* (New York: Praeger, 1968), p. 100.

98. *Une Campagne de 21 ans*, p. 109.

99. Ibid., p. 111.

100. *Mémoires olympiques*, p. 24.

101. *Une Campagne de 21 ans*, pp. 109–11.

102. In 1896, Hungary was to celebrate in Budapest the millennium of the Hungarian people. Kemeny had worked hard to convince Coubertin to hold the first Games there, and according to the baron this would have transpired had the Greek mission fallen through. Ibid. Why Coubertin would have preferred Hungary to the more fully formed proposal of Sweden is unclear. Could he have sensed, through Kemeny, that Hungary was on the eve of a sports florescence and was shortly to become the most rabid Olympic nation in Europe?

103. *Mémoires olympiques*, p. 25.

104. Ibid.

105. Ibid.

106. *Une Campagne de 21 ans*, p. 112.

107. Ibid., pp. 112–13.

108. Emile Durkheim, *The Elementary Forms of the Religious Life*, trans. Joseph Ward Swain (New York: Free Press, 1965), p. 470.

109. *Une Campagne de 21 ans*, p. 113.

110. "A Modern Olympia," p. 34.

111. *Une Campagne de 21 ans*, p. 114.

112. Coubertin pronounced himself "vexed" that his schoolboy Greek was "utterly useless" to him, above all, "thanks to the pronunciation we were taught." *Mémoires olympiques*, p. 26. Did he really think that the main difference between ancient and modern Greek lay in pronunciation? If so, it would be no more astounding than his apparent ignorance of the

fission between *katharevousa* and *demotikē* Greek, created by Europeanized Greeks and French philhellenes like himself, and of the obstacles this imposed for national unity and progress.

113. Who in 1897 replaced Bikelas as Greek member of the I.O.C.

114. *Une Campagne de 21 ans*, p. 110.

115. Ibid., p. 113.

116. Ibid.; *Mémoires olympiques*, p. 28.

117. *Mémoires olympiques*, p. 26.

118. *Une Campagne de 21 ans*, p. 114.

119. *Mémoires olympiques*, p. 26.

120. Campbell and Sherrard, *Modern Greece*, p. 100.

121. *Une Campagne de 21 ans*, p. 115.

122. Ibid. Tricoupis also agreed at this meeting to place the Zappeion at Coubertin's disposal for his meetings.

123. Ibid., p. 113.

124. "Athletics in the Modern World and the Olympic Games," 1894, in *The Olympic Idea*, pp. 7–10.

125. *Une Campagne de 21 ans*, pp. 114–15.

126. *Mémoires olympiques*, p. 27.

127. Athletics: The "Course de Marathon," 100-, 400-, 800-, 1,500-meter flat races, and the 120-meter high hurdles (distances determined by the British Amateur Athletic Association, rules by the U.S.F.S.A.); long jump, high jump, pole vault, discus throw, and shot put (B.A.A.A. rules). Gymnastics: Individual competitions in rope climbing, horizontal bar, parallel bars, rings, horse vaulting, and dumbbell exercises (rules arranged by Strehly at Coubertin's request); and ensemble exercises by teams of ten (a further sop to the Turners). Fencing: contests for amateurs and trainers in foil, saber, and *épee* (French Society for the Encouragement of Fencing rules). Wrestling: Greek and Roman (poorly developed as an amateur sport in Europe, but very popular in the Balkans—here began the tradition of including a favorite sport of the host nation, even if it was not "international"). Shooting: Carbine and pistol. Yachting: 10-mile steam-yacht races (Paris Sailing Circle rules); 5-mile and 10-mile races for 5-, 10-, 20-, and unlimited-ton sailboats (rules and judging by the British Yacht Racing Association). Rowing: 2,000-meter straight races for singles skiffs, doubles gigs and outriggers, and four-man gigs (Italian Rowing Club rules). Swimming: 100, 500, and 1,000 meters. Cycling: 2,000 meters, without trainers; 10,000 meters and 10 kilometers, with trainers (rules of the International Cyclists' Association). Equitation: Jumping, horsemanship (manège); *haute-école* (dressage?); mounted gymnastics. Lawn Tennis: Singles and doubles (rules of the All-England Lawn Tennis Association and the Marylebone Cricket Club). Ibid., p. 31. Coubertin had been unable to convince any but his English-speaking colleagues that boxing, which on occasion he referred to as the "noblest" of sports, was anything more than a barbaric professional entertainment. Much to Coubertin's further chagrin the Greeks later dropped the equestrian events, claiming that there were no suitable horses in Greece. Since no foreign competitors arrived, the rowing was limited to the Greek navy and members of a few local clubs, and with yachting was eventually canceled owing to weather conditions.

128. Ibid., pp. 28, 205–6.

129. Mandell, *The First Modern Olympics*, p. 102.

130. "Olympia," p. 107.

131. Ibid., p. 113.

132. Ibid., p. 107.

133. Ibid., pp. 107–8. For a fuller description of the ceremony, see *Mémoires olympiques*, pp. 205–8. On the monument, he was careful to note, his name was inscribed in French and in Greek.

134. *Mémoires olympiques*, p. 214.

Chapter Seven

1. *Mémoires olympiques*, p. 28.

2. *Une Campagne de 21 ans*, p. 87. This seems poetic justice for Coubertin's refusal to take seriously, years earlier, the hygienists' preoccupation with classroom lighting!

3. *Mémoires olympiques*, p. 9.

4. Ibid., p. 11.

5. *Une Campagne de 21 ans*, p. 117.

6. Ibid.

7. Ibid., p. 116.

8. Ibid., p. 117; *Mémoires olympiques*, p. 30.

9. *Mémoires olympiques*, p. 30.

10. Ibid., p. 29.

11. *Une Campagne de 21 ans*, p. 117.

12. Ibid., p. 119; "Préface des Jeux Olympiques," p. 158.

13. For further details, see Mandell, *The First Modern Olympics*, pp. 104–8. In any event, the restoration was not completed until after the 1896 Olympics. Many spectators occupied the newly graded slopes or temporary wooden benches. But the extraordinary project had progressed sufficiently to guarantee the splendor of the first modern Games.

14. *Mémoires olympiques*, p. 30.

15. Ibid.

16. James D. Bourchier, "History of Modern Greece," *Encyclopaedia Britannica*, 13th ed.

17. *Une Campagne de 21 ans*, p. 121; *Mémoires olympiques*, p. 34.

18. *Une Campagne de 21 ans*, pp. 121–22.

19. At least a portion of their expenses was defrayed by donations collected by Raoul Fabens, secretary of the F.N.O.C. Ibid., p. 123.

20. In the end the "diploma" was designed by the Greek artist Nikolaos Gyzis who, in Coubertin's judgment, "feared to overturn the classical and surrendered himself to a bizarre modernism." Ibid., p. 120.

21. Ibid.

22. Ibid., p. 119.

23. According to the Englishman G. S. Robertson, Cook advertised rooms in Athens at such a "preposterous price" that many foreign visitors were dissuaded from attending. "The newspapers, both in Greece and England, continued, even after the end of the meeting, to estimate the number of foreigners present at 20,000. As a matter of fact, there can be no doubt that 1,000 would be a large estimate." "The Olympic Games: By a Competitor and Prize Winner," *Fortnightly Review* 65 (1896): 955. The director of the American School of Classical Studies, however, numbered the foreigners present for the opening ceremonies in the "few thousands." Rufus B. Richardson, "The New Olympian Games," *Scribner's Magazine* 20 (1896): 275.

24. *Mémoires olympiques*, p. 32.

25. Ibid., pp. 33–34.

26. *Une Campagne de 21 ans*, p. 123.

27. Robertson, "The Olympic Games by a Competitor," p. 948.

28. Ibid., pp. 944–45.

29. Ibid., p. 955. I take this to be a reference to the I.O.C. in Paris and to Coubertin's *Bulletin*.

30. *Une Campagne de 21 ans*, p. 123.

31. Robertson, "The Olympic Games by a Competitor," p. 945.

32. Ibid., pp. 947–48.

33. Ibid., p. 945.

34. "There go eight instead of eighty," muttered one partisan. "Where are all the vaunted

clubs that live on their amateur sporting reputations?" Mandell, *The First Modern Olympics*, p. 116, from unpublished archival material at Princeton.

35. A little knot of noisy supporters sent the team off with college yells, and S. J. Viasco, the editor of a Greek newspaper in New York, presented the athletes with baskets of flowers, but the newspapers gave the departure little play. Ibid., pp. 116–17.

36. Ibid., p. 115.

37. Ellery H. Clark, *Reminiscences of an Athlete* (Boston: Houghton Mifflin, 1911), pp. 123–24.

38. Richardson, "New Olympian Games," p. 272.

39. Quoted in Mandell, *The First Modern Olympics*, p. 116.

40. *Une Campagne de 21 ans*, pp. 123–24.

41. Official I.O.C. records date the appointment to 1895 without further specifics. It would be interesting to know exactly when Coubertin formally approved it, before or after the press controversy?

42. This account from *Une Campagne de 21 ans*, pp. 124–25. Coubertin also mobilized Baron von Rieffenstein, who had been at the Sorbonne congress, and the director of the German periodical *Spiel und Sport*, who had published the congress's results.

43. Ibid., p. 125; *Mémoires olympiques*, p. 36.

44. Gebhardt, "Letter to Coubertin, January 20, 1896," in *Dokumente zur Frühgeschichte der olympischen Spiele* (Cologne: Carl-Diem-Institut, 1970), p. 57.

45. *Une Campagne de 21 ans*, p. 125; *Mémoires olympiques*, p. 36.

46. Gebhardt, "Letter to Coubertin," p. 57.

47. *Une Campagne de 21 ans*, p. 123.

48. Ibid., p. 125.

49. In a review of the fifth volume, *La France et sa politique extérieure en 1867* (Paris: Calmann-Lévy, 1887), L. Chêneboit credited Rothan's "charming style" and "facile exposition" that gave the book "the passionate interest of a tragic novel." The reader was left, he said, with a "sadness rendered more bitter by the clairvoyance shown by several representatives of France in the midst of these events, which nowhere cries out more ardently and piercingly than in the dispatches of the present author." *Annales des science politiques* 3 (1888): 143.

50. *Pierre de Coubertin*, p. 132.

51. The collection is known from the catalogue, printed and bound on the occasion of its sale, the year of Rothan's death. Of the 262 paintings offered up, most were portraits, landscapes, street scenes, and neoclassical compositions, by sixteenth- and seventeenth-century Dutch and Flemish or eighteenth-century French and Italian painters. The paintings were mostly by minor masters, but also included two small Breughels, three Van Dycks, four Fragonards, three Davids, and a Goya miniature. *Catalogue de tableaux anciens formant l'importante collection de M. Gustave Rothan* (Paris: Ménard, 1890). Unfortunately, I have been unable to turn up any record of the proceeds of this sale, which would give some indication of what sort of dowry, if any, Marie Rothan brought to Pierre. Given that the family put the paintings up for sale immediately upon the death of Gustave, and that Paul Mantz, self-described friend of Rothan, felt the need to lament the dispersal of the collection in the preface (p. xiii) to the very catalogue promoting its sale, it is probable that the family was in rather dire financial straits. Circumstances had likely worsened by the date of Marie's betrothal to Pierre, and if she had brothers, we would be further assured that the marriage was not a pleasant economic prospect for the Coubertins.

52. Eyquem, *Pierre de Coubertin*, p. 132, with no cited sources.

53. So far as is known—which is not far at all—Pierre had had no great love affairs, and certainly no engagement, prior to the one with Marie Rothan. However, behind the figure of Mary Herbertson in the "Roman d'un rallié"—who is not, as Yves-Pierre Boulongne thinks

(*La Vie et l'oeuvre*, p. 63) Marie's double, but in many respects her opposite—I suspect the memory of a real flirtation in the States.

54. Eyquem, *Pierre de Coubertin*, p. 141.

55. Boulongne, *La Vie et l'oeuvre*, p. 63.

56. See the photographic evidence in Eyquem, *Pierre de Coubertin*, p. 17.

57. Ibid., pp. 141–42, without citation.

58. Ibid.

59. It was later replaced by the *Revue olympique* in 1906, and *L'Éducation physique* in 1907.

60. October 20, "The Eastern Question"; October 21, "The Anglo-Saxon World"; November 4, "The Spanish Republics," "The Dark Continent"; November 11, "The Far East." Boulongne reprints the full program. *La Vie et l'oeuvre*, p. 467.

61. Albert Shaw, "Introduction" to *The Evolution of France under the Third Republic*, p. xiv. In this text, Shaw reviews Coubertin's career and promotes him as "the De Tocqueville of our day." The book, he said, "is entitled to international recognition" (p. xvi). Shaw was editor of the *American Monthly Review of Reviews*, in which Coubertin published a series of articles beginning in 1897. Though he had, at times, to remonstrate with the baron over the latter's literary ill-discipline (Mandell, *The First Modern Olympics*, p. 65, n. 21), Shaw was sincerely taken with *The Evolution of France* and repeated much of his flattering introduction to the book in his *Review* (17 [1898]: 435–38). Despite this promotion, the book seems to have enjoyed no particular success in the United States.

62. "Introduction," p. xiv.

63. Review of *L'Évolution française sous la Troisième République*, *Revue politique et parlementaire* 11 (1897): 233–34.

64. Review of *L'Évolution française sous la Troisième République*, *La Réforme sociale* 32 (1896): 379–80.

65. Durkheim was gathering materials for his 1898–1900 lectures on "The Nature of Morals and Rights," later published as part of *Professional Ethics and Civic Morals*, trans. Cornelia Brookfield (Glencoe: Free Press, 1959). On the political solution to *anomie* and the reasons for Durkheim's later rejection of it, see the excellent article by Stephen R. Marks, "Durkheim's Theory of Anomie," *American Journal of Sociology* 80 (1974): 329–63.

66. Coubertin had the motto installed on his bookplate alongside the family crest and under the image of an ancient (Greek?) temple. See Boulongne, *La Vie et l'oeuvre*, p. 482.

67. *The Elementary Forms of the Religious Life*, pp. 474ff.

68. Pierre de Coubertin, "The Olympic Games of 1896," *Century Magazine* 53 (1896): 42.

69. Robertson, "The Olympic Games by a Competitor," p. 947.

70. Ibid., p. 949.

71. Richardson, "The New Olympian Games," pp. 268–69.

72. Mandell, *The First Modern Olympics*, p. 119.

73. Richardson, "The New Olympian Games," p. 273.

74. *Les Jeux Olympiques, 776 av. J.C.–1896* (Athens: Beck, 1896), p. 52. This is the "official" report of the Games, printed in Greek and French.

75. Richardson, "The New Olympian Games," p. 273.

76. Nor, arguably, since. In Greece, in 1977, I was asked repeatedly for assurances that the I.O.C. would return the Games to Athens for the centennial celebration in 1996. As at least three individuals pointed out, that date would also mark the twentieth anniversary of the liberation of the country from the military dictatorship. "It is a celebration we Greeks will need after these difficult times." And the campaign to give the Games a permanent Greek home, which, as we shall see, arose for the first time in 1896, has recently been renewed in fervor. See Helen Vlachos, "Return the Olympics to Greece Permanently: They Started There," *New York Times*, August 12, 1979. From President Caramanlis and former President Tsatsos to innumerable American politicians and journalists, the proposal has been

put still more strongly in the wake of the Moscow Olympic controversies. Caramanlis has made an extraordinary proposal to "Vaticanize" some twenty square miles around and including the ancient ruins of Olympia, making the I.O.C. masters of a sovereign state. As this volume goes to press, this proposal is under intense scrutiny by the I.O.C.

77. Richardson, "The New Olympian Games," p. 273.

78. *Les Jeux Olympiques*, p. 50.

79. Ibid.

80. Details of these sessions are to be found in Otto Mayer, *À travers les anneaux olympiques*, pp. 43–44. At a later meeting on the 11th, a resolution was passed requiring the automatic dismissal of any I.O.C. member who did not send in an annual report or absented himself without valid excuse from the Games.

81. Ibid., p. 43. The fact that no decision was reached and that Coubertin had already declared in favor of the United States reveals once again the ceremonial nature of the discussion.

82. *Les Jeux Olympiques*, p. 51.

83. Ibid., p. 52.

84. Richardson, "The New Olympian Games," p. 274. The newspapers called for a reduction in prices on the grounds that a father of a family, even at these modest rates, could not afford to take his brood to the stadium day after day. "But no reduction was made, and when the interest was strong enough the stadium was filled without it."

85. *Les Jeux Olympiques*, p. 52.

86. Ibid., pp. 51–52. These included the crew of the American cruiser *San Francisco*, given generous shore leave, and a number of American tourists diverted from Italy, the Holy Land, and Egypt by the event. Mandell, *The First Modern Olympics*, p. 118.

87. Coubertin, "The Olympic Games of 1896," p. 42. See Castaigne's illustration, ibid., p. 41.

88. Richardson, "The New Olympian Games," p. 272.

89. *Les Jeux Olympiques*, p. 52.

90. Ibid.

91. "The Olympic Games by a Competitor," p. 954.

92. *Les Jeux Olympiques*, p. 52.

93. Coubertin, "The Olympic Games of 1896," p. 40.

94. *Les Jeux Olympiques*, p. 53.

95. The marvelous photographs and illustrations of the scene are, of course, in black and white, but they do not exaggerate the effect. See Yalouris, *The Olympic Games through the Ages*, p. 297; Richardson, "The New Olympian Games," p. 271.

96. Richardson, "The New Olympian Games," p. 275.

97. Ibid., p. 274.

98. Otto Szymiczek, "Athens 1896," in *The Olympic Games*, p. 27.

99. *The First Modern Olympics*, p. 123.

100. Richardson, "The New Olympian Games," p. 270.

101. *Les Jeux Olympiques*, p. 52.

102. Richardson, "The New Olympian Games," p. 268.

103. Coubertin, "The Olympic Games of 1896," p. 44; *Les Jeux Olympiques*, pp. 53–54.

104. Coubertin, "The Olympic Games of 1896," p. 44.

105. *Les Jeux Olympiques*, p. 54.

106. Richardson, "The New Olympian Games," p. 274

107. *Les Jeux Olympiques*, p. 54.

108. Coubertin, "The Olympic Games of 1896," p. 44.

109. *Les Jeux Olympiques*, p. 54.

110. "The Olympic Games of 1896," p. 44.

111. Ibid.

112. *Les Jeux Olympiques*, pp. 54–55.

113. Ibid., p. 55.

114. *Mémoires olympiques*, p. 36.

115. *Les Jeux Olympiques*, p. 55.

116. *Mémoires olympiques*, p. 36.

117. "The Olympic Games of 1896," p. 44.

118. *Mémoires olympiques*, p. 36.

119. *Le Jeux Olympiques*, p. 56.

120. Palamis (1859–1943) had, perhaps, already acceded to the title of "National Poet." He was the leader of that influential Athenian group which had inherited the demotic mantle of the Ionian school of Dionysus Solomas and introduced free verse, symbolism, and the cadence of spoken language into Greek poetry. The classical sentiments of the lyric were neatly complemented by its demotic. For the original Greek, see Yalouris, *The Olympic Games through the Ages*, p. 295.

121. This translation differs a little, in the direction of the Greek, from some of the English texts in use.

122. Szymiczek, "Athens 1896," p. 27; Coubertin, "The Olympic Games of 1896," p. 44.

123. *Les Jeux Olympiques*, pp. 56–57. Coubertin recalled the effect of the Delphic Hymn to Apollo on the Paris congress, where "once before music had been associated with the revival of the Olympic games." "The Olympic Games of 1896," p. 44.

124. *Les Jeux Olympiques*, p. 57.

125. Ibid.

126. "The Olympic Games by a Competitor," p. 956.

127. *Les Jeux Olympiques*, p. 57.

128. Prince George, president; Phokianos, a gymnastics teacher, vice-president; and, as members, Captain Yenisarlis of the army, Professor Politis of Athens University, and Georges Streit, sometime university professor and president of the Students' Club.

129. *Le Voyage d'Athènes*, pp. 50–51.

130. Robertson, "The Olympic Games by a Competitor," pp. 948, 952.

131. Tuffere did 41'8"; Persakis, 41'1", among the few marks creditable by international standards at these Games.

132. George Horton, "The Recent Olympic Games," *Bostonian* 4 (1896): 220; Mandell, *The First Modern Olympics*, pp. 125–26.

133. Yalouris, *The Olympic Games through the Ages*, p. 485.

134. Only then did the closing ceremonies start their slower evolution to the present form which they did not assume until Melbourne in 1956. At Athens, the national anthem does not appear to have been joined with the flag-raising in the victory ceremonies until it was demanded by the crowd for Loues after the Marathon.

135. *Le Voyage d'Athènes*, pp. 92–93.

136. Robertson, "The Olympic Games by a Competitor," p. 952. Mandell makes their number fourteen. *The First Modern Olympics*, p. 126.

137. Thomas P. Curtis, "The Glory that was Greece," *Sportsman* 12 (1932): 22.

138. Mandell, *The First Modern Olympics*, p. 115.

139. Coubertin, *Mémoires olympiques*, p. 41; "The Olympic Games of 1896," p. 45.

140. Richardson, "The New Olympian Games," p. 276.

141. *Mémoires olympiques*, p. 41.

142. "The Olympic Games by a Competitor," pp. 949–50.

143. "The New Olympian Games," p. 276.

144. Ibid., p. 281.

145. According to Robertson, the Americans would have jumped much farther but that

for safety they took off well behind the board. They were unaccustomed to the means of judging fair jumps, which, as it developed, was to become standard practice. "The Olympic Games by a Competitor," p. 952.

146. Richardson, "The New Olympian Games," p. 277.

147. Robertson, "The Olympic Games by a Competitor," p. 949. Instead of a 7-foot circle, the throwers released from a 7-foot square, and this, according to Robertson, kept Garrett two or three feet off form.

148. Richardson, "The New Olympian Games," p. 280.

149. Robertson, "The Olympic Games by a Competitor," p. 954.

150. "The New Olympian Games," pp. 275, 277.

151. *Le Voyage d'Athènes*, p. 43.

152. "The New Olympia Games" (April 11, 1896), pp. 511–12. This anonymous dispatch was clearly written before Loues had won his victory.

153. "The New Olympian Games," pp. 277–78.

154. Ibid., p. 281.

155. *Le Voyage d'Athènes*, pp. 67–68.

156. Coubertin, "The Olympic Games of 1896," p. 47.

157. Not all Greeks were so anxious to see victors other than Americans. A neighbor of Richardson's in the stadium, "an educated Greek, whose notions of geography being derived from schooldays were probably a little vague," insisted on adding Flack's victory to the American roster. "Australian," he said to Richardson, "why that is the same thing." "The New Olympian Games," pp. 276–77.

158. "The Olympic Games of 1896," p. 48.

159. Ibid., p. 45; Mandell, *The First Modern Olympics*, p. 131.

160. I guess it at 2,000, judging from the photograph reproduced in plate 11.

161. Richardson, "The New Olympian Games," p. 272.

162. *Pierre de Coubertin*, p. 153.

163. See the photograph in Yalouris, *The Olympic Games through the Ages*, p. 304. Szymiczek says these courts were "hastily arranged by the temple of Olympian Zeus." "Athens, 1896," p. 28. Coubertin implies that the contests were held on the tennis courts in the center of the velodrome ("The Olympic Games of 1896," p. 42), but the photograph makes this unlikely. It also shows no evidence of any "large, circus-type tent" which Mandell says was erected over the courts. *The First Modern Olympics*, p. 131.

164. Richardson, "The New Olympian Games," p. 273.

165. *Le Voyage d'Athènes*, p. 42. Robertson ("The Olympic Games by a Competitor," p. 947) also reports the cries of *adika*.

166. Richardson, "The New Olympian Games," p. 278.

167. Mandell, *The First Modern Olympics*, p. 133; Robertson, "The Olympic Games by a Competitor," p. 947.

168. Richardson, "The New Olympian Games," p. 279. As I will argue in detail in a subsequent work, athletic contests like the run are at once expressive and inversive of the modern cultural order: expressive, because the competition is not only head-to-head, but subject to exact chronometric measurement, with all its associations to industrial time, work discipline, and quantifiable "production"; inversive, because in the world of sport, there are clear-cut, objective, universally recognized winners and losers. Moreover, the introduction of time- and record-keeping makes it possible to agree on who is the best, not only in particular competitions, but across whole eras. Events like gymnastics, however, are more complicated and model more differentiated and "realistic" social processes in which objective and subjective criteria of performance interpenetrate, and judgment is corporate, consensual, and, therefore, open to dispute. Rules are not as fully explicit, often inscrutable to the

spectatorial mass, and the fate of individual performances is subject to forces beyond the performers' control, such as crowd pressure or judges' personal agendas.

Modern athletics differ from the ancient Greek games not only in the introduction of time- and record-keeping and subjective consensual judging, but also in the reckoning, rewarding, and remembering of second and third places (in Athens, 1896, third place received no awards). In the language of game theory, ancient athletics were "zero-sum" games, whereas modern Olympic contests are three-sum games. In fact, however, they are potentially n-sum games, for time- and record-keeping make it possible for a contestant who does not place to be honored nonetheless for surpassing a personal, age-group, national or other record. Moreover, as Jean Giraudoux profoundly remarked *(Maximes sur le sport*, p. 26), "Alongside the actual winner is always a moral winner." The ancient Greeks found no moral value among losers; at least they cared neither to remember nor to celebrate moral victors who were not victorious. As I will elsewhere show, modern Olympic memory is more perspicacious in this respect.

169. Maurras, *Le Voyage d'Athènes*, pp. 42–43.

170. Robertson, "The Olympic Games by a Competitor," p. 946. In the event, the Germans did not return home "with a halo of glory," at least not with one that many of their countrymen were prepared to acknowledge. Hofmann, Flatow, and the rest were immediately barred from competition by the Turner organizations for defying the ban against the Athens Olympics.

Robertson's comments on gymnastics point up another paradox that I will treat in detail elsewhere. Giraudoux embodied it in two of his wonderful epigrams *(Maximes sur le sport*, p. 26): "Sport is the national occupation of northern peoples. Sport is the esperanto of the races." Even for the northern athlete Robertson, German gymnastics was a "language" he could not comprehend.

171. Richardson, "The New Olympian Games," p. 280.

172. Ibid.

173. Ibid., p. 269.

174. See illustration, ibid., p. 284.

175. Coubertin, "The Olympic Games of 1896," pp. 47–48. The passage goes on: "and harangued them in the tongue of Demosthenes." Note again Coubertin's ignorance of the differences between classical and *demotikē* Greek. All documents and notices were printed exclusively in Greek. This led to no end of confusion for the foreigners but also increased the exotic flavor of their stay and led them into more contacts with their hosts. "That Americans might not be compelled to understand French, or Hungarians forced to speak German, the daily programs of the games, and even invitations to luncheon, were written in Greek. On receipt of these cards, covered with mysterious formulae, where even the date was not clear (the Greek calendar is twelve days behind ours), every man carried them to his hotel porter for elucidation." Ibid.

176. Ibid.

177. Ibid. The king's banquet is described below.

178. "The New Olympian Games," p. 269. In the end, Richardson went so far as to compare the performance disfavorably with the Vassar College *Antigone* of 1893.

179. Ibid.

180. Ibid., p. 270.

181. For a theoretical precis, see my "Olympic Games and the Theory of Spectacle in Complex Society," in *Rite, Drama, Festival, Spectacle*.

182. Finley and Pleket, *The Olympic Games: The First Thousand Years*, p. 35. Maurras, to the contrary, believed that a Marathon race had been instituted in ancient times to commemorate Pheidippides. *Le Voyage d'Athènes*, p. 69.

183. Ion P. Ionnides, "The True Course Run by the Marathon Messenger," in F. Landry

and W. A. R. Orban, eds., *Philosophy, Theology, and History of Sport and of Physical Activity* (Miami: Symposia Specialists, 1978), p. 268, citing Eusebios.

184. *History*, vi, 105. In this reconstruction, I am, for the most part, following Harris, *Greek Athletes and Athletics*, pp. 76–77.

185. Plutarch, *Moralia*, 347 c.

186. Lucian, *A Slip of the Tongue in Greeting* [*Prosagoreusei ptaismatos*], 3. Lucian actually gives the name as "Philippides."

187. "Every man remembers, as a striking feature of his own youth, the story of Marathon and Pheidippides." So said Maurras, *Le Voyage d'Athènes*, p. 69.

188. Ionnides, "The True Course Run by the Marathon Messenger."

189. "The Olympic Games by a Competitor," p. 950.

190. "The New Olympian Games," pp. 280, 281.

191. Ibid., p. 273.

192. "The Olympic Games of 1896," p. 46.

193. *Le Voyage d'Athènes*, pp. 77–78.

194. Ibid., p. 70.

195. "The New Olympian Games," p. 280.

196. *Le Voyage d'Athènes*, p. 70.

197. Coubertin, "The Olympic Games of 1896," p. 46.

198. Ibid.

199. Ibid.

200. Robertson, "The Olympic Games by a Competitor," p. 953.

201. Claude Lévi-Strauss, *The Savage Mind* (Chicago: University of Chicago Press, 1966), pp. 30–33; Marshall Sahlins, *Culture and Practical Reason* (Chicago: University of Chicago Press, 1978), pp. 51–52.

202. *Mémoires olympiques*, p. 40.

203. *Moralia*, 347 D.

204. Richardson, "The New Olympian Games," p. 279.

205. Robertson, "The Olympic Games by a Competitor," p. 947. The Americans found nothing but poetic justice in Goulding's defeat. He was known to them as a swaggering braggart too confident of victory, and, according to Curtis, a poor loser besides, slinking out of the stadium after the race and never seen again. "The Glory That Was Greece," pp. 21–23.

206. "The Olympic Games by a Competitor," p. 951.

207. Richardson, "The New Olympian Games," p. 279.

208. Ibid., p. 280.

209. *Les Jeux Olympiques*, pp. 82–83.

210. Maurras, *Le Voyage d'Athènes*, pp. 70–71.

211. Richardson, "The New Olympian Games," p. 280.

212. *Les Jeux Olympiques*, p. 83. Some place the cannon shot, a signal that the leader had arrived at Ampelokipi, before Papadiamantopoulos' dash into the stadium. Szymiczek, "The Revival of the Olympic Games," p. 302.

213. *Le Voyage d'Athènes*, pp. 70–71.

214. Even mechanical eyes will not do. In Montreal, the victor's approach was televised on a huge screen to the 70,000 awaiting him in the stadium. But even as, on the screen, he dipped down into the tunnel, barely 15 seconds from view, no one could quite fully believe it was Cierpinski until by naked eyes he was seen emerging from the tunnel and running toward the finish line.

215. *Les Jeux Olympiques*, p. 83.

216. Szymiczek, "The Revival of the Olympic Games," p. 302; Maurras, *Le Voyage d'Athènes*, p. 71.

217. *Les Jeux Olympiques*, p. 83.

218. *Le Voyage d'Athènes*, p. 70.

219. *Les Jeux Olympiques*, p. 82.

220. Szymiczek, "The Revival of the Olympic Games," p. 302.

221. *Les Jeux Olympiques*, p. 82.

222. Ibid.

223. Szymiczek, "The Revival of the Olympic Games," p. 302.

224. *Les Jeux Olympiques*, p. 82.

225. Ibid.

226. Ibid.

227. Ibid.

228. Ibid.

229. Ibid.

230. Ibid., p. 84.

231. Coubertin, "The Olympic Games of 1896," p. 46.

232. Coubertin, *Mémoires olympiques*, p. 41.

233. "The Olympic Games by a Competitor," p. 950.

234. Maurras, *Le Voyage d'Athènes*, p. 71.

235. *Les Jeux Olympiques*, p. 83.

236. *Le Voyage d'Athènes*, p. 71.

237. Richardson, "The New Olympian Games," p. 280.

238. *Les Jeux Olympiques*, p. 84.

239. Richardson, "The New Olympian Games," p. 280.

240. Coubertin, *Mémoires olympiques*, p. 40.

241. *Les Jeux Olympiques*, p. 84.

242. Coubertin, "The Olympic Games of 1896," p. 46.

243. *Les Jeux Olympiques*, p. 84.

244. Coubertin, *Mémoires olympiques*, p. 41.

245. *Les Jeux Olympiques*, p. 84. Coubertin, "The Olympic Games of 1896," p. 46.

246. *Le Voyage d'Athènes*, p. 73.

247. Richardson, "The New Olympian Games," pp. 280–81.

248. "The Olympic Games by a Competitor," p. 954.

249. James B. Connolly, "An Olympic Victor," *Scribner's Magazine* 44 (1908): 18–31, 205–17, 357–70.

250. Zeldin, *France 1848–1945*, 2:1147.

251. Ibid.

252. *Le Voyage d'Athènes*, p. 73.

253. "The Olympic Games of 1896," p. 46.

254. *Le Voyage d'Athènes*, p. 72.

255. "The New Olympian Games," p. 281.

256. "The Olympic Games of 1896," p. 46.

257. "They New Olympian Games," p. 282.

258. *Le Voyage d'Athènes*, p. 77.

259. Ibid., pp. 72, 77.

260. *Les Jeux Olympiques*, p. 84.

261. Richardson, "The New Olympian Games," p. 279.

262. *Le Voyage d'Athènes*, pp. 65–66.

263. Mandell, *The First Modern Olympics*, p. 141.

264. Curtis, "The Glory That Was Greece," p. 56.

265. Richardson, "The New Olympian Games," p. 281.

266. Ibid., pp. 281–82. The official report compared Loues' father to Diagoras of Rhodes in his "proud simplicity and emotion." *Les Jeux Olympiques*, p. 98.

267. Ibid., p. 281.
268. Maurras, *Le Voyage d'Athènes*, p. 78; Coubertin, *Mémoires olympiques*, p. 40.
269. Richardson, "The New Olympian Games," p. 281.
270. Ibid.
271. Coubertin, *Mémoires olympiques*, p. 40.
272. Richardson, "The New Olympian Games," p. 281.
273. "An Olympic Victor," p. 25.
274. Ibid., p. 26.
275. Ibid., pp. 206, 30.
276. Ibid., p. 206.
277. Ibid., pp. 211–14.
278. Ibid., pp. 216–17.
279. Ibid., p. 357.
280. Ibid., pp. 359–61.
281. Ibid., p. 366.
282. Ibid., p. 369.
283. Sophia Morgan, pers. comm., 1977.
284. Postponed from Tuesday because of the weather.
285. *Les Jeux Olympiques*, p. 98.
286. Mandell has excavated the French menu from the archives at Princeton University: tranches de poisson frit, à la Colbert; pommes de terre; pilaff à volaille; filet de boeuf rôti; purée d'épinards; jambon et dinde froids à la gelée salade à la russe; crème glacée à l'ananas; and five domestic and foreign wines. *The First Modern Olympics*, p. 148.
287. *Une Campagne de 21 ans*, pp. 125–26.
288. Ibid., p. 126.
289. *Pierre de Coubertin*, pp. 155–56.
290. *Les Jeux Olympiques*, pp. 98–99.
291. Ibid., p. 99.
292. "The Olympic Games of 1896," p. 48.
293. *Les Jeux Olympiques*, p. 99.
294. Ibid., pp. 99–100.
295. Ibid., p. 100.
296. Ibid., p. 101.
297. Ibid., pp. 101–2.
298. The Americans, he said, were serious of purpose, yet amiable, light-hearted, open, and unpretentious. With Garrett's discus victory, he averred (forgetting that Connolly's triple jump was the first Olympic crown): "The new continent, last born into the world, having suffered so much for not having underneath itself any tradition, felt that, by virtue of the Olympic laureate, they became, they too, citizens of the ideal city that dominates in its ruins all civilizations and races." Maurras, as we have seen, interpreted the character and performances of the Americans quite differently, and, while he would have been pleased that his countryman had so thoroughly discovered the virtues of monarchy, devotion to the king of Greece was hardly what Maurras had in mind for the French. Whether or not, as Henry reports (*An Approved History of the Olympic Games*, p. 37), Maurras leaned over to Coubertin in the thrill of Loues' victory and said, "I see that your internationalism of athletics does not kill national spirit, it strengthens it," it is clear from *Le Voyage d'Athènes* that the promotion of nationalism was what Maurras came to value most about the Games. This will be discussed in detail below, along with Maurras's view that "cosmopolitanism" was the most hateful thing of all. Hughes le Roux, on the other hand, referred to the Games as a "cosmopolitan festival," attaching only positive value to the term.
299. The schedule of events is reported inaccurately; Lermusiaux is given victory in the 800 meters, instead of in one of its heats; the Marathon distance is said to be "exactly 48

kilometers," instead of 42; the Marathon field was reported as composed of "8 Greeks, 2 Frenchmen, and 1 Australian."

300. This, on the authority of Reichel, Coubertin's old ally, who was covering the Games for *Vélo.*

301. *Les Jeux Olympiques,* p. 100.

302. Interestingly, the Englishman's dispatches reached London in one day, whereas Hughes le Roux's took four days to reach Paris.

303. *Times* (London), April 11, 1896.

304. Ibid., April 10, April 13. The former also reported that a contingent of Bulgarian athletes arrived late for the Games but participated in some events. Nothing further is heard of them in Olympic accounts, which is a loss, since it would be interesting to know of their reception by the Greek people as the only representatives of a nation with whom Greece had well-publicized political conflicts.

305. *Les Jeux Olympiques,* p. 100.

306. Ibid., pp. 100–101.

307. "The Olympic Games of 1896," p. 48.

308. *Une Campagne de 21 ans,* p. 127; *Mémoires olympiques,* p. 37.

309. The *New York Times* was solely preoccupied with the American victories. Under headlines such as "American Athletes Won," "The Americans Ahead," "Honors for Americans," "Americans Won Most Crowns," the paper reported results, the jubilation at Princeton where students were said to have held a "mass meeting" and to have telegraphed congratulations to Garrett, and a brief background paragraph on this new hero. The editorial on April 12, concerned with the Marathon, again discussed only the athletic significance of Loues' victory, noting that he had silenced critics of Greek physical development and arguing that he should be awarded "the world record" since his time compared favorably with professional and amateur records at lesser distances.

310. *Mémoires olympiques,* p. 39.

311. Richardson, "The New Olympian Games," p. 284.

312. Reproduced ibid.

313. "The Olympic Games by a Competitor," p. 957.

314. *Une Campagne de 21 ans,* p. 127.

315. *Mémoires olympiques,* p. 39.

316. *Une Campagne de 21 ans,* p. 126.

317. Ibid., p. 127.

318. "Les Jeux Olympiques," p. 14. His *Century Magazine* article on the Olympics was "By Their Founder, Baron Pierre de Coubertin, Now President of the International Committee," and its concluding paragraph begins, "It was with these thoughts in mind that *I* sought to revive the Olympic Games. *I* have succeeded after many efforts." "The Olympic Games of 1896," p. 53, emphasis added.

319. Coubertin assigned the toast to "a lunch given by Bikelas" (*Une Campagne de 21 ans,* p. 126) whose date I have been unable to establish. Perhaps it was the same as one of the two events noted by the London *Times* (April 14, 15, 1896): a "lunch at the Crown Prince's" at which Bikelas was present, or more likely a Monday night "dinner given by Mr. Skouzes in honor of Bikelas."

320. *Une Campagne de 21 ans,* pp. 127–28.

321. Ibid., p. 128; "The New Olympian Games," p. 286.

322. Coubertin was forced to fire off a "letter of rectification" to the paper. *Une Campagne de 21 ans,* p. 128.

323. Ibid.

324. Ibid.

325. "The New Olympian Games," p. 286.

326. Coubertin, *Une Campagne de 21 ans,* pp. 9–10.

327. Richardson, "The New Olympian Games," p. 273.

328. *Les Jeux Olympiques*, p. 104.

329. *Le Voyage d'Athènes*, pp. 88–89.

330. *Les Jeux Olympiques*, p. 104.

331. Ibid.

332. *Le Voyage d'Athènes*, p. 89.

333. Ibid.

334. *Les Jeux Olympiques*, p. 104.

335. *Times* (London), April 16, 1896.

336. *Les Jeux Olympiques*, p. 105.

337. "The Olympic Games of 1896," p. 50.

338. Robertson, "The Olympic Games by a Competitor," pp. 956–57.

339. This description is from *Les Jeux Olympiques*, pp. 105–6, from pl. 17, and the illustration in Yalouris, *The Olympic Games through the Ages*, p. 309.

340. Szymiczek, "The Revival of the Olympic Games," p. 308.

341. "The New Olympian Games," p. 282.

342. *Le Voyage d'Athènes*, pp. 90–91.

343. Richardson, "The New Olympian Games," p. 282.

344. Coubertin, "The Olympic Games of 1896," p. 50.

345. These first Olympic medals were not attached by ribbon or pin to the athletes' bodies, showing that their kinship with such medals as those awarded at international expositions was greater than with military decorations. Gold medals for the victors came with the London Games in 1908.

346. *Les Jeux Olympiques*, p. 106. Maurras, in the midst of his conversion to monarchy, was careful to note that the athletes bowed "deeply" to the king. George, according to Maurras, gave each a military salute before shaking his hand. *Le Voyage d'Athènes*, p. 90.

347. *Les Jeux Olympiques*, pp. 106–7.

348. *Times* (London), April 16, 1896.

349. *Les Jeux Olympiques*, p. 107.

350. "The New Olympian Games," p. 282.

351. *Les Jeux Olympiques*, p. 105.

352. "The New Olympian Games," p. 282. Evidently to a philhellenic classicist like Richardson, even heroic Greeks were not entitled to possess the artistic treasures of the ancient, heroic age! Did he fear that Loues would drink soup out of it?

353. *Les Jeux Olympiques*, pp. 107–8.

354. Ibid., p. 108. Coubertin called this "the traditional procession," though it is not clear which "tradition" he was referring to. "The Olympic Games of 1896," p. 50.

355. Maurras, *Le Voyage d'Athènes*, pp. 91–92.

356. *Les Jeux Olympiques*, p. 108. So began yet another familiar Olympic tradition.

357. Coubertin, "The Olympic Games of 1896," p. 50. Where were the rest of the Greeks situated in the procession?

358. *Les Jeux Olympiques*, p. 108.

359. *Times* (London), April 16, 1896; *Les Jeux Olympiques*, p. 108.

Chapter Eight

1. *Les Jeux Olympiques*, p. 108.

2. Ibid.; *Times* (London), April 16, 1896.

3. *Les Jeux Olympiques*, p. 108.

4. "The Olympic Games of 1896," pp. 50–51.

5. Ibid., p. 50.

6. Bourchier, "History of Modern Greece," p. 468.

7. Ibid.

8. Campbell and Sherrard, *Modern Greece*, p. 106.

9. Bourchier, "History of Modern Greece," p. 468.

10. Ibid.

11. *Mémoires olympiques*, pp. 37–38. See also *Une Campagne de 21 ans*, pp. 131–32.

12. Coubertin, *Souvenirs d'Amérique et de Grèce* (Paris: Hachette, 1897). The book received an anonymous notice in the *Century Magazine* 54 (1897): 470, which commented on the contrast between the "triumph" of the Games and the "tragedy" of the war and suggested a connection between them.

13. *Une Campagne de 21 ans*, p. 131.

14. "The Olympic Games of 1896," p. 53.

15. Ibid.

16. Ibid.

17. *Le Voyage d'Athènes*, p. 58.

18. Ibid.

19. Ibid., p. 59.

20. Ibid., p. 68.

21. Ibid., p. 95.

22. Ibid., p. 92.

23. Ibid., p. 93.

24. Coubertin, "Does Cosmopolitan Life Lead to International Friendliness?" *American Monthly Review of Reviews* 17 (1898): 429–34.

25. Ibid., pp. 429–30.

26. Ibid., p. 431.

27. Ibid.

28. Ibid.

29. Ibid., p. 433.

30. Ibid.

31. Ibid., p. 434. It is worth noting that Daniel Boorstin in his much-discussed *The Image: A Guide to Pseudo-Events in America* (New York: Atheneum, 1962) makes exactly the same distinctions between the "traveler" and the "tourist" that Coubertin made sixty-four years before between the "cosmopolitan" and the "internationalist." It is also worth noting that Boorstin exempted amateur athletics from his general critique of alienating imagery in modern life.

32. Coubertin, *Le Respect mutuel* (Paris: Alcan, 1915).

33. Marcel Mauss, "La Nation et l'internationalisme," *Oeuvres*, ed. Victor Karady, vol. 3 (Paris: Éditions de Minuit, 1969): 571–630.

34. Ruth Benedict, *The Crysanthemum and the Sword* (New York: Meridian, 1946), p. 15.

35. Clifford Geertz, "Deep Play: Notes on the Balinese Cockfight." *Daedalus* 101 (1972): 1–38.

36. Coubertin, "Olympia," p. 118.

37. "The New Olympic Games," p. 512.

38. Other kinds of performances, of course, were enmeshed with these four focal types: banquets, street demonstrations, stage plays, café debates, political elections, church rituals, newspaper editorials, and so on.

39. Gregory Bateson, "A Theory of Play and Fantasy," in *Steps to an Ecology of Mind* (New York: Ballantine, 1972). Erving Goffman, *Frame Analysis* (New York: Harper, 1974).

40. Arnold van Gennep, *The Rites of Passage*, trans. Monka B. Vizedom and Gabrielle L. Caffee (Chicago: University of Chicago Press, 1960); Victor Turner, *The Forest of Symbols*, *The Ritual Process*.

41. Coubertin, "Seventh Olympic Letter," 1918, *The Olympic Idea*, p. 57.

42. MacAloon, "Olympic Games and the Theory of Spectacle in Complex Society."

43. *Une Campagne de 21 ans*, p. 128.

44. *Mémoires olympiques*, pp. 41–42.

45. Eyquem, *Pierre de Coubertin*, pp. 155–56.

46. *Mémoires olympiques*, p. 42.

47. All sources agree that the accident happened in 1898. If so, it must have taken place early in the year, when Jacques was at the very most a toddler. One would think, had he been any more developed, that the boy would have saved himself.

48. *Mémoires olympiques*, p. 59.

Bibliography

Acomb, Evelyn M. *The French Laic Laws, 1879–1889*. New York: Columbia University Press, 1941.

Adam, Paul. *La Morale des sports*. Paris: Librairie Mondiale, 1907.

Agulhon, Maurice. *La République au village*. Paris: Plon, 1970.

Ahern, P. H. *The Life of John J. Keane*. Milwaukee: Bruce, 1955.

Altick, Richard D. *The Shows of London*. Cambridge: Harvard University Press, 1978.

Arnold, Matthew. *Democratic Education. The Complete Prose Works of Matthew Arnold*. Ed. R. H. Super. Vol. 2. Ann Arbor: University of Michigan Press, 1962.

———. "Rugby Chapel." *Poems. The Works of Matthew Arnold*. Vol. 1. London: Macmillan, 1903.

———. *Schools and Universities on the Continent. The Complete Prose Works of Matthew Arnold*. Ed. R. H. Super. Vol. 4. Ann Arbor: University of Michigan Press, 1964.

Atlas, Caron. "The Crystal Palace." M.A. thesis. University of Chicago, 1980.

Aubry, Octave. *The Second Empire*. Trans. Arthur Livingston. New York: Lippincott, 1940.

Bamford, T. W. *Thomas Arnold*. London: Cresset, 1960.

Barrès, Maurice. *Le Voyage de Sparte. L'Oeuvre de Maurice Barrès*. Vol. 7. Ed. Club de l'honnête homme. Paris: Plon, 1967.

Barrows, Isabel C., ed. *Physical Training*. Boston: Ellis, 1890.

Barthes, Roland. *La Tour Eiffel*. Paris: Delpire, 1964.

Bateson, Gregory. "A Theory of Play and Fantasy." In *Steps to an Ecology of Mind*. New York: Ballantine, 1972.

Baudelaire, Charles. *Art in Paris 1845–1862: Salons and Other Exhibitions Reviewed by Charles Baudelaire*. Trans. and ed. Jonathan Mayne. London: Phaidon, 1965.

Beau de Loménie, Emmanuel. *La Restauration manquée: L'Affaire du drapeau blanc*. Paris: Éditeurs des Portiques, 1932.

Beauroy, Jacques, et al., eds. *The Wolf and the Lamb: Popular Culture in France from the Old Regime to the Twentieth Century*. Saratoga, Calif.: Anma Libri, 1976.

Benedict, Ruth. *The Chrysanthemum and the Sword*. New York: Meridian, 1946.

Bert, Paul. *La Morale des Jésuites*. 3d ed. Paris: Charpentier, 1880. English trans. by the publisher. *The Doctrine of the Jesuits*. Boston: Bradbury, 1880(?).

Bezucha, Robert J. "The Moralization of Society: The Enemies of Popular Culture in the 19th Century." *The Wolf and the Lamb: Popular Culture in France from the Old Regime to the Twentieth Century*. Ed. Jacques Beauroy, et al. Saratoga, Calif.: Anma Libri, 1976.

Biernakiewiez, Tadeuz. "Un Précurseur de Pierre de Coubertin, Gustav Johan Schartau." *Kultura Fizycna*, September 1964.

Bikelas, Demetrios. *La Grèce byzantine et moderne*. Paris: Fermin-Didot, 1893.

Binet, Alfred, and Henri, V. *La Fatigue intellectuelle*. Paris: Schleicher, 1898.

Boorstin, Daniel. *The Image: A Guide to Pseudo-Events in America*. New York: Atheneum, 1962.

Boulongne, Yves-Pierre. *La Vie et l'oeuvre pédagogique de Pierre de Coubertin, 1863–1937*. Ottawa: Leméac, 1975.

Bourchier, James D. "History of Modern Greece." *Encyclopaedia Britannica*. 13th ed.

Bourdon, Georges. *L'Encyclopédie des sports*. Paris: Librairie de France, 1924.

Boutmy, Émile. *La Développement de la constitution et la société politique en Angleterre*. Paris: Plon et Marescq ainé, 1887.

―――. "Le Gouvernement local et la tutelle de l'état en Angleterre." *Annales des sciences politiques* 1 (1886): 165–203.

―――. "L'Individu et l'état en Angleterre." *Annales des sciences politiques* 2 (1887): 435–522.

Bowra, C. M. *The Odes of Pindar*. Baltimore: Penguin Classics, 1969.

Brailsford, Dennis. *Sport and Society Elizabeth to Anne*. London: Routledge & Kegan Paul, 1969.

Bréal, Michel. *Excursions pédagogiques: Un Voyage scolaire en Allemagne*. Paris: Hachette, 1882.

―――. *Quelques Mots sur l'instruction publique en France*. Paris: Hachette, 1872.

Brogan, D. W. *France under the Republic*. New York & London: Harper, 1940.

Brooke, M. Z. *Le Play: Engineer and Social Scientist*. London: Longman, 1970.

Burchell, S. C. *Imperial Masquerade: The Paris of Napoleon III*. New York: Atheneum, 1971.

Buthman, William Curt. *The Rise of Integral Nationalism in France*. New York: Columbia University Press, 1939.

Butler, E. M. *The Tyranny of Greece over Germany*. Boston: Beacon, 1958.

Campbell, John, and Sherrard, Phillip. *Modern Greece*. New York: Praeger, 1968.

Castagnary, Jules A. *Salons, 1857–1870*. 2 vols. Paris: Charpentier, 1892.

"Catalogue de tableaux anciens formant l'importante collection de M. Gustave Rothan." Preface by Paul Mantz. Paris: Ménard, 1890.

Chêneboit, L. Review of *La France et sa politique extérieure en 1867*, by Gustave Rothan. *Annales des sciences politiques* 3 (1888): 143.

Clark, Ellery H. *Reminiscences of an Athlete*. Boston: Houghton Mifflin, 1911.

"Une Conférence à Londres." *La Réforme sociale* 14 (1887): 621–22.

Connolly, James B. "An Olympic Victor." *Scribner's Magazine* 44 (1908): 18–31, 205–17, 357–70.

Coubertin, Pierre de. "Address Delivered at the Opening of the Prague Olympic Congress, 1925." *The Olympic Idea: Discourses and Essays*. Ed. Carl-Diem-Institut and the Deutschen Sporthochschule, Köln. Rev. Liselot Diem and O. Anderson. Trans. John G. Dixon. Stuttgart: Hofmann, 1967.

―――. "Are the Public Schools a Failure? A French View." *Fortnightly Review* 78 (1902): 979–86.

―――. "Athletics in the Modern World and the Olympic Games." 1894. *The Olympic Idea: Discourses and Essays*. Ed. Carl-Diem-Institut and the Deutschen Sporthochschule, Köln. Rev. Liselot Diem and O. Anderson. Trans. John G. Dixon. Stuttgart: Hofmann, 1967.

―――. *Une Campagne de 21 ans*. Paris: Librairie de l'Éducation Physique, 1908.

―――. "Une Campagne de 35 ans." *Revue de Paris* 30 (June 1, 1923): 688–94.

―――. *La Chronique de France*. 7 vols. Auxerre & Paris: Lanier, 1900–1906.

―――. "Les Collèges anglais: Harrow School." *La Réforme sociale* 12 (1886): 466–73.

―――. "Courrier d'Irlande: Les Difficultés de la situation." *La Réforme sociale* 13 (1887): 235–40.

―――. "Does Cosmopolitan Life Lead to International Friendliness?" *American Monthly Review of Reviews* 17 (1898): 429–34.

―――. "L'Éducation anglaise." *La Réforme sociale* 13 (1887): 632–52.

―――. *L'Éducation anglaise en France*. Paris: Hachette, 1889.

―――. *L'Éducation en Angleterre*. Paris: Hachette, 1888.

―――. *Essais de psychologie sportive*. Lausanne: Payot, 1913.

―――. *L'Évolution française sous la Troisième République*. Paris: Hachette, 1896. *The Evolution of France under the Third Republic.* Trans. Isabel Hapgood. New York: Crowell, 1897.

———. "L'Exposition athlétique." *Revue athlétique* 1 (May 25, 1890).

———. "La Force nationale et le sport." *Revue des deux mondes* 7 (1902): 916–24.

———. *France since 1814.* New York: Macmillan, 1900.

———. "Gladstone, vieux canotier." *Journal des débats* (July 9, 1893).

———. *La Gymnastique utilitaire.* Paris: Alcan 1905.

———. *Histoire universelle.* 4 vols. Aix-en-Provence: Société de l'histoire universelle, 1919.

———. "Les Jeux olympiques 776 av. J.C.—1896." 1896. *The Olympic Idea: Discourses and Essays.* Ed. Carl-Diem-Institut and the Deutschen Sporthochschule. Rev. Liselot Diem and O. Anderson. Trans. John G. Dixon. Stuttgart: Hofmann, 1967.

———. "Les Jeux olympiques de Much Wenlock." *Sports athlétiques* 1 (December 25, 1890).

———. "Le Play: Réformateur et Sociologue." *La Chronique de France* 6 (1906): 158–73.

———. "Lettre aux membres de la Société d'économie sociale et des unions." *La Réforme sociale* 16 (1888): 249–52.

———. *Mémoires olympiques.* Lausanne: Bureau international de pédagogie sportive, 1931.

———. "Mes Mémoires." Ms., 1936. Published in Yves-Pierre Boulongne. *La Vie et l'oeuvre pédagogique de Pierre de Coubertin 1863–1937.* Ottawa: Leméac, 1975.

———. "A Modern Olympia." 1910. *The Olympic Idea: Discourses and Essays.* Ed. Carl-Diem-Institut and the Deutschen Sporthochschule, Köln. Rev. Liselot Diem and O. Anderson. Trans. John G. Dixon. Stuttgart: Hofmann, 1967.

———. *Notes sur l'éducation publique.* Paris: Hachette, 1901.

———. "Olympia." 1929. *The Olympic Idea: Discourses and Essays.* Ed. Carl-Diem-Institut and the Deutschen Sporthochschule, Köln. Rev. Liselot Diem and O. Anderson. Trans. John G. Dixon. Stuttgart: Hofmann, 1967.

———. "The Olympic Games and Gymnastics." 1931. *The Olympic Idea: Discourses and Essays.* Ed. Carl-Diem-Institut and the Deutschen Sporthochschule, Köln. Rev. Liselot Diem and O. Anderson. Trans. John G. Dixon. Stuttgart: Hofmann, 1967.

———. "The Olympic Games of 1896." *Century Magazine* 53 (1896): 39–53.

———. *The Olympic Idea: Discourses and Essays.* Ed. Carl-Diem-Institut and the Deutschen Sporthochschule, Köln. Rev. Liselot Diem and O. Anderson. Trans. John G. Dixon. Stuttgart: Hofmann, 1967.

———. *Pages d'histoire contemporaine.* Paris: Plon, 1908.

———. *Pédagogie sportive.* Paris: Crès, 1922.

———. "The Philosophic Foundations of Modern Olympism." 1935. *The Olympic Idea: Discourses and Essays.* Ed. Carl-Diem-Institut and the Deutschen Sporthochschule, Köln. Rev. Liselot Diem and O. Anderson. Trans. John G. Dixon. Stuttgart: Hofmann, 1967.

———. "Philosophie de l'histoire des États-Unis." *La Revue bleue* 35 (June 4, 1898): 708–15.

———. "Préface des Jeux Olympiques." *Cosmopolis* 2 (1896): 146–59.

———. "Le Remède au surmenage et la transformation des lycées de Paris." *La Réforme sociale* 16 (1888): 241–49.

———. *Le Respect Mutuel.* Paris: Alcan, 1915.

———. "Le Rétablissement des Jeux Olympiques." *Revue de Paris* 1 (May 15, 1894): 170–84.

———. "The Revival of the French Universities." *American Monthly Review of Reviews* 16 (1897): 52–56.

———. "Second Olympic Letter." 1918. *The Olympic Idea: Discourses and Essays.* Ed. Carl-Diem-Institut and the Deutschen Sporthochschule, Köln. Rev. Liselot Diem and O. Anderson. Trans. John G. Dixon. Stuttgart: Hofmann, 1967.

———. "Seventh Olympic Letter." 1918. *The Olympic Idea: Discourses and Essays.* Ed. Carl-Diem-Institut and the Deutschen Sporthochschule, Köln. Rev. Liselot Diem and O. Anderson. Trans. John G. Dixon. Stuttgart: Hofmann, 1967.

———. *Souvenirs d'Amérique et de Grèce.* Paris: Hachette, 1897.

————. "Speech at the Award of the Olympic Diplomas." 1909. *The Olympic Idea: Discourses and Essays*. Ed. Carl-Diem-Institut and the Deutschen Sporthochschule, Köln. Rev. Liselot Diem and O. Anderson. Trans. John G. Dixon. Stuttgart: Hofmann, 1967.

————. "Speech by Baron de Coubertin at the Close of the Berlin Olympic Games." 1936. *The Olympic Idea: Discourses and Essays*. Ed. Carl-Diem-Institut and the Deutschen Sporthochschule, Köln. Rev. Liselot Diem and O. Anderson. Trans. John G. Dixon. Stuttgart: Hofmann, 1967.

————. "Speech by Baron de Coubertin at the Paris Congress, 1894." *The Olympic Idea: Discourses and Essays*. Ed. Carl-Diem-Institut and the Deutschen Sporthochschule, Köln. Rev. Liselot Diem and O. Anderson. Trans. John G. Dixon. Stuttgart: Hofmann, 1967.

————. "Speech to the Conference on Physical Training." *Physical Training*. Ed. Isabel C. Barrows. Boston: Ellis, 1890.

————. "Statistiques irlandaises." *La Réforme sociale* 15 (1888): 661–69.

————. "Toynbee Hall: Le Patronage social à Londres et les étudiants anglais." *La Réforme sociale* 14 (1887): 227–33.

————. "A Typical Englishman: Dr. W. P. Brookes of Wenlock." *American Monthly Review of Reviews* 15 (1897): 62–65.

————. "L'Université catholique de Washington." *La Réforme sociale* 16 (1888): 349–51.

————. "Les Universités anglaises: Cambridge." *La Réforme sociale* 12 (1886): 593–604.

————. "Universités transatlantiques." *La Réforme sociale* 20 (1890): 182–84.

————. *Universités transatlantiques*. Paris: Hachette, 1890.

Curtis, Thomas P. "The Glory that was Greece." *Sportsman* 12 (1932).

Curtius, Ernst. *Olympia: Ein Vortrag*. Berlin: Wilhelm Hertz, 1852.

Curtius, Ernst, and Adler, Friedrich, eds. *Olympia: Die Ergebnisse der von dem Deutschen Reich veranstalteten Ausgrabung*. 5 vols. Berlin: A. Ascher, 1890–1897.

DaMatta, Roberto. "Carnival in Multiple Planes." *Rite, Drama, Festival, Spectacle: Rehearsals toward a Theory of Cultural Performance*. Ed. John J. MacAloon. Philadelphia: Institute for the Study of Human Issues. Forthcoming.

Daryl, Philippe [Paschal Grousset]. *Public Life in England*. Trans. Henry Firth. London: Routledge, 1884.

Deuel, Leo, ed. *The Memoirs of Heinrich Schliemann*. New York: Harper & Row, 1977.

Diem, Carl. "Pierre de Coubertin's Ancestry." *Bulletin du Comité international olympique*, January 15, 1952.

Drees, Ludwig. *Olympia: Gods, Artists, and Athletes*. New York: Praeger, 1968.

Durkheim, Émile. *The Elementary Forms of the Religious Life*. Trans. Joseph Ward Swain. New York: Free Press, 1965.

————. *The Evolution of Educational Thought*. Trans. Peter Collins. London & Boston: Routledge & Kegan Paul, 1977.

————. *Moral Education: A Study in the Theory and Application of the Sociology of Education*. Trans. Everett K. Wilson and Herman Schnurer. Ed. Everett K. Wilson. New York: Free Press, 1961.

————. *Professional Ethics and Civic Morals*. Trans. Cornelia Brookfield. Glencoe: Free Press, 1958.

Duruy, Victor. *Histoire des Grecs*. 3 vols. Paris: Hachette, 1887.

Elder, Glen. *Children of the Great Depression: Social Change in the Life Cycle*. Chicago: University of Chicago Press, 1974.

Engels, Friedrich. *Socialism: Utopian and Scientific*. Chicago: Charles Herr, 1918.

Erikson, Erik. *Childhood and Society*. New York: Norton, 1950.

Eyquem, Marie-Thérèse. *Pierre de Coubertin: L'Épopée olympique*. Paris: Calmann-Lévy, 1966.

Falcucci, Clément. *L'Humanisme dans l'enseignement secondaire en France au XIX siècle*. Toulouse: Edouard Privat, 1939.

Festinger, Leon. *A Theory of Cognitive Dissonance.* Evanston: Row, Peterson, 1957.

Festinger Leon; Riecken, Henry W.; and Schacter, Stanley. *When Prophecy Fails.* Minneapolis: University of Minnesota Press, 1956.

Ffrench, Yvonne. *The Great Exhibition of 1851.* London: David Bogue, 1951.

Finley, M. I., and Pleket, H. W. *The Olympic Games: The First Thousand Years.* New York: Viking, 1976.

Freud, Sigmund. *The Future of an Illusion.* Trans. James Strachey. New York: Norton, 1961.

Gardiner, E. Norman. *Athletics in the Ancient World.* Oxford: Clarendon, 1930.

Gargan, Edward T. "Editor's Introduction." *The Origins of Contemporary France,* by Hippolyte Adolphe Taine. Chicago: University of Chicago Press, 1974.

Gebhardt, Wilhelm. "Letter to Coubertin, January 20, 1896." *Dokumente zur Fruhgeschichte der olympischen Spiele.* Cologne: Carl-Diem-Institut, 1970.

Geertz, Clifford. "Deep Play: Notes on the Balinese Cockfight." *Daedalus* 101 (1972): 1–38.

Gennadius, J. "The Revival of the Olympian Games." *Cosmopolis* 2 (1896): 59–74.

Gennep, Arnold van. *The Rites of Passage.* Trans. Monika B. Vizedom and Gabrielle L. Caffee. Chicago: University of Chicago Press, 1960.

Gibbes-Smith, C. H. *The Great Exhibition of 1851.* London: Victoria & Albert Museum, 1964.

Giraudoux, Jean. *Maximes sur le sport.* Paris: Grasset, 1928.

Goffman, Erving. *Frame Analysis.* New York: Harper, 1974.

———. "Where the Action Is." *Interaction Ritual.* New York: Doubleday Anchor, 1967.

Goguel, François. "Six Authors in Search of National Character." In *In Search of France.* Ed. Stanley Hoffmann, et al. New York: Harper Torchbooks, 1965 (Cambridge: Harvard University Press, 1963).

Goody, Jack. *The Domestication of the Savage Mind.* Cambridge: Cambridge University Press, 1978.

Gosse, Edmund. "Current French Literature." *Cosmopolis* 2 (1896): 660–77.

Gouldner, Alvin. *The Hellenic World: A Sociological Analysis.* New York: Harper Torchbooks, 1969.

Greeley, Horace. *Glances at Europe.* New York: Dewitt Davenport, 1851.

Grombach, John V. *Olympia Cavalcade of Sports.* New York: Ballantine, 1956.

Grousset, Paschal. *La Renaissance physique.* Paris, 1888.

Guts-Muths, J. *Gymnastik für Jugend.* Berlin: Schnepfenthal, 1804.

Halbwachs, Maurice. *L'Évolution des besoins dans les classes ouvrières.* Paris: Alcan, 1933.

Halévy, Daniel. *La Fin des notables.* Paris: Grasset, 1930. Trans. Alain Silvera and June Guichardnaud. *The End of the Notables.* Middletown, Conn.: Wesleyan University Press, 1974.

Harris, H. A. *Greek Athletes and Athletics.* Bloomington, Ind.: Indiana University Press, 1966.

Harris, Neil. "Museums, Merchandising, and Popular Taste: The Struggle for Influence." *Material Culture and the Study of American Life.* Ed. Ian Quimby. New York: Norton, 1978.

Harrison, Brian. "Religion and Recreation in Nineteenth Century England." *Past and Present* 38 (1967): 98–125.

Hébert, Georges. *Le Sport contre l'éducation physique.* Paris: Vuibert, 1925.

Henricks, Thomas. "Sport and Social Distance in Pre-Industrial England." Ph.D. diss., University of Chicago, 1977.

Henry, Bill. *An Approved History of the Olympic Games.* New York: G. P. Putnam's Sons, 1976 [1948].

Hoffmann, Stanley, et al. *In Search of France.* New York: Harper Torchbooks, 1965. (Cambridge: Harvard University Press, 1963.)

Hohrod, Georges [Pierre de Coubertin]. "Le Roman d'un rallié." *La Nouvelle Revue* 116 (February 15, 1899): 577–601; 117 (March 1–April 15, 1899): 44–68, 222–47, 452–82, 650–84.

Horton, George. "The Recent Olympic Games." *Bostonian* 4 (1896).

Hughes, Thomas. *The Manliness of Christ*. London: Macmillan, 1879.

———. *Tom Brown at Oxford*. London: Macmillan, 1861.

———. *Tom Brown's Schooldays*. London: Macmillan, 1857. 6th ed., 1868, 1878.

———. *True Manliness: Selections from the Writings of Thomas Hughes*. Ed. E. E. Brown. Introduction by James Russell Lowell. Boston, 1880.

Institut supérieur de théologie, Enghien, Belgium. *Les Établissements des Jésuites en France depuis quatre siècles*. 5 vols. Wetteren, Belgium: Meester, 1955.

Ionnides, Ion P. "The True Course Run by the Marathon Messenger." *Philosophy, Theology, and History of Sport and of Physical Activity*. Ed. F. Landry and W. A. R. Orban. Miami: Symposia Specialists, 1978.

Isaac, Jules. "Francis I." *Encyclopaedia Britannica*. 13th ed.

Jacquemet, G., ed. *Catholicisme hier, aujourd'hui, demain*. 7 vols. Paris: Letouzey, 1949.

Jardin, André, and Tudesq, André-Jean. *La France des notables*. 2 vols. Paris: Seuil, 1973.

Les Jeux Olympiques, 776 av. J.C.–1896. Athens: Beck, 1896.

Johnson, Rossiter. *A History of the World's Columbian Exposition*. 4 vols. New York: Appleton, 1898.

Jolinon, Jules. *Le Joueur de balle*. Paris: Reider, 1929.

Jones, Chris. *Climbing in North America*. Berkeley & Los Angeles: University of California Press, 1976.

Jones, Ethel. *Les Voyageurs français en Angleterre de 1815 à 1830*. Paris: Boccard, 1930.

Jusserand, J. J. *Sports et jeux d'exercice dans l'ancienne France*. Paris: Plon, 1901.

Killanin, Lord, and Rodda, John, eds. *The Olympic Games*. New York: Collier, 1976.

Kingsley, Charles. *Health and Education*. London: Macmillan; New York: Appleton, 1874.

———. *Westward Ho!* London & Toronto: Dent, 1906. (Orig. pub. London, 1855.)

La Chesnaye-Desbois, F. A. de, ed. *Dictionnaire de la noblesse de France*. 3d ed. Vol. 8. Paris: Schlesinger, 1866.

Lainé, P. *Archives généalogiques et historiques de la noblesse de France ou receuil de preuves, mémoires et notices généalogiques, servant à constater l'origine, la filiation, les alliances et les illustrations religieuses, civiles, et militaires de diverses maisons et familles nobles du royaume*. Vols. I and II. Paris: Chez l'auteur, 1828, 1850.

Landes, David S. *Prometheus Unbound*. Cambridge: Cambridge University Press, 1970.

Laurie, André [Paschal Grousset]. *La Vie de collège en Angleterre*. Paris: Hetzel, 1881.

Leo XIII. *Rerum Novarum*, 1891.

Le Play, Frédéric. *La Constitution d'Angleterre*. 2 vols. 2d ed. Tours: Mame, 1875 [1845].

———. *La Constitution essentielle de l'humanité*. Tours: Mame, 1881.

———. *L'Organisation du travail*. Tours: Mame, 1870.

———. *Les Ouvriers européens*. Paris, 1855.

———. *La Paix sociale après le désastre*. Tours: Mame, 1871.

———. *La Réforme sociale en France*. 3 vols. 4th ed. Tours: Mame, 1872 [1864].

Leroy-Beaulieu, Anatole. *Les Catholiques libéraux: L'Église et le libéralisme de 1830 à nos jours*. Paris: Plon, Nourrit, 1885.

———. *Les Juifs et l'antisemitisme: Israel chez les nations*. Paris: C. Levy, 1893.

Leroy-Beaulieu, Paul. *L'Administration locale en France et en Angleterre*. Paris: Guillaumin, 1872.

Lévi-Strauss, Claude. *The Savage Mind*. Chicago: University of Chicago Press, 1966.

Locke, Robert R. *French Legitimists and the Politics of Moral Order in the Early Third Republic*. Princeton: Princeton University Press, 1974.

Lucas, John Apostal. "Baron Pierre de Coubertin and the Formative Years of the Modern International Olympic Movement, 1883–1896." Ph.D. diss., University of Maryland, 1962.

MacAloon, John J. "Cultural Performances, Culture Theory." "Olympic Games and the Theory of Spectacle in Complex Society." *Rite, Drama, Festival, Spectacle: Rehearsals toward a Theory of Cultural Performances.* Ed. John J. MacAloon. Philadelphia: Institute for the Study of Human Issues. Forthcoming.

———. "Religious Themes and Structures in the Olympic Movement and the Olympic Games." In *Philosophy, Theology, and History of Sport and Physical Activity.* Ed. F. Landry and W. A. R. Orban. Miami: Symposia Specialists, 1978.

MacIntosh, Peter. *Sport and Society.* London: C. A. Watts, 1963.

Mack, Edward C. *Public Schools and British Opinion 1780–1860.* London: Methuen, 1938.

Mack, Edward C., and Armytage, W. H. G. *Thomas Hughes.* London: Ernest Benn, 1952.

Mack, John E. *A Prince of Our Disorder.* New York: Little, Brown, 1976.

Mahaffy, J. P. "The Olympic Games at Athens in 1875." *Macmillan's Magazine* 32 (1875): 324–27.

Malcolmson, Robert. *Popular Recreations in English Society.* Cambridge: Cambridge University Press, 1973.

Manchester, Herbert. *Four Centuries of Sport in America, 1490–1890.* New York: Derrydale, 1931.

Mandell, Richard. *The First Modern Olympics.* Berkeley: University of California Press, 1976.

———. *The Nazi Olympics.* New York: Macmillan, 1971.

———. *Paris 1900: The Great World's Fair.* Toronto: University of Toronto Press, 1967.

Maneuvrier, Édouard. *L'Éducation de la bourgeoisie sous la République.* Paris: Cerf, 1888.

Marks, Stephen R. "Durkheim's Theory of Anomie." *American Journal of Sociology* 80 (1974): 329–63.

Martin, Theodore. *The Life of His Royal Highness The Prince Consort.* 2 vols. New York: Appleton, 1880.

Marx, Karl. "The Civil War in France." *The Karl Marx Library.* ed. and trans. Saul K. Padover. Vol. 1. New York: McGraw-Hill, 1971.

Maurras, Charles. *Anthinéa.* Paris: Flammarion, 1901.

———. "Lettres des Jeux Olympiques." *La Gazette de France.* April 15, 17–20, 22, May 29, 1896.

———. "Les Nouveaux Théoreticiens de l'éducation et l'école de la paix sociale." *La Réforme sociale* 14 (1887): 533–47.

———. "Un Plan de réforme de l'éducation française." *La Réforme sociale* 15 (1888): 475–79.

———. *Le Voyage d'Athènes.* Paris: Flammarion, 1929.

Maurrus, Michael R. "Folklore as an Ethnographic Source: A 'Mise au Point.'" *The Wolf and the Lamb: Popular Culture in France from the Old Regime to the Twentieth Century.* Ed. Jacques Beauroy, et al. Saratoga, Calif.: Anma Libri, 1976.

Mauss, Marcel. "La Nation et l'internationalisme." *Oeuvres.* Ed. Victor Karady. Vol. 3. Paris: Éditions de Minuit, 1969.

Mayer, Otto. *À travers les anneaux olympiques.* Geneva: Callier, 1960.

Mayeur, Jean-Marie. *Les Débuts de la IIIe République 1871–1898.* Paris: Seuil, 1973.

Mayhew, Henry. *1851; Or, The Adventures of Mr. and Mrs. Cursty Sandboys and Family.* London: David Bogue, 1851.

Meyer, Gaston. *Le Phénomène olympique.* Paris: Editions de la Table Ronde, 1960.

Monceaux, Paul. "Fouilles au sanctuaire des jeux isthmiques." *Gazette archéologique* 19 (1884): 273–85, 353–66.

Montherlant, Henri de, *Les Olympiques.* Paris: Gallimard, 1954.

Natan, Alex. "Sport and Politics." *Sport, Culture, and Society.* Ed. J. W. Loy and G. S. Kenyon. Toronto: Macmillan, 1969.

Newman, J. H. *The Idea of a University.* 10th ed. London: Longmans, Green, 1893 [1851].

Newton, Charles Thomas. *Essays on Art and Archeology.* New York: Macmillan, 1880.

Norton, Charles Eliot. "The Dimensions and Proportions of the Temple of Zeus at Olympia." *Proceedings of the American Academy of Arts and Sciences* 5, n.s. (1878): 145–170.

Owen, Robert. *Robert Owen's Journal*. Vol. 1. London: By the author, 1851.

Pareto, Vilfredo. *The Rise and Fall of Elites: An Application of Theoretical Sociology*. Ed. with an Introduction by Hans L. Zetterberg. Totowa, N.J.: Bedminster, 1968.

Parkin, G. R. *Life and Letters of Edward Thring*. 2 vols. London: Macmillan, 1898.

Pitts, Jesse R. "Change in Bourgeois France." In *In Search of France*. Ed. Stanley Hoffmann, et al. New York: Harper Torchbooks, 1965. (Cambridge: Harvard University Press, 1963.)

———. "Frédéric Le Play." *International Encyclopedia of the Social Sciences*. 1968.

Pius X. *Quam singulari*. 1910.

Prévost, Jean. *Plaisirs des sports*. Paris: Nouvelle Revue française, 1926.

Prost, Antoine. *Histoire de l'enseignement en France, 1800–1967*. Paris: Armand Colin, 1968.

Prothero, R. E. [R. E. P. Ernle]. *The Life and Correspondence of A. P. Stanley*. New York: Scribner, 1894.

Ralston, David. *The Army of the Republic*. Cambridge: M.I.T. Press, 1967.

"Ravignan, Gustave François Xavier de." *New Catholic Encyclopedia*. 1967.

Ravignan, Gustave François Xavier de. *Conférences du R. P. Ravignan*. 4 vols. Paris: Poussielgue-Rusand, 1860.

———. *De l'Existence et de l'institut des Jésuites*. Paris: Poussielgue-Rusand, 1844.

Reinach, Théodore. "Une page de musique grec." *Revue de Paris* 1 (May 15, 1894): 204–24.

Reiss, Steven R. "Professional Baseball and American Culture in the Progressive Era." Ph.D. diss., University of Chicago, 1974.

Révérend, A. *Titres, anoblissements, et pairies de la Restauration, 1814–1830*. Vol. 3. Paris: Champion, 1903.

Révérend, A., ed. *Annuaire de la noblesse*. Vol. 49. Paris, 1893.

Review of *L'Évolution française sous la IIIᵉ République*, by Pierre de Coubertin. *La Réforme sociale* 32 (1896): 379–80.

———. *Revue politique et parlementaire* 11 (1897): 233–34.

Richardson, Rufus B. "The New Olympian Games." *Scribner's Magazine* 20 (1896): 267–86.

Robertson, G. S. "The Olympic Games: by a Competitor and Prize Winner." *Fortnightly Review* 65 (1896): 944–57.

Roosevelt, Theodore. *American Ideals and Other Essays Social and Political*. New York: Putnam, 1897.

Rothan, Gustave. *La France et sa politique extérieure en 1867*. Paris: Calmann-Lévy, 1887.

Rouse, W. H. D. *A History of Rugby School*. London: Duckworth, 1898.

Sahlins, Marshall. *Culture and Practical Reason*. Chicago: University of Chicago Press, 1978.

Sainte-Beuve, C.-A. *Nouveaux Lundis*. Vol. 9. Paris: Calmann-Lévy, 1884.

Schechner, Richard. "The Restoration of Behavior." *Rite, Drama, Festival, Spectacle: Rehearsals toward a Theory of Cultural Performance*. Ed. John J. MacAloon. Philadelphia: Institute for the Study of Human Issues. Forthcoming.

Le Second Ordre. Paris: Éditions du Grand Armorial de France, 1947.

Seillières, Ernest de. *Un Artisan d'énergie française, Pierre de Coubertin*. Paris: Henri Didier, 1917.

Sereville, E. de, and Saint-Simon, F. D., eds. *Dictionnaire de la noblesse française*. Paris: Contrepoint, 1975.

Shaw, Albert. "Baron Pierre de Coubertin." *American Monthly Review of Reviews* 17 (1898): 435–38.

Shaw, Albert. Introduction to *The Evolution of France under the Third Republic* by Pierre de Coubertin. Trans. Isabel Hapgood. New York: Crowell, 1897.

Shorey, Paul. "Can We Revive the Olympic Games?" *Forum* 19 (1895): 317–23.

Silverman, Debora. "The 1889 Exhibition: The Crisis of Bourgeois Individualism." *Oppositions* 8 (1977): 71–91.

Simon, Jules. "L'Éducation." *La Réforme sociale* 12 (1887): 676–88.

———. Préface to *L'Éducation anglaise en France*, by Pierre de Coubertin. Paris: Hachette, 1889.

———. *La Réforme de l'enseignement secondaire*. Paris: Hachette, 1874.

Simpson, J. B. Hope. *Rugby since Arnold*. London: Macmillan; New York: St. Martin's, 1967.

Singer, B. H. "The Village Schoolmaster as Outsider." *The Wolf and the Lamb: Popular Culture in France from the Old Regime to the Twentieth Century*. Ed. Jacques Beauroy, et al. Saratoga, Calif.: Anma Libri, 1976.

Sloane, William Milligan. *The French Revolution and Religious Reform*. New York: Scribners, 1901.

———. *How to Bring Out the Ethical Value of History*. Chicago, 1898.

———. *Life of Napoleon Bonaparte*. 4 vols. New York: Century, 1896.

Snodgrass, A. M. *The Dark Age of Greece: An Archeological Survey of the Eleventh to the Eighth Centuries*. Edinburgh: Edinburgh University Press, 1971.

Société des artistes français. *Salon(s), 1846; 1848; 1852; 1853; 1855; 1857; 1861; 1863; 1875; 1876*. Paris: Musée Royal, 1846, 1848, 1852, 1853, 1855, 1857, 1861, 1863, 1875, 1876.

Sorel, Albert. *L'Europe et la révolution française*. Paris: Plon, Nourrit, 1887.

Spencer, Herbert. *Education: Intellectual, Moral, and Physical*. London: Watts, 1861.

Stanley, A. P. *The Life and Correspondence of Thomas Arnold*. New York: Appleton, 1845. (London: Murray, 1844.)

Strachey, Lytton. *Eminent Victorians*. London: Putnam, 1918.

Szymiczek, Otto. "Athens 1896." *The Olympic Games*. Ed. Lord Killanin and John Rodda. New York: Collier, 1976.

———. "The Revival of the Olympic Games." *The Olympic Games through the Ages*. Ed. Nicolaos Yalouris. Athens: Ekdotike Athenon, 1976.

Taine, Hippolyte. *Étienne Mayran*. Ed. Blossom L. Henry. New York: Prentice Hall, 1931.

———. "Fondation de l'École libre des sciences politiques." *Derniers Essais de critique et d'histoire*. Paris: Hachette, 1894.

———. *Notes on England*. Trans. with an introduction by Edward Hyams. London: Thames and Hudson, 1957.

Thieme, Ulrich. *Allgemeines Lexicon der Bildenden Künstler*. Vol. 7. Leipzig, 1912.

Thompson, E. P. *The Making of the English Working Class*. New York: Vintage, 1963.

———. "Patrician Society, Plebian Culture." *Journal of Social History* 7 (1974): 382–405.

———. "Time, Work Discipline, and Industrial Capitalism." *Past and Present* 38 (1967): 56–97.

Thring, Edward. *Education and School*. London: Macmillan, 1867.

Tudesq, André-Jean. *Les Grands Notables en France 1840–1849*. 2 vols. Paris: Presses Universitaires de France, 1964.

Turner, Victor. *Dramas, Fields, and Metaphors*. Ithaca: Cornell University Press, 1974.

———. *The Forest of Symbols*. Ithaca: Cornell University Press, 1967.

———. *The Ritual Process*. Chicago: Aldine, 1969.

———. *Schism and Continuity in an African Society*. Manchester: Manchester University Press, 1957.

Turner, Victor, and Turner, Edith. *Image and Pilgrimage in Christian Culture*. New York: Columbia University Press, 1978.

Ulmann, Jacques. *De la gymnastique aux sports modernes*. Paris: Vrin, 1971.

Van Essen, C. C. "La Découverte du Laocoon." *Mededelingen der Koninklijke Nederlandse Akademie van Wetenschappen* 18 (1955): 291–305.

Vlachos, Helen. "Return the Olympics to Greece Permanently: They Started There." *New York Times*, August 12, 1979.

Wardman, H. W. *Ernest Renan: A Critical Biography*. New York: Humanities Press, 1964.

Weber, Eugen. "Gymnastics and Sports in *Fin-de-siècle* France: Opium of the Classes?" *American Historical Review* 76 (1971): 70–98.

————. *A Modern History of Europe*. New York: Norton, 1971.

————. *Peasants into Frenchmen*. Stanford, Calif.: Stanford University Press, 1976.

————. "Pierre de Coubertin and the Introduction of Organized Sport in France." *Journal of Contemporary History* 5 (1970): 3–26.

————. "Who Sang the Marseillaise?" *The Wolf and the Lamb: Popular Culture in France from the Old Regime to the Twentieth Century*. Ed. Jacques Beauroy, et al. Saratoga, Calif.: Anma Libri, 1976.

Weber, Max. "Bureaucracy." *From Max Weber: Essays in Sociology*. Ed. and trans. H. H. Gerth and C. Wright Mills. New York: Oxford University Press, 1946.

West, Gilbert. *Odes of Pindar: to which is prefixed a Dissertation on the Olympick Games*. 4 vols. London: Willett, 1749.

Whitridge, Arnold. *Dr. Arnold of Rugby*. Introduction by Sir Michael Sadler. New York: Henry Holt, 1928.

Williams, Raymond. *Culture and Society 1780–1950*. New York: Harper & Row, 1966.

Williamson, Eugene L., Jr. *The Liberalism of Thomas Arnold*. University, Ala.: University of Alabama Press, 1964.

Worboise, Emmena Jane. *The Life of Dr. Arnold*. London, 1885.

Yalouris, Nicolaos, ed. *The Olympic Games through the Ages*. Athens: Ekdotike Athenon, 1976.

Zeldin, Theodore. "English Ideals in French Politics." *Cambridge Historical Journal* 1 (1959): 40–58.

————. *France 1848–1945*. Vol. 1: *Ambition, Love, and Politics*. Vol. 2: *Intellect, Taste, and Anxiety*. Oxford: Oxford University Press, 1977.

Index